This companion workbook is meant to be used alongside Thinkwell's web-based Trigonometry text. For more information about this please contact support@thinkwell.com.

Senior Editor:
Sarah Flood Ryland

Text and Cover design:
Peat Duggins, Martin Turzik, Amy Bryant

Production Guru:
Samantha Webber

Technical Guru:
Palo Chalupka

Project Manager:
Amy Bryant

With Special Thanks to:
Hank Cathey
Peat Duggins
Justin Kauffman
Vera Renkiewicz
Kristy Summers
Scout and Bingle

Thinkwell's Trigonometry

with Edward Burger

2008 Update

PREFACE

To The Student:

How to Use this workbook to succeed:

Congratulations! You are about to add a new dimension to your college learning experience - one that is more engaging, more thorough, and more effective than any textbook assignment you've ever received.

This printed workbook is designed to help you take maximum advantage of Thinkwell's Trigonometry by providing a streamlined version of the multimedia content of the Thinkwell text. It also can serve as a useful place to record your own notes, examples, questions, and ideas.

Concepts, theories, and examples from the Trigonometry video lectures are outlined here in order to streamline referencing and reviewing the material. Trigonometry vocabulary terms are defined as they are used, repeated at the end of subchapters, and appear in the glossary at the end of this book. A searchable index is also available on the Thinkwell Trigonometry website.

This workbook is not a substitute for viewing the lectures. It's a tool to help you to navigate the course with maximum success. Many students have found that a workbook helps them follow the video lectures more attentively, allowing them to pause and make their own notes as they watch the videos.

For more help with the online components of Thinkwell's Trigonometry, consult the Student User's Guide, available online in the Help Center, or contact us at technicalsupport@thinkwell.com.

The following tips are offered to help you with the transition from a traditional text to Thinkwell's next-generation textbook. Many of these suggestions, however, are reliable, time-tested study habits that work in just about any situation.

Get Organized:

Survey your coming semester from beginning to end. Using a calendar, make a full-semester study schedule for all of your courses. Include midterms, assignments, and study times. Often, instructors assume that you will spend at least three hours on homework for every hour you spend in class. Find out what your instructors' estimates are for your classes and plan accordingly. Schedule this time on your calendar. Plan to study during those times of the day when you're the least tired and least likely to be distracted. Find a quiet, private place to study to help ensure that noise and surprise distractions will not interrupt you.

Also schedule time to work on long-term assignments and projects. Plan to start working on them as early as possible so that you have plenty of time to ask questions, research, problem-solve, and make any revisions.

View the Thinkwell lectures actively:

Research shows that students who interact with course content, rather than passively reading, listening, or viewing it, are much more likely to gain a far superior understanding of that content. Allow yourself about 30 minutes to view a typical 10-to-15 minute Thinkwell video lecture. This extra time allows you to stop the lecture whenever you feel a need to review the material again or jot down a question or comment. Try watching each lecture once without stopping. Then watch it a second time, using this workbook and taking your own notes. Highlight the key concepts as they are discussed and any important points or details that will help you remember and understand this critical content. Write down new terms along with their definitions.

Also pay close attention to the text and graphic elements of the Thinkwell video lecture on your screen. For instance, the key concept box, contains the main ideas of the lecture around which sub-points, examples, and definitions are built. These key concepts also appear on the subchapter pages of this workbook. Most of the Thinkwell video lectures also contain a definitions area. Here you'll find terms, formulas, laws, or other discipline-specific language you should know.

Finally, the content area, on the right-hand side of your screen, contains some of the same information that appears in the online notes and in this workbook. The text and graphics in this area of the video builds as the Thinkwell presenter delivers the lecture. Pay special attention to headings, charts, bulleted lists, and diagrams, for they contain distillations of important material.

Utilize Thinkwell's Website resources:
Your Thinkwell website contains hundreds of on-line exercises and test questions, which your instructor can activate. Depending on how your instructor uses them, these automatically-graded questions will exercise or test your knowledge of the course content. Many of these exercises contain hints and explanations concerning any questions that you might answer incorrectly.

The Thinkwell website provides you with an online searchable index and glossary of key terms. The searchable index tells you in which lecture or exercise a term appears. The glossary database provides you with the definitions of all key terms. Be sure you know the meaning of all terms introduced in the lectures as well as any additional terms your instructor may have mentioned.

Every lecture also provides you with online notes. These are digital versions of much of the content of this workbook in a lecture-by-lecture format.

Take In-class notes:
If your instructor lectures in class, note-taking is critical. Studies show that you are far more likely to remember and comprehend material if you take notes in addition to listening to a lecture. Try to take notes that are readable and complete, and when possible, structure your notes according to the structure of the lecture. Your instructor may be speaking from prepared notes, so try to listen for the main headings and subheadings. Pay attention to lists and diagrams.

Try to find a moment immediately after the lecture to review and flesh out your notes. Most students' memories of even the major points of a lecture begins to fade after about thirty minutes. This 10-to-20 minute exercise is an extremely good use of time and one that you'll appreciate when you review your notes prior to an exam.

Prepare for exams:
Your notes reflect your ongoing understanding of and progression through the course content. One of the most effective ways to study is to cumulatively outline your notes. This method works best if you write your outlines by hand, even if you took them first on your computer.

Start with the notes you made in class (or from your Thinkwell lectures), and make a new set of notes that summarizes these in outline format. Begin making summary outline notes after the forth or fifth lecture. Try to keep the summary outline notes to three or four pages. Retain important headings, subheadings, lists, and any brief explanations you need to understand each key idea or concept.

After the next four or five lectures, revise your summary outline notes from the first group of lectures, and add your summary outline notes from the next group so that the entire summary outline is still just four pages long. Each time you revise your four-page summary outline, you are organizing and revisiting the important ideas of the coursecand learning them. It might look as though you're trying to distill the essentials of a course down to a few pages, but in fact you will be learning, managing, and understanding the core content of the course.

Another useful study technique is to try to predict the questions that will be on the exam. Base this exercise on the key points from your notes. This isn't as hard as it sounds and is a very good way to prepare. Some instructors may make previous exam questions available. You don't want to be surprised when you sit down to take the exam.

Finally, for problem-solving courses, it's very important to know the method for solving every kind of problem you might encounter on an exam. Work as many practice problems as you can, making sure you haven't forgotten any types or special cases. Most importantly, listen attentively for any guidance that your instructor might provide concerning the types of questions you can expect to see on the exam.

From all of us at Thinkwell who are committed to engaging your interest and ensuring your success, Good luck!

Thinkwell's Trigonometry

with Edward Burger

Table of Contents:

Algebraic Prerequisites

Algebraic Prerequisites

Using the Cartesian System

- **x-Axis**: The horizontal scale for measuring change on a graph.
- **y-Axis**: The vertical scale for measuring change on a graph.
- **Origin**: The point where the two scales cross and both have a value of 0. The coordinates of the origin are **(0,0)**.
- **Cartesian Plane**: The name for the system that uses the *x*- and *y*-axes.
- **Quadrants**: The four areas that are created by drawing *x*- and *y*-axes on a plane.
- **Ordered Pairs**: The address of each point. It states the *x*-value first, then the *y*-value **(x,y)**. By using this protocol, everyone in the world knows to start at the origin, (0,0) and move sideways as indicated by the **x-value** and vertically as indicated by the **y-value**.

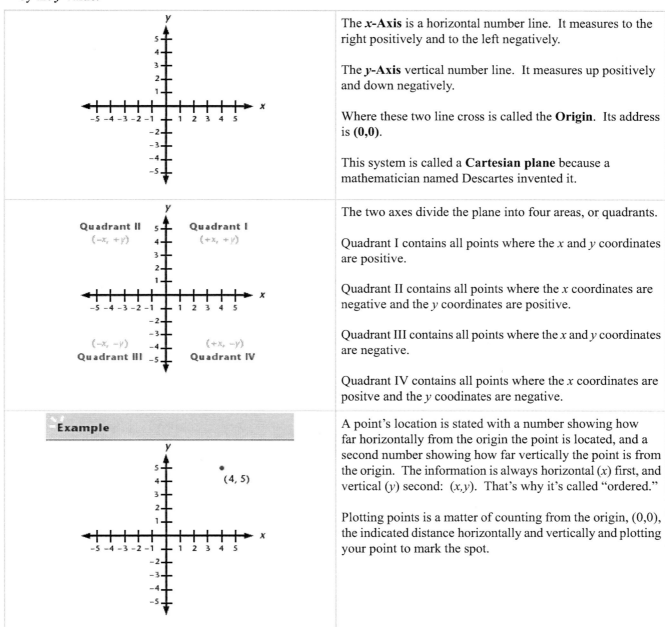

The **x-Axis** is a horizontal number line. It measures to the right positively and to the left negatively.

The **y-Axis** vertical number line. It measures up positively and down negatively.

Where these two line cross is called the **Origin**. Its address is **(0,0)**.

This system is called a **Cartesian plane** because a mathematician named Descartes invented it.

The two axes divide the plane into four areas, or quadrants.

Quadrant I contains all points where the *x* and *y* coordinates are positive.

Quadrant II contains all points where the *x* coordinates are negative and the *y* coordinates are positive.

Quadrant III contains all points where the *x* and *y* coordinates are negative.

Quadrant IV contains all points where the *x* coordinates are positve and the *y* coodinates are negative.

A point's location is stated with a number showing how far horizontally from the origin the point is located, and a second number showing how far vertically the point is from the origin. The information is always horizontal (*x*) first, and vertical (*y*) second: (*x,y*). That's why it's called "ordered."

Plotting points is a matter of counting from the origin, (0,0), the indicated distance horizontally and vertically and plotting your point to mark the spot.

Sample problems:

1. What are the coordinates of a point located in the third quadrant 5 units from each axis?

   Solution: $(-5, -5)$

   Explanation: Points in quadrant III have negative *x* and *y* values. So, a point in quadrant III that is five units from each axis will have the coordinates $(-5, -5)$.

2. What are the coordinates of the resulting point when $(-3, 7)$ is reflected across the x-axis?
   Solution: $(-3, -7)$
   Explanation: A reflection across the x-axis changes only the y-coordinate, so the x-coordinate is still -3. The y-coordinate has the opposite sign. Thus, the result of reflecting $(-3, 7)$ across the x-axis is $(-3, -7)$.

Practice problems: *(Answers on page: 443)*

1. True or false: The point below is located at $(-8, -12)$.

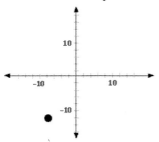

2. In what quadrant is the point $(10.3, -0.2)$ located?

3. What are the coordinates of a point located in the second quadrant and 2 units away from each axis?

Review questions: *(Answers to odd questions on page: 443)*

1. True or false: The point below is located at $(1, -2)$.

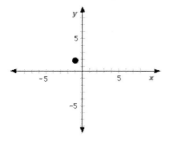

2. True or false: The point below is located at $(-10, 10)$.

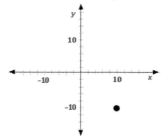

3. What are the coordinates of a point located in the fourth quadrant and 5 units away from each axis?

4. What are the coordinates of a point located in the third quadrant and 4 units away from each axis?

5. In what quadrant does the point $(3, -7)$ lie?

Thinking Visually

- An **axis** is the scale which measures the distance along one dimension, either width, height, or depth.
- The **origin** is the point where the axes of a system intersect.
- A **horizontal axis** measures horizontal distance from the origin on a plane. It is usually designated by x and is referred to as the x-axis.
- A **vertical axis** measures vertical distance from the origin on a plane. It is usually designated by y and is referred to as the y-axis.
- A **plane** is a level surface usually considered to have width and height but no depth. A plane is created whenever two axes intersect.
- A **point** is a specific location with no width, height, or depth on a surface. Its designation and location are given by the ordered pair (x,y) which gives the measurements for both its horizontal and its vertical location from the origin on the plane.
- **Plotting a point** is the process of locating a point on an axis system.
- A **line** is the straight path that passes through and beyond two specific points.
- A **circle** is a completely symmetrical figure which is composed of all the points a fixed distance from a specific point.

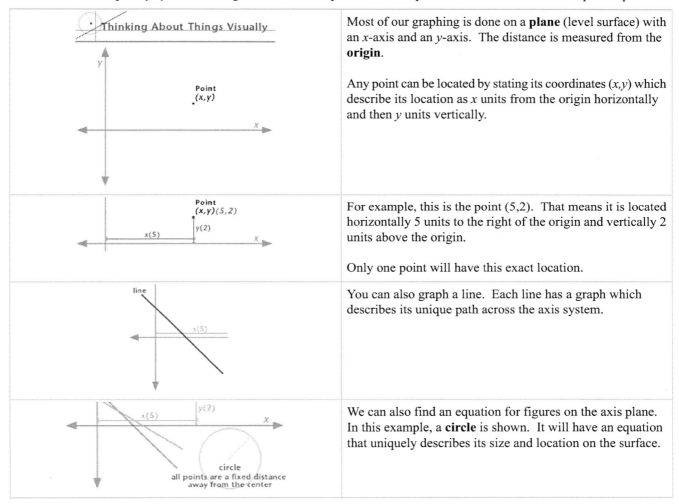

Thinking About Things Visually	Most of our graphing is done on a **plane** (level surface) with an x-axis and an y-axis. The distance is measured from the **origin**. Any point can be located by stating its coordinates (x,y) which describe its location as x units from the origin horizontally and then y units vertically.
Point (x,y) $(5,2)$	For example, this is the point $(5,2)$. That means it is located horizontally 5 units to the right of the origin and vertically 2 units above the origin. Only one point will have this exact location.
line	You can also graph a line. Each line has a graph which describes its unique path across the axis system.
circle — all points are a fixed distance away from the center	We can also find an equation for figures on the axis plane. In this example, a **circle** is shown. It will have an equation that uniquely describes its size and location on the surface.

Finding the Distance between Two Points

- **Distance formula**:

$$d = \sqrt{(x_2 - x_1)^2 + (y_2 - y_1)^2}$$

- The distance formula is an application of the Pythagorean Theorem, which states that the hypotenuse of a right triangle equals the square root of the sum of the other sides squared.
- **Midpoint formula**:

$$(\frac{x_1 + x_2}{2}, \frac{y_1 + y_2}{2})$$

- The midpoint formula determines the point in the middle of the line segment formed by 2 points.

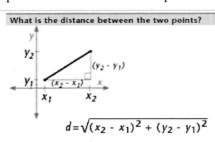

What is the distance between the two points?

$$d = \sqrt{(x_2 - x_1)^2 + (y_2 - y_1)^2}$$

Draw your given line segment first.

Then draw a vertical line from one end and a horizontal line from the other end. This creates a right triangle.

The length of the triangle's horizontal side can be found by taking the difference of the two x-values because they measure horizontal movement.

The length of the vertical side can be found by taking the difference of the two y-values because they measure vertical movement.

Now, using the Pythagorean Theorem,
(first side)^2 + (second side)^2 = (hypotenuse)^2.
$(x_2 - x_1)^2 + (y_2 - y_1)^2 = d^2$. So,
$$d = \sqrt{(x_2 - x_1)^2 + (y_2 - y_1)^2}$$

Example Find the distance between two points

(6,4) and (-8,11)

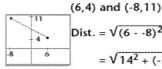

Dist. $= \sqrt{(6 - -8)^2 + (4 - 11)^2}$

$= \sqrt{14^2 + (-7)^2}$

$= \sqrt{196 + 49}$

$= \sqrt{245} = 15.65$

Now that you know the formula, just substitute in the values from each point and solve for your length.

It doesn't matter which point is identified as (x_1, y_1) and (x_2, y_2).

In this case (6, 4) is (x_2, y_2).

Example Find the midpoint

(1, -1) and (5,5)

Midpoint $= (\frac{1 + 5}{2}, \frac{-1 + 5}{2})$

$= (\frac{6}{2}, \frac{4}{2}) = (3,2)$

Finding the midpoint of a line segment means finding the average between the two endpoints:

Add the x-values and divide by 2.

Add the y-values and divide by 2.

These answers are the ordered pair of your midpoint.

Sample problems:

1. Given the points $P = (3,10)$ and $Q = (-1,0)$, find the length of the line segment from P to Q.
   Solution: 10.8

   Explanation: Use the distance formula, $d = \sqrt{(x_2 - x_1)^2 + (y_2 - y_1)^2}$, to find the length of a line segment. Substitute the x and y values into the formula and simplify:
   $d = \sqrt{(-1-3)^2 + (0-10)^2} = \sqrt{(-4)^2 + (-10)^2} = \sqrt{116} = 10.8$.
   In this case point Q was identified as (x_2, y_2). Notice that identifying P as (x_2, y_2)
   yields the same distance: $d = \sqrt{(3--1)^2 + (10-0)^2} = \sqrt{116} = 10.8$.

2. Given the points $A = (-4,10)$ and $B = (2,-6)$, find the coordinates of the point that is one-fourth of the distance from A to B.

   Solution: $\left(-\dfrac{5}{2}, 6\right)$

   Explanation: To find the point that is $\frac{1}{4}$ of the distance from A to B first find the midpoint, C, then find the midpoint between A and C. First, substitute the x and y values from A and B into the midpoint formula: $\left(\dfrac{x_1 + x_2}{2}, \dfrac{y_1 + y_2}{2}\right) \Rightarrow \left(\dfrac{-4+2}{2}, \dfrac{10+-6}{2}\right) = (-1, 2) = C.$

   Next substitute the x and y values from A and C into the midpoint formula: $\left(\dfrac{-4+-1}{2}, \dfrac{10+2}{2}\right) = \left(-\dfrac{5}{2}, 6\right).$

3. A soccer player kicks a ball from the point (10, 12) towards the point (50, 40), but an opponent stops the ball when it is only half way to its destination. How far is the blocker from the kicker? Assume the units are in yards.

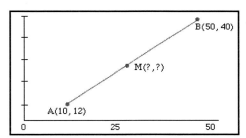

   Solution: 24.4 yards

   Explanation: First, find the coordinates of the midpoint: $\left(\dfrac{10+50}{2}, \dfrac{12+40}{2}\right) = (30, 26)$.
   Then use the distance formula to compute the distance from $A(10,12)$ to the midpoint $(30,26)$: $d = \sqrt{(30-10)^2 + (26-12)^2} = \sqrt{20^2 + 14^2} = \sqrt{400 + 196} = \sqrt{596} = 24.4$.

Practice problems: *(Answers on page: 443)*

1. Given the points $A = (-3.4, -2.7)$ and $B = (10.5, -7.8)$ find the length of the line segment from A to B.

2. Given the points $A = (3\sqrt{2}, -2\sqrt{5})$ and $B = (-2\sqrt{2}, 3\sqrt{5})$, find the distance between A and B.

3. Find the midpoint of the segment AB.

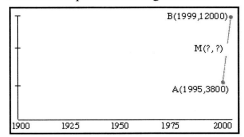

Review questions: *(Answers to odd questions on page: 443)*

1. Find the midpoint between the two intercepts of a line if the intercepts are $(-6, 0)$ and $(0, -14)$.

2. Find the distance between the two points $(-3, 11)$ and $(4, -15)$.

3. Find the length of the line segment between the points $(12.1, -1.1)(-4.7, 3.3)$.

4. Find the distance between the points $(2.2, 3.5)$ and $(1.5, 0.9)$.

5. Find the distance between the points $(-3.4, -2.7)$ and $(10.5, -7.8)$.

Finding the Second Endpoint of a Segment

- **Midpoint formula**: $\left(\frac{x_1 + x_2}{2}, \frac{y_1 + y_2}{2} \right)$

- Any point's location is given by the ordered pair (x, y) where x measures horizontal distance from the origin and y measures vertical distance from the origin.

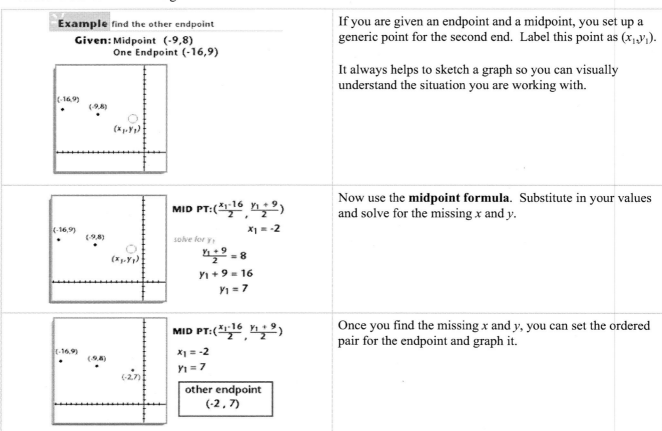

Example find the other endpoint

Given: Midpoint $(-9, 8)$
One Endpoint $(-16, 9)$

If you are given an endpoint and a midpoint, you set up a generic point for the second end. Label this point as (x_1, y_1).

It always helps to sketch a graph so you can visually understand the situation you are working with.

MID PT: $\left(\frac{x_1 - 16}{2}, \frac{y_1 + 9}{2} \right)$

$x_1 = -2$

solve for y,

$\frac{y_1 + 9}{2} = 8$

$y_1 + 9 = 16$

$y_1 = 7$

Now use the **midpoint formula**. Substitute in your values and solve for the missing x and y.

MID PT: $\left(\frac{x_1 - 16}{2}, \frac{y_1 + 9}{2} \right)$

$x_1 = -2$

$y_1 = 7$

other endpoint
$(-2, 7)$

Once you find the missing x and y, you can set the ordered pair for the endpoint and graph it.

Sample problems:

1. The point $(4,-2)$ is the midpoint of line segment AB. If the coordinates of
   B are $\left(\frac{2}{3},-\frac{1}{2}\right)$, find the coordinates of A.

   Solution: $\left(\frac{22}{3},-\frac{7}{2}\right)$

   Explanation: Let the coordinates of A be (x,y).

   Use the midpoint formula to write two equations: $\dfrac{x+\frac{2}{3}}{2}=4$ and $\dfrac{y+-\frac{1}{2}}{2}=-2$.

   Solve for x: $\dfrac{x+\frac{2}{3}}{2}=4$; $x+\frac{2}{3}=8$; $3x+2=24$; $3x=22$; $x=\frac{22}{3}$.

   Solve for y: $\dfrac{y+-\frac{1}{2}}{2}=-2$; $y-\frac{1}{2}=-4$; $2y-1=-8$; $2y=-7$; $y=-\frac{7}{2}$.

   The coordinates of point A are $\left(\frac{22}{3},-\frac{7}{2}\right)$.

2. The point $(5,3)$ is the midpoint of (a,b) and $(-4,2)$. Find the value of $a+b$.

   Solution: 18

   Explanation: Use the midpoint formula to write two equations: $\frac{-4+a}{2}=5$ and $\frac{2+b}{2}=3$.

   Solve for a: $\frac{-4+a}{2}=5$; $-4+a=10$; $a=14$. Solve for b: $\frac{2+b}{2}=3$; $2+b=6$; $b=4$.

   The value for $a+b$ is $14+4=18$.

3. The point $\left(2w,\frac{1}{2}w+4\right)$ is the midpoint of line segment PQ. If the coordinates of
   P are $(3w,7)$, find the coordinates of Q.

   Solution: $(w,w+1)$

   Explanation: Let the coordinates of Q be (x,y). Use the midpoint formula to write

   two equations: $\dfrac{3w+x}{2}=2w$ and $\dfrac{7+y}{2}=\frac{1}{2}w+4$. Solve for x: $\dfrac{3w+x}{2}=2w$;

   $3w+x=4w$; $x=w$. Solve for y: $\dfrac{7+y}{2}=\frac{1}{2}w+4$; $7+y=w+8$; $y=w+1$.

   Thus, the coordinates of Q are $(w,w+1)$.

Practice problems: *(Answers on page: 443)*

1. The point $\left(\frac{11}{4},-\frac{1}{2}\right)$ is the midpoint of line segment AB. If the coordinates of
   A are $(5,0)$, find the coordinates of B.

2. The point $(3,-1)$ is the midpoint of (x,y) and $(-1,1)$. Find the value of $x-y$.

3. The point $\left(n+\frac{3}{2},2n\right)$ is the midpoint of line segment PQ. If the coordinates of
   P are $(2-n,5n)$, find the coordinates of Q.

Review questions: *(Answers to odd questions on page: 443)*

1. The point $\left(-\frac{3}{4},7\right)$ is the midpoint of line segment AB. If the coordinates of
   A are $\left(-\frac{5}{2},2\right)$, find the coordinates of B.

2. The point $(-1,\ 2)$ is the midpoint of (x,y) and $(6,0)$. Find the value of $\frac{x}{y}$.

3. The point $(\frac{3}{2},0)$ is the midpoint of (x,y) and $(5,1)$. Find the value of $y-x$.

4. The point $(d,d+1)$ is the midpoint of line segment AB. If the coordinates of
   A are $(3-d,5d)$, find the coordinates of B.

5. The point $\left(\frac{1}{2} - \frac{1}{6}z, \frac{1}{4}z + \frac{5}{2}\right)$ is the midpoint of line segment AB. If the coordinates of A are $\left(1 - z, \frac{1}{2}z + 5\right)$, find the coordinates of B.

Collinearity and Distance

- Points that fall on the same line are **collinear** points.
- Three points are collinear if, for some pair of lengths between two points, their sum is equal to the remaining third length between two points.
- Three points are not collinear if, for every pair of lengths between two points, their sum is greater than the remaining third length between two points. This result indicates that the points form a triangle.
- **Pythagorean Theorem**: $a^2 + b^2 = c^2$
- If you are given three points and you square the three lengths between pairs of points, you can tell that the points form a right triangle if the sum of any two of the squared lengths equals the third squared length.
- **Distance formula**: $d = \sqrt{\left(x_2 - x_1\right)^2 + \left(y_2 - y_1\right)^2}$
- The distance between any two points is found by squaring the difference in their x-values and adding it to the squared difference in their y-values, then finding the square root of the sum.

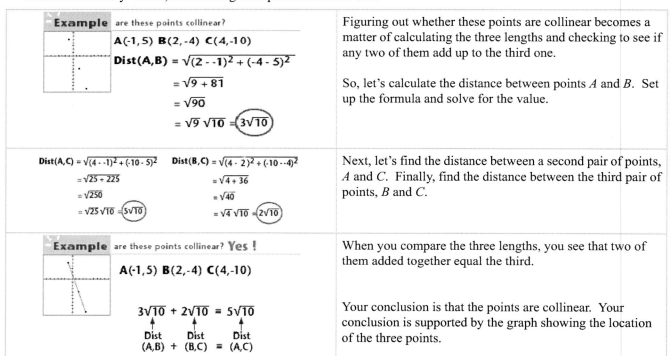

Example are these points collinear? $A(-1, 5)$ $B(2, -4)$ $C(4, -10)$ $\text{Dist}(A, B) = \sqrt{(2 - -1)^2 + (-4 - 5)^2}$ $= \sqrt{9 + 81}$ $= \sqrt{90}$ $= \sqrt{9}\,\sqrt{10} = \boxed{3\sqrt{10}}$	Figuring out whether these points are collinear becomes a matter of calculating the three lengths and checking to see if any two of them add up to the third one. So, let's calculate the distance between points A and B. Set up the formula and solve for the value.
$\text{Dist}(A, C) = \sqrt{(4 - -1)^2 + (-10 - 5)^2}$ $= \sqrt{25 + 225}$ $= \sqrt{250}$ $= \sqrt{25}\,\sqrt{10} = \boxed{5\sqrt{10}}$ $\qquad$ $\text{Dist}(B, C) = \sqrt{(4 - 2)^2 + (-10 - -4)^2}$ $= \sqrt{4 + 36}$ $= \sqrt{40}$ $= \sqrt{4}\,\sqrt{10} = \boxed{2\sqrt{10}}$	Next, let's find the distance between a second pair of points, A and C. Finally, find the distance between the third pair of points, B and C.
Example are these points collinear? **Yes !** $A(-1, 5)$ $B(2, -4)$ $C(4, -10)$ $3\sqrt{10} + 2\sqrt{10} = 5\sqrt{10}$ $\text{Dist}\ \ \ \text{Dist}\ \ \ \text{Dist}$ $(A, B) + (B, C) = (A, C)$	When you compare the three lengths, you see that two of them added together equal the third. Your conclusion is that the points are collinear. Your conclusion is supported by the graph showing the location of the three points.

Sample problems:

1. Are the points $A(-2, -7)$, $B(0, 3)$ and $C(1, 8)$ collinear?

   Solution: yes

   Explanation: The points A, B, and C are collinear if $AB + BC = AC$, so use the distance formula, $d = \sqrt{\left(x_1 - x_2\right)^2 + \left(y_1 - y_2\right)^2}$, to find AB, BC, and AC.

   Find AB: $AB = \sqrt{\left(-2 - 0\right)^2 + \left(-7 - 3\right)^2} = \sqrt{104} = 2\sqrt{26}$.

   Find BC: $BC = \sqrt{\left(0 - 1\right)^2 + \left(3 - 8\right)^2} = \sqrt{26}$.

   Find AC: $AC = \sqrt{\left(-2 - 1\right)^2 + \left(-7 - 8\right)^2} = \sqrt{234} = 3\sqrt{26}$.

   Check that $AB + BC = AC$: $2\sqrt{26} + \sqrt{26} = 3\sqrt{26} = AC$. Thus, the points are collinear.

2. Are the points $A(-8,-12)$, $B(0,0)$ and $C(4,6)$ collinear?

Solution: yes

Explanation: Find AB: $AB = \sqrt{(-8-0)^2 + (-12-0)^2} = \sqrt{208} = 4\sqrt{13}$.

Find BC: $BC = \sqrt{(0-4)^2 + (0-6)^2} = \sqrt{52} = 2\sqrt{13}$.

Find AC: $AC = \sqrt{(-8-4)^2 + (-12-6)^2} = \sqrt{468} = 6\sqrt{13}$.

Check that $AB + BC = AC$: $4\sqrt{13} + 2\sqrt{13} = 6\sqrt{13} = AC$. Thus, the points are collinear.

3. Are the points $A(-\frac{1}{3},2)$, $B(0,1)$ and $C(\frac{5}{3},\frac{2}{3})$ collinear?

Solution: no

Explanation: Find AB: $AB = \sqrt{\left(-\frac{1}{3}-0\right)^2 + (2-1)^2} = \sqrt{\frac{10}{9}} = \frac{\sqrt{10}}{3}$.

Find BC: $BC = \sqrt{\left(0-\frac{5}{3}\right)^2 + \left(1-\frac{2}{3}\right)^2} = \sqrt{\frac{26}{9}} = \frac{\sqrt{26}}{3}$.

Find AC: $AC = \sqrt{\left(-\frac{1}{3}-\frac{5}{3}\right)^2 + \left(2-\frac{2}{3}\right)^2} = \sqrt{\frac{52}{9}} = \frac{2\sqrt{13}}{3}$.

Check that $AB + BC = AC$: $\frac{\sqrt{10}}{3} + \frac{\sqrt{26}}{3} = \frac{\sqrt{10}+\sqrt{26}}{3} \neq AC$. Thus, the points are not collinear.

Practice problems: *(Answers on page: 443)*

1. Are the points $A(2,7)$, $B(0,1)$ and $C(-3,-8)$ collinear?

2. Are the points $A(-9,5)$, $B(-3,1)$ and $C(3,-4)$ collinear?

3. Are the points $A(6,1)$, $B(8,\frac{1}{3})$ and $C(10,-\frac{1}{3})$ collinear?

Review questions: *(Answers to odd questions on page: 443)*

1. Are the points $A(-2,-1)$, $B(-2,\frac{5}{3})$ and $C(-2,6)$ collinear?

2. Are the points $A(5,-7)$, $B(-2,0)$ and $C(-3,0)$ collinear?

3. Are the points $A(-3,7)$, $B(1,3)$ and $C(5,-1)$ collinear?

4. Are the points $A(-2,-17)$, $B(1,-2)$ and $C(3,12)$ collinear?

5. Are the points $A(-3,-5)$, $B(-1,-\frac{5}{3})$ and $C(2,\frac{10}{3})$ collinear?

Triangles

- **Collinear**: any two or more points that fall on the same line.
- **Distance formula**:

$$d = \sqrt{(x_2 - x_1)^2 + (y_2 - y_1)^2}$$

- Three points are collinear any time that the sum of any two lengths between two points is equal to the third length between two points.
- Three points form a triangle any time that the sum of any two lengths between points is longer than the third length between two points.
- **Pythagorean Theorem**:

$$a^2 + b^2 = c^2$$

- Three points form a right triangle any time any two lengths squared add up to the third length squared.

Example are these points collinear? A(-3,-5) B(3, -3) C(0,6) Dist $(A,B) = \sqrt{(3 - -3)^2 + (-3 - -5)^2}$ $= \sqrt{6^2 + 2^2}$ $= \sqrt{36 + 4}$ $= \sqrt{40} = 6.32...$	Calculate the three lengths between each pair of points. Here are the calculations for (A, B).
Dist $(A,C) = \sqrt{(0 - -3)^2 + (6 - -5)^2}$ $= \sqrt{3^2 + 11^2}$ $= \sqrt{9 + 121}$ $= \sqrt{130} = 11.40...$ Dist $(B,C) = \sqrt{(0 - 3)^2 + (6 - -3)^2}$ $= \sqrt{(-3)^2 + 9^2}$ $= \sqrt{9 + 81}$ $= \sqrt{90} = 9.48...$	Here are the calculations for (A, C) and (B, C).
are these points collinear? **No !** A(-3,-5) B(3, -3) C(0,6) $6.32 + 11.40 \neq 9.48$ $9.48 + 11.40 \neq 6.32$ $6.32 + 9.48 \neq 11.40$	These points are not collinear because no two sums add up to the third one.
Example Are the points a right triangle? **Yes!** A(-3,-5) B(3, -3) C(0,6) $(\sqrt{40})^2 + (\sqrt{90})^2 = (\sqrt{130})^2$ $40 + 90 = 130$	The three points meet the test for being a right triangle: two of their lengths squared do add up to the third length squared.

Sample problems:

1. True or false: Triangle ABC is a right triangle.

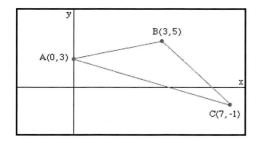

Solution: True

Explanation: Use the Pythagorean Theorem to determine if triangle ABC is a right triangle.

Find the lengths of the three sides: $AC = \sqrt{(0-7)^2 + (3+1)^2} = \sqrt{49+16} = \sqrt{65}$,

$AB = \sqrt{(0-3)^2 + (3-5)^2} = \sqrt{9+4} = \sqrt{13}$, $BC = \sqrt{(3-7)^2 + (5+1)^2} = \sqrt{16+36} = \sqrt{52}$.

Substitute the three lengths into $c^2 = a^2 + b^2$, where c is the hypotenuse and longest side:

$\left(\sqrt{65}\right)^2 = \left(\sqrt{13}\right)^2 + \left(\sqrt{52}\right)^2$; $65 = 13+52$; $65 = 65$, so the triangle is right.

 www.thinkwell.com

2. Do the points $A(-6,-4)$, $B(0,-2)$, and $C(-10,8)$ form the vertices of a right triangle?
   Solution: Yes

   Explanation: Find the lengths of the three sides: $AB = \sqrt{(-6-0)^2 + (-4--2)^2} = \sqrt{40}$,
   $BC = \sqrt{(0--10)^2 + (-2-8)^2} = \sqrt{200}$, $AC = \sqrt{(-6--10)^2 + (-4-8)^2} = \sqrt{160}$.
   Use the Pythagorean Theorem to determine if the three sides form a right triangle:
   $\left(\sqrt{40}\right)^2 + \left(\sqrt{160}\right)^2 = \left(\sqrt{200}\right)^2$; $40 + 160 = 200$, so triangle ABC is a right triangle.

3. Do the points $A(-4,1)$, $B(1,4)$, and $C(-6,-1)$ form the vertices of a right triangle?
   Solution: No

   Explanation: Find the lengths of the three sides: $AB = \sqrt{(-4-1)^2 + (1-4)^2} = \sqrt{34}$,
   $BC = \sqrt{(1--6)^2 + (4--1)^2} = \sqrt{74}$, $AC = \sqrt{(-4--6)^2 + (1--1)^2} = \sqrt{8}$.
   Use the Pythagorean Theorem to determine if the three sides form a right triangle:
   $\left(\sqrt{34}\right)^2 + \left(\sqrt{8}\right)^2 = \left(\sqrt{74}\right)^2$; $34 + 8 \neq 74$, so triangle ABC is not a right triangle.

Practice problems: *(Answers on page: 443)*

1. True or false: Triangle ABC is a right triangle.

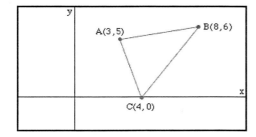

2. Do the points $A(-2,5)$, $B(12,3)$, and $C(10,-11)$ form the vertices of a right triangle?
3. Do the points $A(-5,3)$, $B(6,0)$, and $C(5,7)$ form the vertices of a right triangle?

Review questions: *(Answers to odd questions on page: 443)*

1. Do the points $A(4,-3)$, $B(0,-3)$, and $C(4,2)$ form the vertices of a right triangle?
2. Do the points $A(-2,5)$, $B(1,3)$, and $C(-1,0)$ form the vertices of a right triangle?
3. Do the points $A(0,0)$, $B(2,1)$, and $C(3,-7)$ form the vertices of a right triangle?
4. Do the points $A(-6,3)$, $B(3,-5)$, and $C(-1,5)$ form the vertices of a right triangle?
5. Do the points $A(4,-3)$, $B(7,1)$, and $C(2,1)$ form the vertices of a right triangle?

Finding the Center-Radius Form of the Equation of a Circle

- A **circle** is the set of all points on a plane which are the same distance from a given point, the center of the circle.
- The **center of a circle** is usually given as the ordered pair (h, k) where h is the x-value and k is the y-value of the centerpoint.
- Any point (x, y) mentioned in relation to a circle is found on the circumference of the circle.
- **Radius** is the distance from the center of a circle to any point on its circumference.
- The **equation of a circle** $(x - h)^2 + (y - k)^2 = r^2$

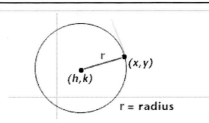

This diagram shows the major parts of a circle.

$$\sqrt{(x - h)^2 + (y - k)^2} = r$$

You can find the length of the radius by using the distance formula with the endpoints (h, k) and (x, y).

Example find the equation for the circle

radius 5 , center (-2,3)

r　　　　h　k

$(x - h)^2 + (y - k)^2 = r^2$

$(x - -2)^2 + (y - 3)^2 = 5^2$

$(x + 2)^2 + (y - 3)^2 = 25$

When you are given the center and the radius, creating the equation for the circle is a matter of substituting into the standard equation for a circle. Here, you're given the center (h, k) is $(-2, 3)$, so we substitute -2 for h and 3 for k into the equation.

Notice: The signs change because h and k are subtracting in the standard equation. You are given the radius is 5 so you substitute that into the equation and square it. The graph shows a sketch of the circle.

Sample problems:

1. Write the equation of a circle if the center is at $(-3, 5)$ and the radius is 6.

    Solution: $(x+3)^2 +(y-5)^2 = 36$

    Explanation: Substitute the radius, 6, and the (h, k) values from the center into the equation of a circle, $(x-h)^2 +(y-k)^2 = r^2$: $(x--3)^2 +(y-5)^2 = 6^2$. Simplify: $(x+3)^2 +(y-5)^2 = 36$.

2. Write the equation of a circle if the center is at the origin and a point on the circle is $\left(0, 2\dfrac{1}{2}\right)$.

    Solution: $x^2 + y^2 = 6\dfrac{1}{4}$

    Explanation: The radius of the circle is the distance between the center of the circle and a point on the circle. In this case, the distance is from the origin, $(0,0)$, and $\left(0, 2\dfrac{1}{2}\right)$, so the radius is $2\dfrac{1}{2}$.

    Substitute that radius and the (h, k) values from the center, $(0, 0)$, into the equation

    of a circle: $(x-0)^2 +(y-0)^2 = \left(2\dfrac{1}{2}\right)^2$. Simplify: $x^2 + y^2 = 6\dfrac{1}{4}$.

3. Write the equation of a circle if the center is at $(1, -2)$ and a point on the circle is $(5, -2)$.

    Solution: $(x-1)^2 +(y+2)^2 = 16$

    Explanation: The radius of the circle is the length of the vertical line between $(1, -2)$ and $(5, -2)$, so $r = 4$. Substitute that radius and the (h, k) values from the center into the equation of a circle, then simplify: $(x-1)^2 +(y--2)^2 = 4^2$; $(x-1)^2 +(y+2)^2 = 16$.

Practice problems: *(Answers on page: 443)*

1. Write the equation of the circle with a center at $(3, -2)$ and radius $\sqrt{5}$.

2. Write the equation of a circle if the center is at the origin and the *diameter* is 10.

3. True or false: The equation $x^2 +(y+2)^2 = 1$ describes a circle with the center at $(0, 2)$ and the radius is 1.

Review questions: *(Answers to odd questions on page: 443)*

1. Write the equation of a circle with a center at $(-4,2)$ and a diameter of 10.

2. Write the equation of a circle with a center at $(0,0)$ and a radius of $\sqrt{7}$.

3. Write the equation of the circle in which the endpoints of its diameter are $A(0,0)$ and $B(0,6)$.

4. Write the equation of the circle with a radius of $\dfrac{5}{2}$ and a center at the origin.

5. Write the equation of the circle with a radius of 3 and a center at $(4,2)$.

Finding the Center and Radius of a Circle

- The **equation of a circle**: $(x-h)^2 + (y-k)^2 = r^2$
- Completing the square:
  - Reduce the equation, if there is a coefficient in front of x^2.
  - Move the constant to the right.
  - Complete the square.
- Watch your signs when stating the center of the circle from the equation.
  The equation reads $(x-h)$ and $(y-k)$ so the signs change from the equation to the ordered pair notation.

Example Find the Center and Radius $x^2 + 6x + y^2 + 8y + 9 = 0$ $x^2 + 6x + y^2 + 8y = -9$ $x^2 + 6x + \underline{9} + y^2 + 8y + \underline{\quad} = -9 + \underline{9} + \underline{\quad}$ *add to both sides* *take $\frac{1}{2}$ and square* $\frac{1}{2} \cdot 6 = 3$ $3^2 = 9$	Frequently you are given an equation that you think is for a circle because it has terms with both x^2 and y^2. Try to convert the equation to your standard form for a circle by completing the square. Do the completing the square process once for the x-terms and a second time for the y-terms. Here note that $6/2 = 3$ and $3^2 = 9$. So 9 is added to the equation for the x-terms.
$x^2 + 6x + \underline{9} + y^2 + 8y + \underline{16} = -9 + \underline{9} + \underline{16}$	Next work with the y-terms. You can see that $8/2 = 4$, and $4^2 = 16$. So, 16 is being added to the equation.
$(x+3)^2 + (y+4)^2 = 16$	Now write the completed squares as binomials and that gives the left side of the circle equation. The total on the right side represents the radius squared.
Center: $(-3,-4)$ **Radius:** $\sqrt{16} = 4$	In this form you know your center and your radius.
Example Find the Center and Radius $x^2 - 4x + y^2 + 12y = -4$ $x^2 - 4x + \underline{4} + y^2 + 12y + \underline{36} = -4 + \underline{4} + \underline{36}$ ↑ watch your signs ! $(x \ominus 2)^2 + (y + 6)^2 = 36$ **Center:** $(+2,-6)$ **Radius:** $\sqrt{36} = 6$	This example works the same way. 1. Complete the square for the x-terms. 2. Complete the square for the y-terms. 3. Write the binomials on the left side. 4. Note the center and the radius.

Sample problems:

1. Determine the center and the radius of the circle described by $3x^2 - 18x + 3y^2 + 30y = -27$.
   <u>Solution</u>: $(3, -5)$; $r = 5$

Explanation: Express the equation $3x^2 - 18x + 3y^2 + 30y = -27$ in the form of the equation of a circle, $(x-h)^2 + (y-k)^2 = r^2$, by completing the square for both x and y.

Divide the equation by 3: $x^2 - 6x + y^2 + 10y = -9$.

Add 9 to both sides, since $\left(\dfrac{-6}{2}\right)^2 = 9$: $(x^2 - 6x + 9) + y^2 + 10y = -9 + 9$.

Add 25 to both sides, since $\left(\dfrac{10}{2}\right)^2 = 25$: $(x^2 - 6x + 9) + (y^2 + 10y + 25) = -9 + 9 + 25$.

Factor each trinomial and simplify the right side: $(x-3)^2 + (y+5)^2 = 25$.

Now, consider the general equation of a circle, $(x-h)^2 + (y-k)^2 = r^2$ to determine the center, (h, k), and the radius. The center is $(3, -5)$ and $r^2 = 25$, so $r = 5$.

2. Determine the center and the radius of the circle described by $x^2 - x + y^2 - 3y = -\dfrac{3}{2}$.

Solution: $\left(\dfrac{1}{2}, \dfrac{3}{2}\right)$; $r = 1$

Explanation: Complete the square of the x-terms by adding $\dfrac{1}{4}$ to both sides, since $\left(\dfrac{-1}{2}\right)^2 = \dfrac{1}{4}$:

$\left(x^2 - x + \dfrac{1}{4}\right) + y^2 - 3y = -\dfrac{3}{2} + \dfrac{1}{4}$. Complete the square of the y-terms by adding $\dfrac{9}{4}$ to both sides,

since $\left(-\dfrac{3}{2}\right)^2 = \dfrac{9}{4}$: $\left(x^2 - x + \dfrac{1}{4}\right) + \left(y^2 - 3y + \dfrac{9}{4}\right) = -\dfrac{3}{2} + \dfrac{1}{4} + \dfrac{9}{4}$. Factor each trinomial and

simplify the right: $\left(x - \dfrac{1}{2}\right)^2 + \left(y - \dfrac{3}{2}\right)^2 = 1$. Determine the center and radius of the circle from

the equation: $\left(\dfrac{1}{2}, \dfrac{3}{2}\right)$ is the center and $r^2 = 1$, so $r = 1$.

3. Determine the center and the radius of the circle described by $x^2 - 2\sqrt{2}x + y^2 - 4\sqrt{2}y = 6$.

Solution: $(\sqrt{2}, 2\sqrt{2})$; $r = 4$

Explanation: Complete the square for x and y: $(x^2 - 2\sqrt{2}x + 2) + (y^2 - 4\sqrt{2}y + 8) = 6 + 2 + 8$.

Factor and simplify: $(x - \sqrt{2})^2 + (y - 2\sqrt{2})^2 = 16$. So the center is at $(\sqrt{2}, 2\sqrt{2})$ and $r^2 = 16$, so $r = \sqrt{16} = 4$.

Practice problems: *(Answers on page: 443)*

1. Determine the center and the radius of the circle described by $4x^2 - 24x + 4y^2 + 8y = 12$.

2. Determine the center and the radius of the circle described by $x^2 - \dfrac{2}{3}x + y^2 - \dfrac{4}{3}y = \dfrac{31}{9}$.

3. Determine the center and the radius of the circle described by $x^2 - \dfrac{4}{3}x + y^2 - y = \dfrac{11}{36}$.

Review questions: *(Answers to odd questions on page: 443)*

1. Determine the center and the radius of the circle described by $x^2 - 6x + y^2 + 8y = 3$.

2. Determine the center and the radius of the circle described by $x^2 - 4x + y^2 - 6y = -9$.

3. Determine the center and the radius of the circle described by $x^2 + 4\sqrt{3}x + y^2 + 2\sqrt{3}y = -6$.

4. Determine the center and the radius of the circle described by $\left(x^2 - 4x + 4\right) + \left(y^2 + 6y + 9\right) = 16$.

5. Determine the center and the radius of the circle described by $x^2 - x - y^2 + \frac{2}{3}y = -\frac{1}{9}$.

Decoding the Circle Formula

- **Equation of a circle**: $(x - h)^2 + (y - k)^2 = r^2$
- The **center of a circle** is represented by the point (h, k).
- The **radius** is the distance from the center of a circle to any point on its circumference.

Example Find the Center and Radius **Suppose:** *you are given a equation* $(x - 4)^2 + (y + 6)^2 = 49$	When you first look at an equation, a natural question is what kind of line or curve is it representing.
Using the Equation for a Circle center is *(h,k)* radius is *r* $(x - 4)^2 + (y + 6)^2 = 49$ $(y - (-6))^2$ *So, we have a Circle* **Center: (4 ,-6)** *take the opposite sign*	An equation that has an x^2 and a y^2 with terms being added together positively will likely be a circle. When defining the center of the circle remember to change the signs from the standard form of the equation. The equation states $(x - h)$ and $(y - k)$, showing both center values as negative, while the ordered pair (h, k) shows both values as positive.
Radius: $\sqrt{49} = 7$ *must be positive*	The radius will be the square root of the constant on the right side of the equation. It will always be positive because it represents a distance.
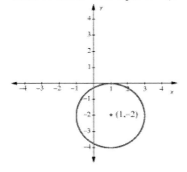	And once you know the center and the radius of a circle, you can easily sketch its graph.

Sample problems:

1. Given the equation $(x + 1)^2 + (y - 5)^2 = 9$, find the center and the radius of the circle.

   <u>Solution:</u> $(-1, 5)$; $r = 3$

   <u>Explanation:</u> Consider the standard form of the equation of a circle: $(x - h)^2 + (y - k)^2 = r^2$.

   Express the given equation in standard form: $(x - (-1))^2 + (y - 5)^2 = 3^2$. Identify the center and radius of the circle from the equation: $(-1, 5)$ and $r = 3$

2. True or false: The equation $(x - 1)^2 + (y + 2)^2 = 4$ describes the graph below.

Solution: True

Explanation: Identify the center and radius from the equation expressed in standard form: $(x-1)^2 + (y-(-2))^2$. So, the center is at $(1, -2)$ and the radius is 2. That center and radius agree with the circle in the graph.

3. True or false: The equation $(x+4)^2 + (y+1)^2 = 4$ describes the graph below.

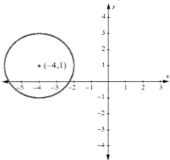

Solution: False

Explanation: Identify the center and radius from the equation expressed in standard form: $(x-(-4))^2 + (y-(-1)^2)$. So, the center of this circle is at $(-4, -1)$, but the center of the graphed circle is at $(-4, 1)$.

Practice problems: *(Answers on page: 443)*

1. Find the center and radius of the circle $(x-2)^2 + y^2 = 9$.

2. Sketch a graph of the equation $(x+1)^2 + (y-2)^2 = 4$.

3. Find the center and radius of the circle $(x+4)^2 + (y-1)^2 = 5$.

Review questions: *(Answers to odd questions on page: 443)*

1. Find the center and radius of the circle $(x+3)^2 + (y-4)^2 = 3$.

2. Find the center and radius of the circle $(x-3)^2 + (y+5)^2 = 27$.

3. Find the center and radius of the circle $(x-9)^2 + (y-3)^2 = 36$.

4. Find the center and radius of the circle $x^2 + y^2 = 4.44$.

5. Find the center and radius of the circle $x^2 + (y+4)^2 = 121$.

Solving Word Problems Involving Circles

- **Equation of a circle:**
  $(x-h)^2 + (y-k)^2 = r^2$
- **Distance Formula:**
  $$d = \sqrt{\left(x_2 - x_1\right)^2 + \left(y_2 - y_1\right)^2}$$
- **Midpoint Formula:**
  $$\left(\frac{x_1 + x_2}{2}, \frac{y_1 + y_2}{2}\right)$$

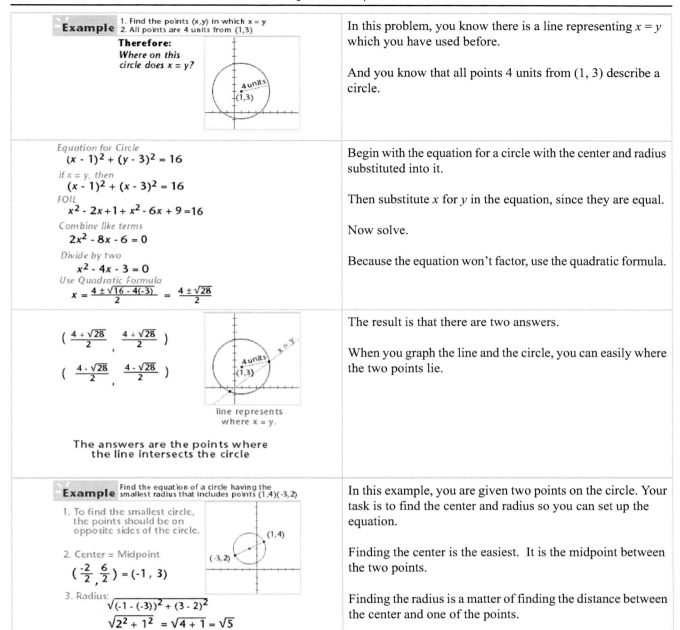

Example 1. Find the points (x,y) in which x = y
2. All points are 4 units from (1,3)

Therefore:
Where on this
circle does x = y?

In this problem, you know there is a line representing $x = y$ which you have used before.

And you know that all points 4 units from (1, 3) describe a circle.

Equation for Circle
$$(x - 1)^2 + (y - 3)^2 = 16$$
if x = y, then
$$(x - 1)^2 + (x - 3)^2 = 16$$
FOIL
$$x^2 - 2x + 1 + x^2 - 6x + 9 = 16$$
Combine like terms
$$2x^2 - 8x - 6 = 0$$
Divide by two
$$x^2 - 4x - 3 = 0$$
Use Quadratic Formula
$$x = \frac{4 \pm \sqrt{16 - 4(-3)}}{2} = \frac{4 \pm \sqrt{28}}{2}$$

Begin with the equation for a circle with the center and radius substituted into it.

Then substitute x for y in the equation, since they are equal.

Now solve.

Because the equation won't factor, use the quadratic formula.

$$\left(\frac{4 + \sqrt{28}}{2}, \frac{4 + \sqrt{28}}{2} \right)$$

$$\left(\frac{4 - \sqrt{28}}{2}, \frac{4 - \sqrt{28}}{2} \right)$$

line represents
where x = y.

The answers are the points where
the line intersects the circle

The result is that there are two answers.

When you graph the line and the circle, you can easily where the two points lie.

Example Find the equation of a circle having the smallest radius that includes points (1,4)(-3,2)

1. To find the smallest circle, the points should be on opposite sides of the circle.

2. Center = Midpoint
$$\left(\frac{-2}{2}, \frac{6}{2} \right) = (-1, 3)$$

3. Radius:
$$\sqrt{(-1 - (-3))^2 + (3 - 2)^2}$$
$$\sqrt{2^2 + 1^2} = \sqrt{4 + 1} = \sqrt{5}$$

4. Find the Equation
$$(x + 1)^2 + (y - 3)^2 = 5$$

In this example, you are given two points on the circle. Your task is to find the center and radius so you can set up the equation.

Finding the center is the easiest. It is the midpoint between the two points.

Finding the radius is a matter of finding the distance between the center and one of the points.

Writing the equation involves substitution.

Sample problems:

1. Find the equation of the circle with the smallest radius that contains the points $(2, 4)$ and $(-4, 2)$.

   Solution: $(x+1)^2 + (y-3)^2 = 10$

   Explanation: The smallest circle that contains these points must have a diameter with $(2,4)$ and $(-4,2)$ as endpoints. So, the midpoint of $(2,4)$ and $(-4,2)$ will be the center of the circle.

   Use the midpoint formula to find the center: $\left(\frac{-4+2}{2}, \frac{2+4}{2} \right) = (-1,3)$.

   To find the radius, compute the distance from the center to either of the given points using the distance formula:

   $r = \sqrt{(2+1)^2 + (4-3)^2} = \sqrt{10}$. Now, substitute $(-1,3)$ for (h,k) and $\sqrt{10}$ for r into the standard equation of a circle,

   $(x-h)^2 + (y-k)^2 = r^2$, and simplify: $(x-(-1))^2 + (y-3)^2 = (\sqrt{10})^2$; $(x+1)^2 + (y-3)^2 = 10$.

2. Given a circle with radius 3 and center $(-2, 5)$, find all points (x, y) on that circle in which $y = -2x$.

   Solution: $(-1.073, 2.146)$ and $(-3.727, 7.454)$

Explanation: All the points on the circle where $y = -2x$ can be represented graphically.
Visualize the graph of the circle and the line $y = -2x$. The points on the circle where $y = -2x$ are the point(s) where the line and circle intersect. Therefore, in order to determine the points where $y = -2x$, solve the system of equations: $(x+2)^2 + (y-5)^2 = 9$ and $y = -2x$.
Solve the system using the substitution method, so substitute $-2x$ into the equation of the circle for y: $(x+2)^2 + (-2x-5)^2 = 9$. Next, simplify: $x^2 + 4x + 4 + 4x^2 + 20x + 25 = 9$; $5x^2 + 24x + 29 = 9$.
Set the equation equal to zero: $5x^2 + 24x + 20 = 0$. Solve for x using the quadratic formula:
$$x = \frac{-24 \pm \sqrt{(24)^2 - 4(5)(20)}}{2(5)} = \frac{-24 \pm \sqrt{176}}{10} = \frac{-24 \pm 13.27}{10} = -1.073 \text{ or } -3.727.$$
So the x-coordinates of the 2 points on the circle where $y = -2x$ are -1.073 and -3.727.
Find the y-coordinates by substituting those x-values into $y = -2x$:
$y = -2(-1.073) = 2.146$ and $y = -2(-3.727) = 7.454$.
So the points on the circle in which $y = -2x$ are $(-1.073, 2.146)$ and $(-3.727, 7.454)$.

3. Let the center of the circle defined by $(x+5)^2 + (y+4)^2 = 1$ be point A.
   And let the center of the circle defined by $(x-3)^2 + (y-2)^2 = 1$ be point B.
   Write the equation of the circle whose diameter endpoints are at A and B.

   Solution: $(x+1)^2 + (y+1)^2 = 25$

   Explanation: Find the coordinates of A and B.
   Point A is the center of the circle whose equation is $(x+5)^2 + (y+4)^2 = 1$, so $A = (-5, -4)$.
   Point B is the center of the circle whose equation is $(x-3)^2 + (y-2)^2 = 1$, so $B = (3, 2)$.
   Use the midpoint formula to determine the center of the new circle, since the center is the midpoint
   between A and B: center $= \left(\dfrac{-5+3}{2}, \dfrac{-4+2}{2} \right) = (-1, -1)$. Substitute the values from the new
   center and either A or B into the distance formula to determine the radius:
   $r = \sqrt{(3--1)^2 + (2--1)^2} = \sqrt{16+9} = \sqrt{25} = 5$. Now, write the equation of the
   circle using the center, $(-1, -1)$ and the radius, 5: $(x+1)^2 + (y+1)^2 = 25$.

Practice problems: *(Answers on page: 444)*

1. Given a circle with center $(5, -1)$ and radius $2\sqrt{10}$, find all points on that circle such that $-x = y$.

2. Write the equation of a circle whose diameter endpoints are
   1) the center of the circle given by the equation $x^2 + y^2 - 2x + 6y = 15$ and
   2) the point $(7, 5)$.

3. Write the equation of a circle whose diameter endpoints are the points on a circle
   with center $(0, 0)$ and radius 1, where $y = 1 - x$.

Review questions: *(Answers to odd questions on page: 444)*

1. Find the equation of a circle whose diameter endpoints are $(1, 7)$ and $(5, 3)$.

2. Find the equation of the circle whose diameter endpoints are $(0, 0)$ and $(4, 6)$.

3. Find the equation of the circle with the smallest possible radius that contains the points
   $(-2, 6)$ and $(4, -10)$.

4. Find the distance from the center of the circle described by $x^2 + y^2 - 2x + 6y = 15$ to
   the point $(3, -2)$.

5. Find the distance between the centers of the two circles whose equations are
   $x^2 + y^2 = 25$ and $x^2 - 32x + y^2 - 24y = -175$.

Graphing Equations by Locating Points

- One way to graph a line is to pick some x-values, substitute them into the function to find the corresponding y-values, and graph the points.
- Whenever you see one variable squared and the other variable not squared, expect your graph to be a parabola. If it is the x that is squared, the parabola will open up or down. If it is the y that is squared, the parabola will open to one side.
- Whenever you see a variable inside an absolute value, expect a V-shaped graph

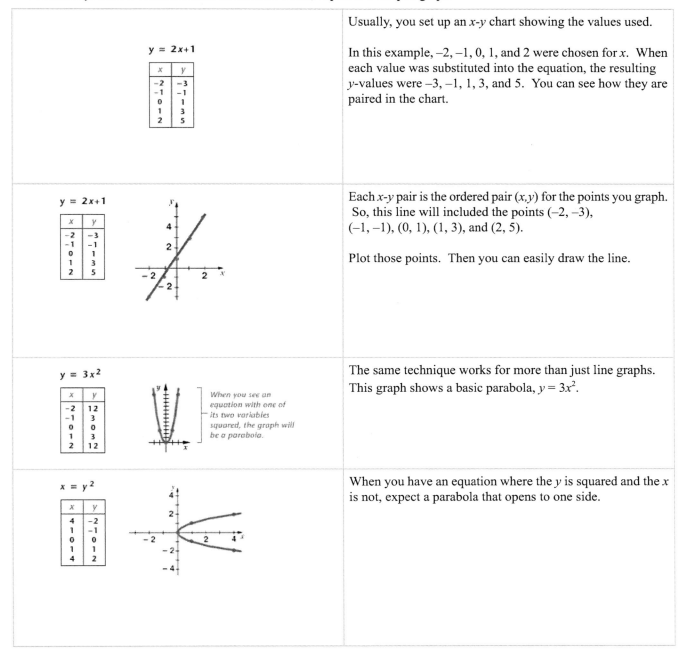

$y = 2x+1$

x	y
-2	-3
-1	-1
0	1
1	3
2	5

Usually, you set up an x-y chart showing the values used.

In this example, $-2, -1, 0, 1,$ and 2 were chosen for x. When each value was substituted into the equation, the resulting y-values were $-3, -1, 1, 3,$ and 5. You can see how they are paired in the chart.

$y = 2x+1$

x	y
-2	-3
-1	-1
0	1
1	3
2	5

Each x-y pair is the ordered pair (x,y) for the points you graph. So, this line will included the points $(-2, -3)$, $(-1, -1)$, $(0, 1)$, $(1, 3)$, and $(2, 5)$.

Plot those points. Then you can easily draw the line.

$y = 3x^2$

x	y
-2	12
-1	3
0	0
1	3
2	12

When you see an equation with one of its two variables squared, the graph will be a parabola.

The same technique works for more than just line graphs. This graph shows a basic parabola, $y = 3x^2$.

$x = y^2$

x	y
4	-2
1	-1
0	0
1	1
4	2

When you have an equation where the y is squared and the x is not, expect a parabola that opens to one side.

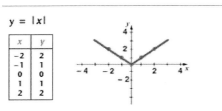

$y = |x|$

Here is an example that graphs as a "V". One example of the effect of the absolute value is to pair both –2 and 2 for x with 2 for y.

Sample problems:

1. Sketch the graph of $y = 5 - |x|$.

   Solution:

   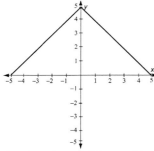

   Explanation: Make a table to determine several coordinate pairs. Any value of x may be used in the table, however typically -2, -1, 0, 1, and 2 are chosen. Substitute each x value into $y = 5 - |x|$:

   $x = -2$: $\quad y = 5 - |-2| = 5 - 2 = 3 \implies (-2,3)$
   $x = -1$: $\quad y = 5 - |-1| = 5 - 1 = 4 \implies (-1,4)$
   $x = 0$: $\quad y = 5 - |0| = 5 - 0 = 5 \implies (0,5)$
   $x = 1$: $\quad y = 5 - |1| = 5 - 1 = 4 \implies (1,4)$
   $x = 2$: $\quad y = 5 - |2| = 5 - 2 = 3 \implies (2,3)$

   Plot the points to sketch the graph.

x	y
-2	3
-1	4
0	5
1	4
2	3

2. Sketch the graph of $x = (y+1)(y+2)$.

   Solution:

   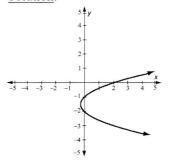

www.thinkwell.com

Explanation: Make a table to determine several coordinate pairs. Since x is a function of y, choose values for y and substitute each one into the equation to find the corresponding x. Plot the points to sketch the graph.

x	y
0	-2
0	-1
2	0
6	1
12	2

3. Sketch the graph of $y = -2(x-1)^2 + 1$.
   Solution:

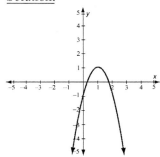

Explanation: Make a table to determine several coordinate pairs. Choose five values for x and substitute each one into the equation to find the corresponding y-values. Plot the points from the table to sketch the graph.

x	y
-2	-17
-1	-7
0	-1
1	1
2	-1

Practice problems: *(Answers on page: 444)*

1. Sketch the graph of $y = 4 - x$.

2. Sketch the graph of $y = x^2 + 3$.

3. Sketch the graph of $x = y^2 - y + 1$.

Review questions: *(Answers to odd questions on page: 444)*

1. Sketch the graph of $y = 5 - 2x$.

2. Sketch the graph of $y = |x - 1|$.

3. Sketch the graph of $y = (x+1)(x-3)$.

4. Sketch the graph of $x = y(y+2)$.

5. Sketch the graph of $x = y^3 - 5$.

Finding the x- and y-Intercepts of an Equation

- An **x-intercept** is a point where a curve crosses the *x*-axis.
- A **y-intercept** is a point where a curve crosses the *y*-axis.
- A line will have one *x*-intercept and one *y*-intercept (with the exception of horizontal or vertical lines).
- A curve may have more than one of either intercept. A curve may have none of either or both intercepts.

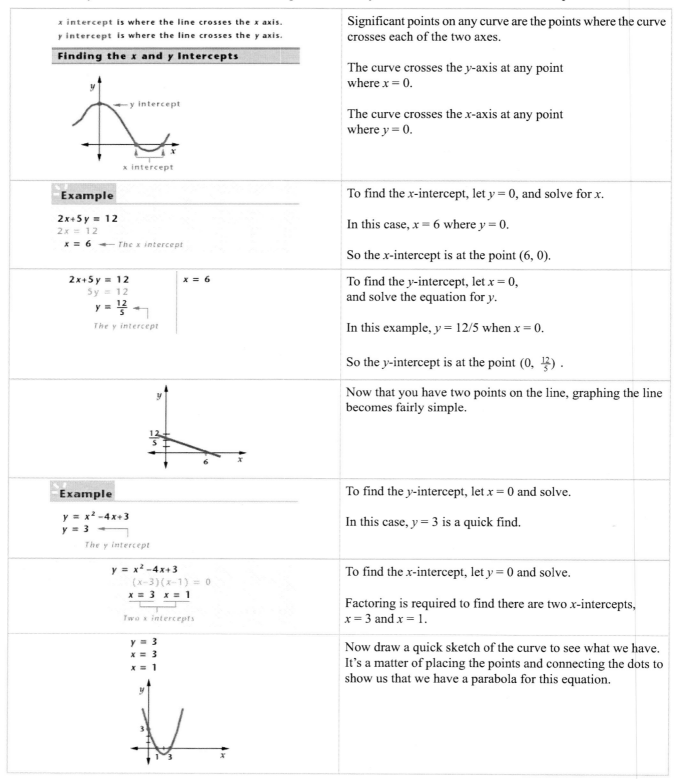

x intercept is where the line crosses the x axis.
y intercept is where the line crosses the y axis.

Finding the *x* and *y* Intercepts

← y intercept

x intercept

Significant points on any curve are the points where the curve crosses each of the two axes.

The curve crosses the *y*-axis at any point where $x = 0$.

The curve crosses the *x*-axis at any point where $y = 0$.

Example

$2x + 5y = 12$
$2x = 12$
$x = 6$ ←— The x intercept

To find the *x*-intercept, let $y = 0$, and solve for *x*.

In this case, $x = 6$ where $y = 0$.

So the *x*-intercept is at the point $(6, 0)$.

$2x + 5y = 12$ $x = 6$
$5y = 12$
$y = \dfrac{12}{5}$ ←

The y intercept

To find the *y*-intercept, let $x = 0$, and solve the equation for *y*.

In this example, $y = 12/5$ when $x = 0$.

So the *y*-intercept is at the point $(0, \frac{12}{5})$.

Now that you have two points on the line, graphing the line becomes fairly simple.

Example

$y = x^2 - 4x + 3$
$y = 3$ ←

The y intercept

To find the *y*-intercept, let $x = 0$ and solve.

In this case, $y = 3$ is a quick find.

$y = x^2 - 4x + 3$
$(x - 3)(x - 1) = 0$
$x = 3 \quad x = 1$

Two x intercepts

To find the *x*-intercept, let $y = 0$ and solve.

Factoring is required to find there are two *x*-intercepts, $x = 3$ and $x = 1$.

$y = 3$
$x = 3$
$x = 1$

Now draw a quick sketch of the curve to see what we have. It's a matter of placing the points and connecting the dots to show us that we have a parabola for this equation.

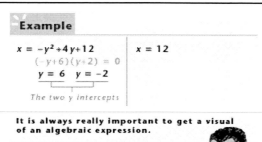

Example

$$x = -y^2 + 4y + 12 \qquad x = 12$$
$$(-y+6)(y+2) = 0$$
$$y = 6 \quad y = -2$$

The two y intercepts

This equation follows the exact same procedures as the two examples above.

Find an x-intercept: when $y = 0$, $x = 12$. Find y-intercepts: when $x = 0$, $y = 6$ and $y = -2$.

It is always really important to get a visual of an algebraic expression.

Finding the x and y Intercepts

Example

$$x = -y^2 + 4y + 12$$
$$(-y+6)(y+2) = 0$$
$$y = 6 \quad y = -2$$

$$x = 12$$
$$y = 6$$
$$y = -2$$

Graphing this one again reveals a parabola, but one opening to the left.

Using these intercepts gives a quick and easy way to sketch the graph of an equation. Using them lets us visually understand what the equation is saying.

Sample problems:

1. Find the y-intercept of $9y = 2x^2 - 18$.

   Solution: $(0, -2)$

   Explanation: To find the y-intercept, substitute $x = 0$ into $9y = 2x^2 - 18$ and solve for y: $9y = 2(0)^2 - 18$; $9y = -18$; $y = -2$. So, the y-intercept is located at $(0, -2)$.

2. Find the x and y-intercepts of $y = 2x^2 + x - 1$.

   Solution: x-intercepts: $\dfrac{1}{2}$ and -1, y-intercepts: -1

   Explanation: To find the x-intercept, substitute $y = 0$ into $y = 2x^2 + x - 1$ and solve for x: $2x^2 + x - 1 = 0$. Solve this equation by factoring the trinomial, then set each factor equal to 0, and then solve each equation for x: $(2x-1)(x+1) = 0$; $2x - 1 = 0$ or $x + 1 = 0$; $2x = 1$ or $x = -1$; $x = \frac{1}{2}$ or $x = -1$. Thus, the x-intercepts are $\frac{1}{2}$ and -1. To find the y-intercept, substitute $x = 0$ into $y = 2x^2 + x - 1$ and solve for y: $y = 2(0)^2 + (0) - 1 = 2(0) + 0 - 1 = -1$. Thus, the y-intercept is -1.

3. Find the x and y-intercepts of $\dfrac{x^2}{4} + \dfrac{y^2}{9} = 1$.

   Solution: x-intercepts: ± 2, y-intercept: ± 3

   Explanation: To find the x-intercept, substitute $y = 0$ into the equation and solve for x: $\frac{x^2}{4} + \frac{(0)^2}{9} = 1$; $\frac{x^2}{4} + 0 = 1$; $\frac{x^2}{4} = 1$; $x^2 = 4$; $\sqrt{x^2} = \sqrt{4}$; $x = \pm 2$. Thus, the x-intercepts are 2 and -2. To find the y-intercept, substitute $x = 0$ into the equation and solve for y: $\frac{(0)^2}{4} + \frac{y^2}{9} = 1$; $0 + \frac{y^2}{9} = 1$; $\frac{y^2}{9} = 1$; $y^2 = 9$; $\sqrt{y^2} = \sqrt{9}$; $y = \pm 3$. Thus, the y-intercepts are 3 and -3.

Practice problems: *(Answers on page: 444)*

1. Find the x-intercepts for the equation $y = x^2 + 2x - 3$.

2. Given the equation $y = -\frac{1}{3}x + \frac{5}{3}$, find the y-intercept.

3. Given the equation $\frac{x^2}{36} + \frac{y^2}{4} = 1$, find a y-intercept.

Review questions: *(Answers to odd questions on page: 444)*

1. Find the y-intercept for the equation $y = x^2 - 8$

2. Find the y-intercept for the equation $y = -x^2 - 2$

3. Find the x-intercepts for the equation $y = 2x^2 - 6x$

4. Find the x-intercepts for the equation $y = x^2 + 6x + 8$

5. Find the y-intercept for the equation $y = 2x^2 + 4x + 3$

Functions and the Vertical Line Test

- A **relation** is a set of ordered pairs in which any given x-value may be paired with more than one y-value.
- A **function** is a set of ordered pairs in which each x-value is matched with exactly one y-value.

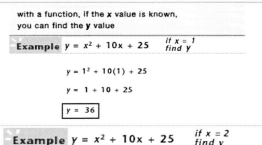

If each time you use a specific value for x in an equation, you get exactly one value for y, then the equation is a function.

In this example, solving for a random value, $x = 1$, you get exactly one answer, $y = 36$. Only one y-value is possible for this or any other x, so the equation qualifies as a function.

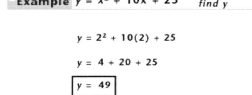

In this example, if you solve for $x = 2$, you get exactly one answer, $y = 49$. Only one y-value is possible for this or any other x, so the equation qualifies as a function.

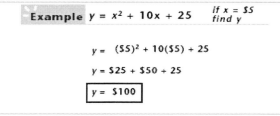

In this example, if you solve for $x = \$5$, you get exactly one answer, $y = \$100$. Only one y-value is possible for this or any other x, so the equation qualifies as a function.

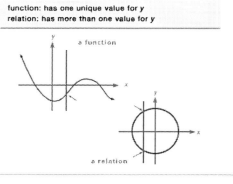

The graph on the left represents a function. No matter where you place the vertical line it passes through only one point on the curve. For each x there is only one (x,y) point.

The graph on the right does not represent a function because the vertical line passes through more than one point. This type of graph represents a relation.

Sample problems:

1. True or false: The following is a graph of a function.

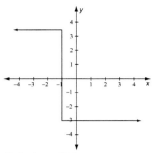

Solution: False

Explanation: Using the vertical line test we can see that at the value $x = -1$, there are multiple values for y. Therefore, it fails the vertical line test and is not a function.

2. True or false: The following is a graph of a function.

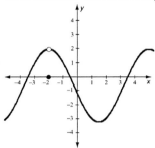

Solution: True

Explanation: Using the vertical line test we can determine that for the given graph every value of x leads to only one value of y (even at $x = -2$ when the function jumps from a height of $y = 2$ down to $y = 0$). Therefore, the given graph is of a function.

3. True or false: The following is a graph of a function.

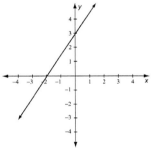

Solution: True

Explanation: Using the vertical line test we can determine that for the given graph every value of x leads to only one value of y. Therefore, the given graph is of a function.

Practice problems: *(Answers on page: 444)*

1. True or false: The following is a graph of a function.

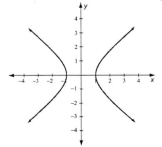

2. True or false: The following is a graph of a function.

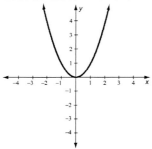

3. True or false: The following is a graph of a function.

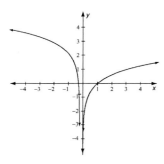

Review questions: *(Answers to odd questions on page: 444)*

1. Let $f = \{(-1,3),(-2,5),(-3,7)\}$. Is f a function?

2. True or false: The following is a graph of a function.

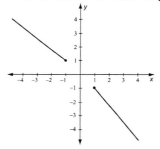

3. True or false: The following is a graph of a function.

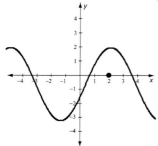

 www.thinkwell.com

4. True or false: The following graph is a function.

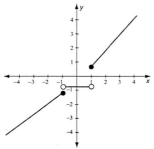

5. True or false: The following table represents a function.

X	y
-2	16
-1	4
0	0
1	4
2	16

Identifying Functions

- A **function** is an equation where you get exactly one result for each value you put in.
- **Vertical line test** for a function of x means that for every value of x there exists at most one value of y.

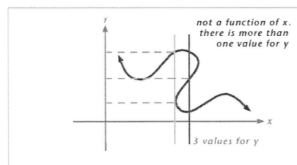

not a function of x.
there is more than
one value for y

3 values for y

For an equation to be a function of x, it must pass the vertical line test. This means that every value of x has no more than one value of y; i.e., a vertical line will intersect a given curve no more than once.

when given an algebraic expression, how do you identify a function?

Example $2x + 3y = 7$ *is this a function of x?*

$$3y = 7 - 2x$$

$$y = \frac{7 - 2x}{3}$$

In identifying a function, the question is whether for every value of x, there is only one or no values of y.

First transform this equation into a statement that shows what y equals in terms of x.

Then, you know that this one is a function of x; no matter what you use for x, you will derive only one y.

Example $y = x^2 - 4$ *is this a function of x?*

yes *ask: when substituting for x do you get one value for y?*

This example meets the function test because, once again, for each value of x you use there will be exactly one value of y.

the function as a graph:

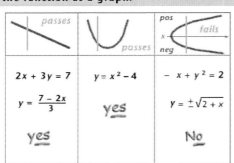

It is easy to check each example using the vertical line test.

The first two examples verify graphically what you found out algebraically. They show there is only one y-value for each x-value; i.e., that a vertical line intersects the curve at most once.

The third example verifies graphically that the curve fails the vertical line test and, therefore, cannot be considered a function of x.

Sample problems:

1. Given $y = \dfrac{1}{x^2}$, determine algebraically if y is a function of x.

   Solution: y is a function of x

   Explanation: Determine if there is more than one y-value for any given x-value. Choose any x-value, for example $x = 3$, and substitute it into the equation to find the corresponding y-value:

   $y = \dfrac{1}{(3)^2} = \dfrac{1}{9}$. Since the x-value produces only one y-value, $y = \dfrac{1}{x^2}$ is a function of x.

2. Given $y - x^3 = 0$, solve for y and determine algebraically if y is a function of x.

   Solution: y is a function of x

   Explanation: Solve the equation for y: $y - x^3 = 0 \Rightarrow y = x^3$. Determine if there is more than one y-value for any given x-value. Choose any x-value, for example $x = -5$, and substitute it into the equation to find the corresponding y-value:

   $y = (-5)^3 = -125$. Since the x-value raised to the third power produces only one y-value as a result, $y - x^3 = 0$ is a function of x.

3. Given $x^4 - y^4 = 1$, solve for y and determine algebraically if y is a function of x.

   Solution: y is not a function of x

   Explanation: Solve the equation for y: $x^4 - y^4 = 1 \Rightarrow y^4 = x^4 - 1;\ y = \pm\sqrt[4]{(x^4 - 1)}$.
   Determine if there is more than one y-value for any given x-value. Choose any x-value, for example $x = 2$, and substitute it into the equation to find the corresponding y-value: $y = \pm\sqrt[4]{(2^4 - 1)} = \pm\sqrt[4]{15}$. Therefore, the equation does not describe a function of x, since there is an x-value that corresponds to two y-values.

Practice problems: *(Answers on page: 444)*

1. Given $y = \dfrac{5}{1 - x}$, determine algebraically if y is a function of x.

2. Given $3x + 2y^2 = 1$, solve for y and determine algebraically if y is a function of x.

3. Given $x^2 - 2y = 0$, solve for y and determine algebraically if y is a function of x.

Review questions: *(Answers to odd questions on page: 444)*

1. Given $y = \dfrac{x+1}{x^2}$, determine algebraically if y is a function of x.

2. Given $y = \sqrt[4]{\dfrac{1}{x}}$, determine algebraically if y is a function of x.

3. Given $\frac{1}{2}x - y^2 = x^2$, solve for y and determine algebraically if y is a function of x.

4. Given $\dfrac{3x^4 - 5y^4}{2} = 1$, solve for y and determine algebraically if y is a function of x.

5. Given $x - \frac{2}{3}y = x^2$, solve for y and determine algebraically if y is a function of x.

Function Notation and Finding Function Values

- **Function notation** replaces the "$y =$" in an equation with "$f(x) =$" which shows that each y-value depends on the value used for x.
- *f(x)* shows the y-value for the given x and shows that the y-value can be found when an x-value is known and used in the equation. Other letters are frequently used as well, so that you may find $g(x)$, $h(x)$, and so on.
- *f(x)* is read "f of x." The expression $f(2)$ is read as "f of 2". $f(2)$ indicates the value that y has in this function when $x = 2$.

$f(x)$ = the value of y written in terms "f of x" of a function of x **Example** $y = 2x^2 - 1$ *what does this mean?* $f(2) =$ *insert 2 for x* $f(2) = 2(2)^2 - 1 = 7$ Original Question: Find the value for y when x = 2 New Notation: Find f of 2	For this function, $f(2)$ means to substitute 2 in each place that you find an x in the expression. Then solve for the value of the expression to determine $f(2)$. $f(2)$ is the y-value for the point where $x = 2$ in this expression. Since this $f(2) = 7$, on a graph, you would find the point (2, 7). This notation replaces the old "$y =$" notation.
$f(1) = 2(1)^2 - 1 = 1$ *plug in 1 for x*	This $f(1)$ uses 1 for every x to determine that $f(1)$, or y, equals 1. On a graph this is the point (1, 1).
$f(0) = 2(0)^2 - 1 = -1$ *plug in 0 for x*	Now $f(0)$ replaces x with 0 and it turns out that $f(0)$ equals -1. On a graph this is the point $(0, -1)$.
Example $g(x) = \dfrac{1}{x+3}$ evaluate: $g(2) = \dfrac{1}{2+3} = \dfrac{1}{5}$ *substitute 2 for x*	For this function, $g(2)$ equals 1/5. On a graph, this is the point (2, 1/5)

Example

$h(x) = \sqrt{x^2 - 1}$

function doesn't have to be f

evaluate:

$h(1) = \sqrt{1^2 - 1}$

$h(1) = \sqrt{0}$

$h(1) = 0$

$h(2) = \sqrt{2^2 - 1}$

$h(2) = \sqrt{3}$

For this function, $h(2)$ equals $\sqrt{3}$. On a graph, this is the point $(2, \sqrt{3})$.

Sample problems:

1. Given $g(x) = \dfrac{x+5}{2}$, find $g(2a-5)$.

   Solution: a

   Explanation: Substitute $2a-5$ for x in $g(x) = \dfrac{x+5}{2}$ and simplify:

   $g(2a-5) = \dfrac{(2a-5)+5}{2} = \dfrac{2a}{2} = a.$

2. Given $f(x) = |2x-5|$, find the value of $f(4) - f(1)$.

   Solution: 0

   Explanation: Substitute 4 and 1 for x in $f(x) = |2x-5|$, simplify each function, and then subtract:

   $f(4) - f(1) = |2(4)-5| - |2(1)-5| = |3| - |-3| = 3 - 3 = 0.$

3. Given $f(x) = 1 - 2x^2$, find $\dfrac{f(x+h) - f(x)}{h}$.

   Solution: $-4x - 2h$

   Explanation: In this problem the function $f(x) = 1 - 2x^2$ is used twice,

   once substituting $(x+h)$ and once as is. Complete the substitution:

   $\dfrac{f(x+h) - f(x)}{h} = \dfrac{[1 - 2(x+h)^2] - [1 - 2x^2]}{h}$. Simplify:

   $\dfrac{[1 - 2x^2 - 4xh - 2h^2] - [1 - 2x^2]}{h} = \dfrac{1 - 2x^2 - 4xh - 2h^2 - 1 + 2x^2}{h} = \dfrac{-4xh - 2h^2}{h} = -4x - 2h.$

Practice problems: *(Answers on page: 444)*

1. Given $h(x) = \dfrac{2}{x} + x$, find $h(a+1)$.

2. Given $f(x) = x^2 - 2x$ find $f(x+h)$.

3. Given $f(x) = x^2 + 3$, find $\dfrac{f(x) - f(x+2)}{-4}$.

Review questions: *(Answers to odd questions on page: 444)*

1. If $f(x) = x^3 - 5x - 2$, find $f(-2)$.

2. If $f(x) = x^3 - 5x - 2$, find $f\left(\dfrac{3}{2}\right)$.

3. If $f(x) = \dfrac{x^3 + 2x}{x-1}$, find $f(-2)$.

4. If $f(x) = (x-2)^2 + 3$, find $f(a+1) - f(1)$.

5. If $f(x) = \dfrac{(3x-1)}{4x+2}$, find $f\left(\dfrac{x-1}{x+2}\right)$.

Determining Intervals Over Which a Function Is Increasing

- A **function is decreasing** if the graph drops as the x-values get larger.
- A **function is increasing** if the graph rises as the x-values get larger.
- A **function is constant** if it is neither increasing nor decreasing over a given interval.
- A **maximum** is a high point that occurs when an increasing curve begins decreasing.
- A **minimum** is a low point that occurs when a decreasing curve begins increasing.
- Whether a function is increasing or decreasing is determined as the graph is viewed from left to right.
- Some functions increase and decrease many times over their curve.

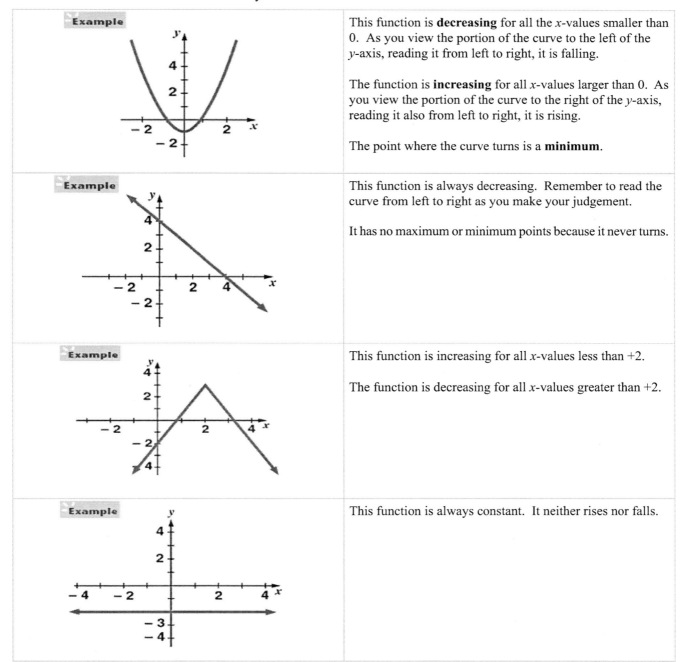

Example

This function is **decreasing** for all the x-values smaller than 0. As you view the portion of the curve to the left of the y-axis, reading it from left to right, it is falling.

The function is **increasing** for all x-values larger than 0. As you view the portion of the curve to the right of the y-axis, reading it also from left to right, it is rising.

The point where the curve turns is a **minimum**.

Example

This function is always decreasing. Remember to read the curve from left to right as you make your judgement.

It has no maximum or minimum points because it never turns.

Example

This function is increasing for all x-values less than +2.

The function is decreasing for all x-values greater than +2.

Example

This function is always constant. It neither rises nor falls.

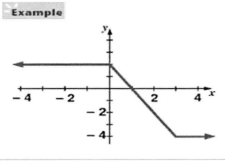

This function is constant for all x-values less than or equal to 0. It is also constant for all x-values greater than or equal to 3.

The function is decreasing over the interval $0 < x < 3$.

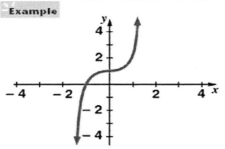

This function is increasing over its entire curve. Remember you are reading from left to right. Your analysis is whether the point to the right is higher than your point of reference for each point on the curve.

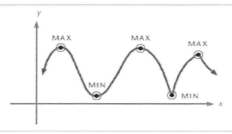

Functions that change between increasing and decreasing have high and low points.

This function has three **maxima** and two **minima** that you can see over the pictured interval. This function is turning frequently.

Sample problems:

1. Given the graph of $f(x) = \dfrac{x^2(8-x^2)}{4}$, determine the interval of x where $f(x)$ is increasing.

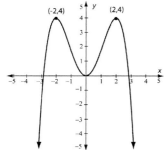

Solution: $(-\infty, -2)$ and $(0,2)$

Explanation: Observe the graph from left to right. The curve rises for x from $-\infty \rightarrow -2$, then begins decreasing. Then again the curve rises for x from $0 \rightarrow 2$, then decreases. Express these x-values in interval notation: $(-\infty, -2)$ and $(0,2)$.

2. Given the graph of $f(x) = \dfrac{x^2 + 4}{2x}$, determine the interval of x where $f(x)$ is increasing.

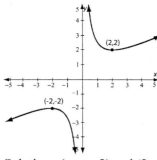

Solution: $(-\infty, -2)$ and $(2, \infty)$

Explanation: The curve rises for x from $-\infty \rightarrow -2$, then again from $2 \rightarrow \infty$. Express these x-values in interval notation: $(-\infty, -2)$ and $(2, \infty)$.

3. Given the graph of $f(x) = x^3 - 3x$, determine the interval of x where $f(x)$ is decreasing and the interval of x where $f(x)$ is constant.

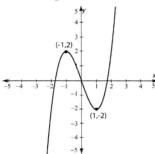

Solution: $(-1, 1)$, $f(x)$ is never constant

Explanation: The curve *decreases* for x from $-1 \rightarrow 1$. Express these x-values in interval notation: $(-1, 1)$. A function is constant where its graph is horizontal, however this function is never constant.

Practice problems: *(Answers on page: 444)*

1. Given the graph of $f(x) = -x^2 + 4$, determine the interval of x where $f(x)$ is decreasing.

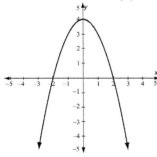

2. Given the graph of $f(x) = x^3 - 2$, determine the interval of x where $f(x)$ is increasing.

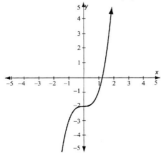

3. Given the graph $f(x)$ below, determine the interval of x where $f(x)$ is constant.

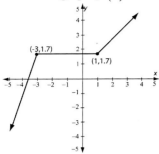

Review questions: *(Answers to odd questions on page: 444)*

1. Given the graph of $f(x) = |x|$, determine the interval of x where $f(x)$ is increasing.

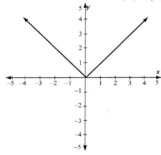

2. Given the graph of $f(x) = 1 - x^3$, determine the interval of x where $f(x)$ is increasing.

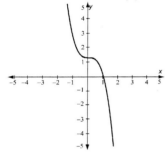

3. Given the graph of $f(x) = \frac{2}{3}x + 1$, determine the interval of x where $f(x)$ is increasing.

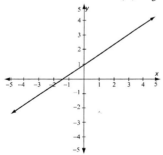

4. Given the graph $f(x)$ below, determine the interval of x where $f(x)$ is decreasing.

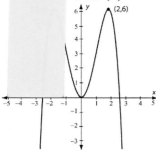

5. Given the graph $f(x)$ below, determine the interval of x where $f(x)$ is constant.

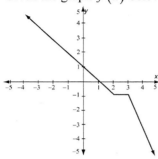

Evaluating Piecewise-Defined Functions for Given Values

- A **piecewise-defined function** is defined using different equations for different intervals in its **domain**.
- To evaluate a piecewise-defined function at a particular x-value, determine the interval that the x-value is in and use the corresponding piece of the function.
- To graph a piecewise-defined function, you combine the graphs of each piece while paying attention to the intervals where the pieces are defined.

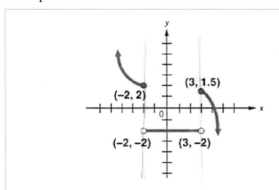

Up to this point you have only seen the graphs of relatively tame functions.

Take a look at the graph of this strange function. It's pretty wild!

After recovering from the shock (or not), you might ask yourself: How can you write down an equation for this function? The answer is to put together three separate functions, one for each piece of the graph.

whether the value is $\geq$ or < 2 will determine which formula to use

Example $f(x) = \begin{cases} 3x^2 + 1 & \text{if } x \geq 2 \\ \frac{-1}{2}x + 14 & \text{if } x < 2 \end{cases}$

evaluate:

$f(5) = 3x^2 + 1 \qquad 5 \geq 2$

$f(2) = 3x^2 + 1 \qquad 2 \geq 2$

$f(0) = \frac{-1}{2}x + 14 \qquad 0 < 2$

Here's an example of a function that pieces together two separate functions; functions defined in this way are called **piecewise-defined functions**.

To evaluate a piecewise-defined function at a particular x-value, you need to know which formula (or piece) to use. In this case, if $x > 2$, you use the first formula. If $x < 2$, you use the second formula.

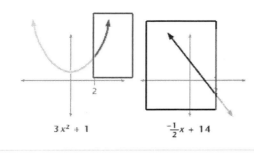

$3x^2 + 1$ $-\frac{1}{2}x + 14$

Here are the graphs of the two pieces each by itself. For the entire piecewise-defined function, you combine the graph of the first function for $x > 2$ with the graph of the second function for $x < 2$.

NOTE: If you aren't comfortable graphing functions yet, don't worry – you'll get to that soon.

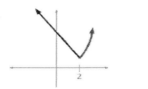

Put the two pieces together and you get the graph of the piecewise-defined function!

Sample problems:

1. Given the function $f(x) = \begin{cases} x+1 \text{ if } x > 2 \\ -2x+5 \text{ if } x \le 2 \end{cases}$, determine the interval of x in which $f(x)$ is decreasing.

   Solution: $(-\infty, 2]$

   Explanation: Consider the graph of the first part, $f(x) = x+1$. The graph is increasing. Consider the graph of the second part, $f(x) = -2x+5$. The graph is decreasing. This part of the function applies when $x \le 2$. Express this inequality in interval notation: $(-\infty, 2]$.

2. Given the function $f(x) = \begin{cases} -2x & \text{if} & x < -3 \\ -3x-1 & \text{if} & -3 \le x \le 2 \\ -4x & \text{if} & x > 2 \end{cases}$, evaluate $f(-1)$.

   Solution: 2

   Explanation: To evaluate $f(-1)$, determine which part of the function is indicated by the given domain value, -1. Since -1 is in $-3 \le x \le 2$, evaluate $f(-1)$ using the second part, $f(x) = -3x - 1$: $f(-1) = -3(-1) - 1 = 2$.

3. Given the function $f(x) = \begin{cases} \frac{1}{2}x^2 & \text{if} & x < -7 \\ 5-x & \text{if} & -7 \le x < 0 \\ x^3 +1 & \text{if} & x \ge 0 \end{cases}$, evaluate $f(0)$.

   Solution: 1

   Explanation: Since 0 is in $x \ge 0$, evaluate $f(0)$ using the third part, $f(x) = x^3 + 1$: $f(0) = 0^3 + 1 = 1$.

Practice problems: *(Answers on page: 444)*

1. Given the function $g(x) = \begin{cases} x^2 \text{ if } x \le -1 \\ x \text{ if } -1 < x < 1 \\ -x \text{ if } x \ge 1 \end{cases}$, determine the interval of x in which $f(x)$ is decreasing.

2. Given the function $f(x) = \begin{cases} x+4 & \text{if } x < -4 \\ \frac{1}{x} & \text{if } -4 \le x \le 0 \\ x^2 - x & \text{if } x > 0 \end{cases}$, evaluate $f(-3)$.

3. Given the function $f(x) = \begin{cases} x^2 +4x+1 & \text{if } x < 2 \\ 5-x & \text{if } x = 2 \\ x^2 -1 & \text{if } x > 2 \end{cases}$, evaluate $f(-1)$.

Review questions: *(Answers to odd questions on page: 444)*

1. Given the function $f(x) = \begin{cases} 3x & \text{if } x \le 0 \\ 2 & \text{if } 0 < x < 1 \\ -x & \text{if } x \ge 1 \end{cases}$, determine the interval of x in which $f(x)$ is constant.

2. Given the function $f(x) = \begin{cases} 4+x & \text{if } x \le -2 \\ x^2 & \text{if } -2 < x < 3 \\ x^3 & \text{if } x \ge 3 \end{cases}$, determine the interval of x in which $f(x)$ is increasing.

3. Given the function $f(x) = \begin{cases} 2x+4 & \text{if } x < -1 \\ x & \text{if } -1 \le x \le 0 \\ x^2 - 3x & \text{if } x > 0 \end{cases}$, evaluate $f(-7)$.

4. Given the function $f(x) = \begin{cases} x^3 & \text{if } x < 5 \\ |x-2| & \text{if } 5 \le x \le 9 \\ 4 & \text{if } x > 9 \end{cases}$, evaluate $f(10)$.

5. Given the function $f(x) = \begin{cases} x^3 & \text{if } x < 5 \\ |x-2| & \text{if } 5 \le x \le 9 \\ 4 & \text{if } x > 9 \end{cases}$, evaluate $f(-2)$.

Solving Word Problems Involving Functions

- Function thinking allows you to solve a problem with two unknowns by setting up an equation with one unknown defined in terms of the other unknown. Then, when you can determine a value for the one unknown, you can solve for the other unknown.
- $f(x)$ means a function defined in terms of x. It also means the value an expression has for a given quantity, x.
- The perimeter of a rectangle equals the sum of the sides.
- The area of a rectangle equals length times width.

A rectangle has a length (L). The perimeter is 50'. What is the width (w) as a function of (L)?	For any rectangle, Perimeter $= 2l + 2w$; Area $= l \cdot w$
width as a function of length $\longrightarrow$ $\boxed{W = 25 - L}$	Once we know that the perimeter equals 50, we know $P = 50 = 2l + 2w$ We can easily solve for w using this information. At any specific length (l) we can now solve for the width (w).

SILVER ↕ w ├── L ──┤ W = 25 − L $A = L(25 - L)$ multiply all terms $A(L) = L(25 - L)$ when: $A(5) = 5ft(25ft - 5ft)$ $= 5ft(20ft)$ $= 100\ ft^2$	Once we have a statement for w, we can define the area in terms of the other variable L. Our notation is $A(L)$ which is read "area in terms of length," or the function "A of L." Then, at any specific length, in this case when $L = 5$, we can calculate the area.

Sample problems:

1. Determine the area of the region that lies between the x-axis and $f(x) = \begin{cases} 7 \text{ for } 0 \le x \le 4 \\ 6 \text{ for } 4 \le x \le 8 \\ 2 \text{ for } 8 \le x \le 10 \end{cases}$.

   Solution: 56 units^2
   Explanation: Sketch the region. The function $f(x)$ produces a set of three rectangles, so find the sum of the areas of each rectangle: $(7)(4) + (6)(4) + (2)(2) = 56$ units^2.

2. A piece of rope that is 10 feet long is cut into two pieces. One piece is used to form a circle and the other is used to form a square. Write a function for the sum of the areas of the square and the circle as a function of the radius of the circle.

   Solution: $\pi r^2 + \left(\frac{5 - \pi r}{2}\right)^2$
   Explanation: Let r be the radius of the circle and s be the length of a side of the square. The circumference of the circle is $2\pi r$ and the perimeter of the square is $4s$. Since the length of the rope is 10 feet, $2\pi r + 4s = 10$. Solve for s: $s = \dfrac{10 - 2\pi r}{4} = \dfrac{5 - \pi r}{2}$.
   Write a function for the sum of the areas of the circle and the square: $A = \pi r^2 + s^2$.
   Substitute the expression for s into the area function: $A = \pi r^2 + \left(\frac{5 - \pi r}{2}\right)^2$.

3. A rectangle is inscribed in a semicircle with its length lying along the diameter of the circle as shown in the figure. The equation of the circle is $x^2 + y^2 = 25$. Write a function for the area of the rectangle in terms of x.

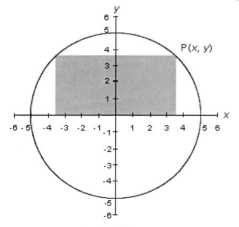

   Solution: $2x\sqrt{25 - x^2}$
   Explanation: The base of the rectangle is $2x$ and the height is y. So, the area of the rectangle is given by $A = 2xy$. Solve the circle equation for y: $y = \sqrt{25 - x^2}$.
   Substitute the expression for y into the area function: $A = 2xy = 2x\sqrt{25 - x^2}$.

Practice problems: *(Answers on page: 445)*

1. Determine the area of the region that lies between the x-axis and $f(x) = \begin{cases} 10 \text{ for } 0 \le x \le 1 \\ 12 \text{ for } 1 \le x \le 5. \\ 3 \text{ for } 5 \le x \le 7 \end{cases}$

2. Write a function for the volume of a sphere in terms of the surface area, S, of the sphere.

3. Write a function for the area of a rectangle in terms of the width, w, if the perimeter of the rectangle is 20 cm.

Review questions: *(Answers to odd questions on page: 445)*

1. Determine the area of the region that lies between the x-axis and $f(x) = \begin{cases} 1 \text{ for } 0 \le x \le 1 \\ 8 \text{ for } 1 \le x \le 7 \\ 2 \text{ for } 7 \le x \le 10 \end{cases}$.

2. The perimeter of the given rectangle is 28 feet. Let y be the width and x the length. Find the area as a function of the length (x).

3. The area of a circle is $A = \pi r^2$ and the circumference is $C = 2\pi r$. Write an equation for the area of a circle as a function of the circumference .

4. A rectangle is in the 1st quadrant with one vertex at the origin, another on the x-axis, a third on the y-axis, and the final vertex on the line $3x + 2y = 6$. Find a formula for the area of the rectangle as a function of x.

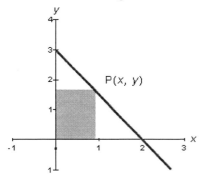

5. A rectangular metal sheet 10 inches by 8 inches is made into an open box by cutting out square corners on all four vertices of length x. Find a formula for the volume of the rectangular box .

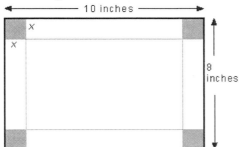

Finding the Domain and Range of a Function

- The **domain** of a function is the set of all x-values that can be used as inputs for the function.
- The **range** of a function is the set of all possible y-values, or outputs, for a function.
- Values excluded from the domain include values that result in a negative number under a square root sign and values that cause a denominator to equal zero.

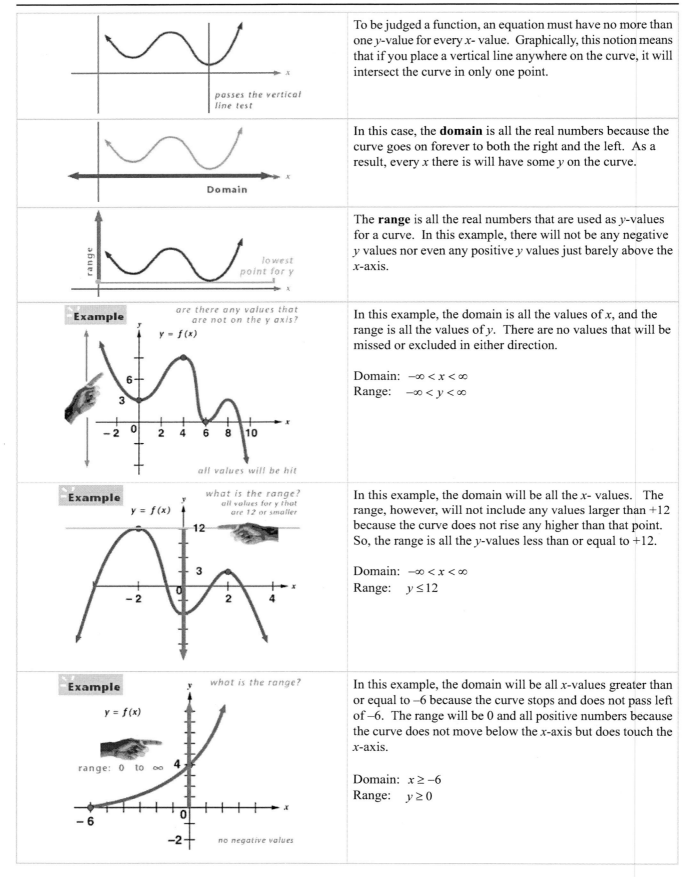

To be judged a function, an equation must have no more than one y-value for every x- value. Graphically, this notion means that if you place a vertical line anywhere on the curve, it will intersect the curve in only one point.

passes the vertical line test

In this case, the **domain** is all the real numbers because the curve goes on forever to both the right and the left. As a result, every x there is will have some y on the curve.

Domain

The **range** is all the real numbers that are used as y-values for a curve. In this example, there will not be any negative y values nor even any positive y values just barely above the x-axis.

range *lowest point for y*

Example *are there any values that are not on the y axis?*

$y = f(x)$

all values will be hit

In this example, the domain is all the values of x, and the range is all the values of y. There are no values that will be missed or excluded in either direction.

Domain: $-\infty < x < \infty$
Range: $-\infty < y < \infty$

Example *what is the range? all values for y that are 12 or smaller*

$y = f(x)$

In this example, the domain will be all the x- values. The range, however, will not include any values larger than +12 because the curve does not rise any higher than that point. So, the range is all the y-values less than or equal to +12.

Domain: $-\infty < x < \infty$
Range: $y \le 12$

Example *what is the range?*

$y = f(x)$

range: 0 to ∞

no negative values

In this example, the domain will be all x-values greater than or equal to –6 because the curve stops and does not pass left of –6. The range will be 0 and all positive numbers because the curve does not move below the x-axis but does touch the x-axis.

Domain: $x \ge -6$
Range: $y \ge 0$

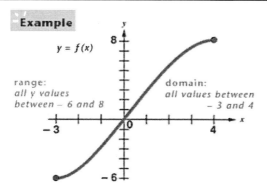

Example $y = f(x)$

range: all y values between – 6 and 8

domain: all values between – 3 and 4

In this example of a curve segment, the endpoints are (–3, –6) and (4, 8). Since the curve is continuous between those two points, all values between the two points are used on the curve. As a result the domain will include all values between –3 and 4. The range will include all values between –6 and 8.

Domain: $-3 \le x \le 4$
Range: $-6 \le y \le 8$

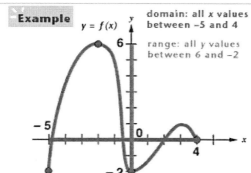

Example $y = f(x)$

domain: all x values between –5 and 4

range: all y values between 6 and –2

This curve is continuous and moves between (–5, –2) and (4, 0). The domain is limited to include all values between or equal to –5, the left end of the curve, and +4, the right end of the curve. The range is limited to include all values between or equal to –2, the lowest point on the curve, and +6, the highest point on the curve.

Domain: $-5 \le x \le 4$
Range: $-2 \le y \le 6$

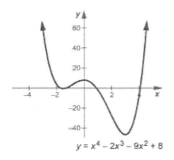

Example $y = f(x)$

domain: – 4 to 3
range: 6 to – 5

This unusual curve has endpoints at (–4, 0) and (3, 4). That fact will limit its values as shown. Its domain will be all the values between or equal to –4 and +3. Its range will be all the values between or equal to –5 and +6.

Domain: $-4 \le x \le 3$
Range: $-5 \le y \le 6$

Sample problems:

1. Find the domain of the function $y = x^4 - 2x^3 - 9x^2 + 8$.

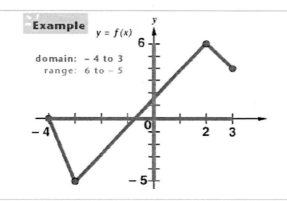

$y = x^4 - 2x^3 - 9x^2 + 8$

<u>Solution:</u> $-\infty < x < \infty$
<u>Explanation:</u> In the graph the arrows indicate that the graph extends infinitely in both the negative and positive directions, thus the possible x values are all real numbers. Additionally, in the equation, x is defined for all real numbers. Therefore, the domain is $-\infty < x < \infty$.

2. Given $y = f(x) = \sqrt{\dfrac{x+8}{2}}$, use this equation and the graph below to find the domain of the function f.

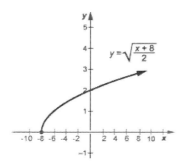

Solution: $x \geq -8$

Explanation: In the graph the possible values of x are any value -8 or larger. Thus, the domain is $x \geq -8$.

3. Find the domain and range of the function graphed below.

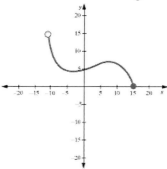

Solution: Domain: $-10 < x \leq 15$

Range: $0 \leq y < 15$

Explanation: The open circle at $(-10, 15)$ indicates that the point is not included in the domain/range. The domain (possible x-values) extends from -10 to 15, including 15, but not -10, or $-10 < x \leq 15$. The range (possible y-values) extends from 0 to 15, but not including 15, or $0 \leq y < 15$.

Practice problems: *(Answers on page: 445)*

1. Find the domain of the function $f(x) = x^2 + 2x - 3$.

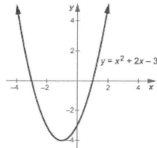

2. What is the domain of the following function?

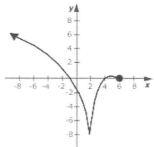

3. Find the domain and range of the function graphed below.

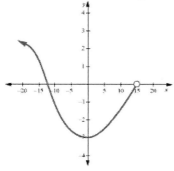

Review questions: *(Answers to odd questions on page: 445)*

1. From the graph of $f(x) = x^2 + 2x - 3$, find the range of f.

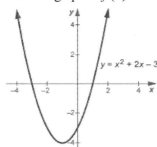

$y = x^2 + 2x - 3$

2. What is the range for the function graphed as shown?

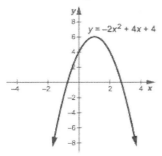

$y = -2x^2 + 4x + 4$

3. What is the domain for the function graphed as shown?

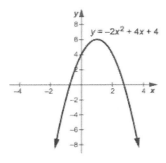

4. What is the domain for the function graphed as shown?

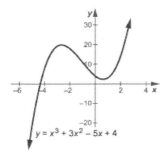

5. What is the range for the function graphed as shown?

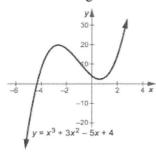

Domain and Range: One Explicit Example

- The **domain** for a function is the set of all real numbers that can be used for x.
- Values must be excluded from the domain if they create either a denominator equal to zero or a negative total under a square root sign.
- The **range** for a function is the set of all real numbers that are possible for y.
- $\mathbb{R}$ is the notational symbol for the set of all real numbers.

Example $f(x) = 2x + 5$ Find the domain *there are no undefined values for x* domain = $\mathbb{R}$ *all x values are allowed*	Any number can be multiplied with 2. There is no denominator to be considered. Therefore, no real numbers are excluded. The domain for this example is the set of all real numbers. Another notation for $-\infty > x < \infty$ is $\mathbb{R}$.

$f(x) = 2x + 5$ **Find the domain** **Find the range** domain = $\mathbb{R}$ can $f(x) = 23$? *check answer:* $2x + 5 = 23$ $f(9) = 2(9) + 5$ $2x = 18$ $= 23$ $x = 9$	Finding the range is a matter of ascertaining what values are possible for y. In this example, is it possible that y could equal 23? It turns out that 23 works nicely. And, in working with 23 you can see that any number placed in that position will work out to involve only real numbers. Therefore, the range for this function is also the set of all real numbers.
$f(x) = 2x + 5$ domain = $\mathbb{R}$ range = $\mathbb{R}$ 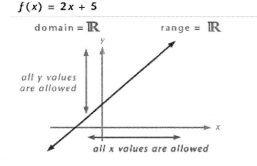 *all y values are allowed* *all x values are allowed*	Looking at your conclusions graphically, you see that the function represents a line that is continuous throughout the plane. With a graph it is easy to visualize the fact that some point on the line will use every possible x-value. Likewise, some point on the line will use every possible y-value. You can visually see that declaring your domain and range each to be the full set of real numbers is the correct conclusion.

Sample problems:

1. Given the function $f(x) = 5 - \dfrac{2x-7}{3x^2}$, find the domain.

   Solution: all real numbers except 0

   Explanation: The domain is the set of all real numbers excluding those values that either: (1) lead to a negative number under a radical, or (2) create a denominator equal to 0. The first condition does not exclude any values in this function because the function does not ask for the square root of any value. The second condition does apply because the denominator contains a variable. Solve the denominator for any value(s) which make it equal 0 and exclude those values: $3x^2 = 0$; $x^2 = 0$; $x = 0$. Therefore, the domain is the set of all real numbers except 0.

2. Given the function $y = \dfrac{x^2 - 3x - 28}{x + 4}$, find the domain.

   Solution: All real numbers except -4

   Explanation: Since the denominator contains a variable, solve the denominator for any value(s) which make it equal 0 and exclude those values from the domain. Set the denominator equal to 0 and solve for x: $x + 4 = 0$; $x = -4$. Therefore, the domain is the set of all real numbers except -4.

3. Given the function $y = \left| x^2 + 4 \right|$, find the domain and range.

   Solution: Domain: $\mathbb{R}$; Range: $y \geq 4$

   Explanation: The domain is all possible x-values. Any number can be squared, thus the domain is all real numbers. The range is all possible y-values. The absolute value of any number is positive, so obviously the range must include only positive numbers. Furthermore, the result of squaring any number is also positive, thus the value inside the absolute value is always greater than or equal to 4. Thus, the range is $y \geq 4$.

Practice problems: *(Answers on page: 445)*

1. Given the function $y = \dfrac{x^2 - 3x - 28}{x + 4}$, find the domain.

2. Given the function $y = \sqrt{x - 5}$, find the domain.

3. Given the function $y = -x^2$, find the domain and range.

Review questions: *(Answers to odd questions on page: 445)*

1. Determine the domain for the following relation: $y = x^2 + 2$

2. Determine the range for the following relation: $y = x^2 + 2$

3. Determine the domain and range for the following relation: $y = x^3 + 1$

4. Determine the domain and range for the following relation: $y = \sqrt{x + 2}$

5. Determine the domain and range for the following relation: $y = \dfrac{1}{x - 3}$

Satisfying the Domain of a Function

- The **domain** is the set of all real number values that can be used for x.
- $\mathbb{R}$ is the notational symbol for the set of all real numbers.
- $\mathbb{R} \setminus \{a_1, a_2, \ldots\}$ is the notation for a domain or range of all real numbers except certain ones.

Example $f(x) = x^2 - x + 1$ *find the domain* *ask: when input into the machine, what are the x values that will produce real numbers?* Domain = $\mathbb{R}$	In this example, all real numbers can be used for x because any number can be squared and then subtracted.
Example $g(x) = \sqrt{3 - 4x}$ *find the domain* $3 - 4x \geq 0$ *solve as an inequality* $\underline{\;-3 \qquad -3\;}$ *subtract 3 from each side* $\dfrac{-4x}{-4} \geq \dfrac{-3}{-4}$ *divide each side by -4* $\boxed{x \leq \dfrac{+3}{4}}$	In this problem if you try using a value larger than ¾, you will have a negative number under the square root sign. The domain does not allow you to include anything like that. It is OK to create 0 under the square root sign because the square root of 0 is 0. So, you are restricted in your domain for this function to numbers that are less than or equal to +3/4, as shown.
Example $h(x) = \dfrac{x - 1}{x^2 - 5x + 6}$ *find the domain* $x^2 - 5x + 6 = 0$ *identify when denominator = 0 first, set to = 0* $(x - 2)(x - 3) = 0$ *factor the denominator* $x = 2 \quad x = 3$ *values that cause the denominator to = 0* domain = all numbers except domain = $\mathbb{R} \setminus \{2, 3\}$ *another way to write it*	This example shows values eliminated from the domain because they create denominators that equal 0. Notice these excluded values for x are discovered by setting the denominator equal to 0 and solving for x by factoring. Here is one notation for the domain when specific values are excluded.

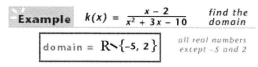

Example $k(x) = \dfrac{x-2}{x^2 + 3x - 10}$ *find the domain*

$$\boxed{\text{domain} = \mathbb{R} \setminus \{-5, 2\}}$$ *all real numbers except –5 and 2*

another way to do the problem:

$k(x) = \dfrac{\cancel{x-2}}{(x+5)(\cancel{x-2})}$ *factor denominator immediately and cancel*

$= \dfrac{1}{x+5}$

$x \ne 5$ $x \ne 2$ *is 2 allowable?*

remember the promise:
you can only cancel when not dividing by 0

In this example, first factor the denominator and notice you can cancel one factor with itself in the numerator.

Remember: Even if an expression is factored out, any value for x that would make the cancelled expression equal 0 must still be excluded.

Any activity performed with a rational expression must clearly state what values are to be excluded.

Sample problems:

1. Given $f(x) = \sqrt{4+2x}$, find the domain for the function f.
   Solution: $x \ge -2$
   Explanation: The domain is the set of all real numbers excluding those values that either: (1) lead to a negative number under a radical, or (2) create a denominator equal to 0. Since the radical contains a variable, determine the value(s) of x that will create a negative number in the radical. Set the expression under the radical greater than or equal to 0 and solve for x: $4 + 2x \ge 0$; $2x \ge -4$; $x \ge -2$. So, the domain is the set of all real numbers greater than or equal to -2.

2. Given $f(x) = \dfrac{2x+5}{x^3 + 6x^2 - 16x}$, find the domain for the function f.
   Solution: $\mathbb{R} \setminus \{-8, 0, 2\}$
   Explanation: Since the denominator contains a variable, determine the value(s) of x that will create 0 in the denominator. Set the denominator equal to 0 and solve for x:
   $x^3 + 6x^2 - 16x = 0$; $x(x+8)(x-2) = 0$; $x = 0$, $x = -8$ or $x = 2$.
   So, the domain is the set of all real numbers except -8, 0, and 2.

3. Given $f(x) = \dfrac{\sqrt{2x-3}}{x^2 - 8x + 15}$, find the domain of the function f.

   Solution: $x \ge \dfrac{3}{2} \setminus \{3, 5\}$

   Explanation: The expression under the radical must be greater than or equal to 0:

   $2x - 3 \ge 0$; $2x \ge 3$; $x \ge \dfrac{3}{2}$. Thus, the domain includes only those values greater than

   or equal to $\dfrac{3}{2}$. However, there are further restrictions since the denominator cannot

   equal 0. Set the expression in the denominator equal to 0 and solve for x:

   $x^2 - 8x + 15 = 0$; $(x-5)(x-3) = 0$; $x = 5$ or $x = 3$. Thus, the domain is all

   real numbers greater than or equal to $\dfrac{3}{2}$, excluding 3 and 5, or $x \ge \dfrac{3}{2} \setminus \{3, 5\}$.

Practice problems: *(Answers on page: 445)*

1. Given $f(x) = \sqrt{x+5}$ find the domain for the function f.

2. Given $f(x) = \dfrac{5x}{x^2 + 6x + 9}$ find the domain for the function f.

3. Given $f(x) = \dfrac{\sqrt{5-x}}{x^2 - x - 20}$, find the domain of the function f.

Review questions: *(Answers to odd questions on page: 445)*

1. Given $f(x) = \dfrac{1}{x-4}$, find its domain.

2. Given $f(x) = \dfrac{1}{x^2 - x}$, find its domain.

3. Given $f(x) = \sqrt{9 - x^2}$, find its domain.

4. Given $f(x) = \dfrac{x}{\sqrt{x+1}}$, find its domain.

5. Given $f(x) = \dfrac{\sqrt{2+x}}{3-x}$, find its domain.

An Introduction to Slope

- The graph of any **linear function** is a straight line.
- In Algebra, the degree of steepness of a line is called its **slope**.

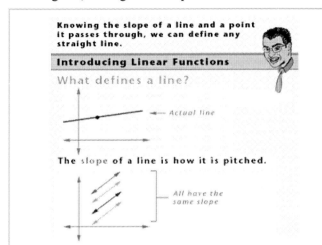

Every line has some degree of steepness, or slope. The degree of steepness ranges from horizontal, or flat, through all the levels to vertical, or upright.

Many lines can have the same slope.

If you know a line's slope and any one point on the line, you can tell exactly where to locate the line on a graph. And that line is a unique line.

Remember: You can identify and locate any unique line by knowing two things about it:
1. its slope, and
2. any one of its points.

Finding the Slope of a Line Given Two Points

- **Slope** is the change from one point to another on a line. It is stated as a ratio (fraction) with change vertically over change horizontally. This is frequently referred to as *rise/run*.
- Slope is the measure of pitch or steepness of a line. The larger the slope the steeper the line. A vertical line is so steep that the sideways change cannot be measured and its slope is undefined.

- **Slope (m)** $= \dfrac{y_2 - y_1}{x_2 - x_1} = \dfrac{\Delta y}{\Delta x} = \dfrac{\text{change in } y\text{s}}{\text{change in } x\text{s}}$. Δ is a notation for "change in".

Example

Suppose we're given 2 points. Find the slope of the line that passes through these points.

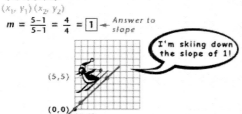

In this example, we find the change between the two points by doing three things:

1. Subtract the two y-values, 5 and 1, and write that as the numerator of our ratio.
2. Subtract the two x-values, 5 and 1, and write that as the denominator of our ratio.
3. Reduce the fraction if possible.

The slope is 1 which tells us that the graph is rising at the same rate it is moving sideways.

Example

Suppose we're given 2 points. Find the slope of the line that passes through these points.

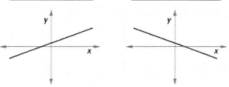

In this example, we follow the same process.

Remember: Decide which point is (x_2, y_2) and be sure to use its coordinates first on both levels. If you don't, your signs will be incorrect.

In this case, we have $-7 - 0 = -7$ over $-3 - 2 = -5$. So, our slope is 7/5. This tells us that the graph is moving up 7 units for each 5 units it moves to the right.

Note: A positive slope indicates a line that is climbing when viewed from left to right.

Note: A negative slope indicates a line that is falling when viewed from left to right.

Sample problems:

1. Find the slope of the line through the two points $(1, -3)$ and $(1, 4)$.

   Solution: Undefined

   Explanation: Substitute the x and y values from the 2 points into the formula, (be consistent with the choice for y_2 and x_2): $m = \dfrac{y_2 - y_1}{x_2 - x_1} = \dfrac{4 - (-3)}{1 - 1} = \dfrac{7}{0} =$ undefined.

2. Find the slope of the line through $\left(-\dfrac{1}{3}, 3\right)$ and $\left(-2, -\dfrac{1}{3}\right)$.

   Solution: 2

   Explanation: Substitute the x & y values into the slope formula:

   $$m = \frac{y_2 - y_1}{x_2 - x_1} = \frac{-\dfrac{1}{3} - 3}{-2 - \left(-\dfrac{1}{3}\right)} = \frac{-\dfrac{10}{3}}{-\dfrac{5}{3}} = -\frac{10}{3} \cdot -\frac{3}{5} = 2.$$

3. If the slope of a line that passes through $(5, 8)$ and $(9, y)$ is $\dfrac{3}{2}$, find the value of y.

   Solution: 14

   Explanation: Substitute the values from the points and the slope into the slope formula and solve for y: $m = \dfrac{y_2 - y_1}{x_2 - x_1} \Rightarrow \dfrac{3}{2} = \dfrac{y - 8}{9 - 5}; \dfrac{3}{2} = \dfrac{y - 8}{4}; (4)\dfrac{3}{2} = y - 8; 6 = y - 8; y = 14.$

Practice problems: *(Answers on page: 445)*

1. Find the slope of the line through the points $(-1, 3)$, $(1, -6)$.

2. Find the slope of the line through the points $(2, 2)$, $(0, 0)$.

3. If the slope of a line that passes through $(x, -4)$ and $(7, 10)$ is $\dfrac{7}{4}$, find the value of x.

Review questions: *(Answers to odd questions on page: 445)*

1. Find the slope of the line through the points $(2, 4)$, $(8, 6)$.

2. Find the slope of the line through the points $(9, 16)$, $(4, 27)$.

3. Find the slope of the line through the points $(22, 7)$, $(0, -6)$.

4. Find the slope of the line through the points $(0, 2)$, $(-4, -6)$.

5. Find the slope of the line through the points $(-8, -6)$, $(-2, -4)$.

Interpreting Slope from a Graph

- **Slope:** $\dfrac{rise}{run} = \dfrac{y_2 - y_1}{x_2 - x_1} = \dfrac{\Delta y}{\Delta x} = pitch$.

- A **positive slope** indicates that a line rises when viewed from left to right.
- A **negative slope** indicates that a line falls when viewed from left to right.
- The steeper a line rises or falls, the larger the absolute value of the slope will be.
- The **slope of a vertical line** is said to be undefined because the denominator of its fraction equals 0 which is an undefined situation in mathematics.
- The **slope of a horizontal line** is said to be 0 because the numerator of its fraction equals 0.

Example	This line has a positive slope because it is tilting upwards when viewed from left to right.
	The greater the tilt, the larger the slope value will be.
Example	The slope for this line is undefined. There is no change left to right from one point to another on the line. So, when you subtract the *x*-values in the denominator, your answer is 0.
Example	The slope of this line is negative because it tilts down when viewed from left to right. Again, the greater the tilt, the larger the absolute value for the slope.

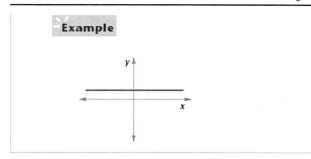

The slope for this line is 0. When you subtract the y-values of any two of its points, you will get 0 because there is no change up and down from one point to another on this line.

Sample problems:

1. If two lines are parallel and the equation of one line is $y = 5$, what is the slope of the other line?
   Solution: 0
   Explanation: The line defined by the equation $y = 5$ is horizontal. Any line parallel to that line will also be horizontal. The slope of any horizontal line is 0.

2. If two lines are perpendicular and the equation of one line is $y = 2x$, does the other line increase or decrease from left to right?
   Solution: Decrease
   Explanation: The line defined by the equation $y = 2x$ has a positive slope (2), so it increases from left to right. A line that is perpendicular to that line will have slope $-\frac{1}{2}$, since perpendicular lines have slopes that are opposite reciprocals. Therefore, the other line will decrease from left to right.

3. If two lines are parallel and the equation of one line is $3x + 2y = 10$, does the other line increase or decrease from left to right?
   Solution: Decrease
   Explanation: Begin by expressing the equation in slope-intercept form so that the slope can be easily identified from the equation. In order to express an equation in slope-intercept form, solve the equation for y:
   $3x + 2y = 10 \Rightarrow 2y = 10 - 3x \Rightarrow y = \frac{10-3x}{2} \Rightarrow y = 5 - \frac{3}{2}x.$
   The line defined by $y = 5 - \frac{3}{2}x$ has a negative slope ($-\frac{3}{2}$), so it decreases from left to right. A line that is parallel to that line will also have slope $-\frac{3}{2}$, since parallel lines have equal slopes. Therefore, both lines will decrease from left to right.

Practice problems: *(Answers on page: 445)*

1. If two lines are parallel and the equation of one line is $x = 5$, what is the slope of the other line?

2. If two lines are perpendicular and the equation of one line is $y = -0.5x$, does the other line increase or decrease from left to right?

3. If two lines are perpendicular and the equation of one line is $x - 5y = 15$, does the other line increase or decrease from left to right?

Review questions: *(Answers to odd questions on page: 445)*

1. If two lines are parallel and the equation of one line is $40x + 5y = 5$
   what is the slope of the other line?

2. If two lines are parallel and the equation of one line is $3x - 2y = 18$
   does the other line increase or decrease from left to right?

3. If two lines are parallel and the equation of one line is $y = 3x + 1$
   does the slope of the other line increase or decrease from left to right?

4. If two lines are perpendicular and the equation of one line is $2x + 3y = 4$ does the slope of the other line increase or decrease from left to right?

5. If two lines are perpendicular and the equation of one line is $3x - 2y = 4$ does the slope of the other line increase or decrease from left to right?

Graphing a Line Using Point and Slope

- **Slope:** $\dfrac{rise}{run} = \dfrac{y_2 - y_1}{x_2 - x_1} = \dfrac{\Delta y}{\Delta x} = pitch$
- A **positive slope** indicates that a line rises when viewed from left to right.
- A **negative slope** indicates that a line falls when viewed from left to right.

Graphing a line using point & slope **Example** 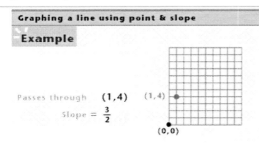 Passes through **(1,4)** Slope $= \dfrac{3}{2}$	When graphing a line using just one point and the slope, your first step is to locate the point. Here, the point (1, 4) means you move from the origin, (0, 0) one space to the right and four spaces up. Then place and label your point.
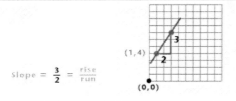 Slope $= \dfrac{3}{2} = \dfrac{rise}{run}$	You can use the slope to determine a second point. In this example, begin at (1, 4). From there, count up 3 and to the right 2. Place your second point. By definition, you have enough information now to draw a line. Just as a check you might count again to a third point to extend the line.
Example Passes through **(−1,−3)** Slope $= \dfrac{-4}{5}$ $\dfrac{rise}{run}$ 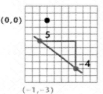 (0,0) 5 -4 (−1,−3)	In this example, first locate the point (−1, −3). The slope is negative, so count down to start instead of up. From (−1, −3), count down 4 and to the right 5 to locate your second point. Finally, draw your line through the points.
Example Passes through **(0,0)** Slope $= -1 = \dfrac{-1}{1}$ $\dfrac{rise}{run}$ Make into fraction (0,0) −1 1	For this line your starting point will be the origin, (0, 0). From there, use your slope to count down 1, then to the right 1, and locate your second point. Finally, draw the line.

Sample problems:

1. Describe the movement indicated when the slope of a line is -3.

   Solution: Move down 3 units, then run to the right 1 unit

   Explanation: The slope of a line is a number that indicates the vertical change and the horizontal change from one point to the next. The numerator of the slope describes the vertical change (the rise) and the denominator describes the horizontal change (the run). The numerator of -3 is -3 and the denominator is 1. Therefore, the movement indicated by the slope is down 3 units, since the number is negative, and over to the right 1 unit.

2. Graph the line with slope $\dfrac{1}{2}$ that passes through the point $(0, -3)$.

   Solution:

   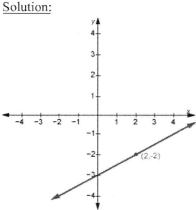

   Explanation: Begin by plotting the given point, $(0, -3)$, on the y-axis. Use the slope to find a second point on the line, $m = \dfrac{\text{rise}}{\text{run}} = \dfrac{1}{2}$. From $(0, -3)$, rise 1, then run 2, and then plot a second point at $(2, -2)$. Draw a line through these two points.

3. What is the x-intercept of the line that passes through $(4, 1)$ with slope $-\dfrac{1}{3}$?

   Solution: $(7, 0)$

   Explanation: To solve this problem graphically, first sketch the graph of this line and then determine the x-intercept. Begin by plotting the point $(4, 1)$ and then use the slope to determine a second point. The slope is $-\dfrac{1}{3}$ which indicates that the vertical change (rise) is down 1 unit from $(4, 1)$. The horizontal change (run) is to the right 3 units. Thus, the second point is at $(7, 0)$ which is located on the x-axis, so it is the x-intercept of the line.

Practice problems: *(Answers on page: 445)*

1. What are the coordinates of the y-intercept of the line that passes through $(-3, 5)$ with slope 1?

2. Graph the line with slope -3 that passes through the point $(2, -5)$.

3. Is $(4, 7)$ a point on the line that passes through the origin with slope 2?

Review questions: *(Answers to odd questions on page: 446)*

1. Graph the line with slope $\dfrac{3}{2}$ that passes through the point $(-2, -1)$.

2. Graph the line with slope $-\dfrac{3}{2}$ that passes through the point $(-2, -1)$.

3. Graph the line with slope -2 that passes through the point $(-2, 3)$.

4. Graph the line with slope $\frac{1}{2}$ that passes through the point (−2, 3).

5. Graph the line with slope $-\frac{1}{2}$ that passes through the point (−2, 3).

Writing an Equation in Slope-Intercept Form

- **Standard equation of a line:** $Ax + By = C$. A linear equation will always have an x to the first power, a y, and some constant.
- **Slope-intercept equation of a line:** $y = mx + b$. The constant, m, represents the slope or rate of change from one point to the next in the line. The constant, b, represents the y-intercept or point where the line crosses the y-axis.
- The **y-intercept** is the point where the line crosses the y-axis. The x-value is always 0. The y-value is represented by the variable b. The point's coordinates are (0, b).
- It is often very useful to express an equation that is given in standard form in slope-intercept form.
- To change a standard equation to a slope-intercept equation solve the equation for y.

Example Find the equation of the line where: (m) Slope = -2 (b) y-intercept = 5 $y = mx + b$ $\boxed{y = -2x + 5}$	You can create the equation for a line if you know the y-intercept and its slope. Start with: $y = mx + b$. Substitute your slope, −2, in for m. Substitute your y-intercept, 5, in for b. You're done.
Example Find the equation of the line where: (m) Slope = $\frac{1}{2}$ (b) y-intercept = -6 $y = mx + b$ $\boxed{y = \frac{1}{2}x - 6}$	Same thing works in this example: Start with: $y = mx + b$. Substitute ½ for m: $y = \frac{1}{2}x + b$. Substitute −6 for b: $y = \frac{1}{2}x - 6$. You're done.
Example Graph this line: $y = \frac{-2}{3}x + 1$ $\quad$ slope $\quad$ y-intercept 	You can also use the slope-intercept form of an equation to create a graph of the line. Start with the equation: $y = -2/3x + 1$. Place the y-intercept: (0, 1). Use the slope: $\quad$ count down −2 and to the right 3. Place a point at that location. Draw the line through the two points.

Example   Graph this line:

$$y = \frac{1}{2}x - 3$$

slope   y-intercept

The same process works here.

Start with the equation: $y = \frac{1}{2}x - 3$.
Place the y-intercept: $(0, -3)$.
Use the slope:
   count up 1 and to the right 2.
Place a point at that location.
Draw the line through the two points. Many people will suggest doing at least three points to reduce the possibility of error.

Sample problems:

1. Write the equation of the line with slope 5 that crosses the y-axis at the origin.

   Solution: $y = 5x$

   Explanation: Use the slope-intercept form of a linear equation, $y = mx + b$, where m is the slope and b is the y-intercept, to write the equation of this line. Substitute the slope into $y = mx + b$ for m: $y = 5x + b$. Next, substitute the y-intercept into $y = 5x + b$ for b. Since the line crosses the y-axis at the origin, the y-intercept is 0. So, the equation of the line is $y = 5x + 0 \implies y = 5x$.

2. Find the slope and y-intercept of the line formed by $5x - 2y = 6$.

   Solution: $m = \frac{5}{2}$ and $b = -3$

   Explanation: Since this equation is in standard form, begin by solving it for y so that it will be expressed in the more useful slope-intercept form: $5x - 2y = 6 \implies -2y = 6 - 5x \implies y = \frac{6-5x}{-2} \implies y = -3 + \frac{5}{2}x = \frac{5}{2}x - 3$. Since the equation is in the form $y = mx + b$, the slope and y-intercept are easily identified. The slope, m, is the coefficient of x and the y-intercept is the constant term. Thus, $m = \frac{5}{2}$ and $b = -3$.

3. Write the equation of the line that passes through the points $(6, -2)$ and $(10, 0)$ with y-intercept -5.

   Solution: $y = \frac{1}{2}x - 5$

   Explanation: The slope and y-intercept must be known to write the equation of a line. The value of b is given, -5, so begin by using the slope formula to find m:
   $m = \frac{y_2 - y_1}{x_2 - x_1} = \frac{0 - (-2)}{10 - 6} = \frac{2}{4} = \frac{1}{2}$. Now write the equation of the line by substituting m and b into $y = mx + b$: $y = \frac{1}{2}x - 5$.

Practice problems: *(Answers on page: 446)*

1. Write the equation of the line with slope $\frac{4}{3}$ that crosses the y-axis at $(0, -1)$.

2. Find the slope and y-intercept of the line formed by $x + y = 2$.

3. Write the equation of the line that passes through the points $(-1, -3)$ and $(2, 6)$ with y-intercept 0.

Review questions: *(Answers to odd questions on page: 446)*

1. Write the equation of the line with slope -3 and y-intercept $(0, 4)$.

2. Write the equation of the line with slope 0 and y-intercept $(0, -3)$.

3. Write the equation of the line with slope $\frac{2}{3}$ and y-intercept $(0, -2)$.

4. Find the slope and y-intercept of the line formed by $x - 3y = 12$.

5. Write the equation of the line that passes through the origin and has the same slope as $y = \frac{1}{3}x - 4$.

Writing an Equation Given Two Points

- **Standard equation of a line:** $Ax + By = C$. A linear equation will always have an x to the first power, a y, and some constant.
- **Slope-intercept equation of a line:** $y = mx + b$. The constant, m, represents the slope or rate of change from one point to the next in the line. The constant, b, represents the y-intercept or point where the line crosses the y-axis.
- The **y-intercept** is the point where the line crosses the y-axis. The x-value is always 0. The y-value is represented by the variable b. The point's coordinates are $(0, b)$.
- It is often very useful to express an equation that is given in standard form in slope-intercept form.
- To change a standard equation to a slope-intercept equation solve the equation for y.

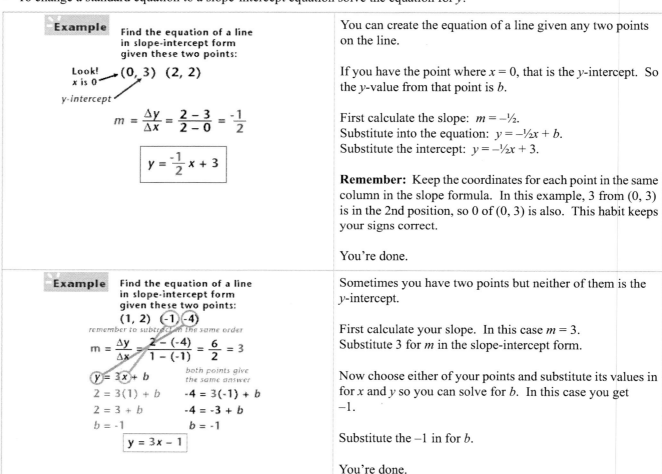

Example Find the equation of a line in slope-intercept form given these two points:

Look! x is 0 → $(0, 3)$ $(2, 2)$
y-intercept

$m = \dfrac{\Delta y}{\Delta x} = \dfrac{2 - 3}{2 - 0} = \dfrac{-1}{2}$

$\boxed{y = \dfrac{-1}{2}x + 3}$

You can create the equation of a line given any two points on the line.

If you have the point where $x = 0$, that is the y-intercept. So the y-value from that point is b.

First calculate the slope: $m = -\frac{1}{2}$.
Substitute into the equation: $y = -\frac{1}{2}x + b$.
Substitute the intercept: $y = -\frac{1}{2}x + 3$.

Remember: Keep the coordinates for each point in the same column in the slope formula. In this example, 3 from $(0, 3)$ is in the 2nd position, so 0 of $(0, 3)$ is also. This habit keeps your signs correct.

You're done.

Example Find the equation of a line in slope-intercept form given these two points:

$(1, 2)$ $(-1, -4)$
remember to subtract in the same order

$m = \dfrac{\Delta y}{\Delta x} = \dfrac{2 - (-4)}{1 - (-1)} = \dfrac{6}{2} = 3$

$y = 3x + b$ both points give the same answer

$2 = 3(1) + b$ $-4 = 3(-1) + b$
$2 = 3 + b$ $-4 = -3 + b$
$b = -1$ $b = -1$

$\boxed{y = 3x - 1}$

Sometimes you have two points but neither of them is the y-intercept.

First calculate your slope. In this case $m = 3$.
Substitute 3 for m in the slope-intercept form.

Now choose either of your points and substitute its values in for x and y so you can solve for b. In this case you get -1.

Substitute the -1 in for b.

You're done.

Sample problems:

1. Write the equation of a line in slope intercept form given the points: $(-2, -2)$ and $(3, 3)$.
   Solution: $y = x$
   Explanation:

   First calculate the slope between the two points: $m = \dfrac{y_2 - y_1}{x_2 - x_1} = \dfrac{(-2) - (3)}{(-2) - (3)} = \dfrac{-5}{-5} = 1$.
   Substitute the slope into slope-intercept form: $y = mx + b \Rightarrow y = 1x + b \Rightarrow y = x + b$.
   Determine b by substituting one of the points into $y = x + b$ and solve for b: $(3) = (3) + b$; $b = 0$.
   Complete the equation by substituting in $b = 0$ into $y = x + b$: $y = x + 0 \Rightarrow y = x$.

2. Write the equation of a line in slope intercept form given the points $(7, 5)$ and $(0, -2)$.
   Solution: $y = x - 2$
   Explanation: First calculate the slope between the two points:

   $m = \dfrac{y_2 - y_1}{x_2 - x_1} = \dfrac{5 - (-2)}{7 - (0)} = \dfrac{7}{7} = 1$. Next, determine b. Notice that the 2nd point is on the
   y-axis, so -2 is the y-intercept. Now write the equation of the line by substituting
   the m and b values into $y = mx + b$: $y = 1x + (-2) \Rightarrow y = x - 2$.

3. Write the equation of a line in slope intercept form given the points $(2, 1)$ and $(-2, -1)$.

   Solution: $y = \dfrac{1}{2}x$
   Explanation: First calculate the slope between the two points:

   $m = \dfrac{y_2 - y_1}{x_2 - x_1} = \dfrac{1 - (-1)}{2 - (-2)} = \dfrac{2}{4} = \dfrac{1}{2}$. Next, determine b by substituting m and the values

   from *either* point into $y = mx + b$, then solve for b: $1 = \dfrac{1}{2}(2) + b$; $b = 0$. Now
   write the equation of the line by substituting the values for m and b into $y = mx + b$:
   $y = \dfrac{1}{2}x + 0 \Rightarrow y = \dfrac{1}{2}x$.

Practice problems: *(Answers on page: 446)*

1. Write the equation of a line in slope intercept form given the points: $(1, 51)$ and $(0, 29)$.

2. Write the equation of a line in slope intercept form given the points: $(-5, 5)$ and $(7, -7)$.

3. Write the equation of a line in slope intercept form given the points: $\left(1, \dfrac{-23}{13}\right)$ and $\left(0, \dfrac{-37}{13}\right)$.

Review questions: *(Answers to odd questions on page: 446)*

1. Write the equation of a line in slope-intercept form given the points $(1, 2)$, $(2, 4)$.

2. Write the equation of a line in slope-intercept form given the points $(1.6, 3)$, $(0.3, 1.4)$.

3. Write the equation of a line in slope-intercept form given the points $(0, 0)$, $(-3, 6)$.

4. Write the equation of a line in slope-intercept form given the points $(10, 2)$, $(5, 2)$.

5. Write the equation of a line in slope-intercept form given the points $(3, 6)$, $(-3, 8)$.

Writing an Equation in Point-Slope Form

- **The point-slope form of an equation:** $y - y_1 = m(x - x_1)$. This equation is created from the slope formula. It allows you to create the equation of a line knowing any one point and the slope.

- **Slope:** $\dfrac{rise}{run} = \dfrac{y_2 - y_1}{x_2 - x_1} = \dfrac{\Delta y}{\Delta x}$

Example

Suppose: You are given the slope and a point

Write the equation of the line in point-slope form.

$$(-1, 3) \qquad m = \frac{-1}{4}$$
$$(x_1, y_1)$$

$$y - y_1 = m(x - x_1)$$

$$\boxed{y - 3 = \frac{-1}{4}(x + 1)}$$

Again, you are substituting values into the general equation.

Your slope is –1/4. Substitute –1/4 for m.
Your point is (–1,3). Substitute its values in for x_1 and y_1.

This formula is valuable if you are given the slope and any one point on a line.

Notice: The signs change as the point values go into the formula. They are subtracting.

You've got your equation. You're done.

Example

Suppose: You are given the equation of a line

What do you know about this line?

$$y - 2 = \frac{2}{3}(x + 1)$$
$$\frac{2}{3}(x - -1)$$

Slope is $\frac{2}{3}$

(-1, 2) is a point on the line

Thinking in reverse, you can look at an equation and discern the details needed to be able to graph a line.

Looking at this equation, you know immediately that the slope, m, is 2/3.

You also know that one point on the line is located at (–1,2).

Remember: change the signs on the numbers from the equation to determine the x- and y-values for the point.

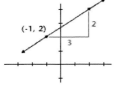

Place the one point you know, (–1,2).
From there count up 2 and to the right 3 to locate the second point.
Draw the line through the two points.
You've got your unique line.

Sample problems:

1. Write the equation in point-slope form of the line that passes through $(-4,-1)$ and has a slope of $\frac{2}{3}$.

   <u>Solution:</u> $y + 1 = \frac{2}{3}(x + 4)$

   <u>Explanation:</u> Substitute $m = \frac{2}{3}$ and the $x-$ and $y-$values from the point $(-4,-1)$ into the point-slope formula, $y - y_1 = m(x - x_1)$ to write the equation of the line:

   $y - (-1) = \frac{2}{3}(x - (-4)); \ y + 1 = \frac{2}{3}(x + 4).$

2. Write the equation in point-slope form of the line that crosses the y-axis at 2 and is parallel to the line described by $3x - 5y = 20$.

   <u>Solution:</u> $y - 2 = \frac{3}{5}x$

   <u>Explanation:</u> Find the slope of $3x - 5y = 20$ by expressing it in slope-intercept form:

   $y = \frac{3}{5}x - 4$, so the $m = \frac{3}{5}$. The slope of the new line is also $\frac{3}{5}$, since the lines are parallel.

   Now, using $m = \frac{3}{5}$, $(0, 2)$ (the y-intercept), and point-slope formula, write the equation of

   the line: $y - 2 = \frac{3}{5}(x - 0); \ y - 2 = \frac{3}{5}x.$

3. Write the equation in point-slope form of the line passing through $(2, -4)$ that is perpendicular to the line described by $3x + 2y = 5$.

Solution: $y + 4 = \dfrac{2}{3}(x - 2)$

Explanation: The slope and a point are needed in order to write the equation of a line in point-slope form. A point on the line $(2, -4)$ is given, so begin by finding the slope. The line is perpendicular to $3x + 2y = 5$, so the lines must have slopes that are negative reciprocals. To find the slope of $3x + 2y = 5$ express the equation in slope-intercept form, $y = mx + b$: $3x + 2y = 5 \Rightarrow 2y = 5 - 3x \Rightarrow y = \dfrac{5 - 3x}{2} \Rightarrow y = \dfrac{5}{2} - \dfrac{3x}{2}$, so the slope is $-\dfrac{3}{2}$. The slope of a line perpendicular to that line is $\dfrac{2}{3}$. Now, substitute the slope and the x and y values from the point into point-slope form, $y - y_1 = m(x - x_1)$: $y - (-4) = \dfrac{2}{3}(x - 2)$. Simplify: $y + 4 = \dfrac{2}{3}(x - 2)$.

Practice problems: *(Answers on page: 446)*

1. Write the equation in point-slope form of the line that crosses the x-axis at 3 with a slope of 4.

2. Write the equation of the line in point-slope form that passes through $(-1, 5)$ and is perpendicular to the line described by $x - 2y = 8$.

3. Write the equation of the line in point-slope form that passes through $(-3, 2)$ and is parallel to the line that passes through $(5, 2)$ and $(7, 8)$.

Review questions: *(Answers to odd questions on page: 446)*

1. Write the equation in point-slope form of the line that contains the point $(2, 5)$ and has a slope of 4.

2. Write the equation in point-slope form of the line that contains the point $(-1, -6)$ and has a slope of $\dfrac{1}{4}$.

3. Write the equation in point-slope form of the line that passes through $(4, 0)$ and is parallel to the line described by $x + y = 3$.

4. Write the equation in point-slope form of the line that passes through $(-3, 7)$ and is perpendicular to the line described by $y = 5 + 2x$.

5. Write the equation in point-slope form of the line that passes through $\left(\dfrac{3}{4}, -\dfrac{2}{3}\right)$ and is perpendicular to $3x + 5y = 10$.

Matching a Slope-Intercept Equation with Its Graph

- **Slope-intercept equation of a line:** $y = mx + b$. The constant, m, represents the slope or rate of change from one point to the next in the line. The constant, b, represents the y-intercept or point where the line crosses the y-axis.
- **The point-slope form of an equation:** $y - y_1 = m(x - x_1)$. This equation is created from the slope equation. It allows you to create the equation of a line knowing any one point and the slope.

Graph:

$$y + 1 = 2(x + 1) \longleftarrow \text{point-slope form}$$
$$y - (-1) = 2(x - (-1))$$

Slope = 2

(-1, -1) is a
point on the line

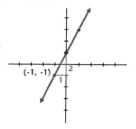

Consider the example given here:
$y + 1 = 2(x + 1)$.

Notice, the equation is in point-slope form. The slope is 2 and the given point is $(-1, -1)$.

Remember: Change the signs for the given point because those coordinates are being subtracted in the formula.

Graph:

$$y = 3$$
$$y = 0x + 3 \longleftarrow \text{slope-intercept form}$$

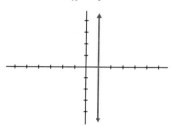

Slope = 0
y-intercept = 3

This equation does not contain x. Therefore the slope is 0, which makes it a horizontal line. Clearly the y-intercept is at 3.

So, you graph a horizontal line at $y = 3$.

Graph:

$$x = 1$$

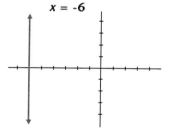

Choose any point on this line. The y can be anything in the real numbers. The $x = 1$.

So, graphing the line shows you it is vertical.

Graph:

$$-2x - 5 = 7 \longleftarrow \begin{array}{l}\text{this is not}\\ \text{slope-intercept}\\ \text{form because}\\ \text{there is no } y\end{array}$$
$$-2x = 12$$
$$x = -6$$

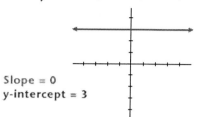

Notice this equation has no y-term.

Solve it for x.
Graph it.

You're done.

Graph:

$$2x - 3y = 1 \longleftarrow \text{ standard form}$$

$$2x = 1 + 3y \quad \text{solve for } y$$

$$2x - 1 = 3y$$

$$\frac{2}{3}x - \frac{1}{3} = y$$

$$y = \frac{2}{3}x - \frac{1}{3}$$

y-intercept $= -\dfrac{1}{3}$

Slope $= \dfrac{2}{3}$

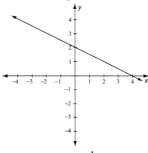

First, solve this equation for y.

Then you see that your slope is 2/3, and your y-intercept is −1/3.

Graph the line. First, locate your y-intercept. Then count up 2 and to the right 3 for the next point. Finally, draw the line.

Sample problems:

1. Write the equation of a line in slope-intercept form that matches the following graph.

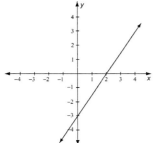

Solution: $y = -\dfrac{1}{2}x + 2$

Explanation: The y intercept of the graph is 2, so $b = 2$. Next, determine the slope. Once again, the x and y-intercepts are easy points to use, so $m = \dfrac{\Delta y}{\Delta x} = \dfrac{-2}{4} = -\dfrac{1}{2}$.

Now substitute m and b into slope-intercept form, $y = mx + b$: $y = -\dfrac{1}{2}x + 2$.

2. Does the equation $3x - 2y = 6$ match the following graph?

Solution: Yes

Explanation: Express $3x - 2y = 6$ in slope-intercept form: $y = \dfrac{3}{2}x - 3$. So, $m = \dfrac{3}{2}$ and $b = -3$. The y-intercept of the graphed line is also -3 & the slope is $\dfrac{3}{2}$.

Thus, the equation matches the graph.

Practice problems: *(Answers on page: 447)*

1. Does the equation $x - 2y = -3$ match the line graphed below?

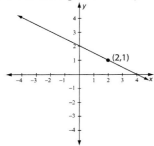

2. Does the equation $x + 2y = 4$ match the following graph?

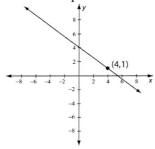

3. Write the equation of a line in slope-intercept form that matches the following graph.

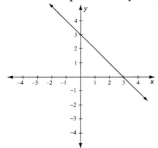

Review questions: *(Answers to odd questions on page: 447)*

1. Does the equation $x + y = 3$ match the following graph?

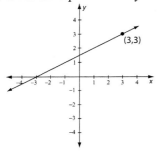

2. Does the equation $x + \dfrac{1}{3}y$ match the following graph?

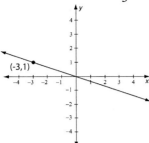

3. Write the equation of a line in slope-intercept form that matches the following graph.

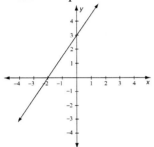

4. Does the equation $x = 4$ match the following graph?

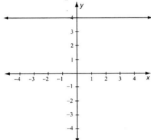

5. Does the equation $3x - 4y = 12$ match the following graph?

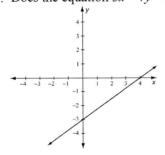

Slope for Parallel and Perpendicular Lines

- Two lines are parallel when they have the same slope and different y-intercepts.
- Two lines are perpendicular when their slopes are the negative reciprocals of each other. Another way to say this is that two lines are perpendicular when the product of their slopes is -1.

Parallel Lines

$$y = \frac{2}{3}x + 1$$

slope   y-intercept

$$y = \frac{2}{3}x - 2$$

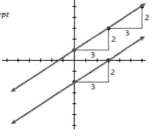

When two lines are parallel, they have exactly the same angle of tilt. They have exactly the same slope with different x- and y-intercepts.

All lines parallel to these two lines will have the same slope with unique x- and y-intercepts.

Perpendicular Lines

$$y = \frac{3}{4}x + 0$$

slope

$$y = \frac{-4}{3}x$$

notice the second slope is a negative reciprocal

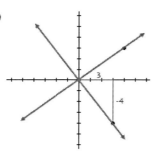

When two lines are perpendicular, they tilt opposite to each other. And, they exactly reverse how their x's and y's change. In this case, every time y changes 3 on the top line, x will change 3 on the second line. And, every time x changes 4 on the top line, y will change 4 on the second line.

Example
Find the equation of the line that passes through the point (1, 3) and is parallel to
$$3x + 4y = -24$$

You've just learned that parallel lines have the same slope. And this gives you a point on the second line. That's all you need.

$$4y = -3x - 24$$

$$y = \frac{-3x - 24}{4}$$

$$y = \frac{-3}{4}x - \frac{24}{4}$$

slope

Your first step is to determine the slope of the parallel line.

point-slope form → $y - y_1 = m(x - x_1)$

$$y - 3 = \frac{-3}{4}(x - 1)$$

Your second and last step is to substitute the coordinates of the point you were given on the parallel line into the point-slope form of an equation. And, there is your equation!

Example
Find the equation of the line that passes through (1, 2) and is perpendicular to

find the slope of the original line $x + y = 4$

$$y = -x + 4 \qquad \text{Slope} = \frac{-1}{1}$$

So, the slope of the ⊥ line $= -\left(\frac{1}{-1}\right) = 1$

point-slope form $y - y_1 = m(x - x_1)$

$$y - 2 = 1(x - 1)$$

$$y - 2 = x - 1$$

slope-intercept form → $y = x + 1$

Use the same steps here as you did above, only this time the slopes are the negative reciprocals of each other:

1. Find the slope of your equation: $m = -1$.
2. Determine the slope of the perpendicular line: $m = +1$.
3. Substitute into the point-slope form.
4. Do the arithmetic to get to the simpler slope-intercept form of the equation.

www.thinkwell.com

Sample problems:

1. What is the slope of a line perpendicular to the line $y = \frac{2}{3}x + 4$?

   Solution: $-\frac{3}{2}$

   Explanation: The slope of the line described by $y = \frac{2}{3}x + 4$ is $\frac{2}{3}$. The slopes of perpendicular lines are always opposite reciprocals. The opposite reciprocal of $\frac{2}{3}$ is $-\frac{3}{2}$.

2. Write the equation of a line through $(0, 7)$ that is parallel to the line described by $y = \frac{4}{3}x + \frac{9}{2}$.

   Solution: $y = \frac{4}{3}x + 7$

   Explanation: The slope of the line described by $y = \frac{4}{3}x + \frac{9}{2}$ is $\frac{4}{3}$. Parallel lines have the same slope, so the slope of the new line is also $\frac{4}{3}$. The lines goes through the point $(0, 7)$, which is the y-intercept, so $b = 7$. Substitute the m and b values into slope-intercept form: $y = \frac{4}{3}x + 7$.

3. Write the equation in slope-intercept form of a line through $(-1, 2)$ that is perpendicular to the line described by $4x - 3y = 8$.

   Solution: $y = -\frac{3}{4}x + \frac{5}{4}$

   Explanation: Express the equation in slope-intercept form, then identify the slope: $4x - 3y = 8 \Rightarrow y = \frac{4}{3}x - \frac{8}{3}$, so the slope is $\frac{4}{3}$. The slope of a line perpendicular to this given line is $-\frac{3}{4}$. Substitute the slope and the point into the point-slope formula to derive the equation: $y - 2 = -\frac{3}{4}(x - (-1))$. Simplify the equation and solve it for y:

   $y - 2 = -\frac{3}{4}(x + 1)$; $y = -\frac{3}{4}x - \frac{3}{4} + 2$; $y = -\frac{3}{4}x + \frac{5}{4}$.

Practice problems: *(Answers on page: 447)*

1. What is the slope of the line parallel to the line $2x - y = 5$?

2. What is the slope of the line perpendicular to line $4x - 8y = -24$?

3. Write the equation in slope-intercept form of a line through $(-2, 8)$ that is perpendicular to the line $-4x + 6y = 24$.

Review questions: *(Answers to odd questions on page: 447)*

1. What is the slope of the line parallel to the line $y = \frac{1}{2}x + 3$?

2. Write the equation in slope-intercept form of the line passing through point $(4, 5)$ that is parallel to the x-axis.

3. Write the equation in slope-intercept form of the line passing through point $(-1, -2)$ that is perpendicular to the the line $2x + 5y + 8 = 0$.

4. Write the equation in slope-intercept form of the line passing through $(-4, 2)$ that is perpendicular to the line described by $y = \frac{4}{3}x + 7$.

5. Write the equation in slope-intercept form of the line passing through point $(1, -6)$ that is parallel to the the line described by $x + 2y = 6$.

Graphing Some Important Functions

- This lecture presents some basic equations with their graphs. Becoming familiar with linear, quadratic, cubic, radical and absolute value equations and their graphs is important.

Example	Consider the equation $f(x) = c$.
$f(x) = c$ c is a constant 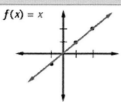	Every point on the line matches some x with the same value for y (or c in this case). The line is not moving at all on the vertical scale; therefore, it is horizontal.

Example	Every point changes x- and y-values exactly the same. So you get a line that divides the matching-signs quadrants exactly in half.
$f(x) = x$ 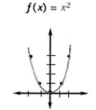	The function of $f(x) = x$ is the linear function.

Example	Parabolas are guaranteed symmetry by the x^2 term which neutralizes the signs of the values for x.
all parabolas will have this same basic shape $f(x) = x^2$ 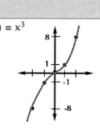	The function $f(x) = x^2$ is the quadratic parent function.

Example	This curve will rise three times faster than it moves sideways thanks to the impact of the x^3 term.
$f(x) = x^3$ 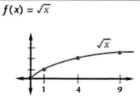	The funtion $f(x) = x^3$ is the cubic parent function.

Example	**Remember:** The value under the radical must be greater than or equal to zero so that a real number root can exist.
$f(x) = \sqrt{x}$	The function $f(x) = \sqrt{x}$ is the radical parent function.

www.thinkwell.com

Example

x	$f(x)$
-2	2
-1	1
0	0
-1	1
2	2

$f(x) = |x|$

Remember: Absolute value is always positive and graphed along the positive axis regardless of the expression within its notation.

The function $f(x) = |x|$ is the absolute value parent function.

Sample problems:

1. True or false: The graph of $y = 3x^3$ is a parabola.
    Solution: False
    Explanation: The function $y = 3x^3$ is cubic. However, parabolas are formed from quadratic functions where the variable is squared, not cubed.

2. Identify the parent function of $f(x) = |x| + 7$.
    Solution: $f(x) = |x|$
    Explanation: The function $f(x) = |x| + 7$ is an absolute value function, so its parent function is the most basic absolute value function $f(x) = |x|$.

3. All points on the graph of $y = x^2 + 2$ are contained in which quadrants?
    Solution: I and II

    Explanation: The domain of $y = x^2 + 2$ is all real numbers, however the graph is not in all four quadrants. The range is $y \geq 2$ (since any number squared then added to two is greater than or equal to 2), so the y-coordinates are only positive numbers. Thus, the graph is contained in the quadrants where x is negative or positive, but y is only positive, or quadrants I and II.

Practice problems: *(Answers on page: 447)*

1. Identify the parent function of $g(x) = 3\sqrt{x}$.

2. Identify the parent function of $y = x^2 + 4$.

3. In which quadrant do the points of the graph of $x = |y| + 1$ occur?

Review questions: *(Answers to odd questions on page: 447)*

1. True or false: The graph $y = -3$ is a vertical line.

2. True or false: The graph of the parent radical function passes through the origin.

3. Identify the parent function of $y = 6 - x$.

4. Identify the parent function of $f(x) = x^3 - 1$.

5. True or false: The graph of $f(x) = \frac{1}{3}x^2$ is a parabola.

Graphing Piecewise-Defined Functions

- **Piecewise functions** are those that are defined differently on different intervals of the x-axis.

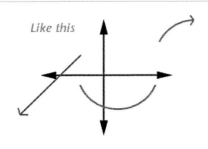

Like this

Piecewise functions can have different shapes from each other in their various parts.

Each part must be graphed separately as you use x-values all along the x-axis.

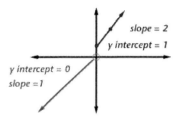

$$f(x) = \begin{cases} 2x+1 & \text{if } x \geq 0 \\ x & \text{if } x < 0 \end{cases}$$

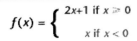

In this case you will use $2x+1$ every time you are considering an x that is equal to or larger than 0.

You will use x every time you are considering an x that is less than 0.

The result in this case is two unrelated lines: one that includes 0 and moves to the right, and one that starts at but does not include 0, and moves to the left. Notice how the endpoints are represented to show whether 0 is included or excluded on each line.

$$f(x) = \begin{cases} x+1 & \text{if } x \leq 3 \\ 4 & \text{if } x > 3 \end{cases}$$

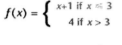

This example graphs y equals 4 for every x greater than +3. Notice the horizontal line that starts at +3 and moves to the right.

The function also includes a graph for $x+1$ for every x that includes and is less than +3. That graphs a downsloping line that includes +3 and moves to the left.

Both lines represent the function.

$$f(x) = \begin{cases} 2+x & \text{if } x < -4 \\ -x & \text{if } -4 \leq x \leq 5 \\ 3x & \text{if } x > 5 \end{cases}$$

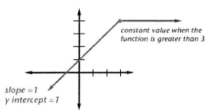

This function uses three different expressions to express itself. The result is three lines each being graphed over its segment of the x-axis.

Notice how the endpoints are represented. Notice that the middle line is a line segment with two definite endpoints. The two outer lines each have one definite endpoint but go on infinitely on their segment of the plane.

Sample problems:

1. What is the domain of $f(x) = \begin{cases} 3x^2 + x & \text{if } x < -2 \\ 4 - x & \text{if } x \geq -2 \end{cases}$?

   Solution: All real numbers
   Explanation: The domain is all possible x values, defined in this function by the two inequalitites $x < -2$ and $x \geq -2$. Together these inequalities include all real numbers.

2. Graph: $f(x) = \begin{cases} x^2 & \text{if } -2 \leq x \leq 2 \\ 4 & \text{if } x \text{ is any other real number} \end{cases}$

   Solution:

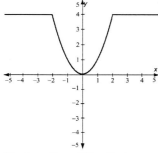

Explanation: The first case defines the function for $-2 < x < 2$. Between the points where $x = -2$ and $x = 2$, the graph is a parabola with its vertex at the origin. The second case defines the function as a straight line at all other points. For values of x that are less than or equal to -2 or greater than or equal to 2, the function is a straight line at $y = 4$. The function is defined at all points. It is represented by the described parabola with specified endpoints and the two rays with specified starting points.

3. Graph: $f(x) = \begin{cases} x+1 \text{ if } x \le 2 \\ x-1 \text{ if } x > 2 \end{cases}$

Solution:

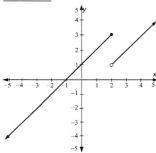

Explanation: The graph of $y = x+1$ when $x \le 2$ is a line that extends downward from the point $(2,3)$, including $x = 2$. The graph of $y = x-1$ if $x > 2$ is a line that extends upward from the point $(2,1)$, not including $x = 2$. The solution includes the point $(2,3)$ and shows the correct lines.

Practice problems: *(Answers on page: 447)*

1. What is the domain of $f(x) = \begin{cases} x^2 - 5 \text{ if } 0 \le x < 1 \\ -x \text{ if } x \ge 1 \end{cases}$?

2. Graph: $f(x) = \begin{cases} 3 \text{ if } x \le 0 \\ x^2 \text{ if } x > 0 \end{cases}$

3. Graph: $f(x) = \begin{cases} x \text{ if } x < -1 \\ -x^2 \text{ if } -1 < x < 1 \\ -1 \text{ if } x > 1 \end{cases}$

Review questions: *(Answers to odd questions on page: 447)*

1. For how many integer values of x is $f(x)$ not defined? $f(x) = \begin{cases} x \text{ if } x > 4 \\ -x + 2 \text{ if } 0 \le x < 4 \\ 2x \text{ if } x \le -3 \end{cases}$

2. What is the range of the function represented by the following graph?

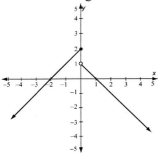

3. What is the domain of $f(x) = \begin{cases} 1 \text{ if } 0 < x < 5 \\ x+1 \text{ if } x \geq 5 \end{cases}$?

4. Graph: $f(x) = \begin{cases} x^2 + 1 \text{ if } x \geq 0 \\ -3 \text{ if } x < 0 \end{cases}$

5. Graph: $f(x) = \begin{cases} 3 - x \text{ if } x < 1 \\ 4 \text{ if } 1 < x \leq 2 \\ x \text{ if } x > 3 \end{cases}$

Matching Equations with Their Graphs

- Each type of equation has its own signature graph. Learn to match graphs with their equations.

What is the equation for this graph? 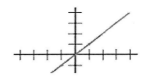	This graph is a straight line with a slope of 1. $y = x$ If you try some points, you will find (1, 1),(–2, –2), (0, 0), all on this line.
What is the equation for this graph? 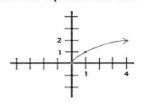	$y = \sqrt{x}$ **Remember:** x must be positive or 0 to be under the radical sign. As a result, the graph does not exist to the left of 0 or below the x-axis. Points you will find on this line include (0, 0), (16, 4), (25, 5) and (4, 2).
What is the equation for this graph? 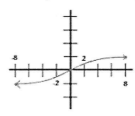	$y = \sqrt[3]{x}$ When you try points with this expression, you will find (1, 1), (–1, –1), (–8, –2), (27, 3) On this graph both coordinates always have the same sign and the x-values grow much faster than the y-values. Those two characteristics place this graph in Quadrants I and III following closely along the x-axis.

What is the equation for this graph?	$x = |y|$
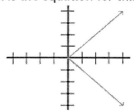	Try some points. You will find $(0, 0)$, $(2, 2)$ and $(2, -2)$, $(5, 5)$ and $(5, -5)$ among the points on this line. There is no way for x to be negative on this graph.
What is the equation for this graph?	$y = x^2$
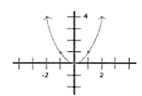	Try some points and you will find $(0, 0)$, $(2, 4)$ and $(-2, 4)$, $(5, 25)$ and $(-5, 25)$. There is no way for y to be negative and the y-values grow much faster than the x-values.

Sample problems:

1. Choose the relation from the following list that best describes the graph below:

$y = \dfrac{1}{x}$; $x = y^2$; $y = \sqrt{x}$; $x = |y|$; $y = x^2$; $y = [x]$; $y = x^3$; $y = |x|$; $y = \sqrt[3]{x}$.

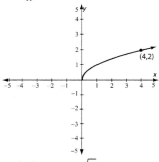

Solution: $y = [x]$

Explanation: The graph shows $y = [x]$. The greatest integer function is a step function, and several values of x give the same value of y, e.g., $[1.1] = [1.5143] = [1.67] = [1.9]$. Each of these pairs with $y = 1$.

2. Choose the relation from the following list that best describes the graph below:

$y = \dfrac{1}{x}$; $x = y^3$; $y = \sqrt{x}$; $x = |y|$; $y = x^2$; $y = [x]$; $y = x^3$; $y = |x|$; $y = \sqrt[3]{x}$.

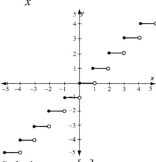

Solution: $y = \sqrt{x}$

Explanation: The domain of the graph shown is $x \geq 0$, which is also the domain of $y = \sqrt{x}$. The point $(4,2)$ is a point on the graph of $y = \sqrt{x}$, since $2 = \sqrt{4}$.

3. Choose the relation from the following list that best describes the graph below:

$y = \dfrac{1}{x}$; $x = y^2$; $y = \sqrt{x}$; $x = |y|$; $y = x^2$; $y = [x]$; $y = x^3$; $y = |x|$; $y = \sqrt[3]{x}$.

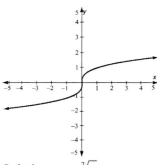

Solution: $y = \sqrt[3]{x}$

Explanation: The graph shows that y equals the cube root of x. This graph passes through the origin, and slowly progresses away from the x-axis in the first and third quadrants.

Practice problems: *(Answers on page: 447)*

1. Choose the relation from the following list that best describes the graph below:

$y = \dfrac{1}{x}; \quad x = y^2; \quad y = \sqrt{x}; \quad x = |y|; \quad y = x^2; \quad y = [x]; \quad y = x^3; \quad y = |x|; \quad y = \sqrt[3]{x}.$

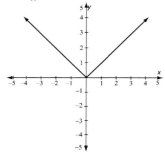

2. Choose the relation from the following list that best describes the graph below:

$y = \dfrac{1}{x}; \quad x = y^2; \quad y = \sqrt{x}; \quad x = |y|; \quad y = x^2; \quad y = [x]; \quad y = x^3; \quad y = |x|; \quad y = \sqrt[3]{x}.$

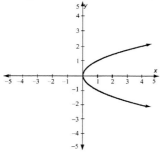

3. Choose the relation from the following list that best describes the graph below:

$y = \dfrac{1}{x}; \quad x = y^2; \quad y = \sqrt{x}; \quad x = |y|; \quad y = x^2; \quad y = [x]; \quad y = x^3; \quad y = |x|; \quad y = \sqrt[3]{x}.$

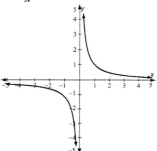

Review questions: *(Answers to odd questions on page: 447)*

1. Choose the relation from the following list that best describes the graph below:

$y = \dfrac{1}{x}$; $\quad x = y^2$; $\quad y = \sqrt{x}$; $\quad x = |y|$; $\quad y = x^2$; $\quad y = [x]$; $\quad y = x^3$; $\quad y = |x|$; $\quad y = \sqrt[3]{x}$.

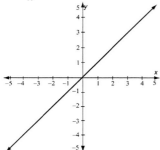

2. Choose the relation from the following list that best describes the graph below:

$y = \dfrac{1}{x}$; $\quad x = y^2$; $\quad y = \sqrt{x}$; $\quad x = |y|$; $\quad y = x^2$; $\quad y = [x]$; $\quad y = x^3$; $\quad y = |x|$; $\quad y = \sqrt[3]{x}$.

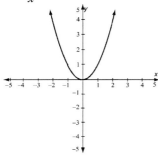

3. Choose the relation from the following list that best describes the graph below:

$y = \dfrac{1}{x}$; $\quad x = y^2$; $\quad y = \sqrt{x}$; $\quad x = |y|$; $\quad y = x^2$; $\quad y = [x]$; $\quad y = x^3$; $\quad y = |x|$; $\quad y = \sqrt[3]{x}$.

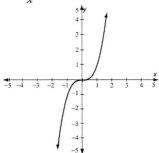

4. Choose the relation from the following list that best describes the graph below:

$y = 2^x$; $\quad x = y^3$; $\quad y = \sqrt{x}$; $\quad x = |y|$; $\quad y = x^2$; $\quad y = [x]$; $\quad y = x^3$; $\quad y = |x|$; $\quad y = \sqrt[3]{x}$.

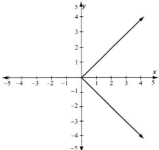

5. Choose the relation from the following list that best describes the graph below:

$$y = 2^x; \quad x = y^3; \quad y = \sqrt{x}; \quad x = |y|; \quad y = x^2; \quad y = [x]; \quad y = x^3; \quad y = |x|; \quad y = \sqrt[3]{x}.$$

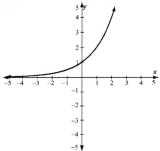

Shifting Curves along Axes

- Shifting a graph up is a matter of adding a value to the expression that produces the y-values. Likewise, shifting a graph down is a matter of subtracting a value from the same expression.
- Shifting a graph to the left on the axes is a matter of adding a value so that the x-values increase, $(x + c)$. Likewise, shifting a graph to the right is a matter of subtracting a value so that the x-values decrease, $(x - c)$.
- **Symmetry** means that half the graph is the exact mirror image of the other half.

Example — how do you modify this equation when it shifts up 1 unit? 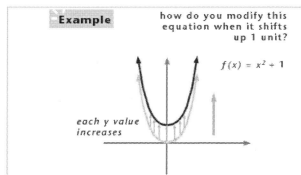 $f(x) = x^2 + 1$ — each y value increases	Moving a graph up on the axes involves adding a value to the expression that produces the y-values. In this example, $f(x) = x^2$ is shown graphed with its vertex at the origin. Then, +1 is added to the expression for $f(x)$, or y. As a result, the entire curve lifts up one unit on the axes. This change is shown by the upper curve on the graph.
Example — how do you modify this equation when it shifts down 1 unit? 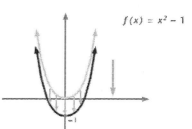 $f(x) = x^2 - 1$	Moving a graph down on the axes involves subtracting a value from the expression that produces the y-values. In this example, $f(x) = x^2$ is shown graphed with its vertex at the origin. Then, −1 is added to the expression for $f(x)$ so that the entire curve shifts down one unit on the axes. This change is shown by the lower curve on the graph.
Example $f(x) = x^2$ shifted to the left or right 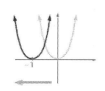 $f(x) = (x + 1)^2 \qquad f(x) = (x - 1)^2$	Movement sideways on a graph involves changing x-values without changing y-values. You generally do it by adding or subtracting some value to the x within parentheses so that the manipulations of the equation include it with the x-values. **NOTE:** The curve moves sideways opposite to the sign of the number added to the x-expression.

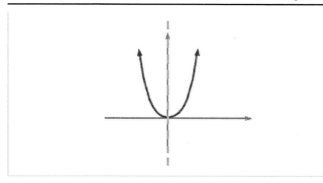

Symmetry means that you can cut a curve in half, flip one half over on top of the other one, and they will exactly match.

Symmetry also means that if you put a mirror at the vertex of a curve, the curve that appears in the mirror will exactly match the portion of the graph that the mirror is covering up.

Sample problems:

1. True or false: The equation $y = (x-4)^2 - 1$ will shift the graph of $y = x^2$ to the left 4 units and down 1 unit.
   Solution: False
   Explanation: Subtracting 1 from the expression shifts the parabola down 1 unit. Subtracting 4 from the x value within the parentheses shifts the parabola to the right 4 units. Remember, the curve moves sideways opposite to the sign of the number added to the x within the parentheses.

2. Write the equation that would move $y = (x+1)^2 + 5$ to the left 3 units and down 7 units.
   Solution: $y = (x+4)^2 - 2$
   Explanation: To move a curve to the left 3 units, add 3 within the parentheses. To move a curve down 7 units subtract 7 outside the parentheses. So, $y = (x+1)^2 + 5$ becomes $y = (x+1+3)^2 + 5 - 7 \Rightarrow y = (x+4)^2 - 2$.

3. Write the equation that would move $y = x^2 - 4$ up 5 units and to the right 3 units.
   Solution: $y = (x-3)^2 + 1$
   Explanation: To shift up 5 units, add 5 outside the parentheses. To shift right 3 units, subtract 3 within the parentheses. Thus, $y = (x-3)^2 - 4 + 5 \Rightarrow y = (x-3)^2 + 1$.

Practice problems: *(Answers on page: 447)*

1. How could you change the function $f(x) = x^2 - 2$ so that its graph will shift up two units?

2. How would you change the function, $f(x) = x^2$, so that its graph would shift 3 units higher?

3. Write the equation that will shift $y = (x-2)^2 - 1$ to the left 2 units and up 1 unit.

Review questions: *(Answers to odd questions on page: 447)*

1. What would you do to $f(x) = 3x^2 - 7$ so that its graph will pass through $(0,0)$?

2. What would you do to the function $f(x) = 2x^3 + 2$ so that its graph will pass through $(0,0)$?

3. True or false: The equation $y = (x+3)^2 + 5$ will shift the graph of $y = x^2$ to the left 3 units and up 5 units.

4. True or false: The equation $y = (x-1)^2 - 7$ will shift the graph of $y = x^2$ to the left 1 unit and down 7 units.

5. Write the equation that will shift the graph of $y = (x-1)^2$ to the right 5 units and down 2 units.

Shifting or Translating Curves along Axes

- Shifting up or down on a graph is a matter of adding or subtracting a value to the expression that gives you the y-values.
- Shifting sideways on a graph is a matter of adding or subtracting within parentheses with the x. Remember shifts move opposite to the signs added in these x-expressions.
- Shift carefully. When you add to y, go high. When you add to x, go west.

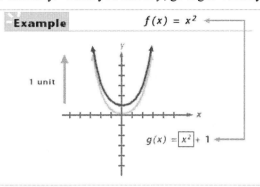

Example $f(x) = x^2$

Consider the example here: graph $g(x) = x^2 + 1$.

In this case, $+1$ was added to the expression used to derive the y-values.

So, the entire curve shifted up one unit on the axes.

This happens because for every point (x, y) on the original curve there exists a point $(x, y + 1)$ on the new curve.

Example $f(x) = x^2$

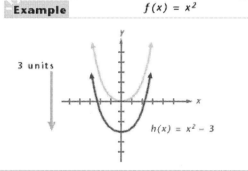

In this example, -3 is added to the expression used to derive the y-values.

The result is that every y is reduced by 3 and the entire curve drops three units on the axes.

In generic terms, for every point (x, y) on the original curve there exists a point $(x, y - 3)$ on the new curve.

$(x + \text{a number})$ ⟵ shift left
$(x - \text{a number})$ ⟶ shift right

Example $f(x) = x^2$

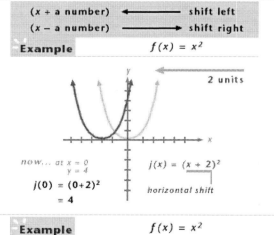

$j(x) = (x + 2)^2$

now... at $x = 0$
$y = 4$
$j(0) = (0+2)^2$
$= 4$

horizontal shift

Shifting sideways is a little more complicated. The value to shift must accompany the x within the parentheses. By doing this, you are really changing the value of x.

Notice that when you add a positive number to x, the graph shifts to the negative, i.e., to the left.

In this example, $(x + 2)^2$ shifts the curve 2 units to the left.

Example $f(x) = x^2$

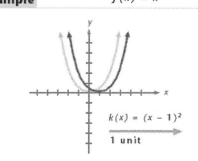

$k(x) = (x - 1)^2$

1 unit

Once again, here is the basic parabola with its vertex at the origin.

In this example, $(x - 1)^2$ shifts the curve 1 unit to the right.

When you add a negative number to x, the graph shifts to the positive, i.e., to the right.

Sample problems:

1. Modify the equation $f(x) = 3(x+2)^2 - \dfrac{4}{5}$ to shift the parabola up $3\dfrac{1}{2}$ units and to the left 7 units.

   <u>Solution:</u> $f(x) = 3(x+9)^2 + 2\dfrac{7}{10}$

   <u>Explanation:</u> Add $3\dfrac{1}{2}$ to $-\dfrac{4}{5}$ to shift the parabola up $3\dfrac{1}{2}$ units, and add 7 to 2 to shift the parabola

   7 units to the left: $f(x) = 3(x+2+7)^2 - \dfrac{4}{5} + 3\dfrac{1}{2} \Rightarrow f(x) = 3(x+9)^2 + 2\dfrac{7}{10}$.

2. Modify the equation $y = -x^2 + \dfrac{2}{3}$ to shift the parabola to the right 5 units and down 2 units.

   <u>Solution:</u> $y = -(x-5)^2 - 1\dfrac{1}{3}$

   <u>Explanation:</u> Subtract 5 from x to shift the parabola to the right 5 units and subtract 2 from $\dfrac{2}{3}$ to

   shift the parabola down 2 units: $y = -(x-5)^2 + \dfrac{2}{3} - 2 \Rightarrow y = -(x-5)^2 - 1\dfrac{1}{3}$.

3. What are the new values of b and c when the graph of $y = x^2 + 4x + 3$ is shifted up 2 units and to the left 3 units? (Recall the standard form of a quadratic: $ax^2 + bx + c$)
   <u>Solution:</u> $b = 10$ and $c = 26$
   <u>Explanation:</u> Express the equation in vertex form by completing the square: $y = (x^2 + 4x + 4) + 3 - 4$;
   $y = (x+2)^2 - 1$. Now add 2 to -1 and add 3 to 2 to do the shifting:
   $y = (x+2+3)^2 - 1 + 2 \Rightarrow y = (x+5)^2 + 1$.
   Next, express the equation in standard form by simplifying:
   $y = (x+5)^2 + 1$; $y = (x^2 + 10x + 25) + 1$; $y = x^2 + 10x + 26$.

Practice problems: *(Answers on page: 448)*

1. Modify the following equation to shift this parabola $2\dfrac{1}{2}$ units down: $f(x) = \dfrac{5}{4}\left(x - \dfrac{9}{2}\right)^2 + \dfrac{17}{4}$

2. Modify the following equation to shift this curve 3 units to the left: $f(x) = 2x^2 - 5$

3. What are the new values of b and c when the graph of $y = x^2 + 6x - 5$ is shifted down 4 units and to the right 1 unit?

Review questions: *(Answers to odd questions on page: 448)*

1. Modify the equation $f(x) = 5(x+3)^2 - 1$ to shift the parabola $5\frac{1}{2}$ units to the right.

2. Modify the equation $f(x) = -4.75(x-0.25)^2 - 2$ to shift the parabola up 3.45 units and to the left 11.8 units.

3. Modify the equation $f(x) = -x^2 + 3$ to shift the parabola $3\frac{2}{5}$ units to the left.

4. Modify the equation $f(x) = -x^2 - 5$ to shift the parabola 4 units to the right and 1 unit down.

5. What are the new values of b and c when the graph of $y = x^2 + 8x - 7$ is shifted down 3 units and to the right 4 units?

Stretching a Graph

- Multiplying the equation of a quadratic function by a coefficient greater than 1 makes the parabola narrower.
- Multiplying the equation of a quadratic function by a coefficient between 0 and 1 makes the parabola wider.

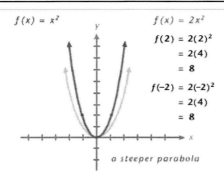

Here the function $f(x) = x^2$ was graphed first.

Then, $f(x) = 2x^2$ was graphed. It is steeper and therefore narrower than the original parabola.

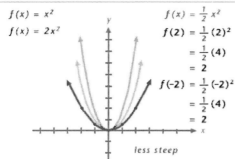

Using the same axes, the curve of $f(x) = \frac{1}{2}x^2$ was added.

This curve is the least steep of the three curves.

Another way of describing this curve is to say that it is the widest and most open.

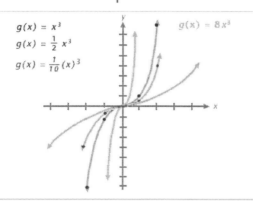

The same pattern holds for curves other than parabolas. On these axes, you have the graph of $g(x) = x^3$.

The steepest graph is that of $g(x) = 8x^3$. The two wider curves on the axes are for $g(x) = \frac{1}{2}x^3$ and $g(x) = \frac{1}{10}x^3$.

Sample problems:

1. True or false: The graph of $f(x) = \frac{1}{4}x^2$ is wider than the graph of $f(x) = x^2$.

    Solution: True

    Explanation: The width of the parabola is described by the value of the coefficient, a. If $|a| > 1$, then the parabola is narrower than $f(x) = x^2$. If $|a| < 1$, then the parabola is wider than $f(x) = x^2$. In the function $f(x) = \frac{1}{4}x^2$, $a = \frac{1}{4}$, so the parabola is wider than $f(x) = x^2$ since $|a| < 1$.

2. True or false: The graph of $f(x) = -\frac{8}{3}x^2$ is wider than the graph of $f(x) = x^2$ and it opens in the opposite direction.

    Solution: False

    Explanation: Since $|a| = \left|-\frac{8}{3}\right| = \frac{8}{3} > 1$, the parabola is narrower than the graph of $f(x) = x^2$.

    However, the parabolas do open in opposite directions since the a values have opposite signs.

3. Write the function that results in the following changes to the graph of $f(x) = x^2$: shifts 2 units to the right, shifts 5 units up, and is 3 times wider.

Solution: $f(x) = \dfrac{1}{3}(x-2)^2 + 5$

Explanation: Shifting the parabola formed by $f(x) = x^2$ to the right 2 units and up 5 units results in a move of the vertex from $(0,0)$ to $(2,5)$. Thus, $h = 2$ and $k = 5$, so the new function is $f(x) = a(x-2)^2 + 5$. The new graph is also 3 times wider, so divide the a value in $f(x) = x^2$ by 3. Thus, $a = \dfrac{1}{3}$ and the complete function is $f(x) = \dfrac{1}{3}(x-2)^2 + 5$.

Practice problems: *(Answers on page: 448)*

1. True or false: The graph of $f(x) = 4x^2$ is wider than the graph of $f(x) = 7x^2$.

2. True of false: If $y = ax^2$ opens up and is wider than $y = x^2$, then $a > 1$.

3. True of false: If $y = ax^2$ opens down and is narrower than $y = 5x^2$, then $a < -5$.

Review questions: *(Answers to odd questions on page: 448)*

1. True or false: The graph of $f(x) = -5x^2$ is narrower than the graph of $f(x) = -3x^2$.

2. Write the function that results in the following changes to the graph of $f(x) = -x^2$: shifts up 2 units, to the left 5 units, and is 3 times as narrow.

3. True or false: The parabola formed by $f(x) = 4x^2$ is 4 times as wide as the parabola formed by $f(x) = x^2$.

4. Write the function that results in the following changes to the graph of $f(x) = -x^2$: flips over and is 3 times wider.

5. If the a value of $f(x) = x^2$ is multiplied by a negative integer other than -1, how is the graph affected?

Graphing Quadratics Using Patterns

- To graph any function, follow these steps:
    1. Determine its basic shape centered at the origin.
    2. Determine its sign so you can sketch how it opens.
    3. Determine its steepness so you can sketch its shape.
    4. Determine its location according to any shift indicated.

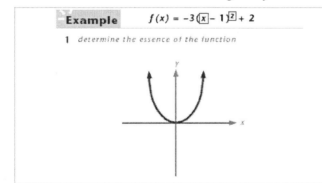

Example $f(x) = -3\,(\boxed{x} - 1)^{\boxed{2}} + 2$

1 *determine the essence of the function*

Your first step is to graph the general shape of the curve centered at the origin.

In this example, only the x is squared, so you will have a parabola as shown.

2 *determine the sign* 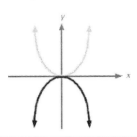	Your next step is to determine which direction the parabola will open. If the coefficient of the x-term is negative, the curve will open downward. Otherwise, it opens upward. In this example, the coefficient is negative, so the curve opens downward, as shown.
3 *determine steepness of the curve* 	The third step is to determine how wide or narrow the curve is; i.e., the curve's steepness or pitch. In this case, the x-term is multiplied by 3 which will make the curve noticeably narrower than the generic parabola, as shown here.
4 *determine any shift* 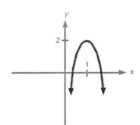	Your final step is to check for any shifts of the vertex away from the origin. In this example, the $(x-1)$ indicates a move to the right 1 unit. The $+2$ indicates a move up 2 units. You can see on the graph that the curve has moved its vertex to the right 1 and up 2.

Sample problems:

1. Write the equation of a parabola that has the vertex at (5,4), is 3 times narrower than $y = x^2$, and opens down along the y-axis.

   Solution: $y = -3(x-5)^2 + 4$

   Explanation: Substitute the (h,k) values from the vertex into vertex form: $y = a(x-5)^2 + 4$.

   To make the parabola 3 times narrower than $y = x^2$, multiply a in $y = x^2$ by 3: $y = 3(x-5)^2 + 4$.

   To produce a parabola that opens down, the sign of a must be negative: $y = -3(x-5)^2 + 4$.

2. Write a function that produces the following changes to $y = x^2$: shifts to the right 7 units, shifts down 1 unit, 4 times wider, and opens in the opposite direction.

   Solution: $y = -\frac{1}{4}(x-7)^2 - 1$

   Explanation: Subtract 7 from x to shift to the right: $y = (x-7)^2$. Subtract 1 to shift down: $y = (x-7)^2 - 1$. To make the parabola 4 times wider, divide a by 4: $y = \frac{1}{4}(x-7)^2 - 1$. Change the sign of a to open the parabola in the opposite direction: $y = -\frac{1}{4}(x-7)^2 - 1$.

3. Write a function that produces the following changes to $y = -5x^2$: shifts to the left 2 units, shifts up 3 units, 2 times wider, and opens in the opposite direction.

   Solution: $y = \frac{5}{2}(x+2)^2 + 3$

   Explanation: Add 2 to x to shift to the left: $y = -5(x+2)^2$. Add 3 to shift up: $y = -5(x+2)^2 + 3$.

   To make the parabola 2 times wider, divide a by 2: $y = -\frac{5}{2}(x+2)^2 + 3$. Change the sign of a to open the parabola in the opposite direction: $y = \frac{5}{2}(x+2)^2 + 3$.

Practice problems: *(Answers on page: 448)*

1. Write the equation of a parabola with vertex at $(-7,0)$ that is 4 times narrower than $y = \frac{5}{6}x^2$.

2. Write a function that produces the following changes to $y = x^2$: shifts to the right 3.25 units and shifts up 1.5 units.

3. Write a function that produces the following changes to $y = 3(x+5)^2 + 1$: shifts to the left 3 units, shifts down 4 units, and is 3 times wider.

Review questions: *(Answers to odd questions on page: 448)*

1. Write the equation of a parabola with vertex at $(-2,5)$ with width that is $\frac{1}{4}$ of the width of $y = x^2$.

2. Write a function that produces the following changes to $y = x^2$: shifts to the right 2 and up 5 units.

3. Write a function that produces the following changes to $y = x^2 + 4$: shifts to the left 3 units and opens in the opposite direction.

4. Write a function that produces the following changes to $y = -2x^2 - 1$: shifts to the right 3 units, shifts up 5 units, opens in the opposite direction, and is 4 times wider.

5. Write a function that produces the following changes to $y = -(x-3)^2 + 1$: shifts down 4 units, to the left 11 units, and opens in a positive direction.

Determining Symmetry

- **Symmetry** indicates that half the graph of a curve is an exact mirror image of the other half of the graph. You can take the right half of the curve and flip it over the y-axis to see the left half of the curve.
- An **even function** is one which exactly maps one half of itself on the right side of its axis and exactly reflects that half on the left side of its axis; i.e., an even function is one which is symmetrical about its axis.
- An even function will pair each y-value used with both x and $-x$ for every value used for x. This means that $f(x) = f(-x)$ for these equations.
- An **odd function** will be symmetrical but in respect to the origin, $(0, 0)$. For an odd function, every point (x, y) will be matched with $(-x, -y)$. You can take the right half of the curve and flip it over the y-axis, then flip it again over the x-axis to see the left half of the curve.
- For an odd function, every $f(-x) = -f(x)$. Every $-x$-value is matched with its $-y$-value.
- A circle is symmetrical with respect to the x-axis, the y-axis and also with the origin. Remember that a circle is not a function because it cannot pass the vertical line test.

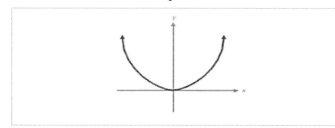

You can graph one side of an even function, and flip that curve over the y-axis to get the rest of the graph. You know that every point (x, y) matches with its own $(-x, y)$.

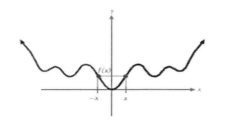

If you work out the curve from (0, 0) to the right of the *y*-axis, you can sketch the left side in mirror image and be done.

What you will notice if you actually work out the points is that for every point (*x*, *y*) that you have, you will also have the point (–*x*, *y*).

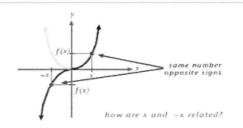

Odd functions flip from one quadrant to the opposite quadrant skipping the one in between.

As you can see in this example, $f(x)$ will pair with $-f(x)$.

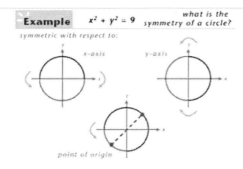

In this example, the circle is centered at the origin and has a radius of 3.

It is not a function because every *x* is paired with more than one *y*.

It is symmetrical several ways. You can flip it over the *y*-axis; you can flip it over the *x*-axis; you can flip it around the origin.

Sample problems:

1. If $f(x)$ is an even function and the points $(1, 2)$, $(3, 10)$, and $(4, 17)$ lie on the graph of $f(x)$, identify three additional points on the graph.
   Solution: $(-1, 2)$, $(-3, 10)$, and $(-4, 17)$
   Explanation: Since $f(x)$ is an even function the graph is symmetrical around the *y*-axis.
   Reflect each given point over the *y*-axis: $(1, 2)$, $(3, 10)$, and $(4, 17) \rightarrow (-1, 2)$, $(-3, 10)$, and $(-4, 17)$.

2. If $f(x)$ is an odd function and the points $(-1, 5)$ and $(0, -1)$ lie on the graph of $f(x)$, identify two additional points on the graph.
   Solution: $(1, -5)$ and $(0, 1)$
   Explanation: Since $f(x)$ is an odd function the graph is symmetrical around the origin.
   To reflect the given points over the origin, switch the sign of each coordinate:
   $(-1, 5)$ and $(0, -1) \rightarrow (1, -5)$ and $(0, 1)$.

3. Determine if the function is even, odd, or neither: $f(x) = x^2 + 1$
   Solution: Even
   Explanation: If $f(x)$ is an even function, then $f(-x) = f(x)$. If $f(x)$ is an odd function, then $f(-x) = -f(x)$. If $f(-x) \neq f(x)$ and $f(-x) \neq -f(x)$, then the function is neither even nor odd.
   Find $f(-x)$: $f(-x) = (-x)^2 + 1 = x^2 + 1 = f(x)$. Thus, $f(x)$ is an even function since $f(-x) = f(x)$.

Practice problems: *(Answers on page: 448)*

1. If $f(x)$ is an even function and the points $(-4, -1)$ and $(5, 0)$ lie on the graph of $f(x)$, identify two additional points on the graph.

2. If $f(x)$ is an odd function and the points $(2, 0)$ and $(-5, -1)$ lie on the graph of $f(x)$, identify two additional points on the graph.

3. Determine if the function is even, odd, or neither: $f(x) = \dfrac{2x + x^3}{3}$

Review questions: *(Answers to odd questions on page: 448)*

1. If $f(x)$ is an even function and the points $(3, -2)$ and $(0, -1)$ lie on the graph of $f(x)$, identify two additional points on the graph.

2. If $f(x)$ is an even function and the points (a, b) and (c, d) lie on the graph of $f(x)$, identify two additional points on the graph.

3. If $f(x)$ is an odd function and the points $(13, -4)$ and $(-7, -1)$ lie on the graph of $f(x)$, identify two additional points on the graph.

4. If $f(x)$ is an odd function and the points $(a, -b)$ and $(-c, d)$ lie on the graph of $f(x)$, identify two additional points on the graph.

5. Determine if the function is even, odd, or neither: $f(x) = x^2 - x^3$

Reflections

- **Reflecting a curve** over the x-axis matches every original (x, y) with its own $(x, -y)$.
- Reflecting a curve over the y-axis matches every (x, y) with its own $(-x, y)$.

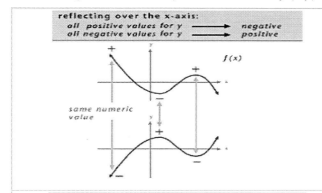

This curve is **reflecting** over the x-axis. You can see visually how every point that was above the x-axis is now the exact same distance below the x-axis and the same distance from the origin.

So, every (x, y) is matched with its $(x, -y)$.

You reflect any curve over the x-axis by changing the sign of the y-value in every point.

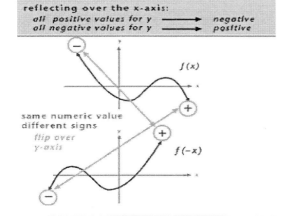

You can see that reflecting over the y-axis works the same way, only now it is the x-values that are affected.

From this graph you can see that every point on the curve has moved at the same height from x units from the origin to $-x$ units from the origin.

So, every (x, y) is now matched with its own $(-x, y)$.

You can achieve a reflection around the y-axis by changing the sign of the x-value for every (x, y) in the curve.

Example

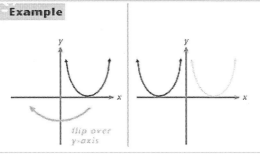

This graph shows an example where the entire curve has shifted around the y-axis. Even though the curve looks like it has merely moved, it really has flipped over as every x-value became a $-x$.

Sample problems:

1. If the points $(1, -3)$, $(0, 5)$, and $(-4, -2)$ lie on the graph of $f(x)$,
   identify three points on the graph when $f(x)$ is reflected across the x-axis.
   <u>Solution:</u> $(1, 3)$, $(0, -5)$, and $(-4, 2)$
   <u>Explanation:</u> When $f(x)$ is reflected across the x-axis, the sign of each y-coordinate
   is switched: $(1, -3)$, $(0, 5)$, and $(-4, -2)$ $\rightarrow$ $(1, 3)$, $(0, -5)$, and $(-4, 2)$.

2. If the points $(-a, b)$ and $(c + d, -e)$ lie on the graph of $f(x)$,
   identify two points on the graph when $f(x)$ is reflected across the y-axis.
   <u>Solution:</u> (a, b) and $(-c - d, -e)$
   <u>Explanation:</u> When $f(x)$ is reflected across the y-axis, the sign of each x-coordinate
   is switched: $(-a, b)$ and $(c + d, -e)$ $\rightarrow$ (a, b) and $(-c - d, -e)$.

3. Sketch a reflection of the graph below across the y-axis.

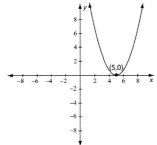

<u>Solution:</u>

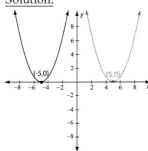

<u>Explanation:</u> To reflect $f(x)$ across the y-axis, switch the sign of each x-coordinate. Choose any point on the graph.
Plot the reflection point: do not shift vertically, shift horizontally an equal distance from the y-axis, but in the
opposite direction. Repeat the pattern for several points.

Practice problems: *(Answers on page: 448)*

1. If the points $(-5, -2)$, $(1, -7)$, and $(0, -2)$ lie on the graph of $f(x)$,
   identify three points on the graph when $f(x)$ is reflected across the x-axis.

2. If the points $(1 - a, b - d)$ and $(c - d, e)$ lie on the graph of $f(x)$,
   identify two points on the graph when $f(x)$ is reflected across the y-axis.

3. Sketch a reflection of the graph below across the x-axis.

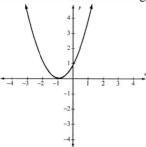

Review questions: *(Answers to odd questions on page: 448)*

1. If the points $(10, -2)$, $(-1, 3)$, and $(0, 0)$ lie on the graph of $f(x)$,
   identify three points on the graph when $f(x)$ is reflected across the y-axis.

2. If the points (x, y) and $(-w, -z)$ lie on the graph of $f(x)$,
   identify two points on the graph when $f(x)$ is reflected across the y-axis.

3. If the points $(2a + x, 1 - y)$ and $(z - w, 1 + z)$ lie on the graph of $f(x)$,
   identify two points on the graph when $f(x)$ is reflected across the x-axis.

4. Sketch a reflection of the graph below across the x-axis.

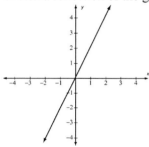

5. Sketch a reflection of the graph below across the y-axis.

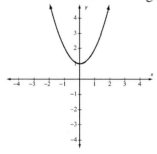

Reflecting Specific Functions

- Reflecting over the x-axis means that the y values will change signs. Any $+y$ will become $-y$ while any $-y$ will become $+y$.
- Reflecting over the y-axis means that the x values will change signs. Any $+x$ will become $-x$ while any $-x$ will become $+x$.
- When reflecting a function across the x-axis, change the sign of every term in the expression because they all are part of finding the y-value.
- When reflecting a function across the y-axis, change only the sign of every x-term because each x is becoming $-x$.

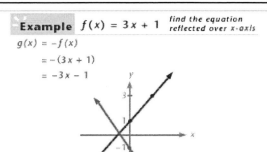

Example $f(x) = 3x + 1$ _find the equation reflected over x-axis_

$g(x) = -f(x)$
$= -(3x + 1)$
$= -3x - 1$

This example shows a reflection across the x-axis. When you compare the original and the reflected lines, you can see that the reflected line has changed all signs for y-values.

This can be easily achieved by changing signs over the entire expression and then finding values in the new expression.

In this example, the $(3x + 1)$ changes to be $-(3x + 1)$, or $-3x - 1$.

You do this because it is the entire expression that gives you each value for y.

This method also gives you the equation of the reflection.

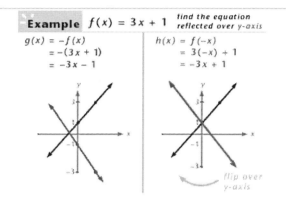

Example $f(x) = 3x + 1$ _find the equation reflected over y-axis_

$g(x) = -f(x)$
$= -(3x + 1)$
$= -3x - 1$

$h(x) = f(-x)$
$= 3(-x) + 1$
$= -3x + 1$

flip over y-axis

Any reflection over the y-axis involves changing the signs for all the x-values.

For every x in the expression, substitute in a $-x$. Then figure the final expression.

Note: To reflect across the y-axis, change the sign of every x in the expression.

Note: To reflect across the x-axis, change the entire expression.

Sample problems:

1. For the function, $y = -\frac{3}{4}x + 1$, find the original and reflected points about the x-axis for the value $x = 8$.

   Solution: $(8, -5)$ and $(8, 5)$

   Explanation: Substitute $x = 8$ into the function and solve for y: $y = -\frac{3}{4}(8) + 1 = -6 + 1 = -5$.
   The original point is $(8, -5)$. To reflect the point about the x-axis, switch the sign of the y-coordinate: $(8, -5) \rightarrow (8, 5)$.

2. Let $g(x)$ be the result when $f(x) = 2x - 5$ is reflected across the x-axis. Find $g(x)$.

   Solution: $g(x) = 5 - 2x$

   Explanation: The reflection of $f(x)$ across the x-axis is $-f(x)$: $g(x) = -f(x) = -(2x - 5) = -2x + 5 = 5 - 2x$.

3. Let $g(x)$ be the result when $f(x) = x^2 + x$ is reflected across the y-axis. Find $g(x)$.

   Solution: $g(x) = x^2 - x$

   Explanation: The reflection of $f(x)$ across the y-axis is $f(-x)$: $g(x) = f(-x) = (-x)^2 + (-x) = x^2 - x$.

Practice problems: _(Answers on page: 448)_

1. For the function, $y = 4 - x^2$, find the original and reflected points about the y-axis for the value $x = -1$.

2. Let $g(x)$ be the result when $f(x) = 2x^2 - x + 1$ is reflected across the x-axis. Find $g(x)$.

3. Let $g(x)$ be the result when $f(x) = \dfrac{1 - x^3}{x^2}$ is reflected across the y-axis. Find $g(x)$.

Review questions: *(Answers to odd questions on page: 448)*

1. For the function, $y = x - x^3$, find the original and reflected points about the y-axis for the value $x = 2$.

2. For the function, $y = 3x - 2$, find the original and reflected points about the x-axis for the value $x = a + 1$.

3. Let $g(x)$ be the result when $f(x) = -x^3 - x^2 + x$ is reflected across the x-axis. Find $g(x)$.

4. Let $g(x)$ be the result when $f(x) = -5x^3 + 2x^2$ is reflected across the y-axis. Find $g(x)$.

5. Let $g(x)$ be the result when $f(x) = 1 - x + x^3$ is reflected across the y-axis. Find $g(x)$.

Deconstructing the Graph of a Quadratic Function

- Quadratic functions:
  1) represent parabolas;
  2) have symmetry;
  3) have a turning point, either a maximum or a minimum.
- The domain for quadratic functions is the set of all real numbers.

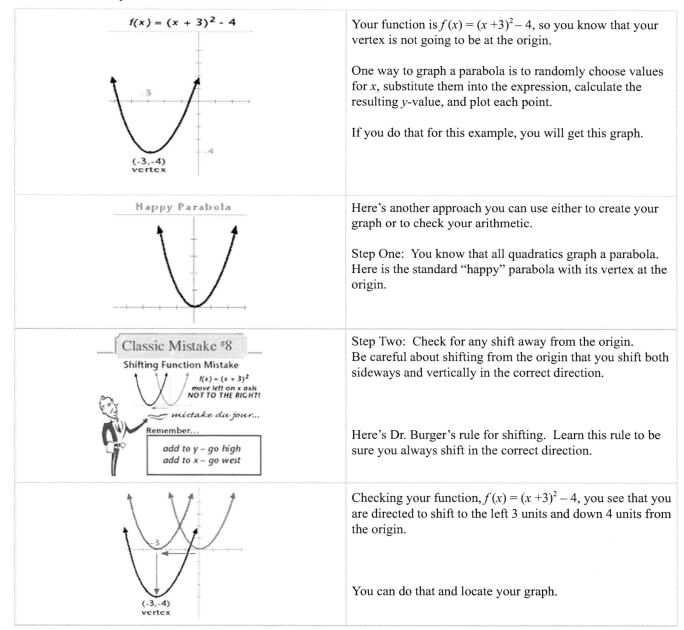

$f(x) = (x + 3)^2 - 4$	Your function is $f(x) = (x+3)^2 - 4$, so you know that your vertex is not going to be at the origin.

One way to graph a parabola is to randomly choose values for x, substitute them into the expression, calculate the resulting y-value, and plot each point.

If you do that for this example, you will get this graph. |
| Happy Parabola | Here's another approach you can use either to create your graph or to check your arithmetic.

Step One: You know that all quadratics graph a parabola. Here is the standard "happy" parabola with its vertex at the origin. |
| Classic Mistake #8

Shifting Function Mistake
$f(x) = (x + 3)^2$
move left on x axis
NOT TO THE RIGHT!

mistake du jour...

Remember...
add to y – go high
add to x – go west | Step Two: Check for any shift away from the origin. Be careful about shifting from the origin that you shift both sideways and vertically in the correct direction.

Here's Dr. Burger's rule for shifting. Learn this rule to be sure you always shift in the correct direction. |
| (-3,-4) vertex | Checking your function, $f(x) = (x+3)^2 - 4$, you see that you are directed to shift to the left 3 units and down 4 units from the origin.

You can do that and locate your graph. |

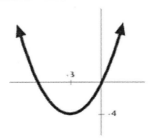

In this example, your domain is the set of all real numbers.

Your range is more limited. The smallest y-value that you will have is the one at the vertex, which is –4. As a result, your range is limited to all the numbers between –4 and $+\infty$.

Sample problems:

1. Describe the shifts made to the graph of $y = x^2$ when $y = (x-5)^2 + 1$ is graphed.
   Solution: 5 units to the right and one unit up
   Explanation: In the function $y = (x-5)^2 + 1$, 5 is subtracted from x which indicates a shift of 5 units to the right and 1 is added which indicates a shift of one unit up. The vertex of this parabola is located at $(5, 1)$ which is 5 units to the right and one unit up from the vertex of $y = x^2$, $(0, 0)$.

2. Identify the vertex of the parabola described by $y = (x+2)^2 - 3$.
   Is the vertex the maximum or minimum of the parabola?
   Solution: $(-2, -3)$, minimum
   Explanation: The vertex of $y = (x+2)^2 - 3$ is 2 units to the left and 3 units down from $(0,0)$, or at $(-2, -3)$. The parabola opens up, so the vertex is the minimum.

3. Determine the range of $y = -(x+1)^2 + 4$.
   Solution: $y \le 4$
   Explanation: The vertex of $y = -(x+1)^2 + 4$ is at $(-1, 4)$. The parabola opens down, so the maximum y-value is 4. Thus, the range is $y \le 4$.

Practice problems: *(Answers on page: 448)*

1. Describe the shifts made to the graph of $y = x^2$ when $y = (x+2)^2 - 1$ is graphed.

2. Identify the vertex of the parabola described by $y = -(x+5)^2$.
   Is the vertex the maximum or minimum of the parabola?

3. Determine the range of $y = (x-6)^2 - 3$.

Review questions: *(Answers to odd questions on page: 448)*

1. Describe the shifts made to the graph of $y = x^2$ when $y = \left(x - \frac{1}{2}\right)^2 + 3$ is graphed.

2. Describe the shifts made to the graph of $y = x^2$ when $y = (x+5)^2 - 2$ is graphed.

3. Identify the vertex of the parabola described by $y = -(x-7)^2 + 1$.
   Is the vertex the maximum or minimum of the parabola?

4. Determine the range of $y = (x-1)^2$.

5. Determine the range of $y = -(x-4)^2 + 2$.

Nice-Looking Parabolas

- **Standard form of a parabola:** $f(x) = ax^2 + bx + c$.
- **Vertex of a parabola:** (h, k).
  - $h = -b/2a$.
  - $k = f(h)$.
- **Standard form for parabola showing vertex:** $f(x) = a(x - h)^2 + k$.

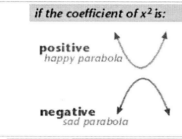

The direction a parabola opens is easy to determine. Look at the coefficient of the squared term in the function.

If the coefficient is positive, the curve opens in the positive direction.

If the coefficient is negative, the curve opens in the negative direction.

Example vertex (h, k)

$f(x) = (x + 3)^2 - 4$

First, consider the standard form of a parabola:
$f(x) = a(x - h)^2 + k$

Then look at this example. The vertex (h, k) is easily determined to be $(-3, -4)$.

Remember: h is subtracting so change the sign of the x-value before using it in the vertex.

match game

Which equation matches the parabola?

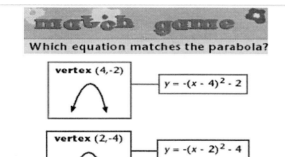

vertex $(4, -2)$ $y = -(x - 4)^2 - 2$

vertex $(2, -4)$ $y = -(x - 2)^2 - 4$

Notice: Downturning parabolas have negative coefficients on the squared term in their equations.

Notice: The x-value changes sign as a coordinate from what is used in the equation.

Sample problems:

1. Determine the direction and vertex of the parabola described by $y = -2(x-1)^2 + 4$.

   Solution: opens down, vertex: $(1, 4)$

   Explanation: This equation is in vertex form: $y = a(x - h)^2 + k \implies$
   $y = -2(x-1)^2 + 4$, so $a = -2$, $h = 1$, and $k = 4$. Since a is negative, the parabola must open down. The vertex is located at the point (h, k), so the vertex of this parabola is at $(1, 4)$.

2. Determine the direction and vertex of the parabola described by $y = 3(x+2)^2 - 4$.

   Solution: opens up, vertex: $(-2, -4)$

   Explanation: This equation is in vertex form: $y = a(x - h)^2 + k \implies$
   $y = 3(x+2)^2 - 4 = 3(x - (-2))^2 + (-4)$, so $a = 3$, $h = -2$, and $k = -4$.
   Since a is positive, the parabola must open up. The vertex is located at the point (h, k), so the vertex is at $(-2, -4)$.

3. True or false: The vertex of the parabola described by $y = (x+5)^2$ is at $(-5,\, 0)$.

Solution: True

Explanation: This equation is in vertex form: $y = a(x-h)^2 + k \implies$
$y = (x+5)^2 = 1(x-(-5))^2 + 0$, $h = -5$, and $k = 0$. The vertex is located at the point $(h,\, k)$, so it is at $(-5,\, 0)$.

Practice problems: *(Answers on page: 448)*

1. Determine the direction and vertex of the parabola described by $y = 5 - x^2$.

2. Determine the direction and vertex of the parabola described by $y = (x-2)^2$.

3. Determine the direction and vertex of the parabola described by $f(x) = \dfrac{1}{2}(x+3)^2 - 7$.

Review questions: *(Answers to odd questions on page: 448)*

1. Determine the direction and vertex of the parabola described by $y = x^2 - 8$.

2. Determine the direction and vertex of the parabola described by $y = -x^2 - 2$.

3. Determine the direction and vertex of the parabola described by $y = -(x-3)^2 - 2$.

4. Determine the direction and vertex of the parabola described by $y = (x+3)^2 - 1$.

5. Determine the direction and vertex of the parabola described by $y = 5(x+1)^2 + 1$.

Using Discriminants to Graph Parabolas

- **Quadratic equation:** $ax^2 + bx + c = 0$.
- **Quadratic formula:**
$$x = \frac{-b \pm \sqrt{b^2 - 4ac}}{2a}.$$
- **Discriminant:** $b^2 - 4ac$. Checking the value of the discriminant tells about the solutions:
  - $b^2 - 4ac > 0$ indicates there are two real solutions.
  - $b^2 - 4ac = 0$ indicates there is only one solution.
  - $b^2 - 4ac < 0$ indicates there are no real solutions.

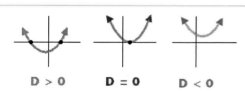 D > 0 D = 0 D < 0	Analyzing the discriminant gives you an idea where to graph the curve of a quadratic function.
Example 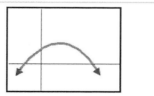	Matching the graph with the elements of its function, this parabola has: • a value of a that is less than 0, because it turns down, • a discriminant greater than 0 because it crosses the x-axis twice and must have two real-number solutions.

Example	This is a positive parabola with one real solution: its $a > 0$, and its discriminant = 0.
Example	This is a positive parabola with two real solutions: its $a > 0$, and its discriminant > 0.
Example	This is a negative parabola with one real solution: its $a < 0$, because it turns down, and its discriminant = 0.
Example	This is a negative parabola with no real solutions: it's $a < 0$, and its discriminant < 0.

Sample problems:

1. Suppose the vertex of a parabola is at (0, 3) and the parabola opens down. What can you determine about the value of the discriminant?

   Solution: the discriminant is > 0

   Explanation: The vertex of the parabola is above the x-axis and the parabola opens down. Thus, the parabola must cross the x-axis twice. Therefore, the discriminant must be a positive number.

2. Suppose a parabola opens up and the vertex is on the x-axis. What can you determine about the value of a and the discriminant?

   Solution: a is positive and the discriminant is 0.

   Explanation: Two aspects of the parabola are given: 1) the parabola opens up and 2) the vertex is on the x-axis. Since the parabola opens up, the value of a is positive. Since the vertex is on the x-axis, the parabola crosses the x-axis only once. Therefore, the discriminant must be 0.

3. Suppose the vertex of a parabola is in the 1st quadrant and the y-value of the y-intercept is greater than the y-value of the vertex. What can you determine about the values of a, c, and the discriminant?

Solution: a is positive, c is positive, and the discriminant is negative

Explanation: Visualize the parabola. The y-intercept must be higher than the vertex since the y-value of the y-intercept is greater than the y-value of the vertex. Since the y-intercept is higher than the vertex the parabola must open up, so a is positive. Additionally, c must be positive. A parabola with the vertex in the 1st quadrant that opens up does not cross the x-axis, so the discriminant must be negative.

Practice problems: *(Answers on page: 449)*

1. True or false: The equation of the following parabola has a negative discriminant.

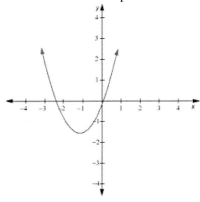

2. Suppose the discriminant of a quadratic equation is 0 and the value of a is less than 0. What can you determine about the parabola defined by this equation?

3. Suppose the vertex of a parabola is in the 4th quadrant and the parabola opens up. What can you determine about the discriminant?

Review questions: *(Answers to odd questions on page: 449)*

1. True or false: The equation of the parabola below has a positive discriminant.

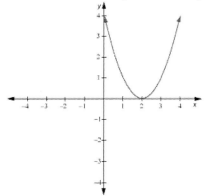

2. True or false: The equation of the parabola below has a negative discriminant.

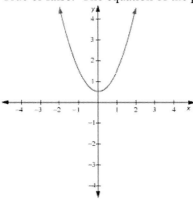

3. True or false: The equation of the parabola below has a positive discriminant.

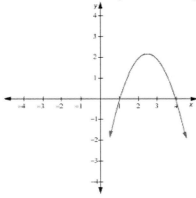

4. Suppose the discriminant of a quadratic equation is 4 and the vertex of the parabola described by this equation is in the 2nd quadrant. What can you determine about the value of the a in the equation?

5. Suppose the vertex of a parabola is on the x-axis and the y-intercept is less than 0. What can you determine about the discriminant and the value of the a?

Maximum Height in the Real World

- **Standard form of a parabola:**

  $f(x) = ax^2 + bx + c.$
- **Vertex of a parabola:**

  (h, k), where $h = \dfrac{-b}{2a}$ and $k = f(h)$.
- **Standard form for parabola showing vertex:**

  $f(x) = a(x - h)^2 + k.$

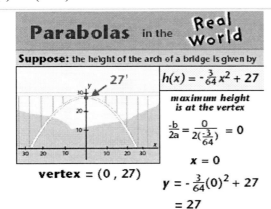

In this example, your x-axis represents the distance in feet that the bridge spans.

The graph is set so that $x = 0$ where the bridge's curve is at its highest; i.e., at the vertex.

So, $h = 0$.

Solve for k, which turns out to be 27 feet.

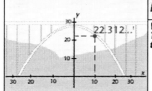

Parabolas in the **Real World**

Suppose: the height of the arch of a bridge is given by

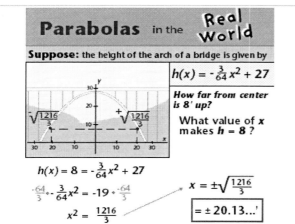

$h(x) = -\frac{3}{64}x^2 + 27$

What is the height 10' to the right of the center?

$h(10) = -\frac{3}{64}(100) + 27$

$= \frac{-75}{16} + \frac{432}{16}$

$= \frac{357}{16} = \boxed{22.312....}$

Now you want to find the height of the span 10 feet on either side of center.

This means $x = 10$.

Substitute 10 into the function for x and solve for the y, or height.

That height is 22.312 feet.

Parabolas in the **Real World**

Suppose: the height of the arch of a bridge is given by

$h(x) = -\frac{3}{64}x^2 + 27$

How far from center is 8' up?

What value of x makes $h = 8$?

$\sqrt{\frac{1216}{3}}$ $\sqrt{\frac{1216}{3}}$

$h(x) = 8 = -\frac{3}{64}x^2 + 27$

$-\frac{64}{3} \cdot -\frac{3}{64}x^2 = -19 \cdot -\frac{64}{3}$

$x^2 = \frac{1216}{3}$

$x = \pm\sqrt{\frac{1216}{3}}$

$= \pm 20.13...'$

Now you want to find the location of a specific height of the span of the bridge.

Set the height to 8 feet; i.e., $h(x) = 8$. That means that the function, $h(x)$, equals 8. Now solve for x.

The edge of the bridge is 8 feet above its base on either side at 20.13 feet from the height of the arch.

Sample problems:

1. A model rocket is shot into the air. Its height in feet, y, after x seconds is given by the function $y = -16x^2 + 128x$. Find the maximum height of the rocket.
   Solution: 256 feet
   Explanation: The maximum height is the y-coordinate of the vertex, (h, k). Find h:
   $h = \dfrac{-b}{2a} = \dfrac{-128}{2(-16)} = 4$. The maximum height of the rocket is 256 feet.

2. Using the situation from sample problem #1, determine how long the rocket stays in the air.
   Solution: 8 seconds
   Explanation: The rocket will stay in the air until the height is 0, so substitute 0 into the equation for y and solve for x: $0 = -16x^2 + 128x$. Divide the equation by -16: $0 = x^2 - 8x$. Factor and solve: $0 = x(x - 8)$; $x = 0$ or $x - 8 = 0$; $x = 0$ or $x = 8$. The height of the rocket is 0 after 0 seconds and after 8 seconds. So the rocket stays in the air for 8 seconds.

3. A batter hits a baseball and the ball, y, after x seconds is given by the function $y = -16x^2 + 58x + 3$. How long does it take for the ball to reach its maximum height?
   Solution: 1.8 seconds
   Explanation: The maximum height of the ball is the y-coordinate of the vertex. But, the time it takes the ball to reach that maximum height is the x-coordinate of the vertex. Find the x-coordinate of the vertex: $h = \dfrac{-b}{2a} = \dfrac{-58}{2(-16)} = 1.8125$. So the ball reaches its maximum height after 1.8 seconds.

Practice problems: *(Answers on page: 449)*

1. In a baseball game, a batter pops a ball straight up in the air as given by the function: $f(x) = -16t^2 + 160t$, where t is in seconds. A seagull is witnessed swooping down and swallowing the ball at an altitude of 300 feet. Find the time, t, when the seagull ate the ball.

2. The ball described in problem #1 will reach its maximum height before being eaten by the seagull. After how many seconds will the ball reach its maximum height and what will that height be?

3. Suppose the ball described in problem #1 was not eaten by the seagull. After how many seconds will the ball hit the ground?

Review questions: *(Answers to odd questions on page: 449)*

1. An electronics company found that for a particular model of television they manufacture the revenue is given by the function $f(x) = 4000p - 4p^2$, where the unit price of the television is p dollars. What unit price should be established for the television to maximize revenue?

2. If a stone is thrown directly upwards from the ground with an initial velocity of 80 feet per second, the height of the stone is $s(t) = -16t^2 + 80t$. Find the maximum height of the stone before it falls back to the ground .

3. If a stone is thrown directly upwards from the ground with an initial velocity of 60 feet per second, the height of the stone is $s(t) = -16t^2 + 60t$. Find how long it would take before the stone reaches maximum height.

4. A one-way tunnel is in the shape of a parabola, $f(x) = -\dfrac{1}{4}x^2 + 9$, where $-6 \le x \le 6$. Find the height of the tallest truck of width 8 feet that can pass through this tunnel.

5. An object is dropped from a height of 100 feet. At any time $t > 0$, the height of the object is given by $f(t) = -16t^2 + 100$. How many seconds will it take for the object to hit the ground?

Finding the Vertex by Completing the Square

- **Standard form of a parabola:** $f(x) = ax^2 + bx + c$.
- **Vertex of a parabola:** (h, k).
  - $h = -b/2a$.
  - $k = f(h)$.
- **Vertex form for parabola :** $f(x) = a(x - h)^2 + k$.
- Completing the square is one method for changing a function into the vertex form in order to be able to graph it easier.

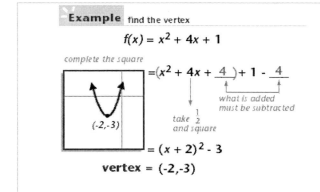

Example find the vertex

$$f(x) = x^2 + 4x + 1$$

complete the square

$$= (x^2 + 4x + \underline{4}) + 1 - \underline{4}$$

what is added
must be subtracted

take $\frac{1}{2}$
and square

(-2,-3)

$$= (x + 2)^2 - 3$$

vertex = (-2,-3)

In this example the x-terms are $(x^2 + 4x)$.

To complete that square, divide the 4 in half, square it, and add it inside the x-term expression so that you have $(x^2 + 4x + 4)$. To maintain the balance of the function, add a -4 outside the x-term expression.

Combine like terms and contract the square.

The vertex is at $(-2, -3)$.

In addition you know this will be a positive parabola.

Your graphing job is easy.

Example

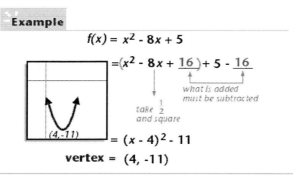

$f(x) = x^2 - 8x + 5$

$= (x^2 - 8x + \underline{16}) + 5 - \underline{16}$

what is added must be subtracted

take $\frac{1}{2}$ and square

$= (x - 4)^2 - 11$

vertex = (4, -11)

Follow the same process for this example as above.

Within the *x*-expression, you'll add 16.
Outside that expression, add −16 for balance.

Factor into squared form and your vertex is (4, −11).

It's a positive parabola.

Example

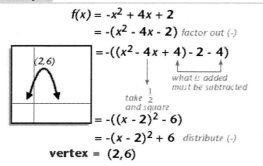

$f(x) = -x^2 + 4x + 2$

$= -(x^2 - 4x - 2)$ *factor out (-)*

$= -((x^2 - 4x + 4) - 2 - 4)$

what is added must be subtracted

take $\frac{1}{2}$ and square

$= -((x - 2)^2 - 6)$

$= -(x - 2)^2 + 6$ *distribute (-)*

vertex = (2,6)

Again, follow the same process as above.

Calculate the value to add and subtract.
Factor into squared form.
Graph the vertex.

Note that this is a negative parabola and graph the curve.

Sample problems:

1. Use the completing the square method to find the vertex of the parabola defined by $y = x^2 + 6x - 5$.
   Solution: $(-3, \ -14)$

   Explanation: Express the equation in vertex form, $y = a(x - h)^2 + k$, by completing the square.

   First, square $\frac{1}{2}$ of the linear coefficient, then add that number <u>and</u> subtract it to balance the equation:
   $y = x^2 + 6x - 5 = (x^2 + 6x) - 5 = (x^2 + 6x + 9) - 5 - 9$. Next, factor the trinomial and simplify:
   $y = (x + 3)^2 - 14$, so the vertex is at $(-3, \ -14)$.

2. Use the completing the square method to find the vertex of $f(x) = -x^2 + 10x - 7$.
   Solution: $(5, \ 18)$
   Explanation: The coefficient of the quadratic term is not 1, so factor -1 from the expression:
   $f(x) = -(x^2 + 10x - 7)$. Next, add and subtract 25 to complete the square inside the parentheses:
   $f(x) = -((x^2 + 10x + 25) + 7 - 25)$. Next, factor and simplify: $f(x) = -((x - 5)^2 - 18)$. Now
   distribute the negative: $f(x) = -(x - 5)^2 + 18$. Thus, the vertex is at $(5, \ 18)$.

3. Find the vertex of the parabola defined by $y = 2x^2 - 8x + 1$ by completing the square.
   Solution: $(2, \ -7)$

   Explanation: Factor 2 from the expression: $y = 2\left(x^2 - 4x + \frac{1}{2}\right)$. Complete the

   square: $y = 2\left(\left(x^2 - 4x + 4\right) + \frac{1}{2} - 4\right)$. Factor, simplify, and then distribute the 2:

   $y = 2\left(\left(x - 2\right)^2 - \frac{7}{2}\right)$; $y = 2(x - 2)^2 - 7$. So the vertex is at $(2, \ -7)$.

Practice problems: *(Answers on page: 449)*

1. Use the completing the square method to find the vertex of $y = -x^2 + \frac{1}{2}x - 1$.

---

2. Use the completing the square method to find the vertex of $y = -2x^2 - 8x + 1$.

3. Use the completing the square method to find the vertex of $y = -4x^2 + 2x - 3$.

Review questions: *(Answers to odd questions on page: 449)*

1. Use the completing the square method to find the vertex of $y = x^2 - 2x + 6$.

2. Use the completing the square method to find the vertex of $y = 2x^2 - 4x + 8$.

3. Use the completing the square method to find the vertex of $f(x) = -x^2 - 2x - 2$.

4. Use the completing the square method to find the vertex of $y = 3x^2 + 3x + \frac{3}{4}$.

5. Use the completing the square method to find the vertex of $f(x) = -5x^2 + 5x - \frac{1}{4}$.

Using the Vertex to Write the Quadratic Equation

*   **Standard form of a parabola:** $f(x) = ax^2 + bx + c$.
*   **Vertex of a parabola:** (h, k).
    * $h = -b/2a$.
    * $k = f(h)$.
*   **Vertex form for a parabola:** $f(x) = a(x - h)^2 + k$.
*   To rewrite an equation in vertex form:
    *   Find the value of h.
    *   Find the value of k.
    *   Substitute these values into vertex form.

$$h = \frac{-b}{2a} \qquad k = f(h)$$ **Example** *write equation in standard form* $$f(x) = \underset{a=1}{x^2} + \underset{b=4}{4x} + \underset{c=1}{1}$$ $$h = \frac{-4}{2} = -2$$ $$k = f(-2) = (-2)^2 + 4(-2) + 1$$ $$= -3$$ $$\text{vertex} = (-2, -3)$$ $$= (x + 2)^2 - 3$$	One way to determine the vertex (h,k) of a parabola is to use the formulas for h and k shown here. In this example, $a = 1$ and $b = 4$. So, $h = -(4)/2(1) = -2$. $k = f(-2) = (-2)^2 + 4(-2) + 1 = -3$ The vertex is (h, k) are now known. Substitute these coordinates to write the equation in standard form.
Example *write equation in standard form* $$f(x) = \underset{a=1}{x^2} - \underset{b=-8}{8x} + \underset{c=5}{5}$$ $$h = \frac{\overset{8}{\cancel{16}}}{2} = 8 \; 4$$ $$k = f(h) = \overset{4}{\cancel{8}}{}^2 - 8(\overset{4}{\cancel{8}}) + 5$$ $$= 5 \; -11$$ $$\text{vertex} = (8, 5)(4, -11)$$ $$= \cancel{(x - 8)^2 + 5}$$ $$= (x - 4)^2 - 11$$	This example points out the value of being accurate and careful in what you are doing. You are following the same process: 1. Determine h and k. (Please use the correct numbers, or .....oops.) 2. Write the vertex. 3. Write the function in standard form showing the vertex.

Example *write equation in standard form*

$f(x) = -x^2 + 4x + 2$
$\quad a=-1 \quad b=4 \quad c=2$

$h = \frac{-4}{-2} = 2$

$k = f(h) = -2^2 + 4(2) + 2$
$\quad = 6$

vertex $= (2,6)$

$\quad = -(x - 2)^2 + 6$

You know that this is a down-turned parabola because x^2 has a negative coefficient.

Find h and k.

Write the equation in standard form.

Be sure to substitute the a value back into vertex form.

Sample problems:

1. Use the vertex to express the equation $f(x) = x^2 + 10x - 12$ in vertex form.

   Solution: $y = (x+5)^2 - 37$

   Explanation: Begin by using the formulas for h and k to find the vertex: $h = \frac{-b}{2a} = \frac{-10}{2(1)} = -5$ and $k = f(h) = f(-5) = (-5)^2 + 10(-5) - 12 = -37$. Next, substitute the a, h, and k values into the vertex form, $y = a(x-h)^2 + k$: $y = 1(x - (-5))^2 + (-37)$. Simplify: $y = (x+5)^2 - 37$.

2. Use the vertex to express the equation $y = -2x^2 - 8x + 1$ in vertex form.

   Solution: $y = -2(x+2)^2 + 9$

   Explanation: Find h and k: $h = \frac{-(-8)}{2(-2)} = -2$ and $k = -2(-2)^2 - 8(-2) + 1 = 9$.

   Now substitute the a, h, and k values into the vertex form: $y = -2(x+2)^2 + 9$.

3. Suppose there is a parabola with the vertex at $(3, 4)$ and $(1, -4)$ is a point on that parabola. Use vertex form to find the value of a, then write the equation that describes this parabola in standard form.

   Solution: $y = -2x^2 + 12x - 14$

   Explanation: First find the value of a by substituting the values from the vertex and the point into the vertex form: $y = a(x-h)^2 + k \Rightarrow -4 = a(1-3)^2 + 4$ since $(3, 4)$ is (h, k) and $(1, -4)$ is (x, y). Simplify and solve the equation: $-4 = a(1-3)^2 + 4$; $-4 = 4a + 4$; $-8 = 4a$; $a = -2$. Next, substitute the a, h, and k values into the vertex form: $y = a(x-h)^2 + k \Rightarrow y = -2(x-3)^2 + 4$. Simplify this equation to express it in standard form: $y = -2(x^2 - 6x + 9) + 4$; $y = (-2x^2 + 12x - 18) + 4$; $y = -2x^2 + 12x - 14$.

Practice problems: *(Answers on page: 449)*

1. Use the vertex to express $y = x^2 - 6x + 10$ in vertex form.

2. Use the vertex to express $f(x) = 2x^2 + 12x + 13$ in vertex form.

3. Write the equation of a parabola that passes through the point $(3, 10)$ and has the same vertex as $y = 5(x-1)^2 - 2$.

Review questions: *(Answers to odd questions on page: 449)*

1. Use the vertex to express $y = x^2 - 8x + 17$ in vertex form.

2. Use the vertex to express $f(x) = -x^2 + 10x - 22$ in vertex form.

3. Use the vertex to express $y = 5x^2 + 10x + 7$ in vertex form.

4. Write the equation of a parabola that passes through the point $(-2, \ 61)$ and has the
    same vertex as $y = \dfrac{1}{2}(x-1)^2 - 2$.

5. Write the equation of a parabola that passes through the point $(5, \ -14)$ and has the
    same vertex as $f(x) = -x^2 + 6x - 35$.

Finding the Maximum or Minimum of a Quadratic

- Every parabola has a turning point, or vertex. This point is the **minimum point** on a positive parabola. It is the
  maximum point on a negative parabola.
- On a parabola opening along the y-axis, the maximum or minimum value relates to the height of the curve. Therefore, it
  is the k-value of the vertex. This maximum or minimum occurs at the point on the curve when x has the h-value of the
  vertex.

<table>
<tr>
<td>

$$h = \tfrac{-b}{2a} \qquad k = f(h)$$

Example find the minimum or maximum

$$f(x) = 2x^2 + 3x + 1$$

find (h,k) $\quad h = \boxed{\dfrac{-3}{4}} \quad k = f(h) = \boxed{-\dfrac{1}{8}}$

$$\text{vertex} = (\tfrac{-3}{4}, \tfrac{-1}{8})$$

minimum $= \dfrac{-1}{8}$ 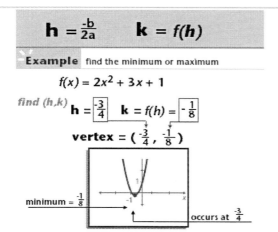 occurs at $\dfrac{-3}{4}$

</td>
<td>

This parabola is positive; it will have a minimum.

The minimum value is $-1/8$ (k). This value occurs at $-3/4$ (h).

Graphing the curve gives us a visual relationship to the changes occurring for various x- and y-values related to this function.

</td>
</tr>
<tr>
<td>

$$h = \tfrac{-b}{2a} \qquad k = f(h)$$

Example find the minimum or maximum

$$f(x) = -x^2 + 4x + 1$$

$$h = \tfrac{-4}{-2} = 2 \quad k = f(h) = 5$$

$$\text{vertex} = (2,5) \quad \textbf{maximum} = 5$$
$$\textbf{at } x = 2$$

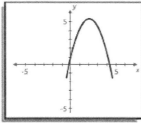

</td>
<td>

This parabola is a negative curve. So, you know that it will have a maximum point.

Doing the arithmetic, you find that the curve's maximum is $5(k)$, reached at the point $2(h)$.

Again, a quick sketch of the curve gives you a visual concept of how values change across the span of this curve.

</td>
</tr>
</table>

Sample problems:

1. Find the maximum value of $f(x) = -x^2 - 5x$.

   Solution: $\dfrac{25}{4}$

   Explanation: Find the vertex, (h, k), using $h = -\frac{b}{2a}$ and $k = f(h)$. Find h: $h = -\frac{b}{2a} = -\frac{-5}{2(-1)} = -\frac{5}{2}$.

   Next, find k: $k = f\left(-\frac{5}{2}\right) = -\left(-\frac{5}{2}\right)^2 - 5\left(-\frac{5}{2}\right) = \frac{25}{4}$. So, the vertex is $\left(-\frac{5}{2}, \frac{25}{4}\right)$. Since the maximum value is the y-coordinate of the vertex, the maximum is $\frac{25}{4}$.

2. True or false: The maximum value of the function $f(x) = 2x^2 - 3x - 1$ is $-\dfrac{17}{8}$.

   Solution: False

   Explanation: Since $a > 0$, the parabola opens up and extends infinitely in the positive direction. Therefore, there is no maximum value. (However, the minimum value is $-\dfrac{17}{8}$.)

3. True or false: The maximum value of the function $f(x) = -\dfrac{1}{4}x^2 + \dfrac{1}{3}x + \dfrac{1}{2}$ is $\dfrac{11}{18}$.

   Solution: True

   Explanation: Since $a < 0$ the parabola opens down, and there is a maximum.

   Find h: $h = -\frac{b}{2a} = -\frac{\frac{1}{3}}{2\left(-\frac{1}{4}\right)} = -\frac{\frac{1}{3}}{-\frac{1}{2}} = \frac{2}{3}$. Since the maximum is the y-coordinate of the vertex, the

   maximum value is found by computing $f\left(\frac{2}{3}\right)$: $f\left(\frac{2}{3}\right) = -\frac{1}{4}\left(\frac{2}{3}\right)^2 + \frac{1}{3}\left(\frac{2}{3}\right) + \frac{1}{2} = \frac{11}{18}$.

Practice problems: *(Answers on page: 449)*

1. Find the maximum or minimum value of the function $f(x) = 4x^2 + 1$.

2. Find the maximum or minimum value of the function $f(x) = \dfrac{1}{3}x^2 - \dfrac{1}{4}x - \dfrac{1}{2}$.

3. True or false: The minimum value of the function $y = x^2 + 6x + 1$ is -8.

Review questions: *(Answers to odd questions on page: 449)*

1. Find the maximum or minimum value of the function $f(x) = -3x^2 + 2$.

2. Find the minimum value of $f(x)$ where $f(x) = 2x^2 - 4x + 1$.

3. Find the minimum value of y where $y = 5x^2 + 11x$.

4. Find the maximum value of y, where $y = -2x^2 + 4x - 1$.

5. Find the maximum or minimum value of the function $f(x) = -\dfrac{3}{4}x^2 + \dfrac{1}{2}x + 2$.

Graphing Parabolas

- **Vertex form for a parabola:** $f(x) = a(x - h)^2 + k$.
- To graph a parabola from a quadratic equation find several useful points (the vertex, x-intercept(s), and y-intercept) then sketch the parabola through these points.
  - First, identify the vertex: *(h, k)*.
  - Second, determine whether the curve is a positive or negative parabola.
  - Finally, set the expression equal to 0 and solve for the x-values. These are the points where the curve crosses the x-axis.
- The **axis of symmetry** is the imaginary line that passes through the vertex and is parallel to the axis along which the curve is opening.

Example graph the equation

$$f(x) = -2(x + 3)^2 + 2$$

vertex = (-3,2)

find x-intercept, set equal to 0

$$-2(x + 3)^2 + 2 = 0$$

factor out 2

$$2(1 - (x + 3)^2) = 0$$

divide by 2

$$1 - (x + 3)^2 = 0$$

factor difference of 2 squares

$$(1 + (x + 3))(1 - (x + 3)) = 0$$

$$x + 4 = 0 \quad 1 - x - 3 = 0$$

$$x = -4 \quad\quad x = -2$$

Parabola should be symmetrical vertex

This example is for a negative parabola – because a coefficient is negative.

The vertex is shown in the expression: $(-3, 2)$.
Remember: the x-value changes sign.

To find the x-intercepts, set everything equal to 0 and solve for x.

These are the points where the curve crosses the x-axis.

Graph everything and you are done.

Example graph the equation

$$f(x) = x^2 - 2x + 3$$

find vertex by using formula

$$x = \frac{2}{2} = 1$$

$$y = f(1) = 1^2 - 2(1) + 3$$

vertex (1 , 2)

find y intercept

$$f(0) = 0^2 - 2(0) + 3$$

$$= 3$$

Since this equation is in standard form, find the vertex using the formulas for h and k:
$$h = -b/2a = -(-2)/2(1) = 1$$
$$k = f(h) = f(1) = 1^2 - 2(1) + 3 = 2$$
So the vertex is at $(1, 2)$.

The parabola opens up since a is positive.

---

vertex

With the vertex above the x-axis and the curve opening upward, you know the curve will never cross the x-axis.

---

find y intercept

$$f(0) = 0^2 - 2(0) + 3$$

$$= 3$$

So look for the y-intercept. Solve $f(x)$ for $x = 0$. This y-value is where the curve will cross the y-axis. In this case, that is the point $(0, 3)$. The y-intercept is always at c.

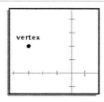

Hint: if you find one point, the axis of symmetry will tell you where another point is

vertex

Now, use the fact that a parabola has symmetry to help locate a second point.

In this example, the y-intercept is to the left 1 unit and up 1 unit from the vertex. So, to graph your matching point, locate the point that is to the right 1 unit and up 1 unit from the vertex.

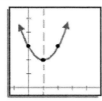

Now your curve is noted and you can draw it.

Sample problems:

1. Find the vertex, direction, x-intercepts (if they exist), and y-intercept for the parabola defined by the function: $f(x) = -3(x-2)^2 - 6$.

   Solution: vertex: $(2, -6)$; direction: down; x-intercept: none exist; y-intercept: $(0, -18)$

   Explanation: Since the equation is in vertex form, $y = a(x-h)^2 + k$, determine the vertex by identifying h and k from the equation: $f(x) = -3(x-2)^2 - 6 \Rightarrow h = 2$ and $k = -6$, so the vertex is at $(2, -6)$. The direction is determined by identifying the value of a. In this equation a is -3, so the parabola opens down. The x-intercepts do not always exist on a parabola. In this case the vertex is below the x-axis and the parabola opens down, so by visualizing the graph it may be determined that there are no x-intercepts. The y-intercept is found by substituting $x = 0$ into the equation, then solving for y:
   $f(x) = -3(0-2)^2 - 6 = -3(-2)^2 - 6 = -3(4) - 6 = -18$. Therefore, the y-intercept is $(0, -18)$.

2. Find the vertex, direction, x-intercepts (if they exist), and y-intercept for the parabola defined by the function $y = (x+5)^2$.

   Solution: vertex: $(-5, 0)$; direction: up; x-intercept: $(-5, 0)$
   y-intercept: $(0, 25)$

   Explanation: Since the equation is in vertex form, $y = a(x-h)^2 + k$, determine the vertex by identifying h and k from the equation: $f(x) = (x+5)^2 = 1(x-(-5))^2 + 0 \Rightarrow$
   $h = -5$ and $k = 0$, so the vertex is at $(-5, 0)$. In this equation a is 1, so the parabola opens up. The vertex is on the x-axis, so the parabola must have only one x-intercept and it is the vertex, so the x-intercept is also at $(-5, 0)$. The y-intercept is found by substituting $x = 0$ into the equation, then solving for y: $y = (0+5)^2 = (5)^2 = 25$. Therefore, the y-intercept is $(0, 25)$.

3. Find the vertex, direction, x-intercepts (if they exist), and y-intercept for the parabola defined by the function $f(x) = x^2 + 6x + 8$.

   Solution: vertex: $(-3, -1)$; direction: up; x-intercept: $(-4, 0)$ and $(-2, 0)$;
   y-intercept: $(0, 8)$

   Explanation: Since the equation is in standard form, determine the vertex by using the formulas for h and k: $h = \dfrac{-b}{2a} = \dfrac{-6}{2(1)} = -3$ and

   $k = f(h) = f(-3) = (-3^2) + 6(-3) + 8 = 9 - 18 + 8 = -1$, so the vertex is $(-3, -1)$. Since a is positive, the parabola opens up. The vertex is below the x-axis and the parabola opens up, so the parabola must have two x-intercepts. Find the x-intercepts by substituting $y = 0$ into the equation, then solve for x: $0 = x^2 + 6x + 8$;
   $0 = (x+4)(x+2)$; $x+4 = 0$ or $x+2 = 0$; $x = -4$ or $x = -2$. So the x-intercept are at $(-4, 0)$ and $(-2, 0)$. Determine the y-intercept by substituting $x = 0$ into the equation: $0^2 + 6(0) + 8 = 8$, so the y-intercept is at $(0, 8)$. (Note: the y-intercept is always c.)

Practice problems: *(Answers on page: 449)*

1. Find the vertex, direction, x-intercepts (if they exist), and y-intercepts for the parabola defined by the function $f(x) = 3x^2$.

2. Find the vertex, direction, x-intercepts (if they exist), and y-intercepts for the parabola defined by the function $y = \dfrac{1}{2}(x-4)^2$

3. Find the vertex, direction, x-intercepts (if they exist) and y-intercept for the parabola defined by the function $g(x) = 5 - 2x - 3x^2$

Review questions: *(Answers to odd questions on page: 449)*

1. Find the vertex, direction, x-intercepts (if they exist) and y-intercept for the parabola

   defined by the function $f(x) = \dfrac{3x^2}{4}$

2. Find the vertex, direction, x-intercepts (if they exist) and y-intercept for the parabola

   defined by the function $f(x) = -(x+3)^2$

3. Find the vertex, direction, x-intercepts (if they exist) and y-intercept for the parabola

   defined by the function $y = x^2 + 2x - 6$

4. Find the vertex, direction, x-intercepts (if they exist) and y-intercept for the parabola

   defined by the function $f(x) = 4x^2 - 4x + 3$

5. Find the vertex, direction, x-intercepts (if they exist) and y-intercept for the parabola

   defined by the function $f(x) = -2x^2 + 6x - 3$

Using Operations on Functions

- Using operations with functions is a useful way to create new functions for new purposes.
- All four of the basic operations can be used to combine two or more functions into a new function.
- Remember to watch signs carefully.
- Remember to change your domains appropriately when functions become denominators.

Example $(f+g)(x)$ $f(x) = 2x+3$ } By combining these $g(x) = 4x+8$ } two functions we created another $(f+g)(x) = 6x+11$	Adding two functions is just a matter of combining like terms. Here you add $2x$ and $4x$ to get $6x$. You add 3 and 8 to get 11. And there you have your $(f+g)(x)$, a whole new function. Subtracting works the same way if you remember to change the signs appropriately before you combine the like terms.
Example $(fg)(x)$ $f(x) = 2x+3$ $g(x) = 4x+8$ $(f+g)(x) = 6x+11$ $(fg)(x) = (4x+8)(2x+3)$ $\qquad = 8x^2 + 28x + 24$	Multiplying two functions is just a matter of combining two expressions. Write your multiplication problem out, then FOIL carefully to get your new function.
Example $\left(\dfrac{f}{g}\right)(x)$ $f(x) = 2x+3$ $g(x) = 4x+8$ $\left(\dfrac{f}{g}\right)(x) = \dfrac{2x+3}{4x+8}$ Must be careful to not have a value that would make the denominator zero Ex: $x = -2$ (not allowed)	We can take the same two functions and set up a division problem. Notice how it looks just like a fraction. If anything can be factored out to "reduce" the fraction, do that too. **Note:** The denominator can never equal 0, so the domain must be defined to exclude any values for x that would set the denominator equal to 0.
Example $\left(\dfrac{g}{f}\right)(x)$ $f(x) = x^2 - 1$ $g(x) = (x+2)^2$ Except $\left(\dfrac{g}{f}\right)(x) = \dfrac{(x+2)^2}{x^2-1}$ } Domain $= \mathbb{R} \setminus \{\pm 1\}$	Each of these curves taken separately is a parabola. Each parabola is defined at every point and its domain is the set of all real numbers. **Note:** two values must be excluded because they cause the denominator to equal 0. Those two values, in this example, are $+1$ and -1.

Sample problems:

1. If $j(x) = 2x^5 - 6x^3 + 7x - 11$ and $k(x) = x^5 + 3x^4 + 3x^3 + 4$, what is $(j - k)(x)$?

   Solution: $x^5 - 3x^4 - 9x^3 + 7x - 15$

   Explanation: The notation $(j - k)(x)$ means subtract the two functions in terms of x.
   Distribute the negative throughout the second function, then combine like terms:
   $$(j - k)(x) = j(x) - k(x)$$
   $$= (2x^5 - 6x^3 + 7x - 11) - (x^5 + 3x^4 + 3x^3 + 4)$$
   $$= 2x^5 - 6x^3 + 7x - 11 - x^5 - 3x^4 - 3x^3 - 4$$
   $$= x^5 - 3x^4 - 9x^3 + 7x - 15.$$

2. If $m(x) = (x + 1)$ and $n(x) = (x^2 - 1)$, what is $\dfrac{m(x)}{n(x)}$?

   Solution: $\dfrac{1}{x - 1}$, $x \neq \pm 1$

   Explanation: The notation $\frac{m(x)}{n(x)}$ means to divide the two functions in terms of x. Write the two functions
   as a fraction: $\frac{m(x)}{n(x)} = \frac{x+1}{x^2-1}$. To simplify, factor then cancel: $\frac{x+1}{x^2-1} = \frac{x+1}{(x+1)(x-1)} = \frac{1}{x-1}$. Determine the domain
   by setting the denominator equal to 0 and solve for x: $(x + 1)(x - 1) = 0$; $x + 1 = 0$ or $x - 1 = 0$;
   $x = -1$ or $x = 1$. So the domain is all real numbers except ± 1.

3. If $f(x) = x^2 - x$ and $g(x) = 7 - 2x$, what is $(g + f)(x - h)$?

   Solution: $x^2 - 3x - 2xh + 3h + h^2 + 7$

   Explanation: $(g + f)(x - h) = g(x - h) + f(x - h) = 7 - 2(x - h) + (x - h)^2 - (x - h)$
   $= 7 - 2x + 2h + x^2 - 2xh + h^2 - x + h = x^2 - 3x - 2xh + 3h + h^2 + 7.$

Practice problems: *(Answers on page: 449)*

1. If $g(x) = 7x^2$ and $h(x) = (4x - 1)$, what is $(gh)(x)$?

2. If $f(x) = 3x - 2$ and $g(x) = 7x + 12$, what is the sum of the two functions?

3. If $f(x) = 3x^2 - 5x$ and $g(x) = 2x + 3$, what is $(f - g)(x + h)$?

Review questions: *(Answers to odd questions on page: 449)*

1. True or false: Given two functions $f(x)$ and $g(x)$, $(f + g)(x) = f(x) + g(x)$.

2. Given $r(x) = 7x - 22$ and $t(x) = x^2 + 3$, express the sum $(r + t)(x)$.

3. If $m(x) = x + 5$ and $n(x) = x^2 - 25$, what is $\dfrac{m(x)}{n(x)}$?

4. If $p(x) = 3x - 1$ and $q(x) = 2x + 5$, what is $(pq)(x)$?

5. If $f(x) = 5x^3 - 6x + 4$ and $g(x) = x^3 + x^2 + x + 1$, what is $(f - g)(x)$?

Composite Functions

- A **composite function** is made up of multiple functions acting on each other in a specified order.
- The benefit of composing functions with each other is that you can follow one input through several processes to reach a final output.
- **Composition notation:** $f \circ g$ indicates that $f(x)$ will be evaluated with the output from $g(x)$.
- Note carefully which function is going to be used first. Make sure that the first function's output is used in the second function.

Example $f(x) = 3x-1$ $g(x) = 2x^2+x+1$	$(g \circ f)(3) = g(f(3))$ $= g(3 \cdot 3 - 1)$ $= g(8)$ $= 2(8)^2 + 8 + 1$ $= 128 + 8 + 1$ $= \boxed{137}$ ← Answer	The composition, g of f, is being evaluated here at $x = 3$. First $f(x)$ is evaluated for $x = 3$. The answer is 8. Next, $g(x)$ is evaluated for $x = 8$. The answer is 137. So, $g \circ f(3) = 137$.
Example $f(x) = 3x-1$ $g(x) = 2x^2+x+1$	$(f \circ g)(3) = f(g(3))$ $= f(2(3)^2 + 3 + 1)$ $= f(22)$ $= 3 \cdot 22 - 1$ $= \boxed{65}$ ← Answer	In this example, the composition is f of g. So, first evaluate $g(x)$ for $x = 3$. The answer is 22. Next evaluate $f(x)$ for $x = 22$. The answer is 65. Therefore, $f \circ g(3) = 65$.

Sample problems:

1. Find $(f \circ g)(3)$ for $f(x) = 4x^2 - 5x$ and $g(x) = x^3 - 2x + 4$.
   Solution: 2375
   Explanation: The notation $(f \circ g)(3)$ means to evaluate the function g for 3, then use that result to evaluate f: $(f \circ g)(3) = f(g(3)) = f((3)^3 - 2(3) + 4) = f(25) = 4(25)^2 - 5(25) = 2375$.

2. Find $(g \circ f)(-1)$ for $f(x) = 2x^7 + x^3$ and $g(x) = x^4 + 2$.
   Solution: 83
   Explanation: The notation $(g \circ f)(-1)$ means to evaluate the function f for -1, then use that result to evaluate g: $(g \circ f)(-1) = g(f(-1)) = g(2(-1)^7 + (-1)^3) = g(-3) = (-3)^4 + 2 = 83$.

3. Find $(f \circ g)(2)$ for $f(x) = \dfrac{x^3 + 5}{x}$ and $g(x) = \sqrt{2x^4 + 4}$.
   Solution: $36\dfrac{5}{6}$
   Explanation: The notation $(f \circ g)(2)$ means to evaluate the function g for 2, then use that result to evaluate f: $(f \circ g)(2) = f(g(2)) = f(\sqrt{2(2)^4 + 4}) = f(6) = \dfrac{(6)^3 + 5}{6} = \dfrac{221}{6} = 36\dfrac{5}{6}$.

Practice problems: *(Answers on page: 449)*

1. Find $(f \circ g)(4)$ for $f(x) = x + 4$ and $g(x) = x^2 - 4$.

2. Find $(g \circ f)(2)$ for $f(x) = 2x$ and $g(x) = 2x + 1$?

3. Find $(g \circ f)\left(\dfrac{1}{2}\right)$ for $f(x) = 8x^2$ and $g(x) = \dfrac{\sqrt{3x^3 + 1}}{2x}$.

Review questions: *(Answers to odd questions on page: 449)*

1. What is $(f \circ g)(5)$ if $f(x) = x^2$ and $g(x) = x - 3$?

2. What is $(f \circ g)(7)$ if $f(x) = x^2$ and $g(x) = x - 3$?

3. Find $(f \circ g)(x)$ if $f(x) = 2x + 1$ and $g(x) = x^2 + 5$

4. Let $f(x) = \dfrac{1}{x^2}$ and $g(x) = x + 2$. Find $(g \circ f)(1)$.

5. Given $p(x) = x^2 - x - 5$ and $r(x) = 2x - 1$, evaluate $(p \circ r)(3)$.

Components of Composite Functions

- The benefit of composing functions with each other is that you can follow one input through several processes to reach a final output.
- **Composition notation:** $f \circ g$ indicates that $f(x)$ will be evaluated with the output from $g(x)$.
- Note carefully which function is going to be used first. Make sure that function's output is used in the second function.

Example	
$f(x) = 3x - 1$ $(f \circ f)(2) = f\big(f(2)\big)$ $= f(5)$ $3(5)-1 = 14$ $= \boxed{14}$ ← Answer	You can even create a composition of a function with itself. In this example, you are asked for $f \circ f$ at $x = 2$. First evaluate $f(x)$ at $x = 2$. The answer is 5. Then evaluate $f(x)$ at $x = 5$. The answer is 14. 14 is the value of $f \circ f$.
$g(x) = 2x^2 + x + 1$ $(g \circ g)(2) = g\big(g(2)\big)$ $= g(11)$ $2(11)^2 + 11 + 1 =$ $= \boxed{254}$ $242+11+1 = 254$ Answer	In this case, you are to evaluate $g \circ g$ when $x = 2$. Evaluate $g(x)$ at $x = 2$. The answer is 11. Then, evaluate $g(x)$ again at $x = 11$. The answer is 254. 254 is the value of $g \circ g$ when $x = 2$.
$f(x) = 3x - 1$ $g(x) = 2x^2 + x + 1$ In General: $(f \circ g)(x) = f\big(g(x)\big)$ $= f(2x^2 + x + 1)$ Plug in stuff to x $= 3(2x^2 + x + 1) - 1$ $= \boxed{6x^2 + 3x + 2}$ ← Answer	In this example, you are to evaluate $f \circ g$ when $x = x$. Following your process, evaluate $g(x)$ when $x = x$. It is given that $g(x) = 2x^2 + x + 1$. Now, substitute all of that into $f(x)$ in place of every x you see. Do any multiplying and combine like terms. You get $6x^2 + 3x + 2$. Therefore, the value of $f \circ g\,(x)$ when $x = x$ is $6x^2 + 3x + 2$.
$f(x) = 3x - 1$ $g(x) = 2x^2 + x + 1$ $(g \circ f)(x) = g\big(f(x)\big)$ $= g(3x - 1)$ Plug in stuff $= 2(3x-1)^2 + (3x-1) + 1$ $= 2(9x^2 - 6x + 1) + 3x$ $(g \circ f)(x) = \boxed{18x^2 - 9x + 2}$ ← Answer	Now, let's reverse the composition. This time, evaluate $g \circ f$ when $x = x$. Starting with $f(x)$ when $x = x$, there is no change. Substitute the entire $f(x)$ expression for every x in $g(x)$ and evaluate. The answer is very different from the answer you found for the composition $f \circ g$.

Sample problems:

1. What is $(f \circ g)(x)$ when $f(x) = 3x^2$ and $g(x) = \dfrac{x}{2}$?

   Solution: $\dfrac{3x^2}{4}$

   Explanation: Evaluate the function g for x, then use that result to evalute f:

   $(f \circ g)(x) = f\big(g(x)\big) = f\left(\frac{x}{2}\right) = 3\left(\frac{x}{2}\right)^2 = \frac{3x^2}{4}$.

2. What is $(g \circ f)(2x+1)$ when $f(x) = 3x+4$ and $g(x) = x^2 - 1$?

   Solution: $36x^2 + 84x + 48$

   Explanation: Evaluate the function f for $2x+1$, then use that result to evalute g:

   $(g \circ f)(2x+1) = g\big(f(2x+1)\big) = g\big(3(2x+1)+4\big) = g(6x+7) = (6x+7)^2 - 1 = 36x^2 + 84x + 48$.

3. Let $f(x) = x^2 + 5$ and $g(x) = x - 1$. Find $(f \circ g)(2a+2)$.

   Solution: $4a^2 + 4a + 6$

   Explanation: Evaluate $g(x)$ for $2a+2$, then use the result to evaluate $f(x)$:

   $(f \circ g)(2a+2) = f\big(g(2a+2)\big) = f\big((2a+2)-1\big) = f(2a+1) = (2a+1)^2 + 5$
   $= 4a^2 + 4a + 1 + 5 = 4a^2 + 4a + 6$.

Practice problems: *(Answers on page: 450)*

1. Let $f(x) = 5x^2$ and $g(x) = 6x + 4$. Find $(f \circ g)(x)$.

2. What is $(f \circ g)(x+1)$ when $f(x) = x^2 + 5$ and $g(x) = 6 - x$?

3. Let $f(x) = 3x^2 - 4$ and $g(x) = 5 - x$. Find $(g \circ f)(x+1)$.

Review questions: *(Answers to odd questions on page: 450)*

1. Find $(g \circ f)(2)$ for $f(x) = -4x^2 + 2x - 3$ and $g(x) = 3x - 5$.

2. What is $(f \circ g)(x)$ when $f(x) = x^2$ and $g(x) = \dfrac{3x}{2}$.

3. Let $f(x) = 2x^2 + 3$ and $g(x) = 3x - 4$. Find $(f \circ g)(x)$.

4. Given $h(x) = 3x^2 + 5x + 7$ and $j(x) = 2x + 1$, express $(j \circ h)(x)$.

5. What is $(g \circ f)(2x)$ when $f(x) = (x+1)^2$ and $g(x) = 3x + 5$?

Finding Functions That Form a Given Composite

- The benefit of composing functions with each other is that you can follow one input through several processes to reach a final output.
- **Composition notation:** $f \circ g$ indicates that $f(x)$ will be evaluated with the output from $g(x)$.
- Note carefully which function is going to be used first. Make sure that function's output is used in the second function.

Please, give your answer in the form of a question.

Give the function of g and f so that the answer we give you is (f ∘ g).

3500.00
$(6x-2)^2$

What is:
$f(x) = x^2$
$g(x) = 6x-2$

$f(x) = x^2$
$g(x) = 6x-2$
$f \circ g (x) = f(g(x))$
$\quad = f(6x-2)$
$f \circ g (x) = (6x-2)^2$

In this example, you are given the composition $f \circ g$ and asked to name the two functions that could have been used to create this composition.

You know that $f \circ g (x) = f[g(x)]$.
In this case the only thing that $g(x)$ could be is the expression $(6x-2)$.
So, set $g(x) = 6x-2$.
That leaves $f(x) = x^2$.

And that agrees with what the screen shows.

Please, give your answer in the form of a question.

Give the function of g and f so that the answer we give you is (f ∘ g).

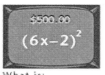
Show me the money!

$g(x) = 4x-1$
$f(x) = 2x^3 - x+3$
$g(x) = f(g(x))$
$\quad = f(4x-1)$

Plug into x

What is:
$g(x) = 4x-1$
$f(x) = 2x^3 - x+3$

$f \circ g(x) = 2(4x-1)^3 - (4x-1)+3$

In this case, you are given that the composition
$f \circ g = 2(4x-1)3 - (4x-1) + 3$.

It would appear that the equivalent of an x-term here is $(4x-1)$.
So, $g(x)$ must equal $(4x-1)$.
If so, replacing every $(4x-1)$ with x, we get $f(x)$ equals $2x^3 - x + 3$.

Sample problems:

1. Find the functions $f(x)$ and $g(x)$ such that $(f \circ g)(x) = \left(x^2 - 3\right)^4 + 1$.

   Solution: $f(x) = x^4 + 1$, $g(x) = x^2 - 3$

   Explanation: Let the expression inside the parentheses be $g(x)$, so $g(x) = x^2 - 3$.
   To find $f(x)$, substitute x into the composite function for $g(x)$:
   $\left(x^2 - 3\right)^4 + 1 \rightarrow (x)^4 + 1$, so $f(x) = x^4 + 1$.

2. Find the functions $f(x)$ and $g(x)$ such that $(f \circ g)(x) = 6\left(x^2\right)^2 - 2\left(x^2\right)$.

   Solution: $g(x) = x^2$, $f(x) = 6x^2 - 2x$

   Explanation: Let the expression inside the parentheses be $g(x)$, so $g(x) = x^2$.
   To find $f(x)$, substitute x into the composite function for $g(x)$:
   $6\left(x^2\right)^2 - 2\left(x^2\right) \rightarrow 6x^2 - 2x$, so $f(x) = 6x^2 - 2x$.

3. Find the functions $f(x)$ and $g(x)$ such that $(f \circ g)(x) = 3x^2 - x^4$.

   Solution: $g(x) = x^2$, $f(x) = 3x - x^2$

   Explanation: Express the composite function as a function with a common expression inside more than one set of parentheses (if possible):
   $x^2 - x^4 = 3\left(x^2\right) - \left(x^2\right)^2$. Let the common expression inside the parentheses
   be $g(x)$, so $g(x) = x^2$. To find $f(x)$, substitute x into the composite function
   for $g(x)$: $3\left(x^2\right) - \left(x^2\right)^2 \rightarrow 3(x) - (x)^2$, so $f(x) = 3x - x^2$.

Practice problems: *(Answers on page: 450)*

1. Find the functions $f(x)$ and $g(x)$ such that $(f \circ g)(x) = 2(3x-1)^2$

2. Find the functions $f(x)$ and $g(x)$ such that $(f \circ g)(x) = -\left(x^2\right)^2 + 5\left(x^2\right)$.

3. Find the functions $f(x)$ and $g(x)$ such that $(f \circ g)(x) = \dfrac{1}{2}x^6 - 3x^3 + 1$.

Review questions: *(Answers to odd questions on page: 450)*

1. Find the functions $f(x)$ and $g(x)$ such that $(f \circ g)(x) = 3(1-x)^5$.

2. Find the functions $f(x)$ and $g(x)$ such that $(f \circ g)(x) = -2\left(x^2 + 1\right)^3 - 5\left(x^2 + 1\right)^2$.

3. Find the functions $f(x)$ and $g(x)$ such that $(f \circ g)(x) = 3(2x)^6 + 3(2x)^3 - (2x)$.

4. Find the functions $f(x)$ and $g(x)$ such that $(f \circ g)(x) = 2x^2 + 4x^4 - 8x^6$.

5. Find the functions $f(x)$ and $g(x)$ such that $(f \circ g)(x) = x^8 - x^4$.

Finding the Difference Quotient of a Function

- Difference quotient:

$$D(x) = \frac{f(x+h) - f(x)}{h}$$

Example	
Example $D(x) = \dfrac{f(x+h)-f(x)}{h}$ $f(x) = 3x-5$ *Substitute* $D(x) = \dfrac{3(x+h)-5-(3x-5)}{h}$	This example shows how the difference quotient formula is used to solve problems. You are given the function $(3x - 5)$. In the formula, replace $f(x + h)$ with $3(x + h) - 5$. Replace $-f(x)$ with $-(3x - 5)$. **Remember:** In the second substitution all the signs will change because you are subtracting.
$= \dfrac{3x+3h-5-3x+5}{h}$ $= \boxed{3} \;\leftarrow\; Answer$ if $h \neq 0$	Then remove your parentheses, combine like terms, and you have your answer. **Note:** Your answer MUST presume that h is not equal to 0.
The difference quotient is just another example of composition that you will see later in calculus. **Example** $D(x) = \dfrac{f(x+h)-f(x)}{h}$ $f(x) = 1-x^2$ *Substitute* $D(x) = \dfrac{1-(x+h)^2-(1-x^2)}{h}$ $= \dfrac{1-(x^2+2hx+h^2)-1+x^2}{h}$ $= \dfrac{-2hx-h^2}{h} = \dfrac{h(-2x-h)}{h} = \boxed{-2x-h}$ $Answer$ if $h \neq 0$	In this example you are given the function $f(x) = 1 - x^2$ and are asked to find the difference quotient. Substitute $(x + h)$ for x. Remove parentheses with a careful regard for signs. Combine like terms and reduce where possible to find your answer. In this case, the difference quotient for the function $f(x) = 1 - x^2$ is $-2x - h$. Assume as a requirement that h cannot equal 0.

Sample problems:

1. Given $f(x) = x^2 - x + 1$, find $f(x+h) - f(x)$.

   Solution: $h^2 - h + 2xh$

   Explanation: $f(x+h) - f(x) = \left[(x+h)^2 - (x+h) + 1\right] - \left[x^2 - x + 1\right] =$

   $\left[(x^2 + 2xh + h^2) - (x+h) + 1\right] - \left[x^2 - x + 1\right] = x^2 + 2xh + h^2 - x - h + 1 - x^2 + x - 1 = h^2 - h + 2xh$

2. Calculate the difference quotient for the function $f(x) = x^2$.

   Solution: $2x + h, \ h \neq 0$

   Explanation: $D(x) = \dfrac{f(x+h) - f(x)}{h} = \dfrac{\left[(x+h)^2\right] - (x^2)}{h} =$

   $\dfrac{\left[x^2 + 2hx + h^2\right] - (x^2)}{h} = \dfrac{2hx + h^2}{h} = \dfrac{h(2x+h)}{h} = 2x + h, \ h \neq 0.$

3. Calculate the difference quotient for the function $f(x) = x^2 - 3x + 2$.

   Solution: $2x + h - 3, \ h \neq 0$

   Explanation: $D(x) = \dfrac{f(x+h) - f(x)}{h} = \dfrac{\left[(x+h)^2 - 3(x+h) + 2\right] - (x^2 - 3x + 2)}{h} =$

   $\dfrac{\left[x^2 + 2hx + h^2 - 3x - 3h + 2\right] - (x^2 - 3x + 2)}{h} = \dfrac{x^2 + 2hx + h^2 - 3x - 3h + 2 - x^2 + 3x - 2}{h} =$

   $\dfrac{2hx + h^2 - 3h}{h} = \dfrac{h(2x + h - 3)}{h} = 2x + h - 3, \ h \neq 0.$

Practice problems: *(Answers on page: 450)*

1. Given $f(x) = 5x^2 + 2x - 1$, find $f(x+h) - f(x)$.

2. Calculate the difference quotient for the function $f(x) = (x+1)^2$.

3. Calculate the difference quotient for the function $f(x) = 2x^2 - 3x$.

Review questions: *(Answers to odd questions on page: 450)*

1. Given $f(x) = x^2 + 1$, find $f(x+h) - f(x)$.

2. Given $f(x) = x - x^2$, find $f(x+h) - f(x)$.

3. Calculate the difference quotient for the function $f(x) = (x-3)^2$.

4. Calculate the difference quotient for the function $f(x) = x^2 - x + 4$.

5. Calculate the difference quotient for the function $f(x) = 5x - x^3$.

Understanding Rational Functions

- **Rational functions** are quotients of polynomials.
- An **asymptote** is a line that the graph of a function approaches but never touches. Asymptotes can be either vertical or horizontal.

What is a Rational Function?	Previously, you studied polynomials and their graphs. **Rational functions** are natural extensions of polynomials. They are functions in the form of a fraction where the numerator and denominator are polynomials.
$\dfrac{\text{polynomial}}{\text{polynomial}}$	

www.thinkwell.com

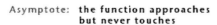

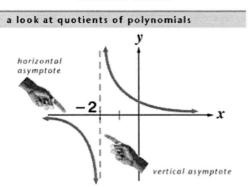

The graphs of rational functions often have asymptotes, or lines that a function gets closer and closer to but never touches. Horizontal asymptotes are horizontal lines, and vertical asymptotes are vertical lines.

This is the graph of a typical rational function. Notice the vertical asymptote at $x = -2$ and the horizontal asymptote at $y = 0$ (the x-axis). The function gets closer and closer to these asymptotes, but it never touches them.

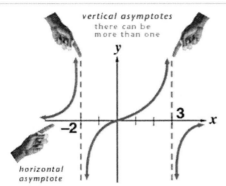

The graph of this rational function has two vertical asymptotes (one at $x = -2$ and one at $x = 3$) and one horizontal asymptote (at $y = 0$, or the x-axis). There is no limit to the number of asymptotes a graph can have.

NOTICE: The function is undefined at the x-values where the vertical asymptotes are located. This happens because the denominator of the function equals zero at these points.

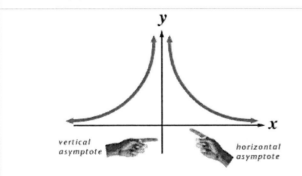

This is another example of the graph of a rational function. It has a vertical asymptote at $x = 0$ (the y-axis) and a horizontal asymptote at $y = 0$ (the x-axis).

Sample problems:

1. What is the domain of this graph?

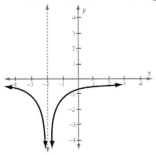

Solution: all real numbers such that $x \neq -2$

Explanation: There is only one vertical asymptote at $x = -2$. Since the curve has no other breaks in it, the domain is all real numbers except -2. In interval notation, this is $(-\infty, -2) \cup (-2, \infty)$.

2. What is the range of this graph?

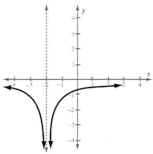

Solution: all real numbers less than 0

Explanation: There is only one horizontal asymptote at the x-axis $(y = 0)$. Since the graph stays below the x-axis, the range is all negative real numbers. In interval notation this is $(-\infty, 0)$.

3. State the horizontal and vertical asymptotes of the graph below.

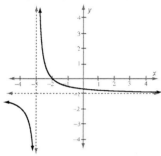

Solution: $y = -1$ and $x = -3$

Explanation: The asymptotes of a graph of a rational function are the values outside of the domain and range. The domain is all real numbers such that $x \neq -3$, so the vertical asymptote is $x = -3$ and the range is all real numbers such that $y \neq -1$, so the horizontal asymptote is $y = -1$.

Practice problems: *(Answers on page: 450)*

1. What is the domain and range of this graph?

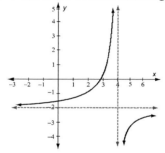

2. What is the domain and range of this graph?

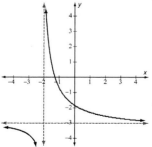

3. State the horizontal and vertical asymptotes of the graph below.

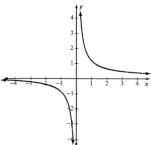

Review questions: *(Answers to odd questions on page: 450)*

1. What is the domain and range of this graph?

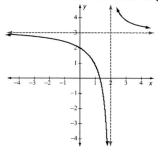

2. What is the domain and range of this graph?

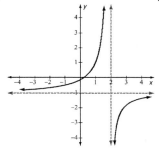

3. What is the domain and range of this graph?

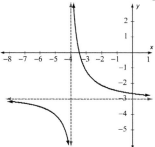

4. State the horizontal and vertical asymptotes of the graph below.

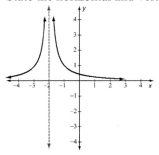

5. State the horizontal and vertical asymptotes of the graph below.

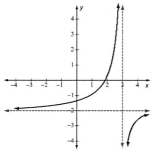

Basic Rational Functions

- **Rational functions** are quotients of polynomials.
- An asymptote is a line that the graph of a function approaches but never touches. Asymptotes can be either vertical or horizontal.

Example $f(x) = \frac{1}{x}$ standard hyperbola

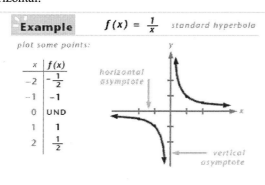

Let's take a look at the graphs of some basic rational functions.

The function $f(x) = 1/x$ is one of the most basic rational functions. Its graph has a vertical asymptote at $x = 0$ (the y-axis) and a horizontal asymptote at $y = 0$ (the x-axis). Notice that $f(x) = 1/x$ is undefined at $x = 0$, where the vertical asymptote is located, because the denominator of the fraction is equal to zero there.

Example $f(x) = \frac{1}{x^2}$

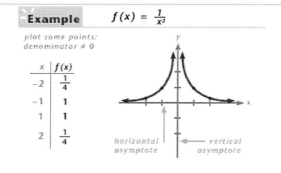

This is the graph of $f(x) = 1/x_2$. It also has a vertical asymptote at $x = 0$ (the y-axis) and a horizontal asymptote at $y = 0$ (the x-axis). Notice, though, that this graph never takes negative y-values.

Example $f(x) = -\frac{1}{x}$ opposite of $\frac{1}{x}$

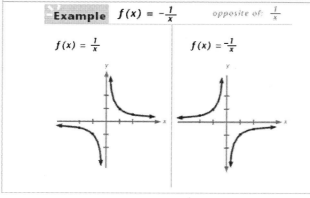

What about the graph of $f(x) = -1/x$? We can graph this rational function by reflecting the graph of $y = 1/x$ over the x-axis.

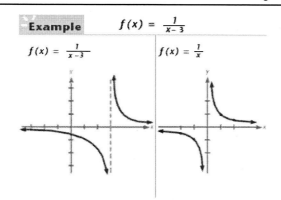

One more example. How can we graph this function? The first step is to graph the function $y = 1/x$. Then, since 3 is subtracted from x in $f(x)$, shift this graph 3 units to the right to find the graph of $f(x)$. Notice that $f(x)$ has a vertical asymptote at $x = 3$, where its denominator is undefined.

REMEMBER: When shifting graphs of functions: "Add to y, go high. Add to x, go west."

Sample problems:

1. Sketch the graph of $f(x) = \dfrac{1}{x} - 2$

   Solution:

   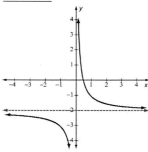

   Explanation: Sketch the graph of $y = \frac{1}{x}$. Shift the entire graph down 2 units. The horizontal asymptote is now $y = -2$ and the vertical asymptote is still the y-axis.

2. Sketch the graph of $f(x) = \dfrac{1}{x-2} + 1$

   Solution:

   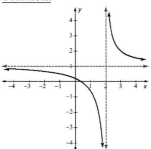

   Explanation: Sketch the graph of $y = \frac{1}{x}$. Shift the entire graph to the right 2 units and up one unit. The vertical asymptote is now $x = 2$ and the horizontal asymptote is now $y = 1$.

3. Sketch the graph of $f(x) = -\dfrac{1}{x+3}$

   Solution:

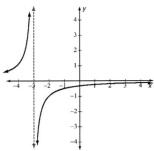

Explanation: Sketch the graph of $y = \dfrac{1}{x}$. Reflect the graph over the x-axis, since

the function is $-\dfrac{1}{x+3}$, and shift the graph 3 units to the left.

Practice problems: *(Answers on page: 450)*

1. Sketch the graph of $f(x) = \dfrac{1}{x} + 3$.

2. Sketch the graph of $f(x) = -\dfrac{1}{x-2}$.

3. Sketch the graph of $f(x) = \dfrac{1}{x+1} - 4$.

Review questions: *(Answers to odd questions on page: 450)*

1. Sketch the graph of $f(x) = \dfrac{1}{x} - 5$.

2. Sketch the graph of $f(x) = -\dfrac{1}{x}$.

3. Sketch the graph of $f(x) = -\dfrac{1}{x+2}$.

4. Sketch the graph of $f(x) = \dfrac{1}{x+2} - 1$.

5. Sketch the graph of $f(x) = \dfrac{1}{x^2}$.

Vertical Asymptotes

- A **vertical asymptote** is a vertical line that the graph of a function approaches but never touches.
- To find the vertical asymptotes of a rational function:
  1. Cancel any common factors in the numerator and denominator to put the fraction in lowest terms.
  2. Set the denominator equal to 0 and solve for x.

Example $p(x) = \dfrac{3}{2x-4}$ *find the vertical asymptote*

$2x - 4 = 0$ ✔ *lowest terms?*   ✔ *set denominator = 0*

$2x = 4$

$\boxed{x = 2}$ vertical asymptote (VA)

Previously, you saw how rational functions often have vertical asymptotes in their graphs. Now you will learn how to find those vertical asymptotes algebraically.

The first step is to reduce the fraction to lowest terms. In this case, this step is not necessary because the fraction is already in lowest terms.

The second step is to set the denominator equal to zero and solve for x. The result is the vertical asymptote.

Example $p(x) = \dfrac{5 + 3x}{x^2 + 4x - 5}$ *find the vertical asymptote*

$\dfrac{5 + 3x}{(x - 1)(x + 5)}$ ✔ *lowest terms!* ✔ *factor denominator*

$\boxed{x = 1, \quad x = -5}$ ✔ *set denominator = 0*

Let's try another problem. After factoring the denominator, you can see that there are no terms to cancel, so the fraction is already in lowest terms. Set the denominator equal to zero, solve for x, and you're done.

Example $f(x) = \dfrac{x^2 - 1}{x + 1}$ *find the vertical asymptote*

$\dfrac{(x + 1)(x - 1)}{(x + 1)}$ ✔ *lowest terms?* ✔ *set denominator = 0*

remember: *only if* $x \neq -1$

$f(x) = x - 1$ ⟵ straight line

no VA !

After factoring the numerator in this problem, you find that the fraction is not in lowest terms because the $(x + 1)$ terms can be cancelled away.

REMEMBER: If you cancel a term from the numerator and denominator of a fraction, you have to promise that the old denominator will never equal zero.

After you cancel the $(x + 1)$ terms, there is no denominator, so there are no vertical asymptotes! The graph of this function is a straight line with a hole in it at $x = -1$.

Example $f(x) = \dfrac{(9x - 1)(x + 3)}{(2x + 6)(x - 5)}$ *find the vertical asymptote*

$f(x) = \dfrac{(9x - 1)(x + 3)}{2(x + 3)(x - 5)}$ ✔ *lowest terms?* ✔ *factor denominator*

only if $x \neq 3$

$= \dfrac{9x - 1}{2(x - 5)}$ ✔ *set denominator = 0*

$\boxed{x = 5}$ VA

One last example. Can you find the vertical asymptotes of this function?

Factor the denominator and cancel the $(x + 3)$ terms. After you have cancelled the terms, the fraction is in lowest terms. Set the denominator equal to zero and solve for x.

Sample problems:

1. Given $f(x) = \dfrac{2}{x - 4}$, find the vertical asymptote(s).

Solution: $x = 4$

Explanation: The expression cannot be simplified, so set the denominator equal to 0 and solve for x: $x - 4 = 0$; $x = 4$. Thus, the vertical asymptote is $x = 4$.

2. Given $f(x) = \dfrac{x}{x^2 - 5x - 6}$, find the vertical asymptote(s).

Solution: $x = 6$ and $x = -1$

Explanation: The expression cannot be simplified, so set the denominator equal to 0 and solve for x: $x^2 - 5x - 6 = 0$; $(x - 6)(x + 1) = 0$. Thus, the graph must have two vertical asymptotes: $x = 6$ and $x = -1$.

3. Given $f(x) = \dfrac{x + 2}{x^2 - 3x - 10}$, find the vertical asymptote(s).

Solution: $x = 5$

Explanation: Simplify the expression: $\dfrac{x + 2}{x^2 - 3x - 10} = \dfrac{x + 2}{(x + 2)(x - 5)} = \dfrac{1}{x - 5}$.

Set the denominator equal to 0 and solve for x: $x - 5 = 0$; $x = 5$. Thus, the vertical asymptote is $x = 5$.

Practice problems: *(Answers on page: 450)*

1. Given $f(x) = \dfrac{1}{x + 7}$, find the vertical asymptote(s).

2. Given $f(x) = \dfrac{x}{x^2 - 9}$, find the vertical asymptote(s).

3. Given $f(x) = \dfrac{x^2 + 5x + 6}{x + 3}$, find the vertical asymptote(s).

Review questions: *(Answers to odd questions on page: 450)*

1. Given $f(x) = \dfrac{6}{x}$, find the vertical asymptote(s).

2. Given $f(x) = \dfrac{3 - x}{x + 5}$, find the vertical asymptote(s).

3. Given $f(x) = \dfrac{1}{x^2 - 25}$, find the vertical asymptote(s).

4. Given $f(x) = \dfrac{x + 7}{x^2 + 9x + 14}$, find the vertical asymptote(s).

5. Given $f(x) = \dfrac{x^2 - 16}{x + 4}$, find the vertical asymptote(s).

Horizontal Asymptotes

- A **horizontal asymptote** is a horizontal line that the graph of a function approaches but never touches.
- To find the horizontal asymptotes of a rational function, consider the largest powers of x in the numerator and denominator:

   1. If the largest power of x is in the denominator, the function has a horizontal asymptote at $y = 0$ (the x-axis).
   2. If the largest power of x is in the numerator, the function has no horizontal asymptote.
   3. If the powers of x are equal in the numerator and denominator, the function has a horizontal asymptote. Divide the coefficients of the largest powers of x to find out where the asymptote is located.

as x goes to ∞ who wins?
numerator or denominator?

When finding the **horizontal asymptotes** of a function, you want to examine what happens to the function as x becomes very large.

You can view this as a race between the numerator and the denominator—which one will get to infinity first?

$f(x) = \dfrac{3}{2x - 4}$ find horizontal asymptote

who will get to ∞ faster?

$f(x) = \dfrac{3}{\boxed{2x} - 4}$ denominator growing faster than numerator

HA $y = 0$

Let's try an example. In this problem, the largest power of x in the denominator, 1, is greater than the largest power of x in the numerator, 0.

This means that the denominator goes to infinity faster than the numerator as x gets large. The denominator wins the race!

$f(x)$ has a horizontal asymptote at $y = 0$.

$f(x) = \dfrac{4x^3 - 3}{2x + 4}$ gets to ∞ faster

no HA

no limits
fraction is getting larger

In this example, the largest power of x in the numerator, 3, is greater than the largest power of x in the denominator, 1. The numerator goes to infinity faster than the denominator as x gets large.

So, as x gets large, $f(x)$ doesn't approach any value. There is no horizontal asymptote.

$$f(x) = \frac{9x - 3x^2}{7x^2 + 103} \quad \text{find horizontal asymptote}$$

$$f(x) = \frac{9x \boxed{-3}x^2}{\boxed{7}x^2 + 103} \quad \text{tie race}$$

$$\boxed{HA \quad y = \frac{-3}{7}}$$

In this problem, the largest power of x in the numerator is equal to the largest power of x in the denominator. This tells you that there is a horizontal asymptote.

To find the asymptote, divide the coefficients of the largest powers of x. The horizontal asymptote in this example is $y = -3/7$.

Sample problems:

1. Give the equation of the horizontal asymptote of the following function: $f(x) = \frac{x-5}{7}$.

   Solution: No horizontal asymptote

   Explanation: The numerator has a degree of 1 and the denominator has a degree of 0. Therefore there is no horizontal asymptote.

2. Given $f(x) = \frac{4x^3 - 7x}{5x^6 + 1}$, find the horizontal asymptote if it exists.

   Solution: $y = 0$

   Explanation: The numerator has a degree of 3 and the denominator has a degree of 6. Therefore, since the degree is greater in the denominator, the equation of the horizontal asymptote is $y = 0$.

3. Given $f(x) = \frac{3 - 2x^3}{5x^3}$, find the horizontal asymptote if it exists.

   Solution: $y = -\frac{2}{5}$

   Explanation: Since the degrees of the numerator and the denominator are equal, the equation of the horizontal asymptote is $y = \frac{a}{b}$, where a and b are the coefficients of the terms with the highest degrees in the numerator and denominator respectively. The coefficient of the highest degree term in the numerator is -2 and the coefficient of the highest degree term in the denominator is 5, so the equation of the horizontal asymptote is $y = -\frac{2}{5}$.

Practice problems: (Answers on page: 451)

1. Given $f(x) = \frac{9}{x-3}$, find the horizontal asymptote if it exists.

2. Given $f(x) = \frac{2x^3 + x - 7}{2x^4 + 1}$, find the horizontal asymptote if it exists.

3. Given $f(x) = \frac{x^4 + 5x + 9}{4x^4 + 3x - 5}$, find the horizontal asymptote if it exists.

Review questions: (Answers to odd questions on page: 451)

1. Given $f(x) = \frac{8}{x-4}$, find the horizontal asymptote if it exists.

2. Given $f(x) = \frac{4x^2 + 5}{5x^5 - 9}$, find the horizontal asymptote if it exists.

3. Given $f(x) = \dfrac{4x^5 + 5}{4x^5 + 2x - 6}$, find the horizontal asymptote if it exists.

4. Given $f(x) = \dfrac{5x^5 - 5}{5x^4 + x + 6}$, find the horizontal asymptote if it exists.

5. Given $f(x) = \dfrac{2x^3 + 7}{5x^2 + 4x + 7}$, find the horizontal asymptote if it exists.

Graphing Rational Functions

- An **asymptote** is a line that the graph of a function approaches but never touches.
- You can use the horizontal and vertical asymptotes of a rational function to help you sketch its graph.

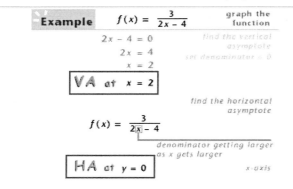

You can use what you have learned about horizontal and vertical asymptotes to graph rational functions.

This question asks you to graph the function $f(x)$.

The first step is to find the vertical asymptotes. The fraction is already in lowest terms, so just set the denominator equal to zero and solve for x.

Now find the horizontal asymptotes. The largest power of x in the denominator is greater than the largest power of x in the numerator, so there is a horizontal asymptote at $y = 0$.

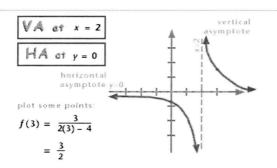

The asymptotes split the plane up into separate regions.

Plot a few points so you know which regions the graph is in and to give you a rough idea of the shape of the curve. Draw a curve that goes through those points and approaches the asymptotes.

This curve is the graph of $f(x)$!

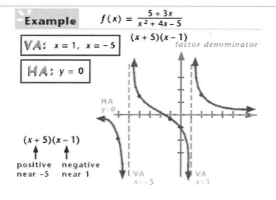

Let's try another example.

The first step is to find the vertical asymptotes. In this case, there are two. Next, find the horizontal asymptotes. Here, there is one at $y = 0$.

Sketch the asymptotes on a graph. They split the plane up into different regions. Plot some points so you know which regions the graph of $f(x)$ is in. Draw a curve that goes through those points and approaches the asymptotes and you're done.

NOTICE: You can also find and plot the x and y-intercepts to help you draw the graph.

Sample problems:

1. Graph: $f(x) = \dfrac{x^2 - 4}{x^2 - 1}$.

   Solution:

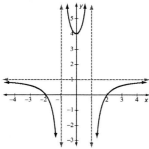

Explanation: Setting the denominator equal to 0 and factoring, we determine that the function has vertical asymptotes at $x = 1$ and $x = -1$. Since the degree of the numerator is equal to the degree of the denominator, the equation of the horizontal asymptote is $y = \dfrac{1}{1} = 1$. Some points in a table of values for $y = \dfrac{x^2 - 4}{x^2 - 1}$ are $(-2, 0)$, $(0, 4)$ and $(2, 0)$. Plot these points and watch for symmetry.

2. Graph: $f(x) = \dfrac{x + 10}{x^2 - 2x - 3}$

Solution:

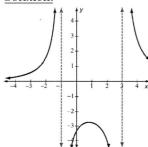

Explanation: Setting the denominator equal to 0 and factoring, we determine that the function has vertical asymptotes at $x = -1$ and $x = 3$. Since the degree of the numerator is less than the degree of the denominator, the equation of the horizontal asymptote is $y = 0$. Some points in a table of values for $y = \dfrac{(x+10)}{(x^2 - 2x - 3)}$ are $\left(-2, \frac{8}{5}\right)$, $\left(0, -\frac{10}{3}\right)$ and $(2, -4)$. Plot these points and watch for symmetry.

3. Graph: $f(x) = \dfrac{x}{x^2 - 4}$.

Solution:

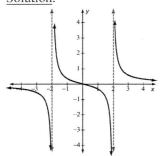

Explanation: Setting the denominator equal to 0 and factoring, we determine that the function has vertical asymptotes at $x = 2$ and $x = -2$. Since the degree of the numerator is less than the degree of the denominator, the equation of the horizontal asymptote is $y = 0$. Some points in a table of values for $y = \dfrac{x}{x^2 - 4}$ are $\left(-3, -\frac{3}{5}\right)$, $(0, 0)$ and $\left(3, \frac{3}{5}\right)$. Plot these points and watch for symmetry.

Practice problems: *(Answers on page: 451)*

1. Graph: $f(x) = \dfrac{3}{x-2}$

2. Graph: $f(x) = \dfrac{5x}{x-1}$

3. Graph: $f(x) = \dfrac{3x}{x^2-4}$

Review questions: *(Answers to odd questions on page: 451)*

1. Graph: $f(x) = \dfrac{-3}{x+1}$

2. Graph: $f(x) = \dfrac{x-2}{x-5}$

3. Graph: $f(x) = \dfrac{x-1}{x-3}$

4. Graph: $f(x) = \dfrac{2x}{x^2-1}$

5. Graph: $f(x) = \dfrac{3x}{x^2-25}$

Graphing Rational Functions: More Examples

- An asymptote is a line that the graph of a function approaches but never touches.
- You can use the horizontal and vertical asymptotes of a rational function to help you sketch its graph.

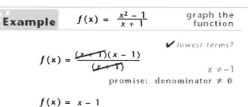

This problem asks you to graph the rational function $f(x)$.

First, find the vertical asymptotes. The $(x + 1)$ terms in the numerator and denominator cancel, so there are none. There are no horizontal asymptotes either.

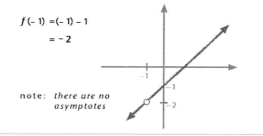

This is an easy one! The function is just a line with a hole in it at $x = -1$.

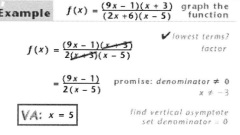

What about this problem? The first step is to find the vertical asymptotes. Factor and cancel some terms to put the fraction in lowest terms. Set the denominator equal to zero and solve for x.

REMEMBER: When you cancel terms in a rational function, you have to promise that the old denominator will never equal zero.

© Thinkwell Corp. www.thinkwell.com

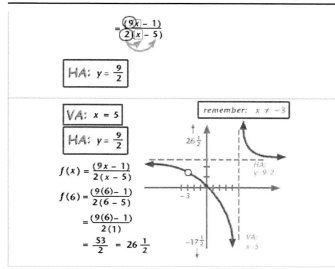

Now find the horizontal asymptotes. The largest power of x in the numerator is equal to the largest power of x in the denominator, so there is a horizontal asymptote located at the quotient of the coefficients.

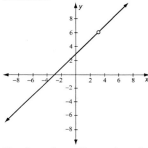

Time to draw the graph. Sketch in the asymptotes, plot a few points, and draw in the curve.

Don't forget about your promise! There is a hole in the graph at $x = -3$.

Sample problems:

1. Graph the following rational function $f(x) = \dfrac{x^2 - 9}{x - 3}$.

Solution:

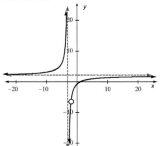

Explanation: Factoring the numerator yields $x - 3$ as a factor common to both the numerator and denominator. Therefore, the graph will have a hole at $x = 3$. The function can be described as $f(x) = x + 3$, for x not equal to 3. Substitute $x = 3$ into the expression $x + 3$ to find the coordinates of the hole, $(3, 6)$. Since the degree of the numerator is greater than the degree of the denominator, there is no horizontal asymptote. Notice that, except for the hole, the graph is a line.

2. Graph the following rational function: $f(x) = \dfrac{(2x + 4)(x - 1)}{(x + 3)(x + 2)}$.

Solution:

Explanation: According to the numerator, we find that $x + 2$ is a common factor between the numerator and denominator. Therefore we have a hole at $x = -2$. Substituting into $\dfrac{2(x-1)}{(x+3)}$, we find that the hole has coordinates $(-2, -6)$. Setting the other factor in the denominator equal to 0, we determine that the function has a vertical asymptote at $x = -3$. Since the degree of the numerator is the same as the degree of the denominator, the equation of the horizontal asymptote is $y = 2$. Graph the function using symmetry.

3. Graph the following rational function: $f(x) = \dfrac{x+1}{x^2+1}$.

Solution:

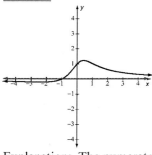

Explanation: The numerator and denominator have no factors in common. Therefore, there are no holes in the graph. Since the denominator never equals 0, the function has no vertical asymptotes. The degree of the numerator is less than the degree of the denominator, so the equation of the horizontal asymptote is $y = 0$. Plot some points and sketch the graph.

Practice problems: *(Answers on page: 451)*

1. Graph: $f(x) = \dfrac{x-5}{x^2 - 6x + 5}$

2. Graph: $f(x) = \dfrac{(-2x-4)(x+4)}{(x+5)(x-2)}$

3. Graph: $f(x) = \dfrac{x^2}{x^2 - 16}$

Review questions: *(Answers to odd questions on page: 451)*

1. Graph: $f(x) = \dfrac{x-4}{x^2 - 2x - 8}$

2. Graph: $f(x) = \dfrac{(-5x-15)(x-2)}{(x+4)(x-5)}$

3. Graph: $f(x) = \dfrac{(4x+12)(x-2)}{(x-5)(x+4)}$

4. Graph: $f(x) = \dfrac{x^2}{x^2 - 9}$

5. Graph: $f(x) = \dfrac{1}{x^2 + 3}$

Understanding Inverse Functions

- An **inverse function** "undoes" another function.

  If $g(x)$ is the inverse function of $f(x)$, then $g\left[\left(f(x)\right)\right] = x$ and $f\left[\left(g(x)\right)\right] = x$.

- Not all functions have inverse functions.

Inverse Function : A function that "undoes" another function.

Suppose you have a function: $f(x)$

$$x \xrightarrow{\ f(x)\ } \text{another number} \xrightarrow{\ g(f(x))\ } x$$

$$(g \circ f)(x) = x$$

$$x \xrightarrow{\ g(x)\ } \text{another number} \xrightarrow{\ f(g(x))\ } x$$

$$(f \circ g)(x) = x$$

We are going to explore the concept of inverse functions.

A function $f(x)$ takes an input, x, and produces an output, $f(x)$. Its inverse function $g(x)$ takes $f(x)$ as its input and outputs x. It "undoes" the action of $f(x)$.

If $g(x)$ is the inverse function of $f(x)$, then $f(x)$ is also the inverse function of $g(x)$. So $f(x)$ undoes the action of $g(x)$, too.

Example

This function undoes the other one

$$f(x) = 2x - 3 \qquad \boxed{g(x) = \dfrac{x + 3}{2}}$$

$$f(1) = -1 \qquad g(-1) = 1$$
$$f(3) = 3 \qquad g(3) = 3$$
$$f(-2) = -7 \qquad g(-7) = -2$$

Now we want to find a function where if we input this, the output is this

$$f \circ g(x) = f(g(x)) =$$
$$2\left(\dfrac{x + 3}{2}\right) - 3 = x$$

That was pretty abstract. Let's try a concrete example.

Consider this function $f(x)$. If you plug in $x = 1$, $f(x)$ outputs -1. If you plug in $x = -2$, $f(x)$ outputs -7, and so on. In order to find the inverse function, you need a function that will "undo" $f(x)$. You need a function that will output 1 when you plug in $x = -1$ and output -2 when you plug in $x = -7$, and so on. Notice that the function $g(x)$ does exactly this.

In fact, if you compute the value of $f[g(x)]$, you find that it is equal to x. The functions really are inverses!

Example

$$f(x) = x^2 \qquad g(x) = \sqrt{x}$$
$$f(2) = 4 \qquad g(4) = 2$$
$$f(-2) = 4$$

The problem is that there are different values of x that lead to the same value of y.

Does the function $f(x) = x^2$ have an inverse?

$g(x) = \sqrt{x}$ looks like a good possibility for the inverse, but notice that $f(-2) = 4$, whereas $g(4) \neq -2$.

The problem is that for $f(x) = x^2$, two different input values lead to the same output value. So given the output value, a hypothetical inverse function wouldn't know which of the two inputs to return! The function $f(x) = x^2$ has no inverse.

REMEMBER: Not all functions have inverses.

Sample problems:

1. Given that $f(5) = 15$, find $f^{-1}(15)$.
   <u>Solution</u>: 5
   <u>Explanation</u>: The inverse function reverses the input and output. So, $f^{-1}(15) = 5$, since $f(5) = 15$.

2. True or false: If $(2,19)$ is a member of f, and f^{-1} exists, then the point $(19,2)$ is a member of f^{-1}.
   <u>Solution</u>: True
   <u>Explanation</u>: If $(2,19)$ is a member of f that means that $f(2) = 19$. The inverse reverses the input and output, so $f^{-1}(19) = 2$. Therefore, $(19,2)$ is a member of f^{-1}.

---

3. Given that $g^{-1}(-4) = 3$, find $g(3)$.

 Solution: -4

 Explanation: The inverse function reverses the input and output. So, $g(3) = -4$, since $g^{-1}(-4) = 3$.

Practice problems: *(Answers on page: 451)*

1. Given that $g^{-1}(x)$ is the inverse of $g(x)$ and that $g^{-1}(-4) = 3$, find $g(3)$.

2. If $(-3, \frac{1}{2})$ is a member of f, and f^{-1} exists, find $f^{-1}(\frac{1}{2})$.

3. Given that $g^{-1}(5) = 2$, find $g(2)$.

Review questions: *(Answers to odd questions on page: 451)*

1. Given that $f(12) = 6$, find $f^{-1}(6)$.

2. Given that $g^{-1}(-3) = 8$, find $g(8)$.

3. Given that $g^{-1}(x)$ is the inverse of $g(x)$ and that $g^{-1}(5) = 2$, find $g(2)$.

4. If $(6.3, 3.2)$ is a member of f, and f^{-1} exists, find $f^{-1}(3.2)$.

5. If $(17.5, -0.2)$ is a member of f, and f^{-1} exists, find $f^{-1}(-0.2)$.

The Horizontal Line Test

- The **horizontal line test**: If the graph of a function intersects every horizontal line at most once, then the function has an inverse.
- A **one-to-one function** is a function that satisfies the horizontal line test. For a one-to-one function, every output y-value comes from exactly one input x-value.

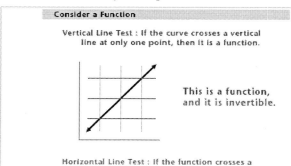

Previously you learned that you could find out whether a graph described a function using the vertical line test.

Now, you can use the **horizontal line test** to determine whether a function has an inverse. If the graph of a function intersects every horizontal line at most once, the function has an inverse. Otherwise, the function has no inverse, because some y-values (outputs) might have more than one corresponding x-value (input).

The horizontal line test tells you that a linear function has an inverse.

A parabola, though, has no inverse because it fails the horizontal line test. Sometimes, two different x-values lead to the same y-value.

Testing Functions			
Vertical Line Test	Horizontal Line Test	Assessment	
✔	✔	This is a function, and it is invertible.	
✔	✘	This is a function, but it has no inverse.	

One-to-One Functions : **Functions where every x goes to only one y, and every y came from only one x.**	

Let's try some more examples.

This cubic function has an inverse. It intersects any horizontal line at exactly one point.

This exotic function fails the horizontal line test and has no inverse.

Functions that pass the horizontal line test are also known as **one-to-one functions**. For a one-to-one function, every x-value goes to only one y-value, and every y-value corresponds to only one x-value. A function has an inverse if it is one-to-one, and a function is one-to-one if it has an inverse.

Sample problems:

1. Does the inverse function of $y = \dfrac{x}{3} + 2$ exist?

   Solution: Yes

   Explanation: An inverse function exists if the graph passes the horizontal line test. To pass the horizontal line test, any horizontal line can intersect the graph no more than one time. The graph of $y = \frac{x}{3} + 2$ is a line since the equation is linear (no exponents), and the line is slanted up since the slope is $\frac{1}{3}$. This graph passes the horizontal line test, so the inverse function of $y = \frac{x}{3} + 2$ exists.

2. True or false: The following graph is a one-to-one function.

   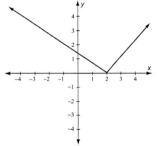

   Solution: False

   Explanation: The graph fails the horizontal line test, therefore it is not one-to-one.

3. True or false: $f(x) = 3 - x^2$ is a one-to-one function.

   Solution: False

   Explanation: The graph of $f(x) = 3 - x^2$ is a parabola since the equation is quadratic (x is squared) and the parabola opens down since the coefficient of x^2 is negative. This graph fails the horizontal line test since many horizontal lines will intersect the parabola twice. Therefore, it is not a one-to-one function.

Practice problems: *(Answers on page: 451)*

1. Does the inverse of $f(x) = 2x + 5$ exist?

2. True or false: The following graph is a one-to-one function.

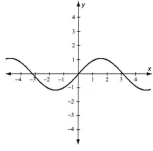

3. True or false: $g(x) = x^3 + 5x - 1$ is a one-to-one function.

Review questions: *(Answers to odd questions on page: 451)*

1. Does the inverse of $h(x) = x^3 - x + 1$ exist?

2. True or false: The following graph is a one-to-one function.

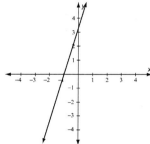

3. True or false: The following graph is a one-to-one function.

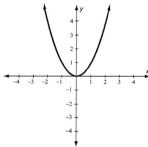

4. True or false: The following graph is a one-to-one function.

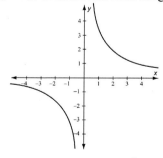

5. True or false: $g(x) = x^3 + 3x - 7$ is a one-to-one function.

Are Two Functions Inverses of Each Other?

- The graphs of inverse functions are reflections of each other across the line $y = x$.

- The notation $f^{-1}(x)$ means "the inverse of the function $f(x)$".

- Inverse functions satisfy the two equations $f \circ f^{-1}(x) = x$ and $f^{-1} \circ f(x) = x$.

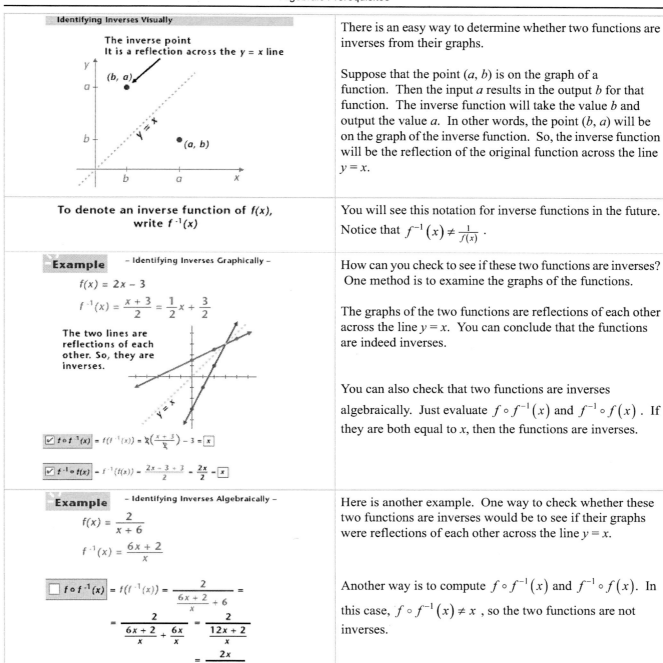

Identifying Inverses Visually

The inverse point
It is a reflection across the $y = x$ line

There is an easy way to determine whether two functions are inverses from their graphs.

Suppose that the point (a, b) is on the graph of a function. Then the input a results in the output b for that function. The inverse function will take the value b and output the value a. In other words, the point (b, a) will be on the graph of the inverse function. So, the inverse function will be the reflection of the original function across the line $y = x$.

To denote an inverse function of $f(x)$, write $f^{-1}(x)$

You will see this notation for inverse functions in the future. Notice that $f^{-1}(x) \neq \frac{1}{f(x)}$.

Example – Identifying Inverses Graphically –

$f(x) = 2x - 3$

$f^{-1}(x) = \frac{x + 3}{2} = \frac{1}{2}x + \frac{3}{2}$

The two lines are reflections of each other. So, they are inverses.

$f \circ f^{-1}(x) = f(f^{-1}(x)) = 2\left(\frac{x+3}{2}\right) - 3 = x$

$f^{-1} \circ f(x) = f^{-1}(f(x)) = \frac{2x - 3 + 3}{2} = \frac{2x}{2} = x$

How can you check to see if these two functions are inverses? One method is to examine the graphs of the functions.

The graphs of the two functions are reflections of each other across the line $y = x$. You can conclude that the functions are indeed inverses.

You can also check that two functions are inverses algebraically. Just evaluate $f \circ f^{-1}(x)$ and $f^{-1} \circ f(x)$. If they are both equal to x, then the functions are inverses.

Example – Identifying Inverses Algebraically –

$f(x) = \frac{2}{x + 6}$

$f^{-1}(x) = \frac{6x + 2}{x}$

$f \circ f^{-1}(x) = f(f^{-1}(x)) = \frac{2}{\frac{6x+2}{x} + 6} =$

$= \frac{2}{\frac{6x+2}{x} + \frac{6x}{x}} = \frac{2}{\frac{12x+2}{x}}$

$= \frac{2x}{12x + 2}$

Here is another example. One way to check whether these two functions are inverses would be to see if their graphs were reflections of each other across the line $y = x$.

Another way is to compute $f \circ f^{-1}(x)$ and $f^{-1} \circ f(x)$. In this case, $f \circ f^{-1}(x) \neq x$, so the two functions are not inverses.

Sample problems:

1. True or false: Given $f(x) = -\frac{2}{x}$ and $g(x) = \frac{2}{x}$, f and g are inverses of one another.

   Solution: False

   Explanation: Evaluate: $f \circ g = f(g(x)) = -\frac{2}{\frac{2}{x}} = -2 \div \frac{2}{x} = -2 \cdot \frac{x}{2} = -x.$ Since $f(g(x)) \neq x$, f and g are not inverse functions.

2. True or false: Given $f(x) = 2 + x^3$ and $g(x) = \sqrt[3]{x - 2}$, f and g are inverses of one another.

Solution: True

Explanation: Evaluate: $f \circ g = f(g(x)) = 2 + \left(\sqrt[3]{x-2}\right)^3 = 2 + (x-2) = 2 + x - 2 = x.$

Evaluate: $g \circ f = g(f(x)) = \sqrt[3]{(2 + x^3) - 2} = \sqrt[3]{2 + x^3 - 2} = \sqrt[3]{x^3} = x.$ Since $f(g(x)) = x$ and $g(f(x)) = x$, f and g are inverses of one another.

3. Determine whether the functions below are inverses of each other by comparing their graphs with the line $y = x$.

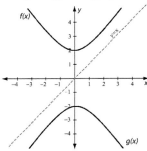

Solution: They are not inverses

Explanation: The two functions are not reflections of each other across the line $y = x$; therefore they are not inverses.

Practice problems: *(Answers on page: 452)*

1. Determine whether the functions below are inverses of each other by comparing their graphs with the line $y = x$.

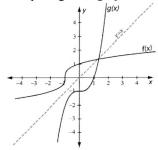

2. True or false: Given $f(x) = \sqrt{4 - x}$, $x \le 4$ and $g(x) = 4 - x^2$, $x > 0$, f and g are inverses of one another.

3. True or false: Given $f(x) = \dfrac{(4x - 2)}{5}$ and $g(x) = \dfrac{(5x + 2)}{4}$, f and g are inverses of one another.

Review questions: *(Answers to odd questions on page: 452)*

1. Given that $f(x) = \dfrac{8x + 3}{7}$ and $g(x) = \dfrac{7x - 3}{8}$, are f and g inverses of one another?

2. Given that $f(x) = \sqrt{4 - x}$, with domain $(-\infty, 4]$ and $g(x) = 4 - x^2$, with domain $(0, \infty)$, are f and g inverses of one another?

3. Given that $f(x) = \dfrac{3}{2 - x}$ and $g(x) = 2 + \dfrac{3}{x}$, are f and g inverses of one another?

4. Determine whether each pair of functions are inverses of each other or not by comparing their graphs with the line $y = x$.

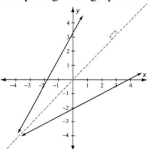

5. True or false: Given $f(x) = 2 + x^3$ and $g(x) = \sqrt[3]{x - 2}$, f and g are inverses of one another.

Graphing the Inverse

- The horizontal line test says that if the graph of a function intersects every horizontal line at most once, then the function has an inverse.
- The graphs of inverse functions are reflections of each other across the line $y = x$.

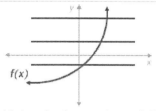

1 Does this function have an inverse? YES
or... Is this a one-to-one function? YES
or... Does it pass the horizontal line test? YES

Take a look at the graph of this function. Does this function have an inverse? You can answer this question using the horizontal line test.

$f(x)$ is one-to-one because it passes the horizontal line test. It has an inverse for the same reason.

Example

Finding the Inverse of a Function

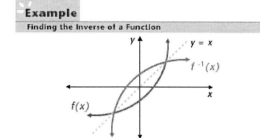

1 Does this function have an inverse? YES
or... Is this a one-to-one function? YES
or... Does it pass the horizontal line test? YES
2 To find the inverse, reflect the curve over the y = x line.

To actually find the inverse function, just reflect the graph of $f(x)$ over the line $y = x$. The result is the graph of $f^{-1}(x)$.

Example

Finding the Inverse of a Function

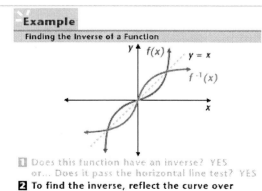

1 Does this function have an inverse? YES
or... Does it pass the horizontal line test? YES
2 To find the inverse, reflect the curve over the y = x line.

In this example, the inverse of the function $f(x)$ has been sketched in along with the graph of $f(x)$. The two graphs are reflections of each other across the line $y = x$.

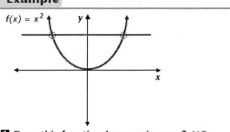

Example

$f(x) = x^2$

1 Does this function have an inverse? NO
or... Is this a one-to-one function? NO
or... Does it pass the horizontal line test? NO

What about this function? Can you sketch its inverse?

This function fails the horizontal line test! It has no inverse.

Sample problems:

1. Graph the inverse f^{-1} (if it exists) of the function f.

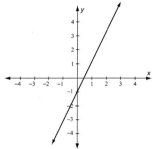

Solution:

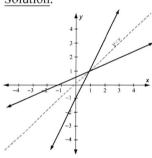

Explanation: The function is one-to-one since it passes the vertical and horizontal line tests. Therefore the inverse function does exist. To graph the inverse, sketch the line $y = x$ then reflect the given line over the line $y = x$.

2. Graph the inverse f^{-1} (if it exists) of the function f.

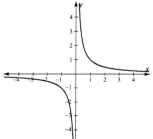

Solution:

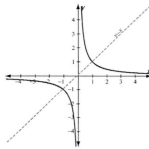

Explanation: The sketched reflection creates a duplicate of the graph. So, the function is its own inverse, $f = f^{-1}$.

3. Graph the inverse f^{-1} (if it exists) of the function f, and find $f^{-1}(1)$.

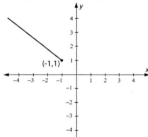

Solution: $f^{-1}(1)$ is -1.

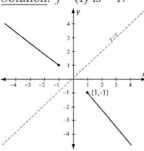

Explanation: Sketch the graph by reflecting the given graph across the line $y = x$. Use the new graph, f^{-1}, to determine $f^{-1}(1)$, the y-value that corresponds with $x = 1$, so $f^{-1}(1) = -1$.

Practice problems: *(Answers on page: 452)*

1. Graph the inverse f^{-1} (if it exists) of the function f.

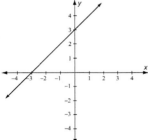

2. Graph the inverse f^{-1} (if it exists) of the function f.

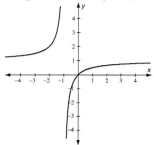

3. Graph the inverse f^{-1} (if it exists) of the function f, and find $f^{-1}(0)$.

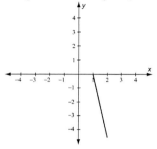

Review questions: *(Answers to odd questions on page: 452)*

1. Graph the inverse f^{-1} (if it exists) of the function f.

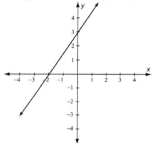

2. Graph the inverse f^{-1} (if it exists) of the function f.

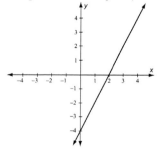

3. Graph the inverse f^{-1} (if it exists) of the function f.

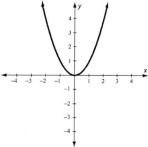

4. Graph the inverse f^{-1} (if it exists) of the function f.

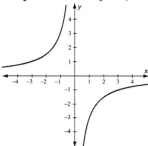

5. Graph the inverse f^{-1} of the function f, and find $f^{-1}(2)$.

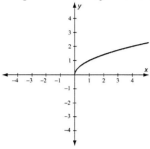

Finding the Inverse of a Function

- To find the inverse of a function algebraically:
    1. Swap the x variables with the y variables.
    2. Solve the new equation for y. If this new equation cannot be solved for y as a function of x, the original function does not have an inverse

---

Example

Finding the Inverse of a Function

$f(x)$ is the same thing as y

$y = 4x - 3 = f(x)$

$x = 4y - 3$

Swap the x and y, then solve for y.

$4y = x + 3$

If you can't solve for y, then the function has no inverse.

$y = \dfrac{x + 3}{4} = f^{-1}(x)$

Previously, you learned how to find the inverse of a function graphically. Now you will learn how to find the inverse of a function algebraically.

To find the inverse of this function, first swap the variable x with the variable y.

Now solve the new equation for y.

The result is the inverse function!

Example Find the inverse of

$y = \dfrac{-6}{x}$

$x = \dfrac{-6}{y}$ *Swap the x and y*

$y\left(x = \dfrac{-6}{y}\right)$

$yx = -6$

$y = \dfrac{-6}{x} = f^{-1}(x)$

Let's try another one. Can you find the inverse of this function?

First, swap the x with the y.

Now solve for y.

You've found the inverse function $f^{-1}(x)$.

Example Find the inverse of

$$f(x) = y = x^2$$

Swap the x and y

$$x = y^2$$

$$y = \boxed{\pm}\sqrt{x}$$

This is not a function, because there are two values for y.

Let's try out our method on this function.

Swap the x with the y. Then solve for y.

Whoops! We don't get a function when we solve for y. This means that the original function does not have an inverse.

REMEMBER: Not all functions have inverses!

Sample problems:

1. Find the inverse of $f(x) = \dfrac{2x-1}{3}$, if it exists.

   Solution: $f^{-1}(x) = \dfrac{3x+1}{2}$

   Explanation: Replace $f(x)$ with y: $y = \frac{2x-1}{3}$. Interchange the x and y variables: $x = \frac{2y-1}{3}$.
   Solve for y: $3x = 2y - 1$; $2y = 3x + 1$; $y = \frac{3x+1}{2}$. Replace y with $f^{-1}(x)$: $f^{-1}(x) = \frac{3x+1}{2}$.
   Check the inverse by evaluating $f^{-1}(f(x))$ and $f(f^{-1}(x))$,
   which should both equal x if they are indeed inverses.

2. Find the inverse of $u(x) = -3\sqrt{\dfrac{x}{3}}$, $x \geq 0$, if it exists, then find $u^{-1}(0)$.

   Solution: $u^{-1}(x) = \dfrac{x^2}{3}$; $u^{-1}(0) = 0$

   Explanation: Since the function is restricted to where $x \geq 0$, it is one-to-one.
   Replace $u(x)$ with y and swap the variables: $y = -3\sqrt{\frac{x}{3}} \Rightarrow x = -3\sqrt{\frac{y}{3}}$.
   Solve for y: $x^2 = (-3\sqrt{\frac{y}{x}})^2$; $x^2 = (-3)^2(\sqrt{\frac{y}{3}})^2$; $x^2 = 9\left(\frac{y}{3}\right)$; $x^2 = 3y$; $y = \frac{x^2}{3}$.
   So, $u^{-1}(x) = \frac{x^2}{3}$, $x \leq 0$. Find $u^{-1}(0)$ by substituting 0 into the inverse function for x:
   $u^{-1}(0) = \frac{(0)}{3} = 0$.

3. The apparent brightness b (in lumens) of a light source is a function of your distance x (in km) from
   the source and is given by $b(x) = \dfrac{32}{x^2}$. Find $b^{-1}(x)$, evaluate $b^{-1}(8)$, and explain the meaning of $b^{-1}(8)$
   in the context of this problem.

   Solution: $b^{-1}(x) = \sqrt{\dfrac{32}{x}}$; $x > 0$; $b^{-1}(8) = 2$; at 2km the brightness of the light is 8 lumens.

   Explanation: Since x represents distance, assume $x \geq 0$, so $b(x)$ is one-to-one. Swap variables and
   solve for y: $b(x) = \frac{32}{x^2}$; $y = \frac{32}{x^2} \Rightarrow x = \frac{32}{y^2}$; $y^2 x = 32$; $y^2 = \frac{32}{x}$; $y = \sqrt{\frac{32}{x}}$. So, $b^{-1} = \sqrt{\frac{32}{x}}$. Evaluate:
   $b^{-1}(8) = \sqrt{\frac{32}{8}} = \sqrt{4} = 2$km, which means that 8 lumens of light are experienced from 2km.

Practice problems: *(Answers on page: 452)*

1. Find the inverse of $g(x) = \dfrac{3(5-2x)}{7}$, and evaluate $g^{-1}(3)$.

2. Algebraically find the equation of the inverse function. If the function is not invertible, state why. $y = \dfrac{4-x^2}{2}$.

3. If x represents the length (in feet) of a pendulum, the period of swing (in seconds) of the pendulum is given
   by $p(x) = \sqrt{\dfrac{x}{5}}$. Find the equation for p^{-1} and compute $p^{-1}(3)$. What does $p^{-1}(3)$ represent?

Review questions: *(Answers to odd questions on page: 452)*

1. Find the inverse of $f(x) = 2x + 1$, if it exists, then find $f^{-1}(5)$.

2. Find the inverse of $f(x) = \dfrac{-5x}{3}$; if it exists, then find $f^{-1}(4)$.

3. Algebraically find the equation of the inverse function. If the function is not invertible, state why. $y = 2x^2 - 5$, $x \geq 0$

4. Find the inverse of $u(x) = -3\sqrt{\dfrac{x}{3}}$, $x \geq 0$; if it exists, then find $u^{-1}(-2)$.

5. The time (in hours) required by a team of rescuers to find a lost hiker depends on the number of rescuers, x, and is given by $t(x) = \dfrac{80}{x}$. What does $t^{-1}(5)$ represent? Now find the equation for $t^{-1}(x)$ and compute $t^{-1}(5)$.

Finding the Inverse of a Function with Higher Powers

- To find the inverse of a function algebraically:
  1. Swap the x variables with the y variables.
  2. Solve the new equation for y. If this new equation cannot be solved for y as a function of x, the original function does not have an inverse.

Remember To find the inverse: Swap the x and y, then solve for y. 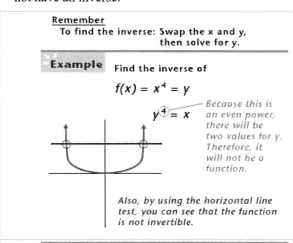	Let's do some practice problems finding the inverses of functions. To find the inverse of this function, just swap the x's and y's and solve for y. In this case, when you solve for y, you do not get a function. This means that $f(x)$ has no inverse. Another way to see why $f(x)$ has no inverse is to graph the original function $f(x)$ and notice that it fails the horizontal line test. $f(x)$ is not one-to-one, so it is not invertible.
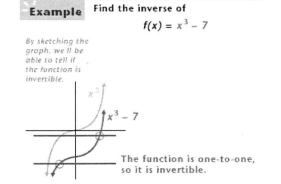	Take a look at this problem. If you want to, you can sketch the graph of $f(x)$ first to make sure that it has an inverse. In this case, the graph of $f(x)$ passes the horizontal line test. It therefore has an inverse function.

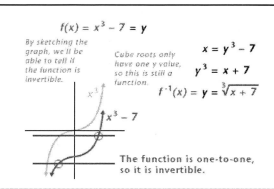

$f(x) = x^3 - 7 = y$

By sketching the graph, we'll be able to tell if the function is invertible.

Cube roots only have one y value, so this is still a function.

$x = y^3 - 7$

$y^3 = x + 7$

$f^{-1}(x) = y = \sqrt[3]{x + 7}$

$x^3 - 7$

The function is one-to-one, so it is invertible.

To find the inverse function, swap the x with the y and solve for y. You can do this by using a cube root.

The result is a function, so there are no problems. You've found the inverse function $f^{-1}(x)$.

Sample problems:

1. Given $m(x) = 2\sqrt[3]{4x - 8}$, write the equation of the inverse of $m(x)$ and find $m^{-1}(2)$.

    <u>Solution:</u> $m^{-1}(x) = \frac{x^3}{32} + 2$ and $m^{-1}(2) = \frac{9}{4}$

    <u>Explanation:</u> Since the function *is* one-to-one, interchange "x" and "y"

    and solve for (the new) y: $y = 2\sqrt[3]{4x - 8} \rightarrow x = 2\sqrt[3]{4y - 8}$;

    $(x)^3 = \left(2\sqrt[3]{4y - 8}\right)^3$; $x^3 = 8(4y - 8)$; $x^3 = 32y - 64$; $32y = x^3 + 64$; $y = \frac{x^3}{32} + 2$.

    Relabel "y" as $m^{-1}(x)$: $m^{-1}(x) = \frac{x^3}{32} + 2$.

    Evaluate the inverse function: $m^{-1}(2) = \frac{(2)^3}{32} + 2 = \frac{9}{4}$.

2. Given $f(x) = 32(x - 1)^5 + 17$, find the equation of the inverse function.
    If the function is not invertible, state why.

    <u>Solution:</u> $f^{-1}(x) = 1 + \dfrac{\sqrt[5]{(x - 17)}}{2}$

    <u>Explanation:</u> Since the function *is* one-to-one, interchange "x" and "y" and solve for y:

    $y = 32(x - 1)^5 + 17 \rightarrow x = 32(y - 1)^5 + 17$; $x - 17 = 32(y - 1)^5$; $\dfrac{x - 17}{32} = (y - 1)^5$;

    $\sqrt[5]{\dfrac{x - 17}{32}} = \sqrt[5]{(y - 1)^5}$; $\dfrac{\sqrt[5]{x - 17}}{2} = y - 1$; $1 + \dfrac{\sqrt[5]{x - 17}}{2} = y$.

    Thus, the inverse is $f^{-1}(x) = 1 + \dfrac{\sqrt[5]{x - 17}}{2}$.

3. Afternoon "monsoon" thunderstorms in the Sonoran desert dramatically cool the atmosphere. The air temperature A (in degrees F) as a function of the time elapsed since the first raindrop fell, t (in hours), is given by $A = \dfrac{10}{\left(t + \frac{1}{2}\right)^2} + 65$.

    Write an equation that expresses t as a function of A.

    <u>Solution:</u> $t = \sqrt{\dfrac{10}{A - 65}} - \dfrac{1}{2}$

    <u>Explanation:</u> Solve for t: $A = \dfrac{10}{\left(t + \frac{1}{2}\right)^2} + 65$; $A - 65 = \dfrac{10}{\left(t + \frac{1}{2}\right)^2}$; $\left(t + \frac{1}{2}\right)^2 = \dfrac{10}{A - 65}$;

    $\sqrt{\left(t + \frac{1}{2}\right)^2} = \sqrt{\dfrac{10}{A - 65}}$; $t + \frac{1}{2} = \sqrt{\dfrac{10}{A - 65}}$; $t = \sqrt{\dfrac{10}{A - 65}} - \frac{1}{2}$.

Practice problems: *(Answers on page: 452)*

1. Given $f(x) = 27(x + 5)^3$, write the equation of the inverse of $f(x)$ and find $f^{-1}(-8)$.

2. Given $f(x) = 32(x - 1)^2 + 17$, find the equation of the inverse function.
    If the function is not invertible, state why.

3. A forensic scientist finds that the time T (in hours) since ingestion of a poison relates to the amount x (in grams) of the poison still in the bloodstream and is given by $T(x) = \sqrt[4]{1000 - 500x}$. What does $T^{-1}(1)$ represent? Now find the equation for $T^{-1}(x)$ and compute $T^{-1}(1)$.

Review questions: *(Answers to odd questions on page: 452)*

1. Given $f(x) = \dfrac{(x-1)^3}{2}$, write the equation of the inverse of $f(x)$ and find $f^{-1}(4)$.

2. Given $f(x) = (x+3)^2 - 5$ for $x \geq -3$, find the equation of the inverse function.
   If the function is not invertible, state why.

3. Given $f(x) = \dfrac{2}{3}(x+7)^6$, find the equation of the inverse function.
   If the function is not invertible, state why.

4. Given $f(x) = 7 - \dfrac{1}{125}(x-3)^3$, find the equation of the inverse function.
   If the function is not invertible, state why.

5. The wind speed S (in mph) needed to produce electric power p (in watts) by a high-tech windmill is given by $S(p) = \sqrt[3]{20p}$. What does $S^{-1}(10)$ represent? Now find the equation for $S^{-1}(p)$ and compute $S^{-1}(10)$.

2

The Trigonometric Functions

Finding the Quadrant in Which an Angle Lies

- Angles are measured from the positive side of the *x*-axis. Positive angles sweep out in a counterclockwise direction and negative angles sweep out in a clockwise direction.
- The plane is split into four regions, or quadrants, in which angles can lie.
- **Acute angles** measure between 0° and 90°.
- **Obtuse angles** measure between 90° and 180°.
- Angles that measure exactly 90° are **right angles**.
- Angles that measure exactly 180° are **straight angles**.
- **Coterminal angles** are angles whose initial sides and terminal sides are the same.

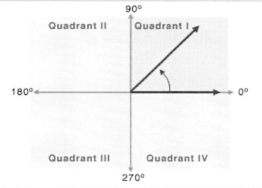

When measureing angles, always begin on the positive side of the *x*-axis.

Positive angles are measured in a counterclockwise direction from the positive *x*-axis and negative angles are measured in a clockwise direction.

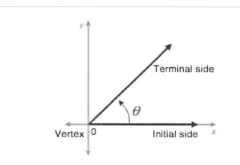

The plane can be broken up into four regions, or quadrants. **Acute angles**, those angles whose measure is less than 90°, lie in quadrant I.

Obtuse angles, those angles whose measure is between 90° and 180°, lie in quadrant II.

Other angles with special names include **right angles**, which measure exactly 90°, and **straight angles**, which measure exactly 180°.

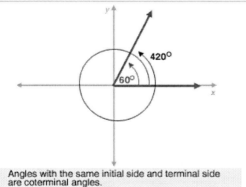

Angles with the same initial side and terminal side are coterminal angles.

The two angles in the diagram on the left measure 60° and 420°. These angles have the same **initial side** and the same **terminal side**, but have different amounts of rotation.

Angles with the same initial and terminal sides are called **coterminal angles**. Thus, 60° and 420° are coterminal angles.

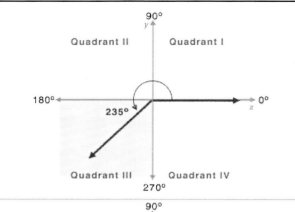

To determine in which region an angle lies, graph the angle.

Since 235° is positive, begin at the positive *x*-axis and move in a counterclockwise direction. Use the axes to estimate the location. The angle with measure 235° is greater than 180° but less than 270°; therefore, 235° is in quadrant III.

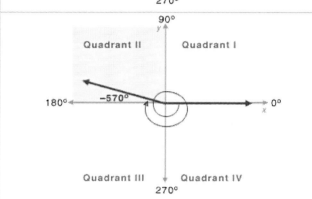

To determine in which region an angle measuring -570° lies, begin at the positive *x*-axis and move in a clockwise direction. Sweep one full cycle, -360°, to return to the positive *x*-axis. Next, move an additional -210° in the clockwise direction to land in quadrant II.

Sample problems:

1. In which quadrant does the terminal side of an angle measuring 133° lie?

Solution: Quadrant II

Explanation: Since 133° is an obtuse angle between 90° and 180°, the terminal side lies in the second quadrant.

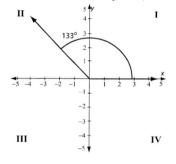

2. In which quadrant would the angle $\theta = -1100°$ be located?

Solution: Quadrant IV

Explanation: Since θ is negative, add 360° to $-1100°$ repeatedly until a number between 0 and 360 is reached: $-1100° + 360° = -740° + 360° = -380 + 360° = -20°$ to produce $-20° + 360° = 340°$. 340° is greater than 270° but less than 360°. Thus, θ lies in the fourth quadrant.

3. True or False: Angle θ could be $-75°$.

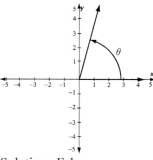

Solution: False

Explanation: The angle θ in the graph is in quadrant I. However, an angle with measure $-75°$ is located in quadrant IV.

Practice problems: *(Answers on page: 453)*

1. In which quadrant would an angle measuring 788° be located?

2. In what quadrant does the terminal side of an angle measuring $-165°$ lie?

3. True or False: Angle θ could be 585°.

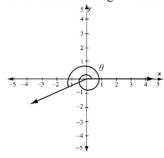

Review questions: *(Answers to odd questions on page: 453)*

1. In what quadrant does the terminal side of an angle measuring 95° lie?

2. In what quadrant does the terminal side of an angle measuring 200° lie?

3. In what quadrant does the terminal side of an angle measuring $-310°$ lie?

4. True or false: Angles measuring 10° and 397° lie in the same quadrant.

5. True or false: Angles measuring 950°, 223° and $-190°$ lie in the same quadrant.

Finding Coterminal Angles

- **Review**: **Coterminal angles** are angles whose **terminal sides** lie in the same place.
- The measures of coterminal angles differ by a multiple of 360°.

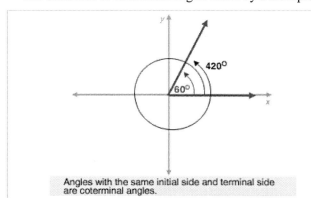

Angles with the same initial side and terminal side are coterminal angles.

Recall that **coterminal angles** are angles that have **terminal sides** in the same location.

The difference of the measures of coterminal angles is a multiple of 360° (some number of full circles).

Example Is 360° coterminal with 0°? 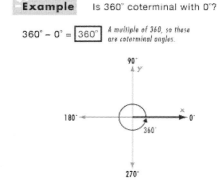	To determine if 360° is coterminal with 0°, find the difference of the measures of the two angles: $$360° - 0° = 360°$$ The difference, 360°, is a multiple of 360°. Thus, 360° is coterminal with 0°.
Example Are −570° and 150° coterminal angles? 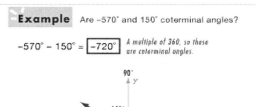	What about − 570° and 150°? Are these two angles coterminal? The difference of the measures of the two angles is − 720°. Since − 720° is a multiple of 360°, they are coterminal angles.
Example Are −800° and −80° coterminal angles? 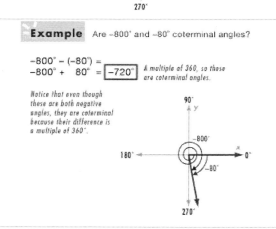	Are .− 800° and − 80° cotermial? Yes, since their measures differ by a multiple of 360° **REMEMBER**: Coterminal angles are not the same angle; they just have terminating sides in the same location.

Sample problems:

1. True or False: If $\theta = 494°$ and $\alpha = -1306°$, then θ and α are coterminal.
   Solution: True
   Explanation: Two angles are coterminal if the difference in their measurements is a multiple of 360. Subtract the angles: $494° - (-1306°) = 1800°$. Divide the difference by 360°: $1800°/360° = 5$. Since there is no remainder, 1800° is a multiple of 360. Thus, θ and α are coterminal.

2. What is the smallest positive angle that is coterminal with 560°?
   Solution: 200°
   Explanation: The smallest postive angle that is coterminal with 560° is 360° less than 560°, or 200°.

3. Find the negative angle closest to zero and coterminal with 655°.
   Solution: − 65°
   Explanation: Subtract 360° from 655° repeatedly until the 1st negative angle measurement is obtained: $655° - 360° = 295° - 360° = -65°$.

Practice problems: *(Answers on page: 453)*

1. True or false: The difference of measures of coterminal angles is always 360°.

2. True or false: If $\theta = -35°$, $\alpha = 1405°$ and $\sigma = 865°$, then θ, α and σ are coterminal.

3. What is the smallest positive angle that is coterminal with $-795°$?

Review questions: *(Answers to odd questions on page: 453)*

1. True or false: For two angles to be coterminal, the difference in their measures must be a multiple of 360.

2. True or false: If $\theta = 125°$ and $\alpha = 465°$, then θ and α are coterminal.

3. True or false: If $\theta = 15°$ and $\alpha = 1095°$, then θ and α are coterminal.

4. True or false: If $\theta = -317°$ and $\alpha = 403°$, then θ and α are coterminal.

5. What is the smallest negative angle that is coterminal with 547°?

Finding the Complement and Supplement of an Angle

- Two positive angles are **complementary** if their measures add up to 90°.
- Two positive angles are **supplementary** if their measures add up to 180°.

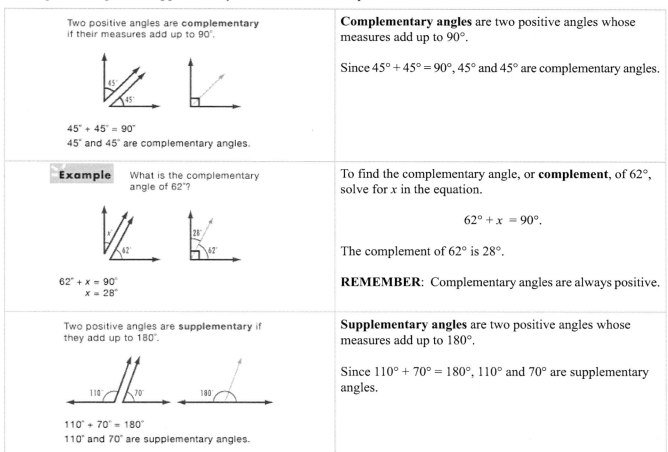

Two positive angles are **complementary** if their measures add up to 90°.

$45° + 45° = 90°$
45° and 45° are complementary angles.

Complementary angles are two positive angles whose measures add up to 90°.

Since $45° + 45° = 90°$, 45° and 45° are complementary angles.

Example What is the complementary angle of 62°?

$62° + x = 90°$
$x = 28°$

To find the complementary angle, or **complement**, of 62°, solve for x in the equation.

$$62° + x = 90°.$$

The complement of 62° is 28°.

REMEMBER: Complementary angles are always positive.

Two positive angles are **supplementary** if they add up to 180°.

$110° + 70° = 180°$
110° and 70° are supplementary angles.

Supplementary angles are two positive angles whose measures add up to 180°.

Since $110° + 70° = 180°$, 110° and 70° are supplementary angles.

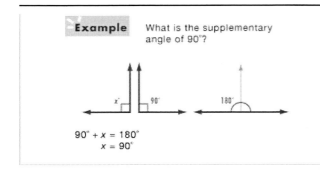

Example What is the supplementary angle of 90°?

To find the **supplement** of 90°, solve for x in the equation $90° + x = 180°$.

Since $90° + 90° = 180°$, 90° and 90° are supplementary angles.

$90° + x = 180°$
$x = 90°$

Sample problems:

1. What is the complementary angle of 2°?
   Solution: 88°
   Explanation: Let x be the complementary angle of 2°. Then $x + 2 = 90°$.
   Solve for x: $x + 2 = 90°$; $x = 88°$.

2. Suppose that angles measuring $2x$ and $4x + 6$ are supplementary. What are the measures of the angles?
   Solution: 58° and 122°
   Explanation: The sum of supplementary angles is 180°, or $(2x) + (4x + 6) = 180$.
   Solve for x: $2x + 4x + 6 = 180$; $6x + 6 = 180$; $6x = 174$; $x = 29$. Substitute 29 into $2x$ and $4x + 6$ to find the measures of the angles: $2(29) = 58$ and $4(29) + 6 = 122$. The two angle measures are 58° and 122°.

3. Suppose that two angles measuring $2a + 7$ and $3a + 4$ degrees are complementary. What are measures of the two angles?
   Solution: 38.6° and 51.4°
   Explanation: Since the two angles are complementary, their sum is 90°, or $(2a + 7) + (3a + 4) = 90$. Solve for a: $(2a + 7) + (3a + 4) = 90$; $5a + 11 = 90$; $5a = 79$; $a = \dfrac{79}{5} = 15.8$. Substitute 15.8 into $2a + 7$ and $3a + 4$ to find the measures of the angles: $2(15.8) + 7 = 38.6$ and $3(15.8) + 4 = 51.4$. The two angle measures are 38.6° and 51.4°.

Practice problems: *(Answers on page: 453)*

1. True or false: Supplementary angles are two angles whose measures add up to 90°.

2. Suppose that an angle measures x (degrees). Write an expression for its supplement in terms of x.

3. The supplement of an angle y measures $10x + 4$ and the complement of the angle measures $4x$. What is the measure of angle y?

Review questions: *(Answers to odd questions on page: 453)*

1. True or false: Complementary angles are two positive angles whose measures add up to 180°.

2. What angle is its own complement?

3. What is the measure of the supplementary angle for an angle of 58°?

4. Suppose two angles are complementary and the measure of one angle is twice the measure of the other. What are the measures of the angles?

5. Suppose that the complement of angle θ measures $5x + 4$ and the supplement of angle θ measures $15x - 6$. Find the measure of θ.

Converting between Degrees and Radians

- Mathematicians prefer to measure angles in **radians**. In **radian measure**, there are 2π radians in one complete circle.
- Use the conversion 2π radians = 360° to convert between degrees and radians.

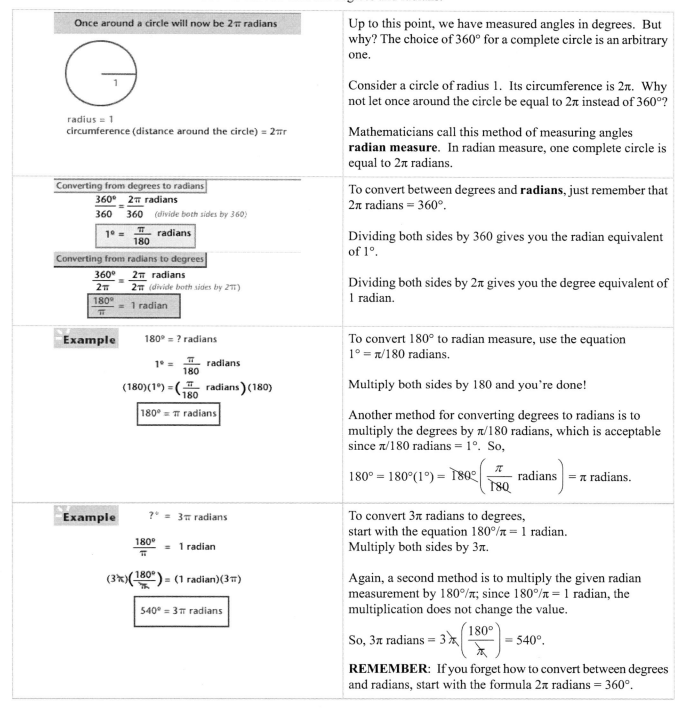

Up to this point, we have measured angles in degrees. But why? The choice of 360° for a complete circle is an arbitrary one.

Consider a circle of radius 1. Its circumference is 2π. Why not let once around the circle be equal to 2π instead of 360°?

Mathematicians call this method of measuring angles **radian measure**. In radian measure, one complete circle is equal to 2π radians.

To convert between degrees and **radians**, just remember that 2π radians = 360°.

Dividing both sides by 360 gives you the radian equivalent of 1°.

Dividing both sides by 2π gives you the degree equivalent of 1 radian.

To convert 180° to radian measure, use the equation $1° = \pi/180$ radians.

Multiply both sides by 180 and you're done!

Another method for converting degrees to radians is to multiply the degrees by $\pi/180$ radians, which is acceptable since $\pi/180$ radians = 1°. So,

$$180° = 180°(1°) = \cancel{180°}\left(\frac{\pi}{\cancel{180}}\ \text{radians}\right) = \pi \text{ radians}.$$

To convert 3π radians to degrees, start with the equation $180°/\pi = 1$ radian. Multiply both sides by 3π.

Again, a second method is to multiply the given radian measurement by $180°/\pi$; since $180°/\pi = 1$ radian, the multiplication does not change the value.

So, 3π radians = $3\cancel{\pi}\left(\dfrac{180°}{\cancel{\pi}}\right) = 540°.$

REMEMBER: If you forget how to convert between degrees and radians, start with the formula 2π radians = 360°.

Sample problems:

1. Convert 20° to radian measure, leave your answer in terms of π.

   Solution: $\dfrac{\pi}{9}$ radians

   Explanation: To convert from degrees to radians, multiply the degree measurement

   by $\dfrac{\pi}{180°}$: $20° \cdot \dfrac{\pi}{180°} = \dfrac{\pi}{9}$.

2. Convert $\dfrac{\pi}{5}$ radians to degree measure.

Solution: $36°$

Explanation: To convert from radians to degrees, multiply the radian measurement

by $\dfrac{180°}{\pi}$: $\dfrac{\pi}{5} \cdot \dfrac{180°}{\pi} = \dfrac{180°}{5} = 36°$.

3. Convert $-\dfrac{80\pi}{7}$ radians to degree measure.

Solution: $-2057.14°$

Explanation: Multiply by $\dfrac{180°}{\pi}$: $\left(-\dfrac{80\pi}{7}\right) \cdot \left(\dfrac{180°}{\pi}\right) = -\dfrac{80(180°)}{7} = -2057.14°$.

Practice problems: *(Answers on page: 453)*

1. How many degrees are there in 3 radians? Leave your answer in terms of π.

2. Convert $-\dfrac{20\pi}{3}$ radians to degree measure.

3. A wall clock reads exactly 4 o'clock. What is the radian measure of the smaller angle formed by the hour and minute hands of the clock?

Review questions: *(Answers to odd questions on page: 453)*

1. Convert $45°$ to radian measure. Leave your answer in terms of π.

2. Convert $\dfrac{7\pi}{8}$ radians to degree measure.

3. Convert $132°$ to radian measure. Leave your answer in terms of π.

4. Convert $\dfrac{5\pi}{12}$ to degree measure.

5. Which angle is greater, $1°$ or 1 radian?

Using the Arc Length Formula

- The **arc length** of an **arc** of a circle is given by the formula $s = r\theta$, where s is the length of the arc, r is the radius of the circle, and θ is the central angle subtended, measured in **radians**.

Arc length: the length of an arc of a circle arc length $s = r\theta$ measured in radians	Measuring **arc length** is one example of why it is often more convenient to measure angles in **radians** instead of degrees. This formula, $s = r\theta$, says that the length of the **arc** of a circle is equal to the radius of the circle times the angle subtended by the arc, measured in radians.
What if $\theta = \pi$? $s = r\theta$ $s = (r)(\pi)$ $s = \pi r$	Try the formula out on an arc that subtends an angle measuring π radians (one-half of the circle). Plug in the known values and solve. The length of this arc is equal to πr, where r is the radius of the circle.

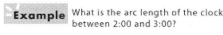

Example What is the arc length of the clock between 2:00 and 3:00? 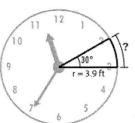	You can use the formula for arc length to find the measure of the arc from 2:00 to 3:00 on the clock illustrated to the left. Use the arc length formula, $s = r\theta$, and plug in the known values.
Remember $1° = \dfrac{\pi}{180}$ Convert to radians using either method: $(30)1° = \dfrac{\pi}{180}(30)$ $30° = \dfrac{\pi}{6}$ OR: $30°\left(\dfrac{\pi}{180}\right) = \dfrac{30\pi}{180} = \dfrac{\pi}{6}$	First, convert 30° to radians so you can use the formula for arc length. There are 2 ways to convert from degrees to radians, use whatever method you find easier. **REMEMBER**: The formula for arc length only works when the angle is measured in radians.
$s = r\theta$ Plug in the known values: $s = (3.9')\dfrac{\pi}{6}$ $s = 2.04'$ 	Plugging into the formula $s = r\theta$ results in measure for the arc length for the clock between 2:00 and 3:00. The arc length of the clock between 2:00 and 3:00 is 2.04 feet.

Sample problems:

1. A string on a pendulum with a length of 2 ft subtends an angle of 35°. Find the length of the arc the pendulum swings through.
   Solution: 1.22 feet
   Explanation: Think of the pendulum as making a circle with a 2 ft. radius. To find the

   arc length, convert 35° to radians: $35° = 35 \cdot \left(\dfrac{\pi}{180}\right) = \dfrac{7\pi}{36}$ radians. Use the arc

   length formula: $s = r\theta = \left(2 \text{ ft}\right)\left(\dfrac{7\pi}{36}\right) = 1.22$ ft. The arc length of the pendulum is 1.22 ft.

2. The cities of Vandora and Lachistan are located on the same longitude, but different latitudes. Vandora is on the latitude 58° N, while Lachistan is at 10° S. What is the distance (along the surface of the Earth) between the two cities? Assume that the radius of the Earth is 3700 miles.
   Solution: 4391 miles
   Explanation: The distance between two cities along the surface of the Earth is an arc of a circle. The angle subtended by the arc is 68°.

   Convert this to radians: $68° = 68 \cdot \left(\dfrac{\pi}{180}\right)$ radians $= \dfrac{17\pi}{45}$ radians.

   Now use the arc length formula: $s = r\theta = \left(3700 \text{ miles}\right)\left(\dfrac{17\pi}{45}\right) = 4391.2$ miles.

3. The wheels on Jan's bicycle have a radius of 50 centimeters. Jan rides her bicycle so that its wheels rotate at 1 revolution per second. Determine Jan's speed in meters per second.

Solution: 3.14 meters/sec

Explanation: In 1 second, the wheels make 1 revolution. A full revolution of a circle is equal to 2π radians, so in 1 second, the wheel rotates $1(2\pi) = 2\pi$ radians. Convert 50 cm to meters: 50 cm = .5m. Use the arc length formula to calculate the linear distance Jan travels in 1 second: $s = r\theta = (0.5 \text{ meters})(2\pi) = 3.14$ meters. In one second, Jan travels 3.14 meters, so she is riding at 3.14 meters/sec.

Practice problems: *(Answers on page: 453)*

1. What is the length of the arc intercepted by an angle of 10° on a circle with a radius of 10 meters?

2. The clock in the tower of City Hall has a circular face that measures 15 feet in diameter. What is the arc length between the number 3 and the number 8 (passing through 4, 5, 6, and 7)?

3. At a birthday party, a circular cake with a diameter of 14 inches is cut into 16 equal pieces. What is the length of the curved end of each piece of cake?

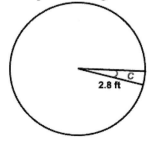

Review questions: *(Answers to odd questions on page: 453)*

1. In the arc length formula, what quantity does s represent?

2. Compute the length of the arc that subtends angle B if its measure is 110°.

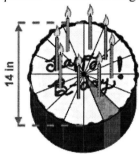

3. Compute the length of the arc that subtends angle C if its measure is 12°.

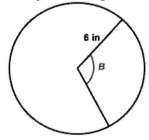

4. On a certain clock, the minute hand is 4.5 inches long. How far does the tip of the minute hand travel in 40 minutes?

5. Find the radius of the circle to the nearest hundredth of an inch.

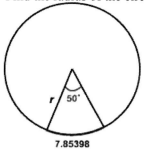

7.85398

An Introduction to the Trigonometric Functions

- The **trigonometric functions** of an angle θ are defined to be the ratios of the side lengths of a right triangle having θ as an angle.
- The three basic trig functions are **sine**, **cosine**, and **tangent**. They are defined as follows:

  - $\sin\theta = \dfrac{opposite}{hypotenuse}$

  - $\cos\theta = \dfrac{adjacent}{hypotenuse}$

  - $\tan\theta = \dfrac{opposite}{adjacent}$

  Their reciprocals are the **cosecant**, **secant**, and **cotangent** functions, respectively.
- Every angle can be expressed in **radians** regardless of starting position.

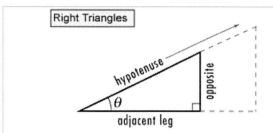

To increase the length of the adjacent leg without changing the angle θ, the opposite leg and hypotenuse must increase proportionally.

If you wish to lengthen the adjacent side without changing the angle θ, you must increase the other two sides of the triangle proportionally.

All right triangles with the same angle θ are **similar**; the lengths of their sides are in the same proportions.

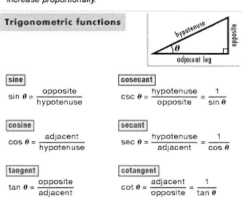

The **trigonometric functions** of an angle θ are defined to be the ratios of the sides of a right triangle having θ for an angle. The three basic trig functions are **sine**, **cosine**, and **tangent**; **cosecant**, **secant**, and **cotangent** are their reciprocals, respectively.

NOTICE: The reciprocal of sine is cosecant, and the reciprocal of cosine is secant. It's easy to mix these up.

sine

$\sin\theta = \dfrac{opposite}{hypotenuse}$

cosecant

$\csc\theta = \dfrac{hypotenuse}{opposite} = \dfrac{1}{\sin\theta}$

cosine

$\cos\theta = \dfrac{adjacent}{hypotenuse}$

secant

$\sec\theta = \dfrac{hypotenuse}{adjacent} = \dfrac{1}{\cos\theta}$

tangent

$\tan\theta = \dfrac{opposite}{adjacent}$

cotangent

$\cot\theta = \dfrac{adjacent}{opposite} = \dfrac{1}{\tan\theta}$

Example

$\sin \theta = \dfrac{\text{opp}}{\text{hyp}} = \dfrac{3}{5}$ $\csc \theta = \dfrac{\text{hyp}}{\text{opp}} = \dfrac{5}{3}$

$\cos \theta = \dfrac{\text{adj}}{\text{hyp}} = \dfrac{4}{5}$ $\sec \theta = \dfrac{\text{hyp}}{\text{adj}} = \dfrac{5}{4}$

$\tan \theta = \dfrac{\text{opp}}{\text{adj}} = \dfrac{3}{4}$ $\cot \theta = \dfrac{\text{adj}}{\text{opp}} = \dfrac{4}{3}$

Compute the trig functions for the angle θ in this 3-4-5 right triangle.

For this triangle, the opposite side has length 3, the adjacent side has length 4, and the hypotenuse has length 5. Substitute these values into the formulas to find the values of the different trig functions.

Example

$\sin \dfrac{\pi}{4} = \dfrac{\text{opp}}{\text{hyp}} = \dfrac{1}{\sqrt{2}} = \dfrac{\sqrt{2}}{2}$ $\csc \dfrac{\pi}{4} = \dfrac{\text{hyp}}{\text{opp}} = \dfrac{\sqrt{2}}{1} = \sqrt{2}$

$\cos \dfrac{\pi}{4} = \dfrac{\text{adj}}{\text{hyp}} = \dfrac{1}{\sqrt{2}} = \dfrac{\sqrt{2}}{2}$ $\sec \dfrac{\pi}{4} = \dfrac{\text{hyp}}{\text{adj}} = \dfrac{\sqrt{2}}{1} = \sqrt{2}$

$\tan \dfrac{\pi}{4} = \dfrac{\text{opp}}{\text{adj}} = \dfrac{1}{1} = 1$ $\cot \dfrac{\pi}{4} = \dfrac{\text{adj}}{\text{opp}} = \dfrac{1}{1} = 1$

Find the trig functions for $\pi/4$ (**radian measure**), the acute angle in an isosceles right triangle.

If each of the legs of the triangle have length 1, use the **Pythagorean theorem** to find the length of the hypotenuse, $\sqrt{2}$.

Substitute to find the values of the trig functions for $\pi/4$.

Example

$\sin \dfrac{\pi}{3} = \dfrac{\text{opp}}{\text{hyp}} = \dfrac{\sqrt{3}}{2}$ $\sin \dfrac{\pi}{6} = \dfrac{\text{opp}}{\text{hyp}} = \dfrac{1}{2}$

$\cos \dfrac{\pi}{3} = \dfrac{\text{adj}}{\text{hyp}} = \dfrac{1}{2}$ $\cos \dfrac{\pi}{6} = \dfrac{\text{adj}}{\text{hyp}} = \dfrac{\sqrt{3}}{2}$

$\tan \dfrac{\pi}{3} = \dfrac{\text{opp}}{\text{adj}} = \dfrac{\sqrt{3}}{1} = \sqrt{3}$ $\tan \dfrac{\pi}{6} = \dfrac{\text{opp}}{\text{adj}} = \dfrac{1}{\sqrt{3}} = \dfrac{\sqrt{3}}{3}$

Find the trig functions for $\pi/6$ **radians** and $\pi/3$ radians.

Use an equilateral triangle with sides of length 2. Drop an altitude, forming two 30°-60°-90° right triangles. Each of these triangles has an angle measuring 30° = $\pi/6$ radians and 60° = $\pi/3$ radians.

It is important to be familiar with the trig functions of the angles $\pi/6$, $\pi/4$, and $\pi/3$ radians.

Sample problems:

1. Given the right triangle below, compute the cosine of angle C.

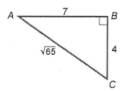

Solution: $\dfrac{4\sqrt{65}}{65}$

Explanation: By definition, $\cos \theta = \dfrac{\text{adjacent}}{\text{hypotenuse}}$. The side adjacent to $\angle C$ is $\overline{BC} = 4$.

The hypotenuse is $\overline{AC} = \sqrt{65}$ Therefore, $\cos C = \dfrac{\text{adj}}{\text{hyp}} = \dfrac{\overline{BC}}{\overline{AC}} = \dfrac{4}{\sqrt{65}}$. Now rationalize:

$\dfrac{4}{\sqrt{65}}\left(\dfrac{\sqrt{65}}{\sqrt{65}}\right) = \dfrac{4\sqrt{65}}{65}$.

2. Given the right triangle below, compute the tangent of angle D.

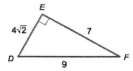

Solution: $\dfrac{7\sqrt{2}}{8}$

Explanation: By definition, $\tan\theta = \dfrac{\text{opposite}}{\text{adjacent}}$. The side opposite $\angle D$ is $\overline{EF} = 7$.

The side adjacent to $\angle D$ is $\overline{DE} = 4\sqrt{2}$. Therefore, $\tan D = \dfrac{7}{4\sqrt{2}}$. Rationalize:

$\dfrac{7}{4\sqrt{2}}\left(\dfrac{\sqrt{2}}{\sqrt{2}}\right) = \dfrac{7\sqrt{2}}{8}$.

3. Given the right triangle below, compute the sine of angle E.

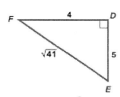

Solution: $\dfrac{4\sqrt{41}}{41}$

Explanation: By definition, $\sin\theta = \dfrac{\text{opposite}}{\text{hypotenuse}}$. The side opposite $\angle E$ is $\overline{DF} = 4$.

The hypotenuse of the triangle is $\overline{EF} = \sqrt{41}$. Therefore, $\sin E = \dfrac{4}{\sqrt{41}}$.

Rationalize: $\dfrac{4}{\sqrt{41}}\left(\dfrac{\sqrt{41}}{\sqrt{41}}\right) = \dfrac{4\sqrt{41}}{41}$.

Practice problems: *(Answers on page: 453)*

1. True or false: The ratio $\dfrac{\overline{AB}}{\overline{BC}}$ represents the tangent of $\angle A$ in the triangle below.

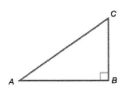

2. Given the triangle below, compute the secant of angle F.

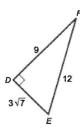

3. What is the value of $\sin\theta$?

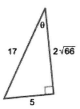

Review questions: *(Answers to odd questions on page: 453)*

1. True or false: The ratio adj/hyp defines the cosine function.

2. What is the value of $\sec\theta$?

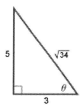

3. What is the value of $\tan\theta$?

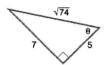

4. Suppose $\csc\theta = \dfrac{\sqrt{265}}{12}$ and $\sec\theta = \dfrac{\sqrt{265}}{11}$, what is the value of $\sin\theta$?

---

5. What is the value of $\cot\theta$?

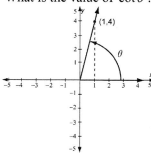

Evaluating Trigonometric Functions for an Angle in a Right Triangle

- Use the **Pythagorean theorem** to find the missing side of a right triangle before computing the **trigonometric functions** for an angle in a given triangle.
- When given the value of a trig function for an **acute angle** θ, find the other trig functions for θ by drawing a right triangle having θ as an angle.

Example Before we can find the trigonometric functions for the angle θ, we must find the length of h using the Pythagorean theorem. In this example: $h^2 = a^2 + b^2$ or $h^2 = 4^2 + 2^2$ $h^2 = 16 + 4$ $h^2 = 20$ $h^2 = \sqrt{20}$ $h^2 = \sqrt{4 \cdot 5}$ $h^2 = \sqrt{4} \cdot \sqrt{5}$ $\boxed{h^2 = 2\sqrt{5}}$	Given the right triangle illustrated here, find the values of the **trigonometric functions** for the angle θ. Before taking the ratios of the sides, find the length of the hypotenuse. Find the length of the hypotenuse using the **Pythagorean theorem**.
Example 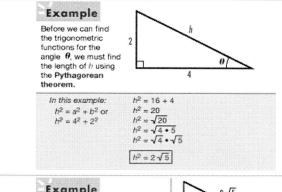 $\sin\theta = \dfrac{\text{opp}}{\text{hyp}} = \dfrac{2}{2\sqrt{5}} = \dfrac{\sqrt{5}}{5}$ $\csc\theta = \dfrac{\text{hyp}}{\text{opp}} = \dfrac{2\sqrt{5}}{2} = \sqrt{5}$ $\cos\theta = \dfrac{\text{adj}}{\text{hyp}} = \dfrac{4}{2\sqrt{5}} = \dfrac{2\sqrt{5}}{5}$ $\sec\theta = \dfrac{\text{hyp}}{\text{adj}} = \dfrac{2\sqrt{5}}{4} = \dfrac{\sqrt{5}}{2}$ $\tan\theta = \dfrac{\text{opp}}{\text{adj}} = \dfrac{2}{4} = \dfrac{1}{2}$ $\cot\theta = \dfrac{\text{adj}}{\text{opp}} = \dfrac{4}{2} = 2$	Once all three sides of the right triangle are known, plug the lengths of the sides into the trig functions to find their values.
REMEMBER $\sin\theta = \dfrac{\text{opp}}{\text{hyp}}$ 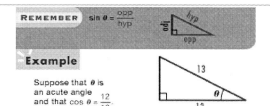 **Example** Suppose that θ is an acute angle and that $\cos\theta = \dfrac{12}{13}$. Find all other trigonometric functions for θ.	Consider the following: given that an angle θ is an **acute angle**, and given that the value for $\cos\theta$ is $12/13$, find the other trig functions for θ. Begin by sketching a right triangle having θ for an angle. Label the side adjacent θ and the hypotenuse using the fact that $\cos\theta = adjacent/hypotenuse = 12/13$.

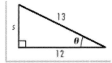

Example

By knowing one trigonometric function of an acute angle we can figure out the others.

$\sin \theta = \dfrac{opp}{hyp} = \dfrac{5}{13}$ $\csc \theta = \dfrac{hyp}{opp} = \dfrac{13}{5}$

$\cos \theta = \dfrac{adj}{hyp} = \dfrac{12}{13}$ $\sec \theta = \dfrac{hyp}{adj} = \dfrac{13}{12}$

$\tan \theta = \dfrac{opp}{adj} = \dfrac{5}{12}$ $\cot \theta = \dfrac{adj}{opp} = \dfrac{12}{5}$

Then use the Pythagorean theorem to find the unknown side of the triangle. In this case, the missing leg has length 5.

Knowing all three sides of the right triangle, plug the lengths of the sides into the trigonometric functions to find their values.

Sample problems:

1. Given the triangle below, compute the cotangent of angle G.

Solution: $\dfrac{2\sqrt{3}}{5}$

Explanation: Find the missing length using the Pythagorean theorem: $a^2 + b^2 = c^2$; $5^2 + b^2 = \left(\sqrt{37}\right)^2$; $25 + b^2 = 37$; $b^2 = 12$; $b = 2\sqrt{3}$. By definition, $\cot \theta = \dfrac{\text{adjacent}}{\text{opposite}}$. The side adjacent to angle G is $\overline{GI}$. The side opposite angle G is $\overline{HI}$. Therefore, $\cot G = \dfrac{\overline{GI}}{\overline{HI}} = \dfrac{2\sqrt{3}}{5}$.

2. Suppose that θ is an acute angle and that $\tan \theta = \dfrac{5}{7}$. Use a right triangle to find the value of $\sin \theta$.

Solution: $\dfrac{5\sqrt{74}}{74}$

Explanation: Since θ is acute, it can be an angle in a right triangle. The value of $\tan \theta$ is $\dfrac{5}{7}$. Although that is a ratio, you can let the side opposite θ be 5 and the side adjacent θ be 7. Use the Pythagorean theorem to find the length of the hypotenuse, h: $7^2 + 5^2 = h^2$; $49 + 25 = h^2$; $74 = h^2$; $h = \sqrt{74}$.

Find $\sin \theta$: $\sin \theta = \dfrac{\text{opposite}}{\text{hypotenuse}} = \dfrac{5}{\sqrt{74}}$. Rationalize: $\dfrac{5\sqrt{74}}{74}$

3. Suppose θ is the angle between AF and the base $BCDF$ in the right triangular prism below. Find $\cos \theta$.

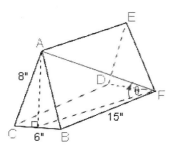

Solution: $\dfrac{3\sqrt{26}}{17}$

Explanation: Let G be the point where the altitude from A intersects the side BC. The angle between AF and the base $BCDF$ is the angle θ in the right triangle AGF. Since cosine relates the adjacent side, GF, and the hypotenuse, AF, use the Pythagorean theorem to calculate the lengths of GF and AF: $(GF)^2 = (BG)^2 + (BF)^2 = 3^2 + 15^2 = 9 + 225 = 234$; $GF = \sqrt{234} = 3\sqrt{26}$. Find the length of AF: $(AB)^2 + (BF)^2 = (AF)^2$; $8^2 + 15^2 = (AF)^2$; $289 = (AF)^2$; $AF = 17$. Therefore, $\cos\theta = \dfrac{3\sqrt{26}}{17}$.

Practice problems: *(Answers on page: 453)*

1. Given the triangle below, compute the cosecant of angle H.

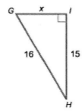

2. Suppose that θ is an acute angle and that $\sec\theta = \dfrac{8}{3}$. Use a right triangle to find the value of $\tan\theta$.

3. Suppose you are given that $\sin\theta = \dfrac{1}{2}$. If the area of the square is 36, what is the area of the triangle?

Review questions: *(Answers to odd questions on page: 453)*

1. Given the triangle below, compute the secant of angle I.

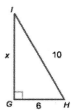

2. What is the value of $\cos\theta$?

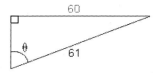

3. Compute the value of $\csc\theta$.

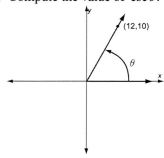

4. What are the ratios of the sides of a right triangle with θ, an acute angle, as one of its angles if $\cos\theta = 25$?

5. True or false: If θ is an acute angle and $\cos\theta = \dfrac{5}{9}$, then $\sin\theta$ is greater than $\tan\theta$.

Finding an Angle Given the Value of a Trigonometric Function

- You can sometimes find the measure of an angle θ given the value of one of its **trigonometric functions** by analyzing a right triangle with θ as one of its angles.

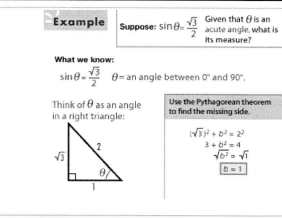

Example Suppose: $\sin\theta = \dfrac{\sqrt{3}}{2}$ Given that θ is an acute angle, what is its measure?

What we know:

$\sin\theta = \dfrac{\sqrt{3}}{2}$ θ = an angle between 0° and 90°.

Think of θ as an angle in a right triangle:

Use the Pythagorean theorem to find the missing side.

$(\sqrt{3})^2 + b^2 = 2^2$
$3 + b^2 = 4$
$\sqrt{b^2} = \sqrt{1}$
$\boxed{b = 1}$

You have learned how to compute **trigonometric functions** given an angle. What about finding an angle given the value of a trig function?

For example, can you find the acute angle θ, given the value of **$\sin\theta$** ?

First, sketch a right triangle having θ as an angle. Use the fact that $\sin\theta = \dfrac{\text{opposite}}{\text{hypotenuse}} = \dfrac{\sqrt{3}}{2}$ to label the legs and hypotenuse of the triangle. Then, use the **Pythagorean theorem** to find the length of the missing leg.

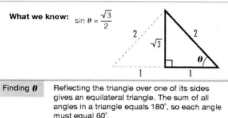

What we know: $\sin\theta = \dfrac{\sqrt{3}}{2}$

Finding θ Reflecting the triangle over one of its sides gives an equilateral triangle. The sum of all angles in a triangle equals 180°, so each angle must equal 60°.

$\theta = 60° = \dfrac{\pi}{3}$ radians

Reflecting the triangle over the side of length $\sqrt{3}$ results in an equilateral triangle.

The angles of an equilateral triangle all measure 60°, or $\pi/3$ **radians**. Therefore, $\theta = 60°$ or $\pi/3$ radians.

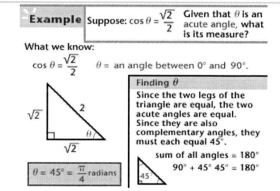

Example Suppose: $\cos\theta = \dfrac{\sqrt{2}}{2}$ Given that θ is an acute angle, what is its measure?

What we know:

$\cos\theta = \dfrac{\sqrt{2}}{2}$ θ = an angle between 0° and 90°.

Finding θ
Since the two legs of the triangle are equal, the two acute angles are equal. Since they are also complementary angles, they must each equal 45°.

sum of all angles = 180°
90° + 45° 45° = 180°

$\theta = 45° = \dfrac{\pi}{4}$ radians

Consider this example: find θ if it is an acute angle whose **cosine** is $\dfrac{\sqrt{2}}{2}$.

Sketch a right triangle with θ as one of its angles. Label the adjacent leg with $\sqrt{2}$ and the hypotenuse with 2. Use the Pythagorean theorem to find that the missing leg.

Since both legs measure $\sqrt{2}$, this right triangle is isosceles. Therefore, $\theta = 45°$ or $\pi/4$ radians.

Sample problems:

1. Suppose $\cot\theta = 1$. Given that θ is an acute angle in a right triangle, what is its measure in radians?

   Solution: $\dfrac{\pi}{4}$

   Explanation: By definition, $\cot\text{angent}\,\theta = \dfrac{\text{adjacent}}{\text{opposite}}$. Since $\cot\theta = 1$, $\dfrac{\text{adjacent}}{\text{opposite}} = 1$.

   Cross-multiply: $\dfrac{\text{adjacent}}{\text{opposite}} = 1$; adjacent = opposite. The sides must be the same length.

   Since the sides are equal, this is an isosceles right triangle. Therefore, $\theta = 45° = \dfrac{\pi}{4}$.

2. Suppose $\sin\theta = \dfrac{\sqrt{2}}{2}$. Given that θ is an acute angle in a right triangle, what is its measure in radians?

Solution: $\dfrac{\pi}{4}$ rad

Explantion: By definition, $\sin\theta = \dfrac{\text{opposite}}{\text{hypotenuse}} = \dfrac{\sqrt{2}}{2}$. Therefore, let the length of the side opposite the angle θ be $\sqrt{2}$, and let the length of the hypotenuse be 2. Use the Pythagorean theorem to find the missing length: $a^2 + b^2 = c^2$; $\left(\sqrt{2}\right)^2 + x^2 = 2^2$; $2 + x^2 = 4$; $x^2 = 2$; $x = \sqrt{2}$. Since both legs of the triangle are equal, the triangle is isosceles. Therefore, $\theta = 45° = \dfrac{\pi}{4}$ rad.

3. Suppose $\cos\theta = \dfrac{\sqrt{3}}{2}$. Given that θ is an acute angle in a right triangle, what is its measure in radians?

Solution: $\dfrac{\pi}{6}$ rad

Explanation: By definition, $\cos\theta = \dfrac{\text{adjacent}}{\text{hypotenuse}} = \dfrac{\sqrt{3}}{2}$. Therefore, let the length of the adjacent side be $\sqrt{3}$, and the length of the hypotenuse be 2. Use the Pythagorean theorem to find the missing length. $a^2 + b^2 = c^2$; $\left(\sqrt{3}\right)^2 + x^2 = 2^2$; $3 + x^2 = 4$; $x^2 = 1$; $x = 1$. The sides are not equal, so reflect the triangle across the leg with the greater length to form an equilateral triangle. An equilateral triangle has equal angles of 60°. Since θ is adjacent to the longer leg, it is added to itself to form one of the 60° angles. Divide by 2 to find the original measure: $\dfrac{60°}{2} = 30° = \dfrac{\pi}{6}$ rad.

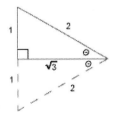

Practice problems: *(Answers on page: 453)*

1. What is the measure of θ if it represents an acute angle in a right triangle with $\sin\theta = \dfrac{1}{2}$?

2. Suppose $\sec\theta = \dfrac{2\sqrt{3}}{3}$. Given that θ is an acute angle in a right triangle, what is its measure in radians?

3. Suppose $\cos\theta = \dfrac{1}{2}$. Given that θ is an acute angle in a right triangle, what is its measure in radians?

Review questions: *(Answers to odd questions on page: 453)*

1. Suppose $\tan\theta = \sqrt{3}$. Given that θ is an acute angle in a right triangle, what is its measure in radians?

2. Suppose $\tan\theta = \dfrac{1}{2}$. Given that θ is an acute angle in a right triangle, what is its measure in radians?

3. Suppose $\csc\theta = \dfrac{2\sqrt{3}}{3}$. Given that θ is an acute angle in a right triangle, what is its measure in radians?

4. What is the measure of θ if it represents an acute angle with $\tan\theta = \dfrac{\sqrt{3}}{3}$?

5. Suppose $\sin\theta = \dfrac{1}{2}$. Given that θ is an acute angle in a right triangle, what is its measure?

Using Trigonometric Functions to Find Unknown Sides of Right Triangles

- You can use trigonometry to solve for an unknown side of a right triangle, given the length of one side and the measure of an angle (other than the right angle, 90°).

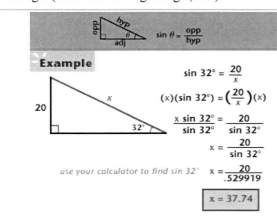

Example

$$\sin 32° = \frac{20}{x}$$

$$(x)(\sin 32°) = \left(\frac{20}{x}\right)(x)$$

$$\frac{x\,\sin 32°}{\sin 32°} = \frac{20}{\sin 32°}$$

$$x = \frac{20}{\sin 32°}$$

use your calculator to find sin 32° $x = \dfrac{20}{.529919}$

$$x = 37.74$$

Consider the triangle illustrated here. To find x, the length of the hypotenuse, use one the of the trigonometric functions.

The **sine** function relates the side opposite the 32° angle to the hypotenuse. Use it to write an equation involving x, then solve for x.

Use a calculator to evaluate sin 32°. (Be sure the calculator is in degree mode)

Example

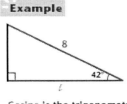

Cosine is the trigonometric function linking the adjacent side to the hypotenuse.

Determine the length of side l for the triangle illustrated here. This time, use the **cosine function**.

Example

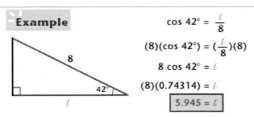

$$\cos 42° = \frac{l}{8}$$

$$(8)(\cos 42°) = \left(\frac{l}{8}\right)(8)$$

$$8\cos 42° = l$$

$$(8)(0.74314) = l$$

$$5.945 = l$$

The side adjacent to the 42° angle is l and the hypotenuse is 8, so $\cos 42° = \dfrac{l}{8}$. Solve this equation for l.

Use a calculator to evaluate the expression.

Sample problems:

1. Given a right triangle with one angle measuring 38° and the opposite side of length 7, find the length x of the side adjacent to the angle.

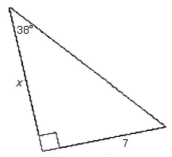

Solution: 8.96

Explanation: The tangent function relates the given angle with the known side and the unknown side. Write an equation using the tangent function and solve for x:

$\tan 38° = \dfrac{7}{x}; \quad x \tan 38° = 7; \quad x = \dfrac{7}{\tan 38°} = 8.96.$

2. A plane is flying over an uncharted island. What is the length of the island (represented by x)?

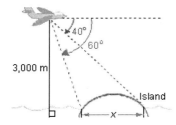

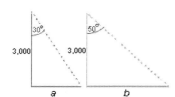

Solution: 1843 m

Explanation: There are two right triangles in the diagram. Using the first, smaller one, find the horizontal distance from the plane to the near side of the island:

$\tan 30° = \dfrac{a}{3,000}; \quad a = 3000 \tan 30° = 1732.$ Using the second, larger, right triangle, find the horizontal distance from the plane to the far side of the island:

$\tan 50° = \dfrac{b}{3,000}; \quad b = 3,000 \tan 50° = 3575.$ The difference of these two distances is the size of the island. The island is 1843 meters across.

3. An isosceles triangle has a base of length 5. The angle opposite the base measures $\dfrac{\pi}{5}$ radians. What are the lengths of the two equal sides?

Solution: 8.1

Explanation: An altitude from the vertex of the triangle to the base forms two congruent right triangles. The base of one of these triangles has length 2.5 and the angle opposite this base is $\dfrac{\pi}{5} \div 2$, or $\dfrac{\pi}{10}$ radians. The sine function relates the known side to the unknown: $\sin \dfrac{\pi}{10} = \dfrac{2.5}{x}$. Solve for x (calculator needs to be in radian mode): $x = \dfrac{2.5}{\sin \dfrac{\pi}{10}} = 8.1.$

Practice problems: *(Answers on page: 453)*

1. Consider the triangle ABC shown below. If $c = 12$, what is the value of a?

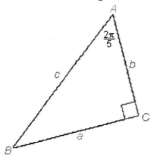

2. Find the missing length x.

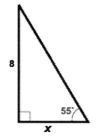

3. A 50 ft ladder is leaning against a wall so that the top of the ladder makes a 20° angle with the wall. How high up the wall does the ladder reach?

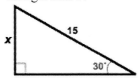

Review questions: *(Answers to odd questions on page: 453)*

1. Which trigonometric function could best be used to find the length x?

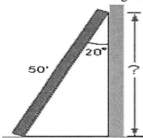

2. True or false: $\sin 30° = \dfrac{x}{15}$ could be used to solve for the unknown length of the triangle below.

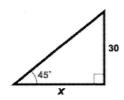

3. Find the missing length x.

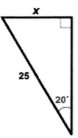

4. What is the length of x?

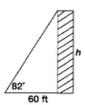

5. A distance of 60 ft is marked off from the foot of a building. The angle of elevation measured to the top of the building from that point is 82°. What is the height of the building to the nearest foot?

Finding the Height of a Building

- **Review:** You can use trigonometry to solve for an unknown side of a right triangle, given the length of one side and the measure of an angle (other than the right angle, 90°).
- Trigonometry has many real-world applications such as finding the height of a building and other tall structures.

Trigonometry can be used to find the height of a building.

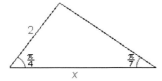

Trigonometry applies directly to the real world; for example, finding the height of a tall building. Simply measuring the building from the bottom to the top isn't always feasible, so we use trigonometric tools instead.

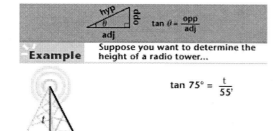

In this example you're asked to find t, the height of the radio tower. From a point on the ground 55 feet away from its base, you measure the angle to the top of the tower to be 75°.

The **tangent** function gives an equation involving t.

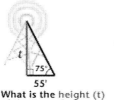

Example — Suppose you want to determine the height of a radio tower...

$$\tan 75° = \frac{t}{55'}$$

What is the height (t) of the tower?

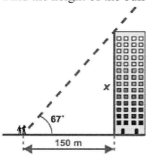

What is the height (t) of the tower?

$$\tan 75° = \frac{t}{55'}$$
$$(55')(\tan 75°) = \left(\frac{t}{55'}\right)(55')$$
$$(55')(\tan 75°) = t$$
$$(55')(3.7320) = t$$
$$\boxed{205.26' = t}$$

Solve the equation for t.

Use a calculator to evaluate $\tan 75°$. (Be sure the calculator is in degree mode!)

The height of the tower is 205.26 ft.

The tower has a height (t) of 205.26 feet.

Sample problems:

1. Find the height of the building.

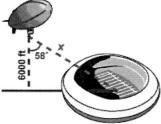

Solution: 353 m

Explanation: The tangent function relates the given angle to the known and unknown side. Use the tangent function to write an equation and solve for x:

$$\tan 67° = \frac{x}{150}; \quad x = 150(\tan 67°) = 353 \text{ m}.$$

2. A blimp is flying at an elevation of 6000 feet. The camera under the blimp has to swivel up 58° from the vertical to focus on the football stadium. What is the distance from the blimp to the stadium?

Solution: 11,322.5 ft

Explanation: Use the cosine function to write an equation and solve for x:

$$\cos 58° = \frac{6000}{x}; \quad x = \frac{6000}{\cos 58°}; \quad x = 11,322.5$$

3. Two buildings are 200 feet apart. If the angle of elevation from the top of the shorter building to the top of the taller building is 8°, what is the difference in the heights of the two buildings?

Solution: 28 feet

Explanation: Let y be the difference in heights between the buildings. From the diagram you can see that $\tan 8° = \frac{\text{opposite}}{\text{adjacent}} = \frac{y}{200}$. Thus $y = 200 \tan 8° \approx 28$. The difference in the heights of the buildings is 28 feet.

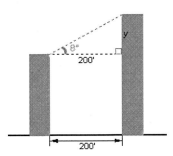

Practice problems: *(Answers on page: 454)*

1. Find the altitude of the airplane.

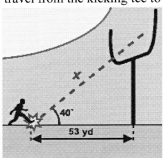

2. In a football game, the field goal kicker has to kick the ball from a point 53 yards from the goalpost at an angle of 40° in order to score points. How far will the ball travel from the kicking tee to the goalpost?

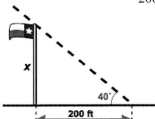

3. The roof of a particular house is 25 feet above the ground. For safety reasons, the angle that a ladder makes with the ground should be no greater than 70 degrees. What is the length of the shortest ladder that will reach the roof of the house safely?

Review questions: *(Answers to odd questions on page: 454)*

1. True or false: $\tan 40° = \dfrac{x}{200}$ can be used to find the height of the flagpole.

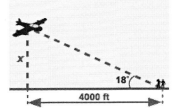

2. Find the height x of the indicated mountain.

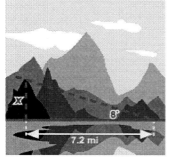

3. Find the altitude of the hot air balloon.

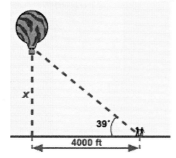

4. Find the distance from the lighthouse to the boat.

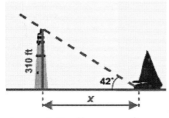

5. A man 1.5 miles away from a rocket launchpad observes a rocket launch. The man determines that the angle of elevation to the rocket is 23°, and then a few moments later he determines the angle of elevation to be 31°. How far did the rocket travel between the two observations? Assume that the rocket travels directly upwards.

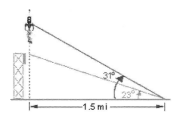

Evaluating Trigonometric Functions for an Angle in the Coordinate Plane

- If (x, y) is a point on the **terminal side** of an angle θ, then

$\sin\theta = \dfrac{y}{r}$, $\cos\theta = \dfrac{x}{r}$, $\tan\theta = \dfrac{y}{x}$, $\csc\theta = \dfrac{r}{y}$, $\sec\theta = \dfrac{r}{x}$, and $\cot\theta = \dfrac{x}{y}$, where $r = \sqrt{x^2 + y^2}$.

- For angles in quadrant I, **A**ll trigonometric functions are positive.
  For angles in quadrant II, only **S**ine and its recipricocal function, cosecant, are positive.
  For angles in quadrant III, only **T**angent and its reciprocal function, cotangent, are positive.
  For angles in quadrant IV, only **C**osine and its reciprocal function, secant, are positive.

  You can remember this with the saying "**A**ll **S**tudents **T**ake **C**alculus."

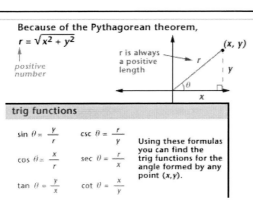

Thus far we have defined the **trigonometric functions** as ratios of sides of right triangles.

The trigonometric functions for an angle can also be defined using a point *(x, y)* on the **terminal side** of the angle.

Using these definitions, the trigonometric functions of any angle can be found.

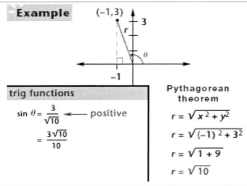

In this example, the terminal side of the angle θ goes through the point $(-1, 3)$. Notice that θ is not an acute angle.

First, find r using the **Pythagorean theorem**. Remember that r is always a positive length.

Then plug in $x = -1$, $y = 3$, and $r = \sqrt{10}$ into the formulas above to get the trig functions for θ.

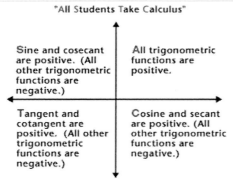

Figure out the signs of the trig functions for angles in each **quadrant**.

For example, for angles that lie in quadrant III, only the **tangent** and **cotangent** functions are positive.

REMEMBER: The saying "All Students Take Calculus" tells which trig functions are positive in each quadrant.

Sample problems:

1. Which trig functions would be positive in the quadrant containing the point $(2, -4)$?
   Solution: Cosine and Secant
   Explanation: In Quadrant IV, x is positive. The ratios for cosine and secant use the values of x and r. Since r is always positive, cosine and secant are positive whenever x is.

2. Find $\cot\theta$ if θ is in the standard position on the coordinate plane and the point $(-4, -2)$ is on the terminal side of θ.
   Solution: 2

   Explanation: By definition, $\cot\theta$ is $\cot\theta = \dfrac{x}{y}$ and $x = -4$ and $y = -2$, so $\cot\theta = \dfrac{-4}{-2} = 2$.

3. Find $\csc\theta$ and $\cot\theta$ if θ is in the standard position on the coordinate plane and the point $(-2, -3)$ is on the terminal side of θ.

   Solution: $\csc\theta = -\dfrac{\sqrt{13}}{3}$; $\cot\theta = \dfrac{2}{3}$

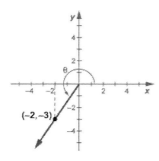

Explanation: Use the basic definition $\csc\theta = \dfrac{r}{y}$. Use the Pythagorean theorem to find the value of the radius: $r = \sqrt{(-2)^2 + (-3)^2} = \sqrt{4+9} = \sqrt{13}$. Thus, $r = \sqrt{13}$ and $y = -3$, so $\csc\theta = \dfrac{\sqrt{13}}{-3}$. For cotangent, substitute the values of x and y into the basic definition: $\cot\theta = \dfrac{x}{y} = \dfrac{-2}{-3} = \dfrac{2}{3}$.

Practice problems: *(Answers on page: 454)*

1. True or false: The point $(3, -2)$ lies in a quadrant where $\csc\theta$ and $\tan\theta$ are both negative.

2. Find $\sin\theta$ if θ is in the standard position on the coordinate plane and the point $(3,4)$ is on the terminal side of θ.

3. Find the values of $\sin\theta$ and $\cos\theta$ for the angle θ in the standard position on the coordinate plane with the point $(6, -3)$ on its terminal side.

Review questions: *(Answers to odd questions on page: 454)*

1. Find $\tan\theta$ if θ is in the standard position on the coordinate plane and the point $(3, 4)$ is on the terminal side of θ.

2. In which quadrant(s) are the values of tangent and cotangent positive?

3. In what quadrant does an angle lie if the sine of the angle is negative and the cosine is positive?

4. What is the value of the tangent of the angle in the standard position on the coordinate axes whose terminal side passes through the point $(6, -3)$?

5. What is the value of $\sin\theta$ if θ is the angle formed by the positive x-axis and a line segment passing through the origin and the point $(-3, 4)$?

Evaluating Trigonometric Functions Using the Reference Angle

- The **reference angle** for an angle θ is the positive, **acute** angle made by the **terminal side** of θ and the x-axis.
- To find the value of a trig function for an angle θ using its reference angle:
    1. Find the value of the trig function for the reference angle.
    2. Change the sign appropriately depending on which **quadrant** θ is in.

The reference angle for an angle θ is the positive, acute angle formed by the x-axis and the terminal side of the angle θ.

Example — Find cos 120°

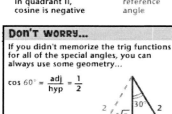

reference angle= 180° – 120° = 60°

cos 120° will equal cos 60° (the reference angle), except, possibly, for the sign.

cos 120° = –cos 60°

In quadrant II, cosine is negative ← reference angle

Don't worry...

If you didn't memorize the trig functions for all of the special angles, you can always use some geometry...

$$\cos 60° = \frac{adj}{hyp} = \frac{1}{2}$$

The notion of a **reference angle** is very useful for computing trigonometric functions.

What is the cosine of 120°? First, find the reference angle by subtracting 120° from 180°.

The cosine of 120° will equal the cosine of the reference angle (in this case, 60°) up to a difference in sign. Determine the sign using the fact that 120° lies in **quadrant II**.

REMEMBER: "All Students Take Calculus."

If you don't have the value of cos 60° memorized, you can figure it out using a 30°-60°-90° right triangle. As you can see, cos 60° = 1/2.

Therefore, cos 120° = –cos 60° =–1/2.

Example — Find tan 300°

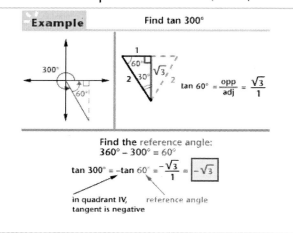

$$\tan 60° = \frac{opp}{adj} = \frac{\sqrt{3}}{1}$$

Find the reference angle:
360° – 300° = 60°

$$\tan 300° = –\tan 60° = \frac{-\sqrt{3}}{1} = \boxed{-\sqrt{3}}$$

in quadrant IV, tangent is negative — reference angle

What is the tangent of 300°?

First find the reference angle for 300°. It is the **acute angle** made by the **terminal side** of 300° and the x-axis. The reference angle measures 60°.

Now find the value of tan 60°. If you don't have it memorized, use some right triangle geometry.

The value of tan 300° is equal to either tan 60° or –tan 60°. Since tangent is negative in quadrant IV,

$$\tan 300° = –\tan 60° = -\sqrt{3} \ .$$

Sample problems:

1. What is the reference angle for the angle $\theta = \dfrac{9\pi}{7}$?

   Solution: $\dfrac{2\pi}{7}$

   Explanation: The reference angle for $\dfrac{9\pi}{7}$ is the acute angle made by the terminal side of θ and the x-axis. This angle is $\dfrac{9\pi}{7} - \pi = \dfrac{2\pi}{7}$.

2. Calculate: $\sin 210°$

   Solution: $-\dfrac{1}{2}$

   Explanation: The angle measuring 210° lies in quadrant III, where sine is negative. Subtract 180° to find the angle formed by the terminal ray of the original angle and the x-axis: $\sin 210° = -\sin 30° = -\left(\dfrac{1}{2}\right) = -\dfrac{1}{2}$

3. Calculate: $\sin\left(-\dfrac{\pi}{3}\right)$

Solution: $-\dfrac{\sqrt{3}}{2}$

Explanation: The reference angle for $-\dfrac{\pi}{3}$ is $\dfrac{\pi}{3}$. The sine function is negative in

the fourth quadrant. Thus, $\sin\left(-\dfrac{\pi}{3}\right) = -\sin\dfrac{\pi}{3} = -\dfrac{\sqrt{3}}{2}$.

Practice problems: *(Answers on page: 454)*

1. Find the reference angle for $\alpha = 890°$.

2. Calculate: $\cos(-60°)$

3. True or false: $\tan\dfrac{7\pi}{8} = -\tan\dfrac{\pi}{8}$

Review questions: *(Answers to odd questions on page: 454)*

1. Determine the reference angle for $\theta = 210°$.

2. Find the reference angle for $460°$.

3. Find the reference angle for $-50°$.

4. Find $\tan 225°$.

5. Evaluate $\cos\left(-\dfrac{7\pi}{3}\right)$ without the use of a calculator.

Finding the Value of Trigonometric Functions Given Information about the Values of Other Trigonometric Functions

- It is possible to find the value of trigonometric functions for an angle θ given only information about other trigonometric functions for θ. Here is one method of solving these problems:
  1. Determine which quadrant θ lies in.
  2. Sketch a picture of θ and its right triangle in the x-y plane.
  3. Use the **Pythagorean theorem** to find the length of the unknown side of the triangle.
  4. Use the triangle to compute the values of the trigonometric functions.

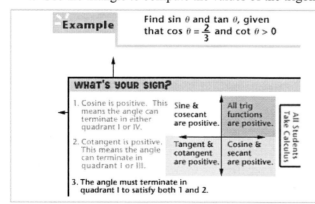

Find the value of $\sin\theta$ and $\tan\theta$ if $\cos\theta = 2/3$ and $\cot\theta > 0$.

The first step is to determine which quadrant θ lies in. Use the fact that both $\cos\theta$ and $\cot\theta$ are positive.

In order for $\cos\theta$ and $\cot\theta$ to both be positive, θ must lie in quadrant I.

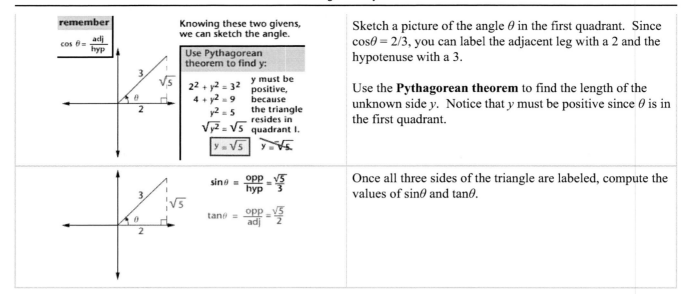

Sketch a picture of the angle θ in the first quadrant. Since $\cos\theta = 2/3$, you can label the adjacent leg with a 2 and the hypotenuse with a 3.

Use the **Pythagorean theorem** to find the length of the unknown side y. Notice that y must be positive since θ is in the first quadrant.

Once all three sides of the triangle are labeled, compute the values of $\sin\theta$ and $\tan\theta$.

Sample problems:

1. Find $\cos\theta$ and $\tan\theta$ given that $\sin\theta = \dfrac{2}{5}$ and $\tan\theta$ is greater than zero.

   Solution: $\cos\theta = \dfrac{\sqrt{21}}{5}$; $\tan\theta = \dfrac{2\sqrt{21}}{21}$

   Explanation: θ must be in quadrant I since $\sin\theta > 0$ and $\tan\theta > 0$.

   Sketch a right triangle and label the opposite side 2 and the hypotenuse 5.

   Use the Pythagorean theorem to find the unknown side, x:

   $x = \sqrt{5^2 - 2^2} = \sqrt{21}$, so $\cos\theta = \dfrac{\sqrt{21}}{5}$; $\tan\theta = \dfrac{2}{\sqrt{21}}$ or $\dfrac{2\sqrt{21}}{21}$.

   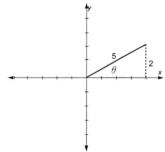

2. If you know $\sin\theta = \dfrac{4}{5}$, can you find $\cos\theta$?

   Solution: No

   Explanation: Using the Pythagorean theorem, we find that $x = 3$ or -3, so both $\cos\theta = \dfrac{3}{5}$ or $\cos\theta = -\dfrac{3}{5}$ are possible, but you do not have enough information to determine which is correct.

3. Suppose that $\sin\theta < 0$ and $\cos\theta = a$, where $0 < a < 1$. Find the value of $\csc\theta$ in terms of a.

   Solution: $-\dfrac{1}{\sqrt{1-a^2}}$

Explanation: First, determine what quadrant θ is in using the facts that $\sin \theta < 0$ and $\cos \theta = a > 0$. Since the sine function is negative in Quadrants III and IV, and the cosine function is positive in Quadrants I and IV, θ must lie in Quadrant IV. Sketch a picture of θ and its reference triangle. Use the fact that

$$\cos \theta = \frac{\text{adjacent}}{\text{hypotenuse}} = a = \frac{a}{1}$$ to label the sides of the triangle. Then use the

Pythagorean theorem to find the length of the unknown side y in terms of a:

$a^2 + y^2 = 1; \;\; y^2 = 1 - a^2; \;\; y = -\sqrt{1-a^2}$. Notice that y is negative because θ lies below the x-axis.

Compute $\csc \theta$: $\csc \theta = \dfrac{\text{hypotenuse}}{\text{opposite}} = \dfrac{1}{-\sqrt{1-a^2}} = -\dfrac{1}{\sqrt{1-a^2}}$.

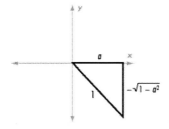

Practice problems: *(Answers on page: 454)*

1. Find $\sin \theta$ and $\cos \theta$ given that $\tan \theta = -\dfrac{12}{5}$ and $\sin \theta < 0$.

2. Find $\sin \theta$ and $\tan \theta$, given that $\cos \theta = -\dfrac{3}{5}$ and $\sin \theta > 0$.

3. Find $\csc \theta$, given that $\cos \theta = -\dfrac{\sqrt{2}}{2}$ and $\cot \theta = 1$.

Review questions: *(Answers to odd questions on page: 454)*

1. In which quadrant(s) are the values of tangent and cotangent positive?

2. In what quadrant does an angle lie if the sine of the angle is negative and the cosine is positive?

3. Find $\tan \theta$ given that $\sin \theta = \dfrac{2}{3}$ and $\cos \theta = \dfrac{\sqrt{5}}{3}$.

4. Find $\cos \theta$, given that $\tan \theta = \dfrac{1}{2}$ and $\cos \theta > 0$.

5. Find $\tan \theta$, given that $\cos \theta = -\dfrac{2}{\sqrt{5}}$ and $\sin \theta < 0$.

Trigonometric Functions of Important Angles

- Memorize the trigonometric functions for important angles: 0, π/6, π/4, π/3, and π/2 (or 0°, 30°, 45°, 60°, and 90°).

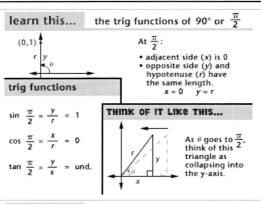

There are some trigonometric values for important angles that should be memorized. One such angle is 90°, or $\pi/2$.

The angle $\pi/2$ lies directly on the y-axis.

Calculate the values of the trig functions using the point $(0, 1)$ on its **terminal side**.

NOTICE: The tangent function for $\pi/2$ is undefined!

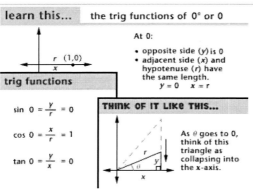

Calculate the trigonometric functions for 0 in the same way.

The angle 0 also has a degenerate right triangle, but like before, calculate its trigonometric functions using the point $(1, 0)$ on its terminal side.

This is a table with the important angles between 0 and $\pi/2$ (or 90°) and their trigonometric functions. These angles and values are worth memorizing-- you'll see them a lot in the future!

By dividing fractions, you can check that the tangent function is equal to the sine function divided by the cosine function.

Sample problems:

1. Find the value of $\sin\dfrac{5\pi}{6}$. (Do not use a calculator.)

   Solution: 1/2

   Explanation: The reference angle for $\dfrac{5\pi}{6}$ is $\dfrac{\pi}{6}$. Since $\sin\dfrac{\pi}{6} = \dfrac{1}{2}$ and since $\dfrac{5\pi}{6}$ is in the second quadrant where the sine function is positive, $\sin\dfrac{5\pi}{6} = \sin\dfrac{\pi}{6} = \dfrac{1}{2}$.

2. Evaluate: $\sin\left(\dfrac{\pi}{6}\right) + \cos\left(\dfrac{\pi}{3}\right) + \tan\left(\dfrac{\pi}{4}\right)$. (Do not use a calculator.)

   Solution: 2

   Explanation: Recall the values of the trigonometric functions for the angles $\dfrac{\pi}{6}$, $\dfrac{\pi}{4}$, and $\dfrac{\pi}{3}$: $\sin\dfrac{\pi}{6} = \dfrac{1}{2}$; $\cos\dfrac{\pi}{3} = \dfrac{1}{2}$; $\tan\dfrac{\pi}{4} = 1$. Therefore,

   $\sin\dfrac{\pi}{6} + \cos\dfrac{\pi}{3} + \tan\dfrac{\pi}{4} = \left(\dfrac{1}{2}\right) + \left(\dfrac{1}{2}\right) + (1) = \dfrac{1}{2} + \dfrac{1}{2} + 1 = 2$.

3. Find the value of $\cos 45°$. (Do not use a calculator.)

Solution: $\dfrac{\sqrt{2}}{2}$

Explanation: The point $(1,1)$ lies on the terminal side of the angle measuring $45°$.

Let $x = 1$ and $y = 1$. Use the Pythagorean theorem to find r: $1^2 + 1^2 = r^2$; $r^2 = 2$;

$r = \sqrt{2}$. Therefore, $\cos 45° = \dfrac{x}{r} = \dfrac{1}{\sqrt{2}} = \dfrac{\sqrt{2}}{2}$.

Practice problems: *(Answers on page: 454)*

1. What is the value of $\tan 45°$? (Do not use a calculator.)

2. What is the exact value of $\tan\left(-\dfrac{4\pi}{3}\right)$? (Do not use a calculator.)

3. What is the value of $\sin\dfrac{\pi}{2}$? (Do not use a calculator.)

Review questions: *(Answers to odd questions on page: 454)*

1. What is the value of $\cos\dfrac{\pi}{2}$? (Do not use a calculator.)

2. What is the value of $\sin\dfrac{\pi}{4}$? (Do not use a calculator.)

3. What is the value of $\sin\dfrac{\pi}{3}$? (Do not use a calculator.)

4. Evaluate $\tan\left(-\dfrac{13\pi}{4}\right)$. (Do not use a calculator.)

5. What is the value of $\tan 30°$? (Do not use a calculator.)

An Introduction to the Graphs of Sine and Cosine Functions

- The graph of the sine function oscillates and repeats without end. The graph of the cosine function is the same as that of the sine function shifted to the left by $\pi/2$ units.
- The **amplitude** of an oscillating function is half the difference between the maximum and minimum values of the function.
- The **period** of an oscillating function is the length of the interval over which the function goes through one full cycle before it repeats.

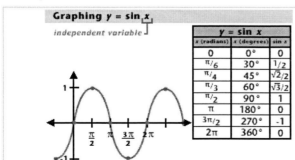

Graphing $y = \sin x$

independent variable

$y = \sin x$		
x (radians)	x (degrees)	sin x
0	0°	0
$\pi/6$	30°	1/2
$\pi/4$	45°	$\sqrt{2}/2$
$\pi/3$	60°	$\sqrt{3}/2$
$\pi/2$	90°	1
π	180°	0
$3\pi/2$	270°	-1
2π	360°	0

Graph the function $y = \sin x$ by making a table of values and plotting the points.

The graph of the sine function is pictured to the left. It repeats itself without stopping.

NOTE: On the graph, x is given in **radians**, not degrees.

Graphing y = sin x

max = 1
min = -1
amplitude = 1
period = 2 π

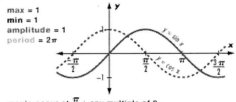

max's occur at $\frac{\pi}{2}$ ± any multiple of 2π.

min's occur at $\frac{3\pi}{2}$ ± any multiple of 2π.

zeros occur at any multiple of π.

There are terms that describe the graphs of oscillating functions like
$y = \sin x$:

1. The **amplitude** is equal to half the difference between the maximum height and the minimum height. For $y = \sin x$, the amplitude is $(1/2)[1 - (-1)] = 1$. You can think of the amplitude as the half of vertical distance that the function covers.

2. The **period** is the length of the largest interval the function covers without repeating. The sine function repeats every 2π radians, so the period of sine is 2π.

Since the sine function repeats every 2π radians, its **maxima**, **minima**, and **zeros** also repeat themselves regularly.

Graphing sin x and cos x

max = 1
min = 1
amplitude = 1
period = 2π

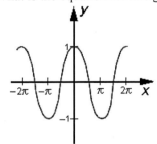

max's occur at $\frac{\pi}{2}$ ± any multiple of 2π.

min's occur at $\frac{3\pi}{2}$ ± any multiple of 2π.

zero's occur at any multiple of π.

Look at the graph of the cosine function $y = \cos x$.

The amplitude, period, and maximum and minimum values of the cosine function are all the same as the corresponding values for the sine function.

Notice, though, that the locations of the maxima, minima, and zeros are different.

Sample problems:

1. What is the equation for this graph?

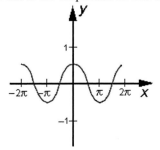

Solution: $y = \cos x$

Explanation: The graph has a maximum value of 1 at $x = 0$, minimum values of -1 at $x = -\pi$ and $x = \pi$, zeros at odd multiples of $\pi/2$, and period of 2π. Thus, the equation is $y = \cos x$.

2. What is the amplitude of this curve?

© Thinkwell Corp. www.thinkwell.com

Solution: $\dfrac{1}{2}$

Explanation: Subtract the minimum value from the maximum value and divide by 2:

$$\dfrac{[\frac{1}{2}-(-\frac{1}{2})]}{2}=\dfrac{1}{2}.$$

3. What is the period of this curve?

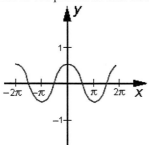

Solution: 2π

Explanation: The period is the length of the largest interval the function covers without repeating. In this graph, the non-repeating interval is from -2π to 0 or from 0 to 2π. Therefore, the period is 2π.

Practice problems: *(Answers on page: 454)*

1. What is the equation for this graph?

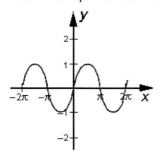

2. What is the amplitude of this sine curve?

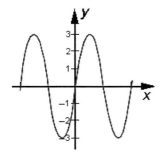

3. What is the period of this curve?

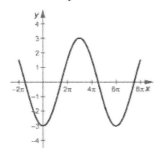

Review questions: *(Answers to odd questions on page: 454)*

1. True or false: The amplitude is the height of the function from the lowest point to its highest point.

2. True or false: The period is the distance in the *x*-direction that covers exactly one repetition of the function.

3. True or false: The amplitudes of $y = \sin x$ and of $y = \cos x$ are the same.

4. True or false: $y = \cos x$ has a zero at 2π.

5. True or false: The maximum value of $y = \cos x$ occurs at 2π.

Graphing Sine or Cosine Functions with Different Coefficients

- The coefficients in the functions $y = a \sin(bx)$ or $y = a \cos(bx)$ determine the **amplitude** and **period** of the functions.
- The amplitude of the function $y = a \sin x$ or $y = a \cos x$ is equal to $|a|$.
-
  The period of the function $y = \sin(bx)$ or $y = \cos(bx)$ is equal to $2\pi / |b|$.

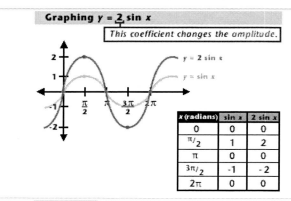

To graph the function $y = 2\sin x$, stretch the graph of $y = \sin x$ vertically by a factor of 2. The **amplitude** of the new graph is 2. A coefficient larger than 1 stretches the graph out vertically (as in this case), and a coefficient smaller than 1 compresses the graph vertically.

In general, the graph of the function $y = a \sin x$ (or $y = a \cos x$) has an amplitude of the **absolute value** of a. Note also that a coefficient that is negative will flip the graph over the *x*-axis.

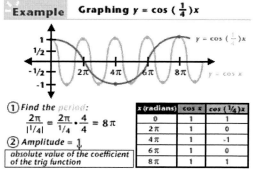

What if the coefficient being changed is inside the **argument** of the function, as in the function $y = \cos(x/4)$?

The coefficient inside the argument changes the **period** of the function. Since the coefficient is smaller than one, it lengthens the period of the graph. If it had been greater than one, it would have shortened the period.

In general, the period of the function $y = \sin(bx)$ or $y = \cos(bx)$ is $2\pi / |b|$.

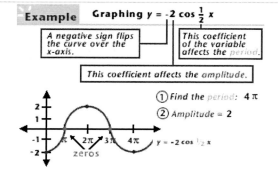

Consider the equation $y = -2\cos 1/2x$. First, graph the regular cosine function $y = \cos x$, then consider the coefficients. The negative sign flips the graph over the *x*-axis. The coefficient of 2 in front stretches the graph vertically so that the amplitude is 2. Finally, the coefficient of 1/2 inside the argument gives the graph a period of 4π instead of 2π. The result is the graph to the left.

Sample problems:

1. What is the amplitude of the function $y = \dfrac{3}{2}\cos 3x$?

   Solution: $\dfrac{3}{2}$

   Explanation: Since the amplitude is equal to the absolute value of the coefficient in front of the trigonometric function, amplitude $= \left|\dfrac{3}{2}\right| = \dfrac{3}{2}$.

2. Identify the period and amplitude of $y = 3\cos 2x$.
   Solution: The period is π, and the amplitude is 3
   Explanation: The period of a function of the form $y = a\cos(bx)$ is 2π divided by the absolute value of the coefficient b. The period of the given function is therefore $\dfrac{2\pi}{|2|} = \pi$. The amplitude of a function of the form $y = a\cos(bx)$ is the absolute value of the coefficient a. The amplitude of the given function is therefore $|3| = 3$.

3. True or false: The equation $y = 3\sin 4x$ is graphed below.

   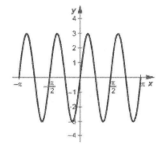

   Solution: True
   Explanation: Compared to the graph of $y = \sin x$, the amplitude of this graph has been increased by a factor of 3. The graph has not been flipped, so the coefficient must be 3 and not -3. Compared to the graph of $y = \sin x$, the period of this graph has been decreased. The period is now $\dfrac{\pi}{2}$ instead of 2π. Thus $\dfrac{2\pi}{b} = \dfrac{\pi}{2}$, so $b = 4$.
   Therefore, the coefficient of the argument is 4.

Practice problems: *(Answers on page: 454)*

1. What is the amplitude of the function $y = -4\sin\dfrac{1}{2}x$?

2. Identify the period and amplitude of $y = -2\sin 5x$.

3. True or false: The equation $y = 3\cos 2x$ is graphed below.

   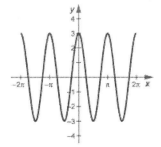

Review questions: *(Answers to odd questions on page: 454)*

1. What is the period of the function $y = -4\sin\dfrac{1}{2}x$?

2. What is the period of the function $y = \dfrac{3}{2}\cos 3x$?

3. What is the amplitude of the function $y = 2\cos x$?

4. Identify the period and amplitude of $y = -\dfrac{1}{2}\cos\dfrac{x}{3}$.

5. True or false: $y = -\sin 2x$ is the equation for the following graph.

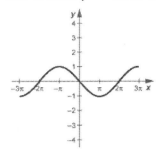

Finding Maximum and Minimum Values and Zeros of Sine and Cosine

- When graphing trigonometric functions, there are points on the graph where important things happen:
  - **Maxima** occur at the highest points of the graph and repeat each **period**.
  - **Minima** occur at the lowest points of the graph and repeat each period.
  - **Zeros** occur where the function crosses the x-axis.
- Adding or subtracting a constant to a trigonometric function produces a vertical shift, moving the graph up or down.

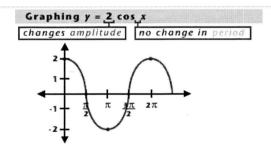

One way to find the important points of a trigonometric function is to graph it.

Consider the function $y = 2\cos x$. The coefficients of the trigonometric function change the appearance of the graph, but the function still looks fundamentally the same.

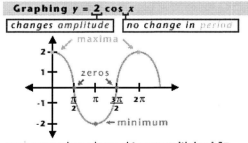

max's occur when x is equal to any multiple of 2π (like 0, 2π, 4π). Even multiples of π.
min's occur when x is equal to any odd multiple of π. (like π, 3π, 5π).
zeros occur when x is equal to any odd multiple of $\frac{\pi}{2}$. (like $\frac{\pi}{2}$, $\frac{3\pi}{2}$, $\frac{5\pi}{2}$).

Three important points you might be asked to find for a trig function are the **maxima**, **minima**, and **zeros**.
- maxima (singular: **maximum**) occur wherever the graph reaches the highest point.
- minima (singular: **minimum**) occur wherever the graph drops to the lowest point.
- Zeros occur where the graph crosses the x-axis (or the y-value equals zero)

Maxima and minima occur once per period for sine and cosine. Per period, zeros can occur twice, once, or not at all, depending on the function and its vertical shift and amplitude.

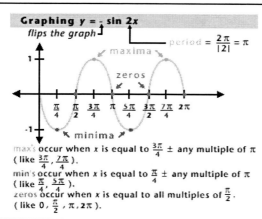

Graphing $y = -\sin 2x$
flips the graph

period $= \dfrac{2\pi}{|2|} = \pi$

maxima

zeros

minima

max's occur when x is equal to $\frac{3\pi}{4} \pm$ any multiple of π
(like $\frac{3\pi}{4}$, $\frac{7\pi}{4}$).
min's occur when x is equal to $\frac{\pi}{4} \pm$ any multiple of π
(like $\frac{\pi}{4}$, $\frac{5\pi}{4}$).
zeros occur when x is equal to all multiples of $\frac{\pi}{2}$.
(like 0, $\frac{\pi}{2}$, π, 2π).

Notice that for this example there are two maxima and two minima in the 2π interval. By reducing the period, the number of times the curve oscillates increases. As such, the curve "tops out" and "bottoms out" more often.

By adding multiples of the period to a maximum or minimum point or to all of the zeros in a single period of the trig function, you can describe all of the maxima, minima, and zeros for a trig function.

Sample problems:

1. Find the maximum for $y = -\dfrac{3}{2}\cos\left(\dfrac{2\pi}{3}x\right)$.

   Solution: $\dfrac{3}{2}$

   Explanation: The amplitude $= \dfrac{3}{2}$, which corresponds to the highest point on the graph and is the maximum.

2. Find the the maximum for $y = 3\sin 2x + 3$.
   Solution: 6
   Explanation: The vertical shift of this function is 3 so the graph moves up 3 units. Since the maximum value is equal to the shift of the sine function plus the amplitude, the result is $3 + 3 = 6$. Notice that the argument does not play any role in finding the maximum value.

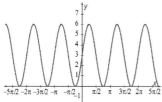

3. A group of scientists conducting a statistical survey found that traffic in a local mall over the course of a day could be estimated by the equation: $P(t) = -3500\cos\left(\dfrac{\pi}{5}t\right) + 3500$ where P is the population and t is the time after the mall opens, in hours. After the mall opens, how much time passes before the number of people in the mall reaches its maximum?
   Solution: 5 hours
   Explanation: Start by finding the maximum number of people, $P(t)$. The maxima is found by adding the vertical shift, 3500, to the amplitude; $\text{max} = 3500 + |-3500| = 3500 + 3500 = 7000$.

   Substitute into the formula and solve for t: $7000 = -3500\cos\left(\dfrac{\pi}{5}t\right) + 3500$;

   $3500 = -3500\cos\left(\dfrac{\pi}{5}t\right)$; $-1 = \cos\left(\dfrac{\pi}{5}t\right)$. Determine when $\cos\left(\dfrac{\pi}{5}t\right)$ equals -1. The value of $\cos x$ is -1 when x is an odd multiple of π. Since you want the time after the mall opens, use the smallest positive value, π, and replace x with $\dfrac{\pi}{5}t$. $x = \pi$; $\dfrac{\pi}{5}t = \pi$; $t = 5$. The number of people in the mall is maximized when $t = 5$.

Practice problems: *(Answers on page: 454)*

1. Estimate the maximum value of this sine wave.

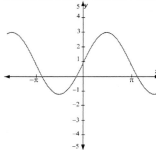

2. Find the minimum value of $y = -\dfrac{1}{2}\sin 3x - \dfrac{3}{2}$.

3. In a particular wildlife refuge, the number of white spotted owls varies according to the following formula where P is the population and t is the time in months since January 1, 1991: $P(t) = 15\sin\left(\dfrac{\pi}{6}t\right) + 20$. What is the maximum population of white spotted owls in the wildlife refuge?

Review questions: *(Answers to odd questions on page: 454)*

1. What is the maximum value of the function $y = 4\cos 3\pi x$?

2. Find the minimum for $y = 3\cos 2x - 5$.

3. Find the maximum for $y = 3\cos 2x$.

4. What is the minimum value of the function $y = 3\cos 2\pi x + 8$?

5. What is the maximum value of the function $y = 5\sin\dfrac{2x}{5}$?

Solving Word Problems Involving Sine or Cosine Functions

- One application of the sine or cosine functions can be seen in wave motion, such as the movement of water and sound. Wave motion can be modeled by these functions. As such, they appear often in word problems.

■ *The waves are traveling at the rate of 540 ft/sec (or 370 mph).*
■ *The peak or height of the wave is 50 ft.*
■ *The time that it take for a wave to complete 1 period is 20 min.*

What is the length between each wave?

Given that a tsunami wave is moving at a rate of 540 feet per second and that the peak of the wave is 50 feet, and given that the time it takes the wave to move one **period** is 20 minutes, find the distance between each wave.

What is the length between each wave?

Tsunami waves, like many waves in nature, are **sinusoidal**. This means that they behave like a sine wave.

If you know the speed of the wave and the time it takes the wave to travel one period, you can find the distance between the waves.

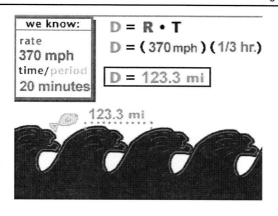

we know:
rate
370 mph
time/period
20 minutes

$D = R \cdot T$

$D = (370\,mph)(1/3\,hr.)$

$D = 123.3\,mi$

123.3 mi

Since rate is equal to the distance divided by time, then distance must be equal to the rate times time. Use 370 mph then convert 20 minutes to 1/3 hour. Plug in the values and simplify.

The waves are 123.3 miles apart!

Notice how we did not need to know the **amplitude** of the sine wave.

Be very careful with your units when solving word problems. Many mistakes made in this type of problem are caused by not canceling units correctly.

Sample problems:

1. The waves of a tsunami have peaks 50 m high and are 200 km apart. They are traveling at a rate of 400 km/hr. How much time does it take to complete one period?
   Solution: 30 min
   Explanation: Substitute the known values into $d = rt$ and solve for t:

   $$200\,km = \frac{400\,km}{1\,hr}t; \quad t = \left(\frac{(200\,\cancel{km})1\,hr}{400\,\cancel{km}}\right) = 0.5\,hr = 30\,minutes.$$

2. A wave in a pond with an amplitude of 3 feet and a period of 6 seconds has an equation at a fixed position of the form $y = A\sin Bt$. How high is the wave from trough to crest?
   Solution: 6 feet
   Explanation: The height from the trough to crest is equal to twice the amplitude. The height is $3(2) = 6$ feet.

3. The temperature of a particular patient in a hospital is modeled by the following function where t is the time in hours: $T(t) = 3\sin\dfrac{\pi t}{14} + 98$. What is the maximum temperature that the patient can attain?
   Solution: 101°F
   Explanation: The sine function ranges from -1 to 1. Multiply that range by the amplitude, which is 3, to obtain the range $[-3,3]$. Finally, add 98 to obtain $[95,101]$. Thus the maximum temperature of the patient will be 101°F.

Practice problems: *(Answers on page: 454)*

1. A surfer is riding a wave with an amplitude of 20 feet and a period of 40 feet. If the wave completes a period in 10 seconds, what is the speed of the surfer?

2. The waves of a tsunami are traveling at 400 ft/sec. The waves are 40 ft high, and their period is 15 min. What is the length of each wave in miles?

3. The temperature of a particular patient in a hospital is modeled by the following function where t is the time in hours: $T(t) = 4\sin\dfrac{\pi t}{7} + 98$. How long will it take for the patient's temperature to reach its first maximum?

Review questions: *(Answers to odd questions on page: 454)*

1. The waves of a tsunami are 50 ft high and 528 miles apart. It takes a wave 20 minutes to complete one period. How fast are the waves traveling?

2. The waves of a tsunami are 50 ft high, 100 miles apart and traveling at a rate of 1000 miles per hour. How long does it take for the waves to complete one period?

3. The waves of a tsunami have peaks 60 m high and 200 km apart. At what speed are the waves traveling?

4. The waves of a tsunami are traveling at 0.1 mi/sec. It takes a wave 20 min to complete one period. What is the length between wave peaks?

5. The temperature of a particular patient in a hospital ranges between 94°F and 100°F as modeled by the following function where t is the time in hours: $T(t) = 3\sin\dfrac{\pi t}{14} + C$. What is the value of C for this function?

Graphing Sine and Cosine Functions with Phase Shifts

- A **phase shift** is a horizontal **translation** of a trig function.
    - Phase shifts occur when adding or subtracting from the x-term in the trig function.
    - A phase shift will move the graph of the function to the left or the right, depending on whether the constant is added or subtracted.
    - Adding or subtracting an entire **period** does not change the appearance of the graph.

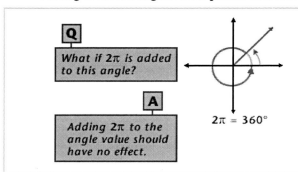

Recall that adding 2π to an angle results in a **coterminal angle**. So, adding 2π to an angle has no effect on the value of trig functions for that angle.

Adding 360° has the same effect as adding 2π.

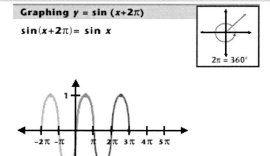

A **phase shift** is a horizontal movement of a trig function. Phase shifts occur any time you add or subtract from the x-term in a trigonometric function.

Since adding or subtracting 2π from an angle doesn't affect the sine of the angle, and since adding any multiple of 2π is the same as adding 2π several times, adding any multiple of 2π to the angle in the **argument** of the sine function doesn't change the appearance of the graph. The graph shifts on top of itself.

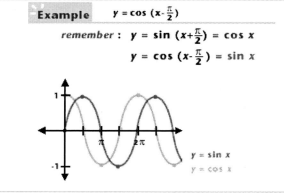

Consider the equation $y = \cos(x - \pi/2)$. Subtracting from the x-term causes a translation in the graph, moving the function to the right.

The new graph should look familiar. Moving the cosine curve to the right $\pi/2$ units, it becomes the sine curve.

By the same logic, moving the sine curve to the left $\pi/2$ units, it becomes the cosine curve.

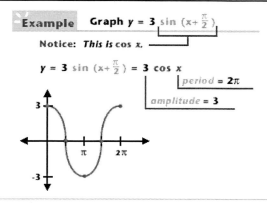

Example   **Graph** $y = 3 \sin (x + \frac{\pi}{2})$

Notice: *This is cos x.*

$y = 3 \sin (x + \frac{\pi}{2}) = 3 \cos x$

period = 2π

amplitude = 3

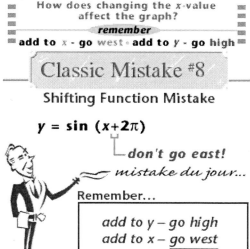

Knowing the patterns of phase shifts can allow for substitution to take place—making the graphing process of the trig functions much easier.

Consider the example illustrated here:
Graph $y = 3 \sin (x + \pi/2)$. Notice that adding $\pi/2$ to the sine curve produces the cosine curve. $\sin (x + \pi/2) = \cos x$

Therefore, substitute $\cos x$ for $\sin (x + \pi/2)$ and graph.

How does changing the *x*-value affect the graph?

remember

add to *x* - **go west** · **add to** *y* - **go high**

Classic Mistake #8

Shifting Function Mistake

$y = \sin (x + 2\pi)$

don't go east!

mistake du jour...

Remember...

> *add to y – go high*
> *add to x – go west*

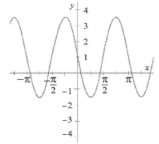

Be careful not to make the common **shifting function mistake**. Many people think that if you add to the *x*-term then the graph moves in the positive direction, which is false.

Remember, if you add to *x*, go west (or left).

If you add to *y*, go high.

Sample problems:

1. What is the phase shift for the function $y = \frac{2}{3} \cos\left(x + \frac{\pi}{4}\right)$?

   Solution: $\frac{\pi}{4}$ to the left

   Explanation: Adding to *x* moves the graph left. In this case, $\frac{\pi}{4}$ is the quantity added to *x*.

2. True or false: The function $y = \frac{5}{2} \sin 2\left(x + \frac{\pi}{2}\right) + 1$ is graphed below.

   Solution: True

   Explanation: The amplitude is $\frac{5}{2}$, the period is π, and the function is shifted upward by 1 unit. There is also a phase shift $\frac{\pi}{2}$ units to the left.

3. True or false: The graph of $y = \cos\left(x + \dfrac{\pi}{2}\right)$ is the graph of $y = \cos x$ shifted $\dfrac{\pi}{2}$ units to the right.

Solution: False

Explanation: Adding a constant to the argument of the cosine function shifts the curve west, or to the left, by that many units.

Practice problems: *(Answers on page: 454)*

1. What is the phase shift of the function $y = \dfrac{\pi}{2}\sin(x - 3)$?

2. True or false: The graph of $y = \sin\left(x + 4\pi\right)$ is the same as the graph of $y = \sin x$.

3. True or false: The graph of $y = \cos(x - \dfrac{\pi}{3})$ is the graph of $y = \cos x$ shifted $\dfrac{\pi}{3}$ units to the right.

Review questions: *(Answers to odd questions on page: 455)*

1. True or false: The function $y = 2\sin\left(x + \dfrac{\pi}{2}\right)$ is graphed below.

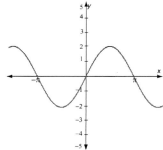

2. True or false: The graphs of $y = -2\cos\left(x - 4\pi\right)$ and $y = -2\cos x$ are identical.

3. What is the phase shift of the function $y = -\dfrac{1}{2}\cos\left(x + \dfrac{\pi}{2}\right)$?

4. What is the phase shift for the function $y = \dfrac{3}{4}\sin\left(x - \dfrac{\pi}{6}\right)$?

5. What is the phase shift for the function $y = \dfrac{\pi}{3}\cos 3\left(x + 4\right)$?

Fancy Graphing: Changes in Period, Amplitude, Vertical Shift, and Phase Shift

- **Review**: Use information about the **period, amplitude, vertical shift**, and **phase shift** to accurately graph very involved sine and cosine functions.
  - Graph the function with just the change in period and amplitude (and any flips) first.
  - Translate the graph appropriately according to the phase shift.
  - Translate the graph appropriately according to the vertical shift.

fancy graphing	Determine the **amplitude, period, vertical shift**, and the **phase shift** to graph trigonometric functions.

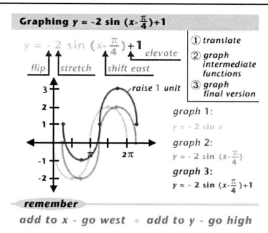

Graphing $y = -2 \sin \left(x - \frac{\pi}{4}\right) + 1$

① translate
② graph intermediate functions
③ graph final version

graph 1:
$y = -2 \sin x$

graph 2:
$y = -2 \sin \left(x - \frac{\pi}{4}\right)$

graph 3:
$y = -2 \sin \left(x - \frac{\pi}{4}\right) + 1$

remember

add to x - go west • add to y - go high

When asked to graph a function with more than one coefficient change, its helpful to draw several intermediate graphs to help keep the information straight.

Remember which constants affect which aspects of the graph:

• Multiplying the trig function by a constant stretches the graph vertically, changing the amplitude.

• Negative signs in front flip the graph upside down. This does not change the amplitude.

• Adding or subtracting from the *x*-term creates a phase shift, moving the graph left or right.

• Adding or subtracting from the entire expression creates a vertical shift.

Graph the function, taking into account any changes in period and amplitude. Then draw another graph taking into account the phase shift. Finally, take the vertical shift into account.

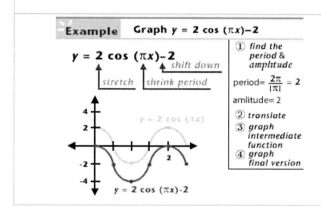

Example Graph $y = 2 \cos (\pi x) - 2$

$y = 2 \cos (\pi x) - 2$

shift down
stretch | shrink period

① find the period & amplitude
period= $\frac{2\pi}{|\pi|} = 2$
amplitude= 2
② translate
③ graph intermediate function
④ graph final version

$y = 2 \cos (\pi x) - 2$

How would you go about graphing this equation:
$y = 2\cos(\pi x) - 2$?

Start by finding the period and amplitude. Notice that the period is equal to 2 radians, *not* 2π radians.

After graphing the function with just the period and amplitude change, translate the graph by the vertical shift (which is -2).

Sample problems:

1. Determine the period of the function $y = \dfrac{3}{\pi} \sin \left(\dfrac{2\pi}{3} x - 1\right) + \dfrac{3}{4}$.

   Solution: 3
   Explanation: To find the period, divide 2π by the absolute value of the coefficient
   of the argument: $2\pi \div \left|\dfrac{2\pi}{3}\right| = 2\pi \left(\dfrac{3}{2\pi}\right) = 3$.

2. Find the amplitude, period, phase shift and vertical shift of $y = -4\sin(3x - \pi) + 1$.

   Solution: amplitude = 4, period $= \dfrac{2\pi}{3}$, phase shift is $\dfrac{\pi}{3}$ to the right, vertical shift is up one.
   Explanation: The absolute value of the constant multiplying the trigonometric function is
   the amplitude, so amplitude $= |-4| = 4$. To find the period, find *b* by factoring the
   coefficient of *x* out of the argument; $(3x - \pi) = 3\left(x - \dfrac{\pi}{3}\right)$, so $b = 3$ and the period is
   $\dfrac{2\pi}{|b|} = \dfrac{2\pi}{3}$. Subtracting a constant from the argument means the functions shifts east
   or to the right. The constant being added to the entire expression is the vertical shift,
   so the graph moves up 1 unit.

3. Give the equation of the graph of $y = 2\cos 3x + 1$ after it has been stretched vertically by a factor of 2, flipped upside down, and stretched horizontally by a factor of 3.

Solution: $y = -4\cos x + 1$

Explanation: To stretch the graph vertically by a factor of 2, multiply the cosine expression by 2. To flip the graph upside down, multiply the cosine expression by -1. To stretch the graph horizontally by a factor of 3, divide the argument of the cosine function by 3.

Practice problems: *(Answers on page: 455)*

1. Determine the phase shift of the function $y = \dfrac{2}{3}\cos\left(x + \dfrac{\pi}{6}\right) - \dfrac{3}{2}$.

2. Give the equation of the graph obtained by shifting $y = 4\cos x$ up 2 units and to the right 3 units.

3. Give the equation of the graph obtained by shifting $y = \sin x$ down 1 unit, to the right π units, and by increasing its amplitude to 3.

Review questions: *(Answers to odd questions on page: 455)*

1. What is the vertical translation of $y = -3\cos 5x - 4$?

2. What is the phase shift of the equation $y = 3\sin(2x - 5) - 3$?

3. True or false: $y = \cos(2x - \pi) - 2$ has a phase shift of $\dfrac{\pi}{2}$ units to the right and a vertical shift of 2 units down.

4. What is the phase shift of $y = 5\sin(\pi + 2x)$?

5. True or false: $y = 2\sin \pi(x - 1) + 2$ is graphed below.

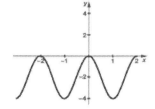

Graphing the Tangent, Secant, Cosecant, and Cotangent Functions

- The **tangent**, **secant**, **cosecant**, and **cotangent** functions are all defined in terms of the **sine** and **cosine** functions. Knowing how to graph sine and cosine empowers you to graph the other four.

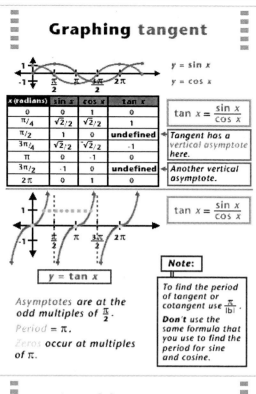

Graphing tangent

$y = \sin x$

$y = \cos x$

x (radians)	sin x	cos x	tan x
0	0	1	0
$\pi/4$	$\sqrt{2}/2$	$\sqrt{2}/2$	1
$\pi/2$	1	0	undefined
$3\pi/4$	$\sqrt{2}/2$	$-\sqrt{2}/2$	-1
π	0	-1	0
$3\pi/2$	-1	0	undefined
2π	0	1	0

$$\tan x = \frac{\sin x}{\cos x}$$

◄ *Tangent has a vertical asymptote here.*

◄ *Another vertical asymptote.*

$$\tan x = \frac{\sin x}{\cos x}$$

$y = \tan x$

Note:

To find the period of tangent or cotangent use $\frac{\pi}{|b|}$.

Don't use the same formula that you use to find the period for sine and cosine.

Asymptotes are at the odd multiples of $\frac{\pi}{2}$.

Period = π.

Zeros occur at multiples of π.

The tangent function is equal to the **sine** function divided by the **cosine** function. Start by making a table of values. For any given *x*-value (in the first column), the value of sine and cosine (in the second and third columns) are known. Divide sine by cosine. This is the value of the tangent function.

For example, if $x = 0$, then $\sin x = 0$, $\cos x = 1$, and $\tan x = 0/1$ or 0.

If the value of the tangent is undefined, that means there is a **vertical asymptote** at that point.

There are asymptotes at every odd multiple of $\pi/2$. Therefore, the tangent function is undefined at these points.

Notice that tangent completes a **period** in π radians instead of 2π radians like sine and cosine. Finding the period of tangent requires the formula $\pi/|b|$.

The **zeros** of the tangent function occur at the multiples of π.

Graphing secant

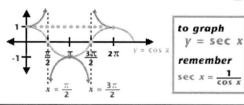

$y = \cos x$

to graph
$$y = \sec x$$
remember
$$\sec x = \frac{1}{\cos x}$$

$x = \frac{\pi}{2}$ $x = \frac{3\pi}{2}$

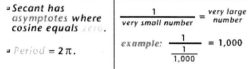

▪ *Secant has asymptotes where cosine equals zero.*

$$\frac{1}{\text{very small number}} = \frac{\text{very large number}}{}$$

example: $\dfrac{1}{\frac{1}{1,000}} = 1,000$

▪ *Period = 2π.*

The **secant** function is defined to be the reciprocal of the cosine function. So, take the values of cosine and put them under 1.

Because secant is defined as the reciprocal of cosine, secant will be undefined wherever cosine is equal to zero. Wherever the cosine is really small, the secant will be really big. Wherever the cosine is one, the secant will be one.

Secant has no zeros unless it is affected by a **vertical shift**. The period is equal to the period of cosine. Secant has asymptotes wherever cosine has zeros.

Graphing cosecant

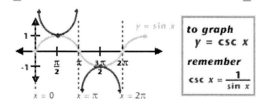

$y = \sin x$

to graph
$$y = \csc x$$
remember
$$\csc x = \frac{1}{\sin x}$$

$x = 0$ $x = \pi$ $x = 2\pi$

Cosecant has asymptotes at zeros of sine.

Notice:
Cosecant graph is identical to secant, but shifted over.
(Just like the sine and cosine relationship)

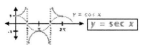

$y = \cos x$

$y = \sec x$

The **cosecant** function is the reciprocal of the sine function. To plot some points take the values of sine and put them under 1.

Just like secant, cosecant is defined to be the reciprocal of a trig function (in this case, the sine function). Wherever sine is really small, the cosecant will be really big. Wherever sine is 1, the cosecant will be 1.

Just like secant, cosecant has no zeros unless it is affected by a vertical shift. The period of cosecant is equal to the period of sine. Cosecant has asymptotes where sine has zeros.

Also, just like the sine and cosine relationship, the secant and cosecant are identical, except that one is shifted over slightly.

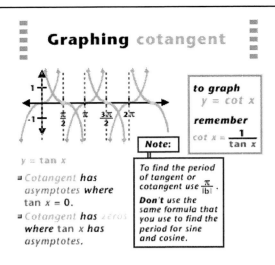

Graphing cotangent

$y = \tan x$

- Cotangent has asymptotes where $\tan x = 0$.
- Cotangent has zeros where $\tan x$ has asymptotes.

to graph
$y = \cot x$
remember
$\cot x = \dfrac{1}{\tan x}$

Note:
To find the period of tangent or cotangent use $\dfrac{\pi}{|b|}$.
Don't use the same formula that you use to find the period for sine and cosine.

The **cotangent** function is the reciprocal of the tangent function.
Wherever the tangent function equals 1, the reciprocal equals 1 as well.

Wherever the tangent function equals zero, the cotangent is undefined and has an asymptote.

Wherever the tangent function is undefined, the cotangent function equals zero.

Just like the tangent curve, cotangent has a period of π.

Be very careful when finding the period of tangent and cotangent —do not use the wrong formula. They get their own formula since their periods are different.

Sample problems:

1. What is the period of $y = \cot x$?
   Solution: π
   Explanation: To determine the period of a tangent or cotangent function,
   use the formula $\dfrac{\pi}{|b|}$: $\dfrac{\pi}{|1|} = \pi$. Thus, the period is π.

2. Where are the vertical asymptotes of the graph of $y = \cot x$?
   Solution: $x = k\pi$ (multiples of π)
   Explanation: Because $\cot x$ is the reciprocal of $\tan x$, its asymptotes occur at values of x
   for which $\tan x = 0$. These are the same values that make $\sin x = 0$. They are given by $x = k\pi$.

3. True or false: The function $y = -\cot x$ is graphed below.

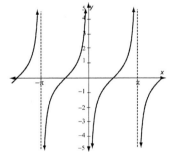

   Solution: True
   Explanation: First graph the function $y = -\tan x$. Wherever $y = -\tan x$ has a zero, $y = -\cot x$ will
   have a vertical asymptote and wherever $y = -\tan x$ has a vertical asymptote, $y = -\cot x$ will
   have a zero.

Practice problems: *(Answers on page: 455)*

1. What is the period of $y = \tan 2x$?

2. Where are the zeros of $y = \tan(x - \pi)$?

 www.thinkwell.com

3. True or false: The function $y = -\sec x$ is graphed below?

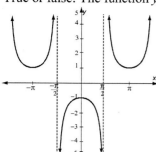

Review questions: *(Answers to odd questions on page: 455)*

1. What is the period of $y = \tan x$?

2. Where are the zeros of $y = \sec x$?

3. Where are the vertical asymptotes of $y = \csc x$?

4. True or false: The function $y = \sec 2x$ has zeros at $x = \dfrac{\pi}{4}$ and $x = \dfrac{3\pi}{4}$.

5. True or false: The function $y = -\tan x$ is graphed below.

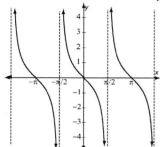

Fancy Graphing: Tangent, Secant, Cosecant, and Cotangent

- Graph **tangent**, **secant**, **cosecant**, and **cotangent** step by step, changing the graph to match the coefficients.
  - First graph the normal version of the function (with the proper period).
  - Alter this graph according to the other coefficients. This step might stretch or compress the graph and/or move it vertically or horizontally.

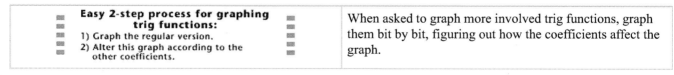

Easy 2-step process for graphing trig functions:	When asked to graph more involved trig functions, graph them bit by bit, figuring out how the coefficients affect the graph.
1) Graph the regular version. 2) Alter this graph according to the other coefficients.	

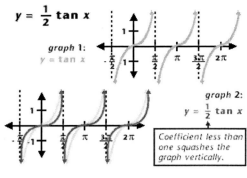

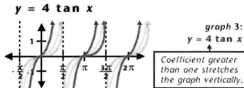

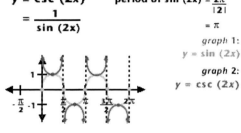

To graph $y = 1/2 \tan x$, start by graphing **tan** x.

The coefficient in front of the tangent will multiply each y-value by one-half; therefore, each point on the graph gets closer to the x-axis. The coefficient compresses the graph.

To graph $y = 4 \tan x$, remember that the coefficient will multiply each y-value by 4; therefore each point on the graph will be stretched upwards. A coefficient that is greater than one will always elongate the graph.

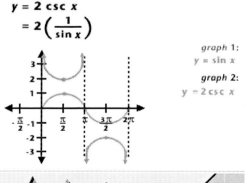

To graph the cosecant function, remember that **cosecant** is the reciprocal of the **sine** function. Start by graphing the sine curve with the proper period.

Now take the reciprocal. Remember that cosecant will have **asymptotes** wherever sine has **zeros**.

Changing the period will compress the graph horizontally.

At first glance, the function of $y = 2 \csc x$ looks a lot like the function of $y = \csc(2x)$, but notice that the coefficient has been moved. Therefore, the graph is going to look very different.

The period of $y = 2 \csc x$ is 2π. Because of the coefficient in front of the trig function, each of the y-terms of the cosecant curve has to be multiplied by 2. So, the cosecant curve moves away from the sine curve.

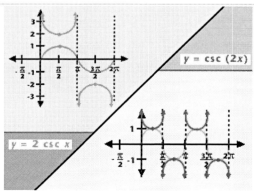

Notice here, the graphs of $y = 2 \csc x$ and $y = \csc(2x)$ are very different. The placement of the coefficient greatly effects the graph.

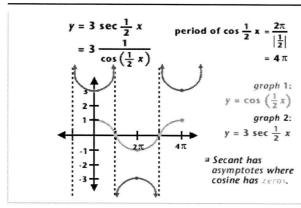

Graph $y = 3 \sec(1/2x)$.

Follow the same steps to graph **secant** that were used to graph cosecant. Start by graphing the cosine function. Remember that secant is the reciprocal of **cosine**.

Then graph the secant function, multiplying it by 3 (stretching it away from the x-axis).

Remember that secant has asymptotes where the cosine curve has zeros.

Sample problems:

1. True or false: The following is a graph of one period of $y = \cot 2x$.

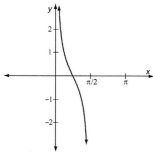

Solution: True

Explanation: The period is $\dfrac{\pi}{2}$ and there are no phase shifts or vertical translations.

2. Describe the steps for graphing $y = \sec 2x$.
   Solution: Find the period, graph $y = \cos 2x$ and then graph the reciprocal

   Explanation: Use the coefficient of x, 2, to calculate the period: $\dfrac{2\pi}{2} = \pi$. Graph $y = \cos 2x$ and then graph its reciprocal.

3. In the graph of $y = 2 \tan \pi x$, where do the zeros occur?
   Solution: At every integer
   Explanation: The period of this function is $\pi / \pi = 1$. Since $\tan 0 = 0$, the zeros occur at every integer.

Practice problems: *(Answers on page: 455)*

1. True or false: One period of $y = \dfrac{1}{2} \csc x + 1$ is graphed below.

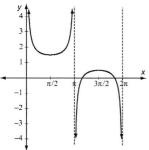

2. What is the period of $y = 2 \tan 3(x - 2) + 7$?

3. How does the graph of $y = 2 \sec x$ differ from the graph of $y = \sec 2x$?

Review questions: *(Answers to odd questions on page: 455)*

1. What is the period of $y = \tan 6x$?

2. True or false: $x = \dfrac{\pi}{2}$ is an equation of a vertical asymptote of $y = \sec x$.

3. True or false: The function $y = 5\tan 4x$ is graphed below.

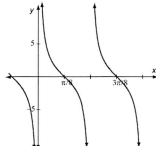

4. Describe the steps for graphing the function $y = \dfrac{1}{2}\csc x$.

5. How does the graph of $y = -3\sec 2x$ differ from the graph of $y = \sec 2x$?

Identifying a Trigonometric Function from its Graph

- To identify which **trig function** a graph might represent, graph the reciprocal of the function.

Identify the function:

Is it:

$y = -2\tan x$

$y = \sec 2x$

$y = \cot x$

$y = -\csc x$

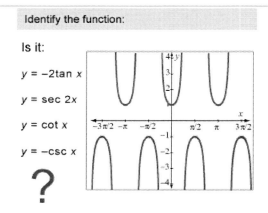

Identifying **trig functions** can be made easier by sketching a graph of the reciprocal of the given function.

Where there are asymptotes in the original function, its reciprocal will have zeros.

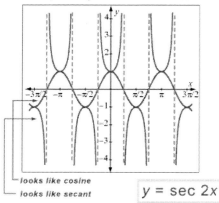

looks like cosine
looks like secant

$y = \sec 2x$

To sketch the reciprocal of the graph you are interested in, remember that **asymptotes** become **zeros** and zeros become asymptotes.

The reciprocal function of the graph given here makes a graph similar to the cosine curve, so the original graph must be a secant curve.

Identify the function:	Identify the trig function that produces this graph.
Is it: $y = -2\tan x$ $y = \sec 2x$ $y = \cot x$ $y = -\csc x$ **?** 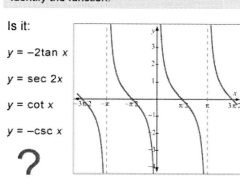	
Where there are asymptotes in the original function, its reciprocal will have zeros. 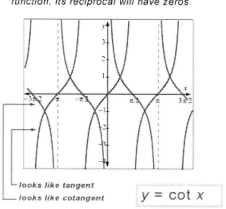 *looks like tangent* *looks like cotangent* $y = \cot x$	First, find the reciprocal graph by turning zeros into asymptotes and asymptotes into zeros. The reciprocal graph looks like the tangent function. So, the original graph must be the cotangent function.

Sample problems:

1. True or false: The function $y = 3\csc\left(x + \dfrac{\pi}{2}\right)$ is graphed below.

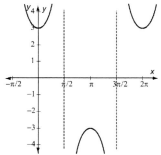

Solution: True

Explanation: The corresponding reciprocal function has an amplitude of 3 and a period of 2π.
The function is either a secant function or a cosecant function shifted to the left by $\pi/2$.

2. Determine the equation of the following graph.

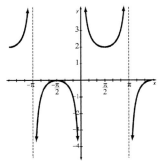

Solution: $y = \csc x + 1$

Explanation: Sketch the graph of the reciprocal function. Use the asymptotes of the function as zeros of the reciprocal function and zeros of the function as asymptotes of the reciprocal function. Because the reciprocal resembles the graph of $y = \sin x$ moved up one unit, the graph must be that of $y = \csc x + 1$.

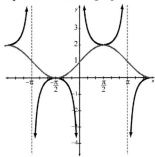

3. True or false: The function $y = \cot 2x$ is graphed below.

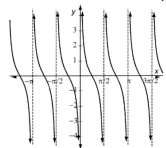

Solution: True

Explanation: Sketch the graph of the reciprocal function. Use the asymptotes of the function as zeros of the reciprocal and the zeros of the function as asymptotes of the reciprocal function. Because the reciprocal resembles the graph of $y = \tan 2x$, the graph must be that of $y = \cot 2x$.

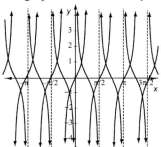

Practice problems: *(Answers on page: 455)*

1. Determine an equation for the graph below.

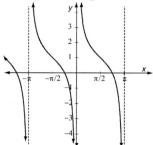

2. True or false: The function $y = -3\cot x$ is graphed below.

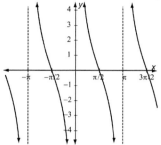

3. True or false: The function $y = 2\sec x$ is graphed below.

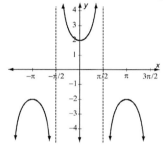

Review questions: *(Answers to odd questions on page: 455)*

1. Determine an equation for the graph below. The graph shows one complete period.

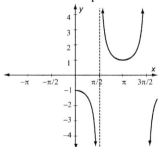

2. Determine an equation for the graph below.

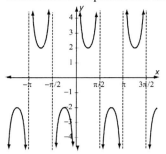

3. Determine an equation for the graph below.

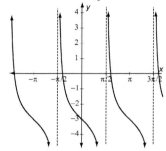

4. True or false: The function $y = \csc x$ is graphed below.

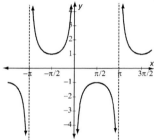

5. True or false: The function $y = -\cot x$ is graphed below.

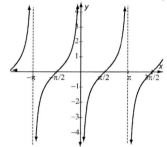

An Introduction to Inverse Trigonometric Functions

- **Review:** In order for a function, $f(x)$, to have an **inverse**, $f^{-1}(x)$, it must be a one-to-one function (ie: it must pass the **horizontal line test**).
- The basic trigonometric functions have inverses if their **domains** are restricted. These inverse functions are known as the **inverse trigonometric functions:**
  - The **inverse sine function** is written $y = \sin^{-1}x$. (Think of $\sin^{-1}x$ as "the angle whose sine is x.")

    The domain for $y = \sin^{-1}x$ is $-1 \le x \le 1$ and the **range** is $-\frac{\pi}{2} \le y \le \frac{\pi}{2}$.

  - The **inverse cosine function** is written $y = \cos^{-1}x$. (Think of $\cos^{-1}x$ as "the angle whose cosine is x.")

    The domain for $y = \cos^{-1}x$ is $-1 \le x \le 1$ and the range is $0 \le y \le \pi$.

  - The **inverse tangent function** is written $y = \tan^{-1}x$. (Think of $\tan^{-1}x$ as "the angle whose tangent is x.")

    The domain for $y = \tan^{-1}x$ is any real number and the range is $-\frac{\pi}{2} \le y \le \frac{\pi}{2}$

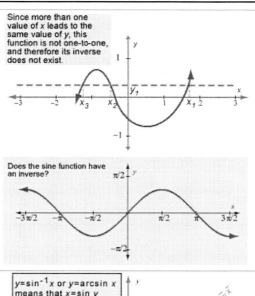

Remember, in order for a function, $f(x)$, to have an inverse, $f^{-1}(x)$, it must pass the horizontal line test. If it fails the horizontal line test, the function is not one-to-one and, therefore, the inverse of that function does not exist.

Consider the sine function, $y = \sin x$. Does $y = \sin^{-1} x$ exist?

From the graph of the sine function, it is clear that $y = \sin x$ is not a one-to-one function, therefore its inverse does not exist.

By restricting the **domain** of the sine function, however, a one-to-one function can be defined.

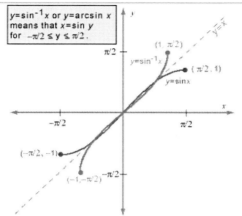

Consider the piece of the sine function between $x = -\pi/2$ and $x = \pi/2$. This piece by itself passes the horizontal line test, so it has an inverse.

Find the inverse by reflecting the restricted piece across the line $y = x$.

The result is the **inverse sine function**, written $y = \sin^{-1}x$.

The meaning of the inverse sine function, $y = \sin^{-1}x$, is "y is the angle whose sine is x," or $x = \sin y$.

Don't forget, $y = \sin^{-1}x$ is NOT the same as $y = \sin x^{-1}$.

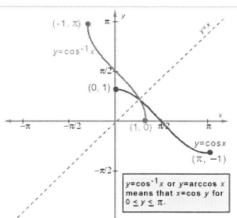

The inverse of the cosine function, $y = \cos^{-1} x$ is defined by restricting the domain of the cosine function, $y = \cos x$, and then by reversing the roles of x and y.

Restrict the domain of the cosine function $y = \cos x$ to x-values between 0 and π.

Reflect this piece of the graph over the line $y = x$. The result is the **inverse cosine function**, written $y = \cos^{-1}x$.

If $y = \cos^{-1}x$, then "y is the angle whose cosine is x," or $\cos y = x$.

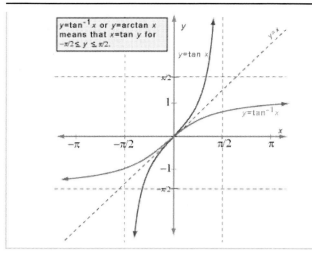

The inverse of the tangent function, $y = \tan^{-1} x$ is defined by restricting the domain of the tangent function, $y = \tan x$, and then by reversing the roles of x and y.

For $y = \tan x$, restrict the domain to the interval between $-\pi/2$ and $\pi/2$ and reflect this piece of the graph over the line $y = x$.

The **inverse tangent function** is notated $y = \tan^{-1}x$, and means "y is the angle whose tangent is x."

Sample problems:

1. What is the range of the inverse cosine function?

   Solution: $0 \le y \le \pi$

   Explanation: In order to produce an inverse function, the domain of cosine must be reduced to $[0, \pi]$. On this interval, cosine passes the horizontal line test. Since this interval is the restricted domain of cosine, it is the range of the inverse cosine function.

2. What is the domain of the inverse tangent function?

   Solution: All real numbers

   Explanation: To pass the horizontal line test, the domain of the tangent function must be restricted to the interval $\left[-\dfrac{\pi}{2}, \dfrac{\pi}{2}\right]$. However, over this restricted domain, the range of tangent is still all real numbers. Thus the domain of the inverse tangent function is also all real numbers.

3. True or false: The inverse tangent function is graphed below.

   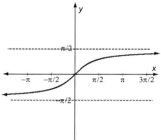

   Solution: True

   Explanation: The domain of this function is any real number, and the range is $-\dfrac{\pi}{2} < y < \dfrac{\pi}{2}$. This is the graph of the inverse tangent function.

Practice problems: (Answers on page: 455)

1. True or false: $\sin x^{-1} = \sin \dfrac{1}{x}$

2. What is the domain of the function $y = 3\sin^{-1} t$?

3. True or false: The function $y = \sin^{-1} x$ is graphed below.

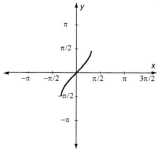

Review questions: *(Answers to odd questions on page: 455)*

1. True or false: The function $y = \dfrac{1}{2}\tan^{-1} x$ is graphed below.

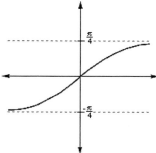

2. True or false: If $\tan^{-1} A = B$, then $\tan B = A$.

3. True or false: The function $y = \cos^{-1} x$ graphed below.

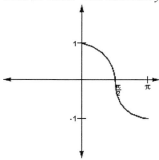

4. What is the range of $y = \cos^{-1} x$?

5. What is the range of $y = \dfrac{1}{3}\tan^{-1} x$?

Evaluating Inverse Trigonometric Functions

- When evaluating an **inverse trigonometric function**:
  - Think of the answer as "the angle whose _____ is...."
    For example, **sin**$^{-1}$ 0.5 is equal to "the angle whose sine is 0.5."
  - Verify that the answer is in the correct **range** for the inverse trig function.
  - The graph of the appropriate trig function is often helpful.

Evaluate: $\sin^{-1}(\frac{\sqrt{3}}{2})$

Q: What is the angle whose sine is $\frac{\sqrt{3}}{2}$? A: $\pi/3$ or 60°

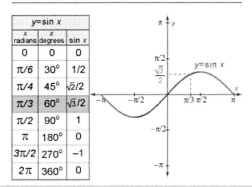

$y=\sin x$		
x radians	x degrees	$\sin x$
0	0	0
$\pi/6$	30°	1/2
$\pi/4$	45°	$\sqrt{2}/2$
$\pi/3$	60°	$\sqrt{3}/2$
$\pi/2$	90°	1
π	180°	0
$3\pi/2$	270°	−1
2π	360°	0

Evaluate: $\sin^{-1}\dfrac{\sqrt{3}}{2}$.

$\sin^{-1}(\dfrac{\sqrt{3}}{2})$ is equal to "the angle whose sine is $\dfrac{\sqrt{3}}{2}$." Notice that the solution must be in the interval $(-\pi/2, \pi/2)$, the **range** of the inverse sine function.

Since $\sin\dfrac{\pi}{3} = \dfrac{\sqrt{3}}{2}$, the solution is $\pi/3$, or 60°.

So, $\sin^{-1} = \dfrac{\sqrt{3}}{2} = \dfrac{\pi}{3}$

Evaluate: $\cos^{-1}(\frac{-1}{2})$

Q: What is the angle whose cosine is $\frac{-1}{2}$? A: $2\pi/3$ or 120°

$y=\cos x$		
x radians	x degrees	$\cos x$
0	0	1
$\pi/6$	30°	$\sqrt{3}/2$
$\pi/4$	45°	$\sqrt{2}/2$
$\pi/3$	60°	1/2
$\pi/2$	90°	0
$2\pi/3$	120°	−1/2
$3\pi/4$	135°	$-\sqrt{2}/2$
$5\pi/6$	150°	$-\sqrt{3}/2$
π	180°	−1

Evaluate: $\cos^{-1}(-\dfrac{1}{2})$.

$\cos^{-1}(-\dfrac{1}{2})$ is "the angle whose cosine is $-1/2$." Notice that the answer must be between 0 and π.

Use the graph of the cosine function and the fact that $\cos\dfrac{\pi}{3} = \dfrac{1}{2}$, to determine that the solution is the angle $2\pi/3$.

Use a calculator in radian mode to find the following:

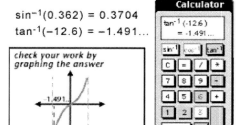

$\sin^{-1}(0.362) = 0.3704$

$\tan^{-1}(-12.6) = -1.491\ldots$

check your work by graphing the answer

It's also possible to compute inverse trig functions using a calculator. Be sure your calculator is in the appropriate mode: degrees or radians.

Use the graph of the appropriate trig function to check the answer.

Sample problems:

1. Use a calculator to evaluate $\cos^{-1} 0.319$ to the nearest degree.
   Solution: 71°
   Explanation: Set the calculator to degree mode.
   For a scientific calculator: 0.319, 2nd, $\cos^{-1}$.
   For a graphing calculator: 2nd, $\cos^{-1}$, 0.319, enter.

2. Use a calculator to evaluate $\sin^{-1}\left(\dfrac{\sqrt{2}}{2}\right)$ in radians to the nearest thousandth.

   Solution: 0.785

   Explanation: Set the calculator to radian mode.

   For a scientific calculator: 2, 2nd, $\sqrt{}$, $\div$, 2, $=$, 2nd, $\sin^{-1}$.

   For a graphing calculator: 2nd, $\sin^{-1}$, 2nd, $\sqrt{}$, 2,), $\div$, 2, enter.

3. Find the exact value of $\tan^{-1}\left(-\sqrt{3}\right)$ in radians.

   Solution: $-\dfrac{\pi}{3}$

   Explanation: The range of the inverse tangent function is $\left[-\dfrac{\pi}{2}, \dfrac{\pi}{2}\right]$. Thus, $\tan^{-1}\left(-\sqrt{3}\right)$ is equal to the angle between $-\dfrac{\pi}{2}$ and $\dfrac{\pi}{2}$ whose tangent is $-\sqrt{3}$. Since $\tan\left(-\dfrac{\pi}{3}\right) = -\sqrt{3}$, and $-\dfrac{\pi}{3}$ is in the correct range of angles, $\tan^{-1}\left(-\sqrt{3}\right) = -\dfrac{\pi}{3}$.

Practice problems: *(Answers on page: 455)*

1. Use a calculator to evaluate $\tan^{-1} 4.65$ to the nearest degree.

2. Use a calculator to evaluate $\cos^{-1}\left(\dfrac{\sqrt{3}}{2}\right)$ to the nearest degree.

3. Find the exact value of $\cos^{-1}\left(-\dfrac{\sqrt{2}}{2}\right)$ in radians.

Review questions: *(Answers to odd questions on page: 455)*

1. Use a calculator to evaluate $\sin^{-1} 0.753$ in radians to the nearest thousandth.

2. Use a calculator to evaluate $\tan^{-1}\left(-\dfrac{\sqrt{3}}{3}\right)$ in radians to five decimal places.

3. Use a calculator to evaluate $\cos^{-1}\left(\dfrac{7\pi}{4}\right)$ in radians to five decimal places.

4. Find the exact value of $\sin^{-1}\left(\dfrac{1}{2}\right)$.

5. Find the exact value of $\tan^{-1} 1$.

Solving an Equation Involving an Inverse Trigonometric Function

- To solve an equation containing an **inverse trigonometric function**:
  - Determine what the equation says by 'untangling' it. Think of the inverse trig function as "the angle whose _____ is...." For example, think of **$\sin^{-1} \dfrac{1}{2}$** as "the angle whose sine is $\dfrac{1}{2}$."
  - After untangling, solve the equation normally.
  - Graph the function to check that all solutions were found.

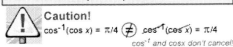

Solve: $\cos^{-1}(\cos x) = \pi/4$

⚠ **Caution!**

$\cos^{-1}(\cos x) = \pi/4 \neq \cos^{-1}(\cos x) = \pi/4$

$\cos^{-1}$ and $\cos x$ don't cancel!

Remember, when solving an equation that contains an inverse trig function, determine what the equation is saying by 'untangling' it.

Take a look at the equation to the left. You might be tempted to cancel the cos and **$\cos^{-1}$** to produce a solution. Unfortunately, the cosine and inverse cosine functions do not cancel in this way!

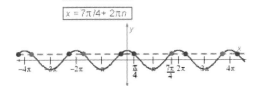

Solve: $\cos^{-1}(\cos x) = \pi/4$

$\boxed{\cos^{-1}(\cos x) = \pi/4}$

translation: $\pi/4$ is the angle whose cosine is $\cos x$

$\cos \pi/4 = \cos x$

$\dfrac{\sqrt{2}}{2} = \cos x$
what are all the x-values whose cosine equals $\dfrac{\sqrt{2}}{2}$?

$\boxed{x = \pi/4 + 2\pi n}$

$\boxed{x = 7\pi/4 + 2\pi n}$

Given the equation to the left:

1. Untangle. $\cos^{-1}(\cos x)$ means "the angle whose cosine is $\cos x$."

2. Determine the value of $\cos\dfrac{\pi}{4}$: $\cos\dfrac{\pi}{4} = \dfrac{\sqrt{2}}{2}$

3. Solve the equation for all possible values of x. There will be two answers per **period**.

4. Check the graph of cosine to make sure your answer is right.

Remember, you can't be too careful when dealing with these functions. Take your time! Many of these solution sets will be infinite--watch out for them.

Sample problems:

1. Find all solutions: $2(\cos x + 1) = 2$

Solution: $\dfrac{\pi}{2} + k\pi$, where k is any integer

Explanation: Simplify: $2(\cos x + 1) = 2$; $2\cos x + 2 = 2$; $2\cos x = 0$; $\cos x = 0$.

Observe from the graph of $y = \cos x$ that $\cos x = 0$ at $\dfrac{\pi}{2}$ and at $-\dfrac{\pi}{2}$.

Additionally, $\cos x = 0$ at $\dfrac{\pi}{2}$ plus any multiple of 2π.

Thus, all solutions can be described as $\dfrac{\pi}{2} + k\pi$, where k is any integer.

2. Find all solutions: $\tan^{-1}(\tan x) = \dfrac{\pi}{6}$

Solution: $x = \dfrac{\pi}{6} + \pi n$

Explanation: Simplify: $\tan^{-1}(\tan x) = \dfrac{\pi}{6}$; $\tan\dfrac{\pi}{6} = \tan x$; $\dfrac{\sqrt{3}}{3} = \tan x$. The x-value

whose tangent is $\dfrac{\sqrt{3}}{3}$ is $\dfrac{\pi}{6}$ given that the period of tangent is π. Therefore, $x = \dfrac{\pi}{6} + \pi n$.

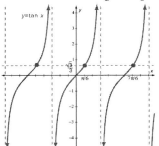

3. Find all solutions: $\tan^{-1}(\sin x) = \dfrac{\pi}{3}$

   <u>Solution</u>: No solution

   <u>Explanation</u>: Simplify: $\tan^{-1}(\sin x) = \dfrac{\pi}{3}$; $\sin x = \tan\dfrac{\pi}{3}$; $\sin x = \sqrt{3}$.
   However, $\sqrt{3} \approx 1.73205$ is not in the range of the sine function. Thus, there is no solution.

Practice problems: *(Answers on page: 455)*

1. Find all solutions: $\sin^{-1}(\sin x) = \dfrac{\pi}{2}$

2. Find all solutions: $\tan^{-1}(\tan x) = -\dfrac{\pi}{4}$

3. Find all solutions: $\cos^{-1}(\cos x) = \dfrac{5\pi}{6}$

Review questions: *(Answers to odd questions on page: 455)*

1. Find all solutions: $\dfrac{4}{3}\tan^{-1}\dfrac{\theta}{2} = \pi$

2. Find all solutions: $\cos^{-1}\left(\cos x\right) = \dfrac{\pi}{3}$

3. Find all solutions: $\sin^{-1}\left(\sin x\right) = 0$

4. Find all solutions: $\cos^{-1}\left(\cos x\right) = \dfrac{2\pi}{3}$

5. Find all solutions: $\sin^{-1}\left(\cos x\right) = \dfrac{\pi}{6}$

Evaluating the Composition of a Trigonometric Function and Its Inverse

- To evaluate a **composite** trigonometric function:
  - First find the value of the inner expression.
  - Then evaluate the outer expression (usually an inverse) at that value.
- Always consider the **range** of the inverses. Certain answers are not allowed when solving an **inverse trig function**.
  - The range of $\sin^{-1}x$ is the interval $[-\pi/2, \pi/2]$.
  - The range of $\cos^{-1}x$ is the interval $[0, \pi]$.
  - The range of $\tan^{-1}x$ is the interval $(-\pi/2, \pi/2)$.

Ranges for inverse trigonometric functions:
$y = \sin^{-1}x$: $-\pi/2 \le y \le \pi/2$
$y = \cos^{-1}x$: $0 \le y \le \pi$
$y = \tan^{-1}x$: $-\pi/2 < y < \pi/2$

To evaluate a composite trig function:
1) Find the value of the inner expression
2) Find the inverse*

*-The solution must be within the range of allowable values for the inverse trig function

To evaluate the **composition** of a trig function and its **inverse**, find the value of the inner expression and then take its inverse.

Remember, the solution for the composite trig function must be within the range of allowable values for the inverse trig function.

Evaluate: $\sin^{-1}(\sin(7\pi/6))$

$\sin^{-1}(\sin(7\pi/6)) \longrightarrow \sin(7\pi/6) = -1/2$
$\sin^{-1}(-1/2) = \boxed{-\pi/6}$

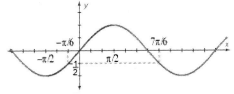

y=sin x		
x radians	x degrees	sin x
0	0	0
π/6	30°	1/2

Consider the composite function, $\sin^{-1}(\sin(7\pi/6))$.

Begin by finding the value of the inner expression, $\sin(7\pi/6)$. The **reference angle** turns out to be $\pi/6$, and sine is negative in the third quadrant, so this value is $-1/2$.

Now find the **inverse sine** of $-1/2$. Remember, the answer has to be between $-\pi/2$ and $\pi/2$, the range of inverse sine.

What is the angle whose sine is $-1/2$? The angle is $-\pi/6$.

Evaluate: $\tan^{-1}(\tan(3\pi/4))$

$\tan^{-1}(\tan(3\pi/4)) \longrightarrow \tan(3\pi/4) = -1$
$\tan^{-1}(-1) = \boxed{-\pi/4}$

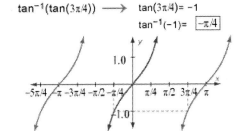

y=tan x		
x radians	x degrees	tan x
0	0	0
π/4	45°	1

Consider the composite function, $\tan^{-1}(\tan(3\pi/4))$.

Begin by finding the value of the inner expression. The reference angle is $\pi/4$, and tangent is negative in the second quadrant, so the inner expression equals -1.

Now take the inverse **tangent** of -1.

What is the angle whose tangent is -1?
The angle is $-\pi/4$. Since the range of inverse tangent is between $-\pi/2$ and $\pi/2$, the answer must be $-\pi/4$.

Evaluate: $\sin\left(\sin^{-1}\frac{1}{2}\right)$

Recall: if f and f^{-1} are inverse functions, then $f(f^{-1}(x))=x$ and $f^{-1}(f(x))=x$

Therefore, $\sin\left(\sin^{-1}\frac{1}{2}\right) = \frac{1}{2}$

check:

$\sin(\text{the angle whose sin is } \frac{1}{2}) \longrightarrow \sin(30°) = \frac{1}{2}$

y=sin x		
x radians	x degrees	sin x
0	0	0
π/6	30°	1/2

Consider the example given here: evaluate $\sin(\sin^{-1} 1/2)$.

Remember the rule that if f and f^{-1} are inverse functions then $f(f^{-1}(x)) = x$ and $f^{-1}(f(x)) = x$; therefore $\sin(\sin^{-1} 1/2) = 1/2$.

You can check this by remembering that $\sin^{-1} 1/2$ means "find the angle whose sine is 1/2." Since you know that $\sin(30°) = 1/2$, then $\sin(\sin^{-1} 1/2) = \sin(30°) = 1/2$.

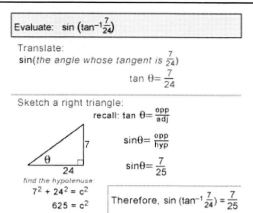

Evaluate: $\sin\left(\tan^{-1}\frac{7}{24}\right)$

Translate:
$\sin(\textit{the angle whose tangent is } \frac{7}{24})$

$$\tan\theta = \frac{7}{24}$$

Sketch a right triangle:

recall: $\tan\theta = \frac{opp}{adj}$

$\sin\theta = \frac{opp}{hyp}$

$\sin\theta = \frac{7}{25}$

find the hypotenuse:
$$7^2 + 24^2 = c^2$$
$$625 = c^2$$
$$25 = c$$

Therefore, $\sin\left(\tan^{-1}\frac{7}{24}\right) = \frac{7}{25}$

Use the right-triangle method to evaluate inverse trig functions when appropriate.

Consider the example illustrated here, $\sin\left(\tan^{-1}\frac{7}{24}\right)$.

The problem is asking you to find the sine of the angle whose tangent is 7/24.

Finding the value of the inner expression is too difficult to do without a calculator. Instead, use the right triangle method to evaluate the expression.

Draw a triangle in the first quadrant (since tangent is positive) and use the Pythagorean theorem to find the hypotenuse.

Knowing all the sides of the triangle, use the trig identities to solve.

Sample problems:

1. Determine the exact value of $\tan(\tan^{-1} 10)$.

   Solution: 10

   Explanation: Remember the rule that if f and f^{-1} are inverse functions then $f(f^{-1}(x)) = x$ and $f^{-1}(f(x)) = x$. So, $\tan(\tan^{-1}10) = 10$. The value 10 is in the domain of the inverse tangent function. Therefore, the tangent of the angle whose tangent is 10 equals 10.

2. Determine the exact value of $\tan\left(\sin^{-1}\frac{3}{5}\right)$.

   Solution: $\frac{3}{4}$

   Explanation: Draw a right triangle with an angle whose measure is equal to $\sin^{-1}\frac{3}{5}$. Since $\frac{3}{5}$ is a ratio, let the opposite side be 3 and the hypotenuse be 5. Use the Pythagorean theorem to find the length of the unknown side. $3^2 + x^2 = 5^2$; $9 + x^2 = 25$; $x^2 = 16$; $x = 4$. Thus, $\tan\left(\sin^{-1}\frac{3}{5}\right) = \frac{\text{opposite}}{\text{adjacent}} = \frac{3}{4}$.

3. Determine the exact value of $\sin^{-1}\left(\sin\left(-\frac{3\pi}{7}\right)\right)$.

   Solution: $-\frac{3\pi}{7}$

   Explanation: The inverse sine function of x produces the angle between $-\frac{\pi}{2}$ and $\frac{\pi}{2}$ whose sine is x. The angle in this expression is in the range of the inverse sine function. $-\frac{\pi}{2} \le -\frac{3\pi}{7} \le \frac{\pi}{2}$. Thus, $\sin^{-1}\left(\sin\left(-\frac{3\pi}{7}\right)\right) = -\frac{3\pi}{7}$.

Practice problems: *(Answers on page: 455)*

1. Determine the exact value of $\sin^{-1}\left(\sin\left(\frac{5\pi}{3}\right)\right)$.

2. Determine the exact value of $\cos^{-1}\left(\cos\left(\dfrac{5\pi}{3}\right)\right)$.

3. Determine the exact value of $\tan^{-1}\left(\tan\left(\dfrac{7\pi}{6}\right)\right)$.

Review questions: *(Answers to odd questions on page: 455)*

1. Determine the exact value of $\cos^{-1}(\cos 1.7)$.

2. Determine the exact value of $\cos^{-1}\left(\cos\left(\dfrac{7\pi}{4}\right)\right)$.

3. Determine the exact value of $\tan^{-1}\left(\tan\left(\dfrac{4\pi}{3}\right)\right)$.

4. Determine the exact value of $\sin^{-1}\left(\sin\left(\dfrac{7\pi}{4}\right)\right)$.

5. Determine the exact value of $\sin^{-1}\left(\sin\left(\dfrac{11\pi}{6}\right)\right)$.

Applying Trigonometric Functions: Is He Speeding?

- **Review:**

$$\sin\theta = \frac{opposite}{hypotenuse} \qquad \cos\theta = \frac{adjacent}{hypotenuse} \qquad \tan\theta = \frac{opposite}{adjacent}$$

- An **angle of depression** is the angle formed by looking straight out to the horizon and then looking down at an object.
- An **angle of elevation** is the angle formed by looking straight out to the horizon and then looking up at an object.
- The angle of depression looking down from a height to a location is the same as the angle of elevation looking up from that location to that height.
- **Review:** *rate = distance /time*

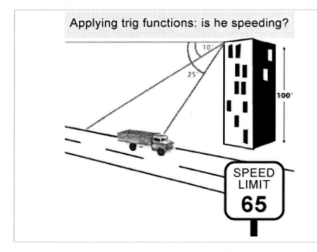

Applying trig functions: is he speeding?

Is the truck illustrated here exceeding the 65 miles per hour speed limit?

To determine that, first find out how far the truck traveled in 3 seconds. From this you can calculate the speed of the truck in miles per hour.

Given the two angles and the height of the building, use the fundamental trig functions to solve.

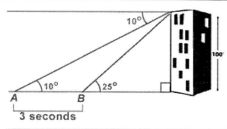

Find the distance from point A to the building

$$\tan 10° = \frac{100}{?}$$

$$? = \frac{100}{\tan 10°}$$

use a calculator $? = 567.13'$

First find the distance from point A to the building.

The angle from point A to the ground is 10° because the angle of elevation is equal to the angle of depression that is given in the example. Also given is the height of the building.

Set up a right triangle diagram to solve.

Given the angle, 10°, and the opposite side length, 100 feet, find the length of the adjacent side. Use the tangent function to solve.

You find that the distance from point A to the building is 567.13 feet.

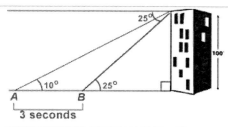

Find the distance from point B to the building

$$\tan 25° = \frac{100}{?}$$

$$?? = \frac{100}{\tan 25°}$$

use a calculator $?? = 214.45'$

Next, find the distance from the point B to the building. This involves the same process as finding the distance from point A— an angle measure and and opposite side length are given, set up a right triangle diagram to solve.

To find the length of the adjacent side, use the tangent function again. Use a calculator to find that the length from point B to the building is 214.45 feet.

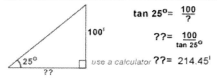

Subtract to find the distance from A to B

$$567.13' - 214.45' = 352.68'$$

convert to miles

352.68 feet = 0.0668 miles

Distance = 0.0668 miles

The distance the truck moved is the difference between these two answers, converted to miles from feet. (Divide the number of feet by 5,280 feet/mile.)

Subtract to find the distance from A to B

$$567.13' - 214.45' = 352.68'$$

convert to miles

352.68 feet = 0.0668 miles

Distance = 0.0668 miles

Find the rate

Use the distance formula:

Distance = Rate × Time

(0.0668 miles) = Rate × (3 seconds)

$$\frac{0.0668}{3 \text{ seconds}} = \text{Rate}$$

$$\frac{0.02226}{\text{second}} = \text{Rate}$$

convert to miles per hour

Rate = 80.15 miles per hour

Finding the truck's speed is a matter of dividing distance traveled by time used.

Use the distance formula to solve.

Convert the answer, 0.02226 miles per second, to miles per hour.

The final answer is 80.15 miles per hour.

Yes, this person was speeding!

80.148 mph is definitely faster than the stated limit of 65 mph.

Give this guy a ticket and tell him to slow down.

Sample problems:

1. A hiker is hiking up a 14° slope. If he hikes at a constant rate of 2 mph, how much altitude does he gain in 4 hours of hiking?

Solution: 1.9 mi

Explanation: Find the distance that he has hiked after 4 hours: $d = rt = 4\text{hr} \cdot 2 \text{ mile/hr} = 8$ miles. Let y be the altitude gained by the hiker. Use the sine function to find the altitude:

$\sin 14° = \dfrac{y}{8}$; $8\sin 14° = y$; $y = 1.9$. The hiker gains 1.9 miles of altitude in his 4 hours of hiking.

2. A motorcyclist traveling along a road can see the top of a 75 foot tall observation tower by looking up at an angle of 7°. Eight seconds later, the same motorcyclist has to crane his neck to an angle of 45° to see the top of the tower. Was the motorcyclist speeding on a road that has a speed limit of 35 mph? What is the difference between the speed of the motorcycle and the speed limit?

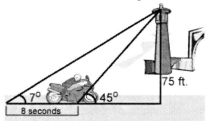

75 ft.

7°   45°

8 seconds

Solution: He is speeding by traveling 10.67 mph over the speed limit.

Explanation: Let x be the distance from the starting point to the tower.

Use the tangent function to find x: $\tan 7° = \dfrac{75}{x}$; $x = \dfrac{75}{\tan 7°}$; $x = 610.83$.

Let y be the distance from the motorcyclist after 8 seconds to the tower.

Use the tangent function to find y: $\tan 45° = \dfrac{75}{y}$; $y = \dfrac{75}{\tan 45°}$; $y = 75$.

Subtract to find the distance traveled by the motorcycle: $610.83 - 75 = 535.83$ ft.

Find the distance in miles: $535.83 \div 5280 = 0.101483$ miles.

Find the speed, r: $r = d/t = 0.101483/8 = 0.012685$ mi/s.

Find the speed in miles per hour: $0.012685 \frac{mi}{s} \times 60 \frac{s}{min} \times 60 \frac{min}{hr} = 45.666$ mph.

Find the miles per hour over the speed limit: $45.666 - 35 = 10.666 \approx 10.67$.

3. A helicopter is hovering 300 feet over the finish line of a boat race. The crew of Boat A can see the helicopter by looking up at an angle of 3°. At that exact same moment, the crew of Boat B has to look at an angle of 3.5° to see the chopper. After 2 minutes, the crew of Boat A has to look at an angle of 32° to see the chopper, while the crew of Boat B has to look at an angle of 32.2° to see it. Assuming that both boats will continue to travel at the same speed they have demonstrated over the last 2 minutes, which boat will win the race, and by how many seconds?

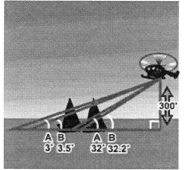

Solution: Boat A by 1.9 seconds

Explanation: Use the tangent function to find the missing distances:

Boat A $\rightarrow \tan 3° = \dfrac{300}{x}$; $x = \dfrac{300}{\tan 3°} = 5724.34$, and $\tan 32° = \dfrac{300}{x}$; $x = \dfrac{300}{\tan 32°} = 480.1$,

so the distance traveled by Boat A is $5724.34 - 480.1 = 5244.24$ ft.

Boat B $\rightarrow \tan 3.5° = \dfrac{300}{x}$; $x = \dfrac{300}{\tan 3.5°} = 4904.96$, and $\tan 32.3° = \dfrac{300}{x}$; $x = \dfrac{300}{\tan 32.2°} = 476.39$,

so the distance traveled is $4904.96 - 476.39 = 4428.57$ ft.

Divide each distance by 120 (120 secs = 2 min) to find the speed for each boat in ft/sec:

Boat A $\rightarrow 5244.24/120 = 43.7$ ft/sec, and Boat B $\rightarrow 4428.57/120 = 36.9$ ft/sec.

Divide the remaining distance for each boat by the speed of each boat to find the time required to finish the race: Boat A $\rightarrow 480.1 \div 43.7 = 10.99$ s, and

Boat B $\rightarrow 476.39 \div 36.9 = 12.91$ s. Thus, Boat A will win the race by 1.9 seconds.

Practice problems: *(Answers on page: 456)*

1. Ada spots the cities of Gary and Smithville from her hot air balloon at an altitude of 3 miles. The angles of depression to the cities are 23° and 60°. How far apart are the cities?

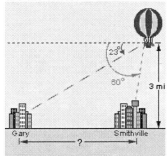

2. A helicopter is hovering 1000 feet above the surface of a lake. The helicopter is observed by the crew of a boat as they look upwards at an angle of 25°. Twenty seconds later, the crew has to look at an angle of 70° to see the helicopter. How fast was the boat traveling?

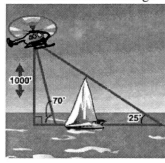

3. An announcer at a race track, sitting on the observation platform 100 feet above the track, spots a horse running on the track. The announcer has to look at an angle of depression of 4°. Some time later during the race (28.6 seconds later to be exact) he spots the same horse. This time he has to look at an angle of depression of 48°. How does the speed of the horse (in miles per hour) compare to that of the horse who set the record for the 1.25 mile Kentucky Derby at 1 minute, 59 seconds?

Review questions: *(Answers to odd questions on page: 456)*

1. A submarine has an enemy battleship in its sights. If the battleship is 800 feet long and subtends an angle of 30°, how far away is the battleship? Assume that the submarine is approaching the exact center of the battleship.

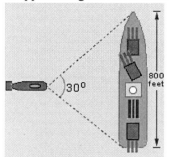

2. What is the height of this building?

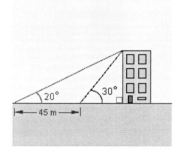

3. Find the distance across the river. Give your answer in miles, rounded to 4 decimal places.

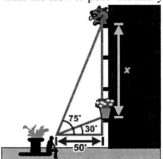

4. A fountain sits in the courtyard 50 feet from a building. A person at the fountain looking up at a 30° angle can see a flower pot in a window. Looking at a 75° angle from the same position, the person sees a dog in a window. How many yards higher is the dog than the flower pot? Round your answer to 2 decimal places.

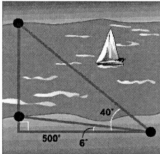

5. A passenger in a car at an intersection sees laundry drying on the roof of a building in the distance. The passenger can see the laundry by looking up at a 10° angle. At the next intersection, the passenger can see the laundry, but only by sticking his head out of the car and looking up at a 35° angle. The car he is riding in had traveled from the first intersection to the second intersection in 5 seconds. What is the difference between the speed of the car and the street speed limit of 25 mph?

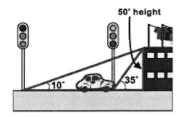

3

Trigonometric Identities

Fundamental Trigonometric Identities

- An **identity** is an equation that is true for all meaningful values of the variable(s) involved.
- Four basic **trigonometric identities**:
  - $\tan\theta = \dfrac{\sin\theta}{\cos\theta}$
  - $\cos^2\theta + \sin^2\theta = 1$ (the **Pythagorean identity**)
  - $1 + \tan^2\theta = \sec^2\theta$
  - $1 + \cot^2\theta = cs\,c^2\,\theta$

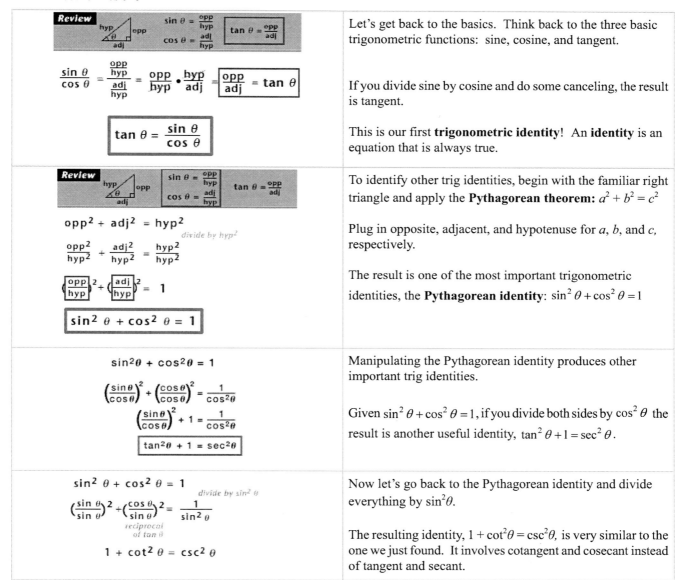

Let's get back to the basics. Think back to the three basic trigonometric functions: sine, cosine, and tangent.

If you divide sine by cosine and do some canceling, the result is tangent.

This is our first **trigonometric identity**! An **identity** is an equation that is always true.

To identify other trig identities, begin with the familiar right triangle and apply the **Pythagorean theorem**: $a^2 + b^2 = c^2$

Plug in opposite, adjacent, and hypotenuse for a, b, and c, respectively.

The result is one of the most important trigonometric identities, the **Pythagorean identity**: $\sin^2\theta + \cos^2\theta = 1$

Manipulating the Pythagorean identity produces other important trig identities.

Given $\sin^2\theta + \cos^2\theta = 1$, if you divide both sides by $\cos^2\theta$ the result is another useful identity, $\tan^2\theta + 1 = \sec^2\theta$.

Now let's go back to the Pythagorean identity and divide everything by $\sin^2\theta$.

The resulting identity, $1 + \cot^2\theta = \csc^2\theta$, is very similar to the one we just found. It involves cotangent and cosecant instead of tangent and secant.

identities

$$\tan \theta = \frac{\sin \theta}{\cos \theta}$$

only these two need to be memorized!

$$\cos^2 \theta + \sin^2 \theta = 1$$

divided by sin² θ =   *divided by cos² θ =*

$$1 + \tan^2 \theta = \sec^2 \theta$$

$$1 + \cot^2 \theta = \csc^2 \theta$$

Notice that you really only need to memorize two of these four identities because the other two are derived from the Pythagorean identity.

Sample problems:

1. True or false: The result of dividing $\text{opp}^2 + \text{adj}^2 = \text{hyp}^2$ by opp^2 is $1 + \cot^2 \theta = \csc^2 \theta$.

   Solution: True

   Explanation: Divide each term by opp^2: $\dfrac{\text{opp}^2}{\text{opp}^2} + \dfrac{\text{adj}^2}{\text{opp}^2} = \dfrac{\text{hyp}^2}{\text{opp}^2}$; $1 + \dfrac{\text{adj}^2}{\text{opp}^2} = \dfrac{\text{hyp}^2}{\text{opp}^2}$. Recall that

   $\dfrac{\text{adj}^2}{\text{opp}^2} = \cot^2 \theta$ and $\dfrac{\text{hyp}^2}{\text{opp}^2} = \csc^2 \theta$, substitute: $1 + \dfrac{\text{adj}^2}{\text{opp}^2} = \dfrac{\text{hyp}^2}{\text{opp}^2} \Rightarrow 1 + \cot^2 \theta = \csc^2 \theta$.

2. True or false: $\tan^2 \theta + 1 = \csc^2 \theta$

   Solution: False

   Explanation: To prove that $\tan^2 \theta + 1 = \csc^2 \theta$ is false, divide the identity $\sin^2 \theta + \cos^2 \theta = 1$

   by $\cos^2 \theta$: $\sin^2 \theta + \cos^2 \theta = 1$; $\dfrac{\sin^2 \theta}{\cos^2 \theta} + \dfrac{\cos^2 \theta}{\cos^2 \theta} = \dfrac{1}{\cos^2 \theta}$. Simplify: $\dfrac{\sin^2 \theta}{\cos^2 \theta} + 1 = \dfrac{1}{\cos^2 \theta}$.

   Recall that $\dfrac{\sin^2 \theta}{\cos^2 \theta} = \tan^2 \theta$ and $\dfrac{1}{\cos^2 \theta} = \sec^2 \theta$, substitute: $\dfrac{\sin^2 \theta}{\cos^2 \theta} + 1 = \dfrac{1}{\cos^2 \theta} \Rightarrow$

   $\tan^2 \theta + 1 = \sec^2 \theta$. Thus, $\tan^2 \theta + 1$ is equal to $\sec^2 \theta$, not $\csc^2 \theta$.

3. Simplify: $\left(\sin^2 \dfrac{\pi}{8} + 3 + \cos^2 \dfrac{\pi}{8} \right)^3$

   Solution: 64

   Explanation: Use the identity $\sin^2 x + \cos^2 x = 1$ to substitute and simplify:

   $\left(\sin^2 \dfrac{\pi}{8} + 3 + \cos^2 \dfrac{\pi}{8} \right)^3 = \left[\left(\sin^2 \dfrac{\pi}{8} + \cos^2 \dfrac{\pi}{8} \right) + 3 \right]^3 = \left[(1) + 3 \right]^3 = 4^3 = 64$.

Practice problems: *(Answers on page: 456)*

1. True or false: The result of dividing $\text{adj}^2 + \text{opp}^2 = \text{hyp}^2$ by adj^2 is $1 + \tan^2 \theta = \sec^2 \theta$.

2. True or false: $\cot^2 \theta + 1 = \sec^2 \theta$

3. Simplify: $\left(2x + \sin^2 \dfrac{2\pi}{3} + 2 + \cos^2 \dfrac{2\pi}{3} \right)^2$

Review questions: *(Answers to odd questions on page: 456)*

1. True or False: The result of dividing $\text{opp}^2 + \text{adj}^2 = \text{hyp}^2$ by hyp^2 is $\sin^2 \theta + \cos^2 \theta = 1$.

2. True or False: $\cot \theta + 1 = \sec^2 \theta$

3. True or False: $\tan^2 \theta = \sec^2 \theta - 1$

4. Simplify: $\left(\cos^2\dfrac{\pi}{2}+5+\sin^2\dfrac{\pi}{2}\right)^2$

5. Simplify: $\left(\sin^2\pi+5x-\left(4-\cos^2\pi\right)\right)^2$

Finding All Function Values

- **Review**: The four basic **trigonometric identities**:

  1. $\tan\theta=\dfrac{\sin\theta}{\cos\theta}$

  2. $\sin^2\theta+\cos^2\theta=1$ (The **Pythagorean identity**)

  3. $1+\tan^2\theta=\sec^2\theta$

  4. $1+\cot^2\theta=\csc^2\theta$

- Given the value of a trigonometric function for an angle and the **quadrant** that the angle lies in, you can use trigonometric identities to find the values of the other trigonometric functions.

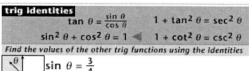

Use the basic trig identities to find the value of trigonometric functions.

Consider the following example,

given $\sin\theta=\dfrac{3}{4}$ and $\dfrac{\pi}{2}<\theta<\pi$, find $\cos\theta$.

Since you are given the value of $\sin\theta$ and the **quadrant** that θ lies in, you can use a basic trig identity to find $\cos\theta$.

Plug $\sin\theta=3/4$ into the **Pythagorean identity** to find $\cos\theta$.

Solving for $\cos\theta$ produces two answers: $+\dfrac{\sqrt{7}}{4}$ and $-\dfrac{\sqrt{7}}{4}$; however, since θ lies in quadrant II, $\cos\theta$ must be negative. Therefore, the answer is the negative square root.

This example asks you to find $\tan\theta$ given

$\sin\theta=\dfrac{3}{4}$ and $\dfrac{\pi}{2}<\theta<\pi$.

Plugging $\sin\theta$ and $\cos\theta$ into the identity

$\tan\theta=\dfrac{\sin\theta}{\cos\theta}$ produces a value of $-\dfrac{3\sqrt{7}}{7}$ for $\tan\theta$.

Finding the values of cosecant, secant, and cotangent simply involves taking the reciprocal of sine, cosine, and tangent repsectively.

Sample problems:

1. If the secant of θ is 2, what is the cosine of θ?

   Solution: $\dfrac{1}{2}$

   Explanation: The cosine of θ is equal to the reciprocal of the secant of θ, or $\cos\theta = \dfrac{1}{\sec\theta}$.

   Thus, $\cos\theta = \dfrac{1}{\sec\theta} = \dfrac{1}{2}$.

2. Find $\cos\theta$, if $\sin\theta = \dfrac{\sqrt{3}}{2}$. (The angle is in the first quadrant).

   Solution: $\dfrac{1}{2}$

   Explanation: Substitute $\sin\theta = \dfrac{\sqrt{3}}{2}$ into the Pythagorean identity and simplify:

   $\sin^2\theta + \cos^2\theta = 1 \Rightarrow \left(\dfrac{\sqrt{3}}{2}\right)^2 + \cos^2\theta = 1;\ \dfrac{3}{4} + \cos^2\theta = 1.$

   Solve for $\cos\theta$: $\dfrac{3}{4} + \cos^2\theta = 1;\ \cos^2\theta = \dfrac{1}{4};\ \sqrt{\cos^2\theta} = \sqrt{\dfrac{1}{4}};\ \cos\theta = \pm\dfrac{1}{2}.$

   Because the angle is in the first quadrant, cosine has to be the positive square root.

   Therefore, $\cos\theta = \dfrac{1}{2}$.

3. If $\sec\theta = 12$, find the value of $\csc\theta$ assuming that $\sin\theta < 0$.

   Solution: $-\dfrac{12\sqrt{143}}{143}$

   Explanation: Since $\sec\theta = 12$ and $\cos\theta = \dfrac{1}{\sec\theta}$, $\cos\theta = \dfrac{1}{12}$.

   Use the Pythagorean identity to find $\sin\theta$:

   $\sin^2\theta + \cos^2\theta = 1;\ \sin^2\theta + \left(\dfrac{1}{12}\right)^2 = 1;\ \sin^2\theta + \dfrac{1}{144} = 1;\ \sin^2\theta = \dfrac{143}{144};\ \sin\theta = \pm\dfrac{\sqrt{143}}{12}.$

   Since $\sin\theta < 0$, $\sin\theta = -\dfrac{\sqrt{143}}{12}$. Thus, $\csc\theta = \dfrac{1}{\sin\theta} = -\dfrac{12}{\sqrt{143}} = -\dfrac{12\sqrt{143}}{143}$.

Practice problems: *(Answers on page: 456)*

1. Find $\cos\theta$, if $\sin\theta = \dfrac{1}{2}$. (The angle is in the first quadrant).

2. If the cotangent of θ is 2 in the first quadrant, what is the secant of θ?

3. Suppose $\csc\theta = 6$ and $\cos\theta < 0$. What is $\cot\theta$?

Review questions: *(Answers to odd questions on page: 456)*

1. If the cosine of θ is $\dfrac{1}{2}$ and the sine of θ is $\dfrac{\sqrt{3}}{2}$, what is the tangent of θ?

2. If $\cos q = 1$, what is the value of $\sin q$?

3. Given that $\sin\theta = .65$ and θ is in the first quadrant, what is the value of $\tan\theta$?

4. What is the cosecant of θ if the cosine of θ is equal to $\dfrac{\sqrt{3}}{2}$ and θ lies in Quadrant I?

5. If $\sec^2 q = 5$, and q lies in Quadrant I, what is the value of $\tan q$?

Simplifying a Trigonometric Expression Using Trigonometric Identities

- **Review**: The four basic **trigonometric identities**:

  1. $\tan\theta = \dfrac{\sin\theta}{\cos\theta}$

  2. $\sin^2\theta + \cos^2\theta = 1$ (the **Pythagorean identity**)

  3. $1 + \tan^2\theta = \sec^2\theta$

  4. $1 + \cot^2\theta = \csc^2\theta$

- You can use trigonometric identities to help you simplify complicated trigonometric expressions.
- Writing a trigonometric function in terms of just sines and cosines often makes it easier to simplify.

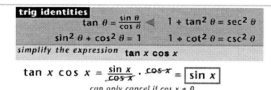

You have seen how using **trigonometric identities** can help you find the values of trigonometric functions. They can also help you simplify complicated trigonometric expressions.

In this example, you can simplify the expression $\tan x \cos x$ by rewriting $\tan x$ as the fraction $\sin x\,/\cos x$.

After canceling and restricting the value of x, $\tan x \cos x$ simplifies to $\sin x$.

---

trig identities
$$\tan\theta = \frac{\sin\theta}{\cos\theta} \qquad 1 + \tan^2\theta = \sec^2\theta$$
$$\sin^2\theta + \cos^2\theta = 1 \qquad 1 + \cot^2\theta = \csc^2\theta$$

simplify the expression

$$\frac{1 + \tan^2\theta}{\csc^2\theta} = \frac{\sec^2\theta}{\csc^2\theta}$$

$$= \frac{1/\cos^2\theta}{1/\sin^2\theta} \qquad \text{convert to sin and cos}$$

$$= \frac{1}{\cos^2\theta} \cdot \frac{\sin^2\theta}{1}$$

$$= \frac{\sin^2\theta}{\cos^2\theta} = \frac{\sin\theta}{\cos\theta} \cdot \frac{\sin\theta}{\cos\theta}$$

$$= \boxed{\tan^2\theta}$$

Consider the example, $\dfrac{1 + \tan^2\theta}{\csc^2\theta}$. To simplify, first rewrite the numerator, $1 + \tan^2\theta$, as $\sec^2\theta$. Next, convert everything to sines and cosines.

REMEMBER: It is often easier to simplify a trigonometric expression when it is written in terms of just sines and cosines.

The answer is pretty simple!

---

simplify the expression

$$\frac{1 - \cos^2 t}{\sin t} = \frac{\sin^2 t}{\sin t}$$

$$= \frac{\sin t \, \sin t}{\sin t}$$

$$= \boxed{\sin t}$$

To simplify the expression given here, first use the **Pythagorean identity** to simplify the numerator.

Next, express the numerator in factored form. Cancel the common factor, $\sin t$, from the numerator and denominator.

NOTICE: You can only cancel terms from the numerator and denominator if you promise that the denominator will never equal 0.

Sample problems:

1. Simplify: $\dfrac{\sin^3 x}{\cos x} + \sin x \cos x$

   Solution: $\tan x$

   Explanation: Find a common denominator and add the terms: $\dfrac{\sin^3 x}{\cos x} + \sin x \cos x = \dfrac{\sin^3 x}{\cos x} + \dfrac{\sin x \cos^2 x}{\cos x} = \dfrac{\sin^3 x + \sin x \cos^2 x}{\cos x}$.

   Factor the numerator: $\dfrac{\sin^3 x + \sin x \cos^2 x}{\cos x} = \dfrac{\sin x (\sin^2 x + \cos^2 x)}{\cos x}$.

   Use the Pythagorean identity to simplify: $\dfrac{\sin x (\sin^2 x + \cos^2 x)}{\cos x} = \dfrac{\sin x (1)}{\cos x} = \dfrac{\sin x}{\cos x} = \tan x$.

2. Simplify: $\dfrac{\sec^2 \theta - \tan^2 \theta}{\cot^2 \theta - \csc^2 \theta}$

   Solution: -1

   Explanation: Use the identities $(1 + \tan^2 \theta = \sec^2 \theta$ and $1 + \cot^2 \theta = \csc^2 \theta)$ to simplify:

   $\dfrac{\sec^2 \theta - \tan^2 \theta}{\cot^2 \theta - \csc^2 \theta} = \dfrac{\left(1 + \tan^2 \theta\right) - \tan^2 \theta}{\cot^2 \theta - \left(1 + \cot^2 \theta\right)} = \dfrac{1}{-1} = -1$.

3. Simplify: $\left(\csc^2 t - 1\right)\left(\csc^2 t \cdot \dfrac{1}{\sec^2 t}\right)$

   Solution: $\cot^4 t$

   Explanation: Rewrite the identity $1 + \cot^2 \theta = \csc^2 \theta$ as $\cot^2 \theta = \csc^2 \theta - 1$ and simplify:

   $\left(\csc^2 t - 1\right)\left(\csc^2 t \cdot \dfrac{1}{\sec^2 t}\right) = \cot^2 t\left(\csc^2 t \cdot \dfrac{1}{\sec^2 t}\right)$, since $\cot^2 t = \csc^2 t - 1$.

   Use the identities $\csc^2 t = \dfrac{1}{\sin^2 t}$ and $\dfrac{1}{\sec^2 t} = \cos^2 t$ to further simplify:

   $\cot^2 t\left(\csc^2 t \cdot \dfrac{1}{\sec^2 t}\right) = \cot^2 t\left(\dfrac{1}{\sin^2 t} \cdot \cos^2 t\right) = \cot^2 t\left(\dfrac{\cos^2 t}{\sin^2 t}\right) = \cot^2 t\left(\cot^2 t\right) = \cot^4 t$.

Practice problems: *(Answers on page: 456)*

1. Simplify: $\dfrac{\sec^2 x - 1}{\sec^2 x}$

2. Simplify: $\sin^2 t \csc^2 t - \cos^2 t$

3. Simplify: $(\sec^2 \theta - 1)(\csc^2 \theta \cos^2 \theta)$

Review questions: *(Answers to odd questions on page: 456)*

1. Simplify: $\csc \theta \tan \theta$

2. Simplify: $\tan^2 x \csc^2 x$

3. Simplify: $\tan x \sin x \sec x$

4. Simplify: $\tan^2 x (1 + \cot^2 x)$

5. Simplify: $\sin^2 x (1 + \cot^2 x)$

Simplifying Trigonometric Expressions Involving Fractions

- **Review**: The four basic **trigonometric identities**:

   1. $\tan \theta = \dfrac{\sin \theta}{\cos \theta}$

   2. $\sin^2 \theta + \cos^2 \theta = 1$ (the **Pythagorean identity**)

   3. $1 + \tan^2 \theta = \sec^2 \theta$

   4. $1 + \cot^2 \theta = \csc^2 \theta$

- **Review**: You can use trigonometric identities to help you simplify complicated trigonometric expressions.
- **Review**: Writing a trig function in terms of just sines and cosines often makes it easier to simplify.

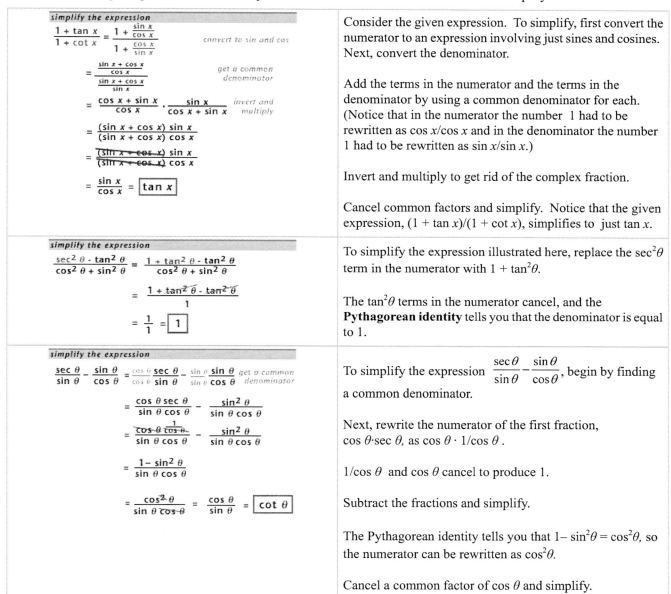

Consider the given expression. To simplify, first convert the numerator to an expression involving just sines and cosines. Next, convert the denominator.

Add the terms in the numerator and the terms in the denominator by using a common denominator for each. (Notice that in the numerator the number 1 had to be rewritten as $\cos x/\cos x$ and in the denominator the number 1 had to be rewritten as $\sin x/\sin x$.)

Invert and multiply to get rid of the complex fraction.

Cancel common factors and simplify. Notice that the given expression, $(1 + \tan x)/(1 + \cot x)$, simplifies to just $\tan x$.

To simplify the expression illustrated here, replace the $\sec^2\theta$ term in the numerator with $1 + \tan^2\theta$.

The $\tan^2\theta$ terms in the numerator cancel, and the **Pythagorean identity** tells you that the denominator is equal to 1.

To simplify the expression $\dfrac{\sec \theta}{\sin \theta} - \dfrac{\sin \theta}{\cos \theta}$, begin by finding a common denominator.

Next, rewrite the numerator of the first fraction, $\cos \theta \cdot \sec \theta$, as $\cos \theta \cdot 1/\cos \theta$.

$1/\cos \theta$ and $\cos \theta$ cancel to produce 1.

Subtract the fractions and simplify.

The Pythagorean identity tells you that $1 - \sin^2\theta = \cos^2\theta$, so the numerator can be rewritten as $\cos^2\theta$.

Cancel a common factor of $\cos \theta$ and simplify.

Sample problems:

1. Simplify: $\dfrac{\sin x - 1}{\cos x} - \dfrac{\cos x}{\sin x - 1}$

   Solution: $2\tan x$

   Explanation: Find a common denominator and subtract:

   $$\dfrac{\sin x - 1}{\cos x}\left(\dfrac{\sin x - 1}{\sin x - 1}\right) - \dfrac{\cos x}{\sin x - 1}\left(\dfrac{\cos x}{\cos x}\right) = \dfrac{(\sin x - 1)^2 - \cos^2 x}{\cos x(\sin x - 1)} = \dfrac{\sin^2 x - 2\sin x + 1 - \cos^2 x}{\cos x(\sin x - 1)}.$$

   Use the Pythagorean identity to substitute $\sin^2 x$ for $1 - \cos^2 x$ and simplify:

   $$\dfrac{\sin^2 x - 2\sin x + (1 - \cos^2 x)}{\cos x(\sin x - 1)} = \dfrac{\sin^2 x - 2\sin x + \sin^2 x}{\cos x(\sin x - 1)} = \dfrac{2\sin^2 x - 2\sin x}{\cos x(\sin x - 1)}.$$

   Factor the numerator and simplify: $\dfrac{2\sin x(\sin x - 1)}{\cos x(\sin x - 1)} = \dfrac{2\sin x}{\cos x} = 2\tan x.$

   (Note that $\sin x \neq 1$ when the factors of $\sin x - 1$ are canceled.)

2. Simplify: $\dfrac{1 - \tan^2 \theta}{1 + \tan^2 \theta}$

   Solution: $\cos^2 \theta - \sin^2 \theta$

   Explanation: Express in terms of $\sin\theta$ and $\cos\theta$: $\dfrac{1 - \tan^2 \theta}{1 + \tan^2 \theta} = \dfrac{1 - \dfrac{\sin^2 \theta}{\cos^2 \theta}}{1 + \dfrac{\sin^2 \theta}{\cos^2 \theta}}.$

   Multiply by $\dfrac{\cos^2\theta}{\cos^2\theta}$ and simplify: $\dfrac{1 - \dfrac{\sin^2 \theta}{\cos^2 \theta}}{1 + \dfrac{\sin^2 \theta}{\cos^2 \theta}} \cdot \dfrac{\cos^2 \theta}{\cos^2 \theta} = \dfrac{\left(1 - \dfrac{\sin^2 \theta}{\cos^2 \theta}\right) \cdot \cos^2 \theta}{\left(1 + \dfrac{\sin^2 \theta}{\cos^2 \theta}\right) \cdot \cos^2 \theta} =$

   $\dfrac{\cos^2 \theta - \sin^2 \theta}{\cos^2 \theta + \sin^2 \theta} = \dfrac{\cos^2 \theta - \sin^2 \theta}{1} = \cos^2 \theta - \sin^2 \theta.$

3. Simplify: $\dfrac{\sec^2 \theta}{1 + \tan^2 \theta} + \dfrac{\tan^2 \theta}{\sec^2 \theta - 1}$

   Solution: 2

   Explanation: Use the Pythagorean identity $(1 + \tan^2 \theta = \sec^2 \theta)$ to substitute:

   $\dfrac{\sec^2 \theta}{1 + \tan^2 \theta} + \dfrac{\tan^2 \theta}{\sec^2 \theta - 1} = \dfrac{\sec^2 \theta}{\sec^2 \theta} + \dfrac{\tan^2 \theta}{\tan^2 \theta} = 1 + 1 = 2.$

Practice problems: *(Answers on page: 456)*

1. Simplify: $\csc\theta\left(\sin\theta + \dfrac{1}{\sec\theta}\right)$

2. Simplify: $\dfrac{(1 + \sin^2 \theta) - (1 - \cos^2 \theta)}{\sec^2 \theta - 1}$

3. Simplify: $\dfrac{\cot^2 x}{(1 - \sin^2 x)} + \dfrac{\tan^2 x}{(1 - \cos^2 x)}$

Review questions: *(Answers to odd questions on page: 456)*

1. Simplify: $\dfrac{\cos x \csc x}{\cot x}$

2. Simplify: $\dfrac{\tan x}{\cos x} \cdot \dfrac{\sec x}{\cot x}$

3. Simplify: $\dfrac{\sec\theta\tan\theta}{\cot\theta\csc\theta}$

4. Simplify: $\dfrac{\tan x + \cot x}{\cot x - \tan x}$

5. Simplify: $\dfrac{\tan^2 t}{\sec^2 t} + \dfrac{\cot^2 t}{\csc^2 t}$

Simplifying Products of Binomials Involving Trigonometric Functions

- **Review:** Four basic **trigonometric identities**:

  - $\tan\theta = \dfrac{\sin\theta}{\cos\theta}$

  - $\cos^2\theta + \sin^2\theta = 1$ (the **Pythagorean identity**)

  - $1 + \tan^2\theta = \sec^2\theta$

  - $1 + \cot^2\theta = \csc^2\theta$

- To simplify a product of trigonometric expressions, first multiply everything out. Then use trig identities to simplify the result.
- **Review:** Rewriting expressions in terms of sines and cosines often makes simplifying easier.

simplify the expression $(\cos\theta + 1)(\cos\theta - 1) = \cos^2\theta + \cos\theta - \cos\theta - 1$ $= \cos^2\theta - 1$ $\cos^2\theta + \sin^2\theta = 1$ $\cos^2\theta + \sin^2\theta - 1 = 0$ $\cos^2\theta - 1 = -\sin^2\theta$ $\boxed{-\sin^2\theta}$	To simplify this product of two binomials, first multiply the terms using the **FOIL** method. Next, use the **Pythagorean identity** to simplify: $\cos^2\theta - 1$ becomes $-\sin\theta$. Therefore, $(\cos\theta + 1)(\cos\theta - 1)$ simplifies to $-\sin^2\theta$.
simplify the expression $(\csc x - \sin x)^2 = (\csc x - \sin x)(\csc x - \sin x)$ $= \csc^2 x - \sin x \csc x - \sin x \csc x + \sin^2 x$ $= \csc^2 x - 2\sin x \csc x + \sin^2 x$ $= \csc^2 x - 2\sin x \cdot \dfrac{1}{\sin x} + \sin^2 x$ $= \csc^2 x - 2(1) + \sin^2 x$ *rewrite in terms of sin x and cos x* $= \dfrac{1}{\sin^2 x} - 2 + \sin^2 x$ *get a common denominator* $= \dfrac{1}{\sin^2 x} + \dfrac{\sin^4 x}{\sin^2 x} - \dfrac{2\sin^2 x}{\sin^2 x}$ $= \dfrac{1 + \sin^4 x - 2\sin^2 x}{\sin^2 x}$ $s^2 - 2s + 1$ $= (s-1)(s-1)$ $= (s-1)^2$ $= \dfrac{(\sin^2 x)^2 - 2(\sin^2 x) + 1}{\sin^2 x}$ $\cos^2 x + \sin^2 x = 1$ $\cos^2 x + \sin^2 x - 1 = 0$ $\sin^2 x - 1 = -\cos^2 x$ $= \dfrac{(\sin^2 x - 1)(\sin^2 x - 1)}{\sin^2 x}$ $= \dfrac{(-\cos^2 x)(-\cos^2 x)}{\sin^2 x}$ $= \dfrac{\cos^4 x}{\sin^2 x}$ *Remember:* $\cot x = \dfrac{\cos x}{\sin x}$ $= \boxed{\cos^2 x \cot^2 x}$	Consider the example illustrated here. Begin rewriting the squared expression as a product of two binomials. Use the FOIL method to multiply. Next, combine like terms. Rewrite $2\sin x \cdot\csc x$ as $2\sin x \cdot 1/\sin x$. Cancel a common factor of $\sin x$ and simplify. Rewrite $\csc^2 x$ as $1/\sin^2 x$. Find a common denominator and combine fractions. Notice, $\sin^4 x$ can be expressed as $(\sin^2 x)^2$. Treat the $\sin^2 x$ terms as you would treat a regular variable, like s, and factor the numerator. Simplify using the Pythagorean identity. Eliminate the fraction by writing the expression using the cotangent function.

simplify the expression $(\csc x - \sin x)^2 = (\frac{1}{\sin x} - \sin x)^2 \quad$ *convert to sin and cos* $= (\frac{1}{\sin x} - \frac{\sin^2 x}{\sin x})^2 \quad$ *get a common denominator* $= (\frac{1 - \sin^2 x}{\sin x})^2$ $= (\frac{\cos^2 x}{\sin x})^2$ $= \frac{\cos^4 x}{\sin^2 x}$ $= \boxed{\cos^2 x \cot^2 x}$	Take a look at that problem again. This time, convert everything to sines and cosines first before doing any simplifying. Combine terms using a common denominator. Use the Pythagorean identity to simplify the numerator. You get the same answer with a lot less work! **REMEMBER:** Converting everything to sines and cosines often makes simplifying a trig function easier.

Sample problems:

1. Simplify: $\dfrac{2}{\sin\theta + 1} - \dfrac{2}{\sin\theta - 1}$

   Solution: $4\sec^2\theta$

   Explanation: Find a common denominator and subtract:

   $$\frac{2}{\sin\theta+1} - \frac{2}{\sin\theta-1} = \frac{2(\sin\theta-1)-2(\sin\theta+1)}{(\sin\theta+1)(\sin\theta-1)} = \frac{2\sin\theta-2-2\sin\theta-2}{(\sin\theta+1)(\sin\theta-1)} = \frac{-4}{(\sin\theta+1)(\sin\theta-1)}.$$

   Multiply the binomials in the denominator and simplify using the Pythagorean identity:

   $$\frac{-4}{(\sin\theta+1)(\sin\theta-1)} = \frac{-4}{\sin^2\theta-1} = \frac{-4}{-\cos^2\theta} = \frac{4}{\cos^2\theta} = 4\sec^2\theta.$$

2. Simplify: $(\csc x + \cot x)(\csc x - \cot x)$

   Solution: 1

   Explanation: Multiply the binomials: $(\csc x + \cot x)(\csc x - \cot x) =$ $\csc^2 x - \csc x \cot x + \cot x \csc x - \cot^2 x = \csc^2 x - \cot^2 x$. Use the identity $\csc^2 x = \cot^2 x + 1$ to simplify: $\csc^2 x - \cot^2 x = \cot^2 x + 1 - \cot^2 x = 1$.

3. Simplify: $[\csc x - (\sec^2 x - \tan^2 x)][\csc x + (\sec^2 x - \tan^2 x)]$

   Solution: $\cot^2 x$

   Explanation: Use the Pythagorean identity to rewrite $(\sec^2 x - \tan^2 x)$ as 1 then multiply the binomials: $[\csc x - (\sec^2 x - \tan^2 x)][\csc x + (\sec^2 x - \tan^2 x)] = (\csc x - 1)(\csc x + 1) = \csc^2 x - 1$. Use the Pythagorean identity to rewrite $\csc^2 x - 1$ as $\cot^2 x$: $\csc^2 x - 1 = \cot^2 x$.

Practice problems: *(Answers on page: 456)*

1. Simplify: $(1 + \sin^2\theta)(1 + \cot^2\theta)$

2. Simplify: $(\cos t - \sec t)^2$

3. Simplify: $[\cot\theta + (\cos^2\theta + \sin^2\theta)][\cot\theta - (\cos^2\theta + \sin^2\theta)]$

Review questions: *(Answers to odd questions on page: 456)*

1. Simplify: $(\sin x - 1)(\sin x + 1)$

2. Simplify: $(\sec t - 1)(\sec t + 1)$

3. Simplify: $(\tan x - \sin x)(\tan x + \sin x)$

4. Simplify: $(\sin\alpha + \cos\alpha)^2$

5. Simplify: $(\cot x - \cos x)(\cot x + \cos x)$

Factoring Trigonometric Expressions

- **Review:** Four basic **trigonometric identities**:
  - $\tan\theta = \dfrac{\sin\theta}{\cos\theta}$
  - $\cos^2\theta + \sin^2\theta = 1$ (the **Pythagorean identity**)
  - $1 + \tan^2\theta = \sec^2\theta$
  - $1 + \cot^2\theta = \csc^2\theta$
- Trigonometric expressions can be **factored** just like **polynomials**. When factoring a trigonometric expression, use trigonometric identities to rewrite or simplify the expression.
- **Review:** Rewriting expressions in terms of sine or cosine often makes simplifying easier.

factor the trig expression $\sin^2\theta + \sin^2\theta\,\tan^2\theta = \sin^2\theta\,(1 + \tan^2\theta)$ $\hspace{3cm}$ *factor out $\sin^2\theta$* $= \sin^2\theta\,\sec^2\theta$ $= \sin^2\theta \cdot \dfrac{1}{\cos^2\theta}$ $= \left(\dfrac{\sin\theta}{\cos\theta}\right)^2$ $= \boxed{\tan^2\theta}$	Just as you can multiply out trigonometric expressions, you can also **factor** them. Consider this example. For the given expression, $\sin^2\theta + \sin^2\theta\cdot\tan^2\theta$, you can factor out $\sin^2\theta$ to produce $\sin^2\theta(1+\tan^2\theta)$. Next, rewrite $1 + \tan^2\theta$ term as $\sec^2$. Simplify further and the final answer is $\tan^2\theta$.
factor the trig expression $\sin x - \cos^2 x - 1 = \sin x - (1 - \sin^2 x) - 1$ *rewrite in terms of $\sin x$* $= \sin x - 1 + \sin^2 x - 1$ $= \sin^2 x + \sin x - 2$ $\begin{array}{l} s^2 + s - 2 \\ =(s + 2)(s - 1) \end{array}$ $\quad = (\sin x + 2)(\sin x - 1)$	The expression given here has sines and cosines in it. How can you possibly factor it? Use the **Pythagorean identity** to write everything in terms of $\sin x$. Then factor as you would factor a regular **polynomial**, treating the $\sin x$ term as you would treat a regular variable.
factor the trig expression $\sin^2 x + \dfrac{2}{\csc x} + 1 = \sin^2 x + \dfrac{2}{1/\sin x} + 1$ $= \sin^2 x + \left(2 \cdot \dfrac{\sin x}{1}\right) + 1$ $= \sin^2 x + 2\sin x + 1$ $= (\sin x + 1)(\sin x + 1)$ $= \boxed{(\sin x + 1)^2}$	To factor this example, first replace $\csc x$ with $\sin x$ so that everything is in terms of sine. This expression factors like a perfect square.

Sample problems:

1. Simplify: $\sec^2 x + 6\tan x + 8$

   Solution: $(\tan x + 3)^2$

   Explanation: Use the identity $\sec^2 x = \tan^2 x + 1$ to write the expression in terms $\tan x$:

   $\sec^2 x + 6\tan x + 8 = \left(\tan^2 x + 1\right) + 6\tan x + 8 = \tan^2 x + 6\tan x + 9$ (which is a perfect square trinomial). Factor: $\tan^2 x + 6\tan x + 9 = \left(\tan x + 3\right)\left(\tan x + 3\right) = \left(\tan x + 3\right)^2$.

2. Simplify: $\dfrac{\sin^3 x + \cos^3 x}{\cos x + \sin x}$

Solution: $1 - \sin x \cos x$

Explanation: The numerator is the sum of two cubes and can be factored:

$$\frac{\sin^3 x + \cos^3 x}{\cos x + \sin x} = \frac{(\sin x + \cos x)(\sin^2 x - \sin x \cos x + \cos^2 x)}{\cos x + \sin x} = \sin^2 x - \sin x \cos x + \cos^2 x.$$

Use the Pythagorean identity:

$$\sin^2 x - \sin x \cos x + \cos^2 x = (\sin^2 x + \cos^2 x) - \sin x \cos x = 1 - \sin x \cos x.$$

(Note: $\cos x + \sin x \neq 0$.)

3. Simplify: $\cos^2 t + 4 + \dfrac{4}{\sec t}$

Solution: $(\cos t + 2)^2$

Explanation: Express in terms of cosine:

$$\cos^2 t + 4 + \frac{4}{\sec t} = \cos^2 t + 4 + \frac{4}{\frac{1}{\cos t}} = \cos^2 t + 4 + 4\cos t.$$

Factor this perfect square trinomial:

$$\cos^2 t + 4\cos t + 4 = (\cos t + 2)(\cos t + 2) = (\cos t + 2)^2.$$

Practice problems: *(Answers on page: 456)*

1. Simplify: $2\cos^2 \theta + 10\cos \theta + 12$

2. Simplify: $\cos\theta \tan\theta + \cos\theta \cot\theta$

3. Simplify: $\dfrac{\sin^2 a - \cos^2 a}{\sin^2 a - \sin a \cos a}$

Review questions: *(Answers to odd questions on page: 456)*

1. Simplify: $\sin^2 q + \cot^2 q \sin^2 q$

2. Simplify: $\sin x - \cos^2 x \sin x$

3. Simplify: $\cos^2 x + \tan^2 x \cos^2 x$

4. Simplify: $\sin^2 x + \sin^2 x \cot^2 x$

5. Simplify: $\csc^2 \theta - \cot^2 \theta$

Determining Whether a Trigonometric Function Is Odd, Even, or Neither

- **Review:** A function $f(x)$ is **odd** if $f(-x) = -f(x)$ and **even** if $f(-x) = f(x)$. The graphs of odd functions are symmetric about the origin and the graphs of even functions are symmetric about the y-axis. A function can also be neither even nor odd.
- The sine and tangent functions are odd and the cosine function is even.

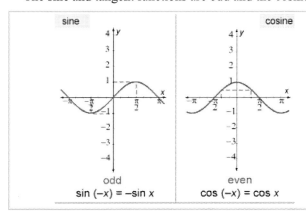

Recall that a function $f(x)$ is **odd** if $f(-x) = -f(x)$ and **even** if $f(-x) = f(x)$. The graphs of odd functions are symmetric about the origin while the graphs of even functions are symmetric about the y-axis.

The sine function is symmetric about the origin; therefore, sine is an odd function.

The cosine function is symmetric across the y-axis; therefore, cosine is an even function.

f(x) = tan x

a) look at the graph.

odd

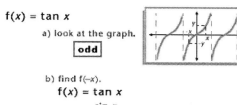

b) find f(-x).

f(x) = tan x

$= \dfrac{\sin x}{\cos x}$ *replace x with -x*

$f(-x) = \dfrac{\sin(-x)}{\cos(-x)}$

$= \dfrac{-\sin x}{\cos x}$

= -tan x = -f(x)

So f(-x) = -f(x), therefore the function is odd.

The graph of $y = \tan x$ is symmetric about the origin. Therefore, the tangent function is an odd function.

Check this algebraically by computing the value of $\tan(-x)$.

The sine function is odd; $\sin(-x) = -\sin x$.
The cosine function is even; $\cos(-x) = \cos x$.

Since $\tan x = \dfrac{\sin x}{\cos x}$, then $\tan(-x) = \dfrac{-\sin x}{\cos x} = -\tan x$; therefore, the tangent function is odd.

Example

$f(x) = \dfrac{\sin x}{x}$

$f(-x) = \dfrac{\sin(-x)}{(-x)}$

$= \dfrac{-\sin x}{-x}$ *(odd)*/*(odd)*

$= \dfrac{\sin x}{x}$

= f(x)

So f(-x) = f(x), therefore the function is even.

$\dfrac{\text{odd}}{\text{odd}} = \text{even}$

Consider the example here: $f(x) = \sin x/x$.

To determine whether the function is odd, even, or neither, compute the value of $f(-x)$.

Substituting $-x$ for x and simplifying yields $f(-x) = f(x)$; therefore, the function is even.

Another way to see this is to note that both $\sin x$ and x are odd functions. Think of them as you would the signs on numbers: negative/negative = positive. In the same way, when dealing with functions, odd/odd = even.

Sample problems:

1. Is the function $f(x) = \sin x + \cos x$ odd, even, or neither?
   Solution: Neither
   Explanation: A function $f(x)$ is even if $f(-x) = f(x)$ and odd if $f(-x) = -f(x)$. Evaluate $f(-x)$: $f(-x) = \sin(-x) + \cos(-x) = -\sin x + \cos x$. Since $f(-x) \neq \sin x + \cos x$ and $f(-x) \neq -(\sin x - \cos x)$, the function is neither even nor odd.

2. Is the function $f(x) = x^2 \sin x \cos x$ odd, even, or neither?
   Solution: Odd
   Explanation: A function $f(x)$ is even if $f(-x) = f(x)$ and odd if $f(-x) = -f(x)$. Evaluate $f(-x)$, remembering that $\sin(-x) = -\sin x$ and $\cos(-x) = \cos x$: $f(-x) = (-x)^2 \sin(-x)\cos(-x) = x^2(-\sin x)(\cos x) = -x^2 \sin x \cos x = -f(x)$. Since $f(-x) = -f(x)$, the function is odd.

3. Is the function $f(x) = \sec x + \sin^2 x$ odd, even, or neither?
   Solution: Even
   Explanation:
   Evaluate $f(-x)$: $f(-x) = \sec(-x) + \sin^2(-x)$

   $= \dfrac{1}{\cos(-x)} + \big(\sin(-x)\big)\big(\sin(-x)\big)$

   $= \dfrac{1}{\cos x} + \big(-\sin x\big)\big(-\sin x\big)$

   $= \sec x + \sin^2 x.$

   Therefore, $f(-x) = f(x)$, so $f(x) = \sec x + \sin^2 x$ is an even function.

Practice problems: *(Answers on page: 456)*

1. Is this the graph of even or odd function?

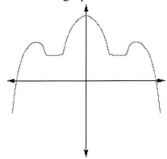

2. Is the function $f(x) = \csc x$ even, odd, or neither?

3. Is the function $f(x) = \tan x \sec x$ even, odd, or neither?

Review questions: *(Answers to odd questions on page: 456)*

1. Is the function $g(x) = 2 \sin x \cos x \tan^2 x$ odd, even or neither?

2. Is the function $f(x) = \csc x \cot x$ odd, even or neither?

3. Is the function $h(x) = \cos x (\sin x + 2)$ odd, even or neither?

4. Is the function $f(x) = 3 \sin x \tan x$ odd, even or neither?

5. Is the function $g(x) = \dfrac{(x-1)^3 \tan^2 x}{\sin^3 x}$ odd, even or neither?

Proving an Identity

- **Review:** An **identity** is a mathematical statement that is true for all meaningful values of the variable(s) involved.
- When proving an identity, treat each side of the equal sign as its own expression. Do not treat the identity as an equality until it is proven that both sides are equal.

Proving an Identity – manipulate each side of the equal sign independently – try to make both sides the same	Often in trigonometry you are given an equation and asked to show whether or not the statement is true. When proving an **identity**, remember to only manipulate one side of the proposed equality at a time.
Fundamental Identities $\qquad \tan \theta = \dfrac{\sin \theta}{\cos \theta}$ $\sec \theta = \dfrac{1}{\cos \theta} \quad \csc \theta = \dfrac{1}{\sin \theta} \quad \sin^2 \theta + \cos^2 \theta = 1$	The four basic trigonometric identities will be used often.

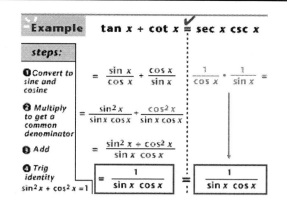

When proving an identity, it is often useful to draw a line down the middle. Only work on one side of the line at a time.

Consider the given example. First express both sides of the identity in terms of sine and cosine.

Next, try to manipulate the left side of the identity until it is identical to the right side of the identity.

Working on the left side of the equal sign, find a common denominator in order to add sin x/cos x + cos x/sin x. Combine like terms.

You can use trig identities to simplify the expression. In this case the numerator, $\sin^2 x + \cos^2 x$, was replaced with the number 1 by the basic identity $\sin^2 x + \cos^2 x = 1$.

Now that both sides of the identity are identical, the proof is finished and the stated identity is true.

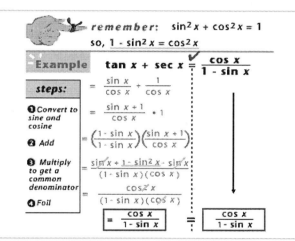

Draw a line down the middle to separate the equality into two expressions.

Change tan x + sec x to an expression in terms of sine and cosine. Add like terms.

Next, multiply by a well-chosen fraction equal to 1 and simplify.

Both sides are the same; therefore the identity must be true.

Sample problems:

1. True or false: $\dfrac{\csc\theta - \cot\theta}{\sec\theta - \tan\theta} = \cot\theta$ is an identity.

   Solution: False

   Explanation:

   Express each side in terms of sine and cosine: $\dfrac{\csc\theta - \cot\theta}{\sec\theta - \tan\theta} = \cot\theta \implies \dfrac{\dfrac{1}{\sin\theta} - \dfrac{\cos\theta}{\sin\theta}}{\dfrac{1}{\cos\theta} - \dfrac{\sin\theta}{\cos\theta}} = \dfrac{\cos\theta}{\sin\theta}$.

   Subtract the terms in the numerator and denominator: $\dfrac{\dfrac{1-\cos\theta}{\sin\theta}}{\dfrac{1-\sin\theta}{\cos\theta}} = \dfrac{\cos\theta}{\sin\theta}$.

   Complete the division on the left side: $\dfrac{1-\cos\theta}{\sin\theta} \cdot \dfrac{\cos\theta}{1-\sin\theta} = \dfrac{\cos\theta}{\sin\theta} \implies \dfrac{1-\cos\theta}{1-\sin\theta} \cdot \dfrac{\cos\theta}{\sin\theta} = \dfrac{\cos\theta}{\sin\theta}$.

   On either side of the equal sign, there is a factor of $\dfrac{\cos\theta}{\sin\theta}$. So, in order for the equation to be an identity, $\dfrac{1-\cos\theta}{1-\sin\theta}$ must equal 1: $\dfrac{1-\cos\theta}{1-\sin\theta} = 1$; $1-\cos\theta = 1-\sin\theta$; $\cos\theta = \sin\theta$.

   Since $\cos\theta$ does not equal $\sin\theta$, $\dfrac{1-\cos\theta}{1-\sin\theta}$ does not equal 1. Therefore, the equation is not an identity.

2. True or false: $\cot x + \csc x = \dfrac{\sin x}{1-\cos x}$ is an identity.

   Solution: True

   Explanation:

   Express the left in terms of sine and cosine: $\cot x + \csc x = \dfrac{\sin x}{1-\cos x}$;

   $\dfrac{\cos x}{\sin x} + \dfrac{1}{\sin x} = \dfrac{\sin x}{1-\cos x}$; $\dfrac{\cos x + 1}{\sin x} = \dfrac{\sin x}{1-\cos x}$.

   Multiply the left hand side of the equation by a well chosen 1: $\dfrac{(1-\cos x)}{(1-\cos x)} \cdot \dfrac{\cos x + 1}{\sin x} = \dfrac{\sin x}{1-\cos x}$.

   Foil the numerator to set $\dfrac{1-\cos^2 x}{\sin x(1-\cos x)} = \dfrac{\sin x}{1-\cos x}$;

   Use the Pythagorean identity: $\dfrac{\sin^2 x}{\sin x(1-\cos x)} = \dfrac{\sin x}{1-\cos x}$.

   Cancel a $\sin x$: $\dfrac{\sin x}{1-\cos x} = \dfrac{\sin x}{1-\cos x}$

   The equation is an identity.

3. True or false: $(\sec\theta - \tan\theta)^2 = \dfrac{(1-\sin\theta)^2}{(1+\sin\theta)^2}$ is an identity.

Solution: False

Explanation:

Express the left in terms of sine and cosine: $\left(\dfrac{1}{\cos\theta} - \dfrac{\sin\theta}{\cos\theta}\right)^2 = \dfrac{(1-\sin\theta)^2}{(1+\sin\theta)^2}$;

$\dfrac{(1-\sin\theta)^2}{\cos^2\theta} = \dfrac{(1-\sin\theta)^2}{(1+\sin\theta)^2}$.

Use the Pythagorian identity: $\dfrac{(1-\sin\theta)^2}{1-\sin^2\theta} = \dfrac{(1-\sin\theta)^2}{(1+\sin\theta)^2}$.

The numerators are the same, so for this statement to be true, $1-\sin^2\theta$ must equal $(1+\sin\theta)^2$; however $1-\sin^2\theta \neq (1+\sin\theta)^2$.

The equation is not an identity.

Practice problems: *(Answers on page: 456)*

1. True or false: $\dfrac{1-\cos t}{\sin t} + \dfrac{\sin t}{1-\cos t} = 2\csc t$ is an identity.

2. True or false: $\dfrac{\csc x}{1+\csc x} = \dfrac{1-\sin x}{\cos^2 x}$ is an identity.

3. True or false: $\dfrac{\csc^2 t + 1 + \cot^2 t}{1 - \sin^2 t} = \dfrac{2}{\sin^2 t \cos^2 t}$ is an identity.

Review questions: *(Answers to odd questions on page: 456)*

1. True or false: $(\sec x \cot x)^2 - 1 = \cot^2 x$ is an identity.

2. True or false: $4\cos^2 t + 3\sin^2 t = 3\cos^2 t + 1$ is an identity.

3. True or false: $\dfrac{2\cot^2\theta}{1+\cot^2\theta} = 2\cos^2\theta$ is an identity.

4. True or false: $(\sin x - \cos x)^2 + (\sin x + \cos x)^2 = 2$ is an identity.

5. True or false: $\dfrac{1-\tan^2\theta}{1-\tan^4\theta} = \dfrac{1}{\sec^2\theta}$ is an identity.

Proving an Identity: Other Examples

- **Review:** An **identity** is a mathematical statement that is true for all meaningful values of the variable(s) involved.
- **Review:** When proving an identity, treat each side of the equal sign as its own expression. Do not treat the identity as an equality until its proven that both sides are equal.

Proving an Identity – manipulate each side of the equal sign independently – try to make both sides the same	To prove an **identity** manipulate the expressions on either side of the equal sign independently. The expression is not an equality until it is proven to be one.
Fundamental Identities $\sec\theta = \dfrac{1}{\cos\theta}$ $\csc\theta = \dfrac{1}{\sin\theta}$ $\tan\theta = \dfrac{\sin\theta}{\cos\theta}$ $\sin^2\theta + \cos^2\theta = 1$	Remember the four basic identities.

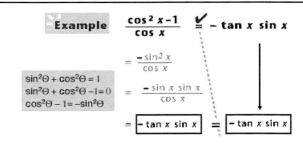

Consider the example illustrated here. Choose one side of the expression to manipulate until it is identical to the expression on the other side of the equal sign.

Use the Pythagorean identity to restate $\cos^2 x - 1$ as $-\sin^2 x$.

Break the sine-squared term into its factors. Put one of the sine terms over the cosine to get an identity (tangent).

Since both sides of the expression are identical, the statement is true; therefore, it is an identity.

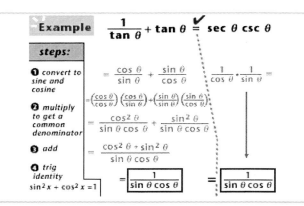

For this example, first put everything in terms of sine and cosine. Then, select one side of the expression to manipulate until it is identical to the other side of the expression.

To add the two fractions on the left-hand side, find a common denominator. Then, combine the like terms.

Use the Pythagorean identity to complete the proof.

Since both sides are identical, the equation is an identity.

Sample problems:

1. Form an identity from the following expression: $\sec^2 \theta - \sec^2 \theta \cos^2 \theta$

   Solution: $\sec^2 \theta - \sec^2 \theta \cos^2 \theta = \tan^2 \theta$

   Explanation: Factor: $\sec^2 \theta - \sec^2 \theta \cos^2 \theta = \sec^2 \theta(1 - \cos^2 \theta)$.

   Use a Pythagorean identity to write $(1 - \cos^2 \theta)$ as $\sin^2 \theta$: $\sec^2 \theta(1 - \cos^2 \theta) = \sec^2 \theta(\sin^2 \theta)$.

   Express in terms of sine and cosine and multiply: $\sec^2 \theta(\sin^2 \theta) = \dfrac{1}{\cos^2 \theta} \cdot \dfrac{\sin^2 \theta}{1} = \dfrac{\sin^2 \theta}{\cos^2 \theta} = \tan^2 \theta$.

   Therefore, $\sec^2 \theta - \sec^2 \theta \cos^2 \theta = \tan^2 \theta$ is an identity.

2. Form an identity from the following expression: $\dfrac{\sin^2 x - 1}{\sin x}$

   Solution: $\dfrac{\sin^2 x - 1}{\sin x} = -\cot x \cos x$

   Explanation: Use the Pythagorean identity: $\dfrac{\sin^2 x - 1}{\sin x} = \dfrac{-\cos^2 x}{\sin x}$.

   Factor $-\cos^2 x$ into $-\cos x$ and $\cos x$: $\dfrac{-\cos^2 x}{\sin x} = \dfrac{-\cos x \cdot \cos x}{\sin x}$.

   Combine one of the $\cos x$ factors with the $\sin x$ factor in the denominator to arrive at a $\cot x$ factor:

   $\dfrac{-\cos x \cdot \cos x}{\sin x} = \dfrac{-\cos x}{\sin x} \cos x = -\cot x \cos x$.

   Therefore $\dfrac{\sin^2 x - 1}{\sin x} = -\cot x \cos x$ is an identity.

3. Form an identity from the following expression: $\tan t \cot t - \sin^2 t$

Solution: $\tan t \cot t - \sin^2 t = \cos^2 t$

Explanation: Express in terms of sine and cosine: $\tan t \cot t - \sin^2 t = \dfrac{\sin t}{\cos t} \cdot \dfrac{\cos t}{\sin t} - \sin^2 t$.

Multiply and cancel like terms: $\dfrac{\sin t}{\cos t} \cdot \dfrac{\cos t}{\sin t} - \sin^2 t = \dfrac{\sin t \cos t}{\sin t \cos t} - \sin^2 t = 1 - \sin^2 t$.

Use a Pythagorean identity: $1 - \sin^2 t = \cos^2 t$. Thus, $\tan t \cot t - \sin^2 t = \cos^2 t$.

Therefore, $\tan t \cot t - \sin^2 t = \cos^2 t$ is an identity.

Practice problems: *(Answers on page: 456)*

1. Form an identity from the following expression: $\csc^2 \theta - \csc^2 \theta \sin \theta$

2. Form an identity from the following expression: $\dfrac{1}{\cot x} + \cot x.$

3. Form an identity from the following expression: $\dfrac{1 + 2\tan^2 x + \tan^4 x}{1 - \tan^2 x}$

Review questions: *(Answers to odd questions on page: 456)*

1. Form an identity from the following expression: $\sec^2 x \cot x - \cot x$

2. Form an identity from the following expression: $\cot^2 \theta \left(\sec^2 \theta - 1 \right)$

3. Form an identity from the following expression: $\left(\sec \theta + \cos \theta \right)\left(\sec \theta - \cos \theta \right)$

4. Form an identity from the following expression: $\dfrac{\csc^4 x - 2\csc^2 x + 1}{\cot^2 x}$

5. Form an identity from the following expression: $\sqrt{\dfrac{\left(1 - \cos \theta\right)^2}{1 - \cos^2 \theta}}$

Solving Trigonometric Equations

- Since trig functions are **periodic**, trig equations will often have many solutions. To find all the possible solutions to a trig equation, first find the solutions for a single period and then add multiples of the period to those solutions.

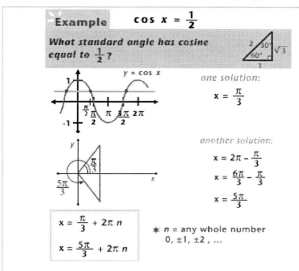

Consider the following question: what standard angle has cosine equal to 1/2?

Cos x is equal to 1/2 every time the graph of $y = \cos x$ intersects the graph of $y = 1/2$.

To find the smallest angle value, think about the angle x in a right triangle; 1 is the adjacent leg and 2 is the hypotenuse. This triangle is the 30:60:90 triangle, and the angle is $\pi/3$ or 60°.

But notice that the graph of cosine is equal to 1/2 more often than just once in a **period**. 1/2 occurs again in the 4th **quadrant**. The distance the angle covers from zero to the first solution is the same as the distance from 2π to the second solution. Subtract that distance from 2π to get the second solution.

These solutions are only for the first period. To get all the solutions, add multiples of the period 2π.

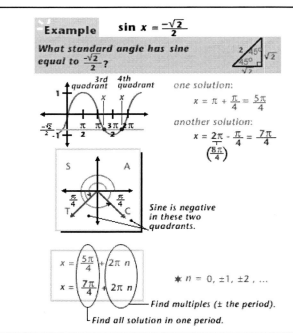

Consider the example given here. First, find the **reference angle** by ignoring the negative sign.

The reference angle is π/4 or 45°. Now, how do you find the actual value of x?

Remember that sine is negative in the third and fourth quadrants and that reference angles are measured from the x-axis.

To find the solution in the third quadrant, add π to the reference angle. To find the solution in the fourth quadrant, subtract the reference angle from 2π.

REMEMBER: This process only gives the answers in the first period of the function. Add multiples of the period to describe all the rest of the solutions.

Sample problems:

1. Find all values of x for which $\sin x = \dfrac{1}{2}$.

   Solution: $x = \dfrac{\pi}{6} + 2\pi n$ or $x = \dfrac{5\pi}{6} + 2\pi n$

   Explanation: $\text{Sin } x > 0$ in quadrant I or quadrant II; therefore, the specific solutions to the equation $\sin x = \dfrac{1}{2}$ must be in the interval $0 \le x \le \pi$. $\text{Sin } 30° = \sin \dfrac{\pi}{6} = \dfrac{1}{2}$ and $\sin 150° = \sin \dfrac{5\pi}{6} = \dfrac{1}{2}$. The period of the sine function is 2π. Adding any multiple of $2\pi \, (2\pi n)$ produces another angle value where $\sin x = \dfrac{1}{2}$.

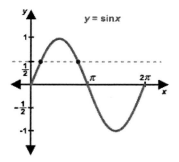

2. Solve for x: $\sin x = 0.8192$

   Solution: $x = 0.96 + 2\pi n$ and $x = 2.18 + 2\pi n$

   Explanation: Notice that the line $y = 0.8192$ passes through the graph of the sine in several places. Looking at the first period you can see that there are two solutions, one in quadrant one and the other in quadrant two. Use the arcsine function to find the value of the reference angle. Subtract that angle from π to determine the solution in the second quadrant. Finally, notice that these solutions repeat in each period, so all of the solutions are given by $x = 0.96 + 2\pi n$ and $x = 2.18 + 2\pi n$ where n is any integer.

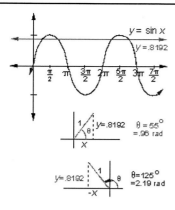

3. Solve for x: $\sin 2x = \dfrac{1}{2}$

   Solution: $x = \dfrac{\pi}{12} + \pi n$ and $x = \dfrac{5\pi}{12} + \pi n$

   Explanation: Notice that the period of sine has changed. Also notice that the line $y = \dfrac{1}{2}$ passes through the graph of $\sin 2x$ at several places. Looking at the first period, there are two solutions. In a triangle, sine is equal to the opposite over the hypotenuse, so the length of the opposite leg is 1 and the hypotenuse 2. This triangle is the 30:60:90 triangle and the angle is $30°$ or $\dfrac{\pi}{6}$. Sine is positive in the first and second quadrant because of the coefficient in the argument, $2 = \dfrac{\pi}{2}$ (in the first quadrant) and $2 = \dfrac{5\pi}{6}$ (in the second quadrant). But notice that the solution repeats each period, so all of the solutions are $x = \dfrac{\pi}{12} \pi n$ and $x = \dfrac{5\pi}{12} + \pi n$ where n is any integer.

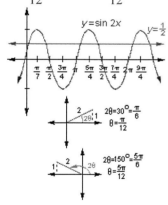

Practice problems: *(Answers on page: 456)*

1. Solve for x: $\cos x = \dfrac{\sqrt{2}}{2}$

2. Solve for x: $\sec x = -1$.

3. Solve for x: $\cos^2 x = 1$

Review questions: *(Answers to odd questions on page: 457)*

1. Find all solutions to the equation $\cos x = -1$.

2. Find all solutions to the equation $\cos x = \dfrac{\sqrt{3}}{2}$.

3. True or false: The equation $\sec x = \dfrac{1}{2}$ has no solutions.

4. Find all solutions to the equation $\sin^2 x = 1$.

5. Find all solutions to the equation $\tan x = 1$.

Solving Trigonometric Equations by Factoring

- When solving trig equations by factoring, try to isolate all the terms on one side of the equation and set it equal to zero. Then, **factor** that side of the equation so that the equation equals zero where the factors equal zero.
- **Review:** Since trig functions are **periodic**, trig equations can have many solutions. To find all the possible solutions to a trig equation, find the solutions for a single period and then add multiples of the **period** to those solutions.

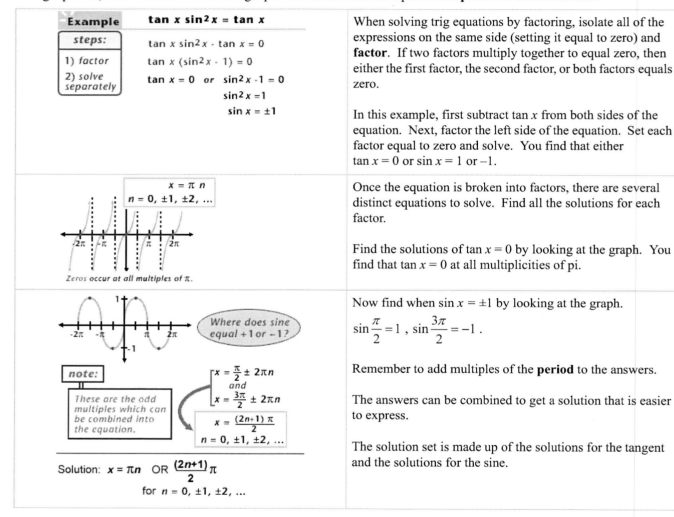

When solving trig equations by factoring, isolate all of the expressions on the same side (setting it equal to zero) and **factor**. If two factors multiply together to equal zero, then either the first factor, the second factor, or both factors equals zero.

In this example, first subtract $\tan x$ from both sides of the equation. Next, factor the left side of the equation. Set each factor equal to zero and solve. You find that either $\tan x = 0$ or $\sin x = 1$ or -1.

Once the equation is broken into factors, there are several distinct equations to solve. Find all the solutions for each factor.

Find the solutions of $\tan x = 0$ by looking at the graph. You find that $\tan x = 0$ at all multiplicities of pi.

Now find when $\sin x = \pm 1$ by looking at the graph.

$\sin \dfrac{\pi}{2} = 1$, $\sin \dfrac{3\pi}{2} = -1$.

Remember to add multiples of the **period** to the answers.

The answers can be combined to get a solution that is easier to express.

The solution set is made up of the solutions for the tangent and the solutions for the sine.

Sample problems:

1. Find all solutions in the interval $[0,2\pi)$ of the equation $2\cos\theta\sin\theta + \cos\theta = 0$.

   Solution: $\theta = \dfrac{\pi}{2}, \dfrac{7\pi}{6}, \dfrac{3\pi}{2}$, or $\dfrac{11\pi}{6}$

   Explanation: Factor: $(\cos\theta)(2\sin\theta + 1) = 0$. Set each factor equal to zero: $\cos\theta = 0$ or $2\sin\theta + 1 = 0$. For the first factor: $\cos\theta = 0$, cosine is equal to zero when θ is equal to $\dfrac{\pi}{2}$ and $\dfrac{3\pi}{2}$. Solve the second factor for θ: $2\sin\theta + 1 = 0$; $2\sin\theta = -1$; $\sin\theta = \dfrac{-1}{2}$, sine is equal to $\dfrac{-1}{2}$ when θ is equal to $\dfrac{7\pi}{6}$ and $\dfrac{11\pi}{6}$. So, the solutions within $[0,2\pi)$ are $\theta = \dfrac{\pi}{2}, \dfrac{7\pi}{6}, \dfrac{3\pi}{2}$, or $\dfrac{11\pi}{6}$.

2. Solve the equation $\sin^2 x + \sin x = 0$ on $[0,2\pi]$.

   Solution: $x = 0, \pi, \dfrac{3\pi}{2}$, or 2π

   Explanation: Factor: $\sin x(\sin x + 1) = 0$. Set each factor equal to zero: $\sin x = 0$ or $(\sin x + 1) = 0$. For the first factor: $\sin x = 0$, therefore $x = 0$, $x = \pi$ or $x = 2\pi$. Solve the second factor for x: $\sin x + 1 = 0$; $\sin x = -1$, therefore $x = \dfrac{3\pi}{2}$. So the solutions are $x = 0$, $x = \pi$, $x = \dfrac{3\pi}{2}$, and $x = 2\pi$.

3. Find all solutions to the equation $2\cos^2 x - 5\cos x = -2$.

   Solution: $x = \dfrac{\pi}{3} + 2\pi n$ or $\dfrac{5\pi}{3} + 2\pi n$

   Explanation: Manipulate the terms: $2\cos^2 x - 5\cos x + 2 = 0$. Factor: $(2\cos x - 1)(\cos x - 2) = 0$. Solve the first factor for x: $2\cos x - 1 = 0$; $\cos x = \dfrac{1}{2}$, then $x = \dfrac{\pi}{3}$ or $x = \dfrac{5\pi}{3}$. Solve the second factor for x: $\cos x - 2 = 0$; $\cos x = 2$, however this is impossible because the range of $\cos x$ is restricted to values between -1 and 1. The general solution is $x = \dfrac{\pi}{3} + 2\pi n$ or $x = \dfrac{5\pi}{3} + 2\pi n$.

Practice problems: *(Answers on page: 457)*

1. Find all solutions in the interval $[0,2\pi)$ of the equation $\sin^2\theta = \dfrac{1}{2}\sin\theta$.

2. Solve the equation $\sin x \tan x = \sin x$ on the interval $[0,2\pi)$.

3. Solve the equation $\tan^2 x \csc x = \tan^2 x$ on $[0,2\pi)$.

Review questions: *(Answers to odd questions on page: 457)*

1. Find all solutions in the interval $[0, 2\pi)$ of the equation $\sin x = \tan x$.

2. Find all solutions in the interval $[0, 2\pi)$ of the equation $\cos^2 x - 1 = -\sin x$.

3. Find all solutions in the interval $[0, 2\pi]$ of the equation $\sin x \cos x = 0$.

4. Find all solutions to the equation $2\sin x \cos x = \sin x$ in $[0, 2\pi)$.

5. Find all solutions to the equation $2\cos^2 x + \cos x = 1$ in $[0, 2\pi)$.

Solving Trigonometric Equations with Coefficients in the Argument

- Coefficients in the **argument** of a trig function change the **period** of the function. To solve an equation involving trig functions with coefficients in the arguments, first solve the equation ignoring the coefficients. Then divide the solutions through by the coefficients appropriately.
- **Review:** Since trig functions are **periodic**, they often have many solutions. To find all the possible solutions to a trig equation, find the solutions for a single period and then add multiples of the period to those solutions.

Example — Find all the solutions for one period of the given function.

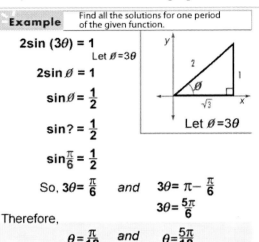

$2\sin(3\theta) = 1$

Let $\emptyset = 3\theta$

$2\sin\emptyset = 1$

$\sin\emptyset = \dfrac{1}{2}$

$\sin? = \dfrac{1}{2}$

$\sin\dfrac{\pi}{6} = \dfrac{1}{2}$

So, $3\theta = \dfrac{\pi}{6}$ and $3\theta = \pi - \dfrac{\pi}{6}$

$3\theta = \dfrac{5\pi}{6}$

Therefore,

$\theta = \dfrac{\pi}{18}$ and $\theta = \dfrac{5\pi}{18}$

To solve trig equations with coefficients in the **argument**, start by factoring (if needed) or isolating the trig function.

NOTICE: In this example we're treating 3θ as if it were a different angle called $\emptyset$ and then finding the values of $\emptyset$ that make $\sin\emptyset = 1/2$.

Divide through by the coefficient of θ to get the answers.

Example — Find all the solutions for **two** periods of the given function.

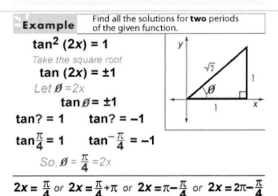

$\tan^2(2x) = 1$

Take the square root

$\tan(2x) = \pm 1$

Let $\emptyset = 2x$

$\tan\emptyset = \pm 1$

$\tan? = 1 \qquad \tan? = -1$

$\tan\dfrac{\pi}{4} = 1 \qquad \tan^{-}\dfrac{\pi}{4} = -1$

So, $\emptyset = \dfrac{\pi}{4} = 2x$

$2x = \dfrac{\pi}{4}$ or $2x = \dfrac{\pi}{4} + \pi$ or $2x = \pi - \dfrac{\pi}{4}$ or $2x = 2\pi - \dfrac{\pi}{4}$

$2x = \dfrac{5\pi}{4} \qquad 2x = \dfrac{3\pi}{4} \qquad 2x = \dfrac{7\pi}{4}$

$x = \dfrac{\pi}{8} \qquad x = \dfrac{5\pi}{8} \qquad x = \dfrac{3\pi}{8} \qquad x = \dfrac{7\pi}{8}$

Consider this example: find all the solutions for two periods of $\tan^2(2x) = 1$.

Begin by taking the square root of both sides.

Solve for the two possible equations: $\tan 2x = 1$ and $\tan 2x = -1$.

The normal tangent curve equals 1 at $\pi/4$ and $5\pi/4$, and it equals -1 at $3\pi/4$ and $7\pi/4$ in the frist two periods.

Divide these answers by the coefficient of the argument to find the solutions.

Example — Find all the solutions in the interval $[0, 2\pi]$ of the given function

$(\sin 2x)(\tan 2x) + \sin 2x = 0$

$(\sin 2x)(\tan 2x + 1) = 0$

$\sin 2x = 0$ or $\tan 2x + 1 = 0$

Substitute $\theta = 2x$

$\sin\theta = 0$ or $\tan\theta = -1$

Interval is $0 < \theta < 4\pi$

So, $\theta = 0, \pi, 2\pi, 3\pi, 4\pi$ or $\theta = \dfrac{3\pi}{4}, \dfrac{7\pi}{4}, \dfrac{11\pi}{4}, \dfrac{15\pi}{4}$

Substitute $\theta = 2x$

$2x = 0, \pi, 2\pi, 3\pi, 4\pi$ or $2x = \dfrac{3\pi}{4}, \dfrac{7\pi}{4}, \dfrac{11\pi}{4}, \dfrac{15\pi}{4}$

Divide by 2

$x = 0, \dfrac{\pi}{2}, \pi, \dfrac{3\pi}{2}, 2\pi \qquad x = \dfrac{3\pi}{8}, \dfrac{7\pi}{8}, \dfrac{11\pi}{8}, \dfrac{15\pi}{8}$

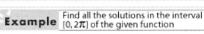

Conisder the example illustrated here: find all solutions in the interval $[0, 2\pi]$ for $(\sin 2x)(\tan 2x) + \sin 2x$.

Since $0 \le x \le 2\pi$, multiply by 2 to find the interval for $2x$: $0 \le 2x \le 4\pi$.

To solve, first factor the equation and then set each factor equal to zero. Let $\theta = 2x$ and solve for θ.

Remember the interval is now $[0, 4\pi]$.

Substitute back $2x$ for θ and divide the answers by 2 to finish the problem.

Sample problems:

1. Solve the equation $\sin 2\theta = 1$ in $[0,2\pi]$.

   Solution: $\dfrac{\pi}{4}$ or $\dfrac{5\pi}{4}$

   Explanation: Since $0 \le \theta \le 2\pi$, multiply by 2 to find the interval for 2θ: $0 \le 2\theta \le 4\pi$.

   Let $x = 2\theta$, and find all values of x on $[0,4\pi]$ where $\sin x = 1$: $x = \dfrac{\pi}{2}$ or $x = \dfrac{5\pi}{2}$.

   Substitute 2θ into each equation and solve for x: $2\theta = \dfrac{\pi}{2}$ or $2\theta = \dfrac{5\pi}{2}$; $\theta = \dfrac{\pi}{4}$

   or $\theta = \dfrac{5\pi}{4}$.

2. Find all solutions to the equation $\tan \dfrac{x}{2} = \sqrt{3}$ on $[0,2\pi]$.

   Solution: $x = \dfrac{2\pi}{3}$

   Explanation: Since $0 \le x \le 2\pi$, divide by 2 to find the interval for $\dfrac{x}{2}$: $0 \le \dfrac{x}{2} \le \pi$.

   Let $\theta = \dfrac{x}{2}$, and find all values of θ on $[0,\pi]$ where $\tan\theta = \sqrt{3}$: $\theta = \dfrac{\pi}{3}$. Substitute

   $\dfrac{x}{2}$ into the equation for θ and solve for x: $\dfrac{x}{2} = \dfrac{\pi}{3}$, then $x = \dfrac{2\pi}{3}$.

3. Find all solutions to the equation $2\cos\left(\dfrac{x}{2}\right) - \sqrt{3} = 0$ on $[0,2\pi]$.

   Solution: $x = \dfrac{\pi}{3}$

   Explanation: Isolate the trig function: $2\cos\left(\dfrac{x}{2}\right) - \sqrt{3} = 0$; $\cos\left(\dfrac{x}{2}\right) = \dfrac{\sqrt{3}}{2}$. Since

   $0 \le x \le 2\pi$, divide by 2 to find the interval for $\dfrac{x}{2}$: $0 \le \left(\dfrac{x}{2}\right) \le \pi$. Let $\dfrac{x}{2} = \theta$ and

   find all values of θ on $[0,\pi]$ where $\cos\theta = \dfrac{\sqrt{3}}{2}$: $\theta = \dfrac{\pi}{6}$. Substitute $\dfrac{x}{2}$ into the

   equation and solve for x: $\dfrac{x}{2} = \dfrac{\pi}{6}$; $x = \dfrac{\pi}{3}$.

Practice problems: *(Answers on page: 457)*

1. Solve the equation $\sin 2\theta = \dfrac{1}{2}$ on $[0,2\pi]$.

2. Find all solutions to the equation $\tan \dfrac{x}{3} = 1$ on $[0,2\pi]$.

3. Solve the equation $\sec \dfrac{3\theta}{2} = -2$ on $[0,2\pi]$.

Review questions: *(Answers to odd questions on page: 457)*

1. Find all solutions in the interval $[0,2\pi)$ of the equation $\sin^2 2\theta = \dfrac{1}{4}$.

2. Find all solutions in the interval $[0,2\pi)$ of the equation $\sin 2\theta = \dfrac{-\sqrt{3}}{2}$.

3. Find all solutions in the interval $[0,2\pi)$ of the equation $2\cos 2\alpha = 1$.

4. Find all solutions in the interval $[0,2\pi)$ of the equation $\sin 3x \cos 2x = 0$.

5. Find all solutions in the interval $[0, 2\pi]$ of the equation $1 - \sin\left(\dfrac{x}{2}\right) = 0$.

Solving Trigonometric Equations Using the Quadratic Formula

- Some quadratic trigonometric equations cannot be easily solved by factoring, so use the **quadratic formula**.
- **Review:** Coefficients in the **argument** of a trig function change the **period** of the function. To solve an equation involving trig functions with coefficients in the arguments, first solve the equation ignoring the coefficients. Then divide the solutions through by the coefficients.
- **Review:** Since trig functions are **periodic**, trig equations often have many solutions. To find all the possible solutions to a trig equation, find the solutions for a single period and then add multiples of the period to those solutions.

If a quadratic trig equation cannot be factored, try using the quadratic formula $\quad x = \dfrac{-b \pm \sqrt{b^2 - 4ac}}{2a}$	If a quadratic trig equation cannot be factored, try using the **quadratic formula**.

Example Solve in the interval $[0, \pi]$

$$3 \sin^2 (2x) + \sin (2x) - 1 = 0$$

if $[S = \sin (2x)] \quad 3 S^2 + S - 1 = 0$

$$a = 3 \quad b = 1 \quad c = -1$$

$S = \dfrac{-1 \pm \sqrt{1 - -12}}{2(3)}$ *Plug into quadratic formula.*

$S = \dfrac{-1 + \sqrt{13}}{6} \quad$ and $\quad S = \dfrac{-1 - \sqrt{13}}{6}$

$S = .43425... \quad$ and $\quad S = -.7675918...$

But, this is only S, we want to find x.

$\sin (2x) = .43425...$ and $\sin (2x) = -.7675918...$

Find the reference angle by finding arc sine on your calculator.

$y = \sin x$

Since $0 \le x \le \pi$, multiply by 2 to find the interval for $2x$: $0 \le 2x \le \pi$.

$\sin (2x) = .43425...$ and $\sin (2x) = -.7675918...$

$\sin^{-1}(.43425) = .4492$	$\sin^{-1}(-.7675918) = -.8751$
$\pi - .4492 = 2.693$	$-.8751 + 2\pi$ or $-.8751 + \pi$
$2x = .4492$ or 2.693	$2x = 5.408$ or 4.0167

therefore,

$x = .2246$ *radians*	$x = 2.704$ *radians*
$x = 1.3462$ *radians*	$x = 2.008$ *radians*

Consider this example:

Solve $3\sin^2(2x) + \sin(2x) - 1 = 0$ for the interval $[0, \pi]$.

Treat the $\sin(2x)$ term like its own variable—so, let $S = \sin x$.

$3\sin^2(2x) + \sin(2x) - 1 = 0$ becomes $S^2 + 2S - 1 = 0$. This expression is quadratic and cannot be easily factored, so use the quadratic formula.

Plug the coefficients into the formula. The result is the solution for S. Substitute $\sin(2x)$ back in for S to solve for x.

Since $0 \le x \le \pi$ multiply by 2 to find the interval for $2x$: $0 \le 2x \le 2\pi$.

Find the **reference angle** in radians by taking the inverse sine on the calculator.

Given the reference angle use the graph of sine to determine the solution. Find all solutions in the given interval.

For the second sine function, notice that the calculator gives a negative answer for the second expression. Add 2π to that answer to move it into the correct interval.

Sample problems:

1. Find all solutions to $\tan^2 x + 2\tan x - 1 = 0$ on $[0, 2\pi]$. (Round solutions to 3 decimal places)
   Solution: $x = 0.393$, 1.963, 3.534, and 5.105
   Explanation: Let $\tan x = z$: $z^2 + 2z - 1 = 0$. Solve using the quadratic formula:
   $$z = \frac{-2 \pm \sqrt{(2)^2 - 4(1)(-1)}}{2(1)} = \frac{-2 \pm \sqrt{4+4}}{2} = \frac{-2 \pm \sqrt{8}}{2} = \frac{-2 \pm 2\sqrt{2}}{2} = -1 \pm \sqrt{2}.$$
   So, $\tan x = -1 \pm \sqrt{2}$. Solve the first equation for x: $x = \tan^{-1}(-1 + \sqrt{2}) = 0.3927$, which is an angle in Quadrant I. Find all solutions in the given interval: since $\tan x$ is also positive in Quadrant III, use 0.3927 as the reference angle to find the quadrant III solution, $\pi + 0.3927 = 3.5343$ (round to three decimal places to get 0.393 and 3.534). Solve the second equation for x: $x = \tan^{-1}(-1 - \sqrt{2}) = -1.1781$, which leads to quadrant II and quadrant IV solutions: $\pi - 1.1787 = 1.963$ and $2\pi - 1.1781 = 5.105$.

2. Find all solutions in the interval $[0, 2\pi)$ of the equation $10\sec^2\theta - 10 = 7\tan\theta + 2$.
   Solution: $\theta = 0.743$, 2.972, 3.884, and 6.069 radians
   Explanation: Use the Pythagorean identity to express $\sec^2\theta$ in terms of tangent, simplify, and set the equation equal to zero: $10\sec^2\theta - 10 = 7\tan\theta + 2$; $10(\tan^2\theta + 1) - 10 = 7\tan\theta + 2$; $10\tan^2\theta + 10 - 10 = 7\tan\theta + 2$; $10\tan^2\theta = 7\tan\theta + 2$; $10\tan^2\theta - 7\tan\theta - 2 = 0$. Use the quadratic formula to solve for $\tan\theta$:
   $$\tan\theta = \frac{-(-7) \pm \sqrt{(-7)^2 - 4(10)(-2)}}{2(10)} = \frac{7 \pm \sqrt{49 + 80}}{20} = \frac{7 \pm \sqrt{129}}{20} = \frac{7 \pm 11.358}{20},$$
   $\tan\theta = 0.9179$ or $\tan\theta = -0.2179$. Solve each equation for θ (use the inverse tangent function and find all solutions in the given interval): $\theta = 0.743$, 2.927, 0.884, and 6.069 radians.

3. Find all solutions in the interval $[0, 2\pi)$ of the equation $5\sin\theta - \cos^2\theta = 1$.
   Solution: $\theta = .382$ and 2.760 radians
   Explanation: Use the Pythagorean identity to substitute sine for cosine, simplify, and set the equation equal to zero: $5\sin\theta - \cos^2\theta = 1$; $5\sin\theta - (1 - \sin^2\theta) = 1$; $5\sin\theta - 1 + \sin^2\theta = 1$; $\sin^2\theta + 5\sin\theta - 2 = 0$. Use the quadratic formula to solve for $\sin\theta$: $\sin\theta = \dfrac{-(5) \pm \sqrt{(5)^2 - 4(1)(-2)}}{2(1)} = \dfrac{-5 \pm \sqrt{25 + 8}}{2} = \dfrac{-5 \pm 5.7446}{2}$, so $\sin\theta = 0.3723$ and -5.3723. The range of sine does not include values less than -1, so discard -5.3723. Therefore, $\sin\theta = 0.3723$. Solve for θ (use the inverse sine function and find all solutions in the given interval): $\theta = .382$ and 2.760 radians.

Practice problems: *(Answers on page: 457)*

1. Find all solutions in the interval $[0, 2\pi)$ of the equation $2\cos^2 3x + 6\cos 3x = 3$.

2. Find all solutions to the equation $5\sin x + 2 = 0$ on $[0, 2\pi]$, rounding your answers to three decimal places.

3. Solve the equation $\sin^2(2x) - 3\sin(2x) + 1 = 0$ on $[0, 2\pi]$, rounding your answers to three decimal places.

Review questions: *(Answers to odd questions on page: 457)*

1. Find all solutions in the interval $[0, 2\pi)$ of the equation $\sin^2 2\theta - 4\sin 2\theta - 3 = 0$.

2. Solve the equation $4\cos x + 3 = 0$ on $[0, 2\pi]$, rounding your answers to three decimal places.

3. True or false: The equation $\sin^2 x - \sin x + 1 = 0$ has no solution on $[0, 2\pi]$.

4. Solve the equation $\sin x^2 + \sin x - 1 = 0$ on $[0, 2\pi]$, rounding your answers to three decimal places.

5. Solve the equation $\cos^2 x - 3\cos x + 1 = 0$ on $[0, 2\pi]$, rounding your answer to three decimal places.

Solving Word Problems Involving Trigonometric Equations

- One application of the trig functions can be seen in **harmonic motion**, such as the movement of a spring. The length or location of the spring can be modeled using trig functions. As such, many word problems involving harmonic motion will require you to solve trigonometric equations.
- **Review**: Since trig functions are **periodic**, they will often have many solutions. To find all the possible solutions to a trig equation, find the solutions for a single period and then add multiples of the period to those solutions.

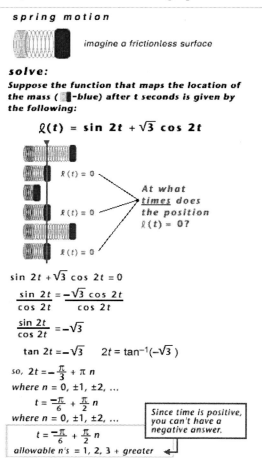

spring motion

imagine a frictionless surface

solve:

Suppose the function that maps the location of the mass (■-blue) after t seconds is given by the following:

$$\ell(t) = \sin 2t + \sqrt{3} \cos 2t$$

$\ell(t) = 0$

$\ell(t) = 0$ — At what **times** does the position $\ell(t) = 0$?

$\ell(t) = 0$

$\ell(t) = 0$

$\sin 2t + \sqrt{3} \cos 2t = 0$

$\dfrac{\sin 2t}{\cos 2t} = \dfrac{-\sqrt{3} \cos 2t}{\cos 2t}$

$\dfrac{\sin 2t}{\cos 2t} = -\sqrt{3}$

$\tan 2t = -\sqrt{3}$ $2t = \tan^{-1}(-\sqrt{3})$

so, $2t = -\dfrac{\pi}{3} + \pi n$
where $n = 0, \pm 1, \pm 2, \ldots$

$t = \dfrac{-\pi}{6} + \dfrac{\pi}{2} n$
where $n = 0, \pm 1, \pm 2, \ldots$

Since time is positive, you can't have a negative answer.

$t = \dfrac{-\pi}{6} + \dfrac{\pi}{2} n$
allowable n's = 1, 2, 3 + greater

There are many applications of trigonometry in the real world. One such application is spring motion.

In this example, you're given the function that maps the location of a spring mass after t seconds. It has an oscillating motion due to the spring. Given this equation, find the times when the **position** equals zero.

Notice that the answer occurs several times because the spring motion is periodic.

To solve, start by setting the position function equal to zero.

Isolate the variables. Notice that sine over cosine is tangent. It is easier to solve an equation with only one trig function than to solve an equation with several.

Find the angle whose tangent is $\sqrt{3}$. (Use a calculator, if necessary.)

Remember, tangent has a period of π, so to list every possible solution add multiples of π to the answer. Now divide by the coefficient of the argument.

Discard any negative answers because a negative time is physically meaningless.

Sample problems:

1. In an electric circuit, the electromotive force is $E(t)$ volts where $E(t) = 2\cos 50\pi t$. Find the smallest positive value of t for which the electromotive force is 2 volts.

   Solution: $\dfrac{1}{25}$

   Explanation: Substitute $E(t) = 2$ and solve for t: $2 = 2\cos 50\pi t$; $1 = \cos 50\pi t$;
   $\cos^{-1}(1) = 50\pi t$. Cosine equals 1 at intervals of 2π, so: $\cos^{-1}(1) = 50\pi t$; $2\pi n = 50\pi t$.

   Solve for t: $t = \dfrac{1}{25} n$, where n is any integer. The smallest possible value of t will occur when $n = 1$, so $t = \dfrac{1}{25}$.

2. An electric generator produces a 30-cycle alternating current described by the equation
$l(t) = 40\sin\left(60\pi\left(t - \dfrac{7}{72}\right)\right)$, where $l(t)$ amps is the current at t seconds. Find the smallest positive value of t for which the current is 20 amps.

Solution: $\dfrac{1}{90}$

Explanation: Substitute $l(t) = 20$ and solve for t: $20 = 40\sin\left(60\pi\left(t - \dfrac{7}{72}\right)\right)$;

$\dfrac{1}{2} = \sin\left(60\pi\left(t - \dfrac{7}{72}\right)\right)$; $60\pi\left(t - \dfrac{7}{72}\right) = \sin^{-1}\left(\dfrac{1}{2}\right)$. The arcsine of $\dfrac{1}{2}$ is $\dfrac{\pi}{2}$ and

$\dfrac{5\pi}{6}$ and occur every period, so add multiples of 2π: $60\pi\left(t - \dfrac{7}{72}\right) = \dfrac{\pi}{6} + 2\pi n$

or $60\pi\left(t - \dfrac{7}{72}\right) = \dfrac{5\pi}{6} + 2\pi n$; $t - \dfrac{7}{72} = \dfrac{1}{360} + \dfrac{1}{30}n$ or $t - \dfrac{7}{72} = \dfrac{1}{72} + \dfrac{1}{30}n$;

$t = \dfrac{1}{10} + \dfrac{1}{30}n$ or $t = \dfrac{1}{9} + \dfrac{1}{30}n$; $t = \dfrac{3}{30} + \dfrac{1}{30}n$ or $t = \dfrac{10}{90} + \dfrac{3}{90}n$, where n can be

any integer. By observation, the smallest positive value of t will occur in the second

equation when $n = -3$, $t = \dfrac{1}{90}$.

3. A weight suspended from a spring is vibrating vertically according to the equation
$y = 2\sin\left(4\pi\left(t + \dfrac{1}{8}\right)\right)$, where y is the distance in cm from the central position t
seconds after the motion is started. Determine the three smallest possible values of t
for which the weight is 1 cm above its central position.

Solution: $\dfrac{1}{12}, \dfrac{5}{12}, \dfrac{7}{12}$

Explanation: To determine the values of t for which the weight is 1 cm above its

central position, let $y = 1$ and solve for t: $1 = 2\sin\left(4\pi\left(t + \dfrac{1}{8}\right)\right)$; $\dfrac{1}{2} = \sin\left(4\pi\left(t + \dfrac{1}{8}\right)\right)$;

$4\pi\left(t + \dfrac{1}{8}\right) = \sin^{-1}\left(\dfrac{1}{2}\right)$; $4\pi\left(t + \dfrac{1}{8}\right) = \dfrac{\pi}{6} + 2\pi n$ or $4\pi\left(t + \dfrac{1}{8}\right) = \dfrac{5\pi}{6} + 2\pi n$;

$t + \dfrac{1}{8} = \dfrac{1}{24} + \dfrac{n}{2}$ or $t + \dfrac{1}{8} = \dfrac{5}{24} + \dfrac{n}{2}$; $t = -\dfrac{1}{12} + \dfrac{n}{2}$ or $t = \dfrac{1}{12} + \dfrac{n}{2}$; so

$t = -\dfrac{1}{12}, \dfrac{5}{12}, \dfrac{11}{12}, \dfrac{17}{12}, \dfrac{23}{12}...$ or $t = \dfrac{1}{12}, \dfrac{7}{12}, \dfrac{13}{12}, \dfrac{19}{12}...$ The three smallest, positive

values are $t = \dfrac{1}{12}, \dfrac{5}{12}, \dfrac{7}{12}$.

Practice problems: *(Answers on page: 457)*

1. A weight suspended from a spring is vibrating vertically according to the equation
$f(t) = 10\sin\left(\dfrac{3}{4}\pi(t - 3)\right)$ where $f(t)$ is the directed distance (in cm) of the weight
from its central position at t seconds. Find the smallest positive value of t for which
the weight will be at its central position.

2. The equation of motion for a weight suspended from a particular spring is given by:
$p(t) = 3\sin\dfrac{t}{2} + 4\cos\dfrac{t}{2}$ where p is the displacement from the equilibrium position in
centimeters and t is the time elapsed in seconds. At what time does the weight first reach
the equilibrium position?

3. The equation of motion for a weight suspended from a particular spring is given by:
$p(t) = -5\cos 2t + 8\sin 2t$ where p is the displacement from the equilibrium position in centimeters and t is the time elapsed in seconds. At what times does the weight pass through the equilibrium position within the first minute?

Review questions: *(Answers to odd questions on page: 457)*

1. A baseball was thrown from first base at an angle q with the horizontal and with an initial velocity of $V_0 = 80$ ft/sec. The ball was caught by the second base player who was 100 ft. away. Find q if the horizontal distance covered by the ball, r, is given by the equation $r = \dfrac{1}{32}V_0^2 \sin 2\theta$. Express the answer in degrees.

2. A weight is oscillating on the end of a spring. The position of the weight relative to the point of the equilibrium is given by the equation $y = \dfrac{1}{12}\left(\sqrt{3}\cos 8t - 3\sin 8t\right)$ where y is the displacement (in meters) and t is the time (in seconds). Find the smallest positive value of t when the weight is at the point of equilibrium.

3. The equation of motion for a weight suspended from a particular spring is $p(t) = 4\sin 2t - 2\cos 2t$ where p is the displacement from the equilibrium position in centimeters and t is the time elapsed in seconds. Find the smallest positive value of t when the weight is at the point of equilibrium. (Use degrees to measure t.)

4. The equation of motion for a weight suspended from a particular spring is given by:
$p(t) = -5\sin 2t - 6\cos 2t$ where p is the displacement from the equilibrium position in centimeters and t is the time elapsed in seconds. When does the weight pass through the equilibrium position within the first three periods?

5. The equation of motion for a weight suspended from a particular spring is given by $p(t) = 2\sin\dfrac{t}{3} + 5\cos\dfrac{t}{3}$, where $p(t)$ is the displacement from the equilibrium position in centimeters and t is the time elapsed in seconds. At what time does the weight first reach the equilibrium position?

Identities for Sums and Differences of Angles

- The **sum and difference identities**:
  - The sine of a sum of angles: $\sin(\theta_1 + \theta_2) = \sin\theta_1 \cos\theta_2 + \cos\theta_1 \sin\theta_2$
  - The sine of a difference of angles: $\sin(\theta_1 - \theta_2) = \sin\theta_1 \cos\theta_2 - \cos\theta_1 \sin\theta_2$
  - The cosine of a sum of angles: $\cos(\theta_1 + \theta_2) = \cos\theta_1 \cos\theta_2 - \sin\theta_1 \sin\theta_2$
  - The cosine of a difference of angles: $\cos(\theta_1 - \theta_2) = \cos\theta_1 \cos\theta_2 + \sin\theta_1 \sin\theta_2$
  - The tangent of a sum of angles: $\tan(\theta_1 + \theta_2) = \dfrac{\tan\theta_1 + \tan\theta_2}{1 - \tan\theta_1 \tan\theta_2}$
  - The tangent of a difference of angles: $\tan(\theta_1 - \theta_2) = \dfrac{\tan\theta_1 - \tan\theta_2}{1 + \tan\theta_1 \tan\theta_2}$

$\sin\left(\dfrac{\pi}{2} + \dfrac{\pi}{2}\right) \overset{?}{=} \sin\left(\dfrac{\pi}{2}\right) + \sin\left(\dfrac{\pi}{2}\right)$ $\sin(\pi) \overset{?}{=} \sin\left(\dfrac{\pi}{2}\right) + \sin\left(\dfrac{\pi}{2}\right)$ $0 \overset{?}{=} 1 + 1$ $0 \neq 2$	This example shows that the sine of a sum of two angles is not equal to the sine of the first angle added to the sine of the second. $\sin(\pi/2 + \pi/2) = 0$, while $\sin(\pi/2) + \sin(\pi/2) = 2$. Therefore, the sine of a sum of two angles does not equal the sine of the first angle plus the sine of the second.

sum of angles formulas:

$$\sin(\Theta_1 + \Theta_2) = \sin\Theta_1\cos\Theta_2 + \cos\Theta_1\sin\Theta_2$$

$$\sin\left(\frac{\pi}{2} + \frac{\pi}{2}\right) = \sin\left(\frac{\pi}{2}\right)\cos\left(\frac{\pi}{2}\right) + \cos\left(\frac{\pi}{2}\right)\sin\left(\frac{\pi}{2}\right)$$

$$\sin(\pi) = (1)(0) + (0)(1)$$

$$0 \overset{\checkmark}{=} 0$$

The example shown is the proper way to find the sine of a sum of angles.

To simplify, first substitute in the values for each trig function.

Then do the arithmetic.

sin is *good*	**cos is** *evil*
• shares the limelight	• it wants it all; needs to be 1st
• signs are the same	• so obnoxious it switches signs

Just memorize tangent.

Here is Dr. Burger's "crutch" for remembering these formulas. They do help.

Memorizing these formulas will save time and will make many problems simple and quick to solve.

Sample problems:

1. Use the subtraction formula for sine to evaluate $\sin 105°$.

   Solution: $\frac{\sqrt{2}+\sqrt{6}}{4}$

   Explanation: Express $105°$ as the difference of two common angles: $\sin 105° = \sin(150° - 45°) = \sin 150° \cos 45° - \cos 150° \sin 45° = \left(\frac{1}{2}\right)\left(\frac{\sqrt{2}}{2}\right) - \left(\frac{-\sqrt{3}}{2}\right)\left(\frac{\sqrt{2}}{2}\right) = \frac{\sqrt{2}}{4} + \frac{\sqrt{6}}{4} = \frac{\sqrt{2}+\sqrt{6}}{4}$.

2. Find $\sin(x + y)$ if $\sin x = -\frac{5}{13}$ and $\cos y = -\frac{3}{5}$ with x and y being in quadrant III.

   Solution: $\frac{63}{65}$

   Explanation: Use the "sine of a sum of angles" formula to expand $\sin(x + y)$: $\sin(x + y) = \sin x \cos y + \cos x \sin y = \left(-\frac{5}{13}\right)\left(-\frac{3}{5}\right) + \cos x \sin y$. Find $\cos x$ and $\sin y$ to complete the formula. Use $\sin x = -\frac{5}{13}$ to find $\cos x$: if $\sin x = -\frac{5}{13}$ then $a^2 + (-5)^2 = 13^2$; $a^2 + 25 = 169$; $a^2 = 144$; $a = 12$, so $\cos x = -\frac{12}{13}$ (since cosine is negative in quadrant III). Use $\cos y = -\frac{3}{5}$ to find $\sin y$: if $\cos y = -\frac{3}{5}$ then $(-3)^2 + b^2 = (5)^2$; $9 + b^2 = 25$; $b^2 = 16$; $b = 4$, so $\sin y = -\frac{4}{5}$ (since sine is negative in quadrant III). Substitute these values into the formula: $\sin x \cos y + \cos x \sin y = \left(-\frac{5}{13}\right)\left(-\frac{3}{5}\right) + \left(-\frac{12}{13}\right)\left(-\frac{4}{5}\right) = \frac{15}{65} + \frac{48}{65} = \frac{63}{65}$.

3. Find $\sin(x - y)$ if $\tan x = -\frac{5}{12}$ and $\cos y = \frac{3}{5}$ with x and y being in quadrant IV.

   Solution: $\frac{33}{65}$

   Explanation: Use the "sine of a difference of angles" formula to expand $\sin(x - y)$: $\sin(x - y) = \sin x \cos y - \cos x \sin y = \sin x\left(\frac{3}{5}\right) - \cos x \sin y$. Find $\sin x$, $\cos x$, and $\sin y$ to complete the formula. Use $\tan x = -\frac{5}{12}$ to find $\sin x$ and $\cos x$: if $\tan x = -\frac{5}{12}$ then $c^2 = (5)^2 + (12)^2$; $c^2 = 25 + 144$; $c^2 = 169$; $c = 13$, so $\sin x = -\frac{5}{13}$ (since sine is negative in quadrant IV) and $\cos x = \frac{12}{13}$ (since cosine is positive in quadrant IV). Use $\cos y = \frac{3}{5}$ to find $\sin y$: if $\cos y = \frac{3}{5}$ then $a^2 + (3)^2 = (5)^2$; $a^2 + 9 = 25$; $a^2 = 16$; $a = 4$, so $\sin y = -\frac{4}{5}$. Substitute these values into the formula: $\sin x \cos y - \cos x \sin y = \left(-\frac{5}{13}\right)\left(\frac{3}{5}\right) - \left(\frac{12}{13}\right)\left(-\frac{4}{5}\right) = -\frac{15}{65} + \frac{48}{65} = \frac{33}{65}$.

Practice problems: *(Answers on page: 457)*

1. Use the addition formula for cosine to evaluate $\cos 105°$.

2. Use the addition of sines identity to evaluate $\sin 255°$.

3. Find $\tan(a+b)$ given that $\cos a = \dfrac{5}{13}$ and $\sin b = \dfrac{\sqrt{3}}{2}$ and both a and b are in quadrant I. (Use a calculator to simplify answer.)

Review questions: *(Answers to odd questions on page: 457)*

1. True or false: You would use the identity $\sin 45° \cos 60° + \cos 45° \sin 60°$ to find $\sin(45° + 60°)$.

2. Use the addition formula for cosine to evaluate $\cos 195°$.

3. Use the addition formula for sine to evaluate $\sin 105°$.

4. Find $\cos(x+y)$ for $\cos x = -\dfrac{4}{5}$ and $\sin y = \dfrac{5}{13}$ with x and y being in quadrant II.

5. Determine $\tan(a-b)$, given that $\cos a = \dfrac{3}{5}$, $\sin b = \dfrac{1}{2}$, and both a and b are in quadrant I. (Use a calculator to simplify answer.)

Using Sum and Difference Identities

- When finding trigonometric function values for an angle, it helps to write the angle as the sum or difference of two angles whose function values are already known. Then, find the desired values using a **sum or difference identity**.

- The sine of a difference of angles: $\sin(\theta_1 - \theta_2) = \sin\theta_1 \cos\theta_2 - \cos\theta_1 \sin\theta_2$.

Difference of Two Sines: $\sin(\theta_1 - \theta_2) = \sin\theta_1 \cos\theta_2 - \cos\theta_1 \sin\theta_2$ **Example** $\sin(15°) =$ *(not a standard formula angle)* $\sin(45° - 30°) =$ *(We know the sine of 45° and 30°)*	In this example you're asked to find the value of $\sin(15°)$. Notice that $15° = 45°-30°$. Substituting $(45°-30°)$ for $15°$ makes it possible to use the difference of angles formula.
$\sin(45° - 30°) =$ $\sin(45°)\cos(30°) - \cos(45°)\sin(30°) =$ $\left(\dfrac{\sqrt{2}}{2}\right)\left(\dfrac{\sqrt{3}}{2}\right) - \left(\dfrac{\sqrt{2}}{2}\right)\left(\dfrac{1}{2}\right)$ <table><tr><td>angles</td><td>0°</td><td>30°</td><td>45°</td><td>60°</td><td>90°</td></tr><tr><td>sine</td><td>0</td><td>$\frac{1}{2}$</td><td>$\frac{\sqrt{2}}{2}$</td><td>$\frac{\sqrt{3}}{2}$</td><td>1</td></tr><tr><td>cosine</td><td>1</td><td>$\frac{\sqrt{3}}{2}$</td><td>$\frac{\sqrt{2}}{2}$</td><td>$\frac{1}{2}$</td><td>0</td></tr></table>	Plug $45°$ and $30°$ into the appropriate places and evaluate.
$= \dfrac{\sqrt{6}}{4} - \dfrac{\sqrt{2}}{4}$ $\sin(15°) = \dfrac{\sqrt{6} - \sqrt{2}}{4}$	Simplify to find that $\sin(15°) = \dfrac{\sqrt{6} - \sqrt{2}}{4}$

> **The power of these sums and difference formulas:**
>
> They allow us to take an angle that we don't know and "decompose" it as either a sum or difference of angles that we do know. Then we can use the sum or difference formulas to calculate the desired value.

This is how to calculate the trigonometric functions for an unusual angle like 15° using the **sum and difference identities.**

Finding the trig functions of different angles will be possible using the sum and difference identities.

Sample problems:

1. Find the exact value of $\cos 15°$.

   <u>Solution:</u> $\frac{\sqrt{6}+\sqrt{2}}{4}$

   <u>Explanation:</u> Use the "cosine of a difference of angles" formula to express the $\cos 15°$ as the difference of two common angles: $\cos(15°) = \cos(45° - 30°) = \cos 45° \cos 30° + \sin 45° \sin 30° =$
   $\left(\frac{\sqrt{2}}{2}\right)\left(\frac{\sqrt{3}}{2}\right) + \left(\frac{\sqrt{2}}{2}\right)\left(\frac{1}{2}\right) = \frac{\sqrt{6}}{4} + \frac{\sqrt{2}}{4} = \frac{\sqrt{6}+\sqrt{2}}{4}$.

2. Find the exact value of $\tan \frac{7\pi}{12}$.

   <u>Solution:</u> $-2 - \sqrt{3}$

   <u>Explanation:</u> Use the "tangent of a sum of angles" formula to express $\tan \frac{7\pi}{12}$ as

   the sum of two common angles: $\tan \frac{7\pi}{12} = \tan\left(\frac{4\pi}{12} + \frac{3\pi}{12}\right) = \tan\left(\frac{\pi}{3} + \frac{\pi}{4}\right)$

   $$= \frac{\tan \frac{\pi}{3} + \tan \frac{\pi}{4}}{1 - \tan \frac{\pi}{3} \tan \frac{\pi}{4}}$$

   $$= \frac{\sqrt{3}+1}{1-(\sqrt{3})(1)} = \frac{\sqrt{3}+1}{1-\sqrt{3}}.$$

   Rationalize the denominator: $\frac{\sqrt{3}+1}{1-\sqrt{3}}\left(\frac{1+\sqrt{3}}{1+\sqrt{3}}\right) = \frac{1+2\sqrt{3}+3}{1+\sqrt{3}-\sqrt{3}-3} = \frac{4+2\sqrt{3}}{-2} = -2 - \sqrt{3}.$

3. If $\cos x = -\frac{4}{5}$ with x in quadrant III and $\cos y = \frac{5}{13}$ with y in quadrant IV, find $\cos(x - y)$.

   <u>Solution:</u> $\frac{16}{65}$

   <u>Explanation:</u> Expand using the cosine of a difference of angles formula:

   $\cos(x - y) = \cos x \cos y + \sin x \sin y \Rightarrow \left(-\frac{4}{5}\right)\left(\frac{5}{13}\right) + \sin x \sin y.$ Find $\sin x$ and $\sin y$.

   Use $\cos x = -\frac{4}{5}$ to find $\sin x$: $a^2 + 4^2 = 5^2$; $a^2 + 16 = 25$; $a^2 = 9$; $a = 3$,

   so $\sin x = -\frac{3}{5}$ (sine is negative since x is in quadrant III). Use $\cos y = \frac{5}{13}$ to find

   $\sin y$: $a^2 + 5^2 = 13^2$; $a^2 + 25 = 169$; $a^2 = 144$; $a = 12$, so $\sin y = -\frac{12}{13}$ (sine is

   negative since y is in quadrant IV). Complete the formula:

   $\cos(x - y) = \cos x \cos y + \sin x \sin y$; $\left(-\frac{4}{5}\right)\left(\frac{5}{13}\right) + \left(-\frac{3}{5}\right)\left(-\frac{12}{13}\right) = \left(-\frac{20}{65}\right) + \left(\frac{36}{65}\right) = \frac{16}{65}.$

Practice problems: *(Answers on page: 457)*

1. Find the exact value of $\sin 75°$.

2. Find the exact value of $\tan \frac{11\pi}{12}$.

3. If $\cos p = -\frac{4}{5}$ with p in quadrant III, and $\cos q = \frac{5}{13}$ with q in quadrant IV, find $\tan(p-q)$.

Review questions: *(Answers to odd questions on page: 457)*

1. Find the exact value of $\cos 75°$.

2. Find the exact value of $\cos 195°$.

3. Find the exact value of $\tan 255°$.

4. Find the exact value of $\cos \dfrac{5\pi}{12}$.

5. If $\sin x = -\dfrac{4}{5}$ with x in quadrant III and $\cos y = \dfrac{5}{13}$ with y in quadrant IV, find $\sin(x+y)$.

Using Sum and Difference Identities to Simplify an Expression

- Sum and difference identities can be useful in simplifying trigonometric expressions.
- **Review:**
  - The sine of a sum of angles: $\sin(\theta_1 + \theta_2) = \sin\theta_1 \cos\theta_2 + \cos\theta_1 \sin\theta_2$
  - The sine of a difference of angles: $\sin(\theta_1 - \theta_2) = \sin\theta_1 \cos\theta_2 - \cos\theta_1 \sin\theta_2$
  - The cosine of a sum of angles: $\cos(\theta_1 + \theta_2) = \cos\theta_1 \cos\theta_2 - \sin\theta_1 \sin\theta_2$
  - The cosine of a difference of angles: $\cos(\theta_1 - \theta_2) = \cos\theta_1 \cos\theta_2 + \sin\theta_1 \sin\theta_2$
  - The tangent of a sum of angles: $\tan(\theta_1 + \theta_2) = \dfrac{\tan\theta_1 + \tan\theta_2}{1 - \tan\theta_1 \tan\theta_2}$
  - The tangent of a difference of angles: $\tan(\theta_1 - \theta_2) = \dfrac{\tan\theta_1 - \tan\theta_2}{1 + \tan\theta_1 \tan\theta_2}$

Example $\sin\dfrac{\pi}{9}\cos\dfrac{7\pi}{18} + \sin\dfrac{7\pi}{18}\cos\dfrac{\pi}{9}$ $= \sin\left(\dfrac{\pi}{9} + \dfrac{7\pi}{18}\right)$	Consider the expression to the left. While it may initially look complicated, further inspection reveals that the expression is equal to the sine of a sum of angles.
$= \sin\left(\dfrac{2\pi}{18} + \dfrac{7\pi}{18}\right)$ $= \sin\left(\dfrac{9\pi}{18}\right)$	To evaluate, first find a common denominator and add the fractions.
$= \sin\left(\dfrac{9\pi}{18}\right)$ $= \sin\dfrac{\pi}{2}$ $= 1$	The expression $\sin\dfrac{9\pi}{18}$ is equivalent to $\sin\dfrac{\pi}{2}$, which is equal to 1. Therefore, $\sin\dfrac{\pi}{9}\cos\dfrac{7\pi}{18} + \sin\dfrac{7\pi}{18}\cos\dfrac{\pi}{9} = 1$.
Example $\dfrac{\tan 47° - \tan 2°}{1 + \tan 47° \tan 2°}$ $= \tan(47° - 2°)$ $= \tan(45°)$ $= 1$	Consider the example illustrated here. The given expression is equal to the tangent of the difference of two angles. The difference is 45° and the tangent of 45° is one.

Sample problems:

1. Simplify: $\sin 20° \cos 80° - \cos 20° \sin 80°$

   Solution: $-\frac{\sqrt{3}}{2}$

   Explanation: Use the sine of a difference of angles formula, $\sin \theta_1 \cos \theta_2 - \cos \theta_1 \sin \theta_2 = \sin(\theta_1 - \theta_2)$,

   to simplify: $\sin 20° \cos 80° - \cos 20° \sin 80° = \sin(20° - 80°) = \sin(-60°) = -\sin 60° = -\frac{\sqrt{3}}{2}$.

2. Simplify: $\dfrac{\tan 20° + \tan 25°}{1 - \tan 20° \tan 25°}$

   Solution: 1

   Explanation: Simplify using the identity for the tangent of a sum, $\tan(\theta_1 + \theta_2) =$
   $\dfrac{\tan \theta_1 + \tan \theta_2}{1 - \tan \theta_1 \tan \theta_2}$: $\dfrac{\tan 20° + \tan 25°}{1 - \tan 20° \tan 25°} = \tan(20° + 25°) = \tan 45° = 1$.

3. Find the exact value of $\cos \frac{5\pi}{12} \cos \frac{7\pi}{12} - \sin \frac{5\pi}{12} \sin \frac{7\pi}{12}$.

   Solution: -1

   Explanation: Use the identity for the cosine of a sum, $\cos(\theta_1 + \theta_2) = \cos \theta_1 \cos \theta_2 - \sin \theta_1 \sin \theta_2$,

   to simplify: $\cos \frac{5\pi}{12} \cos \frac{7\pi}{12} - \sin \frac{5\pi}{12} \sin \frac{7\pi}{12} = \cos\left(\frac{5\pi}{12} + \frac{7\pi}{12}\right) = \cos \pi = -1$.

Practice problems: *(Answers on page: 457)*

1. Simplify: $\cos 70° \cos 20° - \sin 70° \sin 20°$

2. Find the exact value of $\dfrac{\tan 40° - \tan 10°}{1 + \tan 40° \tan 10°}$.

3. Find the exact value of $\cos \dfrac{\pi}{12} \cos \dfrac{5\pi}{12} + \sin \dfrac{\pi}{12} \sin \dfrac{5\pi}{12}$.

Review questions: *(Answers to odd questions on page: 457)*

1. Simplify: $\sin 20° \cos 10° + \cos 20° \sin 10°$

2. Find the exact value of $\cos 40° \cos 10° + \sin 40° \sin 10°$.

3. Find the exact value of $\sin \dfrac{\pi}{18} \cos \dfrac{5\pi}{18} + \cos \dfrac{\pi}{18} \sin \dfrac{5\pi}{18}$.

4. Write $\sin \dfrac{7}{6} \cos \dfrac{1}{6} + \cos \dfrac{7}{6} \sin \dfrac{1}{6}$ as a single sine or cosine term.

5. Express $\cos(x + y) \cos y + \sin(x + y) \sin y$ as a single term.

Confirming a Double-Angle Identity

- The **double-angle identities** arise from the sum identities (from the **sum and difference identities**) when the two angles being added are equal. It is important to remember that one side of the identity refers to double angles while the other side refers to single angles. This shift can be very useful in solving problems.
- The double-angle identities:
  - $\sin 2\theta = 2 \sin\theta \cos\theta$
  - $\cos 2\theta = \cos^2\theta - \sin^2\theta$
  - $\cos 2\theta = 1 - 2\sin^2\theta$
  - $\cos 2\theta = 2\cos^2\theta - 1$
  - $\tan 2\theta = \dfrac{2 \tan \theta}{1 - \tan^2 \theta}$

What if the values of the angles are the same? ($\theta_1 = \theta_2$)

Double Angle Formulas: (only when $\theta_1 = \theta_2$)

• *then* $\tan(\theta_1 + \theta_2) = \dfrac{\tan\theta + \tan\theta}{1 - \tan\theta\,\tan\theta}$

So $\tan(2\theta) = \dfrac{2\tan\theta}{1 - \tan^2\theta}$

If the two angles, θ_1 and θ_2, are the same, then the tangent of $\theta_1 + \theta_2$ is just $2\tan\theta/1-\tan^2\theta$—the **double-angle identity** for tangents.

Double Angle Formulas: $\tan(2\theta) = \dfrac{2\tan\theta}{1 - \tan^2\theta}$
$\sin(2\theta) = 2\sin\theta\cos\theta$
$\cos(2\theta) = \cos^2\theta - \sin^2\theta$

Example
$$\sin\left(\frac{2\pi}{3}\right) = \sin\left[2\left(\frac{\pi}{3}\right)\right]$$
$$= 2\sin\left(\frac{\pi}{3}\right)\cos\left(\frac{\pi}{3}\right)$$

Use a double-angle identity to evaluate this trig function.

Here the sine of $2\pi/3$ (the **double-angle**) can be written in terms of the sine and cosine of $\pi/3$.

$$= 2\left(\frac{\sqrt{3}}{2}\right)\left(\frac{1}{2}\right)$$
$$= \frac{\sqrt{3}}{2}$$

Plug in the values of $\sin(\pi/3)$ and $\cos(\pi/3)$.

Simplify to get the answer.

So, $\sin\dfrac{2\pi}{3} = \dfrac{\sqrt{3}}{2}$.

Double Angle Formulas: $\tan(2\theta) = \dfrac{2\tan\theta}{1 - \tan^2\theta}$
$\sin(2\theta) = 2\sin\theta\cos\theta$
$\cos(2\theta) = \cos^2\theta - \sin^2\theta$

Example
$$\cos\left(\frac{2\pi}{3}\right) = \cos^2\left(\frac{\pi}{3}\right) - \sin^2\left(\frac{\pi}{3}\right)$$
$$= \left(\frac{1}{2}\right)\left(\frac{1}{2}\right) - \left(\frac{\sqrt{3}}{2}\right)\left(\frac{\sqrt{3}}{2}\right)$$
$$= \frac{1}{4} - \frac{3}{4}$$
$$= -\frac{2}{4}$$
$$= -\frac{1}{2}$$

Consider the example illustrated here. Begin with the double-angle identity for cosine.

Substitute in the known values and do the arithmetic.

Sample problems:

1. If $\sin x = \dfrac{3}{5}$ and x is in the first quadrant, find $\sin 2x$.

Solution: $\dfrac{24}{25}$

Explanation: For sine the double angle identity is $\sin 2x = 2\sin x\cos x$; $\sin 2x = 2\left(\dfrac{3}{5}\right)\cos x$.

Use $\sin x = \dfrac{3}{5}$ to find $\cos x$: $5^2 = 3^2 + b^2$; $b^2 = 25 - 9$; $b = 4$, so $\cos x = \dfrac{4}{5}$. Complete

the formula: $\sin 2x = 2\sin x\cos x = 2\left(\dfrac{3}{5}\right)\left(\dfrac{4}{5}\right) = 2\left(\dfrac{12}{25}\right) = \dfrac{24}{25}$.

2. If $\tan x = -\dfrac{5}{12}$ and x is in the second quadrant, find $\sin 2x$.

Solution: $-\dfrac{120}{169}$

Explanation: The double angle identity for sine is $\sin 2x = 2\sin x \cos x$. Use $\tan x = -\dfrac{5}{12}$ to find the values of $\sin x$ and $\cos x$: $c^2 = a^2 + b^2$; $c^2 = 5^2 + 12^2$; $c^2 = 25 + 144$; $c = 13$.
In quadrant II, $\sin x$ is positive and $\cos x$ is negative, so $\sin x = \dfrac{5}{13}$ and $\cos x = -\dfrac{12}{13}$.
Complete the formula: $\sin 2x = 2\sin x \cos x = 2\left(\dfrac{5}{13}\right)\left(-\dfrac{12}{13}\right) = 2\left(-\dfrac{60}{169}\right) = -\dfrac{120}{169}$.

3. Find the exact value of $\cos 2x$ given $\sin\theta = -\dfrac{24}{25}$ and $\cos\theta < 0$.

Solution: $-\dfrac{527}{625}$

Explanation: To solve for $\cos 2x$, use the double angle form that is most appropriate:

$$\cos 2x = 1 - 2\sin^2\theta \Rightarrow \cos 2x = 1 - 2\left(-\dfrac{24}{25}\right)^2 = 1 - 2\left(\dfrac{576}{625}\right) = -\dfrac{527}{625}$$

Practice problems: *(Answers on page: 457)*

1. If $\sin x = \dfrac{1}{2}$ and x is in the first quadrant, find $\tan 2x$.

2. If $\tan x = \frac{3}{2}$ and x is in the first quadrant, find $\sin 2x$.

3. Simplify: $1 - 4\sin^2 x \cos^2 x$

Review questions: *(Answers to odd questions on page: 457)*

1. If $\sin x = \dfrac{\sqrt{2}}{2}$ and x is in the first quadrant, find $\cos 2x$.

2. If $\tan x = \dfrac{24}{7}$ and x is in the first quadrant, find $\cos 2x$.

3. If $\sin x = \dfrac{5}{13}$ and x is in the first quadrant, find $\tan 2x$.

4. If $\cos x = 35$ and x is in the first quadrant, find $\tan 2x$.

5. Find the exact value of $\sin 2x$, given $\sin x = \dfrac{3}{5}$ and $0 < x < \dfrac{\pi}{2}$.

Using Double-Angle Identities

- **Double-angle identities** can help you solve trigonometric equations.
- **Review**: The double-angle identities:
  - $\sin 2\theta = 2\sin\theta\cos\theta$
  - $\cos 2\theta = \cos^2\theta - \sin^2\theta$
  - $\cos 2\theta = 1 - 2\sin^2\theta$
  - $\cos 2\theta = 2\cos^2\theta - 1$
  - $\tan 2\theta = \dfrac{2\tan\theta}{1 - \tan^2\theta}$

Example $\cos 2x = \sin x$ $\quad x \in [0, 2\pi)$ *(find solution for X from 0 to 2π)* $\cos^2 x - \sin^2 x = \sin x$	In this example you are given that $\cos 2x = \sin 2x$ and you are asked to find the solution for x from 0 to 2π. Since this trigonometric equation involves the angle $2x$ and the angle x, use a **double-angle identity** for cosine to simplify the expression. Rewrite $\cos 2x$ as $\cos^2 x - \sin^2 x$.
$1 - \sin^2 x - \sin^2 x = \sin x$ **Pythagorean identity** $\sin^2 x + \cos^2 x = 1$ So $\cos^2 x = 1 - \sin^2 x$	Next, use the **Pythagorean identity** to replace the $\cos^2 x$ term, leaving the equation in terms of $\sin x$.
$1 - 2\sin^2 x = \sin x$ $2\sin^2 x + \sin x - 1 = 0$ $(2\sin x - 1)(\sin x + 1) = 0$ *So either* $(2\sin x - 1) = 0$ $\quad$ OR $\quad (\sin x + 1) = 0$ $\sin x = \frac{1}{2}$ $\qquad\qquad \sin x = -1$	Now follow the usual procedure for solving equations: Combine like terms. Move everything to one side. Factor. Solve for the value of $\sin x$.
$x = \frac{\pi}{6}$ $\quad x = \frac{5\pi}{6}$ $\qquad x = \frac{3\pi}{2}$ $\pi - \frac{\pi}{6} =$ $\frac{6\pi}{6} - \frac{\pi}{6} = \frac{5\pi}{6}$	Check on a graph or a table of trig values to see what angles have these values for their sine. For example, there are two angles, $\pi/6$ and $5\pi/6$, that satisfy $\sin x = 1/2$.
  Remember to check for all values! $x = \frac{\pi}{6}, \frac{5\pi}{6}$ or $\frac{3\pi}{2}$	What is the angle whose sine is -1? $3\pi/2$. So there are three solutions in all: $x = \pi/6$, $5\pi/6$, and $3\pi/2$. Remember to always check for two values when finding the inverse of a function.

Sample problems:

1. Solve $\sin 2t = \cos t$ for t, $t \in [0, 2\pi)$.

   Solution: $\frac{\pi}{2}, \frac{3\pi}{2}, \frac{\pi}{6}, \frac{5\pi}{6}$

   Explanation: Use the double-angle formula for $\sin 2t$: $\sin 2t = \cos t \implies 2\sin t \cos t = \cos t$.
   Set the equation equal to zero, factor and solve each factor for t: $2\sin t \cos t - \cos t = 0$;
   $\cos t(2\sin t - 1) = 0$; $\cos t = 0$ or $2\sin t = 1$; $\cos t = 0$ or $\sin t = \frac{1}{2}$. Thus, $t = \frac{\pi}{2}, \frac{3\pi}{2}, \frac{\pi}{6}, \frac{5\pi}{6}$.

2. Solve $\cos 2t = \cos t$ for t, if t is in the interval $[0, 2\pi)$.

   Solution: $\frac{2\pi}{3}, \frac{4\pi}{3}, 0$

   Explanation: Use the double-angle formula for $\cos 2t$: $\cos 2t = \cos t \implies 2\cos^2 t - 1 = \cos t$. Move
   all terms to the left side: $2\cos^2 t - \cos t - 1 = 0$. Factor and solve each factor for t:
   $(2\cos t + 1)(\cos t - 1) = 0$; $\cos t = -\frac{1}{2}$ or $\cos t = 1$. Thus, $t = \frac{2\pi}{3}, \frac{4\pi}{3}$ or $t = 0$.

3. Solve $\cos 2t = \cos t$ for t, if t is in the interval $[0, 2\pi)$.

Solution: $\dfrac{2\pi}{3}, \dfrac{4\pi}{3}, 0$

Explanation:

Use the most appropriate double-angle formula for $\cos 2t$: $\cos 2t = \cos t \implies 2\cos^2 t - 1 = \cos t$.

Move all of the terms to the left side: $2\cos^2 t - \cos t - 1 = 0$.

Factor and solve each factor for t: $(2\cos t + 1)(\cos t - 1) = 0$; $\cos t = -\dfrac{1}{2}$ or $\cos t = 1$.

Thus, $t = \dfrac{2\pi}{3}, \dfrac{4\pi}{3}$ or $t = 0$.

Practice problems: *(Answers on page: 458)*

1. Solve $\sin 2t = 2\sin t$ for t, $t \in [0, 2\pi)$.

2. Solve $\cos 2t = 1 - \sin t$ for t, $t \in [0, 2\pi)$.

3. Solve $\sin 2t \sin t + \cos 2t \cos t = 1$ for t, $t \in [0, 2\pi)$.

Review questions: *(Answers to odd questions on page: 458)*

1. Solve $\cos 2t = 0$ for t, $t \in [0, 2\pi)$.

2. Solve $(\tan t)(\tan 2t) = 1$ for t, $t \in [0, 2\pi)$.

3. Solve $3\cos 2t - 5\cos t - 1 = 0$ for t, $t \in [0, 2\pi)$.

4. Solve $\cos 2t + 3\cos t = 1$ for t, $t \in [0, 2\pi)$.

5. Find all solutions in the interval $[0, 2\pi)$ for $\cos 4x - 7\cos 2x = 8$.

Solving Word Problems Involving Multiple-Angle Identities

- **Multiple-angle identities** involve trigonometric functions of multiples of an angle θ (such as 2θ or 3θ). The most commonly used multiple angle identities are the **double-angle identities**.
- Trigonometry has many practical applications.
- **Review**: Area of a rectangle: *base · height*
- **Review**:

  Area of a triangle: $\dfrac{1}{2} \cdot base \cdot height$

- **Review**: In the point (x, y), x represents the base, or horizontal distance from a central point, and y represents the height, or vertical distance from that same central point.

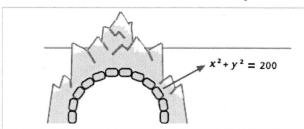

Consider the following application:

An engineer wants to build a tunnel through a mountain with the maximum cross-sectional area possible.

The equation $x^2 + y^2 = 200$ is given to represent the circle, half of which is the arch for the tunnel.

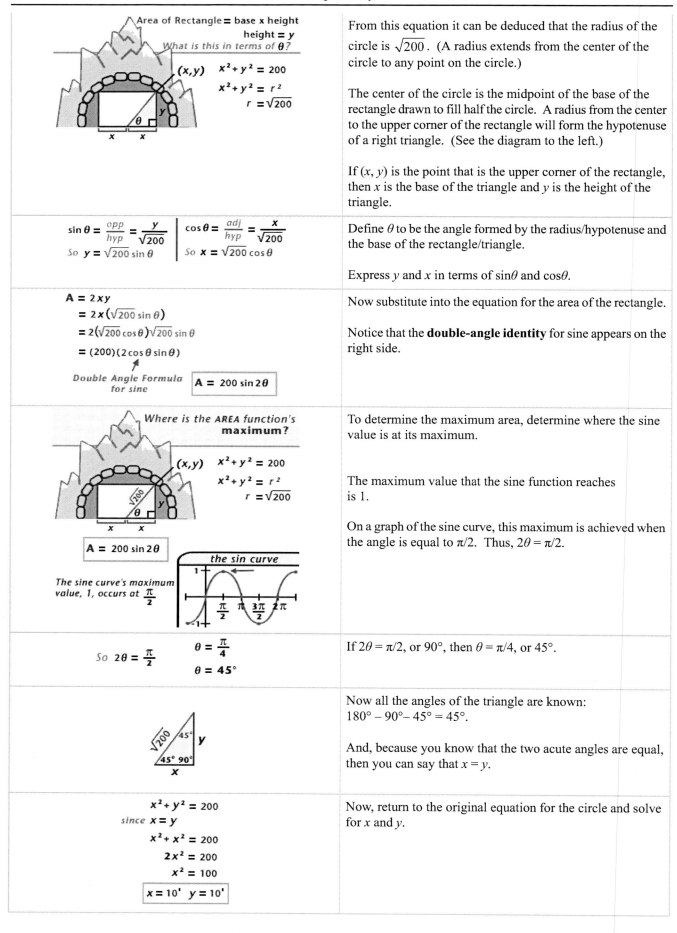

Area of Rectangle = base × height

height = y

What is this in terms of θ?

(x,y) $x^2 + y^2 = 200$

$x^2 + y^2 = r^2$

$r = \sqrt{200}$

From this equation it can be deduced that the radius of the circle is $\sqrt{200}$. (A radius extends from the center of the circle to any point on the circle.)

The center of the circle is the midpoint of the base of the rectangle drawn to fill half the circle. A radius from the center to the upper corner of the rectangle will form the hypotenuse of a right triangle. (See the diagram to the left.)

If (x, y) is the point that is the upper corner of the rectangle, then x is the base of the triangle and y is the height of the triangle.

$\sin\theta = \dfrac{opp}{hyp} = \dfrac{y}{\sqrt{200}}$ $\cos\theta = \dfrac{adj}{hyp} = \dfrac{x}{\sqrt{200}}$

So $y = \sqrt{200}\sin\theta$ So $x = \sqrt{200}\cos\theta$

Define θ to be the angle formed by the radius/hypotenuse and the base of the rectangle/triangle.

Express y and x in terms of $\sin\theta$ and $\cos\theta$.

$A = 2xy$

$= 2x(\sqrt{200}\sin\theta)$

$= 2(\sqrt{200}\cos\theta)\sqrt{200}\sin\theta$

$= (200)(2\cos\theta\sin\theta)$

Double Angle Formula for sine $A = 200\sin 2\theta$

Now substitute into the equation for the area of the rectangle.

Notice that the **double-angle identity** for sine appears on the right side.

Where is the AREA function's **maximum**?

(x,y) $x^2 + y^2 = 200$

$x^2 + y^2 = r^2$

$r = \sqrt{200}$

$A = 200\sin 2\theta$

the sin curve

The sine curve's maximum value, 1, occurs at $\dfrac{\pi}{2}$

To determine the maximum area, determine where the sine value is at its maximum.

The maximum value that the sine function reaches is 1.

On a graph of the sine curve, this maximum is achieved when the angle is equal to $\pi/2$. Thus, $2\theta = \pi/2$.

So $2\theta = \dfrac{\pi}{2}$ $\theta = \dfrac{\pi}{4}$

$\theta = 45°$

If $2\theta = \pi/2$, or 90°, then $\theta = \pi/4$, or 45°.

Now all the angles of the triangle are known:
$180° - 90° - 45° = 45°$.

And, because you know that the two acute angles are equal, then you can say that $x = y$.

$x^2 + y^2 = 200$

since $x = y$

$x^2 + x^2 = 200$

$2x^2 = 200$

$x^2 = 100$

$x = 10' \quad y = 10'$

Now, return to the original equation for the circle and solve for x and y.

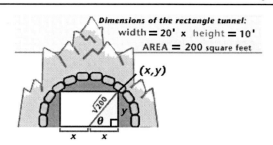

Dimensions of the rectangle tunnel:
width = 20' x height = 10'
AREA = 200 square feet

Substitute x and y into the equation for the area of the rectangle and find the maximum area for the tunnel.

Notice that the width of the rectangle is $2x$ when substituting to find the area.

Sample problems:

1. A function is given by the equation $A = \cos^2 \theta - \sin^2 \theta$. In the interval $0 \le \theta \le 2\pi$, what is the smallest value of A?

   Solution: -1

   Explanation: The expression $\cos^2 \theta - \sin^2 \theta$ is equal to $\cos(2\theta)$, so $A = \cos(2\theta)$. For any equation of the form $y = \cos x$, the minimum value of y is -1.

2. A point (x, y) moves along a circle represented by $x^2 + y^2 = 400$, but never leaves the first quadrant. At any location, the point determines an angle θ. A horizontal line through the point, a vertical line through the point, and a diameter of the circle determine a triangle. Write an expression for the horizontal leg of the triangle.

   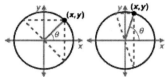

   Solution: $2x$

   Explanation: The horizontal leg connects the two points (x, y) and $(-x, y)$. The distance between those two points is $2x$.

3. A point moves around a circle represented by $x^2 + y^2 = 100$. At any location on the circle, the point determines an angle θ. The points (x, y), $(-x, y)$, $(-x, 0)$, and $(x, 0)$ determine a rectangle. Find an expression that uses only the variable θ to represent the shaded area of the diagram.

   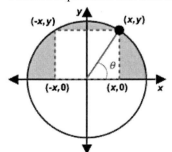

   Solution: $50\pi - 200\sin\theta\cos\theta$

   Explanation: The area of the half circle is $A_1 = \frac{\pi r^2}{2} = \frac{\pi(10^2)}{2} = 50\pi$. The area of the rectangle is $A_2 = lw = (2x)(y)$. Since $x = 10\cos\theta$ and $y = 10\sin\theta$, the area of the rectangle is $A_2 = 2(10\cos\theta)(10\sin\theta) = 200\cos\theta\sin\theta$. So the shaded area is $A = A_1 - A_2 = 50\pi - 200\sin\theta\cos\theta$.

Practice problems: *(Answers on page: 458)*

1. A point (x, y) moves along a circle represented by $x^2 + y^2 = 400$, but never leaves the first quadrant. At any location, the point determines an angle θ. A horizontal line through the point, a vertical line through the point, and a diameter of the circle determine a triangle. Write an expression for the vertical leg of the triangle.

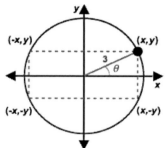

2. The area of a figure is given by the equation $A = \dfrac{(1 + \cos(2\theta))}{2}$. In the interval $0 \le \theta \le \pi$, at what value of θ is the area of the figure equal to zero?

3. A point moves around a circle represented by $x^2 + y^2 = 9$. At any location on the circle, the points (x, y), $(-x, y)$, $(x, -y)$, and $(-x, -y)$ determine a rectangle. Also, for each value of θ, $x = 3\cos\theta$ and $y = 3\sin\theta$. The area of the rectangle can be expressed in terms of θ as $18\sin(2\theta)$. In the interval $0 \le \theta \le \pi$, what is the value of θ that maximizes the area of the rectangle?

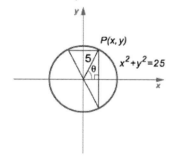

Review questions: *(Answers to odd questions on page: 458)*

1. A point (x, y) moves along a circle represented by $x^2 + y^2 = 25$, but never leaves the first quadrant. At any location, the point determines an angle θ. A horizontal line through the point, a vertical line through the point, and a diameter of the circle determine a triangle. Write x and y in terms of $\sin\theta$ and $\cos\theta$.

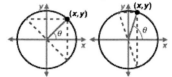

www.thinkwell.com

2. A point (x, y) moves along a circle represented by $x^2 + y^2 = 400$, but never leaves the first quadrant. At any location, the point determines an angle θ. A horizontal line through the point, a vertical line through the point, and a diameter of the circle determine a triangle.

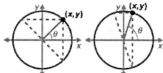

Using the formula for the area of a triangle $A = \left(\dfrac{1}{2}\right)bh$, what is an expression for the area of the triangle formed by the horizontal and vertical lines through (x, y) and the diameter of the circle?

3. A point (x, y) moves along a circle represented by $x^2 + y^2 = 400$, but never leaves the first quadrant. At any location, the point determines an angle θ. A horizontal line through the point, a vertical line through the point, and a diameter of the circle determine a triangle.

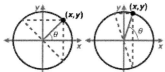

Write x and y in terms of $\sin\theta$ and $\cos\theta$.

4. A point (x, y) moves along a circle represented by $x^2 + y^2 = 400$. At any location on the circle, the point determines an angle θ. A horizontal line through the point, a vertical line through the point, and a diameter of the circle determine a triangle.

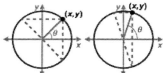

Write an expression that gives the area of the triangle in terms of $\sin\theta$ and $\cos\theta$.

5. A point (a, b) moves along a circle represented by $x^2 + y^2 = 36$, but never leaves the first quadrant. At any location, the point determines an angle q. A horizontal line through the point, a vertical line through the point, and a diameter of the circle determine a triangle. Using the formula for the area of a triangle, $A = (\dfrac{1}{2})(B)(H)$, what is an expression for the area of the triangle in terms of $\sin\theta$ and $\cos\theta$?

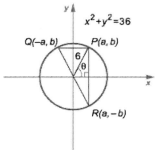

Using a Cofunction Identity

- The **cofunction identities** relate sine to cosine and tangent to cotangent:
  - $\cos(x - \pi/2) = \sin x$
  - $\sin(x - \pi/2) = -\cos x$
  - $\tan(x - \pi/2) = -\cot x$

Example $\cos\left(x - \frac{\pi}{2}\right) \overset{?}{=}$ 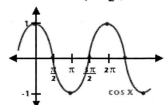	The graph of $\cos x$ is given to the left.

Find the effect of subtracting $\pi/2$ from x. |
| *- Here we're subtracting from x so we shift East.* | Since $\pi/2$ is subtracted from x, the graph is shifted "east," or to the right, of where it used to be.

The new graph looks a lot like the graph of $\sin x$.

How could you determine, algebraically, if the function $\cos(x - \pi/2)$ is the same as $\sin x$? |
| **difference of angles:** $$\cos(\Theta_1 - \Theta_2) = \cos\Theta_1\cos\Theta_2 + \sin\Theta_1\sin\Theta_2$$
 Example $\cos\left(x - \frac{\pi}{2}\right) \overset{?}{=} \sin x$

 $\cos\left(x - \frac{\pi}{2}\right) = \cos x \cos\frac{\pi}{2} + \sin x \sin\frac{\pi}{2}$

 $\quad = \cos x \ (0) \ + \sin x \ (1)$

 $\quad = \sin x$ | Rewrite $\cos(x - \pi/2)$ using the identity for the cosine of a difference of two angles.

Plug in x and $\pi/2$ appropriately into the formula.

Evaluate the trig functions of $\pi/2$: the cosine of $\pi/2$ is 0, and the sine of $\pi/2$ is 1.

$\cos(x - \pi/2)$ simplifies to $\sin x$. |
| $\cos\left(x - \frac{\pi}{2}\right) \overset{\checkmark}{=} \sin x$ $y = \sin x$ | Therefore, the function $\cos x$ shifted to the right $\pi/2$ units is the same as the sine function. |
| **Example** $\sin\left(x - \frac{\pi}{2}\right) \overset{?}{=}$ 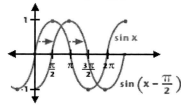 | Now graph $\sin(x - \pi/2)$ and compare it with the graph of $\cos x$.

Again, the curve shifts to the right, or "east." But it doesn't yield the $\cos x$ curve because, for example, the angle 0 is -1 on this new curve while it is 1 on the $\cos x$ curve. However, following the curve, notice that the new curve matches the negative of the cosine curve. |
| **Example** $\sin\left(x - \frac{\pi}{2}\right) \overset{?}{=} -\cos x$

 $\sin\left(x - \frac{\pi}{2}\right) = \sin x \cos\frac{\pi}{2} - \cos x \sin\frac{\pi}{2}$

 $\quad = \sin x \ (0) \ - \cos x \ (1)$

 $\sin\left(x - \frac{\pi}{2}\right) \overset{\checkmark}{=} -\cos x$

 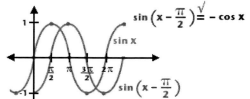 | Can you determine, algebraically, that $\sin(x - \pi/2) = -\cos x$?

Use the identity for the sine of a difference of two angles.

Substitute in known values.

Simplify to find that $\sin(x - \pi/2) = -\cos x$. |

difference of angles:
$$\tan(\theta_1 - \theta_2) = \frac{\tan\theta_1 - \tan\theta_2}{1 + \tan\theta_1 \tan\theta_2}$$

Example $\tan\left(x - \frac{\pi}{2}\right) \stackrel{?}{=} -\cot x$

$$\tan\left(x - \frac{\pi}{2}\right) = \left(\frac{\tan x - \tan\frac{\pi}{2}}{1 + \tan x \tan\frac{\pi}{2}}\right)\left(\frac{\frac{1}{\tan\frac{\pi}{2}}}{\frac{1}{\tan\frac{\pi}{2}}}\right)$$

same as multiplying
by $\frac{1}{1}$

Can you prove algebraically that $\tan(x - \pi/2) = -\cot x$?

First, write out the expression.

Multiply by a fraction equal to 1 to get rid of the undefined value $\tan(\pi/2)$.

$$= \frac{\frac{\tan x}{\tan\frac{\pi}{2}} - 1}{\frac{1}{\tan\frac{\pi}{2}} + \tan x} = \frac{\tan x \cot\frac{\pi}{2} - 1}{\cot\frac{\pi}{2} + \tan x}$$

This is the resulting fraction on the left. Substitute cotangent for tangent in the denominator.

$$= \frac{\tan x(0) - 1}{(0) + \tan x} = \frac{-1}{\tan x} = \boxed{-\cot x}$$

Then substitute known values in wherever possible.

Therefore: $\tan(x - \pi/2) = -\cot x$.

Sample problems:

1. Evaluate $\tan(\theta - 90°)$ if $\tan\theta = \frac{5}{3}$.

Solution: $-\frac{3}{5}$

Explanation: By the cofunction identities, $\tan\left(\theta - \frac{\pi}{2}\right) = -\cot\theta$ and $\frac{\pi}{2} = 90°$,

so $\tan(\theta - 90°) = -\cot\theta = -\frac{1}{\tan\theta} = -\frac{1}{\frac{5}{3}} = -\frac{3}{5}$.

2. Simplify: $\tan\left(x + \frac{\pi}{4}\right)$

Solution: $\frac{1 + \tan x}{1 - \tan x}$

Explanation: Simplify $\tan\left(x + \frac{\pi}{4}\right)$ using the identity for the tangent of a difference of two angles:

$$\tan\left(x + \frac{\pi}{4}\right) = \frac{\tan x + \tan\frac{\pi}{4}}{1 - \tan x \tan\frac{\pi}{4}} = \frac{\tan x + 1}{1 - (\tan x)(1)} = \frac{1 + \tan x}{1 - \tan x}.$$

3. Simplify: $\cos\left(x + \frac{3\pi}{2}\right)$

Solution: $\sin x$

Explanation: Simplify $\cos\left(x + \frac{3\pi}{2}\right)$ using the identity for the cosine of a sum of two angles:

$$\cos\left(x + \frac{3\pi}{2}\right) = \cos x \cos\frac{3\pi}{2} - \sin x \sin\frac{3\pi}{2} = (\cos x)(0) - (\sin x)(-1) = 0 + \sin x = \sin x.$$

Practice problems: *(Answers on page: 458)*

1. Simplify: $\tan(2\pi - x)$

2. Simplify: $\cot\left(\frac{\pi}{2} - x\right)$

3. Simplify: $\sin(x - 3\pi)$

Review questions: *(Answers to odd questions on page: 458)*

1. Simplify: $\cos\left(x - \dfrac{\pi}{2}\right)$

2. Simplify: $\sin\left(x - \dfrac{\pi}{2}\right)$

3. Simplify: $\sin\left(\pi - x\right)$

4. Simplify: $\cos\left(x + \dfrac{\pi}{2}\right)$

5. Simplify: $\cot\left(\dfrac{\pi}{2} + x\right)$

Using a Power-Reducing Identity

- **Power-reducing identities** allow you to write trig expressions with powers as equivalent expressions without powers.
- The power-reducing identities:

  - $\cos^2 \theta = \dfrac{1 + \cos(2\theta)}{2}$

  - $\sin^2 \theta = \dfrac{1 - \cos(2\theta)}{2}$

Example Rewrite: $\sin^4\theta$ $\sin^4\theta = (\sin^2\theta)^2$ $(\sin^2\theta)^2 = \left(\dfrac{1 - \cos(2\theta)}{2}\right)^2$ $\qquad = \dfrac{1}{4}\left[1 - 2\cos(2\theta) + \cos^2(2\theta)\right]$	How would you rewrite the expression $\sin^4 \theta$ without using any powers? Start by writing the original expression as an expression squared. Substitute a **power-reducing** identity for the $\sin^2\theta$ term. Square the resulting expression.
$\qquad = \dfrac{1}{4}\left(\dfrac{2 - 4\cos(2\theta) + 1 + \cos(4\theta)}{2}\right)$ $\sin^4\theta = \boxed{\dfrac{1}{8}\left[3 - 4\cos(2\theta) + \cos(4\theta)\right]}$	Again, substitute the power-reducing identity for the $\cos^2(2\theta)$ term. **REMEMBER**: Double the angle when using a power-reducing identity. Find a common denominator for the expression in the brackets, then simplify.
The Power of Reducing Power Formulas: - *Reduce trig functions with powers to simpler expressions without powers.*	Power-reducing formulas can be really useful—look for opportunities to use them.

Sample problems:

1. Solve for x in the interval $0 < x < \pi$: $\sec^4 2x = 4$

   Solution: $\dfrac{\pi}{8},\ \dfrac{3\pi}{8},\ \dfrac{5\pi}{8},\ \dfrac{7\pi}{8}$

   Explanation: $\sec^4 2x = 4$; $\sqrt{\sec^4 2x} = \sqrt{4}$; $\sec^2 2x = \pm 2$; $\dfrac{1}{\cos^2 2x} = \pm 2$;

   $\cos^2 2x = \pm\dfrac{1}{2}$; $\sqrt{\cos^2 2x} = \pm\sqrt{\dfrac{1}{2}}$; $\cos 2x = \pm\dfrac{\sqrt{2}}{2}$; $2x = \dfrac{\pi}{4},\ \dfrac{3\pi}{4},\ \dfrac{5\pi}{4},$ or $\dfrac{7\pi}{4}$,

   so $x = \dfrac{\pi}{8},\ \dfrac{3\pi}{8},\ \dfrac{5\pi}{8},$ or $\dfrac{7\pi}{8}$.

2. Express $2(\sin^4 t)$ without using any exponents other than 1.

   Solution: $\left(\dfrac{1}{4}\right)(3 - 4\cos 2t + \cos 4t)$

   Explanation: Write the expression in parentheses as a square: $2\left(\sin^4 t\right) = 2\left(\sin^2 t\right)^2$.

   Use the power-reducing identity: $2\left(\sin^2 t\right)^2 = 2\left(\dfrac{1 - \cos 2t}{2}\right)^2 = 2\cdot\left(\dfrac{1}{4}\right)(1 - 2\cos 2t + \cos^2 2t)$.

   Use the power-reducing identity for cosine: $\left(\dfrac{1}{2}\right)(1 - 2\cos 2t + \cos^2 2t) = \left(\dfrac{1}{2}\right)\left(1 - 2\cos 2t + \dfrac{1 + \cos 4t}{2}\right)$

   Find a common denominator and combine like terms: $\left(\dfrac{1}{2}\right)\left(\dfrac{2 - 4\cos 2t + 1 + \cos 4t}{2}\right) = \left(\dfrac{1}{2}\right)\left(\dfrac{3 - 4\cos 2t + \cos 4t}{2}\right)$

   Simplify: $\left(\dfrac{1}{4}\right)(3 - 4\cos 2t + \cos 4t)$.

3. Express $\cos^4 t$ without using any exponents other than 1.

   Solution: $\left(\dfrac{1}{8}\right)(3 + 4\cos 2t + \cos 4t)$

   Explanation: Write the original expression as an expression squared: $\cos^4 t = \left(\cos^2 t\right)^2$.

   Use the power-reducing identity: $\cos^4 t = \left(\cos^2 t\right)^2 = \left(\dfrac{1 + \cos 2t}{2}\right)^2 = \left(\dfrac{1}{4}\right)(1 + 2\cos 2t + \cos^2 2t)$.

   Again, use the power-reducing identity: $\left(\dfrac{1}{4}\right)(1 + 2\cos 2t + \cos^2 2t) = \left(\dfrac{1}{4}\right)\left(1 + 2\cos t + \dfrac{1 + \cos 4t}{2}\right) =$

   $\left(\dfrac{1}{4}\right)\left(\dfrac{2 + 4\cos 2t + 1 + \cos 4t}{2}\right) = \left(\dfrac{1}{8}\right)(3 + 4\cos 2t + \cos 4t)$.

Practice problems: *(Answers on page: 458)*

1. Express $\cos^4 t - \sin^4 t$ without using any exponents other than 1.

2. Solve for x in the interval $0 < x < \pi$: $\tan^2 2x - 1 = 0$

3. Express $\tan^4 t$ without using any exponents other than 1.

Review questions: *(Answers to odd questions on page: 458)*

1. Express $\sin^3 t$ without using any exponents other than 1.

2. Express $\dfrac{\cos^4 t}{16}$ without using any exponents other than 1.

3. Express $\cos^4 t - \cos^2 t$ without using any exponents other than 1.

4. Express $\cos^3 t$ without using any exponents other than 1.

5. Express $\dfrac{\tan^4 t}{4}$ without using any exponents other than 1.

Using Half-Angle Identities to Solve a Trigonometric Equation

- **Half-angle identities** allow you to write trig functions of an angle $x/2$ (half of the angle x) in terms of trig functions of the angle x:

  - $\cos\dfrac{x}{2} = \pm\sqrt{\dfrac{1 + \cos x}{2}}$

  - $\sin\dfrac{x}{2} = \pm\sqrt{\dfrac{1 - \cos x}{2}}$

  - $\tan\dfrac{x}{2} = \pm\dfrac{1 - \cos x}{\sin x}$

Reducing Power Formulas: $$\cos^2\theta = \frac{\cos(2\theta) + 1}{2} \quad \bigg| \quad \sin^2\theta = \frac{1 - \cos(2\theta)}{2}$$	To derive the **half-angle identities**, start with the **power-reducing identities**. Note that the squared side is in terms of θ while the unsquared side is in terms of 2θ.
Half-Angle Formulas: $$\cos\left(\frac{x}{2}\right) = \pm\sqrt{\frac{1 + \cos x}{2}} \quad \bigg| \quad \sin\left(\frac{x}{2}\right) = \pm\sqrt{\frac{1 - \cos x}{2}}$$	Take the square roots of both sides of the identities. 2θ is represented as x, and therefore θ is $x/2$. **NOTE:** In the half-angle formulas, the angles are represented by $x/2$ and x instead of θ and 2θ. The angle on the right is still twice the angle on the left.
$$\tan\left(\frac{x}{2}\right) = \frac{1 - \cos x}{\sin x}$$	Using the two identities above, the half-angle identity for tangent is derived.
Choose the sign $(+\ -)$ of your trig function based on the quadrant your angle lies in. Students ← All, Take → Calculus. sine positive / All trig functions are S / A + , T / C, tangent positive / cosine positive	Pay special attention to the signs for your answer. **REMEMBER:** The quadrant that an angle is in determines the signs of its trig functions.
Example $\sin 15° = \sin\left(\dfrac{30°}{2}\right)$ $\sin\left(\dfrac{30°}{2}\right) = \sqrt{\dfrac{1 - \cos(30°)}{2}}$	Consider the given example: find the value of $\sin 15°$. Since $15° = 30°/2$, use a half-angle identity.
$= \sqrt{\dfrac{1 - \sqrt{3}/2}{2}}$ $= \sqrt{\dfrac{\frac{2}{2} - \sqrt{3}/2}{2}}$ $= \sqrt{\dfrac{2 - \sqrt{3}}{4}}$ $\boxed{\sin 15° = \dfrac{\sqrt{2 - \sqrt{3}}}{2}}$	Now substitute in the known values. Find a common denominator. Do the arithmetic to find the answer.

Sample problems:

1. Find the exact value of $\tan 67.5°$.

   Solution: $1 + \sqrt{2}$

   Explanation: Express $67.5°$ as a fraction with a denominator of 2: $\tan 67.5° = \tan \dfrac{135°}{2}$.

   Use a half-angle identity to simplify: $\tan \dfrac{135°}{2} = \dfrac{1 - \cos 135°}{\sin 135°} = \dfrac{1 - \dfrac{\left(-\sqrt{2}\right)}{2}}{\dfrac{\sqrt{2}}{2}}$

   $$= \dfrac{\dfrac{2}{2} + \dfrac{\sqrt{2}}{2}}{\dfrac{\sqrt{2}}{2}} = \dfrac{2 + \sqrt{2}}{\sqrt{2}} \cdot \dfrac{\sqrt{2}}{\sqrt{2}}$$

   $$= \dfrac{\left(2\sqrt{2}\right) + 2}{2} = \sqrt{2} + 1.$$

2. Find the exaxt value of $\tan \dfrac{\pi}{12}$.

   Solution: $2 - \sqrt{3}$

   Explanation: Express $\dfrac{\pi}{12}$ as a fraction with a denominator of 2: $\tan \dfrac{\pi}{12} = \tan \dfrac{\frac{\pi}{6}}{2}$.

   Use a half-angle identity to simplify: $\tan \dfrac{\frac{\pi}{6}}{2} = \dfrac{1 - \cos \frac{\pi}{6}}{\sin \frac{\pi}{6}} = \dfrac{1 - \frac{\sqrt{3}}{2}}{\frac{1}{2}} = 2 - \sqrt{3}$.

3. Find the value of $\cos x$ for $x = 67.5$ to four decimal places.

   Solution: 0.3827

   Explanation: Substitute using the half-angle formula:

   $$\cos(67.5) = \cos\left(\dfrac{135}{2}\right) = \sqrt{\dfrac{1 + \cos 135}{2}}.$$

   (Note: use the positive square root since 67.5 is in the first quadrant).

   $$\sqrt{\dfrac{1 + \cos 135}{2}} = \sqrt{\dfrac{1 + \left(-\dfrac{\sqrt{2}}{2}\right)}{2}} = \sqrt{\dfrac{2 - \sqrt{2}}{4}} = \dfrac{\sqrt{2 - \sqrt{2}}}{2} \approx 0.3827$$

Practice problems: *(Answers on page: 458)*

1. Find the exact value for $\tan \dfrac{x}{2}$ given $\cos x = \dfrac{24}{25}$ and $\sin x > 0$.

2. Find $\sin \dfrac{a}{2}$ if $\cos a = \dfrac{12}{13}$ for $0° \le a \le 90°$.

3. Find the exact value of $\sin 7.5°$.

Review questions: *(Answers to odd questions on page: 458)*

1. Find the exact value of $\cos 15°$.

2. Find the exact value of $\sin 22.5°$.

3. Find the exact value of $\tan 22.5°$.

4. Find the exact value of $\sin 67.5°$.

5. Find the exact value of $\cos 22.5°$.

4

Applications of Trigonometry

The Law of Sines

- The **law of sines** allows you to solve for sides or angles of triangles that are not right triangles.
- The law of sines:

  In a triangle with sides a, b, and c opposite angles α, β, and γ, $\dfrac{\sin\alpha}{a} = \dfrac{\sin\beta}{b} = \dfrac{\sin\gamma}{c}$.

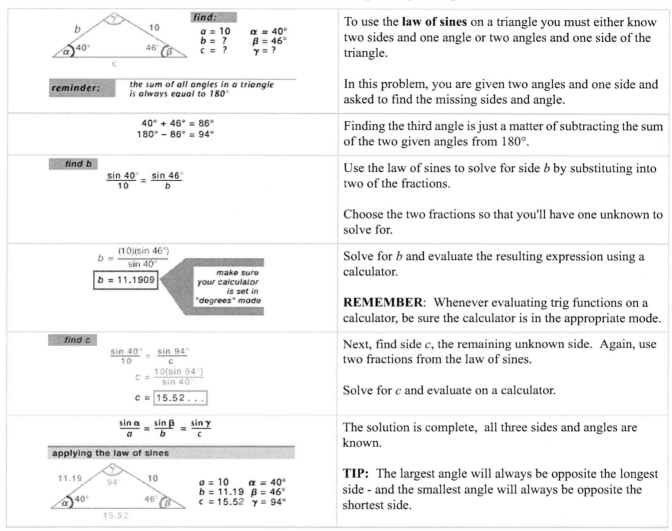

find: $a = 10$ $\alpha = 40°$ $b = ?$ $\beta = 46°$ $c = ?$ $\gamma = ?$ **reminder:** the sum of all angles in a triangle is always equal to $180°$	To use the **law of sines** on a triangle you must either know two sides and one angle or two angles and one side of the triangle. In this problem, you are given two angles and one side and asked to find the missing sides and angle.
$40° + 46° = 86°$ $180° − 86° = 94°$	Finding the third angle is just a matter of subtracting the sum of the two given angles from $180°$.
find b $\dfrac{\sin 40°}{10} = \dfrac{\sin 46°}{b}$	Use the law of sines to solve for side b by substituting into two of the fractions. Choose the two fractions so that you'll have one unknown to solve for.
$b = \dfrac{(10)(\sin 46°)}{\sin 40°}$ $\boxed{b = 11.1909}$ make sure your calculator is set in "degrees" mode	Solve for b and evaluate the resulting expression using a calculator. **REMEMBER**: Whenever evaluating trig functions on a calculator, be sure the calculator is in the appropriate mode.
find c $\dfrac{\sin 40°}{10} = \dfrac{\sin 94°}{c}$ $c = \dfrac{10(\sin 94°)}{\sin 40°}$ $c = \boxed{15.52 \ldots}$	Next, find side c, the remaining unknown side. Again, use two fractions from the law of sines. Solve for c and evaluate on a calculator.
$\dfrac{\sin\alpha}{a} = \dfrac{\sin\beta}{b} = \dfrac{\sin\gamma}{c}$ **applying the law of sines** $a = 10$ $\alpha = 40°$ $b = 11.19$ $\beta = 46°$ $c = 15.52$ $\gamma = 94°$	The solution is complete, all three sides and angles are known. **TIP:** The largest angle will always be opposite the longest side - and the smallest angle will always be opposite the shortest side.

Sample problems:

1. An isosceles triangle has a base of length 49.28 meters and the angle opposite the base is 58.746°. Find the length of the legs of the triangle.
   Solution: 50.23m
   Explanation: Begin by finding the two missing angles (they are equal because the triangle is defined as being isosceles): $180° - 58.746° = 121.254° / 2 = 60.627°$.

   Use the law of sines to find the length of the legs: $\dfrac{a}{\sin A} = \dfrac{c}{\sin C}$; $\dfrac{49.28}{\sin 58.746°} = \dfrac{c}{\sin 60.627°}$; $c = \dfrac{49.28(0.8714)}{(0.8549)} = 50.23$.

2. In the triangle $\angle 1 = \angle 2$, $\overline{CD}$ bisects $\angle ACB$, and $\overline{AD} = 224$. Find $\overline{BD}$.

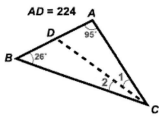

AD = 224

Solution: 509

Explanation: Find $\angle 1$ and $\angle 2$: $\angle 1 + \angle 2 = 180° - (95° + 26°)$; $\angle 1 + \angle 2 = 59°$,

so $\angle 1 = \angle 2 = 29.5°$. Use the law of sines to find $\overline{CD}$: $\dfrac{\sin 95°}{\overline{CD}} = \dfrac{\sin 29.5°}{224}$;

$\overline{CD} = \dfrac{224 \sin 95°}{\sin 29.5} = 453.2$. Find $\overline{BD}$: $\dfrac{\sin 29.5°}{\overline{BD}} = \dfrac{\sin 26°}{453.2}$;

$\overline{BD} = \dfrac{453.2 \sin 29.5°}{\sin 26°} = 509$.

3. The three angles in a triangle correspond to the ratio $5:6:9$. The shortest side of the triangle is 3.25 inches. Find the length of the longest side of the triangle to the nearest hundredth.

Solution: 4.54

Explanation: Find the three angles. The angles can be represented as $5x$, $6x$, and $9x$. The sum of the angles is 180°, so $20x = 180°$ or $x = 9°$, thus the three angles are 45°, 54°, and 81°. The shortest side of the triangle is 3.25, which must be opposite the smallest angle. The longest side is opposite the 81° angle . Use the law of sines: $\dfrac{\sin 81°}{a} = \dfrac{\sin 45°}{3.25}$; $a = \dfrac{3.25(\sin 81°)}{\sin 45°} = 4.54$.

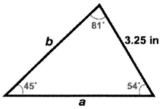

Practice problems: *(Answers on page: 458)*

1. Find the lengths a and b to the nearest millimeter.

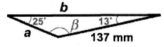

2. The angles of a triangle correspond to the ratio 3:4:5. If the longest side of the triangle is 324 mm, find the length of the shortest side.

3. The vertex angle of an isosceles triangle is 25°, and the legs of the triangle are each 10.0 in. Find the length of the third side of the triangle to the nearest tenth.

Review questions: *(Answers to odd questions on page: 458)*

1. Given that one angle of a triangle is 110°, another angle is 30°, and the side opposite the 30° angle measures 10.5 meters, find the side opposite the unknown angle.

2. AB is a line 652 feet long on one bank of a stream. C is a point on the opposite bank. Angle $A = 50°$ while angle $B = 48°$. Find the width of the stream from C to AB .

3. What is the length of side b?

4. Determine the measure of angle α.

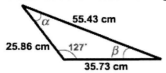

5. The base angles of an isosceles triangle are 73° and the base is 12.86 in. Find the length of the two legs of the triangle to the nearest tenth of an inch.

Solving a Triangle Given Two Sides and One Angle

- **Review**: The **law of sines** solves for sides or angles of triangles that are not right triangles.
- **Review**:

The law of sines: $\dfrac{\sin \alpha}{a} = \dfrac{\sin \beta}{b} = \dfrac{\sin \gamma}{c}$.

applying the law of sines **given: α, a, b** **find: β, γ, c** $\alpha = 50°$ $a = 10$ $\beta = ?$ $b = 8$ $\gamma = ?$ $c = ?$	Given two sides and one angle, use the **law of sines** to solve the triangle.
finding β $\dfrac{\sin 50°}{10} = \dfrac{\sin \beta}{8}$	Start by finding the angle β. Choose the two fractions from the law of sines that leave just one unknown and plug in what is known.
$\sin \beta = \dfrac{8 \sin 50°}{10}$ $\sin \beta = .6128\ldots$ *take inverse sin of β (or arcsin)* $\boxed{\beta = 37.8°}$	Solve the equation for $\sin \beta$. Evaluate the expression using a calculator. Use the **inverse sine function** to find β.
finding γ $\alpha + \beta + \gamma = 180°$ $50° + 37.8° + \gamma = 180°$ $\gamma = \boxed{92.2°}$	To find the third angle, subtract the known angles from 180°.
finding c $\dfrac{\sin 50°}{10} = \dfrac{\sin 92.2°}{c}$ $c = \dfrac{10 \sin 92.2°}{\sin 50°}$ $c = \boxed{13.044\ldots}$	Now solve for the missing side c: Set up two fractions from the law of sines. Cross-multiply, then solve for c. Evaluate the expression.
$\alpha = 50°$ $a = 10$ $\beta = 37.8°$ $b = 8$ $\gamma = 92.2°$ $c = 13$	In summary, here are the findings.
tip *the largest angle will always be opposite the longest side - and the smallest angle will always be opposite the shortest side*	**REMEMBER:** the largest angle will always be opposite the longest side. The smallest angle will always be opposite the shortest side.

Sample problems:

1. Given a triangle with side $a = 91$m, side $b = 73.5$m, and angle $A = 39°$, find angle B.

   Solution: 30.55°

   Explanation: Substitute into the law of sines: $\dfrac{\sin A}{a} = \dfrac{\sin B}{b}$; $\dfrac{\sin 39°}{91} = \dfrac{\sin B}{73.5}$;

   $\dfrac{91}{\sin 39} = \dfrac{73.5}{\sin B}$; $\sin B = \dfrac{(\sin 39)(73.5)}{(91)} = 0.5083$. Use the arcsin function on a

   calculator: $B = 30.55°$.

2. Use the law of sines to find angle α to the nearest tenth.

   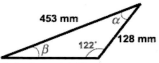

   Solution: 44.1°

   Explanation: Use the law of sines to find β: $\dfrac{\sin \beta}{128} = \dfrac{\sin 122°}{453}$; $\sin \beta = \dfrac{(128(\sin 122°)}{453} =$

   0.2396, $\beta = 13.9°$. Find α: $\alpha = 180° - (122° + \beta) = 180° - (122° + 13.9°) = 44.1°$.

3. Find the missing side of the triangle.

   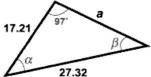

   Solution: 19.22

   Explanation: Find angle β: $\dfrac{\sin 97°}{27.32} = \dfrac{\sin \beta}{17.21}$; $\sin \beta = \dfrac{(17.21)(\sin 97°)}{27.32} = 0.6252$,

   $\beta = 38.7$. Find α: $\alpha = 180° - (97° + 38.7°) = 44.3°$. Find a: $\dfrac{\sin 44.3°}{a} = \dfrac{\sin 97°}{27.32}$;

   $a = \dfrac{(27.32)(\sin 44.3°)}{(\sin 97°)} = 19.22$.

Practice problems: *(Answers on page: 458)*

1. Given a triangle with side $b = 76.45$m, angle $B = 105°$ and side $a = 60$m, find angle C.

2. Use the law of sines to find the measure of angle β to the nearest degree.

   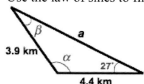

3. Find the lengths of sides a and b, each to the nearest tenth.

   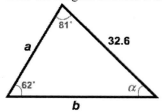

Review questions: *(Answers to odd questions on page: 458)*

1. Given the acute triangle $\triangle ABC$ with side $a = 67$ cm, side $c = 49.8$ cm, and angle $C = 42°$, find angle A.

2. Given $\triangle ABC$ with side $a = 68$ m, angle $A = 62.3°$, and side $c = 57.2$ m, find angle B.

3. In $\triangle ABC$, all angles are acute. Find side a and angle A, given that angle C is $61°$, side c is 21 in, and side b is 15 inches.

4. Given a triangle with angle $B = 110°$, side $b = 22.55$ feet, and side $c = 12$ feet, find angle C and side a.

5. Find side b and angle B given angle A is $42°$, side $a = 14$ inches, side $c = 18$ inches, and all angles are acute.

Solving a Triangle (SAS): Another Example

- **Review**:

  The law of sines: $\dfrac{\sin\alpha}{a} = \dfrac{\sin\beta}{b} = \dfrac{\sin\gamma}{c}$.

- If the side opposite the given angle is shorter than the adjacent side, there may be two triangles. If so, solve for both sets of possibilities. The possibilities are:
  - The opposite side is shorter than the altitude. If so, no triangle exists.
  - The opposite side is longer than the altitude and shorter than the adjacent side. If so, two triangles may be possible.
  - The opposite side is longer than the adjacent side. If so, one triangle is possible.

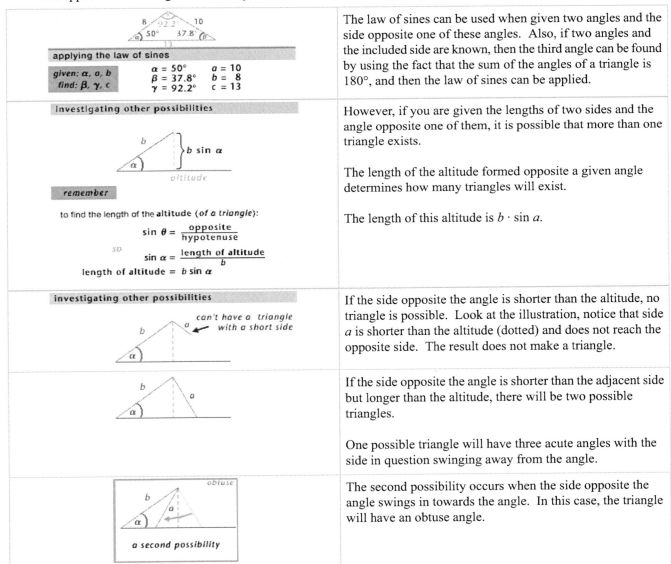

applying the law of sines given: α, a, b α = 50° a = 10 find: β, γ, c β = 37.8° b = 8 γ = 92.2° c = 13	The law of sines can be used when given two angles and the side opposite one of these angles. Also, if two angles and the included side are known, then the third angle can be found by using the fact that the sum of the angles of a triangle is $180°$, and then the law of sines can be applied.
investigating other possibilities $b\sin\alpha$ altitude **remember** to find the length of the altitude (of a triangle): $\sin\theta = \dfrac{\text{opposite}}{\text{hypotenuse}}$ so $\sin\alpha = \dfrac{\text{length of altitude}}{b}$ length of altitude $= b\sin\alpha$	However, if you are given the lengths of two sides and the angle opposite one of them, it is possible that more than one triangle exists. The length of the altitude formed opposite a given angle determines how many triangles will exist. The length of this altitude is $b \cdot \sin a$.
investigating other possibilities can't have a triangle with a short side	If the side opposite the angle is shorter than the altitude, no triangle is possible. Look at the illustration, notice that side a is shorter than the altitude (dotted) and does not reach the opposite side. The result does not make a triangle.
	If the side opposite the angle is shorter than the adjacent side but longer than the altitude, there will be two possible triangles. One possible triangle will have three acute angles with the side in question swinging away from the angle.
a second possibility	The second possibility occurs when the side opposite the angle swings in towards the angle. In this case, the triangle will have an obtuse angle.

$b \leqslant a$ $1 \triangle$ possible *only one possibility*	When the side opposite the angle is longer than the adjacent side, only one triangle is possible.
Example *suppose:* $\alpha = 50°$ $a = 8$ $b = 10$ *find: how will side a fall?* there are 2 possibilities: *acute* *obtuse*	Consider the given example: suppose $\alpha = 50°$, $a = 8$, and $b = 10$. Find all the possible triangles. The altitude is $b \cdot \sin a = (10)(\sin 50) = 7.6$. Since $a = 8$ and $b = 10$, a is longer than the altitude but shorter than b. So, two triangles are possible.
acute $\beta = 73.25°$ *so:* $\gamma = 180° - (73.25° + 50°)$ $= 56.75°$ **remember** the sum of the angles of a triangle always equals $180°$ $\dfrac{\sin 50°}{8} = \dfrac{\sin \beta}{10}$ $\sin \beta = \dfrac{10 \sin 50°}{8}$ $\sin \beta = .95755$	Consider one of the possibilities for β. Use the **law of sines** to solve for angle β. Now find γ by subtracting α and β from $180°$.
find c $\dfrac{\sin 50°}{8} = \dfrac{\sin 56.75°}{c}$ $c = 8.733$	Finally, return again to the law of sines to solve for side c. The triangle is solved. All three sides and all three angles are known.
obtuse $\gamma = 180° - (106.75° + 50°)$ $\gamma = 23.25°$ **remember** the sum of the angles of a triangle always equals $180°$ $\beta = 180° - 73.25°$ $\beta = 106.75°$	Now, solve for the second possible triangle. Start by finding β again. This time β must be obtuse, so the angle will be $180° - 73.25° = 106.75°$. Having found β, find the third angle by subtracting the two angles known for the triangle from $180°$.
find c $\dfrac{\sin 23.25°}{c} = \dfrac{\sin 50°}{8}$ $c = 4.12$	Finally, solve for the third side and then the triangle is solved.
note *if the side opposite the angle given is shorter than the adjacent side, you may have 2 triangles*	Always consider the possibility that two triangles might exist.

Sample problems:

1. In the diagram, $QS = QR$. Find $\angle 4$.

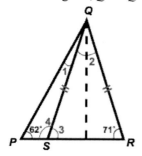

Solution: $109°$

Explanation: In triangle QRS, $QS = QR$ so $\angle 3 = 71°$. $\angle 4$ and $\angle 3$ are supplementary, so $\angle 4 + \angle 3 = 180°$ and $\angle 4 = 180° - 71° = 109°$.

---

2. Given the triangle FGH find angle H given that side $f = 11$ km, side $g = 15$ km and angle $G = 33°$.

Solution: $123.46°$

Explanation:

Find angle F using the law of sines: $\dfrac{\sin F}{11} = \dfrac{\sin 33°}{15}$; $\dfrac{\sin F}{11} = \dfrac{0.5446}{15}$;

$\sin F = \dfrac{(11)(0.5446)}{(15)} = 0.3994$, $F = 23.54°$.

Find angle H: $H = 180° - (33° + 23.54°) = 123.46°$.

3. In these triangles, $\alpha = 41°$, $b = 15.56$ mm, and $a = 13.05$ mm. Find the measures of $\angle 1$ and $\angle 2$ to the nearest degree.

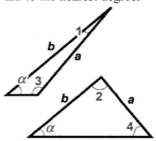

Solution: $\angle 1 = 10°$, $\angle 2 = 88°$

Explanation: Find $\angle 4$, the acute angle opposite b: $\dfrac{\sin 41°}{13.05} = \dfrac{\sin \angle 4}{15.56}$; $\sin \angle 4 =$

$\dfrac{(15.56)(\sin 41°)}{13.05} = 0.7822$, $\angle 4 = 51°$. Find the remaining angles: $\angle 2 = 180° - (41° + 51°) = 88°$;

$\angle 3$ and $\angle 4$ are supplementary, so $\angle 3 = 180° - 51° = 129°$; $\angle 1 = 180° - (\alpha + \angle 3) =$

$180° - (41° + 129°) = 10°$.

Practice problems: *(Answers on page: 458)*

1. In these two triangles, $\alpha = 52°$, $b = 22.71$ cm, and $a = 18.95$ cm.

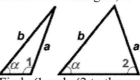

Find $\angle 1$ and $\angle 2$ to the nearest degree.

2. In triangle ABC, angle $B = 27°$, side $a = 8.2'$, and side $b = 5'$. Find two possibilities for angle C.

3. One angle of a triangle is given to be $54.93°$ and a side adjacent to that angle is 15.75 in. If there are two possible triangles, write an inequality to express the possible lengths for the side opposite the given angle.

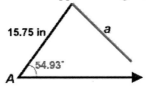

Review questions: *(Answers to odd questions on page: 458)*

1. In $\triangle ABC$, angle $A = 103°$, side $a = 37.48$ ft, and side $c = 29.73$ ft. Find angle C and side b.

2. In $\triangle RST$, angle $R = 41°$, side $r = 18$ cm, and side $s = 57$ cm. Find all possible measures for angle S.

3. In $\triangle ABC$, find angle B, given that angle $C = 31°$, side $a = 9.4$ ft, and side $c = 7$ ft. If two possibilities exist, state both of them.

4. Given triangle FGH, find side h when angle $F = 43°$, side $f = 12$cm and side $g = 9$cm.

5. In triangle PQR, angle $P = 37°$, side $p = 45$cm and side $q = 85$cm. Find all possible measures for angle Q.

The Law of Sines: An Application

Review: The **law of sines**: $\dfrac{\sin \alpha}{a} = \dfrac{\sin \beta}{b} = \dfrac{\sin \gamma}{c}$.

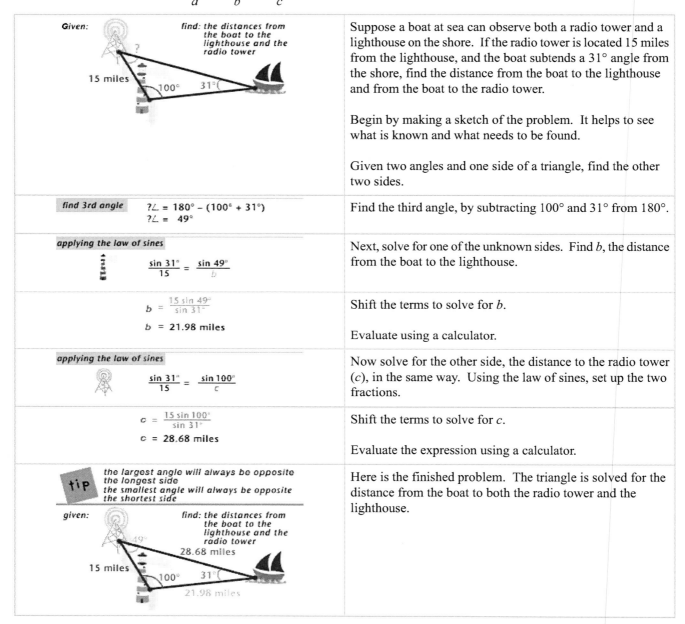

Given: find: the distances from the boat to the lighthouse and the radio tower 15 miles 100° 31°	Suppose a boat at sea can observe both a radio tower and a lighthouse on the shore. If the radio tower is located 15 miles from the lighthouse, and the boat subtends a 31° angle from the shore, find the distance from the boat to the lighthouse and from the boat to the radio tower. Begin by making a sketch of the problem. It helps to see what is known and what needs to be found. Given two angles and one side of a triangle, find the other two sides.
find 3rd angle $?\angle = 180° - (100° + 31°)$ $?\angle = 49°$	Find the third angle, by subtracting 100° and 31° from 180°.
applying the law of sines $\dfrac{\sin 31°}{15} = \dfrac{\sin 49°}{b}$	Next, solve for one of the unknown sides. Find b, the distance from the boat to the lighthouse.
$b = \dfrac{15 \sin 49°}{\sin 31°}$ $b = 21.98$ miles	Shift the terms to solve for b. Evaluate using a calculator.
applying the law of sines $\dfrac{\sin 31°}{15} = \dfrac{\sin 100°}{c}$	Now solve for the other side, the distance to the radio tower (c), in the same way. Using the law of sines, set up the two fractions.
$c = \dfrac{15 \sin 100°}{\sin 31°}$ $c = 28.68$ miles	Shift the terms to solve for c. Evaluate the expression using a calculator.
tip the largest angle will always be opposite the longest side the smallest angle will always be opposite the shortest side given: find: the distances from the boat to the lighthouse and the radio tower 49° 28.68 miles 15 miles 100° 31° 21.98 miles	Here is the finished problem. The triangle is solved for the distance from the boat to both the radio tower and the lighthouse.

Sample problems:

1. Two wires are part of the supports of a tall pole. One wire forms an angle of 53° with the ground and the other wire forms an angle of 78° with the ground. The distance between the feet of the wires is 25 m. Find the height of the pole CD.

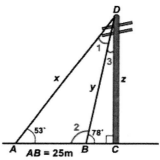

Solution: 46 m

Explanation: Start by finding the other angles in the diagram: $\angle 3=180°-(90°+78°)=12°$; $\angle 2=180°-78°=102°$; $\angle 1=180°-(53°+102°)=25°$. Use the law of sines to

find x: $\dfrac{\sin 25°}{25}=\dfrac{\sin 102°}{x}$; $x=\dfrac{25(\sin 102°)}{\sin 25°}=57.86$. Use the law of sines again

to find z: $\dfrac{\sin 90°}{57.86}=\dfrac{\sin 53°}{z}$; $z=46.2$. Thus, the height of the pole is 46.2 feet.

2. Two wireless telephone transmission centers are 35 km apart. A cell phone user is 19 km from one of the centers. At the cell phone user, the angle formed by the two centers is 101°. Find the distance between the cell phone user and the other transmission center.

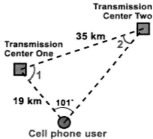

Solution: 26 km

Explanation: Let d be the distance between the cell phone user and the second

transmission center. Find the two unknown angles in the triangle: $\dfrac{\sin \angle 2}{19}=\dfrac{\sin 101°}{35}$;

$\sin \angle 2=\dfrac{(19)(\sin 101°)}{35}=0.5328$, so $\angle 2=32°$. Then $\angle 1=180°-(101°+32°)=47°$.

Find the distance: $\dfrac{\sin 47°}{d}=\dfrac{\sin 101°}{35}$; $d=\dfrac{(35)(\sin 47°)}{\sin 101°}=26$. The distance between the cell phone user and the other tower is 26 km.

3. Two ships are 272 km apart. A submarine lies directly below the line passing through the two ships. From the submarine, the angle formed by the ships is 41° while from ship A the angle formed by ship B and the submarine is 97°. How much farther is ship B from the submarine than ship A?

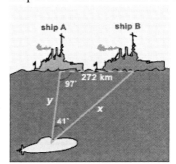

Solution: 134 km

Explanation: Find the distance from the submarine to each ship. For ship B:

$$\frac{\sin 97°}{x} = \frac{\sin 41°}{272}; \ x = \frac{(272)(\sin 97°)}{\sin 41°} = 411.5. \text{ For ship A: } 180° - (41° + 97°) = 42°;$$

$$\frac{\sin 42°}{y} = \frac{\sin 41°}{272}; \ y = \frac{(272)(\sin 42°)}{\sin 41°} = 277.4. \text{ The difference is } 411.5 - 277.4 = 134.1 \text{ km.}$$

Practice problems: *(Answers on page: 458)*

1. A Scout traveled 100 m from Troop Headquarters. For the Scout, the angle formed by the Target and Headquarters was 63°. From Headquarters, the angle formed by the Target and the Scout was 58°.

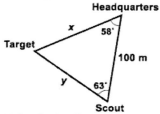

   What is the distance between Headquarters and the Target?

2. Flying above the straight line segment connecting one city to another, an airplane is 174 miles from the first city and 71 miles from the second. From the first city, the angle formed by the airplane and the ground is 22°. Find the distance between the two cities.

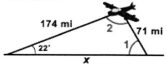

3. A radio tower sits on top of a hill. The distance along the hill from its base to the tower is 212 feet. The angle of elevation from the base of the hill to the top of the tower is 27.2°. The hill itself makes an angle of 14.3° with the horizontal. Find the height of the tower.

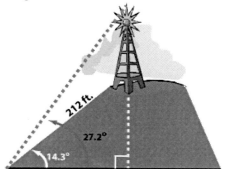

Review questions: *(Answers to odd questions on page: 458)*

1. A pilot in a helicopter sights an ambulance heading toward an accident scene. He measures the angles of depression to the ambulance and the accident to be 21° and 15°, respectively. If the helicopter is 4000 ft from the ambulance, how far does the ambulance have to travel to get to the accident?

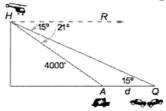

2. A person has a kite out on 1650 feet of string at an angle of 72° with the ground. An observer notes that the angle formed by the kite and the flier is 103°. Find the distance between the observer and the kite flier.

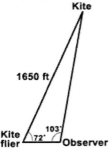

3. Smokey Bear standing on a hill can see two firewatch towers in the distance. He knows that the two towers are 8 miles from each other. He thinks he is approximately 4.8 miles from one tower. He roughly calculates the angle between his two lines of sight to the towers to be 34.6°. How far is he from the second tower?

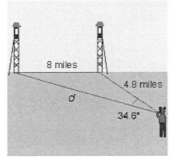

4. Ted was flying his Lear jet over Waikiki when he noticed a party on a yacht. His angle of depression was 17.5°. Then he noticed the surfer on a huge pipeline wave. His angle of depression to the surfer was 24.2°. His navigating copilot told him he was 5120 feet from the yacht. How far was he from the surfer? (Assume that all three characters are in a vertical plane.)

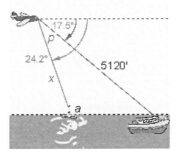

5. Troop A left base camp and hiked 6 hours at 4.4 mph. Troop B left the same camp and hiked 7 hours at 4.2 mph. That evening, Troop A noticed that the angle formed by beacons at the base camp and at Troop B's camp was 87°. Find the distance between Troop A and Troop B.

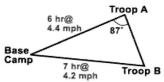

The Law of Cosines

- Like the **law of sines**, the **law of cosines** is a formula that solves for angles and sides for any given triangle, even those that are not right triangles. It is derived from the **Pythagorean theorem**.
- The law of cosines is used to solve a triangle when given three sides of a triangle or two sides plus the included angle.
- The law of cosines has three forms. In every case, the last term is 2 times the product of the two sides with the cosine of the included angle. The single term on the left is always the square of the side opposite the angle. Use the form of the identity that fits what is known about the triangle.

In a triangle with sides a, b, c, and opposite angles α, β, γ:

$$a^2 = b^2 + c^2 - 2bc\cos\alpha \qquad b^2 = a^2 + c^2 - 2ac\cos\beta \qquad c^2 = a^2 + b^2 - 2ab\cos\gamma$$

Pythagorean Theorem: $a^2 + b^2 = c^2$ how is the Pythagorean theorem extended to triangles that aren't right?	The **Pythagorean theorem** applies only to right triangles, although its influences are seen in many of the definitions and identities developed for trigonometry. It has been extended to apply to general triangles with no right angle.
solving for: α use: $a^2 = b^2 + c^2 - 2bc\cos\alpha$	For any non-right triangle, to solve for side a or its angle, α, use this version of the **law of cosines:** $a^2 = b^2 + c^2 - 2bc\cos\alpha$.
solving for: β use: $b^2 = a^2 + c^2 - 2ac\cos\beta$	To solve for side b or its angle, β, use this version of the law of cosines: $b^2 = a^2 + c^2 - 2ac\cos\beta$.
solving for: γ use: $c^2 = a^2 + b^2 - 2ab\cos\gamma$	To solve for side c or its angle, γ, use this version of the law of cosines: $c^2 = a^2 + b^2 - 2ab\cos\gamma$.
the general rule $(\text{opposite side})^2 = \text{sum of the squares of adjacent sides} - 2 \cdot (\text{product adjacent sides})(\cos \text{ of desired angle})$	This is a general way to state the law of cosines: $(\text{opposite side})^2$ = the sum of the squares of adjacent sides − 2 times the product of the adjacent sides times the cosine of the desired angle. **REMEMBER:** the angle must be the angle included between two known sides.
Pythagorean Theorem: $a^2 + b^2 = c^2$ law of cosines applied to a right triangle $c^2 = a^2 + b^2 - 2ab\cos\gamma$ (cos 90° = 0) special angle = 90°	In a right triangle, the law of cosines solves for c, the hypotenuse. In a right triangle, $\cos\gamma = \cos 90° = 0$. If you plug 0 in for $\cos\gamma$, the result is that the entire $-2ab\cos\gamma$ term drops out and what's left is the Pythagorean theorem.

Sample problems:

1. True or false: The equation $a^2 = 64 + 144 - 192\cos 62°$ may be used to find the missing side of the triangle below.

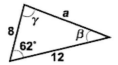

Solution: True

Explanation: In the law of cosines, $a^2 = b^2 + c^2 - 2bc\cos\alpha$, side a is the side opposite angle α, and the other two sides are b and c. Let $\alpha = 62°$, then $b = 8$ and $c = 12$. Substitute these values into the law of cosines and simplify: $a^2 = b^2 + c^2 - 2bc\cos\alpha \Rightarrow$ $a^2 = 8^2 + 12^2 - 2(8)(12)\cos 62°$; $a^2 = 64 + 144 - 192\cos 62°$, which is the equation given in the question.

2. Find the missing side for triangle FGH, if $\angle FGH = 55°$, $FG = 8.6$ cm and $GH = 5.7$cm.
   Solution: 7.09 cm
   Explanation: Use the law of cosines, $a^2 = b^2 + c^2 - 2bc\cos A$, to find the missing side, FH. Let $a = FH$, $b = 8.6$, $c = 5.7$, and $\angle A = 55°$. Substitute these values into the law of cosines $\left(\text{solved for } a\right)$ and simplify: $a = \sqrt{b^2 + c^2 - 2bc\cos A} \Rightarrow FH = $ $\sqrt{8.6^2 + 5.7^2 - 2(8.6)(5.7)(\cos 55°)} = \sqrt{50.22} = 7.09$. Thus, $FH = 7.09$cm.

3. Find the missing side of triangle RST given that $\angle T = 87°$, $ST = 16$mm, and $RT = 23$mm.
   Solution: 27.3mm
   Explanation: Use the law of cosines $a = \sqrt{b^2 + c^2 - 2bc\cos A}$, where $a = RS$, $b = 16$, $c = 23$, and $A = 87°$: $a = \sqrt{16^2 + 23^2 - 2(16)(23)\cos 87°} = \sqrt{256 + 529 - 736(0.0523)} = \sqrt{746.51} = 27.3$.

Practice problems: *(Answers on page: 458)*

1. What must be known about a triangle in order to use the law of cosines to find a missing side?

2. Find the missing side for triangle DEF given that $\angle D = 30°$, $DE = 8$ and $DF = 10$.

3. Find the missing side for triangle ABC given that $\angle B = 110°$, side $a = 4$ and side $c = 4$.

Review questions: *(Answers to odd questions on page: 458)*

1. Find the missing side of the triangle below.

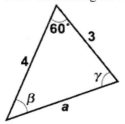

2. Find the missing side of the triangle below.

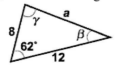

3. Find the missing side of $\triangle ABC$, given that angle C=113°, side $a = 7$, and side $b = 7$.

4. Find the missing side for $\triangle RST$ if you are given $\angle RST = 63°$, $SR = 9.3$ cm, and $ST = 6.9$ cm.

5. Find the missing side for $\triangle EFG$ if you are given $\angle F = 60°$, $EF = 11$ m, and $FG = 13$ m.

The Law of Cosines (SSS)

- **Review**: The **law of cosines** has three forms. Use the form that fits the triangle:

$$a^2 = b^2 + c^2 - 2bc\cos\alpha \quad b^2 = a^2 + c^2 - 2ac\cos\beta \quad c^2 = a^2 + b^2 - 2ab\cos\gamma$$

- **Review**: The law of cosines is used to solve a triangle when given three sides of a triangle or two sides plus the included angle.
- **Review**:

The law of sines: $\dfrac{\sin\alpha}{a} = \dfrac{\sin\beta}{b} = \dfrac{\sin\gamma}{c}$.

given: $a = 8$, $b = 3$, $c = 10$ **find:** $\alpha = ?$, $\beta = ?$, $\gamma = ?$	Given three sides of a triangle, $a = 8$, $b = 3$, $c = 10$, find all three angles, α, β, and γ.
$c^2 = a^2 + b^2 - 2ab\cos\gamma$ $10^2 = 8^2 + 3^2 - 2(8)(3) \cdot \cos\gamma$	First find γ. Use the version of the **law of cosines** which includes this angle: $c^2 = a^2 + b^2 - 2ab\cos\gamma$.
$100 = 73 - 48\cos\gamma$ *subtract 73 from both sides* $\dfrac{27}{-48} = \cos\gamma$ *divide through by -48* $-.5625 = \cos\gamma$	Now, substitute in all the known values and solve for the angle.
$\gamma = 124.23°$	Use the **inverse cosine function** to solve for γ.
remember *sine is positive* *cosine is negative* $\begin{array}{c|c} S & A \\ \hline T & C \end{array}$	Since the cosine of γ is negative, γ should lie between 90° and 180°.
$\dfrac{\sin 124.2°}{10} = \dfrac{\sin\beta}{3}$	To find the second angle, use the **law of sines**. (It is possible to use the law of cosines again, but the arithmetic is easier when using the law of sines.)
$\sin\beta = \dfrac{3\sin 124.2°}{10}$ $\sin\beta = .24806$ $\beta = 14.37°$	Solve for $\sin\beta$. Then find the **inverse sine** to solve for β.
$180° = \alpha + \beta + \gamma$ $\alpha = 180° - \beta - \gamma$ $\alpha = 180° - 124.23° - 14.37°$ $\alpha = 41.40°$	Subtract the two known angles from 180° to find the third angle.
given: $a = 8$, $b = 3$, $c = 10$ **find:** $\alpha = 41.40°$, $\beta = 14.37°$, $\gamma = 124.2°$	Here is the triangle fully solved.

Sample problems:

1. Use the law of cosines to prove that triangle XYZ does not exist, given that $x = 2.5$ cm, $y = 15.0$ cm, and $z = 4.5$ cm.

   Solution: -8.8222 is not in the domain of cosine

   Explanation: Substitute the known values into the law of cosines: $y^2 = x^2 + z^2 - 2xz\cos Y \Rightarrow$ $(15)^2 = (2.5)^2 + (4.5)^2 - 2(2.5)(4.5)\cos Y$; $225 = 6.25 + 20.25 - 22.5\cos Y$; $198.5 = -22.5\cos Y$; $\cos Y = \dfrac{198.5}{-22.5} = -8.8222$. This is impossible, since -8.8222 is not in cosine's domain.

2. In the triangle below, $a = 4$, $b = 6$, and $c = 8$. Find angle β.

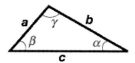

Solution: 46.57°

Explanation: Use the law of cosines to find an unknown angle when given the three sides.

Substitute the values of the sides into $b^2 = a^2 + c^2 - 2ac\cos\beta$ and solve for β:

$(6)^2 = (4)^2 + (8)^2 - 2(4)(8)\cos\beta$; $\quad 36 = 80 - 64\cos\beta$; $\quad \dfrac{-44}{-64} = \cos\beta$; $\quad 0.6875 = \cos\beta$;

$\beta = 46.57°$.

3. To straighten a tree, an 8.4 ft guide wire is stretched from the top of the tree trunk (6.8 ft) to a stake in the ground that is 4.9 ft from the base of the tree. What is the angle of elevation between the ground and the guide wire?

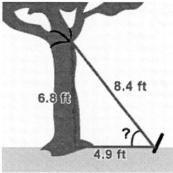

Solution: 54.05°

Explanation: Use the law of cosines to find the measure of the missing angle, x:

$(6.8)^2 = (4.9)^2 + (8.4)^2 - 2(4.9)(8.4)\cos x$; $\quad 46.24 = 94.57 - 82.32\cos\beta$;

$\dfrac{-48.33}{-82.32} = \cos\beta$; $\quad 0.587 = \cos\beta$; $\quad \beta = 54.05°$.

Practice problems: *(Answers on page: 458)*

1. In the triangle below, $a = 5$, $b = 7$, and $c = 10.5$. Find angle β.

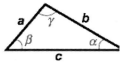

2. In triangle DEF, solve for $\angle D$ given that side $d = 80mm$, $e = 60mm$, and $f = 100mm$.

3. The triangle below has sides with lengths of 5, 9, and 12. Find the measures of all three angles.

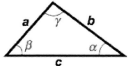

Given $a = 5$, $b = 9$, and $c = 12$, find α, β, and γ.

Review questions: *(Answers to odd questions on page: 459)*

1. For triangle PQR , find angle R given side $p = 5'$, $q = 4'$, and $r = 2'$.

2. In $\triangle ABC$ solve for B given that side $a = 20'$, $b = 25'$, and $c = 30'$.

3. The sides of a parallelogram are 40 feet and 70 feet. The length of the longer diagonal is 105 feet. What is the measure of the smaller angle in the parallelogram?

4. The triangle below has sides with lengths of $a = 50$, $b = 70$, and $c = 85$. Find the measure of the largest angle.

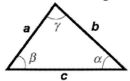

5. Find the smallest angle, given that $a : b : c = 4 : 5 : 7$.

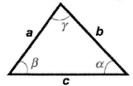

The Law of Cosines (SAS): An Application

- **Review**: The **law of cosines** has three forms depending on which angle is known:
  $$a^2 = b^2 + c^2 - 2bc\cos\alpha \quad b^2 = a^2 + c^2 - 2ac\cos\beta \quad c^2 = a^2 + b^2 - 2ab\cos\gamma$$
- **Review**: The law of cosines is used to solve a triangle when given three sides of a triangle, or two sides plus the included angle.
- **Review**:

  The **law of sines**: $\dfrac{\sin\alpha}{a} = \dfrac{\sin\beta}{b} = \dfrac{\sin\gamma}{c}$.

	Consider the example given here: find the length of the tunnel given two sides and the included angle of a triangle.
$t^2 = a^2 + b^2 - 2ab\cos\gamma$ $t^2 = 7^2 + 5^2 - 2(7)(5) \cdot \cos 28°$ $t^2 = 7^2 + 5^2 - 2(35) \cdot \cos 28°$	Find the third side of the triangle by letting t be the length of the tunnel and plugging it into the law of cosines.
$t^2 = 7^2 + 5^2 - 2(35) \cdot \cos 28°$ $t^2 = 49 + 25 - 70 \cdot \cos 28°$ $t^2 = 12.193$ $t = \sqrt{12.193}$ $\boxed{t = 3.491 \text{ miles}}$ 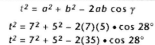	Do the arithmetic to find t^2. Take the square root to find the length of the tunnel, t. The length of the tunnel is 3.491 miles.

www.thinkwell.com

Sample problems:

1. A piece of wire is bent into the shape of a triangle. Two sides have lengths of 18 inches and 22 inches. The angle between these two sides is 45°. What is the total length of the wire?
   Solution: 55.7 inches
   Explanation: Use the law of cosines where a is the unknown side, $b = 18$, $c = 22$, and $\alpha = \cos 45°$:
   $a = \sqrt{b^2 + c^2 - 2bc \cos\alpha} = \sqrt{247.97} = 15.7$. Add the three lengths: $15.7 + 18 + 22 = 55.7$.

2. Two runners began running at the same time, but at a 100° angle from each other. One runner averages 10 mph, the other averages 6.5 mph. How far apart are the runners after one hour?
   Solution: 12.8 miles
   Explanation: After one hour, the first runner will have run 10 mi, and the second one will have run 6.5 mi, these two distances form the sides of the triangle. Use the law of cosines to find the distance between the two runners after one hour:
   $a = \sqrt{(6.5)^2 + (10)^2 - 2(6.5)(10)\cos 100°} = \sqrt{164.8} = 12.8$.

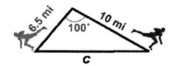

3. The lengths of the diagonals of a parallelogram are 10 feet and 16 feet. Find the lengths of the short sides of the parallelogram if the diagonals intersect at an angle of 28°.
   Solution: 4.3 feet
   Explanation: A triangle is formed by the short side of the parallelogram and half of each diagonal. Find the length of the sides of the triangle, a and b, formed by half of the diagonals: $a = \dfrac{16}{2} = 8$ and $b = \dfrac{10}{2} = 5$. Find c, the short side of the parallelogram, using the law of cosines, where a and b are the sides adjacent to the 28° angle:
   $c = \sqrt{8^2 + 5^2 - 2(8)(5)\cos 28°} = \sqrt{18.4} = \sqrt{18.4} = 4.3$.

Practice problems: *(Answers on page: 459)*

1. Two sides of a triangle each measure 4 mm. The angle between these two sides has a measure of 50°. What is the length of the third side of the triangle?

2. The sides of a parallelogram are 10 cm and 5 cm, and the smallest angle has a measure of 30°. Find the length of the longer diagonal.

3. Two boats leave a dock together. Each travels in a straight line. The angle between their courses measures 54.2°. One boat travels 36.2 km/hr and the other travels 45.6 km/hr. How far apart will they be after three hours?

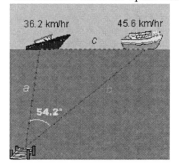

Review questions: *(Answers to odd questions on page: 459)*

1. Determine the length of Lake Manyhaha knowing the following information. A surveyor is standing at a point south of the lake. After measuring he finds he is 2125 meters from the western end of the lake and 3250 meters from the eastern end of the lake. The angle between the lines-of-sight to the two ends of the lake is 77°.

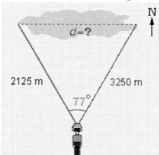

2. One angle of a triangular field measures 82°. The sides that meet at this angle are 100 meters and 120 meters long. How long is the third side?

3. Find the length of *a* in the figure below.

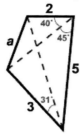

4. The two diagonals of a parallelogram meet at a 60° angle. The diagonals are 10 cm and 6 cm long. Find the lengths of the sides of the parallelogram.

5. A Chinese satellite (*C*) in circular orbit around the earth is sighted by a Russian tracking station (*R*). Radar indicates that the satellite is 734 km from the station. The angle of elevation from ground level to the satellite is 32.7°. How high is the satellite above the earth at this point? [The radius of the earth is 6393.5 km .]

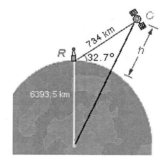

Heron's Formula

- To find the area of any triangle given its three sides, use **Heron's formula**.
- Heron's formula has two parts. For a triangle with sides *a*, *b*, and *c*:

- Calculate *s*, 1/2 of the perimeter of the triangle, called the semi-perimeter: $s = \dfrac{a+b+c}{2}$.

- Calculate the area of the triangle using *s* and the three sides: $A = \sqrt{s(s-a)(s-b)(s-c)}$

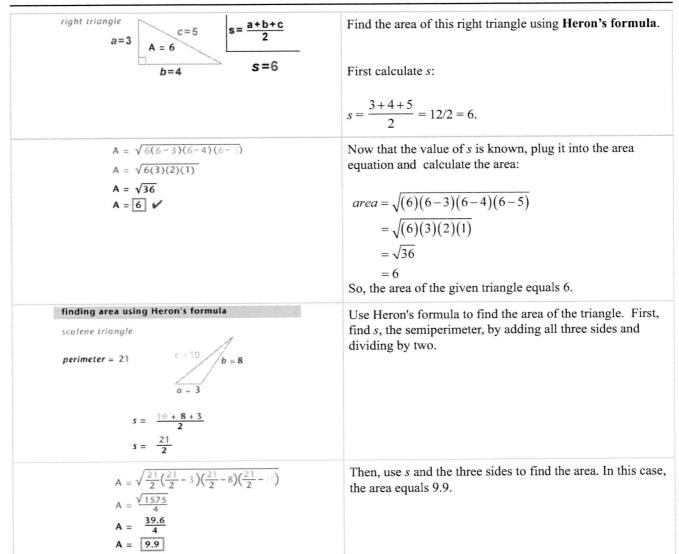

Find the area of this right triangle using **Heron's formula**.

First calculate s:

$$s = \frac{3+4+5}{2} = 12/2 = 6.$$

Now that the value of s is known, plug it into the area equation and calculate the area:

$$area = \sqrt{(6)(6-3)(6-4)(6-5)}$$
$$= \sqrt{(6)(3)(2)(1)}$$
$$= \sqrt{36}$$
$$= 6$$

So, the area of the given triangle equals 6.

Use Heron's formula to find the area of the triangle. First, find s, the semiperimeter, by adding all three sides and dividing by two.

Then, use s and the three sides to find the area. In this case, the area equals 9.9.

Sample problems:

1. Find the area of triangle JHI given that $j = 17$, $h = 18$, and $i = 19$ meters.
   Solution: 139.4 sq. m.

   Explanation: Find the semi-perimeter, s: $s = \frac{P}{2} = \left(\frac{17+18+19}{2}\right) = 27$. Substitute the known values into Heron's formula and simplify: $A = \sqrt{s(s-j)(s-h)(s-i)} = \sqrt{27(27-17)(27-18)(27-19)} = \sqrt{27(10)(9)(8)} = \sqrt{19440} = 139.4 \text{ m}^2$.

2. Find the area of the figure below.

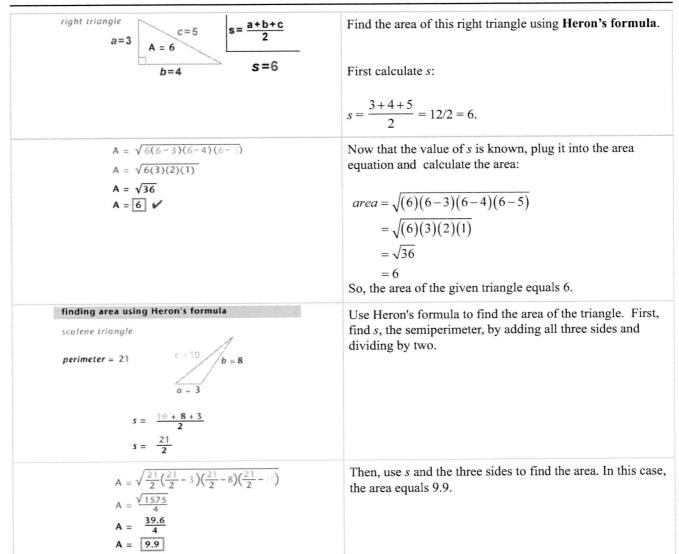

Solution: 70.2 m^2

Explanation: Divide the figure into two figures. The third side of the triangle is the same as the length of the rectangle. Find the semi-perimeter, s: $P = 22$, so $s = \frac{22}{2} = 11$.

Use Heron's area formula to find the area of the triangle:

$A = \sqrt{11(11-8)(11-8)(11-6)} = \sqrt{11(3)(3)(5)} = \sqrt{495} = 22.2$ m^2.

Find the area of the rectangle: $8 \cdot 6 = 48$ m^2. The total area of the figure is the sum of the two areas: 48 m$^2 + 22.2$ m$^2 = 70.2$ m^2.

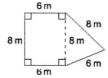

3. What is the area of a triangle with sides measuring 26, 26, and 17 inches?

Solution: 208.9 in^2

Explanation: Find the semi-perimeter, s, of the triangle: $P = 69$, so $s = \frac{69}{2} = 34.5$.

To find the area, substitute the values for s, a, b, and c into Heron's area formula, $A = \sqrt{s(s-a)(s-b)(s-c)}$, and simplify: $A = \sqrt{34.5(34.5 - 26)(34.5 - 26)(34.5 - 17)}$

$$= \sqrt{34.5(8.5)(8.5)(17.5)} = \sqrt{43620.9375}$$
$$= 208.9 \text{ in}^2.$$

Practice problems: *(Answers on page: 459)*

1. For the triangle below, what is the value of s in Heron's area formula?

2. Find the area of triangle PQR given that side $p = 21$ in, side $r = 29$ in and $\angle Q = 53°$.

3. Find the area of the parallelogram.

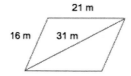

Review questions: *(Answers to odd questions on page: 459)*

1. What is the area of a triangle with sides measuring 15 inches, 12 inches, and 9 inches?

2. A triangular garden has sides that measure 35 ft, 45 ft, and 50 ft. What is the area of the garden?

3. The perimeter of a triangle is 42 cm. Two sides of the triangle have lengths of 15 cm and 20 cm. What is the area of the triangle?

4. Find the height, h, of the triangle below.

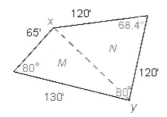

5. A lot has the shape of a quadrilateral as shown in the figure. What is its area?

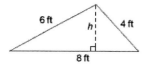

An Introduction to Vectors

- A **vector** is a mathematical object consisting of two parts: a **magnitude** and a direction.

Defining vectors Vectors: *[illustration of car labeled "20 mph northwest"]*	A **vector** is a mathematical object with a **magnitude** and direction. Velocity can be expressed as a vector.
Defining vectors • Vectors are only equal if they have the same magnitude and direction. **Example** *[diagram of equal vectors]*	For two vectors to be equal, they must have the same length and point in the same direction. Putting one on top of the other, they would look exactly the same. So, vectors are only equal if they have the same magnitude and direction.
Defining vectors $\vec{v} = <x, y>$ $\|\vec{v}\| = \sqrt{x^2 + y^2}$ $|\vec{v}| = $ Magnitude of the vector	To describe a vector, list the distance it moves in the x-direction and then the distance it moves in the y-direction. These pairs of numbers look a lot like points, so mathematicians use $<x, y>$ instead of (x, y) to write them. The magnitude of a vector is another name for its length.

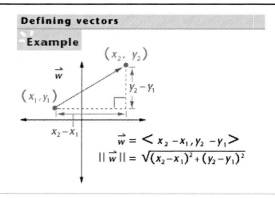

Defining vectors

Example

$$\vec{w} = \ <x_2 - x_1, y_2 - y_1>$$
$$\|\vec{w}\| = \sqrt{(x_2 - x_1)^2 + (y_2 - y_1)^2}$$

It is common to graph vectors by putting their base at the origin. Even if the vector is not lined up there, it is still possible to determine its **components**. To determine the components of a vector not on the origin, find the distance moved in the *x*-direction and then the distance moved in the *y*-direction. The magnitude of a sector is similar to the distance formula used in graphing lines.

Sample problems:

1. Find the component form of the illustrated vector.

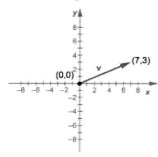

Solution: $\langle 7,3 \rangle$

Explanation: The components of the vector are found by taking the components of the terminal point and subtracting the corresponding components of the initial point. Since the terminal point is $(7,3)$ and the initial point is $(0,0)$, the vector's components are $\langle 7 - 0, 3 - 0 \rangle = \langle 7,3 \rangle$

2. What are the components of the vector below?

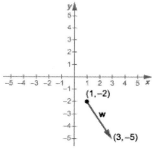

Solution: $<2, -3>$

Explanation: Use the ordered pairs at the beginning and end of vector w, $(1,-2)$ and $(3,-5)$.
Let $(1,-2)$ be (x_1, y_1) and $(3,-5)$ be (x_2, y_2): $w = \langle x_2 - x_1, y_2 - y_1 \rangle = \langle 3 - 1, -5 - (-2) \rangle = \langle 2, -3 \rangle$.

3. Find $\|w\|$ to the nearest whole number.

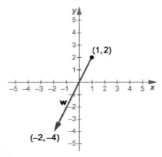

Solution: 7

Explanation: To find the magnitude, or length, of vector w, let the starting point $(1,2)$ be (x_1, y_1) and ending point $(-2,-4)$ be (x_2, y_2).

Use the distance formula:
$$\|w\| = \sqrt{(x_2 - x_1)^2 + (y_2 - y_1)^2}$$
$$= \sqrt{(-2-1)^2 + (-4-2)^2}$$
$$= \sqrt{(-3)^2 + (-6)^2}$$
$$= \sqrt{9 + 36} = \sqrt{45} = 3\sqrt{5}, \text{ so } \|w\| = 6.7, \text{ which rounds to 7.}$$

Practice problems: *(Answers on page: 459)*

1. What are the components of the vector shown below?

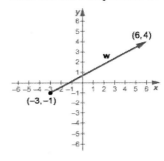

2. Consider the vectors shown below. Which two vectors are equal?

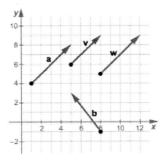

3. Find the component form of the illustrated vector.

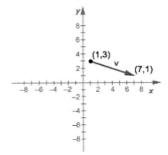

Review questions: *(Answers to odd questions on page: 459)*

1. Find the component form of the illustrated vector.

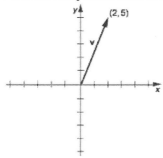

2. Find the component form of the illustrated vector.

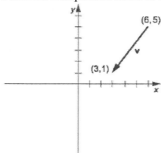

3. Find the component form of the illustrated vector.

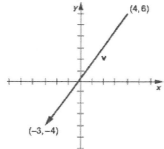

4. Find the component form of the illustrated vector.

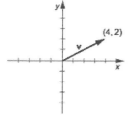

5. Find the component form of the illustrated vector.

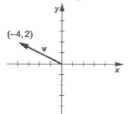

www.thinkwell.com

Finding the Magnitude and Direction of a Vector

- The **magnitude** of a **vector** is its length.

  The magnitude of a vector $\vec{v} = \langle v_1, v_2 \rangle$, denoted $\left\| \vec{v} \right\|$,

  is given by the formula $\left\| \vec{v} \right\| = \sqrt{v_1^2 + v_2^2}$.

- The **direction angle** of a vector is the angle measured from the positive side of the x-axis counterclockwise to the vector.

Example 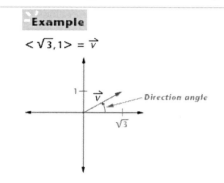	Two pieces of information that describe a **vector** are its **magnitude** and its **direction angle**. Magnitude is just another way of saying length. For example, the magnitude of the vector $\vec{v}$ graphed to the left is the length of the arrow representing $\vec{v}$. The direction angle of $\vec{v}$ is the angle from the positive side of the x-axis up to $\vec{v}$. Measuring direction angles is just like measuring angles in trigonometry.
Example 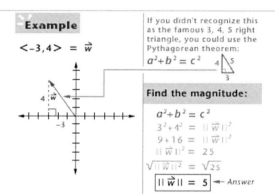	Consider the example illustrated here. How would you find the magnitude of vector $\vec{w}$? Think of the vector as the hypotenuse of a right triangle. The x-component of the vector is one leg of the triangle and the y-component is the other leg. Find the hypotenuse of the right triangle using the Pythagorean theorem. This length is the vector's magnitude.
Example 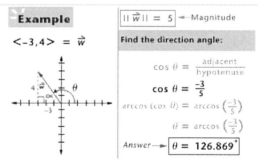	To find the **direction angle** of the vector, use the basic right-angle trigonometry rules. The right triangle graphed here provides the values of the trig functions for the direction angle. Use any one of the trig functions to set up an equation. In this example, we used the cosine function to determine that the cosine of the direction angle is $-3/5$. To solve for θ, take the **inverse cosine** of both sides of the equation. Evaluate using a calculator. The direction angle of vector $\vec{w}$ is $126.869°$

Sample problems:

1. What is the magnitude of the vector $\langle 5, -3 \rangle$?

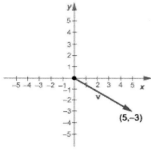

Solution: $\sqrt{34}$ or 5.8

Explanation: The vector forms a right triangle where the components are the legs and the magnitude is the hypotenuse . Use the Pythagorean theorem to determine the magnitude:

$c = \sqrt{a^2 + b^2} = \sqrt{5^2 + (-3)^2} = \sqrt{25 + 9} = \sqrt{34} = 5.8$.

2. What is the magnitude and direction angle of the vector $\langle 3, 6 \rangle$?

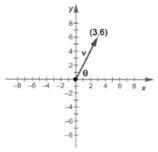

Solution: 6.7, 63.4°

Explanation: Use the Pythagorean theorem to find the magnitude: $c = \sqrt{3^2 + 6^2} = \sqrt{45}$ or 6.7.

Use a trigonometric function to set up an equation to find θ: $\tan\theta = \dfrac{\text{opposite}}{\text{adjacent}} = \dfrac{6}{3} = 2$, $\theta = 63.4°$.

The magnitude is 6.7 and the angle of direction is 63.4°.

3. What is the direction angle of the vector $v = \langle -10, -60 \rangle$?

Solution: 260.5°

Explanation: Use a trigonometric function to find the direction angle α:

$\tan\alpha = \dfrac{\text{opposite}}{\text{adjacent}} = \dfrac{-60}{-10} = 6$; $\alpha = 80.5\%$. Since θ is in the third quadrant, you need to add

the value of the reference angle to $180°$: $180° + \alpha = \theta$; $180° + 80.5° = \theta$; $260.5° = \theta$.

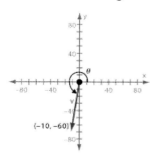

Practice problems: *(Answers on page: 459)*

1. What is the direction angle of the vector $\langle 5, -3 \rangle$?

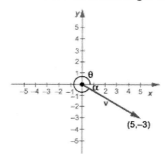

2. What is the direction angle of the vector $v = \langle 2, -30 \rangle$?

3. The direction angle of a vector is 135°. The x-component of the vector is -3. What is the y-component of this vector?

Review questions: *(Answers to odd questions on page: 459)*

1. Find the magnitude of the vector represented by $\langle 4, 5 \rangle$.

2. Find the magnitude of the vector $v = \langle -6, 8 \rangle$.

3. Find the magnitude of the vector $w = \langle -3, 3 \rangle$.

4. Find the direction angle of the vector $m = \langle 12, 5 \rangle$.

5. Determine the direction angle of the vector $u = \langle -5, -7 \rangle$.

Vector Addition and Scalar Multiplication

- A number that is multiplied into a **vector** is called a **scalar**. **Scalar multiplication** is the process of multiplying a vector by a scalar.
- Scalar multiplication can change the **magnitude** of a vector. To perform scalar multiplication, multiply each of the vector's **components** by the scalar.
- The process of adding two vectors together is called **vector addition**. To perform vector addition for two vectors, just add the x-components together and add the y-components together.

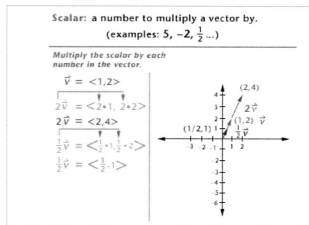

A **scalar** is a number used to multiply a **vector**. To perform **scalar multiplication**, multiply each **component** of the vector by the scalar.

Scalars greater than 1 elongate the vector, increasing the **magnitude**. Look at the illustration, notice how the vector is stretched but the **direction angle** does not change.

Scalars less than 1 but greater than 0 shrink the vector, decreasing the magnitude. Once again, the vector's length changes but the direction angle remains the same.

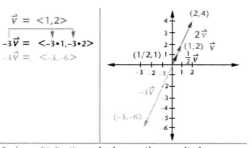

$\vec{v} = \langle 1,2 \rangle$

$-3\vec{v} = \langle -3 \cdot 1, -3 \cdot 2 \rangle$

$-3\vec{v} = \langle -3, -6 \rangle$

Scalar multiplication only changes the magnitude of the vector or flips it across the origin.

Negative scalars flip the vector across the origin.

The absolute value of the scalar still stretches or shrinks the vector in the same manner as above.

Example Adding vectors

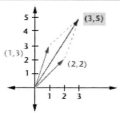

add

$\langle 1,3 \rangle + \langle 2,2 \rangle = \langle 3,5 \rangle$

add

To add two vectors together using **vector addition**, add the x-components together to get the new x-component. Then, add the y-components together to get the new y-component.

---

add

$\langle 1,3 \rangle + \langle 2,2 \rangle = \langle 3,5 \rangle$

add

Vector addition can also be described graphically.

Start by drawing both vectors stemming from the origin.

Draw a parallelogram treating the vectors like adjacent sides of the parallelogram.

The diagonal that starts at the origin matches the graph of the new vector.

Example Subtracting vectors

$\overset{\vec{w}}{\langle 3,2 \rangle} - \overset{\vec{v}}{\langle 1,4 \rangle} = \langle 3,2 \rangle + (-\langle 1,4 \rangle)$

$= \langle 3,2 \rangle + \langle -1,-4 \rangle$

$= \langle 2,-2 \rangle$

When asked to subtract vectors, simply subtract their respective components. Remember to take the component from the first vector minus the component from the second vector both times.

$\overset{\vec{w}}{\langle 3,2 \rangle} - \overset{\vec{v}}{\langle 1,4 \rangle} = \langle 3,2 \rangle + (-\langle 1,4 \rangle)$

$= \langle 3,2 \rangle + \langle -1,-4 \rangle$

$= \langle 2,-2 \rangle$

Vector subtraction can be described graphically.

Start the same way as in vector addition by putting both vectors on the origin.

Flip the vector that's being subtracted across the origin, just as if it had been multiplied by the scalar -1.

Complete the parallelogram created by the first vector and this new vector.

Summary

Scalar multiplication

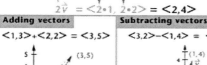

$2\vec{v} = \langle 2 \cdot 1, 2 \cdot 2 \rangle = \langle 2,4 \rangle$

Adding vectors   **Subtracting vectors**

$\langle 1,3 \rangle + \langle 2,2 \rangle = \langle 3,5 \rangle$ $\langle 3,2 \rangle - \langle 1,4 \rangle = \langle 2,-2 \rangle$

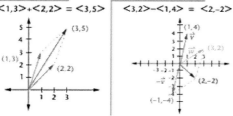

REMEMBER:

When multiplying a vector by a scalar, multiply both of the vector's components by the scalar.

When adding or subtracting vectors, combine the respective components. Do not switch them around or add x-components to y-components, keep them in order.

Graph the new vector by plotting the point or completing the parallelogram.

A SIDEBAR: You can't add a scalar to a vector since scalars do not have direction.

Sample problems:

1. If $v = \langle -6, 8 \rangle$, find the value of $\frac{1}{2}v$.

    Solution: $\langle -3, 4 \rangle$

    Explanation: A scalar is simply a number used to multiply a vector. Multiply each

    component of the vector by the scalar $\frac{1}{2}$: $\frac{1}{2}v = \frac{1}{2}\langle -6, 8 \rangle = \left\langle \frac{1}{2} \cdot (-6), \frac{1}{2} \cdot 8 \right\rangle = \langle -3, 4 \rangle$.

2. Add the vectors $\langle 8, -12 \rangle$ and $\langle 4, 7 \rangle$.

    Solution: $\langle 12, -5 \rangle$

    Explanation: Add the x-components together to get the new x-component and add

    the y-components together to get the new y-component: $\langle 8, -12 \rangle + \langle 4, 7 \rangle = \langle 8 + 4, -12 + 7 \rangle$
    $$= \langle 12, -5 \rangle.$$

3. Given the vectors $u = \langle 3, -2 \rangle$ and $v = \langle 2, 1 \rangle$, determine the components of $3u + v$.

    Solution: $\langle 11, -5 \rangle$

    Explanation: Perform the scalar multiplication: $3u = 3\langle 3, -2 \rangle = \langle 9, -6 \rangle$. Add the vectors:
    $3u + v = \langle 9, -6 \rangle + \langle 2, 1 \rangle = \langle 9 + 2, -6 + 1 \rangle = \langle 11, -5 \rangle$.

Practice problems: *(Answers on page: 459)*

1. If $\vec{v} = \langle 4.5, -5.5 \rangle$, find the value of $-4\vec{v}$.

2. Subtract: $\langle -3, 10 \rangle - \langle 1, -6 \rangle$

3. Given the vectors $r = \langle -1, -1 \rangle$ and $s = \langle -2, 4 \rangle$, determine the components of $2r - s$.

Review questions: *(Answers to odd questions on page: 459)*

1. Given the vector $u = \langle 3, -7 \rangle$, determine the components of $3u$.

2. Given vectors $u = \langle 4, 1 \rangle$, $v = \langle 2, -1 \rangle$, and $w = \langle -2, 3 \rangle$, determine the components of $u + v + w$.

3. Given vectors $u = \langle 4, -3 \rangle$ and $v = \langle 2, 3 \rangle$, determine the components of $2u - v$.

4. Given vectors $r = \langle -2, 2 \rangle$ and $s = \langle 3, -1 \rangle$, determine the components of $3r - s$.

5. Given vectors $u = \langle 4, -3 \rangle$ and $v = \langle 3, 2 \rangle$, determine the components of $5u + v$.

Finding the Components of a Vector

- When given a vector's **magnitude** and **direction** angle, it is possible to determine its **components** by using the **trigonometric functions**.

Example

$\vec{v} = <x,y>$

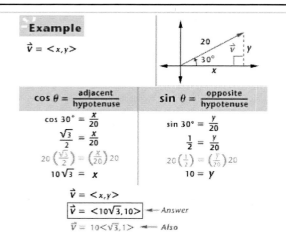

$$\cos \theta = \frac{\text{adjacent}}{\text{hypotenuse}}$$

$$\cos 30° = \frac{x}{20}$$

$$\frac{\sqrt{3}}{2} = \frac{x}{20}$$

$$20\left(\frac{\sqrt{3}}{2}\right) = \left(\frac{x}{20}\right)20$$

$$10\sqrt{3} = x$$

$$\sin \theta = \frac{\text{opposite}}{\text{hypotenuse}}$$

$$\sin 30° = \frac{y}{20}$$

$$\frac{1}{2} = \frac{y}{20}$$

$$20\left(\frac{1}{2}\right) = \left(\frac{y}{20}\right)20$$

$$10 = y$$

$$\vec{v} = <x,y>$$

$$\boxed{\vec{v} = <10\sqrt{3}, 10>} \longleftarrow Answer$$

$$\vec{v} = 10<\sqrt{3}, 1> \longleftarrow Also$$

Suppose you are told that a given vector has a **magnitude** of 20 and a **direction angle** that measures 30°. How would you find its x- and y-**components**?

Using the basic trig functions can help you determine the components of a vector.

To determine the components of the vector given here, use the fact that the **cosine** of the vector's direction angle is defined as the adjacent side over the hypotenuse. For a **vector**, the adjacent side is equal to the x-component. Since the direction angle is known, find the value of the trig function and set it equal to the x-component over the magnitude.

The same thing works for **sine** and the y-component.

Write the answer in vector component form and factor out a **scalar**. (Factoring is not a requirement.)

Example

$\vec{v} = <x,y>$

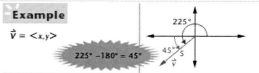

$225° - 180° = 45°$

Remember: in a right triangle, if one angle is 45°, then the remaining angle must be 45°, resulting in an isosceles right triangle.

$$s^2 + s^2 = 5^2$$

$$2s^2 = 25$$

$$\frac{2s^2}{2} = \frac{25}{2}$$

$$s^2 = \frac{25}{2}$$

$$\sqrt{s^2} = \sqrt{\frac{25}{2}}$$

$$s = \frac{5}{\sqrt{2}}$$

$$s = \frac{5\sqrt{2}}{2}$$

$$\vec{v} = <x,y>$$

$$\boxed{\vec{v} = <-\frac{5\sqrt{2}}{2}, -\frac{5\sqrt{2}}{2}>} \longleftarrow Answer$$

Don't forget your negative signs!

Given a vector with magnitude equal to 5 and a direction angle of 225°, find the components.

Notice that the **reference angle** is equal to 45°.

Consider the right triangle for this vector. Since one angle is 90° and the next is 45°, the last angle must be 45° as well. That fact makes the triangle an isosceles right triangle, which means the sides are equal.

Notice, it was not necessary to use the trig functions for this example. Knowing that the sides are equal and applying the Pythagorean theorem will produce the length for all the sides. Adjust the answer so that negative signs are on the correct terms given the location of the vector.

Sample problems:

1. Find the x- and y-components of a vector of magnitude $\sqrt{2}$ and at an angle 45° from the origin.

Solution: $\langle 1,1 \rangle$

Explanation: The magnitude of the vector is the hypotenuse of a triangle where the legs are the x- and y-components. Furthermore, the 45° angle means that the triangle is isosceles. Use the Pythagorean theorem, where a and b are equal and $c = \sqrt{2}$, to find the length of the legs:

$c^2 = a^2 + b^2 \Rightarrow \left(\sqrt{2}\right)^2 = 2\left(a^2\right)$; $2 = 2\left(a^2\right)$; $1 = a^2$; $a = \sqrt{1} = 1$. Thus the legs are each 1, so the x- and y-components are $\langle 1,1 \rangle$.

2. What are the x- and y-components of a vector with a magnitude of 40 and a direction angle of 390°?

<u>Solution:</u> $\langle 20\sqrt{3}, 20 \rangle$

<u>Explanation:</u> Because the vector angle is greater than 360°, it rotates around the coordinate plane once. The vector ends up 30° above the x-axis in the first quadrant. Use a trig function to find the y-component: $\sin 30° = \dfrac{y}{40}$; $y = 40(\sin 30°)$; $y = 40\left(\dfrac{1}{2}\right)$; $y = 20$.

Use the Pythagorean theorem to find the length of the third side, x:
$40^2 = 20^2 + x^2$; $x = \sqrt{1600 - 400} = \sqrt{1200} = 20\sqrt{3}$.

Thus, the x- and y-components are $\langle 20\sqrt{3}, 20 \rangle$.

3. Express the vector in component form.

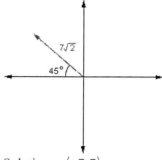

<u>Solution:</u> $\langle -7, 7 \rangle$

<u>Explanation:</u> Use a trig function to find the y-component: $\sin 45° = \dfrac{y}{7\sqrt{2}}$;

$y = 7\sqrt{2}(\sin 45°) = 7$. Since the angle is 45° the triangle must be isosceles. Thus, the x- and y-components are both 7. However, the angle is in quadrant II, so x is negative: $\langle -7, 7 \rangle$.

Practice problems: *(Answers on page: 459)*

1. What are the x- and y-components for a vector with a magnitude of 2 and at an angle 210° from the origin?

2. What are the x- and y-components of a vector with a magnitude of $15\sqrt{2}$ and at an angle of 135° from the origin?

3. Express the vector in component form.

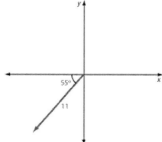

Review questions: *(Answers to odd questions on page: 459)*

1. Express the vector in component form.

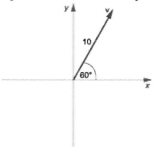

2. Express the vector in component form.

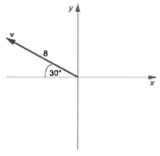

3. Express the vector in component form.

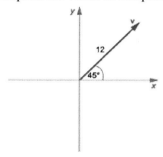

4. Express the vector in component form.

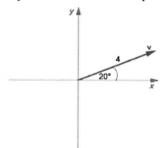

 www.thinkwell.com

5. Express the vector in component form.

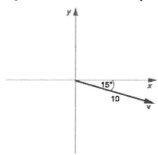

Finding a Unit Vector

- A **unit vector** is a **vector** with a **magnitude** of 1. Unit vectors are used when distance is not important and only the direction is in question.

- The unit vector in the direction of a vector $\vec{v}$ is given by the equation $\vec{u} = \dfrac{1}{\|\vec{v}\|}\vec{v}$.

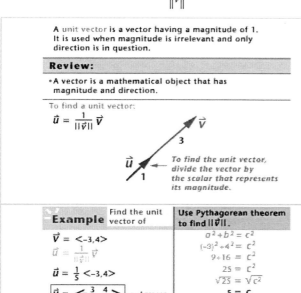

A **vector** whose **magnitude** is equal to 1 is called a **unit vector**. All vectors have corresponding unit vectors, even if the unit vector is bigger than the original vector.

To find the unit vector that corresponds to a particular vector, use **scalar multiplication** to multiply the vector by the reciprocal of its magnitude (in other words, divide by the magnitude). The result is a vector in the same direction with a magnitude of 1.

Consider the following: given the **components** $\langle-3, 4\rangle$ of a vector, find its corresponding unit vector.

REMEMBER: The unit vector is equal to the vector divided by the magnitude, so find the magnitude first.

Find the magnitude by using the Pythagorean theorem. Plug in -3 for a and 4 for b. The hypotenuse, c, is equal to 5.

Next, divide the components of the original vector by 5. The result is the unit vector in the direction of the original vector.

In this example it might appear that the given vector is already a unit vector, but remember, a vector's magnitude is equal to the square root of the sum of the squares of the components.

First, find the magnitude by plugging the vector's components into the Pythagorean theorem. The magnitude for the given vector is $\sqrt{2}$.

Next, divide the components by the magnitude. What you find is that the unit vector for this example is $\left\langle \dfrac{\sqrt{2}}{2}, \dfrac{\sqrt{2}}{2} \right\rangle$.

Sample problems:

1. Find a unit vector with the same directions as $w = \langle 5,12 \rangle$.

Solution: $\left\langle \dfrac{5}{13}, \dfrac{12}{13} \right\rangle$

Explanation: Start by finding the magnitude of the vector: $\|w\| = \sqrt{5^2 + 12^2} = \sqrt{169} = 13$. Now divide the magnitude into each of the vector's components to get the unit vector, u : $u = \left\langle \dfrac{5}{13}, \dfrac{12}{13} \right\rangle$.

2. Find a unit vector with the same direction as $r = \left\langle \dfrac{1}{2}, \dfrac{-2}{5} \right\rangle$.

Solution: $\left\langle \dfrac{5\sqrt{41}}{41}, \dfrac{-4\sqrt{41}}{41} \right\rangle$

Explanation: Start by finding the magnitude of the vector: $\|r\| = \sqrt{\left(\dfrac{1}{2}\right)^2 + \left(-\dfrac{2}{5}\right)^2}$

$$= \sqrt{\dfrac{1}{4} + \dfrac{4}{25}}$$

$$= \sqrt{\dfrac{25}{100} + \dfrac{16}{100}}$$

$$= \sqrt{\dfrac{41}{100}} = \dfrac{\sqrt{41}}{10}.$$

Now divide the magnitude into each of the vector's components to get the unit vector, u :

$$u = \left\langle \dfrac{\frac{1}{2}}{\frac{\sqrt{41}}{10}}, \dfrac{-\frac{2}{5}}{\frac{\sqrt{41}}{10}} \right\rangle$$

$$= \left\langle \dfrac{1}{2} \cdot \dfrac{10}{\sqrt{41}}, -\dfrac{2}{5} \cdot \dfrac{10}{\sqrt{41}} \right\rangle$$

$$= \left\langle \dfrac{1}{2} \cdot \dfrac{10}{\sqrt{41}}, -\dfrac{2}{5} \cdot \dfrac{10}{\sqrt{41}} \right\rangle$$

$$= \left\langle \dfrac{5}{\sqrt{41}}, \dfrac{-4}{\sqrt{41}} \right\rangle$$

$$= \left\langle \dfrac{5\sqrt{41}}{41}, \dfrac{-4\sqrt{41}}{41} \right\rangle$$

3. What is the magnitude of a unit vector that is oriented in the same direction as a vector with a magnitude of 10?
Solution: 1
Explanation: A unit vector is produced by dividing a given vector by its magnitude. Thus, unit vectors have a magnitude of 1.

Practice problems: *(Answers on page: 459)*

1. Find a unit vector with the same direction as $t = \langle -3, -7 \rangle$.

2. Find a unit vector with the same direction as $t = \left\langle \dfrac{\pi}{2}, 0 \right\rangle$.

3. What is the magnitude of a unit vector in the direction of a vector with a magnitude of 472?

Review questions: *(Answers to odd questions on page: 459)*

1. True or false: A unit vector is a vector with magnitude equal to 1.

2. Find a unit vector with the same direction as $v = \langle -5, 12 \rangle$.

3. Find a unit vector with the same direction as $w = \langle -1, 1 \rangle$.

4. Find a unit vector with the same direction as $w = \left\langle \dfrac{3}{\sqrt{13}}, \dfrac{-2}{\sqrt{13}} \right\rangle$.

5. Find a unit vector with the same direction as $w = \langle 7, -24 \rangle$.

Solving Word Problems Involving Velocity or Forces

- **Velocity** can be expressed as a direction and a speed; therefore, velocity is a **vector**.
- Degree measure starts at the positive x-axis and moves counterclockwise. **Compass direction** (or **bearing**) starts at north and moves clockwise.

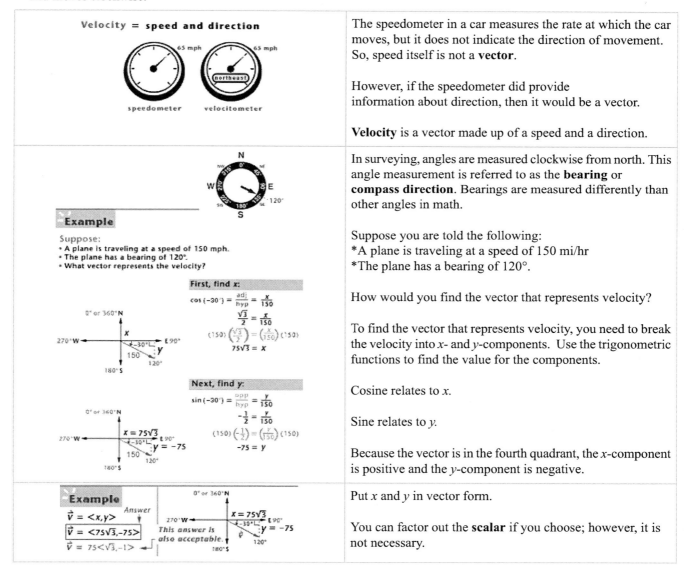

The speedometer in a car measures the rate at which the car moves, but it does not indicate the direction of movement. So, speed itself is not a **vector**.

However, if the speedometer did provide information about direction, then it would be a vector.

Velocity is a vector made up of a speed and a direction.

In surveying, angles are measured clockwise from north. This angle measurement is referred to as the **bearing** or **compass direction**. Bearings are measured differently than other angles in math.

Suppose you are told the following:
*A plane is traveling at a speed of 150 mi/hr
*The plane has a bearing of 120°.

How would you find the vector that represents velocity?

To find the vector that represents velocity, you need to break the velocity into x- and y-components. Use the trigonometric functions to find the value for the components.

Cosine relates to x.

Sine relates to y.

Because the vector is in the fourth quadrant, the x-component is positive and the y-component is negative.

Put x and y in vector form.

You can factor out the **scalar** if you choose; however, it is not necessary.

Sample problems:

1. A boat is traveling at a speed of 48 mph. The boat has a bearing of 135°. What vector represents the velocity?

   Solution: $24\langle \sqrt{2}, -\sqrt{2} \rangle$

   Explanation: First, find x: $\cos(-45°) = \dfrac{x}{48}$; $\dfrac{\sqrt{2}}{2} = \dfrac{x}{48}$; $24\sqrt{2} = x$. Next, find y:

   $\cos(-45°) = \dfrac{x}{48}$; $-\dfrac{\sqrt{2}}{2} = \dfrac{y}{48}$; $-24\sqrt{2} = y$. Because the vector is in the fourth

   quadrant, the x-component is positive and the y-component is negative.

   Therefore, the vector is $\langle 24\sqrt{2}, -24\sqrt{2} \rangle$ or $24\langle \sqrt{2}, -\sqrt{2} \rangle$.

2. A bus is traveling at a speed of 60 mph. The vector that represents the velocity is $30\langle -1, \sqrt{3} \rangle$.

   What is the bearing of the bus?

   Solution: 330°

   Explanation: Since the x-component is negative and the y-component is positive, the

   vector must be in the second quadrant. Distribute the 30 into the vector to get $\langle -30, 30\sqrt{3} \rangle$.

   Use the x component for the cosine trig function: $\cos x = -\dfrac{30}{60}$; $\cos x = -\dfrac{1}{2}$; $x = 120°$. This

   angle has a reference angle of 60° and lies in the second quadrant. The bearing is $270° + 60°$, or 330°.

3. A ship sails 50 mph on a bearing of 20° for one hour and then turns and sails 30 mph on a bearing of 80° for another hour. What vector represents the velocity and what is its magnitude?

   Solution: $\langle 46.6, 52.2 \rangle$ $\bar{v} = 70$

   Explanation: Find the x-component for the ship's first hour of travel:

   $\cos 70 = \dfrac{x}{50}$; $50 \cos 70 = x$; $x = 17.1$. Now find y: $\sin 70 = \dfrac{4}{50}$; $y = 47$. Find the

   components for the second hour (start where the first vector stopped): $\cos 10 = \dfrac{x}{30}$; $x = 29.5$:

   $\sin 10 = \dfrac{y}{30}$; $y = 5.2$. Add the two vectors: $\langle 17.1, 47 \rangle + \langle 29.5, 5.2 \rangle$. The velocity vector

   is $\langle 46.6, 52.2 \rangle$ Magnitude $\bar{v} = \sqrt{46.6^2 + 52.2^2} = 70$.

Practice problems: (Answers on page: 459)

1. A plane is traveling at a speed of 180 mph with a bearing of 300°. What vector represents the velocity?

2. A boat is traveling at a speed of 40 mph. The vector that represents the velocity is $20\langle -\sqrt{2}, -\sqrt{2} \rangle$. What is the bearing of the boat?

3. A scuba diver swims 100 ft/min on a bearing of 170°. The water is moving with a current of 30 ft/min on a bearing of 115°. Find the diver's resultant velocity.

Review questions: *(Answers to odd questions on page: 459)*

1. A plane is traveling at a speed of 250 mph. The plane has a bearing of 30° east of north. Find the vector that represents the velocity of the plane.

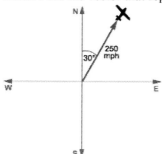

2. A plane is traveling at a speed of 400 mph on a bearing of 150°. Express the velocity of the plane as a vector.

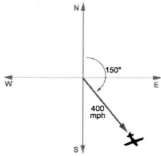

3. A baseball player throws a ball with a velocity of 30 ft/sec at an angle of 65° with the horizontal. Express the velocity of the ball as a vector. Round components to the nearest tenth.

4. A plane leaves an airport on a bearing of 130°, traveling at 450 mph. What is the velocity of the plane as a vector? Express the components to the nearest tenth.

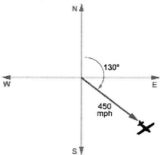

5. A plane leaves the airport on a bearing of 30° traveling at 500 mph. The wind is blowing at a bearing of 135° at a speed of 30 mph. What is the actual velocity of the plane?

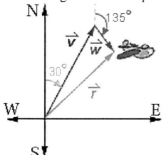

5

Complex Numbers and Polar Coordinates

Introducing and Writing Complex Numbers

- Numbers like $\sqrt{-4}$ or $\sqrt{-9.5}$ that involve the square root of a negative number are called **imaginary numbers**.
- Imaginary numbers can be written in terms of the number i, which is equal to the square root of -1: $i = \sqrt{-1}$.
- A **complex number** has the form $a + bi$ where a is a real number and bi is some number multiplying with i, an imaginary number.

$\sqrt{-9}$ *not real*	When you see a number under a square root sign, you are being asked for the value that multiplied with itself to give the number under the radical sign; i.e., the root that produced the number under the radical sign. There is no real number that multiplies with itself and gives a negative answer. So, the square root of any negative number must be an imaginary number.
$\sqrt{-9} = \sqrt{(-1)(9)}$	You can easily factor the negative out of a number.
$= \sqrt{-1}\sqrt{9}$	Then you can separate the factors so that you have a positive square root to find and the square root of the -1.
$\sqrt{-1} = i$	Because the square root of any negative number is **imaginary**, mathematicians have developed a special set of numbers.
Example $\sqrt{-9} = \sqrt{(-1)(9)}$ $= \sqrt{-1}\sqrt{9}$ $= 3i$	The -1 is represented in the answer by i. The square root of 9 is the 3. Without the use of i, we would be unable to eliminate this radical.

Sample problems:

1. Simplify: $\sqrt{-36}$

   <u>Solution</u>: $6i$

   <u>Explanation</u>: Begin by factoring the radicand: $\sqrt{-36} = \sqrt{(6)^2} \cdot \sqrt{-1}$. Next, find the square root of each factor: $\sqrt{(6)^2} \cdot \sqrt{-1} = 6i$.

2. Simplify: $\sqrt{-49} + 2$

   <u>Solution</u>: $7i + 2$

   <u>Explanation</u>: Factor the randicand then find the root of each factor:

   $\sqrt{-49} + 2 = \left(\sqrt{7 \cdot 7} \cdot \sqrt{-1}\right) + 2 = 7i + 2$

3. Simplify: $5\sqrt{-200} + \sqrt{-32}$

   <u>Solution</u>: $54i\sqrt{2}$

   <u>Explanation</u>: Simplify each radical:

   $5\sqrt{-200} + \sqrt{-32} = 5\sqrt{2 \cdot 100 \cdot -1} + \sqrt{2 \cdot 16 \cdot -1}$
   $= 5(\sqrt{2})(\sqrt{100})(\sqrt{-1}) + (\sqrt{2})(\sqrt{16})(\sqrt{-1})$
   $= 5(\sqrt{2})(10)(i) + (\sqrt{2})(4)(i)$
   $= 50i\sqrt{2} + 4i\sqrt{2} = 54i\sqrt{2}.$

Practice problems: *(Answers on page: 459)*

1. Simplify: $\sqrt{-20}$

2. Simplify: $9 + \sqrt{-18}$

3. Simplify: $\sqrt{-300} + 4\sqrt{-75}$

Review questions: *(Answers to odd questions on page: 459)*

1. Simplify: $\sqrt{-121}$

2. Simplify: $3 - \sqrt[3]{-27}$

3. Simplify: $\sqrt{-1} + 7$

4. Simplify: $4 + \sqrt{-325}$

5. Simplify: $2\sqrt{-125} + 7\sqrt{20}$

Rewriting Powers of i

- $i = \sqrt{-1}$. The number i is an example of an **imaginary number**.
- $i^2 = -1$.
- $i^3 = i \cdot i^2 = i \cdot -1 = -i$.
- $i^4 = (i^2)^2 = -1 \cdot -1 = 1$.
- Every power of i is equal to one of these four values: i, -1, $-i$, or 1.

$i = \sqrt{-1}$	i is called an **imaginary number** because in our number system there is no number which can multiply by itself and still be negative.
$i^2 = -1$	i^2 turns that imaginary number, i, into an imaginary number with a real number value, not by any magic, but by using normal multiplication rules: $$\sqrt{-1} \cdot \sqrt{-1} = (\sqrt{-1})^2 = -1$$
$i^3 = i^2 \bullet i = -i$	i^3 can be read as $i \cdot i^2$. That's a good idea since we know the value of both of those. Substituting -1 for i^2, gives us our value.
$i^4 = 1$	i^4 equals $i^2 \cdot i^2$, which is $-1 -1$. Doing the multiplication, you get 1 as the product. There are no more values beyond i^4. i and i^2 are defined. i^3 and i^4 are combinations of i and i^2 that provide unique answers.
To find the equivalent to any power of i : • divide the power by four • your answer will = $i^{\text{(remainder)}}$ $i = \sqrt{-1}$ $i^2 = -1$ $i^3 = -i$ $i^4 = 1$ **Example** $i^{40} = i^{4 \bullet 10} = (i^4)^{10} = 1^{10} = 1$ **Example** $i^{223} = i^{4 \bullet 55 + 3} = (i^4)^{55} \bullet i^3$ $= (1)^{55} \bullet -i$ $= -i$	Starting with i^5, the values start over because everything is some combination of the first four values. The values make a loop that starts over every four terms. Your value will always be wherever you fall in that loop. Divide the power given for i in your problem by 4. The value you need will be the value for i using the remainder as your power.

Sample problems:

1. Simplify: i^{10}

   Solution: -1

   Explanation: Divide the exponent by 4 (the answer will be $i^{(\text{remainder})}$):

   $i^{10} = i^{4 \cdot 2 + 2} = (i^4)^2 \cdot i^2$.

   Recall that $i^4 = 1$: $(i^4)^2 \cdot i^2 = (1)^2 \cdot i^2 = 1 \cdot i^2 = i^2$.

   Recall that $i^2 = -1$. Thus, $i^{10} = -1$.

2. Simplify: i^{-22}

   Solution: -1

   Explanation: Express i^{-22} with a positive exponent: $i^{-22} = \frac{1}{i^{22}}$.

   Divide the exponent by 4 (the answer will be $i^{(\text{remainder})}$):

   $\frac{1}{i^{22}} = \frac{1}{i^{4 \cdot 5 + 2}} = \frac{1}{(i^4)^5 \cdot i^2} = \frac{1}{(1)^5 \cdot i^2} = \frac{1}{1 \cdot i^2} = \frac{1}{i^2}$.

   Recall that $i^2 = -1$: $\frac{1}{i^2} = \frac{1}{-1} = -1$. Thus, $i^{-22} = -1$.

3. Simplify: $-i^{-494}$

   Solution: 1

   Explanation: Express $-i^{-494}$ with a positive exponent: $-i^{-494} = -\frac{1}{i^{494}}$.

   Divide the exponent by 4: $-\frac{1}{i^{494}} = -\frac{1}{i^{4 \cdot 123 + 2}} = -\frac{1}{(i^4)^{123} \cdot i^2} = -\frac{1}{(1)^{123} \cdot i^2}$

   $= \frac{1}{i^2} = -\frac{1}{-1} = -(-1) = 1$.

Practice problems: *(Answers on page: 459)*

1. Simplify: i^{-3}

2. Simplify: i^{-33}

3. Simplify: $-i^{-168}$

Review questions: *(Answers to odd questions on page: 460)*

1. Simplify: i^4

2. Simplify: i^{15}

3. Simplify: i^{23}

4. Simplify: i^{-35}

5. Simplify: i^{122}

Adding and Subtracting Complex Numbers

- A **Complex Number** is a binomial composed of a variable or constant with an imaginary, or i-number, being added or subtracted.
- When **adding complex numbers**, add like terms according to the normal rules. Add constants to constants, variables to variables, and imaginary numbers to imaginary numbers.
- When **subtracting complex numbers**, subtract like terms according to the normal rules, paying attention to sign changes across parentheses as you combine constants with constants, variables with variables, and imaginary numbers with imaginary numbers.

Example $(5–i) + (9–2i) = 14–3i$ $\begin{aligned} 5-&i \\ +\ 9-&2i \\ \hline 14-&3i \end{aligned}$	**Adding complex numbers** means that you add like terms: • Variables with variables • i's with i's • Constants with constants
Example $(7–3i) – (-5–i) = 12–2i$ $\begin{aligned} 7-&3i \\ -\ (-5-&i\ ) \\ \hline 12-&2i \end{aligned}$	**Subtracting complex numbers** follows the same rules: • Variables with variables • i's with i's • Constants with constants **Remember:** Watch your signs and use your parentheses correctly. It may even pay to write out the numbers with their signs changed before you do any combining. This one mistake creates more errors with this type of numbers than any other action.

Sample problems:

1. Simplify: $5 + 3(1 - 8i) - 10i$
   Solution: $8 - 34i$
   Explanation: Use the distributive property, then combine like terms:
   $5 + 3(1 - 8i) - 10i = 5 + 3 - 24i - 10i = 8 - 34i$.

2. Simplify: $(5 + 9i) - (12 + 13i)$
   Solution: $-7 - 4i$
   Explanation: Distribute the negative, then combine like terms:
   $(5 + 9i) - (12 + 13i) = 5 + 9i - 12 - 13i = -7 - 4i$.

3. Simplify: $(1 - 10i) + 2(5 + 9i) - 5(2 + 3i)$
   Solution: $1 - 7i$
   Explanation: Distribute the 2 and the negative, then combine like terms:
   $(1 - 10i) + 2(5 + 9i) - 5(2 + 3i) = 1 - 10i + 10 + 18i - 10 - 15i = 1 - 7i$.

Practice problems: *(Answers on page: 460)*

1. Simplify: $(6i + 4) + (2i - 7)$

2. Simplify: $(i + 2) - (5i - 1)$

3. Simplify: $(6i + 1) - 2(i - 3) + 5(2i + 7)$

Review questions: *(Answers to odd questions on page: 460)*

1. Simplify: $(6 - i) + (-3 + i)$

2. Simplify: $(5 - 2i) + (3 + 7i)$

3. Simplify: $(2 - 5i) - (5 + 2i)$

4. Simplify: $(11 + 2i) - (9 - 4i)$

5. Simplify: $2(2 - 3i) - (4 + 8i) + 15i$

Multiplying Complex Numbers

- $i = \sqrt{-1}$. This is called an imaginary number because there are no examples of a number which multiplies with itself to produce a negative number. Therefore, no one knows what the square root of a negative might be; it must be **imaginary**.
- $i^2 = -1$. This follows from the definition of a square root. If you multiply a square root times itself, you get the base being rooted.
- **FOIL**: Multiply binomials by multiplying
  First terms together
  Outer terms together
  Inside terms
  Last terms, and adding all the products together.

$i = \sqrt{-1}$ $i^2 = -1$	Here are i and i^2 defined for you. Learn them. They turn up wherever complex numbers turn up.
Example $(2+3i)(6-5i)$ $12+18i-10i-15i^2(-1)$ $=27+8i$	Multiplying with complex numbers works just like **FOIL** with a binomial. Note the i^2 becomes -1 which means that the -15 becomes $+15$.
Example $(3+5i)^2 =$ $(3+5i)(3+5i) =$ $9+15i+15i+25i^2 - 25$ $=-16+30i$	The only new thing to remember is that when you get an i^2 change it to -1. The net effect is to create a constant with the opposite sign. Once you've done that, if there are other constants, combine them.

Sample problems:

1. Express the following complex number in standard form: $(3-i)^2$
   Solution: $8-6i$
   Explanation: Use the FOIL method to multiply: $(3-i)^2 = (3-i)(3-i) = 9 - 6i + i^2$.
   Use $i^2 = -1$ to further simplify the expression: $9 - 6i + i^2 = 9 - 6i + (-1) = 8 - 6i$.

2. Express the following complex number in standard form: $\left(\sqrt{3} + 2i\right)\left(\sqrt{3} - 2i\right)$
   Solution: 7
   Explanation: Multiply: $\left(\sqrt{3} + 2i\right)\left(\sqrt{3} - 2i\right) = \sqrt{9} - 2i\sqrt{3} + 2i\sqrt{3} - 4i^2 = 3 - 4i^2$.
   Use $i^2 = -1$ to further simplify: $3 - 4i^2 = 3 - 4(-1) = 3 + 4 = 7$.

3. Express the following complex number in standard form: $i(5 - 2i)(i + 4)$
   Solution: $3 + 22i$
   Explanation: FOIL the binomials: $i(5 - 2i)(i + 4) = i(5i + 20 - 2i^2 - 8i)$. Distribute the i and
   simplify: $i(5i + 20 - 2i^2 - 8i) = 5i^2 + 20i - 2i^3 - 8i^2 = -3i^2 + 20i - 2i^3 = -3(-1) + 20i - 2(-1)i = 3 + 20i + 2i = 3 + 22i$.

Practice problems: *(Answers on page: 460)*

1. Express the following complex number in standard form: $(5 + 2i)^2$

2. Express the following complex number in standard form: $\left(\sqrt{5} + i\right)\left(\sqrt{5} - i\right)$

3. Express the following complex number in standard form: $i(5 + 2i)(i - 1)$

Review questions: *(Answers to odd questions on page: 460)*

1. Express the following in standard form: $(1+i)^2$

2. Express the following in standard form: $(-1-5i)^2$

3. Express the following in standard form: $(2-2i)(-3+3i)$

4. Express the following in standard form: $i(4-i)(5+2i)$

5. Express the following in standard form: $(4+i)(2+i)$

Dividing Complex Numbers

- Clearing a denominator of radicals means to multiply the fraction by a version of 1. Your version of 1 will be the radical over itself. So, the denominator multiplies out the radical to clear it, and the numerator gets a radical.
- A **conjugate** is used when fractions have radicals or imaginary numbers in their denominators as a means of clearing those values from the denominators, or **rationalizing the denominator**.
- $i = \sqrt{-1}$
- $i^2 = -1$

Example $$\frac{4+i}{3+5i} = \left(\frac{(4+i)}{(3+5i)}\right) \cdot \left(\frac{(3-5i)}{(3-5i)}\right) =$$ $$\frac{12+3i-20i+5}{9-15i+15i+25} = \frac{17-17i}{34}$$	The first step in dividing with complex numbers is to clear the complex values from the denominator. So, multiply both top and bottom of the fraction by the **conjugate** of the denominator. This process leaves all real numbers in the denominator and adds a complex number to the numerator.
$$= \frac{17(1-i)}{34}$$ $$= \frac{1-i}{2}$$ $$real \quad = \frac{1}{2} - \frac{1}{2}i$$ $$imaginary$$	Once you've cleared the undesirable numbers from the denominator, you can easily solve the problem.
Example $$\frac{1}{2+i}\left(\frac{(2-i)}{(2-i)}\right) = \frac{2-i}{4-2i+2i-i^2} = \frac{2-i}{4+1}$$ $$= \frac{2-i}{5}$$ $$= \frac{2}{5} - \frac{1}{5}i$$	Let's try another one. Multiply the top and bottom of the fraction by $2 - i$, the conjugate of the denominator. This one leads you into the paths that are common with imaginary numbers and radicals. It's not difficult, but the answer is unexpected.

Sample problems:

1. Express the following complex number in standard form: $\dfrac{15-9i}{3i}$

   Solution: $-3-5i$

   Explanation: To express a complex number in standard form, $a+bi$, simplify and write the constant term then the imaginary term. Notice that a 3 will factor from the numerator: $\dfrac{15-9i}{3i} = \dfrac{3(5-3i)}{3i} = \dfrac{5-3i}{i}$. Next, since there is an imaginary number in the denominator, rationalize the denominator by multiplying the expression by $\dfrac{i}{i}$:

   $\dfrac{5-3i}{i} = \dfrac{5-3i}{i} \cdot \dfrac{i}{i} = \dfrac{i(5-3i)}{i^2} = \dfrac{5i-3i^2}{i^2}$. Substitute -1 in for i^2 to further simplify:

   $\dfrac{5i-3i^2}{i^2} = \dfrac{5i-3(-1)}{(-1)} = \dfrac{5i+3}{(-1)} = -3-5i$.

2. Express the following complex number in standard form: $\dfrac{8}{9+4i}$

   Solution: $\dfrac{72}{97} - \dfrac{32}{97}i$

   Explanation: The denominator is a binomial with an imaginary number, so in order to simplify first rationalize this denominator by multiplying the expression by the conjugate over itself, $\dfrac{9-4i}{9-4i}$: $\dfrac{8}{9+4i} = \dfrac{8}{9+4i} \cdot \dfrac{9-4i}{9-4i} = \dfrac{8(9-4i)}{(9+4i)(9-4i)} = \dfrac{72-32i}{81-16i^2}$. Further simplify by substituting -1 for i^2: $\dfrac{72-32i}{81-16i^2} = \dfrac{72-32i}{81-16(-1)} = \dfrac{72-32i}{97}$.

   The standard form of a complex number is $a+bi$, so express as $\dfrac{72}{97} - \dfrac{32}{97}i$.

3. Express the following complex number in standard form: $\dfrac{7+2i}{3+5i}$

   Solution: $\dfrac{31}{34} - \dfrac{29}{34}i$

   Explanation: Multiply by the conjugate to rationalize the denominator, then simplify: $\dfrac{7+2i}{3+5i} = \dfrac{7+2i}{3+5i} \cdot \dfrac{3-5i}{3-5i} = \dfrac{21-29i-10i^2}{9-25i^2}$. Further simplify by substituting -1 for i^2: $\dfrac{21-29i-10(-1)}{9-25(-1)} = \dfrac{21-29i-10(-1)}{9-25(-1)} = \dfrac{21-29i+10}{9+25} = \dfrac{31-29i}{34}$.

   The standard form of a complex number is $a+bi$, so express as $\dfrac{31}{34} - \dfrac{29}{34}i$.

Practice problems: *(Answers on page: 460)*

1. Express the following complex number in standard form: $\dfrac{2+3i}{3+2i}$

2. Express the following complex number in standard form: $\dfrac{-5+2i}{-1+3i}$

3. Express the following complex number in standard form: $\dfrac{-4-5i}{-8-7i}$

Review questions: *(Answers to odd questions on page: 460)*

1. Express the following in standard form: $\dfrac{1+i}{5}$

2. Express the following in standard form: $\dfrac{2}{4-7i}$

3. Express the following in standard form: $\dfrac{2-i}{2+i}$

4. Express the following in standard form: $\dfrac{1+3i}{5-i}$

5. Express the following in standard form: $\dfrac{5+i}{11-i}$

Graphing a Complex Number and Finding Its Absolute Value

- **Review**: A **complex number** $x + yi$ has a **real part**, x, and an **imaginary part**, y. The **imaginary number i** represents the quantity $\sqrt{-1}$.
- Complex numbers can be graphed in the **complex plane** just like points are graphed in the coordinate plane. The horizontal axis of the complex plane measures the real part of the complex number and the vertical axis measures the imaginary part.
- The **absolute value** or **modulus** of a complex number $z = x + yi$ is denoted $|z|$. It represents the distance of z from the origin in the complex plane. Calculate it using the **Pythagorean theorem**: $|z| = |x + yi| = \sqrt{x^2 + y^2}$.

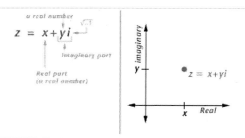

Visualize complex numbers by graphing them in the **complex plane** just as you would graph **ordered pairs**. The horizontal axis is the real axis and the vertical axis is the imaginary axis.

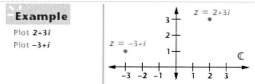

The complex numbers $-3 + i$ and $2 + 3i$ have been graphed in the complex plane on the left.

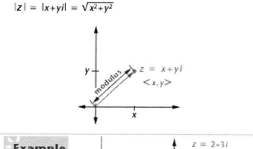

Notice that a point in the complex plane has two coordinates just like a vector does.

The absolute value or modulus of a complex number is analogous to the magnitude of a vector; calculate it using the Pythagorean theorem.

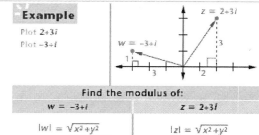

Calculate the moduli of the two complex numbers given here.

Use the Pythagorean theorem and plug in the known values. For the complex number $-3 + i$ plug in -3 for x and i for y. Remember $i^2 = 1$. You find that the modulus for the complex number $-3 + i = \sqrt{10}$.

The modulus is just the distance from a point to the origin.

Sample problems:

1. Determine the modulus of the complex number $-5i$.

    Solution: 5

    Explanation: Compute the modulus of $-5i$: $\sqrt{(0)^2 + (-5)^2} = \sqrt{0 + 25} = \sqrt{25} = 5.$

2. Determine the modulus of the complex number $-4+3i$.

   Solution: 5

   Explanation: Compute the modulus of $-4+3i$ using the formula $|z| = \sqrt{a^2 + b^2}$:

   $|z| = \sqrt{(-4)^2 + (3)^2} = \sqrt{16+9} = \sqrt{25} = 5$.

3. True or false: The complex number $-3-2i$ is graphed below.

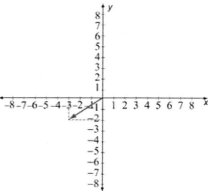

   Solution: True

   Explanation: Move 3 units to the left, according to the real number -3, and move 2 units down, according to the imaginary number $-2i$.

Practice problems: *(Answers on page: 460)*

1. What is the modulus of the complex number, $3+4i$?

2. True or false: The complex number $-4+3i$ is graphed below.

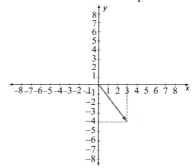

3. What is the modulus of the complex number $(3+4i)(1-2i)$?

Review questions: *(Answers to odd questions on page: 460)*

1. True or false: The absolute value of the complex number $-8i$ is 8.

2. True or false: The complex number $3+4i$ is graphed below.

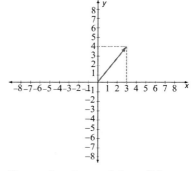

3. Determine the modulus of the complex number $6-8i$.

4. Determine the modulus of the complex number $7 + 3i$.

5. Determine the modulus of the complex number $(5 + 2i)(3 - i)$.

Expressing a Complex Number in Trigonometric or Polar Form

- To express a **complex number** z in **trigonometric form** or **polar form**:
  - Start by sketching the complex number.
  - Find r, the **absolute value**, and θ, the angle from the x-axis.
  - Plug these values into the polar form: $z = r(\cos\theta + i\sin\theta)$.
- **Review**: The **standard form** of a complex number z follows the formula: $z = x + yi$

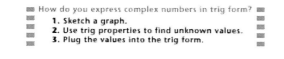

Given a **complex number** in **standard form**, $z = x + yi$, you can express that number in trigonometric or polar form by following these basic steps:

1. Sketch a graph of the complex number
2. Use trig properties to find unknown values
3. Plug the values into the trig form.

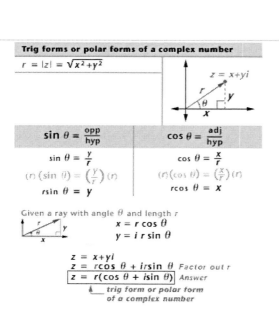

Given the complex number $z = x + yi$, first sketch a graph of the number in the complex plane.

To find r, the modulus of the complex number, use the Pythagorean theorem. The value of r will equal the square root of $x^2 + y^2$.

Now consider the angle θ. Knowing that $\cos\theta = {x}/{r}$, you can find x by multiplying both sides by r. So, $x = r\cos\theta$.

Also notice that $\sin\theta = {y}/{r}$, so $y = r\sin\theta$.

Substituting these values for x and y into the original complex number will give you that complex number expressed in terms of r and θ. This is the **trigonometric form** or **polar form** of the complex number: $z = r(\cos\theta + i\sin\theta)$.

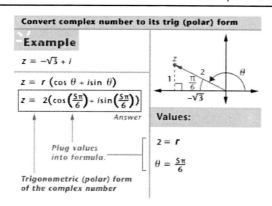

Convert complex number to its trig (polar) form

Example

$z = -\sqrt{3} + i$

$z = r\left(\cos\theta + i\sin\theta\right)$

$\boxed{z = 2\left(\cos\left(\tfrac{5\pi}{6}\right) + i\sin\left(\tfrac{5\pi}{6}\right)\right)}$

Answer

*Plug values
into formula.*

*Trigonometric (polar) form
of the complex number*

Values:

$2 = r$

$\theta = \dfrac{5\pi}{6}$

Consider the complex number $z = -\sqrt{3} + i$.

How would you express this number in polar (or trig) form?

First, sketch a graph of the complex number. Next, find the value of r, the modulus of the complex number. Remember that r is equal to the absolute value, or length, of the complex number.

Plugging the x and y values of the complex number into the Phythagorean theorem, you find that $r = 2$.

Next, find the value of θ as measured from the positive real axis. Given that the angles for a $1 - 2 - \sqrt{3}$ triangle measure $30°$, $60°$, and $90°$, you can label the angle formed with the negative real axis $\pi/6$. Therefore, θ equals $5\pi/6$.

Plug r and θ into the trig (or polar) form of the complex number.

So, the complex number in standard form, $z = -\sqrt{3} + i$, is equal to the complex

number $z = 2\left(\cos\left(5\pi/6\right) + i\sin\left(5\pi/6\right)\right)$ in polar form.

Sample problems:

1. Convert the polar number $4(\cos 90° + i\sin 90°)$ to complex form.
    Solution: $4i$
    Explanation: Evaluate each trig function and simplify:
    $4\left(\cos 90° + i\sin 90°\right) = 4\cos 90° + 4i\sin 90° = 4(0) + 4i(1) = 4i.$

2. Convert the complex number $-3i$ to polar form.
    Solution: $3(\cos 270° + i\sin 270°)$
    Explanation: The polar form is $r\left(\cos\theta + i\sin\theta\right)$.
    Find r: $r = \sqrt{x^2 + y^2} = \sqrt{(0)^2 + (-3)^2} = \sqrt{9} = 3.$
    Find x and y: $-3i = 0 - 3i;$ so, $x = 0$ and $y = -3$, which means $\cos\theta = 0$ and $\sin\theta = -1$.
    Therefore, $\theta = 270°$. Thus, $-3i = r\left(\cos\theta + i\sin\theta\right) = 3\left(\cos 270° + i\sin 270°\right).$

3. What is the polar form of the complex number represented as point A in the graph of the complex plane below?

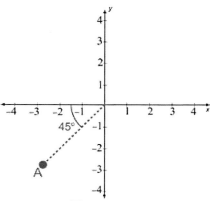

Solution: $3\sqrt{2}\left(\cos 225° + i\sin 225°\right)$

Explanation: The reference angle is 45° and is in the third quadrant. Therefore, $\theta = 225°$. Since both legs of the reference triangle are of length 3, the modulus is $3\sqrt{2}$.

Practice problems: *(Answers on page: 460)*

1. What is the polar form of the complex number $-7i$?

2. Convert the complex number $-5 + 5i$ to polar form.

3. Convert the polar number $4\left(\cos 225° + i\sin 225°\right)$ to complex form.

Review questions: *(Answers to odd questions on page: 460)*

1. Convert the complex number $z = 4 + 4i$ to polar form.

2. Convert the complex number $z = \sqrt{3} + i$ to trigonometric form.

3. Convert the complex number $z = 9i$ to polar form.

4. Convert the trigonometric form of the complex number $z = 6(\cos 60° + i\sin 60°)$ to standard form.

5. Convert the polar form of the complex number $z = 3(\cos 180° + i\sin 180°)$ to standard form.

Multiplying and Dividing Complex Numbers in Trigonometric or Polar Form

- To multiply two complex numbers:
  - Start by putting the complex numbers in **polar form**.
  - Multiply the r-terms and add the θ-terms: $z_1 z_2 = r_1 r_2\left[\cos\left(\theta_1 + \theta_2\right) + i\sin\left(\theta_1 + \theta_2\right)\right.$
- To divide two complex numbers:
  - Start by putting the complex numbers in polar form.
  - Divide the r-terms and subtract the θ-terms:

$$\frac{z_1}{z_2} = \frac{r_1}{r_2}\left[\cos\left(\theta_1 - \theta_2\right) + i\sin\left(\theta_1 - \theta_2\right)\right.$$

Multiply these two complex numbers in polar form:

$$z_1 z_2 = (r_1 \cos \theta_1 + i r_1 \sin \theta_1)(r_2 \cos \theta_2 + i r_2 \sin \theta_2)$$

$$z_1 z_2 = \underbrace{r_1 r_2 \cos \theta_1 \cos \theta_2}_{First} - \underbrace{r_1 r_2 \sin \theta_1 \sin \theta_2}_{Last}$$

$$+ i \underbrace{r_1 r_2 \sin \theta_1 \cos \theta_2}_{Inner} + i \underbrace{r_1 r_2 \cos \theta_1 \sin \theta_2}_{Outer}$$

$$z_1 z_2 = r_1 r_2 [\cos \theta_1 \cos \theta_2 - \sin \theta_1 \sin \theta_2$$
$$+ i (\sin \theta_1 \cos \theta_2 + \cos \theta_1 \sin \theta_2)]$$

$$\boxed{z_1 z_2 = r_1 r_2 [\cos(\theta_1 + \theta_2) + i \sin (\theta_1 + \theta_2)]} \longleftarrow Answer$$

$$\sin \theta_1 \cos \theta_2 + \cos \theta_1 \sin \theta_2 = \sin (\theta_1 + \theta_2)$$

$$z_1 = r_1 (\cos \theta_1 + i \sin \theta_1)$$

$$z_2 = r_2 (\cos \theta_2 + i \sin \theta_2)$$

$$z_1 z_2 = r_1 r_2 [\cos(\theta_1 + \theta_2) + i \sin (\theta_1 + \theta_2)] \longleftarrow Answer$$

Multiply   Add the angles
the moduli

To multiply two complex numbers in polar form
1. Multiply the moduli
2. Add the angles
$$z_1 z_2 = r_1 r_2 [\cos(\theta_1 + \theta_2) + i \sin (\theta_1 + \theta_2)]$$

Multiplying two complex numbers using FOIL is complicated. Instead, look for a pattern.

Notice that when taking the product of the two complex numbers, the polar form of the result has an absolute value of $r_1 r_2$ and an angle of $\theta_1 \theta_2$.

When multiplying two complex numbers, use this shortcut: convert the complex numbers to **polar form**, then multiply the r-terms and add the θ-terms.

Trig (polar) form of a complex number:
$$z = r(\cos \theta + i \sin \theta)$$

Divide the two complex numbers in polar form:

$$z_1 = r_1 (\cos \theta_1 + i \sin \theta_1)$$

$$z_2 = r_2 (\cos \theta_2 + i \sin \theta_2)$$

$$\frac{z_1}{z_2} = \frac{r_1}{r_2} [\cos (\theta_1 - \theta_2) + i \sin (\theta_1 - \theta_2)]$$

To divide two complex numbers in polar form
1. Divide the moduli
2. Subtract the angles
$$\frac{z_1}{z_2} = \frac{r_1}{r_2} [\cos (\theta_1 - \theta_2) + i \sin (\theta_1 - \theta_2)]$$

There is also a shortcut for complex number division.

To divide two complex numbers, divide the r-terms and subtract the θ-terms.

Trig (polar) form of a complex number:
$$z = r(\cos \theta + i \sin \theta)$$

Example Multiply:

$$z_1 = 6(\cos 105° + i \sin 105°)$$

$$z_2 = 3(\cos 15° + i \sin 15°)$$

$$z_1 z_2 = r_1 r_2 [\cos (\theta_1 + \theta_2) + i \sin (\theta_1 + \theta_2)]$$

$$z_1 z_2 = 6 \cdot 3 [\cos(105° + 15°) + i \sin(105° + 15°)]$$

$$\boxed{z_1 z_2 = 18 (\cos 120° + i \sin 120°)} \longleftarrow Answer$$

Consider this example: find the product of z_1 and z_2.

The complex number is already in polar form, so first multiply the r terms, and then add the θ terms.

REMEMBER: To multiply two complex numbers in polar form, multiply the r-terms together and add the θ-terms together.

Trig (polar) form of a complex number:
$$z = r(\cos \theta + i \sin \theta)$$

Example Divide:

$$z_1 = 6 (\cos 105° + i \sin 105°)$$

$$z_2 = 3 (\cos 15° + i \sin 15°)$$

$$\boxed{\frac{z_1}{z_2} = 2 (\cos 90° + i \sin 90°)} \longleftarrow \begin{array}{l}\textit{Answer in trig}\\ \textit{(polar) form}\end{array}$$

Simplifying further:

$$\frac{z_1}{z_2} = 2 (0 + i 1)$$

$$\boxed{\frac{z_1}{z_2} = 0 + 2i} = 2i$$

Answer

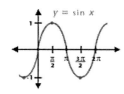

Consider the example illustrated here.

To solve, divide the first complex number by the second.

Next, divide the r-terms.

Finally, subtract the θ-terms.

The answer in polar form, $2(\cos 90° + i \sin 90°)$, can be simplified. Since the sine of 90° is 1, and the cosine of 90° is 0, the final answer is $2i$.

Multiplying and dividing complex numbers in polar form is pretty straightforward—just remember the shortcuts!

To multiply two complex numbers in polar form
1. Multiply the moduli
2. Add the angles

$$z_1 z_2 = r_1 r_2 \left[\cos\left(\theta_1 + \theta_2\right) + i \sin\left(\theta_1 + \theta_2\right)\right]$$

To divide two complex numbers in polar form
1. Divide the moduli
2. Subtract the angles

$$\frac{z_1}{z_2} = \frac{r_1}{r_2}\left[\cos\left(\theta_1 - \theta_2\right) + i \sin\left(\theta_1 - \theta_2\right)\right]$$

Sample problems:

1. If $z_1 = \left[5\left(\cos 90° + i\sin 90°\right)\right]$ and $z_2 = \left[6\left(\cos 180° + i\sin 180°\right)\right]$, find the product of $z_1 z_2$. Express your answer in polar form.

   Solution: $30\left(\cos 270° + i\sin 270°\right)$

   Explanation: To multiply the two complex numbers in trigonometric form, multiply the coefficients and add the angles:

   $$z_1 z_2 = (5 \cdot 6)\left[\cos\left(90° + 180°\right) + i\sin\left(90° + 180°\right)\right] = 30\left(\cos 270° + i\sin 270°\right).$$

2. Find $\dfrac{z_1}{z_2}$ when $z_1 = 12(\cos 60° + i\sin 60°)$ and $z_2 = 3(\cos 20° + i\sin 20°)$.

   Express your answer in polar form.

   Solution: $4(\cos 40° + i\sin 40°)$

   Explanation: Divide the coefficients and subtract the angles:

   $$\frac{z_1}{z_2} = \frac{12(\cos 60° + i\sin 60°)}{3(\cos 20° + i\sin 20°)} = \left(\frac{12}{3}\right)\left[\cos\left(60° - 20°\right) + i\sin\left(60° - 20°\right)\right] = 4(\cos 40° + i\sin 40°).$$

3. What is the product of the three complex numbers $2(\cos 15° + i\sin 15°)$, $3(\cos 30° + i\sin 30°)$, and $4(\cos 45° + i\sin 45°)$? Express your answer in standard form.

   Solution: $24i$

   Explanation: The product of the first two numbers is $(2)(3)\left(\cos 45° + i\sin 45°\right) = 6\left(\cos 45° + i\sin 45°\right)$. Multiply this with the third number to get

   $$(6)(4)\left(\cos\left(45° + 45°\right) + i\sin\left(45° + 45°\right)\right) = 24\left(\cos(90°) + i\sin(90°)\right) = 24\left(0 + i\right) = 24i.$$

Practice problems: *(Answers on page: 460)*

1. If $z_1 = 2(\cos 60° + i\sin 60°)$ and $z_2 = 4(\cos 150° + i\sin 150°)$ find the product of $z_1 z_2$. Express your answer in polar form.

2. If $z_1 = 6\left(\cos 60° + i\sin 60°\right)$ and $z_2 = 2\left(\cos 300° + i\sin 300°\right)$, find the quotient $\dfrac{z_1}{z_2}$. Express your answer in polar form.

3. What is the value of the expression $\dfrac{16(\cos 300° + i\sin 300°)}{8(\cos 60° + i\sin 60°)}$? Express your answer in standard form.

Review questions: *(Answers to odd questions on page: 460)*

1. If $z_1 = 4(\cos 60° + i\sin 60°)$ and $z_2 = 3(\cos 90° + i\sin 90°)$, find the product $z_1 z_2$.

2. Find $\dfrac{z_1}{z_2}$ where $z_1 = 20\left(\cos 120° + i\sin 120°\right)$ and $z_2 = 4\left(\cos 30° + i\sin 30°\right)$.

3. If $z_1 = 3(\cos 20° + i\sin 20°)$ and $z_2 = 5(\cos 70° + i\sin 70°)$, find the product $z_1 z_2$ in polar form.

4. Find the quotient $\dfrac{z_1}{z_2}$ in trigonometric form when $z_1 = 12(\cos 80° + i\sin 80°)$ and $z_2 = 6(\cos 30° + i\sin 30°)$.

5. If $z_1 = 3\sqrt{2}(\cos 135° + i\sin 135°)$ and $z_2 = 4\sqrt{2}(\cos 45° + i\sin 45°)$, find the product $z_1 z_2$ and express the answer in standard form.

Using DeMoivre's Theorem to Raise a Complex Number to a Power

- **Review**: A complex number in polar form is expressed as $r(\cos\theta + i\sin\theta)$, where r is the absolute value of the number and θ is its angle from the x-axis
- You can raise a complex number z in **polar form** to any power n using

  DeMoivre's theorem: $z^n = r^n\left[\cos(n\theta) + i\sin(n\theta)\right]$.

To Square a Complex Number in Polar Form: ① square the modulus ② double the angle $z^2 = zz = r^2\left[\cos(2\theta) + i\sin(2\theta)\right]$ What if you take z and raise it to the n (positive integer) power? 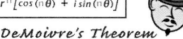 $z^n = r^n\left[\cos(n\theta) + i\sin(n\theta)\right]$ *DeMoivre's Theorem* **Formula for raising a complex number (in polar form) to any power.**	To square a complex number in **polar form**, multiply the number by itself. To raise a complex number to a power other than two, use **DeMoivre's theorem**. DeMoivre's theorem is a formula for raising a complex number z in polar form to the nth power.
Example *Simplify* $(\sqrt{3} + i)^3$ 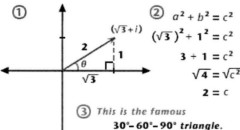 ② $a^2 + b^2 = c^2$ $(\sqrt{3})^2 + 1^2 = c^2$ $3 + 1 = c^2$ $\sqrt{4} = \sqrt{c^2}$ $2 = c$ ③ *This is the famous* **30°–60°–90° triangle.** *So,* $\theta = 30°$ *or* $\dfrac{\pi}{6}$	Use DeMoivre's theorem to raise this complex number to the third power. First, convert the number into polar form: **Step 1**: Graph the complex number. **Step 2**: Find the **modulus**. **Step 3**: Find the angle θ.
Example *Simplify* $(\sqrt{3} + i)^3$ ④ $(\sqrt{3} + i)^3 = \left[2\left(\cos\dfrac{\pi}{6} + i\sin\dfrac{\pi}{6}\right)\right]^3$ ⑤ $= 2^3\left[\cos\left(3\cdot\dfrac{\pi}{6}\right) + i\sin\left(3\cdot\dfrac{\pi}{6}\right)\right]$ $= 8\left(\cos\dfrac{\pi}{2} + i\sin\dfrac{\pi}{2}\right)$ $= 8(0 + i)$ $(\sqrt{3} + i)^3 = \boxed{8i}$	**Step 4**: Plug these values into the polar form $r(\cos\theta + i\sin\theta)$. **Step 5**: Apply DeMoivre's theorem and simplify.

Sample problems:

1. Use DeMoivre's theorem to express the following power in trigonometric form:

$$\left[3\left(\cos 100° + i\sin 100°\right)\right]^4$$

Solution: $81(\cos 400° + i\sin 400°)$

Explanation: $\left[3\left(\cos 100° + i\sin 100°\right)\right]^4 = 3^4\left[\cos\left(4\cdot 100°\right) + i\sin\left(4\cdot 100°\right)\right] = 81(\cos 400° + i\sin 400°)$

2. Find $\left(-1-i\right)^4$ using DeMoivre's theorem.

Solution: $4\left(\cos 900° + i\sin 900°\right)$

Explanation: Convert $-1-i$ to trig form: $x = -1$ and $y = -1$, so

$r = \sqrt{\left(-1\right)^2 + \left(-1\right)^2} = \sqrt{1+1} = \sqrt{2}$, so $\cos\theta = \dfrac{-\sqrt{2}}{2}$ and $\sin\theta = \dfrac{-\sqrt{2}}{2}$, therefore,

$\theta = 225°$. Thus, $-1-i = \left(\sqrt{2}\right)\left[\cos\left(225°\right) + i\sin\left(225°\right)\right]$. Apply DeMoivre's theorem:

$\left(-1-i\right)^4 = \left(\sqrt{2}\right)^4\left[\cos 4\left(225°\right) + i\sin 4\left(225°\right)\right] = 4\left(\cos 900° + i\sin 900°\right)$.

3. Find $\left(2\sqrt{2}\left(\cos 10° + i\sin 10°\right)\right)^4$

Solution: $64(\cos 40° + i\sin 40°)$

Explanation: $\left(2\sqrt{2}\right)^4\left(\cos\left(4\cdot 10\right) + i\sin\left(4\cdot 10\right)\right) = \left(\sqrt{8}\right)^4\left(\cos 40 + i\sin 40\right)$
$$= 8^2\left(\cos 40 + i\sin 40\right)$$
$$= 64\left(\cos 40 + i\sin 40\right)$$

Practice problems: *(Answers on page: 460)*

1. Use DeMoivre's theorem to express the following power in trigonometric form:

$$\left[2\left(\cos 20° + i\sin 20°\right)\right]^6$$

2. Find $\left(\sqrt{3}+i\right)^5$ using DeMoivre's theorem.

3. Compute $(1+i)^6$.

Review questions: *(Answers to odd questions on page: 460)*

1. Use DeMoivre's theorem to express the following power in trigonometric form:
   $[2(\cos 125° + i\sin 125°)]^4$

2. Use DeMoivre's theorem to express the following power in trigonometric form:
   $[3(\cos 40° + i\sin 40°)]^5$

3. Find $\left(1 - \sqrt{3i}\right)^4$ using DeMoivre's theorem, expressing the answer in trigonometric form.

4. Use DeMoivre's theorem to express the following power in trigonometric form: $(-2+2i)^6$.

5. Compute $(4(\cos 80° + i\sin 80°))^3$.

Roots of Complex Numbers

- **Review**: A complex number in **polar form** is expressed as $r(\cos\theta + i\sin\theta)$, where r is the **absolute value** of the number and θ is its angle from the x-axis.
- **Review**: Use **DeMoivre's theorem** to raise a complex number in polar form to a power:

$$z_n = r^n \left[\cos(n\theta) = i\sin(n\theta) \right]$$

- Also use DeMoivre's theorem to find the **nth roots** of a complex number in polar form. The nth roots of the complex number $z = r(\cos\theta + i\sin\theta)$ are given by the formula $\sqrt[n]{r}\left[\cos\left(\dfrac{\theta+2\pi k}{n}\right) + i\sin\left(\dfrac{\theta+2\pi k}{n}\right)\right]$, for $k = 0,1...,(n-1)$.

Find all the solutions to $z^4 = 16$ • There will be 4 roots (even if some of them are complex numbers).	Consider the example here: find all the solutions for $z^4 = 16$. Notice, since z is raised to the fourth power, there will be four solutions to this equation.
$z = \sqrt[4]{16} \longrightarrow z^4 = 16$ $z^4 - 16 = 0$ factor $(z^2 - 4)(z^2 + 4) = 0$	One way to approach the problem would be to move all the terms to one side and factor.
$(z-2)(z+2)(z^2+4) = 0$ $(z-2) = 0 \quad (z+2) = 0$ $z = 2 \qquad z = -2$	Find two real-number roots.
$(z+2)(z^2+4) = 0 \quad (z^2+4) = 0$ $z^2 = -4$ $z = \pm\sqrt{-4}$ $z = \pm 2i$	Then, using the third factor, find two **imaginary roots**.
4 Roots: **2, -2, 2i, -2i**	All four roots for the equation $z^4 = 16$ have been found. They are $2, -2, 2i, -2i$.
Take the nth root of $z = r(\cos\theta + i\sin\theta)$ There will be n roots. $\sqrt[n]{z} = \sqrt[n]{r}\left[\cos\left(\dfrac{\theta+2\pi k}{n}\right) + i\sin\left(\dfrac{\theta+2\pi k}{n}\right)\right]$	Consider another way to solve this problem. Convert the number to **polar form** and find the roots using **DeMoivre's theorem**.
Example Simplify $z^4 = 16$ $z^4 = 16(\cos 0 + i\sin 0)$ So: $z = \sqrt[4]{16}\left[\cos\left(\dfrac{0+2\pi k}{4}\right) + i\sin\left(\dfrac{0+2\pi k}{4}\right)\right]$	To convert to polar form, notice that $r = 16$ and the angle θ is $0°$. Now plug into the formula for the nth roots of a complex number with $n = 4$. Let k equal 0, 1, 2, and 3 to find the four roots. Each value of k will give you one root.
when $k = 0$ $z = 2\left[\cos\left(\dfrac{0+2\pi\cdot 0}{4}\right) + i\sin\left(\dfrac{0+2\pi\cdot 0}{4}\right)\right]$ $z = 2(\cos 0 + i\sin 0)$ $z = 2(1+0)$ $\boxed{z = 2}$	Start with $k = 0$. Calculate the angle, evaluate the trigonometric functions, and simplify. The result is the first root, $z = 2$.

when $k=1$	Next, let $k=1$. Again,
$z = 2\left[\cos\left(\frac{0+2\pi\cdot 1}{4}\right) + i\sin\left(\frac{0+2\pi\cdot 1}{4}\right)\right]$	• calculate the angle,
$z = 2\left(\cos\frac{\pi}{2} + i\sin\frac{\pi}{2}\right)$	• evaluate the trigonometric functions,
$z = 2(0 + i)$	• and simplify.
$z = 2i$	When $k=1$, $z = 2i$.
when $k=2$	Continuing on, plug in $k=2$ into the formula.
$z = 2\left[\cos\left(\frac{0+2\pi\cdot 2}{4}\right) + i\sin\left(\frac{0+2\pi\cdot 2}{4}\right)\right]$	Follow the routine.
$z = 2(\cos\pi + i\sin\pi)$	When $k=2$, $z = -2$.
$z = 2(-1 + 0)$	
$z = -2$	
when $k=3$	Finally, plug in $k=3$.
$z = 2\left[\cos\left(\frac{0+2\pi\cdot 3}{4}\right) + i\sin\left(\frac{0+2\pi\cdot 3}{4}\right)\right]$	This gives the fourth and final root, $z = -2i$.
$z = 2\left(\cos\frac{3\pi}{2} + i\sin\frac{3\pi}{2}\right)$	
$z = 2(0 - i)$	
$z = -2i$	
Four Roots: 2,-2, 2i,-2i **4 Roots:** **2,-2, 2i,-2i**	Notice that the four roots found using DeMoivre's formula are the same as the four roots found by factoring. **REMEMBER:** When solving math problems, use the technique that is simplest for you unless you are directed to use a particular method.

Sample problems:

1. Find the fourth roots of -81. List the roots in complex form.

Solution: $\dfrac{3\sqrt{2} + 3i\sqrt{2}}{2}$, $\dfrac{-3\sqrt{2} + 3i\sqrt{2}}{2}$, $\dfrac{-3\sqrt{2} - 3i\sqrt{2}}{2}$, $\dfrac{3\sqrt{2} - 3i\sqrt{2}}{2}$

Explanation: Express -81 in polar form: $-81 = 81(\cos \pi + i \sin \pi)$. Use the formula,

$\sqrt[n]{r}\left[\cos\left(\dfrac{\theta + 2\pi k}{n}\right) + i \sin\left(\dfrac{\theta + 2\pi k}{n}\right)\right]$ where $n = 4$, $r = 81$, $\theta = \pi$, and $k = 0, 1, 2,$ and 3, to find the

fourth roots of -81. Substitute the values for n, r, and θ into the formula and simplify:

$\sqrt[4]{81}\left[\cos\left(\dfrac{\pi + 2\pi k}{4}\right) + i \sin\left(\dfrac{\pi + 2\pi k}{4}\right)\right] = 3\left[\cos\left(\dfrac{\pi + 2\pi k}{4}\right) + i \sin\left(\dfrac{\pi + 2\pi k}{4}\right)\right]$.

Evaluate the expression for $k = 0, 1, 2,$ and 3:

$k = 0$: $3\left[\cos\left(\dfrac{\pi + 2\pi(0)}{4}\right) + i \sin\left(\dfrac{\pi + 2\pi(0)}{4}\right)\right] = 3\left[\cos\left(\dfrac{\pi}{4}\right) + i \sin\left(\dfrac{\pi}{4}\right)\right]$

$= 3\left[\left(\dfrac{\sqrt{2}}{2}\right) + i\left(\dfrac{\sqrt{2}}{2}\right)\right] = \dfrac{3\sqrt{2} + 3i\sqrt{2}}{2}$

$k = 1$: $3\left[\cos\left(\dfrac{\pi + 2\pi(1)}{4}\right) + i \sin\left(\dfrac{\pi + 2\pi(1)}{4}\right)\right] = 3\left[\cos\left(\dfrac{3\pi}{4}\right) + i \sin\left(\dfrac{3\pi}{4}\right)\right]$

$= 3\left[\left(\dfrac{-\sqrt{2}}{2}\right) + i\left(\dfrac{\sqrt{2}}{2}\right)\right] = \dfrac{-3\sqrt{2} + 3i\sqrt{2}}{2}$

$k = 2$: $3\left[\cos\left(\dfrac{\pi + 2\pi(2)}{4}\right) + i \sin\left(\dfrac{\pi + 2\pi(2)}{4}\right)\right] = 3\left[\cos\left(\dfrac{5\pi}{4}\right) + i \sin\left(\dfrac{5\pi}{4}\right)\right]$

$= 3\left[\left(\dfrac{-\sqrt{2}}{2}\right) + i\left(\dfrac{-\sqrt{2}}{2}\right)\right] = \dfrac{-3\sqrt{2} - 3i\sqrt{2}}{2}$

$k = 3$: $3\left[\cos\left(\dfrac{\pi + 2\pi(3)}{4}\right) + i \sin\left(\dfrac{\pi + 2\pi(3)}{4}\right)\right] = 3\left[\cos\left(\dfrac{7\pi}{4}\right) + i \sin\left(\dfrac{7\pi}{4}\right)\right]$

$= 3\left[\left(\dfrac{\sqrt{2}}{2}\right) + i\left(\dfrac{-\sqrt{2}}{2}\right)\right] = \dfrac{3\sqrt{2} - 3i\sqrt{2}}{2}$

2. Find the cube roots of $2 - 2i$.

Solution: $\sqrt{2}\left[\cos\left(\dfrac{7\pi}{12}\right) + i\sin\left(\dfrac{7\pi}{12}\right)\right]$, $\sqrt{2}\left[\cos\left(\dfrac{5\pi}{4}\right) + i\sin\left(\dfrac{5\pi}{4}\right)\right]$, $\sqrt{2}\left[\cos\left(\dfrac{23\pi}{12}\right) + i\sin\left(\dfrac{23\pi}{12}\right)\right]$

Explanation: Express $2 - 2i$ in polar form: $2 - 2i = 2\sqrt{2}\left(\cos\dfrac{7\pi}{4} + i\sin\dfrac{7\pi}{4}\right)$. Use the formula,

$\sqrt[n]{r}\left[\cos\left(\dfrac{\theta + 2\pi k}{n}\right) + i\sin\left(\dfrac{\theta + 2\pi k}{n}\right)\right]$ where $n = 3$, $r = 2\sqrt{2}$, $\theta = \dfrac{7\pi}{4}$, and $k = 0, 1$ and 2, to

find the cube roots of $2 - 2i$. Substitute the values for n, r, and θ into the formula and simplify:

$$\sqrt[3]{\left(2\sqrt{2}\right)}\left[\cos\left(\dfrac{\frac{7\pi}{4} + 2\pi k}{3}\right) + i\sin\left(\dfrac{\frac{7\pi}{4} + 2\pi k}{3}\right)\right] = \sqrt{2}\left[\cos\left(\dfrac{\frac{7\pi}{4} + 2\pi k}{3}\right) + i\sin\left(\dfrac{\frac{7\pi}{4} + 2\pi k}{3}\right)\right].$$

Evaluate the expression for $k = 0, 1$ and 2:

$k = 0$: $\sqrt{2}\left[\cos\left(\dfrac{\frac{7\pi}{4} + 2\pi(0)}{3}\right) + i\sin\left(\dfrac{\frac{7\pi}{4} + 2\pi(0)}{3}\right)\right] = \sqrt{2}\left[\cos\left(\dfrac{7\pi}{12}\right) + i\sin\left(\dfrac{7\pi}{12}\right)\right]$

$k = 1$: $\sqrt{2}\left[\cos\left(\dfrac{\frac{7\pi}{4} + 2\pi(1)}{3}\right) + i\sin\left(\dfrac{\frac{7\pi}{4} + 2\pi(1)}{3}\right)\right] = \sqrt{2}\left[\cos\left(\dfrac{5\pi}{4}\right) + i\sin\left(\dfrac{5\pi}{4}\right)\right]$

$k = 2$: $\sqrt{2}\left[\cos\left(\dfrac{\frac{7\pi}{4} + 2\pi(2)}{3}\right) + i\sin\left(\dfrac{\frac{7\pi}{4} + 2\pi(2)}{3}\right)\right] = \sqrt{2}\left[\cos\left(\dfrac{23\pi}{12}\right) + i\sin\left(\dfrac{23\pi}{12}\right)\right]$

3. Find the square roots of $8\sqrt{2} + 8i\sqrt{2}$.

Solution: $4\left[\cos\left(\dfrac{\pi}{8}\right) + i\sin\left(\dfrac{\pi}{8}\right)\right]$, $4\left[\cos\left(\dfrac{9\pi}{8}\right) + i\sin\left(\dfrac{9\pi}{8}\right)\right]$

Explanation:

Express $8\sqrt{2} + 8i\sqrt{2}$ in polar form: $8\sqrt{2} + 8i\sqrt{2} = 16\left(\cos\dfrac{\pi}{4} + i\sin\dfrac{\pi}{4}\right)$. Use the formula,

$\sqrt[n]{r}\left[\cos\left(\dfrac{\theta + 2\pi k}{n}\right) + i\sin\left(\dfrac{\theta + 2\pi k}{n}\right)\right]$ where $n = 2$, $r = 16$, $\theta = \dfrac{\pi}{4}$, and $k = 0$ and 1, to find the

square roots of $8\sqrt{2} + 8i\sqrt{2}$. Substitute the values for n, r, and θ into the formula and simplify:

$$\sqrt[2]{16}\left[\cos\left(\dfrac{\frac{\pi}{4} + 2\pi k}{2}\right) + i\sin\left(\dfrac{\frac{\pi}{4} + 2\pi k}{2}\right)\right] = 4\left[\cos\left(\dfrac{\frac{\pi}{4} + 2\pi k}{2}\right) + i\sin\left(\dfrac{\frac{\pi}{4} + 2\pi k}{2}\right)\right].$$

Evaluate the expression for $k = 0$ and 1:

$k = 0$: $4\left[\cos\left(\dfrac{\frac{\pi}{4} + 2\pi(0)}{2}\right) + i\sin\left(\dfrac{\frac{\pi}{4} + 2\pi(0)}{2}\right)\right] = 4\left[\cos\left(\dfrac{\pi}{8}\right) + i\sin\left(\dfrac{\pi}{8}\right)\right]$

$k = 1$: $4\left[\cos\left(\dfrac{\frac{\pi}{4} + 2\pi(1)}{2}\right) + i\sin\left(\dfrac{\frac{\pi}{4} + 2\pi(1)}{2}\right)\right] = 4\left[\cos\left(\dfrac{9\pi}{8}\right) + i\sin\left(\dfrac{9\pi}{8}\right)\right]$

Practice problems: *(Answers on page: 460)*

1. Find the cube roots of 125. List the roots in complex form.

2. Find the sixth roots of $-2i$.

3. Find the fourth roots of $-81 + 81i$.

Review questions: *(Answers to odd questions on page: 460)*

1. True or false: $\sqrt[3]{2}\left(\cos 100° + i\sin 100°\right)$ is a third root of $1 - i\sqrt{3}$.

2. Find the non-real fourth roots of $16 + 0i$ in trigonometric form.

3. Find the cube roots of 8. Which one is in quadrant II?

4. Find the cube roots of $2 + 2i$.

5. Find the cube roots of $1 - i$.

More Roots of Complex Numbers

- **Review**: The *n*th roots of the complex number $z = r(\cos\theta + i\sin\theta)$ are given by the formula $\sqrt[n]{r}\left[\cos\left(\dfrac{\theta + 2\pi k}{n}\right) + i\sin\left(\dfrac{\theta + 2\pi k}{n}\right)\right].$

- **Review**: Complex roots always come in **conjugate pairs**. If one of the roots is in the form $a + bi$, there will always be a second root in the form $a - bi$.

Example *Find the cube roots of -27* • There will be 3 roots. • One of the roots will be -3, because $(-3)(-3)(-3) = 9(-3) = \boxed{-27}$ • The other roots are complex.	Consider the example given here: find the cube roots of -27. One root, -3, is easy to find. How do you find the other roots?
① *Write -27 in polar form.* $\theta = \pi$ $-27 \quad r = 27$ (length) $z = r(\cos\theta + i\sin\theta)$ $z = 27(\cos\pi + i\sin\pi)$	First, find the **polar form** of the number -27. The best first step is a quick sketch. Notice that $\theta = \pi$ and $r = 27$. **REMEMBER**: $r = 27$, not -27, because length is never negative.
② *Use formula.* $\sqrt[n]{r}\left[\cos\left(\dfrac{\theta + 2\pi k}{n}\right) + i\sin\left(\dfrac{\theta + 2\pi k}{n}\right)\right]$	To find the complex roots, use the formula. **REMEMBER**: The values for k start at 0, not 1, and end at $n - 1$, not at n. In this example, k takes on the values 0, 1, and 2.
when $k = 0$ $3\left[\cos\left(\dfrac{\pi + 2\pi \cdot 0}{3}\right) + i\sin\left(\dfrac{\pi + 2\pi \cdot 0}{3}\right)\right]$ $= 3\left(\cos\dfrac{\pi}{3} + i\sin\dfrac{\pi}{3}\right)$ $= 3\left(\dfrac{1}{2} + i\dfrac{\sqrt{3}}{2}\right) = \boxed{\dfrac{3}{2} + \dfrac{3\sqrt{3}}{2}i}$	When $k = 0$, the angle is $60°$, or $\pi/3$. Substitute the values for $\cos(\pi/3)$ and $\sin(\pi/3)$ and note the root.
when $k = 1$ $3\left[\cos\left(\dfrac{\pi + 2\pi \cdot 1}{3}\right) + i\sin\left(\dfrac{\pi + 2\pi \cdot 1}{3}\right)\right]$ $= 3\left(\cos\dfrac{3\pi}{3} + i\sin\dfrac{3\pi}{3}\right)$ $= 3(\cos\pi + i\sin\pi)$ $= 3[-1 + i(0)]$ $= \boxed{-3}$	When $k = 1$: The angle is $180°$, or π. $\sin\pi = 0$, so $i\sin\pi = 0$. $\cos\pi = -1$. Do the arithmetic. The result, -3, is the only real number root.

when $k = 2$ $$3\left[\cos\left(\frac{\pi + 2\pi \cdot 2}{3}\right) + i\sin\left(\frac{\pi + 2\pi \cdot 2}{3}\right)\right]$$ $$= 3\left(\cos\frac{5\pi}{3} + i\sin\frac{5\pi}{3}\right)$$ $$= 3\left(\frac{1}{2} - i\frac{\sqrt{3}}{2}\right)$$ $$= \boxed{\frac{3}{2} - \frac{3\sqrt{3}}{2}i}$$	Finally, plug in $k = 2$. Once again, substitute in the sine and cosine values and simplify. Notice that this root is the conjugate of the first root found.

Sample problems:

1. Find all roots of $x^3 - 8 = 0$ with answers written in complex form.

    Solution: $2,\ -1 + i\sqrt{3},\ -1 - i\sqrt{3}$

    Explanation: If $x^3 - 8 = 0$ then $x^3 = 8$. Express 8 in polar form: $8 = 8(\cos 0 + i\sin 0)$.

    Use the formula, $\sqrt[n]{r}\left[\cos\left(\frac{\theta + 2\pi k}{n}\right) + i\sin\left(\frac{\theta + 2\pi k}{n}\right)\right]$ where $n = 3$, $r = 8$, $\theta = 0$,

    and $k = 0, 1$ and 2, to find the roots of $x^3 - 8 = 0$. Substitute the values for n, r, and θ

    into the formula and simplify:

    $$\sqrt[3]{8}\left[\cos\left(\frac{0 + 2\pi k}{3}\right) + i\sin\left(\frac{0 + 2\pi k}{3}\right)\right] = 2\left[\cos\left(\frac{0 + 2\pi k}{3}\right) + i\sin\left(\frac{0 + 2\pi k}{3}\right)\right].$$

    Evaluate the expression for $k = 0, 1$ and 2:

    $k = 0$: $2\left[\cos(0) + i\sin(0)\right] = 2\left[1 + i(0)\right] = 2,$

    $k = 1$: $2\left[\cos\left(\frac{2\pi}{3}\right) + i\sin\left(\frac{2\pi}{3}\right)\right] = 2\left[-\frac{1}{2} + i\left(\frac{\sqrt{3}}{2}\right)\right] = -1 + i\sqrt{3},$

    $k = 2$: $2\left[\cos\left(\frac{4\pi}{3}\right) + i\sin\left(\frac{4\pi}{3}\right)\right] = 2\left[-\frac{1}{2} + i\left(-\frac{\sqrt{3}}{2}\right)\right] = -1 - i\sqrt{3}.$

    Thus, $x = 2,\ -1 + i\sqrt{3}$, or $-1 - i\sqrt{3}$

2. Find all roots of $x^2 + i = 0$ with answers written in complex form.

    Solution: $\dfrac{-\sqrt{2} + i\sqrt{2}}{2}$ or $\dfrac{\sqrt{2} - i\sqrt{2}}{2}$

    Explanation: If $x^2 + i = 0$ then $x^2 = -i$. Express $-i$ in polar form: $-i = \left(\cos\dfrac{3\pi}{2} + i\sin\dfrac{3\pi}{2}\right)$.

    Find the square roots of $-i$ using the formula $\sqrt[n]{r}\left[\cos\left(\dfrac{\frac{3\pi}{2} + 2\pi k}{n}\right) + i\sin\left(\dfrac{\frac{3\pi}{2} + 2\pi k}{n}\right)\right]$:

    $k = 0$: $\left[\cos\left(\frac{3\pi}{4}\right) + i\sin\left(\frac{3\pi}{4}\right)\right] = -\frac{\sqrt{2}}{2} + i\left(\frac{\sqrt{2}}{2}\right) = \frac{-\sqrt{2} + i\sqrt{2}}{2},$

    $k = 1$: $\left[\cos\left(\frac{7\pi}{4}\right) + i\sin\left(\frac{7\pi}{4}\right)\right] = \frac{\sqrt{2}}{2} + i\left(-\frac{\sqrt{2}}{2}\right) = \frac{\sqrt{2} - i\sqrt{2}}{2}.$

    Thus, $x = \dfrac{-\sqrt{2} + i\sqrt{2}}{2}$ or $x = \dfrac{\sqrt{2} - i\sqrt{2}}{2}$.

3. Find all roots of $x^3 - 12 = 0$ with answers written in complex form.

Solution: 2.289, $-1.145 + 1.982i$, or $-1.145 - 1.982i$

Explanation: If $x^3 - 12 = 0$ then $x^3 = 12$. Express 12 polar form: $12 = 12(\cos 0 + i \sin 0)$.

Find the cube roots of 12:

$k = 0$: $\sqrt[3]{12}\left[\cos(0) + i\sin(0)\right] = \left(\sqrt[3]{12}\left[1 + i(0)\right]\right) = 2.289$,

$k = 1$: $\sqrt[3]{12}\left[\cos\left(\dfrac{2\pi}{3}\right) + i\sin\left(\dfrac{2\pi}{3}\right)\right] = \left(2.289\left[(-0.5) + i(0.866)\right]\right) = -1.145 + 1.982i$,

$k = 2$: $\sqrt[3]{12}\left[\cos\left(\dfrac{4\pi}{3}\right) + i\sin\left(\dfrac{4\pi}{3}\right)\right] = 2.289\left[(-0.5) + i(-0.866)\right] = -1.145 - 1.982i$.

Thus, $x = 2.289$, $-1.145 + 1.982i$, or $-1.145 - 1.982i$.

Practice problems: *(Answers on page: 461)*

1. Find all roots of $x^4 - 16 = 0$ with answers written in complex form.

2. Find all roots of $x^3 + 125 = 0$ with answers written in complex form.

3. Find all roots of $x^6 - 1 = 0$ with answers written in complex form.

Review questions: *(Answers to odd questions on page: 461)*

1. Find all roots of $x^4 - 1 = 0$ with answers written in complex form.

2. Find all roots of $x^4 + 1 = 0$ with answers written in complex form.

3. Find all roots of $x^3 + 64 = 0$ with answers written in complex form.

4. Find all solutions to $x^5 - 1 = 0$. Express solutions in complex form with a and b computed to three decimal places.

5. Find all solutions to $x^3 + 5 = 0$. Express solutions in complex form with a and b computed to three decimal places.

Roots of Unity

- **Review**: The nth roots of the complex number $z = r(\cos\theta + i\sin\theta)$ are given by the formula for $k = 0, 1 \ldots, (n-1)$:

$$\sqrt[n]{r}\left[\cos\left(\frac{\theta + 2\pi k}{n}\right) + i\sin\left(\frac{\theta + 2\pi k}{n}\right)\right].$$

- The **roots of unity** are the complex roots of 1.

Roots of Unity are the complex roots of 1.
1 in polar form is $1(\cos 0 + i \sin 0)$

Example *Find the 8th roots of unity:*

$$\sqrt[n]{r}\left[\cos\left(\frac{\theta + 2\pi k}{n}\right) + i\sin\left(\frac{\theta + 2\pi k}{n}\right)\right]$$

where $k = 0, 1, 2, \ldots, n-1$

$$= 1\left[\cos\left(\frac{0 + 2\pi k}{8}\right) + i\sin\left(\frac{0 + 2\pi k}{8}\right)\right]$$

$$= \cos\frac{2\pi k}{8} + i\sin\frac{2\pi k}{8}$$

where $k = 0, 1, 2, 3, 4, 5, 6, 7$

The nth roots of the number 1 are called the **roots of unity**.

Consider the example here, find the 8th roots of unity.

Find them using the formula for finding the roots of complex numbers.

Notice that there will be eight 8th roots of unity.

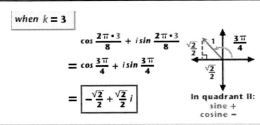

To find the roots, plug in $k = 0, 1, 2, ..., 7$ into the formula.

Here are the calculations for $k = 3$.

The answer is one of the 8th roots of unity.

The 8th Roots of Unity:

$$1, \frac{\sqrt{2}}{2} + \frac{\sqrt{2}}{2}i, i, -\frac{\sqrt{2}}{2} + \frac{\sqrt{2}}{2}i, -1, -\frac{\sqrt{2}}{2} - \frac{\sqrt{2}}{2}i, -i, \frac{\sqrt{2}}{2} - \frac{\sqrt{2}}{2}i$$

Graphing:
- the 8th roots of unity live on the circle centered at the origin of radius $\sqrt[8]{1} = 1$

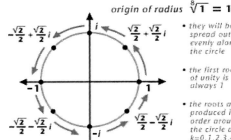

- they will be spread out evenly along the circle
- the first root of unity is always 1
- the roots are produced in order around the circle as $k = 0, 1, 2, 3, 4, 5, 6,$ and 7

Here are all eight of the 8th roots of unity.

Look at the graph of these roots in the complex plane. Notice they are evenly spread out along the circle of radius 1 centered at the origin.

This will always happen whenever graphing the roots of unity.

Sample problems:

1. Find the five fifth roots of unity. Express the roots in polar form.

   Solution: 1, $\cos 72° + i \sin 72°$, $\cos 144° + i \sin 144°$, $\cos 216° + i \sin 216°$, and $\cos 288° + i \sin 288°$

   Explanation: Evaluate the formula for finding roots of complex numbers, where $\theta = 0$ and $n = 5$, for $k = 0,1,2,3,4$:

   $k = 0:$ $\left[\cos \left(\frac{0 + 2\pi(0)}{5} \right) + i \sin \left(\frac{0 + 2\pi(0)}{5} \right) \right] = \cos 0° + i \sin 0° = \left[(1) + i(0) \right] = 1.$

   $k = 1:$ $\left[\cos \left(\frac{2\pi}{5} \right) + i \sin \left(\frac{2\pi}{5} \right) \right] = (\cos 72° + i \sin 72°).$

   $k = 2:$ $\left[\cos \left(\frac{4\pi}{5} \right) + i \sin \left(\frac{4\pi}{5} \right) \right] = (\cos 144° + i \sin 144°).$

   $k = 3:$ $\left[\cos \left(\frac{6\pi}{5} \right) + i \sin \left(\frac{6\pi}{5} \right) \right] = (\cos 216° + i \sin 216°).$

   $k = 4:$ $\left[\cos \left(\frac{8\pi}{5} \right) + i \sin \left(\frac{8\pi}{5} \right) \right] = (\cos 288° + i \sin 288°).$

   The five fifth roots of 1 are 1, $\cos 72° + i \sin 72°$, $\cos 144° + i \sin 144°$, $\cos 216° + i \sin 216°$, and $\cos 288° + i \sin 288°$.

2. You know that all the roots of unity are spread evenly around the circle. Calculate the value of the root to which the arrow is pointing.

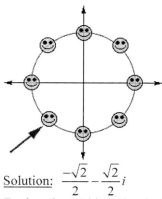

Solution: $\dfrac{-\sqrt{2}}{2} - \dfrac{\sqrt{2}}{2}i$

Explanation: This is the sixth root out of 8 indicated on this circle. It therefore corresponds to $k = 5$ in the formula for finding the eighth roots of 1:

$$\cos\left(\frac{0+2\pi(5)}{8}\right) + i\sin\left(\frac{0+2\pi(5)}{8}\right) = \cos\frac{5\pi}{4} + i\sin\frac{5\pi}{4} = \frac{-\sqrt{2}}{2} - \frac{\sqrt{2}}{2}i$$

3. Use the unit circle on the complex plane to find the fourth roots of unity.
   Solution: $1, i, -1, -i$
   Explanation: This will give the four points that lie on the axes on the unit circle in the complex plane.

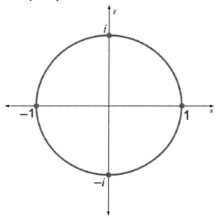

Practice problems: *(Answers on page: 461)*

1. Find the three third roots of unity. Express the roots in complex form.

2. You know that all the roots of unity are spread evenly around the unit circle. Calculate the value of the root to which the arrow is pointing.

3. You know that all the roots of unity are spread evenly around the unit circle. Calculate the value of the root to which the arrow is pointing.

Review questions: *(Answers to odd questions on page: 461)*

1. Find the ten tenth roots of unity. Express the roots in trigonometric form.

2. Find the fifth root of unity that is in the third quadrant.

3. Find the sixth root of unity that is in the second quadrant. Express the answer in complex number form.

4. True or false: 1 is a square root of unity and a cube root of unity.

5. If we graph the ninth roots of unity in the complex plane, how many of them would lie in the second quadrant?

An Introduction to Polar Coordinates

- Instead of describing points using **Cartesian** or **rectangular coordinates**, you can use **polar coordinates** to describe points based on their distance from the origin and their angle from the **polar axis**.
- In polar coordinates, a point is specified by an ordered pair (r, θ), where r is the distance of the point from the origin and θ is the angle of the point from the polar axis. The polar axis is located in the same place as the positive x-axis of a **rectangular coordinate system**.

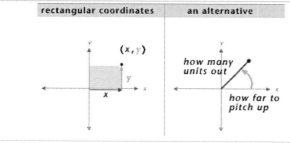

There are many situations where the traditional way of thinking about a rectangular coordinate system is not practical. Consider a radar tower tracking an incoming airplane. The radar tower doesn't calculate the x- and y-components of the plane; instead, it finds the distance of the plane from the tower and its direction from the tower. The radar tower uses what is called **polar coordinates**.

to find point (r, θ):
❶ *sweep counterclockwise θ radians from the positive side of the x-axis*
❷ *move r units out from the origin along the radial arm of θ*

polar coordinates

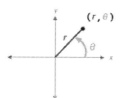

θ: *pitch of angle*
r: *distance from origin*

To find the **polar coordinates** of a point, calculate r, the distance of the point from the origin, and θ, the angle from a set axis known as the **polar axis**.

The polar axis is in the same location as the positive x-axis of the **rectangular coordinate plane**. This is so that the coordinates of the polar graph will match up to the angles of the unit circle.

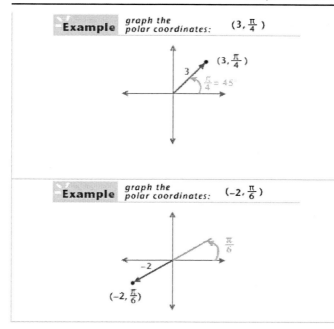

Example graph the polar coordinates: $\left(3, \frac{\pi}{4}\right)$	To graph a point in polar coordinates, start by finding the direction of the point from the origin using the angle θ.

Then move a distance of r in that direction.

In this example you're asked to graph the polar coordinate, $(3, \pi/4)$.

Begin by sweeping up $\pi/4$, or $45°$. Then, move a distance of 3. |
| **Example** graph the polar coordinates: $\left(-2, \frac{\pi}{6}\right)$ | If the r-term is negative, then move in the opposite direction (along the same line) as the angle. Still move the same number of units despite the fact that the value is negative. |

Sample problems:

1. State the location of the point defined by the following polar coordinates: $\left(4, \frac{\pi}{3}\right)$

   Solution: Quadrant I

   Explanation: $\frac{\pi}{3}$ is $60°$ from the positive $x-$axis and in the 1st quadrant. The first coordinate defines the distance from the origin. Since 4 is positive, the point is 4 units from the origin along that $60°$ ray. Thus, $\left(4, \frac{\pi}{3}\right)$ is in quadrant I.

2. State the location of the point defined by the following polar coordinates: $\left(-1, \frac{5\pi}{6}\right)$

   Solution: Quadrant IV

   Explanation: $\frac{5\pi}{6}$ is $150°$ from the positive $x-$axis and in the 2nd quadrant. However, the first coordinate is negative, indicating the reverse direction along the $150°$ ray. Thus, $\left(-1, \frac{5\pi}{6}\right)$ is in quadrant IV.

3. State the location of the point defined by the following polar coordinates: $\left(-3, 2\pi\right)$

   Solution: negative $x-$axis

   Explanation: 2π indicates that the angle is on the $x-$axis and -3 indicates a reverse of direction. Thus, $\left(-3, 2\pi\right)$ is on the negative side of the $x-$axis.

Practice problems: *(Answers on page: 461)*

1. State the location of the point defined by the following polar coordinates: $\left(5, \pi\right)$

2. State the location of the point defined by the following polar coordinates: $\left(-1, \frac{5\pi}{3}\right)$

3. State the location of the point defined by the following polar coordinates: $\left(0.5, \frac{\pi}{6}\right)$

Review questions: *(Answers to odd questions on page: 461)*

1. Plot the point $P\left(3, \frac{\pi}{2}\right)$ in a polar coordinate system.

2. Plot the point $R\left(-2, \frac{\pi}{2}\right)$ in a polar coordinate system.

3. State the location of the point defined by the following polar coordinates: $\left(3, \frac{11\pi}{6}\right)$

4. State the location of the point defined by the following polar coordinates: $(-2, \pi)$

5. State the location of the point defined by the following polar coordinates: $\left(-1, \frac{7\pi}{6}\right)$

Converting between Polar and Rectangular Coordinates

- To convert from **polar coordinates** to **rectangular coordinates**, use the following: $x = r \cos \theta$, $y = r \sin \theta$.
- To convert from rectangular coordinates to polar coordinates, use the following formula:

$$r = \sqrt{x^2 + y^2}, \ \theta = \arctan\left(\frac{y}{x}\right).$$

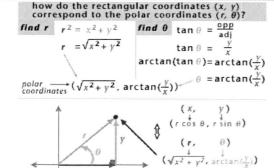	**Polar coordinates** and **rectangular coordinates** both describe points in the plane.
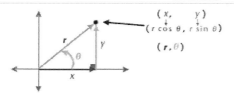	To convert from polar coordinates to rectangular coordinates, use the formulas $x = r \cos \theta$ and $y = r \sin \theta$. In other words, a point with polar coordinates (r, θ) has rectangular coordinates $(r \cos \theta, r \sin \theta)$.
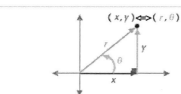	To convert from rectangular coordinates to polar coordinates, use the Pythagorean theorem and one of the **inverse trig functions**. Use the formulas $r = \sqrt{x^2 + y^2}$ and $\theta = \arctan\left(\frac{y}{x}\right)$. Plug the *x*- and *y*-terms into the formula and simplify. The results are the polar coordinates for the point.

 www.thinkwell.com

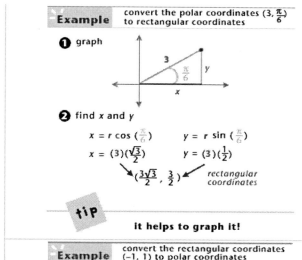

Consider this example, convert the polar coordinates $\left(3, \pi/6\right)$ to rectangular coordinates.

Use the formula for polar coordinates, $(r \cos \theta, r \sin \theta)$. Plug in 3 for r and $\pi/6$ for θ.

Evaluate for cosine and sine and then simplify.

Graphing the point helps identify if the trig functions have the correct signs.

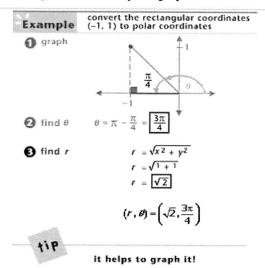

Now try this one: convert the point $(-1, 1)$ from rectangular coordinates to polar coordinates.

Plug the appropriate values into the formula.

Then simplify.

Put the r in the first position and θ in the second position to get the polar coordinates for the point.

Sample problems:

1. Convert the polar coordinates $(-2, -36°)$ to rectangular coordinates.

   Solution: $(-1.6, 1.2)$

   Explanation: Find the x-coordinate: $x = r \cos \theta = -2 \cos(-36°) = -2(.8090) = -1.618$. Find the y-coordinate: $y = r \sin \theta = -2 \sin(-36°) = -2(-.5878) = 1.176$. Thus, the rectangular coordinates are $(-1.6, 1.2)$.

2. Give polar coordinates of a point whose Cartesian coordinates are $(4, -2)$.

   Solution: $(2\sqrt{5}, 333.4°)$

   Explanation: Find r: $r = \sqrt{x^2 + y^2} = \sqrt{16 + 4} = \sqrt{20} = 2\sqrt{5}$. Find θ: $y = \tan^{-1}\left(\dfrac{y}{x}\right) = \tan^{-1}\left(\dfrac{-2}{4}\right) = -26.565° = 333.435°$. Thus, the polar coordinates are $\left(2\sqrt{5}, 333.4°\right)$.

Practice problems: *(Answers on page: 461)*

1. Give polar coordinates of a point whose Cartesian coordinates are $(-3, -3)$.

   $\left(3\sqrt{2}, \dfrac{5\pi}{4}\right)$

2. Give the rectangular coordinates of the point whose polar coordinates are $(3, 217°)$.

Review questions: *(Answers to odd questions on page: 461)*

1. Give polar coordinates of a point whose Cartesian coordinates are $(2,2)$.

2. Give polar coordinates of a point whose Cartesian coordinates are $\left(\sqrt{3},-1\right)$.

3. Give the rectangular coordinates of the point P whose polar coordinates are $\left(4,\dfrac{\pi}{3}\right)$.

4. Give the rectangular coordinates of the point P whose polar coordinates are $(5,220°)$.

5. True or false: The rectangular coordinates of the point $P(4,30°)$ are $x = 2\sqrt{3}$ and $y = 2$.

Graphing Simple Polar Equations

- When graphing in **polar coordinates**:
    - Setting r equal to a constant (as in the equation $r = k$) generates a circle around the origin.
    - Setting θ equal to a constant (as in the equation $\theta = k$) generates a line through the origin.
    - Setting r equal to θ (as in the equation $r = \theta$) generates a spiral.
- To graph a **polar equation** first convert it to **rectangular form**.

drawing a graph using rectangular coordinates 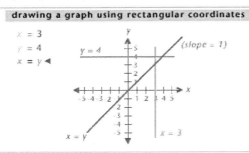	When graphing in **rectangular coordinates**, setting x or y equal to a constant (as in the equations $x = 3$ or $y = 4$) results in a vertical or horizontal line. Setting the two variables equal to each other generates a line that passes through the origin with a pitch of 45° (or a slope of 1).

drawing a graph using polar coordinates

graph the function $r = 16 \cos \theta$

❶ convert to rectangular coordinates

$r = 16 \cos \theta$

$r^2 = 16\,r \cos \theta$ multiply r to both sides

$x^2 + y^2 = 16x$ substitute

$x^2 - 16x + y^2 = 0$

$x^2 - 16x + 64 + y^2 = 0 + 64$ complete the square

$(x - 8)^2 + y^2 = 64$ factor

$(8,0)$ center of circle $\sqrt{64} = 8$ radius

❷ graph

center = $(8,0)$
radius = 8

center of circle
rectangular coordinates: $(8,0)$
polar coordinates: $(8,0)$

How would you go about graphing $r = 16 \cos \theta$?

One way is to first convert the equation to **rectangular coordinates**. Remember that $r \cos \theta = x$ and $r^2 = x^2 + y^2$.

Simplify the expression.

Complete the square for x and y. The result is the equation of a circle with center $(8,0)$ and radius 8.

Graph the center point, find the proper radius, and graph the circle.

Sample problems:

1. Convert $r = 36 \sin \theta$ to rectangular form.

    Solution: $x^2 + \left(y - 18\right)^2 = 324$

    Explanation: Multiply both sides of the equation by r : $r^2 = 36r \sin \theta$. Substitute $r^2 = x^2 + y^2$ and $y = r \sin \theta$: $x^2 + y^2 = 36y$. Set equal to zero and complete the square: $x^2 + y^2 - 36y = 0$; $x^2 + y^2 - 36y + 324 = 324$; $x^2 + \left(y - 18\right)^2 = 324$.

2. Sketch the polar coordinate graph of $r = 3$.
   Solution:

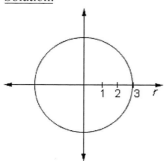

Explanation: Since r is a constant, the distance of the graph from the origin will not change. The angle θ is not restricted though, and can assume any values. Therefore, the equation graphs a circle with its center at the origin and a radius of 3 units.

Practice problems: *(Answers on page: 461)*

1. Convert $r = 4\cos\theta$ to rectangular form.

2. Sketch the polar coordinate graph of $\theta = \dfrac{\pi}{4}$.

Review questions: *(Answers to odd questions on page: 462)*

1. True or false: The graph of $r = 9\sin\theta$ is a circle with a center or $(3,0)$ and radius 3.

2. Convert $r = 10\sin\theta$ to rectangular form.

3. Convert $r = 12\sin\theta$ to rectangular form.

4. Convert $r = 25\sin\theta$ to rectangular form.

5. Sketch the polar coordinate graph of $r = \dfrac{1}{2}$.

6

Exponential and Logarithmic Functions

An Introduction to Exponential Functions

- **Exponential functions** are functions where the variable is in the exponent or power.

Exponential functions Recall: A polynomial has the basic shape: x^3 An exponential function has the basic shape: 3^x Compare by plugging in: $\quad x^3 \qquad\quad 3^x$ $(2)^3 = 8 \quad 3^{(2)} = 9$ $(3)^3 = 27 \quad 3^{(3)} = 27$ $(4)^3 = 64 \quad 3^{(4)} = 81$ $\qquad x^3 < 3^x$	By now you are pretty familiar with polynomials and polynomial functions. When dealing with polynomials, a variable like x is raised to some power. What if the variable is in the exponent? These functions are called exponential functions. The polynomial x^3 and the exponential function 3^x are very different, as this table demonstrates. In fact, it turns out that 3^x is larger than x^3 for almost all values of x.
Example Negative number exponents $3^{-2} = \dfrac{1}{3^2} = \boxed{\dfrac{1}{9}} \leftarrow$ Answer $\qquad\quad \llcorner$ Flipped	You can evaluate an exponential function like 3^x at negative values of x. Just remember the properties of exponents.
Example Fraction number exponents $3^{\frac{3}{2}} = (\sqrt{3})^3$ $\quad = \boxed{3\sqrt{3}} \leftarrow$ Answer	Fractional exponents like 3/2 are no problem either. Just convert the expression with a fractional exponent into an expression with a radical sign.
Example $2^{\sqrt{5}} = ?$ $\sqrt{5} = 2.2360\ldots$ and so on $2^{2.236} = 2^{\frac{2236}{1000}} = \left(\sqrt[1000]{2}\right)^{2236}$ Approximate Answer $\qquad\quad = \boxed{4.7105\ldots}$ and so on	What if the exponent is a number that cannot be written as a fraction, like $\sqrt{5}$? In this case, approximate the value of the radical using the decimal. In this example, $2^{\sqrt{5}}$ is approximately equal to $2^{2.236}$.
More exact answer: $\qquad\quad = 4.71111313332\ldots$ and so on	You can approximate the value of $2^{\sqrt{5}}$ more accurately by using more digits in the decimal form. As the approximation increases in accuracy, it approaches some number. The value of $2^{\sqrt{5}}$ is this number.
What are exponential functions good for? Answer: exponential functions are used in our real world to measure growth, interest rates, and items that have half lives.	Why study exponential functions? As it turns out, they show up everywhere!

Sample problems:

1. True or False: $3^{\frac{\sqrt{7}}{2}} \approx 4.29$.

   Solution: True

   Explanation: Use a calculator to find $\sqrt{7}$: $3^{\frac{2.65}{2}}$. Simplify exponents: $3^{1.325}$.

   Use the calculator to simplify: $3^{1.325} = 4.29$. Or, enter the entire problem into the graphing calculator using the following key sequences:

   ⊡3 ⊡∧ ⊡((⊡√(⊡7 ⊡)) ⊡/ ⊡2 ⊡)) ⊡Enter, which gives 4.278.

2. Which one of the following is <u>not</u> an exponential function? $a(x) = 7^{2x+3}$, $b(x) = \dfrac{5^{x-1}}{2}$, $c(x) = 1^{5x}$.

Solution: $c(x)$

Explanation: There are three requirements for exponential functions: 1) the base must be a positive real number; 2) the base cannot equal 1; 3) exponents must include a variable. Therefore, $c(x) = 1^{5x}$ is not an exponential function since the base is 1.

3. Given the functions $f(x) = x^4$ and $g(x) = 4^x$, which function increases faster as x increases?

Solution: $g(x) = 4^x$

Explanation: Substitute several increasing x values into the function, for example 2, 3, and 4: $f(2) = 16$, $f(3) = 81$, $f(4) = 256$ and $g(2) = 16$, $g(3) = 64$, $g(4) = 256$. So, it appears that they increase in a similar way. However, try a few more increasing x values: $f(5) = 625$, $f(6) = 1296$, $f(7) = 2401$ and $g(5) = 1024$, $g(6) = 4096$, $g(7) = 16,384$. Now, it is apparent that $g(x)$ increases faster than $f(x)$ as x increases.

Practice problems: *(Answers on page: 462)*

1. True or False: $7^{-\sqrt{2}} = 0.064$.

2. Which one of the following is <u>not</u> an exponential function? $a(x) = -(6)^x$, $b(x) = 3^{\pi x}$, $c(x) = 4x^{\sqrt{3}}$.

3. Given the functions $f(x) = \left(\dfrac{1}{x}\right)^5$ and $g(x) = 5^{\frac{1}{x}}$, which function decreases faster as x increases?

Review questions: *(Answers to odd questions on page: 462)*

1. Simplify: $5^{-\sqrt{3}}$

2. Simplify: $7^{\frac{\pi}{\sqrt{5}}}$

3. True or false: $f(x) = 1^x$ is an exponential function.

4. Which of the following is not an exponential function? $f(x) = 3^{\pi x}$, $g(x) = -(6)^x$, $h(x) = (-6)^x$

5. Given the functions $f(x) = x^{\frac{1}{3}}$ and $g(x) = \dfrac{1}{3}^x$, which function decreases as x increases?

Graphing Exponential Functions: Useful Patterns

- Exponential functions are functions where the variable is in the exponent.
- The graphs of exponential functions like $y = a^x$ where $a > 1$ all have the same basic shape. The graph grows rapidly for positive x and shrinks gradually to zero for negative x. The x-axis is a horizontal asymptote.
- The larger the base of an exponential function, the more rapidly it grows for positive values of x and the more rapidly it decreases for negative values of x.

Example

$f(x) = 2^x$

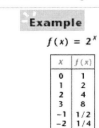
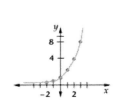

Let's graph an exponential function to get an idea of what they look like.

As you can see from the graph of $f(x) = 2^x$, exponential functions grow quickly for positive values of x and gradually approach zero for negative values of x.

The x-axis is a horizontal asymptote for all exponential functions.

Notice that exponential functions are never zero or negative; they are always positive.

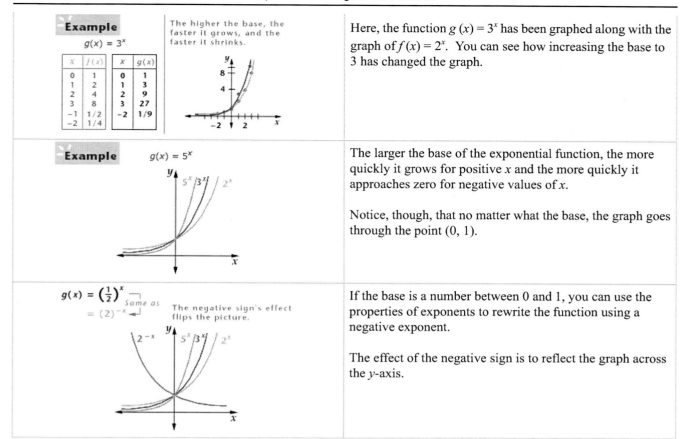

Example $g(x) = 3^x$

The higher the base, the faster it grows, and the faster it shrinks.

x	$f(x)$		x	$g(x)$
0	1		0	1
1	2		1	3
2	4		2	9
3	8		3	27
-1	1/2		-2	1/9
-2	1/4			

Here, the function $g(x) = 3^x$ has been graphed along with the graph of $f(x) = 2^x$. You can see how increasing the base to 3 has changed the graph.

Example $g(x) = 5^x$

The larger the base of the exponential function, the more quickly it grows for positive x and the more quickly it approaches zero for negative values of x.

Notice, though, that no matter what the base, the graph goes through the point (0, 1).

$g(x) = \left(\frac{1}{2}\right)^x$ Same as $= (2)^{-x}$

The negative sign's effect flips the picture.

If the base is a number between 0 and 1, you can use the properties of exponents to rewrite the function using a negative exponent.

The effect of the negative sign is to reflect the graph across the y-axis.

Sample problems:

1. True or false: The function $u(x) = \left(\frac{1}{2}\right)^x$ increases as x increases.

   <u>Solution</u>: False

   <u>Explanation</u>: It appears that $u(x)$ increases as x increase since the exponent is a positive x.

   However, $u(x) = \left(\frac{1}{2}\right)^x$ is not in standard form since a is not greater than 1.

   Express the function in standard form, $y = a^x$, where $a > 0$ by rewriting the base to the -1 power:

   $u(x) = \left(\frac{1}{2}\right)^x = (2^{-1})^x = 2^{-x}$. For all exponential functions in standard form, $y = a^x$, where $a > 1$, if the exponent is a negative x, then the function decreases as x increases.

   So, $u(x)$ does not increase as x increases.

2. Given the functions $f(x) = \left(\frac{4}{5}\right)^x$ and $g(x) = \left(\frac{5}{4}\right)^x$, which function increases as x increases?

   <u>Solution</u>: $g(x)$

   <u>Explanation</u>: $g(x)$ is already in standard form, $y = a^x$, where $a > 1$. So, since the exponent is a positive x, $g(x)$ increases as x increases. It appears that $f(x)$ also increases, but express it in standard form: $f(x) = (\frac{4}{5})^x = \left((\frac{5}{4})^{-1}\right)^x = \frac{5}{4}^{-x}$.

   In standard form the exponent is a negative, so $f(x)$ decreases as x increases.

3. Given the functions $c(x) = \left(\frac{1}{3}\right)^x$ or $d(x) = \left(\frac{1}{3}\right)^{-x}$, which function decreases as x increases?

   Solution: $c(x)$

   Explanation: Express both functions in standard form, $y = a^x$, where $a > 1$: $c(x) = (\frac{1}{3})^x = (3^{-1})^x = 3^{-x}$ and $d(x) = (\frac{1}{3})^x = (3^{-1})^{-x} = 3^x$. Therefore, since the exponent is a negative x in $c(x)$, the function decreases as x increases.

Practice problems: *(Answers on page: 462)*

1. Given the functions $h(x) = 5^{-x}$ or $k(x) = \left(\frac{1}{5}\right)^x$, which function increases as x increases?

2. To the right of the y-axis, which graph rises faster, $m(x) = 5^x$ or $h(x) = 8^x$?

3. For which x-values is the graph of $y = 4^x$ above the x-axis?

Review questions: *(Answers to odd questions on page: 462)*

1. To the right of the y-axis, which graph rises faster, $m(x) = 5^x$ or $h(x) = 6^x$?

2. To the right of the y-axis, which graph rises faster, $f(x) = 5x$ or $g(x) = 2x$?

3. Which of the following functions rises to the right of the y-axis: $f(x) = 4^x$ or $g(x) = \left(\frac{1}{4}\right)^x$?

4. Which of the following functions rises to the left of the y-axis: $f(x) = \left(\frac{8}{1}\right)^x$ or $g(x) = \left(\frac{1}{8}\right)^x$?

5. Given the functions $f(x) = \left(\frac{2}{3}\right)^x$ and $g(x) = \left(\frac{3}{2}\right)^x$, which function increases as x increases?

Graphing Exponential Functions: More Examples

- Exponential functions are functions where the variable is in the exponent.
- You can graph many exponential functions by translating or reflecting the graphs of basic exponential functions like $f(x) = a^x$.
- The base of an exponential function can never be negative.

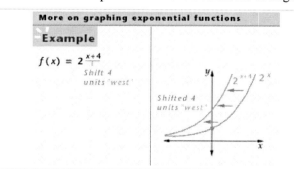	To graph this exponential function, first graph the simpler function $y = 2^x$ and then shift the graph 4 units to the left. **REMEMBER:** "Add to x, go west."
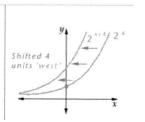	Another way you could graph $f(x)$ is to use the properties of exponents. In this example, rewrite the function as a constant times the function 2^x. The constant stretches the graph of $y = 2^x$ out in the vertical direction.

Example

$g(x) = 2^x + 4$

Now, take that same example and move the constant out of the exponent.

You can graph this function by shifting the graph of the function $y = 2^x$ upwards by 4 units.

NOTICE: The graphs of the functions $f(x) = 2^{x+4}$ and $g(x) = 2^x + 4$ are not the same!

Example

$f(x) = (-3)^x$ ⟵ Will Never graph!!

$= (-3)^2 = 9$

$= (-3)^{\frac{1}{2}} = \sqrt{-3}$

Not a real number

What happens if the base of an exponential function is a negative number?

If the base is a negative number, then the exponential function will be undefined for many values of x. So, exponential functions are not allowed to have negative bases.

$f(x) = (-3)^x \neq 3^{-x}$

Sorry, Two different things!!

Don't confuse these two expressions! They are not the same.

Sample problems:

1. What change is made to the graph of $f(x) = 7^x$ when the function $g(x) = 7^{x+10}$ is graphed?
   Solution: the graph shifted to the left 10 units
   Explanation: In $g(x)$ the exponent is $x + 10$. Since this function has 10 added to x, the graph of $f(x)$ should be shifted to the left 10 units to form the graph of $g(x)$.

2. True or false: the graph of $a(x) = 5^{x+2}$ is the same as the graph of $n(x) = 25 \cdot 5^x$.
   Solution: True
   Explanation: Use the rules of exponents to split up the exponent in $a(x)$:
   $a(x) = 5^{x+2} = 5^x(5^2) = 25 \cdot 5^x$. The graphs are the same since $a(x) = n(x)$.

3. What is the resulting function if the graph of $y = 2^x$ is shifted up 5 units?
   Solution: $y = 2^x + 5$
   Explanation: To shift a graph vertically add or subtract to the entire equation, so to shift the graph up 5 units, add 5 to 2^x: $y = 2^x + 5$.

Practice problems: *(Answers on page: 462)*

1. True or false: the graph of $w(x) = 3^{x+2}$ is the same as the graph of $v(x) = 9 \cdot 3^x$.

2. What change do you have to make to the graph of $v(x) = 2.5^x$ in order to graph the function $w(x) = 2.5^{x+1} + 3$?

3. What is the resulting function if the graph of $y = 4^x$ is shifted up 2 units?

Review questions: *(Answers to odd questions on page: 462)*

1. Which of the following functions will have the same graph as $w(x) = 3^{x+2}$?
   a) $a(x) = 9^x$ b) $b(x) = 9 \cdot 3^x$ c) $c(x) = 3^x + 2$ d) $d(x) = 3x + 2$

2. True or false: the graph of $g(x) = 9^{x+2}$ is the same as the graph of $h(x) = 18 \cdot 9^x$

3. What change is made to the graph of $f(x) = 6^x$ when the function $g(x) = 6^{x+8}$ is graphed?

4. What is the resulting function if the graph of $y = 10^x$ is shifted 1 unit up and 2 units left?

5. What is the resulting function if the graph of $y = 2^x$ is shifted 6 units down and 1 unit right?

Using Properties of Exponents to Solve Exponential Equations

- Exponential equations are equations where the variable is in the exponent.
- You can solve many exponential equations by writing everything in terms of a common base.

Where the unknown is in exponents **Example** $2^x = 4$ $2^x = 4 = 2^2$ *Now the bases are the same* $x = \boxed{2}$ ← *Answer*	One method you can use to solve exponential equations is to express both sides of the equality in terms of the same base. Take a look at this example problem. You can write the right-hand side of the equation using base 2. When the bases are the same, the exponents must also be the same. Use this fact to solve for x.
Example $8^x = 2$ $8^x = (2^3)^x = 2^{3x}$ $2^{3x} = 2^1$ $3x = 1$ *To check answer, plug into x* $x = \boxed{\frac{1}{3}}$ ← *Answer* ✔	In this example, you can use the laws of exponents to write the left-hand side of the equation using base 2. After writing both sides of the equality using the common base, set the exponents equal to each other and solve for x. **REMEMBER:** You can always check your answer by plugging back into the original equation.
Example $8^x = 4$ $2^{3x} = 2^2$ $x = \boxed{\frac{2}{3}}$ ← *Answer*	You need to change the bases of both the left-hand and right-hand side of the equality in this example. After the bases are the same, set the exponents equal to each other and solve for x.
Example $\left(\frac{1}{3}\right)^x = 27$ $3^{-x} = 3^3$ $x = \boxed{-3}$ ← *Answer*	Follow the same procedure to solve this problem. Remember that exponents can be negative as well as positive.
Example $x^{\frac{1}{3}} = 27$ $\left(x^{\frac{1}{3}}\right)^3 = (27)^3$ $x = \boxed{19,683}$ ← *Answer*	What about this problem? It looks very similar to the last one. Be careful! The variable is in the base, not the exponent. To solve this equation for x, just raise both sides of the equation to the third power.

Sample problems:

1. Solve for x: $4^{2x+1} = 64$.

    Solution: $x = 1$

    Explanation: Express each side with a common base: $4^{2x+1} = 4^3$. Set the exponents equal to each other and solve for x: $2x + 1 = 3$; $2x = 2$; $x = 1$.

2. Solve for x: $\left(\frac{3}{5}\right)^{x+7} = \frac{9}{25}$.

Solution: $x = -5$

Explanation: Express each side with a common base. $\left(\frac{3}{5}\right)^{x+7} = \left(\frac{3}{5}\right)^2$. Set the exponents equal to each other and solve for x: $x + 7 = 2$; $x = -5$.

3. Solve for x: $27^{x+2} = 81^{1-x}$.

Solution: $x = -\frac{2}{7}$

Explanation: Express each side with a common base: $3^{3(x+2)} = 3^{4(1-x)}$. Set the exponents equal to each other and solve for x: $3(x + 2) = 4(1 - x)$; $3x + 6 = 4 - 4x$; $7x = -2$; $x = -\frac{2}{7}$.

Practice problems: *(Answers on page: 462)*

1. Solve for x: $10^{7x+1} = 10,000$

2. Solve for x: $5^{x-6} = 25$

3. Solve for x: $c^{9x+2} = c^{3-x}$

Review questions: *(Answers to odd questions on page: 462)*

1. Solve for h: $h^{\frac{4}{3}} = 16$.

2. Solve for r: $\frac{4}{9} = r^{\frac{2}{5}}$.

3. Solve $\left(\frac{100}{9}\right)^x = \left(\frac{1000}{27}\right)^{x+2}$.

4. Solve $8^{2x+6} = 16^{7-x}$.

5. Solve $100^{x-4} = 0.01^{2x}$.

Finding Present Value and Future Value

- The value of an investment over time is described by an exponential equation.
- The **compound interest formula**: $A = P\left[1 + \frac{r}{m}\right]^{mt}$.

- You can use the compound interest formula to find the present and future values of investments.

Present & future values	
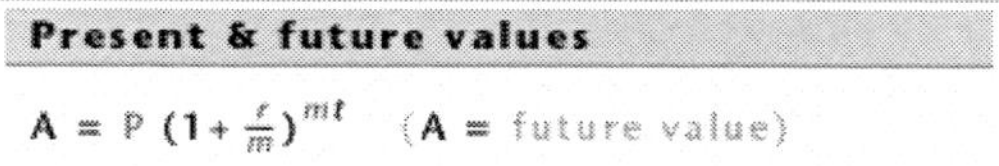 $A = P\left(1 + \frac{r}{m}\right)^{mt}$ (A = future value)	You can use this formula to solve for the present and future values of investments. A is the future value of the investment. P is the present, or initial, value of the investment. r is the rate of interest. m is the number of interest payments, or compoundings, per year. t is the number of years the money is invested.

Example

Suppose you put $9,000 into a 5% bearing interest account that compounded semi-annually (2 times per year). How much money would be in the account at the end of 9 years?

$$A = 9,000 \left(1 + \frac{.05}{2}\right)^{18}$$

$$A = \boxed{14,036.93}$$

Here is a typical problem. You are asked how much money the account will have after nine years.

To find out, plug the information you are given into the formula:

$P = 9,000$ $\quad$ $r = .05$

$m = 2$ $\quad$ $t = 9$

Evaluate the exponential expression and the result is your answer.

NOTICE: The rate is 5%, so $r = .05$, not 5!

Suppose: The account compounded quarterly.

$$A = 9,000 \left(1 + \frac{.05}{4}\right)^{36}$$

$$A = \boxed{14,075.49} \leftarrow \text{Answer}$$

A noticeable difference

What happens if the same account is compounded quarterly instead of semiannually?

Everything in the formula stays the same except for m, the number of interest payments per year; m is now equal to 4.

Notice the difference in the future values of these two very similar investments!

Example

Suppose that in 10 years you want to have $25,000 in a 6% bearing interest account that compounds monthly. How much should you initially put into the account?

$$25,000 = P\left(1 + \frac{.06}{12}\right)^{120}$$

$$P = 25,000 \left(1 + \frac{.06}{12}\right)^{-120}$$

$$= \boxed{13,740.82} \leftarrow \text{Answer}$$

This problem asks you to find the initial value of an investment given that the future value is $25,000.

Plug everything you know into the formula and solve for P. The result is the initial value of the investment.

Sample problems:

1. Suppose you charged an entertainment system for $449 and paid it off at the end of three years with 16.5% accumulated interest. How much did you pay if the interest was compounded monthly?

   Solution: $734.10

   Explanation: Substitute $P = 449$, $r = 0.165$, $m = 12$, and $t = 3$ into the formula

   $A = P\left(1 + \dfrac{r}{m}\right)^{mt}$ and simplify: $A = 449\left(1 + \dfrac{0.165}{12}\right)^{12 \cdot 3}$; $\quad A = 449\left(1 + \dfrac{0.165}{12}\right)^{36}$;

   $A = 449\left(1 + 0.01375\right)^{36}$; $\quad A = 449\left(1.01375\right)^{36}$; $\quad A = 449\left(1.634975\right)$;

   $A = 734.10$. The amount paid is $734.10.

2. A teacher in London wants to end up with $64,000 at retirement, 23 years away, by making a one-time contribution to a 7.2% trust fund today. Use the compound interest formula to determine the amount of his one-time contribution if the fund compounds interest annually.

   Solution: $12,933.02

   Explanation: Identify the values of the known variables: $A = 64,000$, $r = .072$, $m = 1$,

   and $t = 23$. Substitute these values into the compound interest formula, $A = P\left(1 + \dfrac{r}{m}\right)^{mt}$:

   $64,000 = P\left(1 + \dfrac{.072}{1}\right)^{1 \cdot 23}$. Simplify and solve for P: $64,000 = P(1 + .072)^{23}$;

   $P = \dfrac{64,000}{(1 + .072)^{23}} = \dfrac{64,000}{4.94857393} = 12933.02$. So, he must contribute $12,933.02.

---

3. A couple wish to move to Palm Springs 14 years from now. They'll need $1,000,000 at that time. How much must they invest now, at 6.4% compounded monthly, to reach their goal?

Solution: $411,454.91

Explanation: Substitute the values from the problem into the compound interest

formula: $1,000,000 = P\left(1 + \dfrac{.064}{12}\right)^{12(14)}$.

Simplify and solve for P: $1,000,000 = P(1.0053)^{168}$; $1,000,000 = 2.4304P$; $P = 411,454.91$.
So, they must invest $411,454.91.

Practice problems: *(Answers on page: 462)*

1. A fisherman borrows 213,480 yen over 75 months at 17% compounded monthly. How much will he have to pay back?

2. You charge a $769.41 washer at 3.95% over $10\dfrac{1}{2}$ years. How much will that washer really cost if interest is compounded twice a year?

3. A 5% car loan runs for 57 months, with daily compounding of interest. Find the amount the car cost originally if the amount paid back was $20,651.66.

Review questions: *(Answers to odd questions on page: 462)*

1. Fifteen years from now Juanita Bushlueter wants to buy the farm she and her husband are now leasing. She figures they will need $485,000 to make this purchase. How much should they invest now, at 5.5% compounded daily, to reach their goal?

2. How much money should a mother now place in a 9% college trust fund (compounded twice a year), for her daughter, if she wants it to grow to $40,000 12 years from now?

3. Mr. McGoo wants to accumulate $7,500 for his LASIK eye surgery 8 years from now, by making a one-time contribution to a 6% trust fund today. What is McGoo's contribution if interest is compounded monthly?

4. A worker wants to end up with $150,000 at retirement, 20 years away, by making a one-time contribution to a 6% charitable gift annuity today. What is that one-time contribution if the charity compounds interest quarterly?

5. It is Jan 1 of a leap year (like 2008). Charles Keating invests $92,707.64 at 7.99% compounded daily. How much will he have in exactly one year?

Finding an Interest Rate to Match Given Goals

- The value of an investment over time is described by an exponential equation.
-
  The compound interest formula: $A = P\left[1 + \dfrac{r}{m}\right]^{mt}$.

- You can use the compound interest formula to solve for interest rates given goals for the future value of an investment.

Formula for finding interest rate: $A = P\left(1 + \frac{r}{m}\right)^{tm}$	This formula is designed to find the present and future values of investments. It can also be used to find interest rates.

Example

You want to invest $100,000 for 6 months into an account that compounds monthly, and at the end you want to have $102,000. What does the account's interest rate need to be?

$$102,000 = 100,000 \left(1 + \frac{r}{12}\right)^6$$

This example problem asks you to find the interest rate necessary for your $100,000 investment to reach a value of $102,000 after six months.

To solve this problem, substitute into the formula:
   You start with $100,000, so **P** = 100,000.
   You want to end with $102,000, so **A** = 102,000.
   The length of time for the investment is six months, or half a year, so **t** = 0.5.
   The account compounds monthly, or twelve times a year, so **m** = 12.

$$\frac{102}{100} = \left(1 + \frac{r}{12}\right)^6$$

$$\sqrt[6]{\frac{102}{100}} = 1 + \frac{r}{12}$$

$$\frac{r}{12} = \sqrt[6]{\frac{102}{100}} - 1$$

$$r = 12 \left(\sqrt[6]{\frac{102}{100}} - 1\right)$$

$$r = .03967$$

Now solve for **r**.

Evaluate this expression to find the value of **r**.

$$r = \boxed{3.967\%} \leftarrow Answer$$

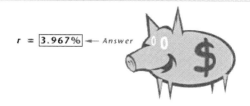

And your rate as a percentage moves the decimal two places, 3.967%.

Sample problems:

1. Suppose you want to invest $75,000 into an account that compounds semi-annually, and at the end of 63 months you want to have $100,000. What does the account's interest rate need to be?
   Solution: 5.6%
   Explanation: Substitute values from the problem into the compound interest formula:
   $100,000 = 75,000\left(1 + \frac{r}{2}\right)^{2(5.25)}$, (63 months = $\frac{63}{12}$ years = 5.25 years). Simplify
   and solve for r : $1.333 = \left(1 + \frac{r}{2}\right)^{10.5}$; $\sqrt[10.5]{1.333} = 1 + \frac{r}{2}$; $1.028 = 1 + \frac{r}{2}$;
   $\frac{r}{2} = .028$; $r = .056$. So the interest rate needs to be 5.6%

2. Suppose $220.80 is compounded annually for 3 years. At what rate would it need to be invested to yield $330? Express your answer to the nearest hundredth of a percent.
   Solution: 14.33%
   Explanation: Substitute the given values into $A = P\left(1 + \frac{r}{m}\right)^{mt}$: $330 = 220.80(1 + r)^3$;
   $(1 + r)^3 = \frac{330}{220.80}$; $1 + r = \left(\frac{330}{220.80}\right)^{\frac{1}{3}}$; $r = \left(\frac{330}{220.80}\right)^{\frac{1}{3}} - 1$; $r = 0.1433$. Thus, the answer is 14.33%.

3. Suppose you want to invest $5,000 into an account that compounds quarterly, and at the end of $2\frac{1}{2}$ years you want to have $6,000. What does the account's interest rate need to be?
   Solution: 7.36%
   Explanation: Substitute $A = 6,000$, $P = 5,000$, $m = 4$, and $t = 2.5$ into the compound interest formula:
   $A = P\left(1 + \frac{r}{m}\right)^{mt}$; $6,000 = 5,000\left(1 + \frac{r}{4}\right)^{4(2.5)}$. Simplify and solve for r : $6,000 = 5,000\left(1 + \frac{r}{4}\right)^{10}$;
   $\frac{6,000}{5,000} = \left(1 + \frac{r}{4}\right)^{10}$; $1.2 = \left(1 + \frac{r}{4}\right)^{10}$; $\sqrt[10]{1.2} = 1 + \frac{r}{4}$; $1.0184 = 1 + \frac{r}{4}$; $\frac{r}{4} = .0184$; $r = .0736$. So the account's interest rate needs to be 7.36%.

Practice problems: *(Answers on page: 462)*

1. Suppose $100 is compounded twice a year for 12 years. At what rate would it need to be invested to achieve a balance of $236.13? Express your answer to the nearest hundredth of a percent.

2. Suppose $4386 is compounded annually for 4 years. At what rate would it need to be invested to yield $9652.90? Express your answer to the nearest tenth of a percent.

3. Suppose $80,000 is compounded monthly for 42 months. At what rate would it need to be invested to achieve a balance of $90,000. Express your answer to the nearest hundredth of a percent.

Review questions: *(Answers to odd questions on page: 462)*

1. $2 million is compounded quarterly for 22 years at what rate to yield $ 5 million?
   Express your answer to the nearest hundredth of a percent.

2. $1750 is compounded daily for 2 years at what rate to rise to $ 1891.96?
   Express your answer to the nearest tenth of a percent.

3. $721.88 is compounded quarterly for 8 years at what rate to reach $2455.63?
   Express your answer to the nearest tenth of a percent.

4. $2507 is compounded quarterly for 5 years at what rate to yield $3725.28?

5. $650 is compounded monthly for 9 years at what rate to rise to $1084.38?
   Express your answer to the nearest tenth of a percent.

e

- The **number** e is approximately equal to 2.71828.
- The number e is very important for measuring population growth and decay, among many other things.

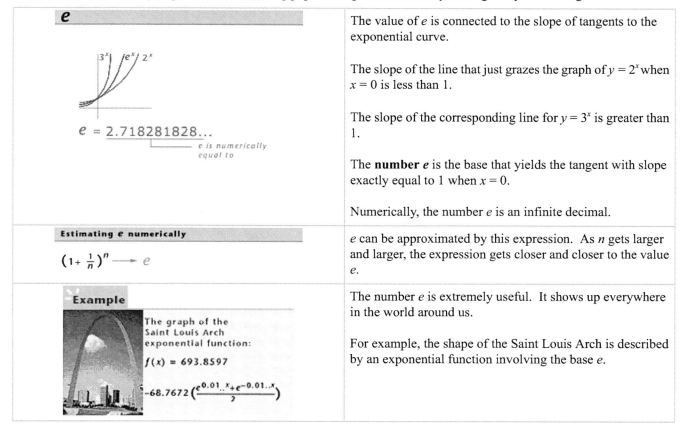

e $e = 2.718281828\ldots$ *e is numerically equal to*	The value of e is connected to the slope of tangents to the exponential curve. The slope of the line that just grazes the graph of $y = 2^x$ when $x = 0$ is less than 1. The slope of the corresponding line for $y = 3^x$ is greater than 1. The **number** e is the base that yields the tangent with slope exactly equal to 1 when $x = 0$. Numerically, the number e is an infinite decimal.
Estimating e numerically $\left(1 + \frac{1}{n}\right)^n \longrightarrow e$	e can be approximated by this expression. As n gets larger and larger, the expression gets closer and closer to the value e.
Example The graph of the Saint Louis Arch exponential function: $f(x) = 693.8597$ $-68.7672\left(\dfrac{e^{0.01\ldots x} + e^{-0.01\ldots x}}{2}\right)$	The number e is extremely useful. It shows up everywhere in the world around us. For example, the shape of the Saint Louis Arch is described by an exponential function involving the base e.

Example

The more population you have, the greater the rate of population growth.

This also indirectly involves the notion of e.

Boing!

The number e is also used to predict population growth or, working backwards, to calculate probable populations during specific historical eras.

The rate of population growth is proportional to population; that is, the more people there are, the faster the population will grow.

As it turns out, population growth (and decay) is described by exponential functions and the number e.

Applying Exponential Functions

- The number e is approximately equal to 2.71828.
- The number e is very important for measuring population growth and decay.
- The population of the world can be modeled using an exponential function with base e.

$e = 2.71828169\ldots$ e is numerically equal to	Exponential functions and the number e are very important in mathematically describing population growth.
Applying exponential functions **Example** $P(t) = 2600e^{.018t}$ t = Years after 1950	Here, $P(t)$ describes the world's population as a function of time, where t is the number of years after 1950.
Applying exponential functions with e will give highly accurate models of population growth for future planning. **Applying exponential functions** **Example** $P(t) = 2600e^{.018t}$ $P(20) = 2600e^{(.018)(20)}$ ← in 1970 $\quad = 3726.65$ $\quad \approx \boxed{3700 \text{ million}}$ ← Real Answer	You can use the formula from above to calculate the number of people in the world in 1970. Since 1970 is twenty years after 1950, just plug in $t = 20$. Using the formula results in an answer very close to the actual population of the world in 1970. The exponential model does a good job!
$P(t) = 2600e^{.018t}$ $P(40) = 2600e^{(.018)(40)}$ ← in 1990 $\quad = 5341.5$ $\quad \approx \boxed{5320 \text{ million}}$ ← Real Answer	You can also calculate the model's prediction for the world's population for any other year after 1950. For 1990, just plug in $t = 40$ (because 1990 is forty years after 1950). The model does a good job here too.

Sample problems:

1. The number of milligrams of a certain drug that remain in a person's bloodstream after h hours is given by the exponential function $D = 5e^{-0.4h}$. Find the number of milligrams present after 5 hours.

   Solution: 0.68 milligrams

   Explanation: Substitute $h = 5$ into the function and simplify: $D = 5e^{-0.4h} = 5e^{-0.4(5)} = 5e^{-2} = 0.68$.

2. The number of milligrams of a certain drug that remain in a person's bloodstream after h hours is given by the exponential function $D = 5e^{-0.4h}$. Find the number of milligrams present after 2 hours and 30 minutes.
   Solution: 1.84 milligrams
   Explanation: Substitute $h = 2.5$ into the function and simplify: $D = 5e^{-0.4h} = 5e^{-0.4(2.5)} = 5e^{-1} = 1.84$.

3. In a population of size P, the number of people who have heard a rumor d days since the rumor began is given by the function $N = P\left(1 - e^{-0.15d}\right)$. In a population of 350 people, how many will have heard the rumor after 2 days?
   Solution: 91 people
   Explanation: Substitute $P = 350$ and $d = 2$ into the function and simplify:
   $N = P\left(1 - e^{-0.15d}\right) = 350\left(1 - e^{-0.15(2)}\right) = 350\left(1 - e^{-0.3}\right) = 90.7$.
   So, after 2 days 91 people will have heard the rumor.

Practice problems: *(Answers on page: 462)*

1. In a population of size P, the number of people who have heard a rumor d days since the rumor began is given by the function $N = P\left(1 - e^{-0.15d}\right)$. In a population of 700 people, how many will have heard the rumor after 3 days?

2. The probability that a customer will arrive t minutes before closing time at a certain store is given by the function $F(t) = 1 - e^{-0.006t}$. Find the probability that a customer will arrive 15 minutes before closing.

3. The probability that a customer will arrive t minutes before closing time at a certain store is given by the function $F(t) = 1 - e^{-0.006t}$. Find the probability that a customer will arrive 20 minutes before closing.

Review questions: *(Answers to odd questions on page: 462)*

1. The number of debit card transactions expected in a certain year in the U.S. can be approximated by the function $y = 0.08e^{0.42x}$, where $x = 0$ corresponds to 1990 and y is in billions. Find the number of debit card transactions in 1996.

2. The number of debit card transactions expected in a certain year in the U.S. can be approximated by the function $y = 0.08e^{0.42x}$, where $x = 0$ corresponds to 1990 and y is in billions. Predict the number of debit card transactions in 2010.

3. The percentage of U.S. households whose members are related by marriage, birth, or adoption is given by the function $p = 89.7e^{-0.0058t}$, where t is the number of years since 1950. What was the percentage of U.S. households whose members were related by marriage, birth, or adoption in 1965?

4. The percentage of U.S. households whose members are related by marriage, birth, or adoption is given by the function $p = 89.7e^{-0.0058t}$, where t is the number of years since 1950. Predict the percentage of U.S. households whose members will be related by marriage, birth, or adoption in 2009.

5. The percentage of U.S. households whose members are related by marriage, birth, or adoption is given by the function $p = 89.7e^{-0.0058t}$, where t is the number of years since 1950. Predict the percentage of U.S. households whose members will be related by marriage, birth, or adoption in 2020.

An Introduction to Logarithmic Functions

- **Logarithms** and exponential functions are inverses of each other. You can use logs to "untangle" expressions involving exponential functions.
- A log is an exponent: the statement $y = \log_b x$ is equivalent to the statement $b^y = x$.

log = exponent	Logs are nothing to be afraid of. Remember the chant: "A log is an exponent."
Example $\log_2 8 = ?$ $\iff$ $2^? = 8$ *log is the exponent that 2 is raised to equal 8.* $? = 3$ $2^{③} = 8$ $\log_2 8 = ③$	What is the value of $\log_2 8$? "A log is an exponent." $\log_2 8$ is the exponent that 2 is raised to in order to get 8. Since 2 raised to the third power is equal to 8, $\log_2 8 = 3$. The log is the exponent, or in this case, 3.
$y = \log_b x$ $\iff$ $b^y = x$	In general, if $y = \log_b x$, then y is equal to the exponent that b is raised to in order to get x. In other words, $b^y = x$.
Example $\log_2 \frac{1}{4} = ?$ $2^? = \frac{1}{4}$ $? = -2$ ✓**work** $2^{-2} = \frac{1}{2^2} = \frac{1}{4}$	How can you evaluate the expression $\log_2 \frac{1}{4}$? "A log is an exponent." $\log_2 \frac{1}{4}$ is equal to the exponent that 2 is raised to in order to get $\frac{1}{4}$. $2^{-2} = \frac{1}{4}$ Therefore, $\log_2 \frac{1}{4} = -2$. **Check your answer:** Raise the base to your log value. If it is correct, you will derive your x-value, in this case $\frac{1}{4}$.
Example $\log_2 (-3) = ?$ *Never take logs* $2^?$ *of Negatives !* *What does ? equal*	Can you evaluate the expression $\log_2(-3)$? 2 raised to any power will always be positive. Thus, the log expression $\log_2(-3)$ is meaningless. **REMEMBER:** Never take the log of a negative number!

Sample problems:

1. True or False: If $w = \log_b z$ then $b^z = w$.
   Solution: False
   Explanation: The statement "If $w = \log_b z$" means: assume that $w = \log_b z$ is true. So, apply the rule of logarithms which states that when $y = \log_b x$, $b^y = x$ must also be true, and vice versa. Thus, if $w = \log_b z$ then $b^w = z$, not $b^z = w$.

2. Evaluate: $\log_3 81$.
   Solution: 4
   Explanation: To evaluate $\log_3 81$, find the exponent that applies to 3 to get 81: $3^x = 81$. To solve this exponential function express each side with a common base: $3^x = 3^4$. So, $x = 4$.

3. Evaluate: $\log_2 \dfrac{1}{8}$.

   Solution: -3

   Explanation: Apply the rule of logarithms: $\log_2 \dfrac{1}{8} = x \Rightarrow 2^x = \frac{1}{8}$. Rewrite the fraction with a negative exponent: $2^x = 8^{-1}$. Express each side with a common base: $2^x = 2^{-3}$. So $x = -3$.

Practice problems: *(Answers on page: 462)*

1. Evaluate: $\log_4 \dfrac{1}{4}$.

2. True or False: If $\log_b c = a$, then $b^a = c$.

3. Evaluate: $\log_5 \dfrac{1}{125}$.

Review questions: *(Answers to odd questions on page: 463)*

1. Evaluate: $\log_6 36$

2. Evaluate: $\log_2 32$

3. Evaluate: $\log_3 \dfrac{1}{27}$

4. Evaluate: $\log_2 \dfrac{1}{16}$

5. Evaluate: $\log_8 4$

Converting between Exponential and Logarithmic Functions

- When converting from logarithmic form to exponential form, remember that "a log is an exponent." This means that the number the log is equal to becomes the exponent in the new form. The base of the log is the base of the exponent too.

A log is an exponent $y = \log_b x \iff b^y = x$	An easy way to remember how logarithms and exponents convert is to remember the statement "a log is an exponent." Whatever is on the other side of the equal sign in the logarithmic form becomes the exponent of the base in the exponential form.
Example *Rewrite as a log statement* $2^5 = 32$ $5 = \log_2 32$ 5 *(log)* is what 2 *(base)* needs to be raised to equal 32	Let's look at this idea in action. Since a log is an exponent, the exponent of this expression will become the log's answer. The bases stay the same. The exponent moves to the other side of the equal sign. The other number fills in the hole.
Example *Rewrite as a log statement* $\left(\frac{2}{3}\right)^{-2} = \frac{9}{4}$ $-2 = \log_{\frac{2}{3}} \frac{9}{4}$ -2 log, base $\frac{2}{3}$ of $\frac{9}{4}$	Now let's try a harder example. Since a log is an exponent, the exponent of this expression will become the log value alone on one side of the equal sign. The base doesn't change from one form to the other. The value of the base raised to the exponent fills its hole.

Example *Rewrite as an exponential statement*	This time we will work the other way.
$\log_6 6 = 1 \iff 6^1 = 6$	A log is an exponent. So the exponent is 1. The base is 6.
	The other number fills in its hole.
Example *Rewrite as an exponential statement*	Let's look at one last example.
$\log_{\sqrt{3}} 9 = 4 \iff (\sqrt{3})^4 = 9$	A log is an exponent. So the exponent is 4.
$\quad\quad\quad\quad = ((\sqrt{3})^2)^2$	The base is $\sqrt{3}$.
$\quad\quad\quad\quad = 3^2 = 9$	The final number fills in its hole.
	Simplifying the expression leaves you with 3^2, which is equal to 9.

Sample problems:

1. Express $3^4 = 81$ in logarithmic form.
   Solution: $\log_3 81 = 4$
   Explanation: Apply the law of logarithms: $b^y = x \Rightarrow \log_b x = y$. So, $3^4 = 81 \Rightarrow \log_3 81 = 4$

2. Convert $\log_p q = r$ into an exponential equation.
   Solution: $p^r = q$
   Explanation: Apply the law of logarithms: $\log_b x = y \Rightarrow b^y = x$. So, $\log_p q = r \Rightarrow p^r = q$.

3. Express $\log_4 1024 = 5$ in an exponential form.
   Solution: $4^5 = 1024$
   Explanation: Apply the law of logarithms: $\log_b x = y \Rightarrow b^y = x$. So, $\log_4 1024 = 5 \Rightarrow 4^5 = 1024$.

Practice problems: *(Answers on page: 463)*

1. Express $6^2 = 36$ in logarithmic form.

2. Express $m^z = k$ in exponential form.

3. Express $\log_{16} 2 = \dfrac{1}{4}$ in exponential form.

Review questions: *(Answers to odd questions on page: 463)*

1. Express $\log_7 1 = 0$ in exponential form.

2. Express $7^3 = 343$ in logarithmic form.

3. Express $\log_{10} 0.01 = -2$ in exponential form.

4. Express $\log_3 2187 = 7$ in exponential form.

5. Express $4^{-\frac{3}{2}} = 0.125$ in logarithmic form.

Finding the Value of a Logarithmic Function

- When calculating logs, think of the expression in terms of the exponential form. Ask yourself "what exponent would I need to make this statement true."

More log Problems

Example *solve the log*

$$\log_6 36 = 2$$

$$6^? = 36$$

To solve logs, convert them to exponential form and see if you know what exponent you will need.

6 raised to what power is 36?
$6^2 = 36$. The second power!

~~More~~ log Problems *hard*

Example *solve the log*

$$\log_4\left(\dfrac{\sqrt[3]{4}}{2}\right)$$

write everything as $\sqrt{4}$ *change roots to exponents*

$$\dfrac{\sqrt[3]{4}}{\sqrt{4}} = \dfrac{4^{1/3}}{4^{1/2}} = 4^{1/3 - 1/2} = 4^{-1/6}$$

$$\log_4 \dfrac{\sqrt[3]{4}}{2} = \log_4 4^{-1/6} = ?$$

$$\Rightarrow 4^? = 4^{-t}, \text{ so } ? = \dfrac{-1}{6}$$

$$\boxed{\log_4 \dfrac{\sqrt[3]{4}}{2} = \dfrac{-1}{6}}$$

In some problems, you will need to simplify pieces of the logarithm in order to see a good answer.

You can't see what the question is asking for when the expressions aren't simplified. Make it your first priority to try to reduce them so you can work the problem.

Notice that this radical expression simplifies to $4^{-1/6}$.

Substituting that into the log problem makes it a lot easier: what exponent do you raise 4 to if you want $4^{-1/6}$? To $-1/6$!

~~More~~ log Problems *really hard*

solve the log

$$6^{\log_6 28}$$

· **express the exponential expression as a logarithmic expression**

$$6^{\log_6 28} = ?$$

$$\log_6 ? = \log_6 28$$

$$? = 28$$

$$\boxed{6^{\log_6 28} = 28}$$

In this problem, the log statement is the exponent.
Look for a way to simplify things.
The statement $\log_6 28$ equals some value:
$$\log_6 28 = ?$$
or in exponential form:
$$6^? = 28.$$
With this information, you realize you are looking for the exponent for 6 that produces 28.

Sample problems:

1. Find the value of the logarithmic expression $\log_2 32$ without using a calculator.
   Solution: 5
   Explanation: Express the logarithmic equation $\log_2 32 = x$ as an exponential equation: $2^x = 32$.
   To solve for x, express each side with a common base: $2^x = 2^5$, so $x = 5$. Thus, $\log_2 32 = 5$.

2. Find the value of the logarithmic expression $\log_{10} 0.0001$ without using a calculator.
   Solution: -4
   Explanation: Express the logarithmic equation $\log_{10} 0.0001 = x$ as an exponential equation
   using 10 as the base: $10^x = 0.0001$. To solve for x, express each side with a common base:
   $10^x = 10^{-4}$, so $x = -4$. Thus, $\log_{10} 0.0001 = -4$.

3. Find the value of the logarithmic expression $\log_8\left(\dfrac{\sqrt[5]{16}}{2}\right)$, without using a calculator.

Solution: $-\dfrac{1}{15}$

Explanation: Begin by simplifying the expression inside the parentheses:

$\dfrac{\sqrt[5]{16}}{2} = \dfrac{16^{\frac{1}{5}}}{2} = \dfrac{\left(2^4\right)^{\frac{1}{5}}}{2} = \dfrac{2^{\frac{4}{5}}}{2} = 2^{\frac{4}{5}-1} = 2^{-\frac{1}{5}}$. So, $\log_8\left(\dfrac{\sqrt[5]{16}}{2}\right) = \log_8\left(2^{-\frac{1}{5}}\right)$.

Express the logarithmic equation $\log_8\left(2^{-\frac{1}{5}}\right) = x$ as an exponential equation: $8^x = 2^{-\frac{1}{5}}$.

To solve for x, express each side with a common base: $2^{3x} = 2^{-\frac{1}{5}}$; $3x = -\frac{1}{5}$; $x = -\frac{1}{15}$.

Practice problems: *(Answers on page: 463)*

1. Find the value of the logarithmic expression $\log_7\left(\dfrac{1}{49}\right)$ without using a calculator.

2. Find the value of the logarithmic expression $\log 1,000,000$ without using a calculator.

3. Find the value of the logarithmic expression $\log_9\left(\dfrac{\sqrt[4]{27}}{3}\right)$ without using a calculator.

Review questions: *(Answers to odd questions on page: 463)*

1. Find the value of $\log_{10} 10,000,000$ without using a calculator.

2. Find the value of $\log_8 64$ without using a calculator.

3. Find the value of $\log_9 9$ without using a calculator.

4. Find the value of $\log_3\left(\dfrac{1}{27}\right)$ without using a calculator.

5. Find the value of $\log_5 0.2$ without using a calculator.

Solving for x in Logarithmic Equations

- When solving logarithmic equations, convert them back to exponential form and figure out what the missing piece should be to make the statement true.

Example **Find Your** $\mathcal{X}$	
$x = \log_2 32$	To solve logs, convert them to exponential form and see if you know what the x-value should be.
$2^x = 32$	
$x = 5$	What power do you have to raise 2 to get 32?
	2 raised to the fifth power is 32.
$\log_x 25 = -2$	Here is a slightly trickier problem.
$x^{-2} = 25$	
$\dfrac{1}{x^2} = 5^2$	Convert the logarithm to an exponential equation first. It is a good idea to simplify expressions with strange pieces.
multiply through by x $\quad 1 = 5^2 x^2$	
divide both sides by 5^2 $\quad \dfrac{1}{5^2} = x^2$	Cross-multiply to isolate the x, then take the square root of each side.
take square roots $\quad x = \dfrac{\pm 1}{5}$	
Remember: the base of a log MUST be positive! $\boxed{x = \dfrac{1}{5}}$	Since the base of a logarithm must be non-negative, $x=1/5$ only.

$$\log_x \left(\tfrac{1}{16}\right) = -2$$

Here's another example.

$$x^{-2} = \tfrac{1}{16}$$

Convert the log to exponential form.

$$x^2 = 16$$

Simplify the negative exponent.

$$x = \pm 4$$

Solve the equation.

$$\boxed{x = 4}$$

Taking the square root gives a positive and negative answer.

✓ **Check your work!**

It is always a good idea to check your work.

Sample problems:

1. Solve for x: $\log_x(-25) = 2$, if $x > 0$.

   Solution: No real solution

   Explanation: The log of a negative number does not exist, regardless of the base. So, there is no solution.

2. Solve for x: $\log_x \left(\dfrac{1}{64}\right) = 2$, if $x > 0$.

   Solution: $x = \dfrac{1}{8}$

   Explanation: Express the logarithmic equation as an exponential equation: $x^2 = \tfrac{1}{64}$. Solve for x: $\sqrt{x^2} = \sqrt{\tfrac{1}{64}}$; $x = \pm\tfrac{1}{8}$. Theoretically there are two solutions, but $x = -\tfrac{1}{8}$ must be rejected because there cannot be a negative base in the logarithmic equation. Thus, $x = \tfrac{1}{8}$.

3. Solve for x: $4x = \log_{\sqrt{3}} 27$.

   Solution: $x = \dfrac{3}{2}$

   Explanation: Express the logarithmic equation as an exponential equation: $\sqrt{3}^{\,4x} = 27$.

   Convert the radical to a fractional exponent, then simplify the exponents: $3^{\frac{1}{2}\cdot 4x} = 27$; $3^{2x} = 27$. To solve for x, express each side with a common base: $3^{2x} = 3^3$; $2x = 3$; $x = \tfrac{3}{2}$.

Practice problems: *(Answers on page: 463)*

1. Solve for x: $\log_x 0 = 5$, if $x > 0$.

2. Solve for x: $5x = \log_3 81$.

3. Solve for x: $3x = \log_{\sqrt{5}} 25$.

Review questions: *(Answers to odd questions on page: 463)*

1. Solve $\log_x 1000 = 3$, if $x > 0$.

2. Solve $\log_8 2x = -1$, if $x > 0$.

3. Solve $\log_5 125 = 11 - x$.

4. Solve $\log_{10} x = 4$, if $x > 0$.

5. Solve $\log_{16} 2 = x$.

Graphing Logarithmic Functions

- **Graphs of logarithmic functions** all have the same basic shape. One of the ways you can make them different is by changing the base.

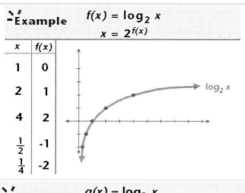

Example $f(x) = \log_2 x$
$x = 2^{f(x)}$

x	f(x)
1	0
2	1
4	2
$\frac{1}{2}$	-1
$\frac{1}{4}$	-2

Now you can begin investigating how logarithmic functions behave graphically.

Set up a table to plot some points.

Notice that the curve does not touch the y-axis. This is because exponential functions never equal zero.

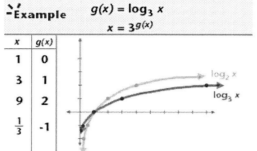

Example $g(x) = \log_3 x$
$x = 3^{g(x)}$

x	g(x)
1	0
3	1
9	2
$\frac{1}{3}$	-1

Compare the graph of $\log_2 x$ with $\log_3 x$.

Once again, the graph never crosses the y-axis.

In addition, notice how the graph with the larger base is greater then the graph with the smaller base until $x = 1$, then they switch.

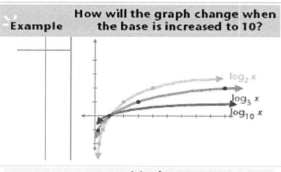

Example How will the graph change when the base is increased to 10?

Consider when the base is equal to 10.

Reading from left to right, the graph with the larger base is greater (higher) than the smaller base until $x = 1$.

After $x = 1$, the graph with the larger base is lower than the graph with the smaller base.

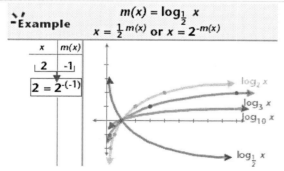

Example $m(x) = \log_{\frac{1}{2}} x$
$x = \frac{1}{2}^{m(x)}$ or $x = 2^{-m(x)}$

x	m(x)
2	-1

$2 = 2^{-(-1)}$

What about fractional bases?

Try plotting some points.

Notice that the graph of $\log_{\frac{1}{2}} x$ is the reflection of $\log_2 x$ across the x-axis.

Sample problems:

1. Where does the graph of $f(x) = \log_2 x$ intersect the graph of $g(x) = \log_5 x$?
   Solution: $(1, 0)$

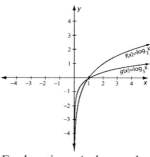

Explanation: As base values increase, the graph of $\log_b x$ changes in two ways:
1) it increases faster when the domain is greater than 0, but less than 1 and
2) it increases slower when the domain is greater than 1.
But for all base values greater than 1, $\log_b x$ passes through $(1, 0)$.
Therefore, the graphs of $f(x)$ and $g(x)$ intersect at $(1, 0)$.

2. True or False: If $f(x) = \log_b x$ increases faster than $g(x) = \log_4 x$ when the domain is greater than 1, then $b > 4$.

Solution: False

Explanation: As base values increase, the graph of $\log_b x$ gets closer to the $x-$axis when the domain is greater than 1. So, to create a logarithmic function that increases faster than $\log_4 x$ when the domain is greater than 1, the base value must be less than 4.

3. Describe the graph of $f(x) = \log_3 x$ as compared to the graph of $g(x) = \log_{\frac{1}{3}} x$.

Solution: $f(x)$ is the reflection of $g(x)$ across the $x-$axis
Explanation: Evaluate each function for several x values:

Find $f(1)$: $3^y = 1$; $y = 0$, so $f(1) = 0$. Find $f(2)$: $3^y = 2$, that's too hard, try another x value.
Find $f(3)$: $3^y = 3$; $y = 1$, so $f(3) = 1$. Use another easy x value, find $f(9)$: $3^y = 9$; $y = 2$, so $f(9) = 2$.

$f(x) = \log_3 x$

x	$y = \log_3 x$ or $3^y = x$	y	point
1	$3^y = 1$	0	(1,0)
3	$3^y = 3$	1	(3,1)
9	$3^y = 9$	2	(9,2)
27	$3^y = 27$	3	(27,3)

$g(x) = \log_{1/3} x$

x	$y = \log_{1/3} x$ or $1/3^y = x$	y	point
1	$1/3^y = 1$	0	(1,0)
3	$1/3^y = 3$	1	(3,1)
9	$1/3^y = 9$	2	(9,2)
27	$1/3^y = 27$	3	(27,3)

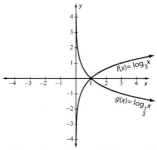

The points from $f(x)$ are all reflections across the $x-$axis of $g(x)$ since the $x-$coordinates are the same and the $y-$coordinates are always opposites. Therefore, the graph of $f(x)$ is the reflection of $g(x)$ across the $x-$axis.

Practice problems: *(Answers on page: 463)*

1. True or False: For $0 < x < 1$; $f(x) = \log_9 x$ increases faster than $g(x) = \log_7 x$.

2. Where do the graphs of $f(x) = \log_2 x$ and $f(x) = \log_{\frac{1}{4}} x$ intersect?

3. Given the function $f(x) = \log_a x$ and $g(x) = \log_{\frac{1}{2}} x$, when $a > 1$, suppose that $f(4) = 7$. Find $g(4)$.

Review questions: *(Answers to odd questions on page: 463)*

1. Graph $f(x) = \log_{\frac{1}{4}} x$.

2. Graph $f(x) = \log_4 x$.

3. Where does the graph of $f(x) = \log_5 x$ intersect the graph of $g(x) = \log_9 x$?

4. How does the graph of $g(x) = \log_2 x$ compare to the graph of $f(x) = \log_{\frac{1}{2}} x$?

5. Which graph increases faster as x increases, when $x > 0$, $f(x) \log_{10} x$ or $g(x) \log_{20} x$?

Matching Logarithmic Functions with Their Graphs

- Since all **logarithmic functions** have the same basic shape, all you really need to know is where the graph crosses the x-axis and approximately how high it gets.

Example 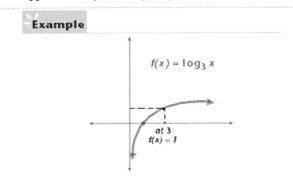	One of the key pieces of information about logarithms is the point where they cross the x-axis (sometimes called the x-intercept). To find the x-intercept: set the log equal to zero and solve: $\quad f(x) = \log_3 x = 0$. That means: $3^0 = x$ leading to $x = 1$ when $y = 0$. In this particular graph, the x-intercept is equal to 1.
Example 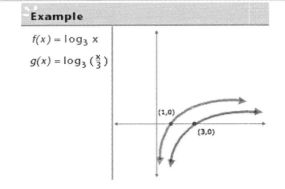	If you change the x-term, you can change the x-intercept. Building on the first example, replace x with $x/3$. Now repeat your process from the first example: $\quad$ Set $f(x) = 0$: $f(x) = \log_3 (x/3) = 0$ $\quad$ leading to: $3^0 = x/3$ $\quad\quad\quad\quad\quad 1 = x/3$ $\quad\quad\quad\quad\quad x = 3$ when $y = 0$. With this change, you move the x-intercept from $x = 1$ to $x = 3$. The new intercept is three times farther from the origin. Dividing by 3 also flattened the curve out some. It still gets infinitely large, but not as fast as the first curve.

Example

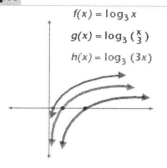

$f(x) = \log_3 x$

$g(x) = \log_3 \left(\frac{x}{3}\right)$

$h(x) = \log_3 (3x)$

Again building on the first example, what happens when you multiply the x-term by 3?

Repeat your process again:

Set $f(x) = 0$: $f(x) = \log_3 3x = 0$

leading to: $3^0 = 3x$

$1 = 3x$

$x = 1/3$ when $y = 0$.

With this change the x-intercept is three times closer to the origin than in the first example.

The graph also gets larger more quickly.

Example

$f(x) = \log_3 x$

$s(x) = \log_3 (x{-}2)$

*(x-2) creates a
shift on the x-axis*

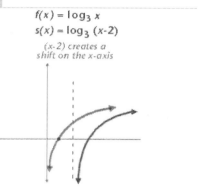

You can do more to a variable than just multiply.

What happens if you subtract 2 from the x ?

Repeat your process again:

Set $f(x) = 0$: $f(x) = \log_3 (x - 2) = 0$

leading to: $3^0 = x - 2$

$1 = x - 2$

$x = 3$ when $y = 0$.

This change has added 2 to the x-value for each y-value. The entire graph shifts 2 units to the right. This is called a translation.

The graph will have the same basic shape as the main graph. It will just be 2 units farther away.

Example

$f(x) = \log_3 x$

$s(x) = \log_3 (x{-}2)$

$l(x) = \log_3 (-x)$

$f(x) = \log_3 1$
$x = 0$

$f(x) = \log_3 (- -1)$
$x = 0$

*creates a
mirror image*

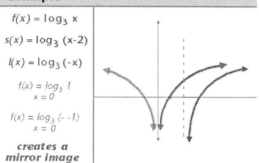

Finally, what happens if you multiply the x by a negative number?

Logarithms normally only work for values greater than 0. But if you multiply by negative one, they work only for x-values less than zero!

Use your process to see how it works:

Set $f(x) = 0$: $f(x) = \log_3 (x - 2) = 0$

leading to: $3^0 = -x$

$1 = -x$

$x = -1$ when $y = 0$.

In fact, the graph of the log of negative x is like a mirror image across the y-axis of the log of x.

Sample problems:

1. Determine the x-intercept of the graph $y = \log_7 \dfrac{x}{4}$?

   Solution: 4

   Explanation: The x-intercept is the point where the graph intersects the x – axis, thus where $y = 0$. So, substitute 0 into the equation for y: $0 = \log_7 \frac{x}{4}$. Apply the law of logarithms, $y = \log_b x \Rightarrow b^y = x$, to express the logarithmic equation as an exponential equation: $0 = \log_7 \frac{x}{4} \Rightarrow 7^0 = \frac{x}{4}$. Solve for x: $1 = \frac{x}{4}$; $x = 4$. So, the x-intercept is 4 or the point $(4, 0)$.

2. Given the functions $f(x) = \log_2 \dfrac{5x}{3}$ and $g(x) = \log_2(5x-3)$, which function has the largest x-intercept?

Solution: $g(x)$

Explanation: Find the x-intercept of $f(x)$ by substituting 0 for $f(x)$, expressing the logarithmic equation as an exponential equation, and solving for x:
$0 = \log_2 \frac{5x}{3} \Rightarrow 2^0 = \frac{5x}{3}$; $1 = \frac{5x}{3}$; $3 = 5x$; $x = \frac{3}{5}$. So the x-intercept of $f(x)$ is $\frac{3}{5}$.
Find the x-intercept of $g(x)$: $0 = \log_2(5x-3) \Rightarrow 2^0 = 5x - 3$; $1 = 5x - 3$; $4 = 5x$; $x = \frac{4}{5}$.
Therefore, the x-intercept of $g(x)$ is larger.

3. From the graph below, which curve accurately represents the graph of $\log_8(x-3)$: $g(x)$ or $h(x)$?

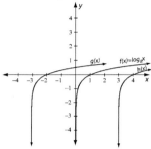

Solution: $h(x)$

Explanation: If $f(x)$ is $\log_8 x$, then $h(x)$ represents the graph of $\log_8(x-3)$ because it is shifted three units to the right. Remember: "add to x, go west". Since 3 is being subtracted from x, go east (right) 3 units.

Practice problems: *(Answers on page: 463)*

1. Which of these equations will produce a curve with the smallest x-intercept: $y = \log_9(7x)$ or $y = \log_{10}(2x)$?

2. How is the curve of $j(x) = \log_8(x-2)$ different from that of $f(x) = \log_8 x$?

3. Determine the x-intercept of the graph of $f(x) = \log_5\left(\dfrac{3x+1}{4}\right)$.

Review questions: *(Answers to odd questions on page: 463)*

1. True or false: All logarithmic functions pass through the point (0, 1).

2. Which of these equations will produce a curve with the largest x-intercept?

   a) $y = \log_6(\dfrac{x}{2})$ b) $y = \log_8(6x)$ c) $y = \log_9(8x)$ d) $y = \log_7(\dfrac{x}{4})$

3. If $f(x) = \log_4 x$, graph $2 + \log_4 x$.

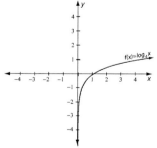

4. If $f(x) = \log_4 x$, graph $\log_4(x-2)$.

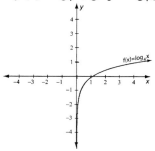

5. If $f(x) = \log_8 x$, graph $\log_8(x+1)$.

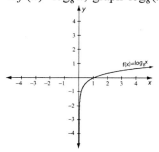

Properties of Logarithms

- The properties of **logarithms** follow directly from the properties of exponents. Keep in mind that "a log is an exponent."
- **REMEMBER:** A log is an exponent!

The log of a product $$\log_b(xy) = \log_b x + \log_b y$$ *sum of two logs*	When dealing with a product of exponents of the same base, you add the exponents. When dealing with the log of a product, you add the logs.
The log of a quotient $$\log_b\left(\tfrac{x}{y}\right) = \log_b x - \log_b y$$ *difference of two logs*	When you have a quotient of bases raised to different exponents, you subtract the exponents. When you have the log of a quotient, you subtract the logs.
The log of a power $$\log_b(x^y) = y\log_b x$$	When you raise a number with an exponent to another power, you multiply the exponents. When taking the log of a number raised to another power, you multiply that number by the log.
$$\log_b b = 1 \qquad b^1 = b$$	Here is another useful property of logs. **REMEMBER:** $\log_b b = x$ means $b^x = b$. The only exponent that produces its base is 1. So, the $\log b$ that produces b has to be 1.
$$\log_b 1 = 0 \qquad b^0 = 1$$	**CHECK THIS OUT:** $\log_b 1 = x$ means $b^x = 1$. The only exponent that lets $b = 1$ is 0. So the log of 1 is 0!

False Formulas

$$\log(x+y) \neq \log x + \log y$$

no standard form for adding

False Formulas

$$\log_b\left(\frac{\log x}{\log y}\right) \neq \log x - \log y$$

the quotient of two logs

NEVER USE THESE FORMULAS! They are examples of some common log mistakes!

The log of a sum is **NOT** equal to the sum of the logs! You add two logs when you are dealing with a product of two numbers.

The quotient of two logs is **NOT** equal to the difference of the logs! You subtract two logs when you are dealing with two numbers dividing, not two logs dividing.

Sample problems:

1. Expand: $\log_{10}(0.75 \cdot 293)$

   <u>Solution</u>: $\log_{10} 0.75 + \log_{10} 293$

   <u>Explanation</u>: Apply the log of a product property, $\log_b(xy) = \log_b x + \log_b y$:

   $\log_{10}(0.75 \cdot 293) = \log_{10} 0.75 + \log_{10} 293$.

2. Expand: $\log_5(7.6 + m)$

   <u>Solution</u>: Cannot be expanded

   <u>Explanation</u>: There is no rule for taking the log of a sum.

3. Expand: $\log_8\left(\dfrac{\sqrt[3]{x}}{y^2}\right)$

   <u>Solution</u>: $\dfrac{1}{3}\log_8 x - 2\log_8 y$

   <u>Explanation</u>: Express the radical as an exponent: $\log_8\left(\dfrac{\sqrt[3]{x}}{y^2}\right) = \log_8 \dfrac{x^{\frac{1}{3}}}{y^2}$.

   Apply the log of a quotient property, $\log_b\left(\dfrac{x}{y}\right) = \log_b x - \log_b y$: $\log_8 \dfrac{x^{\frac{1}{3}}}{y^2} = \log_8 x^{\frac{1}{3}} - \log_8 y^2$.

   Apply the log of a power property, $\log_b\left(x^y\right) = y\log_b x$: $\dfrac{1}{3}\log_8 x - 2\log_8 y$.

Practice problems: *(Answers on page: 463)*

1. Expand: $\log_1 xy^3$

2. Expand: $\log_2 \dfrac{2p}{q}$

3. Expand: $\log_6 \dfrac{x-2}{y}$

Review questions: *(Answers to odd questions on page: 463)*

1. Expand: $\log_4 j\sqrt[6]{k}$

2. Expand: $\log_e(w - 4)$

3. Expand: $\log_5 \dfrac{x^3}{5}$

4. Expand: $\log_{10}\left(\dfrac{xy^2}{\sqrt{z}}\right)$

5. Expand: $\log_2\left(\dfrac{t}{8}\right)$

Expanding a Logarithmic Expression Using Properties

- To simplify logs, expand them out using the log properties.

log properties: • $\log_b b = 1$ • $\log_b 1 = 0$ • $\log_b (xy) = \log_b x + \log_b y$ • $\log_b \left(\frac{x}{y}\right) = \log_b x - \log_b y$ • $\log_b (x^y) = y\log_b x$	Here is a quick list of the properties of logs.
Example *simplify log* $\log_3\left(\frac{3A}{B}\right) =$ $\boxed{\log_3 3A} - \log_3 B =$ $\boxed{\log_3 3} + \log_3 A - \log_3 B =$ $1 + \log_3 A - \log_3 B$	Use the properties of logs to create as many small pieces as possible. The log of a quotient is equal to the difference of the logs. The log of a product is equal to the sum of the logs. The log of a value equal to the base is equal to 1. Now you've simplified the log!
Example *simplify log* $\log_6\left(\frac{6\sqrt{5}}{\sqrt{6}}\right)$ $= \boxed{\log_6(6\sqrt{5})} - \log_6\sqrt{6}$ $= \boxed{\log_6 6} + \log_6\sqrt{5} - \log_6\sqrt{6}$ $= 1 + \log_6\left(5^{\frac{1}{2}}\right) - \log_6\left(6^{\frac{1}{2}}\right)$ $= 1 + \frac{1}{2}\log_6 5 - \frac{1}{2}\log_6 6\,\left(\left(\frac{1}{2}\right)(1)\right)$ $\boxed{\frac{1}{2} + \frac{1}{2}\log_6 5}$	Again, simplify by creating small pieces. Rewrite a quotient as the difference of the logs. Rewrite a product as the sum of the logs. Rewrite square roots as exponents. Then simplify some more. Where possible, do some arithmetic. Then, you're done.
Example *simplify log* $\log_3(A + 3B)$ * *cannot be simplified any further*	**REMEMBER:** The log of a sum cannot be simplified. Don't make the classic mistake!

Example *simplify log*

$$\log_{10} \sqrt[5]{\frac{A^2 B^4}{C^3}}$$

$$= \frac{1}{5}\log_{10}\left(\frac{A^2 B^4}{C^3}\right) = \log_{10}\left(\left(\frac{A^2 B^4}{C^3}\right)^{\frac{1}{5}}\right)$$

$$= \frac{1}{5}[\log_{10}(A^2 B^4) - \log_{10} C^3]$$

$$= \frac{1}{5}[\log_{10} A^2 + \log_{10} B^4 - \log_{10} C^3]$$

$$= \frac{1}{5}[2\log_{10} A + 4\log_{10} B - 3\log_{10} C]$$

$$\boxed{= \frac{2}{5}\log_{10} A + \frac{4}{5}\log_{10} B - \frac{3}{5}\log_{10} C}$$

Problems that look horribly complex can actually be manipulated much more easily with the log properties.

Because products and quotients are so easy to work, they don't cause cancellation errors.

Exponents are even easier. See?

Now the problem is simplified!

Sample problems:

1. Expand and simplify $\log_{10}(10^7 c^{24})$. Assume all variables represent positive real numbers.

   Solution: $\log_{10}(10^7 c^{24}) = 7 + 24\log c$

   Explanation: Apply property $\underline{\log_{10} 10^7 c^{24}}$

         log of a product: $\log_{10} 10^7 + \log_{10} c^{24}$

         log of a power: $7\log_{10} 10 + 24\log_{10} c$

         $\log_b b = 1$: $7 \cdot 1 + 24\log_{10} c$

   So, $\log_{10}(10^7 c^{24}) = 7 + 24\log_{10} c$.

2. Expand and simplify $\log_5\left[\frac{(a+3)}{(a-4)}\right]$. Assume all variables represent positive real numbers.

   Solution: $\log_5(a+3) - \log_5(a-4)$

   Explanation: Apply "the log of a quotient" property: $\log_5\left[\frac{(a+3)}{(a-4)}\right] = \log_5(a+3) - \log_5(a-4)$.
   There is no "log of a sum" property, so the equation cannot be simplified any further.

3. Expand and simplify $\log_3\left(\frac{x\sqrt{y}}{3}\right)$. Assume all variables represent positive real numbers.

   Solution: $\log_3 x + \frac{1}{2}\log_3 y - 1$

   Explanation: Apply property: $\underline{\log_3 \frac{x\sqrt{y}}{3}}$

         log of a quotient: $\log_3 x\sqrt{y} - \log_3 3$

         $\log_b b = 1$: $\log_3 x\sqrt{y} - 1$

         log of a product: $\log_3 x + \log_3 \sqrt{y} - 1$

         $\sqrt{y} = y^{\frac{1}{2}}$: $\log_3 x + \log_3 y^{\frac{1}{2}} - 1$

         log of a power: $\log_3 x + \frac{1}{2}\log_3 y - 1$

Practice problems: *(Answers on page: 463)*

1. Expand and simplify $\log_{10} \frac{\sqrt{2p}}{h^6}$. Assume all variables represent positive real numbers.

2. Expand and simplify $\log_2(8x^2 - y^2)$. Assume all variables represent positive real numbers.

3. Expand and simplify $\log_2\left(\frac{8t^4}{3n^2}\right)$. Assume all variables represent positive real numbers.

Review questions: *(Answers to odd questions on page: 464)*

1. Expand and simplify $\log_4\left(\dfrac{d^2 g^7}{4m^3}\right)$. Assume all variables represent positive real numbers.

2. Expand and simplify $\log_6\left(\dfrac{19c}{36}\right)$. Assume all variables represent positive real numbers.

3. Expand and simplify $\log_7\left(\sqrt[6]{ab} + \sqrt{49}\right)$. Assume all variables represent positive real numbers.

4. Expand and simplify $\log_b\left(a^5 k^7\right)$. Assume all variables represent positive real numbers.

5. Expand and simplify $\log_e \sqrt[3]{\dfrac{a}{b}}$. Assume all variables represent positive real numbers.

Combining Logarithmic Expressions

- To combine logarithms, use their properties backward to convert addition and subtraction into multiplication and division.
- A **common logarithm** is one with no base stated. The base is understood to be 10.
- A **natural logarithm** (ln) has e as its base.

log properties: • $\log_b b = 1$ • $\log_b 1 = 0$ • $\log_b (xy) = \log_b x + \log_b y$ • $\log_b \left(\frac{x}{y}\right) = \log_b x - \log_b y$ • $\log_b (x^y) = y\log_b x$	Here is a quick review of the log properties.
Note: Naked log is $\log x = \log_{10} x$	When you encounter a logarithm without a base listed, it is understood to be the common log or base 10.
Example *Convert into 1 log* $\log_{10}(x+5) + 2\log_{10} x$ $= \log(x+5) + \log x^2$ * bases must match up in order to combine the logs! $= \log((x+5)(x^2))$	Sometimes you will be asked to convert multiple logs into one statement. To do so, use the multiplication and division properties to work backwards. The bases **must** be the same! In this example, since the expression is the sum of two logs, you can combine them into the log of a product.
Example *Convert into 1 log* $3\log_4 x - 2\log_4 z + 2\log_4 w$ $= \log_4 x^3 - \log_4 z^2 + \log_4 w^2$ *difference of 2 logs* $= \boxed{\log_4\left(\frac{x^3}{z^2}\right)} + \log_4 w^2$ *sum of 2 logs* $= \boxed{\log_4\left(\frac{x^3}{z^2}\right)(w^2)}$ $= \log_4\left(\frac{x^3 w^2}{z^2}\right)$	Multiple terms aren't any harder. The difference of two logs is equal to the log of their quotient. The sum of two logs is equal to the log of their product. Simplify the expression next. Now you are done!
Note: Natural log is $\log_e x = \ln x$	The natural log occurs so often that mathematicians use $\ln x$ as a shortcut.

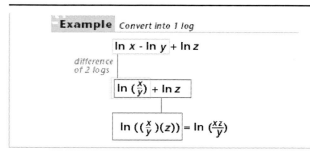

Example *Convert into 1 log*

$\ln x - \ln y + \ln z$

difference of 2 logs

$\ln \left(\frac{x}{y}\right) + \ln z$

$\ln \left(\left(\frac{x}{y}\right)(z)\right) = \ln \left(\frac{xz}{y}\right)$

Remember: $\ln x = \log_e x$

Use your properties again:
The difference of logs becomes a quotient.
The sum of logs becomes a product.

Simplify and you're done!

Sample problems:

1. Write $3\log_2 y + \log_2(y-3) + \log_2 8$ as a single log and simplify if possible. Assume all variables represent positive real numbers.

Solution: $\log_2[y^3(y-3)] + 3$

Explanation:

Apply property	$3\log_2 y + \log_2(y-3) + \log_2 8$
log of a power:	$\log_2 y^3 + \log_2(y-3) + \log_2 8$
evaluate $\log_2 8$:	$\log_2 y^3 + \log_2(y-3) + 3$
log of a product:	$\log_2[y^3(y-3)] + 3$

2. Write $\dfrac{1}{2}\log(x+1) + \dfrac{1}{2}\log(x-1)$ as a single log and simplify if possible. Assume all variables represent positive real numbers.

Solution: $\log\sqrt{(x^2-1)}$

Explanation: Move the $\frac{1}{2}$'s to exponents using the "log of a power" property: $\log(x+1)^{\frac{1}{2}} + \log(x-1)^{\frac{1}{2}}$. Combine the terms using the "log of a product" property: $\log(x+1)^{\frac{1}{2}}(x-1)^{\frac{1}{2}}$. Now that the expression is a single log, simplify further if possible: $\log\left[(x+1)(x-1)\right]^{\frac{1}{2}} = \log\sqrt{(x^2-1)}$. Note: the base in this logarithmic expression is 10.

3. Write $\ln\left(\dfrac{y^7}{z^2}\right) - \ln\left(\dfrac{y^3}{z}\right) - \ln\left(\dfrac{y^4}{z}\right)$ as a single log and simplify if possible. Assume all variables represent positive real numbers.

Solution: 0

Explanation: Combine the first 2 terms using the "log of a quotient" property: $\ln\left(\dfrac{y^7}{z^2} \Big/ \dfrac{y^3}{z}\right) - \ln\left(\dfrac{y^4}{z}\right)$. To divide the rationals, multiply by the reciprocal: $\ln\left(\dfrac{y^7}{z^2} \cdot \dfrac{z}{y^3}\right) - \ln\dfrac{y^4}{z} = \ln\dfrac{y^4}{z} - \ln\dfrac{y^4}{z}$. The two remaining terms are identical, thus the expression simplifies to 0.

Practice problems: *(Answers on page: 464)*

1. Write $\dfrac{2\log a + \log x}{4} - \log 1000$ as a single log and simplify if possible. Assume all variables represent positive real numbers.

2. Write $3\log_6 y - \log_6(y+5) + \log_6 36$ as a single log and simplify if possible. Assume all variables represent positive real numbers.

3. Write $5\ln x - \ln 8 + \ln e$ as a single log and simplify if possible. Assume all variables represent positive real numbers.

Review questions: *(Answers to odd questions on page: 464)*

1. Write the expression $\log_b\left(a^2 - t^2\right) - \log_b\left(a + t\right)$ as a single log and simplify.

   Assume all variables represent positive real numbers.

2. Write the expression $\dfrac{\log(x - 5) - \log y - 2\log z}{3}$ as a single log and simplify.

   Use radicals instead of fractional exponents and assume all variables represent positive real numbers.

3. Write the expression $\left(\dfrac{3}{2}\right)\log_2 u + \left(\dfrac{3}{4}\right)\log_2 w$ as a single log and simplify.

   Use radicals instead of fractional exponents and assume all variables represent positive real numbers.

4. Write the expression $2\log_{10} 5x + \log_{10} 4$ as a single log and simplify if possible.

   Assume all variables represent positive real numbers.

5. Write the expression $2\ln x + 4\ln y - 3\ln z$ as a single log and simplify if possible.

   Assume all variables represent positive real numbers.

Evaluating Logarithmic Functions Using a Calculator

- When using a calculator to find the value of a logarithmic function, use the log properties to make your work easier.

$\boxed{\textbf{log}} = \log_{10}$ $\boxed{\textbf{ln}} = \log_e$	When finding logarithms with a calculator, you will need to find these two keys first.
Example 1.689... $\log 50 = 1.689...$ $10^? = 50$ estimate: $10^1 = 10$ $10^2 = 100$	Start by finding the common log of 50. To make sure that the calculator answer makes sense, it is probably a good idea to estimate first. What exponent would you need to raise the base, 10, to get 50? Somewhere between 1 and 2. Punch in 50 and hit $\boxed{\log}$. The answer, 1.689, fits into your range of 1 to 2.
Example 3.912... $\ln 50 = 3.912...$ estimate: $e = 2.7...$ round to 3 $3^3 = 27$ $3^4 = 81$	Estimating natural logs is trickier, but you can do it by figuring e about equal to 3. Notice that 50 is between 3^3 and 3^4. Punch in 50. Hit $\boxed{\ln}$. The answer, 3.912, fits into your range of 3 to 4. **WARNING:** Some calculators work a little bit differently. You might have to hit $\boxed{\ln}$ *before* you punch in 50.

Example
 0.8685...
 	
 $\log e^2 = 0.8685...$
 or $2\log e$
	To find the log of e-squared, you can **either** find e-squared first and then hit $\boxed{\log}$:
	     Punch in 2.7 and multiply by 2.7,
	     then hit $\boxed{\log}$.
	 or use the exponent rule and move the exponent outside the logarithm:
	     Punch in 2.7, hit $\boxed{\log}$,
	     then multiply that by 2.

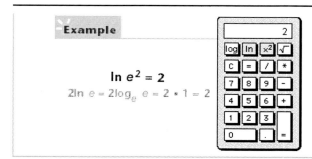

Example

$$\ln e^2 = 2$$

$$2\ln e = 2\log_e e = 2 \cdot 1 = 2$$

Finding the natural log of *e*-squared is actually pretty easy.

Punch in $\boxed{e}$. Square it. Hit $\boxed{\ln}$.

Notice how the answer matches what you could find using the logarithm properties. You know that $\ln e = 1$ and $1 \cdot 2 = 2$.

Sample problems:

1. Use a calculator to evaluate $\log 0.257$ to four decimal places.
   Solution: -0.5901
   Explanation: Complete the following key sequence for most scientific calculators: .257, LOG.
   So, $\log 0.257 = -0.5901$. Complete the following key sequence for a graphing calculator:
   LOG, 0.257, ENTER. Again, $\log 0.257 = -0.5901$.

2. Use a calculator to evaluate $\log 1,000,000$ (the log of a million) to four decimal places.
   Solution: 6
   Explanation: Complete the following key sequence for most scientific calculators:
   1000000, LOG. So, $\log 1,000,000 = 6$. Complete the following key sequence for a graphing
   calculator: LOG, 1000000, ENTER. Again, $\log 1,000,000 = 6$.

3. Use a calculator to evaluate $\ln\left(\dfrac{5}{2}\right)$ to four decimal places.

   Solution: 0.9163
   Explanation: Complete the following key sequence for most scientific calculators: 5, $\div$, 2, =, LN.
   So, $\ln\left(\frac{5}{2}\right) = 0.9163$ when rounded to four decimal places. Complete the following key sequence
   for a graphing calculator: LN, (, 5, / , 2,), ENTER. Again, $\ln\left(\frac{5}{2}\right) = 0.9163$.

Practice problems: *(Answers on page: 464)*

1. Use a calculator to evaluate $\log\left(5\dfrac{3}{4}\right)$ to four decimal places.

2. Use a calculator to evaluate $\log 25,300$ to four decimal places.

3. Use a calculator to evaluate $\ln 0.0104$ to four decimal places.

Review questions: *(Answers to odd questions on page: 464)*

1. Use a calculator to evaluate $\log 35.2$ to four decimal places.

2. Use a calculator to evaluate $\log 65.200$ to four decimal places.

3. Use a calculator to evaluate $\log\left(\dfrac{2}{3}\right)$ to four decimal places.

4. Use a calculator to evaluate $\log\left(\dfrac{6}{7}\right)$ to four decimal places.

5. Use a calculator to evaluate $\ln 25.3$ to four decimal places.

Using the Change of Base Formula

- The **change of base formula**: $\log_b x = \dfrac{\log_a x}{\log_a b}$.

- When a log has a base different from 10 or e, it can be difficult to manipulate. But you can use the **change of base formula** to make the problem easier.

$\log_7 12$ $\log_3 \frac{1}{2}$ $\log_{\frac{3}{2}} 2$ **How would you calculate these?**	Calculating logarithms with base 10 or e is fairly straightforward. But what about logs with different bases? You can't figure these on your calculator. But there must be a way to work with strange bases.
Change of Base Formula $\log_b x = \dfrac{\log_a x}{\log_a b}$ *changing base b to base a*	And here it is! The change of base formula will enable you to turn one log of a given base into a quotient of logs with a different base (a). Notice how you can choose anything for a.

Proving the change of base formula
 let $y = \log_b x \longleftrightarrow b^y = x$
 $\log_a (b^y) = \log_a x$
 $y\log_a b = \log_a x$
 $\boxed{y = \dfrac{\log_a x}{\log_a b}}$
	In case you are skeptical, let's look at how the change of base formula is derived.
	
	    The log equation can be rewritten as an exponential equation.
	    Take the log base a of both sides.
	    Use the log properties to simplify.
	    Solve for y.

Example *solve these logs using change of base formula* A) $\log_3 \frac{1}{2} = \dfrac{\ln \frac{1}{2}}{\ln 3} = -.6309...$ B) $\log_{\frac{3}{2}} 2 = \dfrac{\log 2}{\log \frac{3}{2}} = 1.7095$ ☺ **log and ln can be used interchangably**	Examples show the change of base formula at work. In this problem the base is changed from 3 to e and the problem is easily solved. This example changes the base from 3/2 to 10 and is just as straightforward as the first example. Notice you can use 10 or e as bases easily and in any problem.

Sample problems:

1. True or False: $\log_7 12 = \dfrac{\log 7}{\log 12}$.

   Solution: False

   Explanation: Use the change of base formula, $\log_b x = \frac{\log_a x}{\log_a b}$, where $b = 7$ and $x = 12$, to change the base from 7 to 10, so $a = 10$: $\log_7 12 = \frac{\log_{10} 12}{\log_{10} 7} = \frac{\log 12}{\log 7}$, not $\frac{\log 7}{\log 12}$.

2. Express $\log_{\sqrt{3}} 4$ as a quotient of common logs.

   Solution: $\dfrac{\log 4}{\log \sqrt{3}}$

   Explanation: A common log is a log where the base is understood to be 10 and does not need to be stated. Use the change of base formula to change the base from $\sqrt{3}$ to 10: $\log_{\sqrt{3}} 4 = \dfrac{\log 4}{\log \sqrt{3}}$.

3. Express $\log_{\frac{1}{2}} \sqrt{5}$ as a quotient of natural logs.

Solution: $\dfrac{\ln \sqrt{5}}{\ln \frac{1}{2}}$

Explanation: A natural log is a log with base e, expressed ln. Use the change of base formula to change

the base from $\frac{1}{2}$ to e: $\log_{\frac{1}{2}} \sqrt{5} = \dfrac{\ln \sqrt{5}}{\ln \frac{1}{2}}$.

Practice problems: *(Answers on page: 464)*

1. Express $\log_{20}\left(\dfrac{1541}{3.29}\right)$ as a quotient of common logs.

2. Express $\log_4 0.287$ as a quotient of natural logs.

3. True or False: $\log_{\sqrt{3}} 5 = \dfrac{\log_2 5}{\log_2 \sqrt{3}}$

Review questions: *(Answers to odd questions on page: 464)*

1. Express $\log_9 20$ as a quotient of natural logs.

2. Express $\log_5 3$ as a quotient of natural logs.

3. Express $\log_9 35$ as a quotient of common logs.

4. Express $\log_6 5$ as a quotient of common logs.

5. Express $\log_{\frac{1}{2}} 8$ as a quotient of common logs.

The Richter Scale

- The Richter scale formula: $R = \log \dfrac{I}{I_0}$.

Since logarithms give you an easy way to manipulate exponents, they turn out to have hundreds of real world applications.

One of the real world applications is in seismology, dealing with the intensity of earthquakes. You have probably heard of the **Richter scale**. The Richter scale is how scientists rate the severity of earthquakes.

The Richter scale is a logarithmic scale found by taking the log of the intensity of the earthquake divided by the intensity of normal seismic activity.

$398{,}107{,}000\, I_0$

$R = \log\left(\dfrac{398{,}107{,}000\, I_0}{I_0}\right)$

$R = \log(398{,}107{,}000)$

$R = \boxed{8.599...}$ ← Answer

For one particular earthquake, scientists recorded an intensity of $398{,}107{,}000 I_0$, meaning $398{,}107{,}000$ times normal intensity.

They can find this earthquake's value on the Richter scale by substituting this value in for I.

Then they do the calculations.

That was a pretty severe earthquake!

 www.thinkwell.com

Sample problems:

1. The Richter scale magnitude R of an earthquake of intensity I is defined as $R = \log\left(\frac{I}{I_0}\right)$, where I_0 is a small threshold intensity. Find the magnitude of an earthquake if the intensity is 68 million I_0.
   Solution: 7.83
   Explanation: Use the formula $R = \log\left(\frac{I}{I_0}\right) = \log\left(\frac{68\text{ million }I_0}{I_0}\right) = \log(68\text{ million}) = 7.83$.

2. The Richter scale magnitude R of an earthquake of intensity I is defined as $R = \log\left(\frac{I}{I_o}\right)$, where I_0 is a small threshold intensity. Find the magnitude of an earthquake if the intensity is 10.5 million I_0.
   Solution: 7.02
   Explanation: Use the formula $R = \log\left(\frac{I}{I_0}\right) = \log\left(\frac{10.5\text{ million }I_0}{I_0}\right) = \log(10,500,000) = 7.02$.

3. The Richter scale magnitude R of an earthquake of intensity I is defined as $R = \log\left(\frac{I}{I_o}\right)$, where I_0 is a small threshold intensity. Find the magnitude of an earthquake if the intensity is 205 million I_0.
   Solution: 8.3
   Explanation: Use the formula $R = \log\left(\frac{I}{I_0}\right) = \log\left(\frac{205\text{ million }I_0}{I_0}\right) = \log(205,000,000) = 8.3$.

Practice problems: *(Answers on page: 464)*

1. The Richter scale magnitude R of an earthquake of intensity I is defined as $R = \log\left(\frac{I}{I_o}\right)$, where I_0 is a small threshold intensity. Find the magnitude of an earthquake if the intensity is 9 million I_0.

2. The Richter scale magnitude R of an earthquake of intensity I is defined as $R = \log\left(\frac{I}{I_o}\right)$, where I_0 is a small threshold intensity. Find the magnitude of an earthquake if the intensity is 74 million I_0.

3. The Richter scale magnitude R of an earthquake of intensity I is defined as $R = \log\left(\frac{I}{I_o}\right)$, where I_0 is a small threshold intensity. Find the magnitude of an earthquake if the intensity is 5.4 million I_0.

Review questions: *(Answers to odd questions on page: 464)*

1. The Richter scale magnitude R of an earthquake of intensity I is defined as $R = \log\left(\frac{I}{I_o}\right)$, where I_0 is a small threshold intensity. Find the magnitude of an earthquake if the intensity is 3 million I_0.

2. The Richter scale magnitude R of an earthquake of intensity I is defined as $R = \log\left(\frac{I}{I_o}\right)$, where I_0 is a small threshold intensity. Find the magnitude of an earthquake if the intensity is 15 million I_0.

3. The Richter scale magnitude R of an earthquake of intensity I is defined as $R = \log\left(\frac{I}{I_o}\right)$, where I_0 is a small threshold intensity. Find the magnitude of an earthquake if the intensity is 20.5 million I_0.

4. The Richter scale magnitude R of an earthquake of intensity I is defined as $R = \log\left(\frac{I}{I_o}\right)$, where I_0 is a small threshold intensity. Find the magnitude of an earthquake if the intensity is 0.2 million I_0.

5. The Richter scale magnitude R of an earthquake of intensity I is defined as $R = \log\left(\frac{I}{I_o}\right)$, where I_0 is a small threshold intensity. Find the magnitude of an earthquake if the intensity is 180 million I_0.

The Distance Modulus Formula

- The **distance modulus formula**: $M = 5 \log r - 5$.
- The variables in the distance modulus formula are:
    - **M**, for magnitude, which uses a star's brightness as measured by the observer to calculate its distance from the observer.
    - **r**, the star's distance measured in parsecs, a value equal to approximately 3.3 light years.
- The distance modulus formula is used to calculate high distances.

solving real world problems **Solving real world problems with logs**	Since logarithms empower you to manipulate exponents with great ease and efficiency, they turn out to have numerous real world applications.
Example Given a distance of 1.5 (based on Magnitude) for the star below, find it's distance from Earth in light years. Distance? Earth Star **Sun**	The numbers involved in astronomy are very large. In fact, they are so large that astronomers do not discuss them in terms of traditional units like seconds and miles. The large numbers involved in astronomy create a perfect opportunity for logarithms to help make calculations easier.
To compute distances we can use the distance modulus formula. $M = 5 \log r - 5$ The distance we're told is: $M = 1.5$ We want to find: $M = 1.5$ r Earth Star	Given one of the variables of the distance modulus formula, you can use the logarithm properties to solve for the other variables. In this example, you are told the distance based on magnitude, or brightness of the star to the observer. You are asked to find the distance in light years.
$M = 1.5 = 5 \log r - 5$ | 1 parsec = 3.3 light years $6.5 = 5 \log r$ $\frac{6.5}{5} = \log r$ So: $r = 10^{\frac{6.5}{5}}$ $= 10^{1.3}$ *Answer* $= \boxed{19.95...\text{parsecs}}$ 1 parsec = 3.3 light years $= \boxed{65.84}$ *Answer in light years*	Substitute in what you know and try to isolate the log term. Once you have done this, convert back to exponential form and solve. The answer to the distance modulus formula is in parsecs. You can convert the answer to light-years by multiplying by 3.3.

Sample problems:

1. The distance modulus, M, of a star is given by the formula $M = 5 \log r - 5$, where r is the distance from Earth to the star measured in parsecs. If a star is 153 parsecs away, what is its distance modulus?
   Solution: 5.925
   Explanation: $M = 5 \log r - 5 = 5 \log(153) - 5 = 5(2.185) - 5 = 5.925$.

2. The distance r to a star is measured in parsecs and can be obtained by solving the distance modulus formula $M = 5 \log r - 5$ for r. If Vega has a distance modulus M of -0.48, how far is Vega from Earth?
   Solution: 8.02 parsecs
   Explanation: Substitute $M = -0.48$ into the distance modulus formula and solve for r:
   $-0.48 = 5 \log r - 5$; $4.52 = 5 \log r$; $\frac{4.52}{5} = \log r$; $0.904 = \log r$; $r = 10^{0.904} = 8.02$.

3. The distance r to a star is measured in parsecs and can be obtained by solving the distance modulus formula $M = 5\log r - 5$ for r. If Proxima Centauri has a distance modulus of -4.466, how far is Proxima Centauri from Earth in light years?

Solution: 4.22 light years

Explanation: Substitute $M = -4.466$ into the distance modulus formula and solve for r:

$-4.466 = 5\log r - 5$; $0.534 = 5\log r$; $\frac{0.534}{5} = \log r$; $0.1068 = \log r$; $r = 10^{0.1068} = 1.2788$.

Convert 1.2788 parsecs to light years: $1.2788(3.3) = 4.22$ light years.

Practice problems: *(Answers on page: 464)*

1. The distance modulus , M, of a star is given by the formula $M = 5\log r - 5$, where r is the distance from Earth to the star measured in parsecs. If a star is 79.5 parsecs away, what is its distance modulus?

2. The distance r to a star is measured in parsecs and can be obtained by solving the distance modulus formula $M = 5\log r - 5$ for r. If a star has a distance modulus M of -1.27, how far is the star from Earth?

3. The distance r to a star is measured in parsecs and can be obtained by solving the distance modulus formula $M = 5\log r - 5$ for r. If the Andromeda Galaxy has a distance modulus of 24.12, how far is the Andromeda Galaxy from Earth in light years?

Review questions: *(Answers to odd questions on page: 464)*

1. The distance modulus , M, of a star is given by the formula $M = 5\log r - 5$, where r is the distance from Earth to the star measured in parsecs. If a star is 105.2 parsecs away, what is its distance modulus?

2. The distance r to a star is measured in parsecs and can be obtained by solving the distance modulus formula $M = 5\log r - 5$ for r. If a star has a distance modulus M of -0.65, how far is the star from Earth?

3. The distance r to a star is measured in parsecs and can be obtained by solving the distance modulus formula $M = 5\log r - 5$ for r. If a star has a distance modulus M of 2.31, how far is the star from Earth?

4. The distance r to a star is measured in parsecs and can be obtained by solving the distance modulus formula $M = 5\log r - 5$ for r. If the Magellanic Clouds have a distance modulus of 18.56, how far are the Magellanic Clouds from Earth in light years?

5. The distance r to a star is measured in parsecs and can be obtained by solving the distance modulus formula $M = 5\log r - 5$ for r. If a star has a distance modulus of 32.25, how far is the star from Earth in light years?

Solving Exponential Equations

- When solving for variables in the exponents, either the bases will be the same or they will be different.
  - When the bases are the same, you can set the exponents equal to each other.
  - When the bases are different, you must use logarithms to turn the exponents into coefficients. Then isolate for your variable by using the logarithm properties.

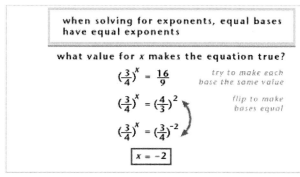

When you are asked to solve equations with variables in the exponents, start by checking the bases. If they are the same, you can set the exponents equal to each other.

It is often a good idea to try to manipulate the bases using exponential properties to make them the same. This process can save you time later.

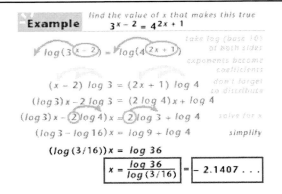

When the bases are not the same, you can still solve the equation.

Since the two expressions are equal, you can equate the logs of both sides and solve for x.

By using the logarithmic properties, you can transform the exponents into coefficients. Use parentheses, especially when variables are nearby.

Distribute across the parentheses. Isolate x.

If you want to clear the logs from your answer, plug these values into your calculator.

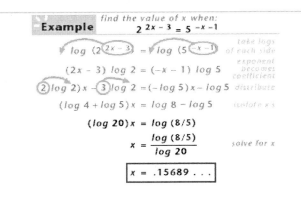

The expressions are equal so you can set up the logs of both sides.

Move the exponents down to be coefficients.

Distribute, being very careful.

Isolate the x-terms.

Solve for x.

Plug the values into your calculator.

Sample problems:

1. Solve for x: $7^{3x^2-12} = 1$

   Solution: $x = \pm 2$.

   Explanation: NOTE: $1 = 7^0$. Express each side with equal bases: $7^{3x^2-12} = 7^0$. Since equal bases have equal exponents, equate the exponents and solve for x: $3x^2 - 12 = 0$; $3x^2 = 12$; $x^2 = 4$; $x = \pm\sqrt{4} = \pm 2$.

2. Solve for x: $3^{4x} = 7^{x+2}$

   Solution: $x = 1.589$

   Explanation: This equation cannot be expressed with equal bases, so equate the logs and apply the logarithmic properties: $\log 3^{4x} = \log 7^{x+2}$; $4x \log 3 = (x+2) \log 7$; $4x \log 3 = x \log 7 + 2 \log 7$. Subtract $x \log 7$ from both sides: $4x \log 3 - x \log 7 = 2 \log 7$. Factor out the x: $x(4 \log 3 - \log 7) = 2 \log 7$. Divide each side by $(4 \log 3 - \log 7)$: $x = \frac{2 \log 7}{4 \log 3 - \log 7} = \frac{1.69}{1.9085 - .8451} = 1.589$.

3. Solve for x: $5^{7x-4} = 3^{2x+1}$

   Solution: $x = 0.831$

   Explanation: This equation cannot be expressed with equal bases, so equate the logs and apply the logarithmic properties: $\log 5^{7x-4} = \log 3^{2x+1}$; $(7x-4) \log 5 = (2x+1) \log 3$; $7x \log 5 - 4 \log 5 = 2x \log 3 + \log 3$. Subtract $2x \log 3$ from both sides and add $4 \log 5$ to both sides: $7x \log 5 - 2x \log 3 = \log 3 + 4 \log 5$. Factor out the x: $x(7 \log 5 - 2 \log 3) = \log 3 + 4 \log 5$. Divide each side by $(7 \log 5 - 2 \log 3)$: $x = \frac{\log 3 + 4 \log 5}{7 \log 5 - 2 \log 3} = \frac{.477 + 2.796}{4.893 - .954} = 0.831$.

Practice problems: *(Answers on page: 464)*

1. Solve for x: $\left(\dfrac{7}{10}\right)^{3x^2-10} = 0.49$

2. Solve for x: $6^{1-4x} = 319$

3. Solve for x: $2^{5x+1} = 3^{2x-4}$

Review questions: *(Answers to odd questions on page: 464)*

1. Solve for x: $2^{3x+1} = 128$

2. Solve for x: $5^{2-x} = 125$

3. Solve for x: $\left(\dfrac{5}{2}\right)^{4x-1} = \dfrac{8}{125}$

4. Solve for x: $3^{\,x} = \dfrac{5}{8}$

5. Solve for x: $5^{x-2} = 3^{3x+2}$

Solving Logarithmic Equations

- When solving an equation made up of logarithms, isolate the logs and then convert to exponential form.
- Always check your answers for extraneous roots. Remember that you can only take the log of positive numbers.

$\log_b (x/y) = \log_b x - \log_b y$ log of quotient = difference of logs **Example** solve for x: $\log(5x-1) = 2 + \log(x-2)$ $\log(5x-1) - \log(x-2) = 2$ *make 1 big log* $\log\left(\dfrac{5x-1}{x-2}\right) = 2$ $\log_{10}\left(\dfrac{5x-1}{x-2}\right) = 2$ $\dfrac{5x-1}{x-2} = 10^2 = 100$ *write log as exponent* $5x-1 = 100(x-2)$ *simplify* *multiply each side by (x-2)* $5x-1 = 100x - 200$ $-95x = -199$ $95x = 199$ $\boxed{x = \dfrac{199}{95}}$	When solving log equations, start by isolating the logs on one side of the equal sign. Next, combine the logs using the log properties. Now write the statement in exponent form. Simplify by cross-multiplying. Finally, solve for x.
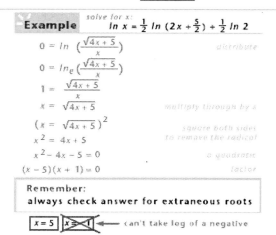 **Example** solve for x: $\ln x = \frac{1}{2}\ln\left(2x + \frac{5}{2}\right) + \frac{1}{2}\ln 2$ $0 = \ln\left(\dfrac{\sqrt{4x+5}}{x}\right)$ *distribute* $0 = \ln_e\left(\dfrac{\sqrt{4x+5}}{x}\right)$ $1 = \dfrac{\sqrt{4x+5}}{x}$ $x = \sqrt{4x+5}$ *multiply through by x* $\left(x = \sqrt{4x+5}\right)^2$ *square both sides to remove the radical* $x^2 = 4x + 5$ $x^2 - 4x - 5 = 0$ *a quadratic* $(x-5)(x+1) = 0$ *factor* **Remember:** always check answer for extraneous roots $\boxed{x=5}$ $\boxed{\cancel{x=1}}$ ← can't take log of a negative	Start by simplifying things if you see an easy way.. Then move all the logs on one side of the equal sign and combine the logs. Convert to exponential form and solve for x. **Remember:** Your log statement is telling you that e^0 equals the radical expression. You know that $e^0 = 1$. After you have found the roots, verify that they are answers for the equation. With logarithms, you have to make sure that the roots do not require you to take the log of a negative number.

Sample problems:

1. Solve for x: $\log x + \log(x+15) = 2$

   Solution: 5

   Explanation: Use the logarithmic properties to combine the logs: $\log x(x+15) = 2$. Express the log as an exponential equation: $10^2 = x(x+15)$. Simplify and manipulate the equation until it is equal to 0: $100 = x^2 + 15x$; $0 = x^2 + 15x - 100$. Factor and solve for x: $0 = (x-5)(x+20)$; $x = 5$ or $x = -20$. But -20 is an extraneous root, so $x = 5$.

2. Solve for x: $\log_7(x^2 - x - 6) - \log_7(x+2) = 1$

   Solution: 10

   Explanation: Use the logarithmic properties to combine the logs: $\log_7 \frac{x^2-x-6}{x+2} = 1$. Express the log as an exponential equation: $7^1 = \frac{x^2-x-6}{x+2}$. Factor the trinomial in the numerator and cancel any common factors: $7 = \frac{(x-3)(x+2)}{x+2}$; $7 = x - 3$. Solve for x: $x = 10$.

3. Solve for x: $2\ln(x-3) = \ln(x+5) + \ln 4$

   Solution: 11

   Explanation: Use the logarithmic properties to combine the logs and move the coefficient: $\ln(x-3)^2 = \ln 4(x+5)$. Simplify and manipulate the equation until it is equal to 0: $\ln(x-3)^2 - \ln(4x+20) = 0$. Use the logarithmic properties again to combine the logs: $\ln \frac{(x-3)^2}{4x+20} = 0$. Express as an exponential equation: $e^0 = \frac{(x-3)^2}{4x+20}$. Simplify and manipulate the equation until it is equal to 0: $1 = \frac{(x-3)^2}{4x+20}$; $4x + 20 = (x-3)^2$; $4x + 20 = x^2 - 6x + 9$; $0 = x^2 - 10x - 11$. Factor and solve for x: $0 = (x+1)(x-11)$; $x = -1$ or $x = 11$. But $x = -1$ is an extraneous root, so $x = 11$.

Practice problems: *(Answers on page: 464)*

1. Solve for x: $\ln(x^2 - x - 12) - \ln(2x+6) = \ln\frac{1}{2}$

2. Solve for x: $\log(x-3) = 1 - \log x$

3. Solve for x: $\log_2(x+1) + \log_2(x-1) = 3$

Review questions: *(Answers to odd questions on page: 464)*

1. Solve for x: $\log_2(25-x) = 3$

2. Solve for x: $\log_2(x+2) = 5$

3. Solve for x: $\log(x+2) + \log(x-1) = 1$

4. Solve for x: $4 + 3\log(2x) = 16$

5. Solve for x: $2 - \ln(3-x) = 0$

Solving Equations with Logarithmic Exponents

- When working with equations with logarithmic expressions, you can use the fact that a logarithm is an exponent to untangle the log pieces and simplify the equation.

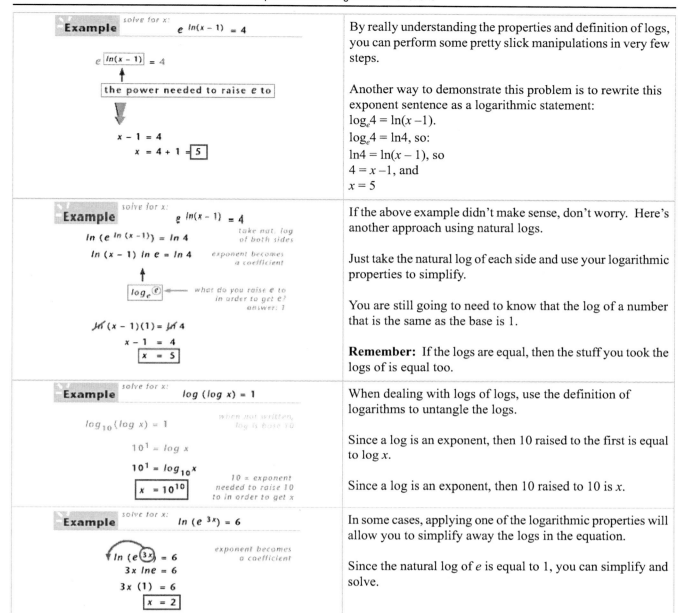

Example solve for x: $e^{\ln(x-1)} = 4$

By really understanding the properties and definition of logs, you can perform some pretty slick manipulations in very few steps.

Another way to demonstrate this problem is to rewrite this exponent sentence as a logarithmic statement:
$\log_e 4 = \ln(x-1)$.
$\log_e 4 = \ln 4$, so:
$\ln 4 = \ln(x-1)$, so
$4 = x - 1$, and
$x = 5$

Example solve for x: $e^{\ln(x-1)} = 4$

If the above example didn't make sense, don't worry. Here's another approach using natural logs.

Just take the natural log of each side and use your logarithmic properties to simplify.

You are still going to need to know that the log of a number that is the same as the base is 1.

Remember: If the logs are equal, then the stuff you took the logs of is equal too.

Example solve for x: $\log(\log x) = 1$

When dealing with logs of logs, use the definition of logarithms to untangle the logs.

Since a log is an exponent, then 10 raised to the first is equal to $\log x$.

Since a log is an exponent, then 10 raised to 10 is x.

Example solve for x: $\ln(e^{3x}) = 6$

In some cases, applying one of the logarithmic properties will allow you to simplify away the logs in the equation.

Since the natural log of e is equal to 1, you can simplify and solve.

Sample problems:

1. Solve for x: $e^{\ln(x-3)} = 9 - 2x$

   Solution: 4

   Explanation: Since $e^{\ln x} = x$, $e^{\ln(x-3)} = 9 - 2x$; $x - 3 = 9 - 2x$. Solve for x: $3x = 12$; $x = 4$.

2. Solve for x: $\ln(e^{5x+1}) = 7x$

   Solution: $\dfrac{1}{2}$

   Explanation: Apply the logarithmic property of exponents: $\ln(e^{5x+1}) = 7x$; $5x + 1(\ln e) = 7x$. Since $\ln e = 1$: $5x + 1 = 7x$. Solve for x: $1 = 2x$; $x = \frac{1}{2}$.

3. Solve for x: $1 = \log_2(\log_2 3x)$

Solution: $\dfrac{4}{3}$

Explanation: Express the log as an exponential equation: $2^1 = \log_2 3x$. Again, express the log as an exponential equation: $2^2 = 3x$. Solve for x: $4 = 3x$; $x = \frac{4}{3}$.

Practice problems: *(Answers on page: 464)*

1. Solve for x: $e^{\ln(4-x)} = 2x + 1$

2. Solve for x: $1 + x = e^{\ln(4x)}$

3. Solve for x: $\log_{\frac{1}{2}}(\log_{\frac{1}{2}} 5x - 1) = 0$

Review questions: *(Answers to odd questions on page: 464)*

1. Solve for x: $e^{\ln(x+4)} = 10 - x$

2. Solve for x: $\ln\left(e^{2x}\right) = x + 5$

3. Solve for x: $3x + 7 = \ln\left(e^{x+10}\right)$

4. Solve for x: $3 = \log_2\left(\log_2 4x\right)$

5. Solve for x: $2 = \log_3\left(\log_2\left(5x - 3\right)\right)$

Compound Interest

The **compound interest formula**: $A = P\left(1 + \left(\dfrac{r}{m}\right)\right)^{tm}$.

Example Professor Burger's Car Problem Professor Burger wants to buy a car. It costs $30,000, and he only has $27,000. If he invests it in a bank account at 6% interest compounded quarterly, how long will he have to wait before it matures to $30,000? Burger's Dreamboat	To solve this problem, you will need to use the techniques for solving exponential equations. You are asked to find out how many years it will take for Dr. Burger to accumulate the necessary funds.
Logarithmic formula: $A = P\left(1 + \left(\frac{r}{m}\right)\right)^{tm}$ A = The future value P = Present value r = The interest rate m = Number of compounding per year t = Number of years	The **compound interest formula** is designed for such situations. Substitute in the facts you know and you will be able to determine what you want to know.
$30,000 = 27,000\left(1 + \frac{.06}{4}\right)^{4t}$ *Do not know the number of years we invest*	After all the facts are substituted, the only variable left is t for the amount of time required.
$\dfrac{30,000}{27,000} = \left(1 + \frac{.06}{4}\right)^{4t}$ *Now to get coefficients, take logs of both sides*	Begin to solve. Isolate the exponential term. Simplify the fraction because you can.
$\ln\left(\frac{30}{27}\right) = \ln\left(\left(1 + \frac{.06}{4}\right)^{4t}\right)$ *Becomes a coefficient*	Now take the natural log of both sides.

$\ln\left(\frac{30}{27}\right) = 4t\ln\left(1+\frac{.06}{4}\right)$ ◄— *now solve for t*

$t = \dfrac{\ln\left(\frac{30}{27}\right)}{4\ln\left(1+\frac{.06}{4}\right)}$

Using the log properties, transform the exponent to be a coefficient.

Simplify for *t* and solve with your calculator.

$t = \boxed{1.769...\text{years}}$ ◄— *Answer*

Burger's Dreamboat

You are proudly able to announce to Dr. Burger that he will need 1.769 years if he follows this plan to save up the money for his dream car.

Sample problems:

1. Suppose you invest $3,000 into an account with a 7.5% interest rate where the interest is compounded monthly. What will the balance be after 9 months?
   Solution: $3,173.03
   Explanation: Substitute $P = 3,000$; $r = 7.5\% = .075$; $m = 12$; and $t = 9$ months (0.75 years) into the compound interest formula, $A = P\left(1+\dfrac{r}{m}\right)^{tm}$ and simplify:

   $A = 3,000\left(1+\dfrac{0.075}{12}\right)^{0.75(12)} = 3,000(1.00625)^9 = 3,000(1.057676951) = 3173.03.$
   So, the balance will be $3,173.03.

2. If you take out a loan of $19,000 at 12% interest, compounded daily, after how many years would the balance owed become $25,000?
   Solution: 2.29 years
   Explanation: From the problem: $P = 19,000$; $r = 12\% = .12$; $m = 365$; $A = 25,000$. Substitute these values into the compound interest formula: $A = P\left(1+\frac{r}{m}\right)^{tm} \Rightarrow 25,000 = 19,000\left(1+\frac{12}{365}\right)^{365t}$.
   Solve for t, divide each side by 19,000 and simplify within the parentheses: $\frac{25}{19} = 1.000329^{365t}$.
   Take a natural log of each side: $\ln\frac{25}{19} = \ln 1.000329^{365t}$. Apply the log of a power property:
   $\ln\frac{25}{19} = 365t(\ln 1.000329)$. Find each natural log with a calculator: $.27443685 = 365t(.00032895)$.
   Solve for t: $365t = 834.28135$; $t = 2.29$.

3. Suppose you invested $5,000 into an account where the interest was compounded weekly. If after 35 years you had $116,500, what was the interest rate?
   Solution: 9%
   Explanation: Substitute the values from the problem into the compound interest formula:
   $116,500 = 5,000\left(1+\frac{x}{52}\right)^{52(35)}$. Simplify and solve for x: $\frac{116,500}{5,000} = \left(1+\frac{x}{52}\right)^{1820}$;
   $23.3 = \left(1+\frac{x}{52}\right)^{1820}$; $\sqrt[1820]{23.3} = 1+\frac{x}{52}$; $1.001731417 = 1+\frac{x}{52}$; $\frac{x}{52} = 0.001731417$;
   $x = .09$. So the interest rate was 9%.

Practice problems: *(Answers on page: 464)*

1. Using the compound interest formula, how much would you need to invest at 6.5% interest to have $200,000 in 6 years, compounded monthly?

2. If Nick has $2,500 to invest and he wants to invest in a program that compounds twice a year so that he will have $3,000 in 3 years, what rate of interest must he find for his investment to be successful?

3. If you invest $10,000 at 9.5% interest, compounded semi-monthly, how long will it take for the balance to reach $50,000?

Review questions: *(Answers to odd questions on page: 464)*

1. Suppose you invest $5,000 at 9% interest. How long would it take your money to double if the interest is compounded semiannually (twice a year)?

2. Using the compound interest formula, how much would you have to invest at 7% interest, compounded quarterly, to have $15,000 in 20 years?

3. If you take out a loan of $19,000 at 12% interest, compounded daily, in how many years would it accumulate to a $25,000 loan?

4. Kris invests $800 at 3% compounded monthly. How long will it take her investment to reach $930?

5. How much should be deposited in an account paying 4% interest compounded monthly in order to have a balance of $14,500 after 6 years?

Predicting Change

- When working with equations with log expressions, you can use the definition of logarithms to untangle the log and simplify the equation.

Example The Used Car Dealership Problem 	Here is another practice problem to show you how to manipulate equations that have logarithmic parts. **THE SET-UP:** Dr. Burger conjectures that the number of used car dealers in a town increases logarithmically in relation to the amount of time since the first used car dealership was introduced.
$P = 500 \log(2t + 3)$ ← *Solve for t* $P =$ Number of used cars dealers $t =$ Number of months since 1st car dealership was introduced	This is the equation Dr. Burger gives. Anytime you get a scientific equation it is a very good idea to make sure you know what all the variables represent. A list is a great way to check.
$P = 500 \log(2t + 3)$ $\dfrac{P}{500} = \log_{10}(2t + 3)$ $10^{P/500} = 2t + 3$ $10^{P/500} - 3 = 2t$ $\boxed{t = \dfrac{10^{P/500} - 3}{2}}$ ← *Answer*	The equation is set up to solve for P. If you wanted to find the t, you would rewrite the equation in terms of P. You are going to need your log properties to do that.
How long will it take for 600 car dealers to come about? $\boxed{t = \dfrac{10^{P/500} - 3}{2}}$ ← *Answer* $t = \dfrac{10^{\frac{600}{500}} - 3}{2}$ $= \dfrac{10^{\frac{6}{5}} - 3}{2}$ 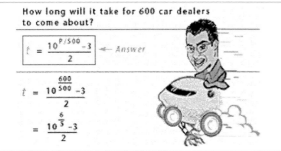	You are asked to determine how long it will be until there are 600 used car salesmen living in your town. Substitute in the value of P and solve for t. Simplify the equation. Let your calculator help you with the final answer.
$t = \boxed{6.4244...\text{months}}$ ← *Answer*	After a little manipulation, your answer is 6.4244 months. That isn't very much time for 600 car dealers to move to their new homes!

Sample problems:

1. The longevity (in years) of ancient empires can be estimated by $T = (500)\ln\dfrac{F}{B}$, where B and F are the populations at the beginning and end of the empire, respectively. One of the Han dynasties lasted for 550 years and the beginning population was 100,000. Estimate the end population of that Han dynasty.

   Solution: 300,417

   Explanation: Substitute $T = 550$ and $B = 100,000$ into the equation $T = (500)\ln\frac{F}{B}$:

   $550 = (500)\ln\frac{F}{100,000}$. Solve for F: $\frac{550}{500} = \ln\frac{F}{100,000}$; $1.1 = \ln\frac{F}{100,000}$; $e^{1.1} = e^{\ln\frac{F}{100,000}}$; $3.004166 = \frac{F}{100,000}$; $F = 300,416.6024$. So the end population is estimated to have been 300,417.

2. The population of Boomtown has been rising according to the model $A = pe^{0.03t}$, where p is the population in 1998 and A is the population t years later. The population in 1998 was 10,000. According to this model, how many years should it take for the population to increase by 9,350?

   Solution: 22

   Explanation: From the problem, $p = 10,000$ and $A = 10,000 + 9,350 = 19,350$. Substitute the value into $A = pe^{0.03t}$ and solve for t: $19,350 = 10,000e^{0.03t}$; $e^{0.03t} = \frac{19,350}{10,000}$; $e^{0.03t} = 1.935$; $\ln e^{0.03t} = \ln 1.935$; $0.03t = .660107$; $t = 22$. So, after 22 years the population will increase by 9,350.

3. A certain model of car depreciates according to the function $V = Ne^{-0.23t}$, where N is the cost of the car when it was new and V is its value t years later. How old is a car of this type if it cost $18,000 new and is now worth $2,000?

   Solution: $9\dfrac{1}{2}$

   Explanation: Substitute $N = 18,000$ and $V = 2,000$ into $V = Ne^{-0.23t}$ and solve for t: $2,000 = 18,000e^{-0.23t}$; $e^{-0.23t} = \frac{2,000}{18,000}$; $e^{-0.23t} = \frac{1}{9}$; $\ln e^{-0.23t} = \ln\frac{1}{9}$; $-0.23t = -2.1972246$; $t = 9.55$. So, the car is worth $2,000 after 9.55, or about $9\frac{1}{2}$ years.

Practice problems: *(Answers on page: 464)*

1. In chemistry, pH is given by the formula: $pH = -\log[H_3O^+]$, where H_3O^+ is the hydronium ion concentration in moles per liter. Given that the pH of hydrochloric acid is equal to 2.0, what is the concentration of the hydronium ion in moles per liter?

2. In recent years the number of cell phones c (in millions) in use in the U.S. has followed the exponential curve $c = 2150(1 - e^{-0.017t})$, where t is the number of years since 1998. Predict the year in which cell phone usage will reach 208.5 million.

3. The percent of children growing up in the U.S. without a father in the years since 1900 can be represented by this formula: $f(x) = \dfrac{25}{1 + 1364.3e^{-\frac{x}{9.316}}}$ such that $x =$ number of years since 1900 and $f(x) =$ the number of children as a percent who are growing up without a father. Predict the year in which 24.1% of the children in the U.S. will be without a father.

Review questions: *(Answers to odd questions on page: 464)*

1. The trout population in an Alaskan lake is increasing according to $f = 8000/(1 + 18e - 0.2t)$, where t is the number of months since the ice broke. How many trout f are there in that lake 6 months after the ice broke?

2. The number of Allied troops that landed in France in World War II, beginning with June 6, 1944 ('D Day'), follows the logistics curve $A = 2,000,000(1 - e - 0.217t)$, where t is the number of months after D Day. Find the number of troops landed by the Battle of the Bulge (6 months after D Day).

3. In an amplifier, the power gain, P, is given by the function $P = 10 \log \dfrac{P_{OUT}}{P_{IN}}$ where P_{IN} is the power input in watts and P_{OUT} is the power output in watts. If an amplifier has a power gain of 20 watts and the input power was .15 watts, find the power output in watts.

4. According to Dr . Burger's model, the population of used car salesmen in a city increases according to the following formula: $P = 500 \log(2t + 3)$, where P is the population of used car salesmen and t is the time in months since the first used car dealership opens. When will the population of used car salesmen equal 300?

5. The garment industry approximates the percentage P (between 1 and 100) of young adult women who are x inches tall or less by $P = \dfrac{100}{[1 + e(43 + 0.67x)]}$. Find the percentage of women who are 5'5" tall or less.

An Introduction to Exponential Growth and Decay

- Population growth is one example of an exponential function. Radioactive decay is also an exponential function.
- When working with exponential functions, use logarithms to turn exponents into coefficients.

Any kind of population growth is exponential growth. **The amount of growth that is occurring depends upon the size of the population at that moment.** • Larger population • More reproduction • More growth • Smaller population • Less reproduction • Less growth	Populations tend to increase exponentially. The reason for this is that when populations are larger, there are more members producing more offspring. Smaller populations have to grow more slowly since they don't have as many members to reproduce.
Decay is also exponential.	In radioactive decay, radioactive materials have something called a half-life. This is the amount of time it takes for the material to reduce in radioactivity by half. Each time this interval of time passes, the material becomes half as much radioactive. Notice that it never becomes non-radioactive.

Example

Population of Williamstown, MA

Model: $P(t) = 12,400(1.14)^t$

A) What is the population in 3 years?

$P(3) = 12,400(1.14)^3$

$\approx 18,371$

Given this formula, calculate the population after three years.

This question is pretty basic. You can just substitute and solve.

B) What is the population in 4.25 years?

$p(4.25) = 12,400(1.14)^{4.25}$

An exponent within a log can be pulled out as a coefficient of that log. $= 12,400\left(e^{\ln\left((1.14)^{4.25}\right)}\right)$

Now you can use your calculator. $= 12,400\left(e^{4.25 \ln 1.14}\right)$

$\approx 21,640$

Here is the formula used another way.

By setting 1.14 raised to 4.25 equal to its natural log all to base e, you gain the ability to use the log properties on the exponent.

Now solving the equation is much easier!

Sample problems:

1. The number of streptococcus bacteria in a petri dish, kept in a medical laboratory, is $A = pe^{0.047t}$, where p is the initial number (when the culture was first brought in) and A is the final number of bacteria after t hours. If a culture containing 40,000 bacteria was brought in, how many will there be after 10 hours? After a week?
Solution: 64,000 and 107,460,590
Explanation: To determine the number of bacteria in the dish after 10 hours, substitute $t = 10$ and $p = 40,000$ into $A = pe^{0.047t}$ and simplify:
$A = 40,000e^{0.047(10)} = 40,000e^{0.47} = 40,000(1.599994193) = 63,999.8 \approx 64,000$.
So, after 10 hours there are about 64,000 bacteria in the dish. After a week ($24 \cdot 7 = 168$ hours):
$A = 40,000e^{0.047(168)} = 40,000e^{7.896} = 40,000(2,686.514748) = 107,460,589.9$.
So, after a week there are 107,460,590 bacteria in the dish.

2. The population of a certain city is given by the function $P(t) = 45,000e^{0.05t}$, where t is the time in years. How many years will it take for the city's population to reach 90,000?
Solution: 14
Explanation: Substitute $P(t) = 90,000$ into $P(t) = 45,000e^{0.05t}$ and solve for t:
$90,000 = 45,000e^{0.05t}$; $e^{0.05t} = 2$; $\ln e^{0.05t} = \ln 2$; $0.05t = 0.6931471806$;
$t = 13.86 \approx 14$. So, the population will reach 90,000 after 14 years.

3. The number of streptococcus bacteria in a Petri dish kept in a medical laboratory is $A = pe^{0.047t}$ where p is the initial number (when the culture was first brought in) and A is the final number of bacteria after t hours. If a culture has grown from 75,000 to 2.2 million, how long did that take?
Solution: 72
Explanation: Substitute $p = 75,000$ and $A = 2.2$ million $= 2,200,000$ into $A = pe^{0.047t}$ and solve
for t: $2,200,000 = 75,000e^{0.047t}$; $e^{0.047t} = \frac{88}{3}$; $\ln e^{0.047t} = \ln(\frac{88}{3})$; $0.047t = 3.378724526$;
$t = 71.89 \approx 72$. To grow from 75,000 to 2.2 million took almost 72 hours.

Practice problems: *(Answers on page: 465)*

1. The population of a certain city is given by the function $P(t) = 45,000e^{0.05t}$, where t is the time in years. What is the population of the city when $t = 6$?

2. The number of deer in a wildlife preserve is given by the function $D(t) = 184 \cdot (1.1)^{0.5t}$, where p is the population in 1990 and t is the number of years after 1990. If the population in 1990 was 184, how long will it take for the population to double?

3. Suppose that the population of New York City between the years of 1950 and 1960 can be approximated by the function $P(t) = 1050 \cdot (1.005)^t$, where t is in years, $t = 0$ corresponds to 1950, and $P(t)$ is in the thousands. Between what 2 years from 1950 and 1960 was the population of NYC 1.09 million?

Review questions: *(Answers to odd questions on page: 465)*

1. If not refrigerated, a perishable food item, t days after packing, reaches a bacteria count b according to the formula $b = 5000e^{0.1t}$. How many bacteria will there be in 18 days?

2. A semi-perishable food item should no longer be consumed if its bacteria count b reaches 2.8 million. How long will this take if $b = 500e^{0.1t}$, where t is the number of days since the food was packed?

3. The growth of a city is described by the population function $P(t) = P_0 e^{kt}$, where P_0 is the initial population of the city, t is the time in years, and k is a constant. If the population of the city at $t = 0$ is 13,000 and the population of the city at $t = 2$ is 16,000, what is the population of the city at $t = 4$?

4. Suppose that the population of New York City from 1990 to the present can be modelled by the function $P(t) = 9013 \cdot e^{.08t}$, where t is in years, $t = 0$ corresponds to 1990, and $P(t)$ is in thousands. Assuming that New York City continues to grow at this rate, when will its population reach 25 million?

5. The weight of a certain growing walrus between one and five years old is described by the function $W(t) = 135 \cdot (1.22)2t$, where t is its age in years and $W(t)$ is in pounds. How much weight does the walrus gain over the four year period between $t = 1$ and $t = 5$?

Half-Life

- The **half-life** of a substance is the amount of time it takes for a radioactive material to decay to half of itself. Radioactive decay is an exponential function.

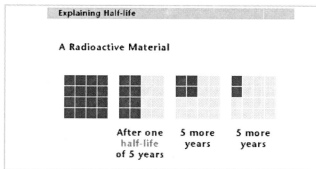

Explaining Half-life

A Radioactive Material

After one half-life of 5 years   5 more years   5 more years

The **half-life** tells you how much time has to pass for a radioactive material to reduce to half of its current mass.

Each time the half-life interval passes, you lose one-half of the material that you had at the beginning of the interval. Think of it like a store that drops its prices 50% every two hours. The price will never equal zero although it will get darn close!

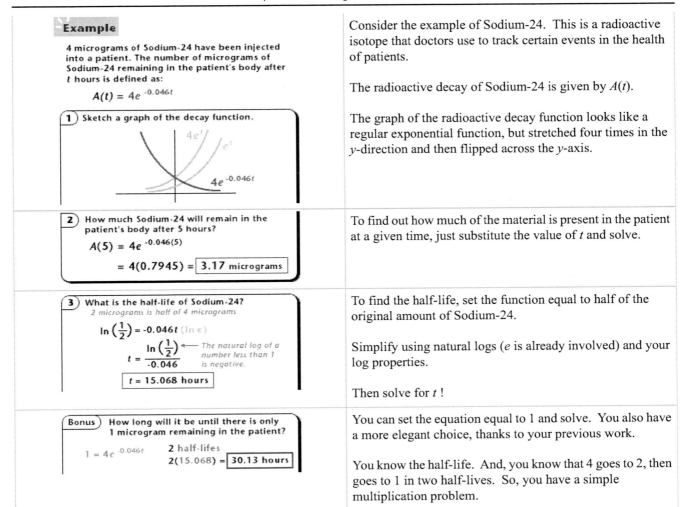

Example

4 micrograms of Sodium-24 have been injected into a patient. The number of micrograms of Sodium-24 remaining in the patient's body after t hours is defined as:

$$A(t) = 4e^{-0.046t}$$

(1) Sketch a graph of the decay function.

$4e^{-0.046t}$

Consider the example of Sodium-24. This is a radioactive isotope that doctors use to track certain events in the health of patients.

The radioactive decay of Sodium-24 is given by $A(t)$.

The graph of the radioactive decay function looks like a regular exponential function, but stretched four times in the y-direction and then flipped across the y-axis.

(2) How much Sodium-24 will remain in the patient's body after 5 hours?

$$A(5) = 4e^{-0.046(5)}$$
$$= 4(0.7945) = \boxed{3.17 \text{ micrograms}}$$

To find out how much of the material is present in the patient at a given time, just substitute the value of t and solve.

(3) What is the half-life of Sodium-24?
2 micrograms is half of 4 micrograms

$$\ln\left(\frac{1}{2}\right) = -0.046t \quad (\ln e)$$

$$t = \frac{\ln\left(\frac{1}{2}\right)}{-0.046} \quad \longleftarrow \text{The natural log of a number less than 1 is negative.}$$

$$\boxed{t = 15.068 \text{ hours}}$$

To find the half-life, set the function equal to half of the original amount of Sodium-24.

Simplify using natural logs (e is already involved) and your log properties.

Then solve for t !

Bonus How long will it be until there is only 1 microgram remaining in the patient?

$$1 = 4e^{-0.046t} \qquad \begin{array}{l} \text{2 half-lifes} \\ 2(15.068) = \boxed{30.13 \text{ hours}} \end{array}$$

You can set the equation equal to 1 and solve. You also have a more elegant choice, thanks to your previous work.

You know the half-life. And, you know that 4 goes to 2, then goes to 1 in two half-lives. So, you have a simple multiplication problem.

Sample problems:

1. The age t (in years) of mummified organic materials can be determined by the function:
    $t = (8300)\ln\dfrac{100}{x}$, where x is the percentage of carbon-14 still remaining. (For example, if $\dfrac{1}{4}$ remains, then $x = 25$). Find the age of a mummified Egyptian ruler if 61% of the carbon-14 remains in his burial wrappings.
    Solution: 4103
    Explanation: Substitute $x = 61$ into $t = (8300)\ln\frac{100}{x}$ and simplify:
    $t = (8300)\ln\frac{100}{61} = (8300)(.4942963218) = 4102.66 \approx 4103$.
    The mummy is 4,103 years old.

2. Carbon-14 is a radioactive substance used by scientists to determine the age of objects. When a plant or animal dies, the carbon-14 within its system begins decaying. The amount of carbon-14 remaining is given by $A = Ce^{-kt}$, where C is the initial amount of carbon-14 in the plant or animal t years after it dies. Given that the half-life of carbon-14 is about 5500 years, how old is a fossilized plant when it has 80% of its original carbon-14 remaining?
    Solution: 1,771

3. Polonium radioactively decays from 410 grams to 0.4 grams in 35 years. What is its half - life (the number of years it takes until half of it remains)? Use the formula $A = pe^{-kt}$, where p is the initial amount, t is the time in years, and A the (smaller) final amount .

Solution: 3.5

Explanation: Begin by finding k. Substitute $A = 0.4$, $p = 410$, and $t = 35$ into $A = pe^{-kt}$ and solve for k: $0.4 = 410e^{-k(35)}$; $\frac{0.4}{410} = e^{-35k}$; $e^{-35k} = .00097561$; $\ln e^{-35k} = \ln .00097561$; $-35k = -6.93245$; $k = 0.19807$. But that is not the answer to the question. Find the half-life by substituting $k = 0.19807$, $p = 410$, and $A = \frac{410}{2} = 205$ (because that is half the original amount) into $A = pe^{-kt}$ and solve for t: $205 = 410e^{-0.19807t}$; $.5 = e^{-0.19807t}$; $\ln e^{-0.19807t} = \ln .5$; $-0.19807t = -0.6931472$; $t = 3.4995 \approx 3.5$. So the half-life is 3.5 years.

Practice problems: *(Answers on page: 465)*

1. Suppose that the decay of polonium, a radioactive element, is described by the function $P(t) = P_0 \cdot (.5)^{.047t}$, where t is the time in years and P_0 is the initial amount of polonium in grams. What percentage of a sample of polonium will remain after 4 years?

2. Sodium-24 is a radioactive substance used for medical purposes. Suppose that a patient is injected with 5mg of sodium-24 at $t = 0$ and that the amount of sodium-24 in the patient's body in milligrams is given by $S(t) = 5e^{-.35t}$, where t is the time in hours. What is the half-life of sodium-24?

3. The amount of radium in a sample after t years is given by the equation $A = pe^{-kt}$, where p is the initial amount of radium in the sample. If the half-life of radium is 1690 years and a sample contains 10g of radium, how much radium will remain after 50 years?

Review questions: *(Answers to odd questions on page: 465)*

1. The half-life of strontium-90 is 25 years. How long will it take a 50 mg sample to decay to a mass of 32 mg?

2. The decay of a radioactive substance is described by the function $A(t) = 5e^{-.1t}$, where t is the time in minutes and $A(t)$ is the mass of the substance in ounces. How many ounces of the substance are left at $t = 8$ minutes?

3. The age t (in years) of an ancient icebound corpse can be determined by the function $t = 7950 \ln\left(\frac{100}{x}\right)$ where x is 100 times the percentage of carbon-14 still remaining in its bones . (For example, if $\frac{1}{2}$ remains, then $x = 50$). Find the percentage of carbon-14 remaining in the bones of the 6,200 year-old Alpine ice man.

4. If 40 milligrams of strontium-90 radioactively decays to 12 milligrams in 30 years, find its half-life (the number of years it takes until half of it remains). Use the formula $A = p \cdot e^{-kt}$, where p is the amount and A the (smaller) final amount.

5. A certain radioactive element has a half-life of 120 years. At $t = 0$ an 80 pound chunk of the element begins decaying away. Find the function $A(t)$ that gives the amount of the element remaining after t years.

Newton's Law of Cooling

• Exponential and logarithmic equations occur frequently in real-world applications. Even refrigeration happens according to an exponential equation.

• **Newton's law of cooling**: $T(t) = A + (T_0 - A)e^{-kt}$.

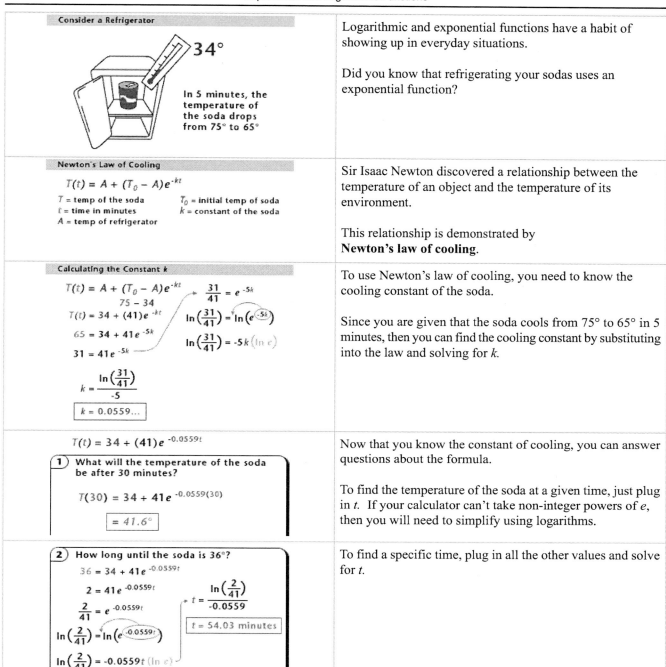

Consider a Refrigerator	Logarithmic and exponential functions have a habit of showing up in everyday situations.
34° — In 5 minutes, the temperature of the soda drops from 75° to 65°	Did you know that refrigerating your sodas uses an exponential function?

Newton's Law of Cooling

$$T(t) = A + (T_0 - A)e^{-kt}$$

T = temp of the soda T_0 = initial temp of soda
t = time in minutes k = constant of the soda
A = temp of refrigerator

Sir Isaac Newton discovered a relationship between the temperature of an object and the temperature of its environment.

This relationship is demonstrated by **Newton's law of cooling**.

Calculating the Constant k

$$T(t) = A + (T_0 - A)e^{-kt}$$
$$75 - 34$$
$$T(t) = 34 + (41)e^{-kt}$$
$$65 = 34 + 41e^{-5k}$$
$$31 = 41e^{-5k}$$

$$\frac{31}{41} = e^{-5k}$$
$$\ln\left(\frac{31}{41}\right) = \ln\left(e^{-5k}\right)$$
$$\ln\left(\frac{31}{41}\right) = -5k\,(\ln e)$$

$$k = \frac{\ln\left(\frac{31}{41}\right)}{-5}$$
$$k = 0.0559\ldots$$

To use Newton's law of cooling, you need to know the cooling constant of the soda.

Since you are given that the soda cools from 75° to 65° in 5 minutes, then you can find the cooling constant by substituting into the law and solving for k.

$$T(t) = 34 + (41)e^{-0.0559t}$$

(1) What will the temperature of the soda be after 30 minutes?

$$T(30) = 34 + 41e^{-0.0559(30)}$$
$$= 41.6°$$

Now that you know the constant of cooling, you can answer questions about the formula.

To find the temperature of the soda at a given time, just plug in t. If your calculator can't take non-integer powers of e, then you will need to simplify using logarithms.

(2) How long until the soda is 36°?

$$36 = 34 + 41e^{-0.0559t}$$
$$2 = 41e^{-0.0559t}$$
$$\frac{2}{41} = e^{-0.0559t}$$
$$\ln\left(\frac{2}{41}\right) = \ln\left(e^{-0.0559t}\right)$$
$$\ln\left(\frac{2}{41}\right) = -0.0559t\,(\ln e)$$

$$t = \frac{\ln\left(\frac{2}{41}\right)}{-0.0559}$$
$$t = 54.03 \text{ minutes}$$

To find a specific time, plug in all the other values and solve for t.

Sample problems:

1. The temperature of a 16 pound turkey in a 325° oven after t minutes is given by the function $T(t) = 325 - 260e^{-0.001822t}$. Find the temperature of the turkey after 2 hours.

   Solution: 141°

   Explanation: Substitute $t = 2$ hours $= 120$ minutes into $T(t) = 355 - 260e^{-0.001822t}$ and simplify:

   $T(120) = 355 - 260e^{-0.001822(120)} = 350 - 260e^{-0.21864} = 350 - 260(0.803612) = 350 - 208.94$
   $= 141.06 \approx 141°$. So the turkey will be 141° after 2 hours.

2. According to Julia Child's The Way to Cook a turkey must be cooked to 165°F. The temperature of a 16 pound turkey in a 325° oven after t minutes is given by the function $T(t) = 325 - 260e^{-0.001822t}$. If Beth wants to serve the turkey at 6:00pm, after letting it cool for 1 hour, what time should she put the turkey in the 325° oven?

    Solution: 12:30pm

    Explanation: Find the time it takes for the turkey to reach 165° by substituting $T(t) = 165$ into $T(t) = 325 - 260e^{-0.001822t}$ and solve for t: $165 = 325 - 260e^{-0.001822t}$; $-160 = -260e^{-0.001822t}$; $\frac{8}{13} = e^{-0.001822t}$; $\ln\frac{8}{13} = \ln e^{-0.001822t}$; $-0.001822t = \ln\frac{8}{13}$; $t = \dfrac{\ln\frac{8}{13}}{-0.001822} = 266.5$. The turkey must cook for about 267 minutes, or 4.45 hours $\approx 4\frac{1}{2}$ hours. She needs to put the turkey in the oven $4\frac{1}{2}$ cook time and 1 cool time $= 5\frac{1}{2}$ hours before 6:00, or at 12:30pm.

3. Suppose a pie is removed from an oven when it reaches 350°F. The pie is let to cool in a room that is 70°F. After 45 minutes, the pie cools to 150°F. Use Newton's Law of cooling to write a function that gives the temperature of the pie, T, as a function of time, t.

    Solution: $T(t) = 70 + 280e^{-0.02784t}$

Practice problems: *(Answers on page: 465)*

1. A soda is placed in a refrigerator maintaining a constant temperature of 36 degrees F at time $t = 0$. The temperature of the soda after t minutes in the refrigerator is described by the function $S(t) = 36 + 34e^{-0.021t}$. Based on this model, how cold will the soda be after 45 minutes?

2. A soda is placed in a refrigerator maintaining a constant temperature of 36 degrees F at time $t = 0$. The temperature of the soda after t minutes in the refrigerator is described by the function $S(t) = 36 + 34e^{-0.021t}$. Based on this model, how long will it take for the soda to reach 40°?

3. Suppose a juice box that is 75° is placed into a 40° refrigerator. After 30 minutes the juice had cooled to 60°. Write a function for the temperature of the juice as a function of time.

Review questions: *(Answers to odd questions on page: 465)*

1. A cup of tea with a temperature of 200° Fahrenheit is placed in a room that has a temperature of 70°F. After 10 minutes the tea's temperature has cooled to 150°F. What is the tea's temperature after 15 minutes? Use the formula $T(t) = T_s + D_0e^{-kt}$.

2. A 150° cup of tea cools to 140° in a 70° room after one minute. How long will it take for the tea to cool to 91°?

3. A chocolate chip cookie is removed from the oven when it is 170°. The cookie cools to 145° after two minutes in a 72° room. What is the temperature of the cookie 15 minutes after it is removed from the oven?

4. When a can of soda is placed in a 30° freezer for 5 minutes, the temperature decreases from 70° to 67°. How long must the soda remain in the freezer before the temperature decreases to 40°?

5. The temperature of a soda t minutes after it is placed in a refrigerator is given by the function $S(t) = 36 + 34e^{-0.021t}$. Based on this model, how long will it take for the temperature of the soda to reach 46 degrees?

Continuously Compounded Interest

*   Another real-world application of exponential formulas can be found in the world of finance. Banks use exponential equations to continuously compound interest.

*   **Continuously compounded interest formula**: $A = Pe^{rt}$.

The Compounded Interest Formula

$$A = P\left(1 + \frac{r}{m}\right)^{tm}$$

$$A = P\left(1 + \frac{r}{m}\right)^{tm}$$

$$\left(1 + \frac{1}{n}\right)^{n} \longrightarrow e$$

Putting in larger and larger values of n, you approach e.

$$e = 2.718...$$

The more often a bank compounds the interest on your money, the more money you will make. Wouldn't it be nice if they compounded the interest continuously instead of quarterly or annually?

Using the definition of the number e, you can find a formula that computes the interest compounded continuously.

The Compounded Interest Formula

$$A = Pe^{rt} \quad \begin{array}{l}\text{formula for continuously}\\ \text{compounded interest}\end{array}$$

A = amount accumulated
P = principal t = number of years
r = interest rate m = compoundings per year

So the formula for **continuously compounded interest** looks easier than the compound interest formula.

Solving continuously compounded interest questions will often require that you use logarithms to "bring down" the exponents.

Keep in mind that $\ln e$ is the same as $\log_e e$. They are both equal to 1.

Example Suppose you invest $300 into an account that compounds continuously at 5.25%. How long would you have to wait to double your money?

$$A = Pe^{rt}$$
$$2P = Pe^{0.0525t}$$
$$2 = e^{0.0525t}$$
$$\ln 2 = \ln(e^{0.0525t})$$
$$\ln 2 = 0.0525t \,(\ln e)$$
$$t = \frac{\ln 2}{0.0525} = \boxed{13.202 \text{ years}}$$

In this example, you are asked to find how long it will take to double your money.

Write the formula.
Substitute in the known facts.

Note how a potentially frustrating problem simplifies when you convert it to a logarithm problem. Then solve, as requested, for t.

In 13.202 years, you will double the money you invested in your continuously compounding bank account.

Sample problems:

1. The government of Monaco borrowed $10,000,000 from the U.S. at 6%. How much will Monaco owe the U.S. in 20 years, continuously compounded?
   Solution: $33,201,169
   Explanation: Substitute $P = 10,000,000$, $r = 6\% = .06$, and $t = 20$ into $A = Pe^{rt}$ and
   simplify: $A = 10,000,000e^{(.06)(20)} = 10,000,000(3.320116923) = 33,201,169.23$.
   So, Monaco will owe the US $33,201,169 after 20 years.

2. Manuel is considering investing some money in an account where the interest is compounded continuously at 10%. How long would it take for his investment to double?
   Solution: Almost 7 years
   Explanation: It may appear that there is not enough information to answer this question, but if the investment is doubled then $A = 2P$. Substitute $A = 2P$ and $r = 10\% = .1$ into $A = Pe^{rt}$ and solve for t:
   $2P = Pe^{.1t}$; $\frac{2P}{P} = e^{.1t}$; $2 = e^{.1t}$; $\ln 2 = \ln e^{.1t}$; $.1t = \ln 2$; $t = \frac{\ln 2}{.1} = 6.93 \approx 7$. So, it takes almost 7 years for an investment to double in this account.

3. Suppose $12,000 is invested at 9%. If the interest is compounded continuously, how long will it take for the investment to mature to $13,000?

Solution: Almost a year

Explanation: Substitute $A = 13,000$, $P = 12,000$, and $r = 9\% = .09$ into $A = Pe^{rt}$ and solve

for t: $13,000 = 12,000e^{.09t}$; $\frac{13}{12} = e^{.09t}$; $\ln\frac{13}{12} = \ln e^{.09t}$; $.09t = \ln\frac{13}{12}$; $t = \dfrac{\ln\frac{13}{12}}{.09} = .89 \approx 1$.

So, the investment will mature to $13,000 after almost 1 year.

Practice problems: *(Answers on page: 465)*

1. If $24,000 is invested at an annual interest rate of 8.5% and the interest compounds continuously, find the balance after 6 years.

2. If $5,000 is invested in an account with 7.5% interest compounded continuously, how long will it take for the investment to increase by $2,000?

3. Suppose an account offers 15.5% interest compounded continuously. How long does it take for investments in this account to triple?

Review questions: *(Answers to odd questions on page: 465)*

1. If you want to invest $6,000 and have it increase to $7,500 in 3 years, what rate of interest is necessary if your investment is compounded continuously?

2. Joe invests $25,000 at 4.25% compounded continuously. How long will it take for the money to double? Use $A = Pe^{rt}$.

3. If you want to invest $2,500 and have it grow to be $3,000 in two years, what rate of interest is necessary if your investment is compounding continuously.

4. Suppose an account offers 8.9% interest compounded continuously. How long does it take for investments in this account to quadruple?

5. In which account will a given balance double faster, an account that is compounded monthly at 8% or an account that is compounded continuously at 7%?

Conic Sections

An Introduction to Conic Sections

- A **conic section** is a curve made by intersecting a cone with a plane. The conic sections include the **point**, **line**, **circle**, **ellipse**, **parabola**, and **hyperbola**.

		By slicing a cone with a plane in different ways, you can generate various **conic sections**. Here the cone is sliced at its very tip. The result is a single **point**.
		If the cone is sliced alone its side, the result is a **line**.
		Here the cone is sliced horizontally. The result is a **circle**.
		If the cone is sliced at an angle, the result is not a circle but an **ellipse**.
		If the slice is made parallel to the side of the cone, then the result is a **parabola**.
		When the slice is made vertically, the result is a **hyperbola**.

An Introduction to Parabolas

- A parabola consists of the set of points that are equidistant from a point called the **focus** and a line called the **directrix**.

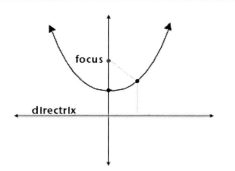

Associated with every parabola is a point called the focus and a line called the directrix.

The parabola itself is the set of points equidistant from the focus and the directrix. Any point on the parabola is as far away from the focus as it is from the directrix. Notice how the focus is inside the curve of the parabola and the directrix is outside.

Parabolas have many interesting properties. For example, if a light is placed at the focus of a reflective parabola, the parabola will reflect the light rays directly outwards. This fact is put to good use in flashlights, satellite dishes, and other objects in the real world.

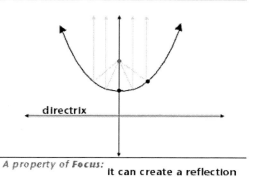

As you probably recall, parabolas are described algebraically by quadratic functions. This example is described by the equation, $y = (x + 1)^2 - 3$.

The curve of a parabola graphed in the Cartesian plane is the same as the curve of a parabola generated by slicing a cone!

Sample problems:

1. Describe the graph of $y = (x - 3)^2 + 5$ in terms of the parabola's direction and vertex.

   <u>Solution</u>: direction: parabola opens up, vertex: (3, 5).

   <u>Explanation</u>: The equation is in vertex form, $y = a(x - h)^2 + k$, so $a = 1$, $h = 3$, and $k = 5$. The direction of a parabola is described by the value of a: if a is positive, the parabola opens up, if a is negative, the parabola opens down. Thus the parabola opens up since a is positive. The vertex is located at (h, k), so the vertex is at (3, 5).

2. True or false: The graph of $y = -x^2 + 2x - 1$ is a parabola that opens down, the vertex is at $(1,0)$, the y-intercept is -1, and it has 2 roots.

Solution: False

Explanation: The equation is in standard form, $y = ax^2 + bx + c$, so $a = -1$, $b = 2$, and $c = -1$. Since a is negative the parabola does open down. The vertex of a parabola in standard form is at (h, k) where $h = \dfrac{-b}{2a}$ and $k = f(h)$. Find the vertex: $h = \dfrac{-2}{2(-1)} = 1$ and $k = -(1)^2 + 2(1) - 1 = 0$, so $(1, 0)$ is the vertex. The y-intercept is the value of y when $x = 0$, or c for all quadratic equations in standard form, so the y-intercept is -1. The root of the parabola is the x-intercept(s). The vertex of this parabola is on the x-axis, therefore there is only one x-intercept, or one root, not two.

3. Does the equation $y = x^2 + 2$ match the following graph?

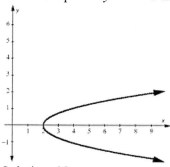

Solution: No

Explanation: The parabola opens sideways, so the y term in the equation must be squared, not the x term.

Practice problems: *(Answers on page: 465)*

1. True or false: The graph of $f(x) = 3x^2$ is a parabola that opens up with its vertex is at $(0,0)$.

2. Graph $y = x^2$.

3. True or false: The following graph represents the equation $y^2 + 2y + x = 0$.

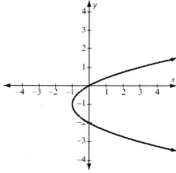

Review questions: *(Answers to odd questions on page: 465)*

1. Describe the graph of $y = (x+1)^2$ in terms of the parabola's direction and vertex.

2. True or false: The graph of $y = -x^2 + 4x + 3$ is a parabola that opens down, the vertex is at $(2, 7)$, and the y-intercept is -3.

3. True or false: The graph of $y = 4x^2 + 6x - 1$ is a parabola that opens up, the vertex is at $\left(-\frac{3}{4}, \frac{13}{4}\right)$, and the y-intercept is -1.

4. True or false: The graph of $x = -\frac{1}{2}y^2$ is a parabola that opens sideways.

5. True or false: The graph of $y = -x^2 + 6x - 1$ is a parabola that opens down, the vertex is at $(3,8)$, the y-intercept is -1, and it has 2 roots.

Determining Information about a Parabola from Its Equation

- A parabola consists of the set of points that are equidistant from a point called the focus and a line called the directrix.
- A parabola of the form $y = cx^2$ has its focus at the point $\left(0, \frac{1}{4c}\right)$ and its directrix along the line $y = -\frac{1}{4c}$.

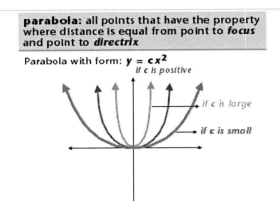

REMEMBER: If $|c| > 1$, then the parabola is narrow as compared to $y = x^2$. If $|c| < 1$, then the parabola is wider than $y = x^2$.

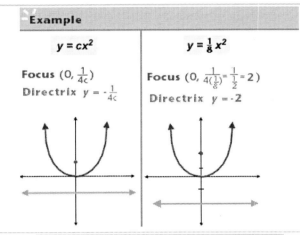

It is relatively easy to find the focus and directrix of a parabola of the form $y = cx^2$. In general, for a parabola of the form $y = cx^2$, the focus is located at the point $\left(0, \frac{1}{4c}\right)$ and the directrix is the line described by the equation $y = -\frac{1}{4c}$.

You can apply these general formulas for a specific parabola like $y = \frac{1}{8}x^2$.

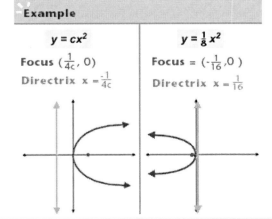

Similar formulas exist for the focus and directrix of a parabola of the form $x = cy^2$.

For a parabola of the form $x = cy^2$, the focus is located at the point $\left(\frac{1}{4c}, 0\right)$ and the directrix is the line $x = -\frac{1}{4c}$.

Sample problems:

1. Identify the focus and directrix of the parabola described by $x = -\frac{5}{6}y^2$.

   Solution: Focus: $\left(-\frac{3}{10}, 0\right)$, directrix: $x = \frac{3}{10}$

   Explanation: The graph of $x = -\frac{5}{6}y^2$ is a parabola of the form $y = cy^2$, so the focus is at $\left(\frac{1}{4c}, 0\right)$ and the directrix is the line $x = -\frac{1}{4c}$. Find the focus: $\frac{1}{4c} = \frac{1}{4\left(-\frac{5}{6}\right)} = -\frac{1}{2\left(\frac{5}{3}\right)} = -\frac{1}{\frac{10}{3}} = -\frac{3}{10}$, so the focus is the point $\left(-\frac{3}{10}, 0\right)$. Find the directrix: $-\frac{1}{4c} = -\left(-\frac{3}{10}\right) = \frac{3}{10}$, so the directrix is the line $x = \frac{3}{10}$.

2. Consider a parabola with the vertex at the origin, that opens up, and that passes through the point $(-3, 18)$. Find the focus of that parabola.

   Solution: $\left(0, \frac{1}{8}\right)$

   Explanation: To determine the focus, first write the equation that describes that parabola using vertex form. Substitute the (h, k) values from the vertex and the (x, y) values from the point into $y = a(x - h)^2 + k$ (this is the correct form since the parabola opens up, not sideways): $18 = a(-3 - 0)^2 + 0$. Solve for a: $18 = 9a$; $a = 2$. Next substitute a, h, and k back into vertex form to write the equation of the parabola: $y = 2(x - 0)^2 + 0$; $y = 2x^2$. Now, substitute that coefficient into the formula for the focus: $\frac{1}{4c} = \frac{1}{4(2)} = \frac{1}{8}$, so the focus is at $\left(0, \frac{1}{8}\right)$.

3. Identify the focus and directrix of the parabola whose equation is $y = 3x^2$.

   Solution: Focus: $\left(0, \frac{1}{12}\right)$, directrix: $y = -\frac{1}{12}$

   Explanation: The graph of $y = 3x^2$ is a parabola of the form $y = cx^2$, so the focus is at $\left(0, \frac{1}{4c}\right)$ and the directrix is the line $y = -\frac{1}{4c}$. Find the focus: $\frac{1}{4c} = \frac{1}{4 \cdot 3} = \frac{1}{12}$, so the focus is the point $\left(0, \frac{1}{12}\right)$. Find the directrix: $y = -\frac{1}{4c} = -\frac{1}{12}$, so the directrix is the line $y = -\frac{1}{12}$.

Practice problems: *(Answers on page: 465)*

1. Consider the parabola $x = \frac{2}{3}y^2$. Identify the vertex and the focus.

2. Consider the parabola $y = -\frac{1}{4}x^2$. Identify the focus and the directrix.

3. Consider a parabola with the vertex at the origin, that opens sideways, and passes through the point $(8, 4)$. Identify the focus.

Review questions: *(Answers to odd questions on page: 465)*

1. Consider the parabola $8x^2 = y$. Identify the vertex and focus.

2. Consider the parabola $x = -\frac{1}{3}y^2$. Identify the vertex and focus.

3. Consider the parabola $y = -\frac{3}{4}x^2$. Identify the focus and the directrix.

4. Consider a parabola with the vertex at the origin, that opens up, and that passes through the point $(6,18)$. Find the focus of that parabola.

5. Consider a parabola with the vertex at the origin, that opens to the right, and that passes through the point $(-12,-6)$. Find the focus of that parabola.

Writing an Equation for a Parabola

- A parabola consists of the set of points that are equidistant from a point called the focus and a line called the directrix.
- The vertex of a parabola is the point where the curve of the parabola changes direction. It is either the highest or lowest point of the parabola (or the leftmost or rightmost point, depending on the direction that the parabola opens).
- A parabola with vertex at (h, k) and focus at a distance of $\pm p$ from the vertex is described by the equation $(x - h)^2 = 4p\,(y - k)$ or $(y - k)^2 = 4p\,(x - h)$, depending on the direction that the parabola opens.

vertex (h,k) **Focus distance $\pm p$ away then:** $(x - h)^2 = 4p(y - k)$ $\smile$ $p > 0$ $\frown$ $p < 0$ $(y - k)^2 = 4p(x - h)$ $\subset$ $p > 0$ $\supset$ $p < 0$	You probably recall that the vertex of a parabola is the point where the curve of the parabola changes direction. For a parabola that opens up or down, it is the lowest or highest point on the graph, respectively. For a parabola that opens left or right, it is the rightmost or leftmost point, respectively. Using these general equations, it is possible to write the equation for a specific parabola given its vertex and focus.
Example *write an equation for a parabola* $V = (0,0)$ $F = (4,0)$ $(y - 0)^2 = 4p(x - 0)$ $y^2 = 4 \cdot 4(x)$ $\boxed{y^2 = 16x}$	It's always a good idea to sketch a rough picture first. Since the vertex is at $(0, 0)$, $h = 0$ and $k = 0$. The focus is 4 units away from the vertex and the parabola opens to the right, so $p = 4$. (If the parabola opened to the left, then p would equal –4). Substitute these values into the general equation and the result is the equation for this specific parabola.
Example *write an equation for a parabola* $V = (4,3)$ $F = (4,0)$ $(x - 4)^2 = 4 \cdot -3(y - 3)$ $\boxed{(x - 4)^2 = -12(y - 3)}$	The first step is to sketch a picture. You can see that this parabola opens downwards. Since the parabola opens downwards and the distance between the vertex and the focus is 3, $p = -3$. Since the vertex is at $(4, 3)$, $h = 4$ and $k = 3$. Substitute into the formula to find the equation for the parabola.

Sample problems:

1. Identify the vertex and focus of the parabola whose equation is $(x - 2)^2 = -8(y - 1)$.

   Solution: vertex: $(2,1)$, focus: $(2,-1)$

   Explanation: This equation is in the form $(x - h)^2 = 4p(y - k)$, so the vertex, (h, k), is at $(2,1)$. The focus is p units away from the vertex, so find p: $4p = -8$; $p = -2$. Therefore, the focus is two units below the vertex, so it is at $(2,-1)$.

2. Find the equation for the parabola with its vertex on the origin and its focus at $(0,3)$.

   Solution: $y = \frac{1}{12} x^2$

   Explanation: The parabola opens up, so use standard form $(x - h)^2 = 4p(y - k)$ to write the equation. Determine p: the focus is at $(0,3)$ which is 3 units away from the vertex, so $p = 3$. Now substitute the values of p and (h, k) (from the vertex) into $(x - h)^2 = 4p(y - k)$, simplify, and solve for y: $(x - 0)^2 = 4 \cdot 3(y - 0)$; $x^2 = 12y$; $y = \frac{1}{12} x^2$.

3. Find the equation for the parabola with its vertex at $(-2,5)$ and its focus at $(-6,5)$.

  <u>Solution:</u> $(y-5)^2 = -16(x+2)$

  <u>Explanation:</u> The parabola opens to the left, so use $(y-k)^2 = 4p(x-h)$ to write the equation. Find p: the focus is -4 units away from the vertex, so $p = -4$. Now substitute the values of p and (h,k) into $(y-k)^2 = 4p(x-h)$ and simplify: $(y-5)^2 = 4(-4)(x-(-2))$; $(y-5)^2 = -16(x+2)$.

Practice problems: *(Answers on page: 465)*

1. Find the equation for the parabola with its vertex on the origin and its focus at $(-3,0)$.

2. Write the equation for the parabola whose vertex is at $(3,5)$ and focus is at $(3,7)$.

3. Identify the vertex and focus of the parabola whose equation is $(y+5)^2 = 4(x-3)$.

Review questions: *(Answers to odd questions on page: 465)*

1. Find the equation for the parabola with its vertex on the origin and its focus at $\left(0, \frac{3}{2}\right)$.

2. Find the equation for the parabola with its vertex on the origin and its focus at $(-5,0)$.

3. Determine the vertex of the parabola $(y-3)^2 = -8(x-2)$.

4. Write an equation for the parabola with vertex $(3,5)$ and focus $(3,1)$.

5. Write an equation for the parabola with vertex $(2,-5)$ and focus $(7,-5)$.

An Introduction to Ellipses

- An ellipse consists of the set of points, the sum of whose distances from two fixed points is always the same. The two fixed points are called the **foci** of the ellipse. The singular form of **foci** is focus.

- The standard equation for an ellipse centered at the origin is $\dfrac{x^2}{a^2} + \dfrac{y^2}{b^2} = 1$, where the x-intercepts are at $\pm a$ and the y-intercepts are at $\pm b$.

- The standard equation for an ellipse centered at (h, k) is $\dfrac{(x-h)^2}{a^2} + \dfrac{(y-k)^2}{b^2} = 1$.

- The long axis of an ellipse is called the **major axis**. The short axis of an ellipse is called the **minor axis**.

A piece of string between 2 foci can be "swept out" to make a perfect ellipse  **An ellipse is a collection of points whose distance from 2 fixed points is always the same.**	Since it is a conic section, an ellipse can be obtained by intersecting a plane with a cone. However, an ellipse can also be defined as a locus of points in the plane: Every ellipse is the set of points whose total distance from two fixed points, called the foci, is the same. You can construct an ellipse using a piece of string and a pencil.

An analytical point of view of an ellipse

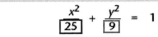

$$\frac{x^2}{\boxed{25}} + \frac{y^2}{\boxed{9}} = 1$$

x intercepts $= \pm \sqrt{25}$ y intercepts $= \pm \sqrt{9}$

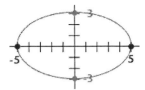

Here is a typical equation describing an ellipse centered at the origin.

An easy way to graph the ellipse described by this equation is to find the x and y-intercepts. You can find them by taking the plus and minus square roots of the coefficients under the x^2 and y^2 terms.

The long axis of the ellipse is called the major axis. In this case the major axis has a length of 10. The endpoints of the ellipse along the major axis are referred to as the vertices of the ellipse. The vertices of the ellipse are located at $(-5, 0)$ and $(5, 0)$. The short axis, called the minor axis, has a length of 6. The endpoints of the ellipse along the minor axis are referred to as the co-vertices of the ellipse. The co-vertices of the ellipse are located at $(-3, 0)$ and $(3, 0)$.

What if the ellipse is not centered at the origin?

center = (h, k)

$$\frac{(x - h)^2}{a^2} + \frac{(y - k)^2}{\boxed{b^2}} = 1$$

The major axis can be the y axis if this number is larger.

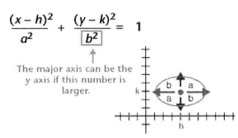

What if the ellipse is centered at (h, k) instead of the origin?

This is the standard equation describing an ellipse centered at (h, k).

To graph the ellipse described by this equation, first find the center of the ellipse. Then you can go a units to the left and right to find the left and right ends of the ellipse. Similarly, you can go b units up and down to find the vertical ends of the ellipse.

Finding the Focus Equation of an Ellipse

$$9x^2 + 4y^2 + 72x - 48y + 144 = 0$$
$$9x^2 + 72x + 4y^2 - 48y = -144$$
$$9(x^2 + 8x) + 4(y^2 - 12y) = -144$$
$$9(x^2 + 8x + \quad) + 4(y^2 - 12y + \quad) = -144 + 9(\quad) + 4(\quad)$$
$$9(x^2 + 8x + 16) + 4(y^2 - 12y + 36) = -144 + 9(16) + 4(36)$$
$$9(x + 4)^2 + 4(y - 6)^2 = 144$$
$$\frac{(x + 4)^2}{16} + \frac{(y - 6)^2}{36} = 1$$

This is the equation of the ellipse

Line 1 is the equation of an ellipse in standard form.

First, subtract the constant term from both sides, and group the x-terms and the y-terms.

Then, factor out the constant on the squared terms.

Leave space to complete the squares on the left side, and add blank terms on the right, multiplied by the coefficients outside the x- and y-terms on the left.

Complete the squares by taking half the coefficients of the first-degree terms, squaring them, and add the squares into the appropriate blanks on both sides of the equation.

Convert to squared form on the left, and simplify on the right.

Last, because 9 and 4 are factors of 144, divide through by 144.

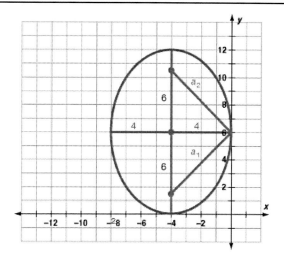

This ellipse has a center of (-4, 6). The minor axis is parallel to the x-axis, with a length of 8, and the major axis is parallel to the y-axis with length 12.

Along the major axis, the distance from one focus, to the ellipse and back to the other focus is the same as the length of the major axis. So, in this example, that distance is 12. Since the distance from one focus to any point on the ellipse and back to the other focus is the same, the equation, $a_1 + a_2 = 12$, can be used to find the foci.

Consider the case when the lines are drawn from the foci to the covertices (the endpoint along the minor axis).

At the covertices, the distance a_1 is equal to a_2. If their sum is 12, then $a_1 = a_2 = 6$. To find y_0, the distance from the center to a focus, use the Pythagorean Theorem and the right triangle formed by the focus, the center, and the covertices.

$$a^2 + b^2 = c^2$$
$$(y_0)^2 + 4^2 = 6^2$$
$$(y_0)^2 + 16 = 36$$
$$(y_0)^2 = 20$$
$$y_0 = 2\sqrt{5}$$

First, substitute y_0 for a and 4 for b in the Pythagorean Theorem. Next, evaluate the exponents. Subtract 16 from both sides, then take the square root of both sides.

The center of the ellipse is (-4, 6), so the foci are along the major axis at (-4, 6 - y_0) and (-4, 6 + y_0). Thus, the foci are

$$\left(-4, 6 - 2\sqrt{5}\right) \text{ and } \left(-4, 6 + 2\sqrt{5}\right).$$

Using the Pythagorean Theorem to generalize a formula for the foci from the ellipse equation, we find:

- if $a \geq b$ (the major axis is along the x-axis), the foci can be found using $c^2 = a^2 - b^2$
- if $a \leq b$ (the major axis is along the y-axis), the foci can be found using $c^2 = b^2 - a^2$

Sample problems:

1. Identify the center and x and y-intercepts of the ellipse described by $\dfrac{x^2}{16} + \dfrac{y^2}{36} = 1$.

   Solution: Center: (0, 0); x-intercepts: ± 4; y-intercepts: ± 6

   Explanation: Since the equation $\dfrac{x^2}{16} + \dfrac{y^2}{36} = 1$ is in the standard form of an ellipse, $\dfrac{x^2}{a^2} + \dfrac{y^2}{b^2} = 1$, the center must be the origin, (0, 0).
   The x-intercepts are at $\pm a$: $a^2 = 16$; $a = \sqrt{16} = \pm 4$.
   The y-intercepts are at $\pm b$: $b^2 = 36$; $b = \sqrt{36} = \pm 6$.

2. Express the equation $4x^2 + 3y^2 + 8x - 6y - 29 = 0$ in the standard form of an ellipse, then identify the center of the ellipse.

   Solution: $\dfrac{(x+1)^2}{9} + \dfrac{(y-1)^2}{12} = 1$; center: (-1, 1)

Explanation: Group the x-terms and y-terms on the left and the constant on the right: $4x^2 + 8x + 3y^2 - 6y = 29$. Factor a 4 from the x-terms and a 3 from the y-terms: $4(x^2 + 2x) + 3(y^2 - 2y) = 29$. Complete the square for x and y (remember to add the product of the constant and the factor to the right side to keep the equation balanced): $4(x^2 + 2x + \_\_) + 3(y^2 - 2y + \_\_) = 29 + 4(\_) + 3(\_)$; $4(x^2 + 2x + 1) + 3(y^2 - 2y + 1) = 29 + 4 \cdot 1 + 3 \cdot 1$.
Factor and simplify: $4(x+1)^2 + 3(y-1)^2 = 36$.

Consider the standard form of an ellipse: $\dfrac{(x-h)^2}{a^2} + \dfrac{(y-k)^2}{b^2} = 1$. Notice that in standard form the right side is 1, so divide the equation by 36 to produce 1 on the right side: $\dfrac{4(x+1)^2}{36} + \dfrac{3(y-1)^2}{36} = \dfrac{36}{36}$; $\dfrac{(x+1)^2}{9} + \dfrac{(y-1)^2}{12} = 1$.
Now the equation is expressed in standard form. Identify the center, or the $(h,\ k)$, values in the equation: $(-1,\ 1)$.

3. Given the ellipse $\dfrac{(x-3)^2}{4} + \dfrac{(y+1)^2}{9} = 1$, find the endpoints of the major axis and the endpoints of the minor axis.

   Solution: Major axis: $(3, 2)$ and $(3, -4)$; minor axis: $(5, -1)$ and $(1, -1)$

   Explanation: Identify the center, $(h,\ k)$ from the equation: $(3, -1)$. The endpoints of the major and minor axes are located $\pm a$ units horizontally and $\pm b$ units vertically from the center. Find a and b: $a^2 = 4$; $a = \sqrt{4} = \pm 2$ and $b^2 = 9$; $b = \sqrt{9} = \pm 3$. Since $b > a$ the vertical axis is the major axis. Find the endpoints of the major axis by moving vertically ± 3 units from the center: $(3, -1+3)$ and $(3, -1-3)$; $(3, 2)$ and $(3, -4)$. Find the endpoints of the minor axis by moving horizontally ± 2 units from the center: $(3+2, -1)$ and $(3-2, -1)$; $(5, -1)$ and $(1, -1)$.

Practice problems: *(Answers on page: 465)*

1. Find the center and the length of the minor axis of the ellipse described by $\dfrac{(x-4)^2}{9} + (y+3)^2 = 1$.

2. Find the center and the lengths of the major and minor axes of the ellipse described by: $7x^2 + 28x + 4y^2 = 0$.

3. Sketch the graph of $\dfrac{x^2}{4} + \dfrac{y^2}{16} = 1$.

Review questions: *(Answers to odd questions on page: 466)*

1. Express the equation $4x^2 + y^2 - 40x + 6y + 105 = 0$ in the standard form of an ellipse and identify the center of the ellipse.

2. Identify the center and x and y-intercepts of the ellipse described by $\dfrac{x^2}{25} + y^2 = 1$.

3. Find the lengths of the major and minor axes of the ellipse represented by this equation: $\dfrac{(x+2)^2}{15} + \dfrac{y^2}{64} = 1$.

4. Given $\dfrac{(x-1)^2}{9} + \dfrac{(y+3)^2}{16} = 1$, state the center and intercepts for this graph.

5. Identify the center of the ellipse described by $5x^2 + 40x + 3y^2 - 6y + 68 = 0$.

Finding the Equation for an Ellipse

- An ellipse consists of the set of points, the sum of whose distances from two fixed points is always the same. The two fixed points are called the foci of the ellipse.
-
   The standard equation for an ellipse centered at (h, k) is $\dfrac{(x-h)^2}{a^2} + \dfrac{(y-k)^2}{b^2} = 1$.

Example

x intercept = ± 5   Foci (–3, 0) (3, 0)

What is the equation for this ellipse?

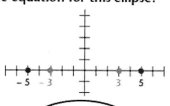

Remember:

$a_1 + a_2 = b_1 + b_2$

How can you find the equation for this ellipse given its *x*-intercepts and foci?

By plotting the *x*-intercepts and foci, you can see that the ellipse is centered at the origin. If you can find the *y*-intercepts of the ellipse, you will know everything you need to know to write its equation.

The key to finding the *y*-intercepts is to remember that for any point on an ellipse, the sum of the distances from that point to the two foci is a constant.

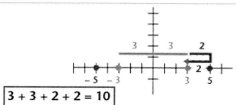

$3 + 3 + 2 + 2 = 10$

What would the length of the string be from the first focus, out to the +5x intercept, and back to the second focus?

Since you know that the point (5,0) is on the ellipse, you can calculate the sum of the distances from that point to the two foci.

If you remember how you can create an ellipse using a piece of string and a pencil, you can think of this distance as the length of that string.

In this case, the sum is equal to 2 + 8, or 10.

Where does the string cross on the y axis?

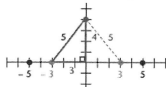

Use the Pythagorean Theorem to find the height of the ellipse.

$3^2 + 4^2 = 5^2$

The sum of the distances from a y-intercept of the ellipse to the two foci will also equal 10. Since the two distances are the same for a *y*-intercept of the ellipse because it is centered at (0,0), the distance from the y-intercept to each of the foci is 5.

You can calculate the location of the y-intercept using the Pythagorean theorem. You place it at (0,±4).

$$\frac{x^2}{a^2} + \frac{y^2}{b^2} = 1$$

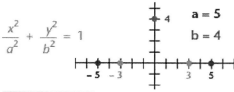

a = 5

b = 4

$$\frac{x^2}{25} + \frac{y^2}{16} = 1$$

Now just substitute into the standard equation for an ellipse centered at the origin.

This is the equation describing the ellipse.

Sample problems:

1. The foci of an ellipse are at $(-8,0)$ and $(8, 0)$ and the *x*-intercepts are at ± 10. Write the equation of this ellipse.

    Solution: $\dfrac{x^2}{100} + \dfrac{y^2}{36} = 1$

Explanation: Since the foci are centered around the origin, the center of the ellipse must be $(0, 0)$.

Therefore, the equation is in the form $\frac{x^2}{a^2} + \frac{y^2}{b^2} = 1$, where a represents the x-intercepts, so $a \pm 10$.

Find b, the y-intercepts. The total distance from any point to the foci must be 20, since $8 + 8 + 2 + 2 = 20$. Since the 2 distances are the same for the y-intercepts, the distance from the focus $(8, 0)$ to the positive y-intercept is 10 (half of 20). Set up a right triangle and use the Pythagorean Theorem to solve for b, the y-intercept: $8^2 + b^2 = 10^2$; $b^2 = 100 - 64$; $b^2 = 36$; $b = \sqrt{36} = \pm 6$. Substitute the a and b values into the standard equation of an ellipse: $\frac{x^2}{(\pm 10)^2} + \frac{y^2}{(\pm 6)^2} = 1$; $\frac{x^2}{100} + \frac{y^2}{36} = 1$.

2. The foci of an ellipse are at $(0, 3)$ and $(0, -3)$ and the y-intercepts are at ± 5. Write the equation of this ellipse.

Solution: $\frac{x^2}{16} + \frac{y^2}{25} = 1$

Explanation: Set up a right triangle and use the Pythagorean Theorem to find the x-intercepts: $a^2 + 9 = 25$; $a^2 = 16$; $a = \pm 4$. Substitute the a and b values into the standard form of an ellipse, $\frac{x^2}{a^2} + \frac{y^2}{b^2} = 1$; $\frac{x^2}{(\pm 4)^2} + \frac{y^2}{25} = 1$; $\frac{x^2}{16} + \frac{y^2}{25} = 1$.

3. True or false: The equation $(x-4)^2 + \frac{(y+5)^2}{4} = 1$ describes an ellipse centered at $(4, -5)$.

Solution: True

Explanation: The equation $(x-4)^2 + \frac{(y+5)^2}{4} = 1$ is expressed in the standard form of an ellipse, $\frac{(x-h)^2}{a^2} + \frac{(y-k)^2}{b^2} = 1$, centered at (h, k). Thus, the center is indeed $(4, -5)$.

Practice problems: *(Answers on page: 466)*

1. The foci of an ellipse are at $(-5, 0)$ and $(5, 0)$ and the x-intercepts are at ± 13. Write the equation of this ellipse.

2. The x-intercepts of an ellipse are at ± 2 and the y-intercepts are at ± 3. Write the equation of this ellipse.

3. Find center of the ellipse described by $\frac{(x+4)^2}{9} + \frac{y^2}{5} = 1$.

Review questions: *(Answers to odd questions on page: 466)*

1. Find the foci of the ellipse represented by the equation $\frac{x^2}{10} + \frac{y^2}{7} = 1$.

2. Find the equation of an ellipse with y-intercepts at ± 4 and x-intercepts at ± 2.

3. The foci of an ellipse are at $(0, -4)$ and $(0, 4)$ and the y-intercepts are at ± 5. Write the equation of this ellipse.

4. The foci of an ellipse are at $(-\sqrt{21}, 0)$ and $(\sqrt{21}, 0)$ and the x-intercepts are at ± 5. Write the equation of this ellipse.

5. Find center of the ellipse described by $(x-1)^2 + \frac{y^2}{3} = 1$.

Applying Ellipses: Satellites

- The standard equation for an ellipse centered at the origin is $\dfrac{x^2}{a^2} + \dfrac{y^2}{b^2} = 1$, where the x-intercepts are at $\pm a$ and the y-intercepts are at $\pm b$. If $a \geq b$, the foci of the ellipse are located at $(\pm c, 0)$, where $c^2 = a^2 - b^2$. If $b < c$, the foci of the ellipse are located at $(0, \pm c)$, where $c^2 = b^2 - a^2$.

The generic formula for an ellipse $\quad \dfrac{x^2}{a^2} + \dfrac{y^2}{b^2} = 1$ **If a ≥ b, then the foci are (±c, 0).** 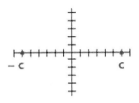 $c^2 = a^2 - b^2$	Previously you learned the general equation describing an ellipse centered at the origin. If a is greater than or equal to b in the equation, then the foci are located on the x-axis at $(+c, 0)$, and $(-c, 0)$. You can calculate where the foci are located exactly using this formula for c^2.
If b ≥ a, then the foci are (0, ±c). 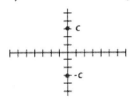 $c^2 = b^2 - a^2$	If b is greater than a in the equation, then the foci are located on the y-axis at $(0, \pm c)$. Use the formula $c^2 = b^2 - a^2$ to find c when $b > a$.
Example **Consider space:** The coordinates for the satellite (in miles) can be described by the regular equation for an ellipse. $\dfrac{x^2}{a^2} + \dfrac{y^2}{b^2} = 1 \qquad \begin{array}{l} a = 4465 \text{ miles} \\ b = 4462 \text{ miles} \end{array}$ 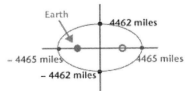	Try this real-world problem. Suppose that an ellipse describes the orbit of a satellite around the Earth with the Earth at a focus. What are the maximum and minimum distances between the satellite and the Earth?
Plug a and b into the generic equation for the ellipse. $\dfrac{x^2}{4465^2} + \dfrac{y^2}{4462^2} = 1$	First, find the equation of the ellipse describing the satellite's orbit using the x- and y-intercepts.
Find the foci by using the formula: $c^2 = a^2 - b^2$ Use a calculator to find: $c^2 = 4465^2 - 4462^2$ $c^2 = 26781$ $\boxed{c = 163.64}$	Now you can find the location of the Earth by finding the location of the foci using the formula from above.

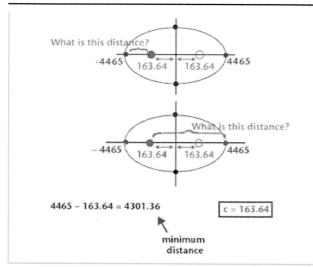

Once you know where the Earth is located, just do a little adding and subtracting to find the maximum and minimum distances between the Earth and the satellite.

Ellipses come up frequently in the real world!

Sample problems:

1. Given $x^2 + \dfrac{y^2}{16} = 1$, where are the foci of the ellipse?

   Solution: $(0, -\sqrt{15})$ and $(0, \sqrt{15})$

   Explanation: Identify a and b from the equation: $a^2 = 1$; $a = \sqrt{1} = \pm 1$ and $b^2 = 16$; $b = \sqrt{16} = \pm 4$. Since $b > a$ the foci are at $(0, \pm c)$. use the formula $c^2 = b^2 - a^2$ to determine c: $c^2 = 16 - 1$; $c^2 = 15$; $c = \sqrt{15}$. So the foci are at $(0, -\sqrt{15})$ and $(0, \sqrt{15})$.

2. Given the ellipse $\dfrac{x^2}{25} + \dfrac{y^2}{9} = 1$, what are the curve's foci?

   Solution: $(4, 0)$ and $(-4, 0)$

   Explanation: Since $a \geq b$, the foci are $(\pm\sqrt{c}, 0)$, where $c^2 = a^2 - b^2$. Use the equation to find c: $c^2 = 25 - 9$; $c = \sqrt{16} = \pm 4$. Therefore, the foci are at $(4, 0)$ and $(-4, 0)$.

3. Suppose that an ellipse describes the orbit of a satellite around the Earth with the Earth at a focus. If horizontal and vertical axes are centered through the orbit, the satellite passes through (5000, 0) and (0, 4500). Find the minimum distance between the satellite and the Earth.

   Solution: 2324.55

   Explanation: Substitute 5,000 and 4,500 into the standard equation of an ellipse for a and b respectively: $\dfrac{x^2}{(5,000)} + \dfrac{y^2}{(4,500)} = 1$. Since $a \geq b$, use the equation $c^2 = a^2 - b^2$ to find c: $c^2 = (5,000)^2 - (4,500)^2$; $c^2 = 4,750,000$; $c = \pm 2179.45$. So the minimum distance must be $4,500 - 2179.45 = 2324.55$ miles.

Practice problems: (Answers on page: 466)

1. Given $\dfrac{x^2}{36} + \dfrac{y^2}{9} = 1$, where are the foci of the ellipse?

2. Given $\dfrac{x^2}{20} + \dfrac{y^2}{45} = 1$, where are the foci of the ellipse?

3. Suppose that an ellipse describes the orbit of a satellite around the Earth with the Earth at a focus. If horizontal and vertical axes are centered through the orbit, the satellite passes through (0, 3800) and (4000, 0). Find the maximum distance between the satellite and the Earth.

Review questions: *(Answers to odd questions on page: 466)*

1. Given $\dfrac{x^2}{100}+\dfrac{y^2}{36}=1$, where are the foci of the ellipse?

2. Given $\dfrac{(x-6)^2}{64}+\dfrac{y^2}{6.25}=1$, where are the foci of the ellipse?

3. Given $\dfrac{(x-4)^2}{9}+(y+3)^2=1$, where are the foci of the ellipse?

4. A room is elliptical. If it is 40 feet long and 20 feet wide, how far apart would two people be if they are standing at the foci?

5. The Oval Office of the President of the US is in the shape of an ellipse. The room is 36 feet long by 28 feet wide. Write the equation for this ellipse.

An Introduction to Hyperbolas

- A **hyperbola** consists of the set of points, the difference of whose distances from two fixed points is a constant. The two fixed points are called the **foci** of the hyperbola. The singular form of foci is focus.

- The standard equation for a hyperbola centered at the origin that opens to the left and right is $\dfrac{x^2}{a^2}-\dfrac{y^2}{b^2}=1$ where the x-intercepts are at $\pm a$. The foci of the hyperbola are located at $(\pm c, 0)$, where $c^2 = a^2 + b^2$.

- The standard equation for a hyperbola centered at the origin that open up and down is $\dfrac{y^2}{b^2}-\dfrac{x^2}{a^2}=1$ where the y-intercepts are at $\pm b$. The foci of the hyperbola are located at $(0, \pm c)$, where $c^2 = a^2 + b^2$.

- In either case, the hyperbola has asymptotes along the lines $y = \pm \dfrac{b}{a} x$.

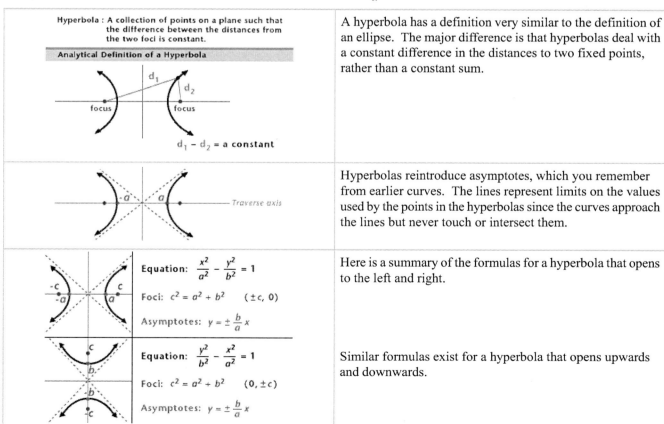

Hyperbola : A collection of points on a plane such that the difference between the distances from the two foci is constant. Analytical Definition of a Hyperbola. $d_1 - d_2 =$ a constant	A hyperbola has a definition very similar to the definition of an ellipse. The major difference is that hyperbolas deal with a constant difference in the distances to two fixed points, rather than a constant sum.
Traverse axis	Hyperbolas reintroduce asymptotes, which you remember from earlier curves. The lines represent limits on the values used by the points in the hyperbolas since the curves approach the lines but never touch or intersect them.
Equation: $\dfrac{x^2}{a^2}-\dfrac{y^2}{b^2}=1$ Foci: $c^2 = a^2 + b^2$ $(\pm c, 0)$ Asymptotes: $y = \pm \dfrac{b}{a}x$	Here is a summary of the formulas for a hyperbola that opens to the left and right.
Equation: $\dfrac{y^2}{b^2}-\dfrac{x^2}{a^2}=1$ Foci: $c^2 = a^2 + b^2$ $(0, \pm c)$ Asymptotes: $y = \pm \dfrac{b}{a}x$	Similar formulas exist for a hyperbola that opens upwards and downwards.

Sample problems:

1. State the equations for the asymptotes of the hyperbola: $\dfrac{y^2}{36} - \dfrac{x^2}{25} = 1$.

   Solution: $y = \pm\dfrac{6}{5}x$

   Explanation: The hyperbola defined by $\dfrac{y^2}{36} - \dfrac{x^2}{25} = 1$ is a up/down hyperbola centered at the origin. Therefore, to find the equations of the asymptotes, use the formula $y = \pm\dfrac{b}{a}x$. Consider the standard form of a hyperbola, $\dfrac{y^2}{b^2} - \dfrac{x^2}{a^2} = 1$ to identify a and b: $a^2 = 25$; $a = \sqrt{25} = \pm 5$ and $b^2 = 36$; $b = \sqrt{36} = \pm 6$. Substitute a and b into $y = \pm\dfrac{b}{a}x$: $y = \pm\dfrac{6}{5}x$.

2. State the foci of the hyperbola: $\dfrac{x^2}{15} - \dfrac{y^2}{5} = 1$.

   Solution: $(\pm 2\sqrt{5},\ 0)$

   Explanation: The equation $\dfrac{x^2}{15} - \dfrac{y^2}{5} = 1$ is in the standard form of a left/right hyperbola, so the foci are located at $(\pm c,\ 0)$ where $c^2 = a^2 + b^2$. Identify $a^2 + b^2$ from the equation, $a^2 = 15$ and $b^2 = 5$. Substitute the $a^2 + b^2$ values into $c^2 = a^2 + b^2$ to determine c: $c^2 = 15 + 5$; $c^2 = 20$; $c = \sqrt{20}$; $c = 2\sqrt{5}$. So the foci are at $(\pm 2\sqrt{5},\ 0)$.

3. State the foci and equation for the asymptotes of the hyperbola: $4y^2 - 9x^2 = 36$.

   Solution: foci: $(0, \pm\sqrt{13})$; asymptotes: $y = \pm\dfrac{3}{2}x$

   Explanation: Express the equation in standard form by dividing by 36: $\dfrac{4y^2}{36} - \dfrac{9x^2}{36} = \dfrac{36}{36}$; $\dfrac{y^2}{9} - \dfrac{x^2}{4} = 1$. Determine c to locate the foci: $c^2 = a^2 + b^2$; $c^2 = 4 + 9$; $c^2 = 13$; $c = \sqrt{13}$. So, the foci are at $(0, \pm\sqrt{13})$ since this is a up/down hyperbola. Find the equation of the asymptotes: $y = \pm\dfrac{b}{a}x$; $y = \pm\dfrac{3}{2}$.

Practice problems: *(Answers on page: 466)*

1. State the equations for the asymptotes of the hyperbola: $x^2 - \dfrac{y^2}{25} = 1$.

2. State the foci of the hyperbola: $y^2 - 25x^2 = 100$.

3. State the foci and the equations for the asymptotes of the hyperbola: $4x^2 - y^2 = 16$.

Review questions: *(Answers to odd questions on page: 466)*

1. State the foci of the hyperbola: $\dfrac{x^2}{9} - \dfrac{y^2}{25} = 1$.

2. State the foci of the hyperbola: $\dfrac{y^2}{36} - \dfrac{x^2}{1} = 1$.

3. State the foci of the hyperbola: $\dfrac{x^2}{7} - \dfrac{y^2}{2} = 1$.

4. State the equations for the asymptotes of the hyperbola: $9x^2 - 4y^2 = 36$.

5. State the foci of the hyperbola: $5y^2 - 4x^2 = 20$.

Finding the Equation for a Hyperbola

- The standard equation for a hyperbola centered at the origin that opens to the left and right is $\dfrac{x^2}{a^2} - \dfrac{y^2}{b^2} = 1$ where the x-intercepts are at $\pm a$. The foci of the hyperbola are located at $(\pm c, 0)$, where $c^2 = a^2 + b^2$.

- The standard equation for a hyperbola centered at the origin that open up and down is $\dfrac{y^2}{b^2} - \dfrac{x^2}{a^2} = 1$, where the y-intercepts are at $\pm b$. The foci of the hyperbola are located at $(0, \pm c)$, where $c^2 = a^2 + b^2$.

- In either case, the hyperbola has asymptotes along the lines $y = \pm \dfrac{b}{a} x$.

Example Write the hyperbola's equation, given:

x intercept $= \pm 4$

Foci at $(\pm 5, 0)$

$\dfrac{x^2}{16} - \dfrac{y^2}{b^2} = 1$

In this example problem, you are asked to write the equation describing a hyperbola given the location of its x-intercepts and foci.

A good first step is to draw a rough sketch of the hyperbola.

You can see that the hyperbola opens to the left and right, so the general equation is $\dfrac{x^2}{a^2} - \dfrac{y^2}{b^2} = 1$.

Since you already know the value of a in the standard equation for a hyperbola, all you need to find is the value of b^2.

$c^2 = a^2 + b^2$

$25 = 16 + b^2$

$9 = b^2$

$\dfrac{x^2}{16} - \dfrac{y^2}{b^2} = 1$ → $\boxed{\dfrac{x^2}{16} - \dfrac{y^2}{9} = 1}$

To find the value of b^2, use the formula $c^2 = a^2 + b^2$.

Substitute b^2 into the standard equation for a hyperbola that opens to the left and right and you're done.

Example Write the hyperbola's equation, given:

y intercept $= \pm 9$

Foci at $(0, \pm 15)$

$c^2 = a^2 + b^2$

$225 = a^2 + 81$

$144 = a^2$

$\dfrac{y^2}{81} - \dfrac{x^2}{a^2} = 1$ → $\boxed{\dfrac{y^2}{81} - \dfrac{x^2}{144} = 1}$

Here is another problem along the same lines.

First sketch a rough picture. This hyperbola opens upwards and downwards, so the general equation is $\dfrac{y^2}{b^2} - \dfrac{x^2}{a^2} = 1$.

Now find the value of a^2 using $c^2 = a^2 + b^2$.

Substitute into the standard equation for a hyperbola that opens upwards and downwards.

Sample problems:

1. Write the equation of a hyperbola given that the y-intercepts are ± 4 and the foci are at $(0, \pm 9)$.

    Solution: $\dfrac{y^2}{16} - \dfrac{x^2}{65} = 1$

    Explanation: Sketch the hyperbola. The general form of the equation is $\dfrac{y^2}{b^2} - \dfrac{x^2}{a^2} = 1$, since it is

    an up/down hyperbola. Substitute 4 into the equation for b: $\dfrac{y^2}{4^2} - \dfrac{x^2}{a^2} = 1$. Use the equation

    $c^2 = a^2 + b^2$ to determine a: $9^2 = a^2 + 4^2$; $81 = a^2 + 16$; $a^2 = 65$; $a = \sqrt{65}$. Substitute $\sqrt{65}$

    into the equation of the hyperbola for a and simplify: $\dfrac{y^2}{4^2} - \dfrac{x^2}{\sqrt{65}^2} = 1$; $\dfrac{y^2}{16} - \dfrac{x^2}{65} = 1$.

2. Write the equation of a hyperbola given that the x-intercepts are ± 2 and the foci are at $(\pm 5, 0)$.

    Solution: $\dfrac{x^2}{4} - \dfrac{y^2}{21} = 1$

    Explanation: Since this is a left/right hyperbola, the general equation is $\dfrac{x^2}{a^2} - \dfrac{y^2}{b^2} = 1$, where the

    x-intercepts are $\pm a$. Substitute 2 into the equation for a: $\dfrac{x^2}{2^2} - \dfrac{y^2}{b^2} = 1$. Find b: $c^2 = a^2 + b^2$;

    $5^2 = 2^2 + b^2$; $25 = 4 + b^2$; $b^2 = 21$; $b = \sqrt{21}$. Therefore, the equation of the hyperbola is

    $\dfrac{x^2}{4} - \dfrac{y^2}{21} = 1$.

3. Write the equation of a hyperbola given that the x-intercepts are ± 4 and it passes through the point $(5, 3.75)$.

    Solution: $\dfrac{x^2}{16} - \dfrac{y^2}{25} = 1$

    Explanation: Since the x-intercepts are ± 4, begin with the equation $\dfrac{x^2}{16} - \dfrac{y^2}{b^2} = 1$. Find b by

    substituting the x and y-values from the point $(5, 3.75)$ into the equation and solving for b:

    $\dfrac{(5)^2}{16} - \dfrac{(3.75)^2}{b^2} = 1$; $\dfrac{25}{16} - \dfrac{14.0625}{b^2} = 1$; $-\dfrac{14.0625}{b^2} = 1 - \dfrac{25}{16}$; $-\dfrac{14.0625}{b^2} = -\dfrac{9}{6}$; $9b^2 = 16(14.0625)$; $b^2 = 25$;

    $b = \sqrt{25}$; $b = \pm 5$. So the equation of the hyperbola is $\dfrac{x^2}{16} - \dfrac{y^2}{25} = 1$.

Practice problems: *(Answers on page: 466)*

1. Write the equation of a hyperbola given that the x-intercepts are ± 6 and the foci are at $(\pm 10, 0)$.

2. Write the equation of a hyperbola given that the y-intercepts are ± 1 and the foci are at $(0, \pm 3)$.

3. A hyperbola's x-intercepts are located at $(4, 0)$ and $(-4, 0)$, and it passes through the point $(-5, 5)$. Write the equation of this hyperbola.

Review questions: *(Answers to odd questions on page: 466)*

1. Write the equation of a hyperbola given that the y-intercepts are $(0, 2)$ and $(0, -2)$ and the foci are at $(0, 3)$ and $(0, -3)$.

2. Write the equation of a hyperbola given that the x-intercepts are $(7, 0)$ and $(-7, 0)$ and the foci are at $(10, 0)$ and $(-10, 0)$.

3. Write the equation of a hyperbola given that the y-intercepts are $(0, 3)$ and $(0, -3)$ that passes through the point $(-2, 5)$.

4. Write the equation of a hyperbola given that the x-intercepts are $(2,0)$ and $(-2,0)$ that passes through the point $(3,\sqrt{3})$.

5. Write the equation of a hyperbola given that the x-intercepts are $(4,0)$ and $(-4,0)$ that passes through the point $(\sqrt{32},1)$.

Applying Hyperbolas: Navigation

- Hyperbolas are useful in many real-world situations. One such situation is the navigation of ships at sea.

- The standard equation for a hyperbola centered at the origin that opens to the left and right is $\dfrac{x^2}{a^2} - \dfrac{y^2}{b^2} = 1$, where the x-intercepts are at $\pm a$. The foci of the hyperbola are located at $(\pm c, 0)$, where $c^2 = a^2 + b^2$.

- The standard equation for a hyperbola centered at the origin that open up and down is $\dfrac{y^2}{b^2} - \dfrac{x^2}{a^2} = 1$, where the y-intercepts are at $\pm b$. The foci of the hyperbola are located at $(0, \pm c)$, where $c^2 = a^2 + b^2$.

- In either case, the hyperbola has asymptotes along the lines $y = \pm \dfrac{b}{a} x$.

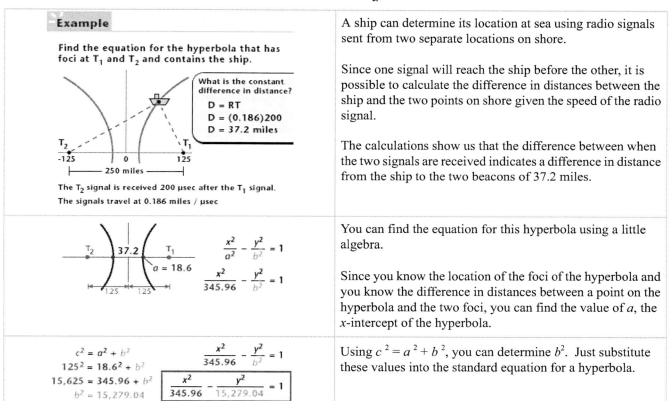

Example

Find the equation for the hyperbola that has foci at T_1 and T_2 and contains the ship.

What is the constant difference in distance?

D = RT
D = (0.186)200
D = 37.2 miles

The T_2 signal is received 200 μsec after the T_1 signal.
The signals travel at 0.186 miles / μsec

A ship can determine its location at sea using radio signals sent from two separate locations on shore.

Since one signal will reach the ship before the other, it is possible to calculate the difference in distances between the ship and the two points on shore given the speed of the radio signal.

The calculations show us that the difference between when the two signals are received indicates a difference in distance from the ship to the two beacons of 37.2 miles.

$$\dfrac{x^2}{a^2} - \dfrac{y^2}{b^2} = 1$$

$$\dfrac{x^2}{345.96} - \dfrac{y^2}{b^2} = 1$$

You can find the equation for this hyperbola using a little algebra.

Since you know the location of the foci of the hyperbola and you know the difference in distances between a point on the hyperbola and the two foci, you can find the value of a, the x-intercept of the hyperbola.

$c^2 = a^2 + b^2$
$125^2 = 18.6^2 + b^2$
$15{,}625 = 345.96 + b^2$
$b^2 = 15{,}279.04$

$$\dfrac{x^2}{345.96} - \dfrac{y^2}{b^2} = 1$$

$$\dfrac{x^2}{345.96} - \dfrac{y^2}{15{,}279.04} = 1$$

Using $c^2 = a^2 + b^2$, you can determine b^2. Just substitute these values into the standard equation for a hyperbola.

Example

If the ship is 100 miles east of the y axis, then how far is it from shore (the x axis)?

$$\frac{x^2}{345.96} - \frac{y^2}{15,279.04} = 1 \qquad \textit{Just plug in 100 for x.}$$

$$\frac{10,000}{345.96} - \frac{y^2}{15,279.04} = 1$$

$$\frac{y^2}{15,279.04} = \frac{10,000}{345.96} - 1$$

$$\frac{y^2}{15,279.04} = 27.9...$$

$$y^2 = 426,362.7...$$

$$\boxed{y = 652.9 \text{ miles}}$$

Once you have found the equation for the hyperbola, it is easy to answer the question to the left. Just plug in $x = 100$ and solve for y.

Bring the constants to one side to isolate the y variable.

Do you see how hyperbolas can be very useful in the real world?

Sample problems:

1. Suppose 2 Loran stations, T_1 and T_2, are positioned 200 miles apart and the signals they are sending travel 186,000 miles per second. A ship, traveling along a hyperbola with the stations as a foci, records a .00038 second time difference between the signals. Write the equation of the hyperbola that contains the ship.

   Solution: $\dfrac{x^2}{1248.92} - \dfrac{y^2}{8751.08} = 1$

   Explanation: The shore and the stations are on the x-axis and the center of the stations is the origin. Since the stations are 200 miles apart, the foci must be $T_1 = (-100, 0)$ and $T_2 = (100, 0)$. Use $d = rt$ to determine the constant difference in distance: $d = (186,000)(.00038) = 70.68$. Therefore, the distance between the x-intercepts must also be 70.68. Since the x-intercepts are centered around the origin and the distance between them is 70.68, the x-intercepts are located at $\pm\dfrac{70.68}{2}$, or ± 35.35. So, $a = 35.35$ and $a^2 = 1248.92$. Determine b^2 using $c^2 = a^2 + b^2$: $100^2 = 1248.92 + b^2$; $b^2 = 8751.08$. Substitute a^2 and b^2 into the standard equation of a hyperbola, $\dfrac{x^2}{a^2} - \dfrac{y^2}{b^2} = 1$: $\dfrac{x^2}{1248.92} - \dfrac{y^2}{8751.08} = 1$.

2. Use the situation in sample problem #1 to determine the distance of the ship from the shore when it is 50 miles east of the y-axis.

   Solution: Approximately 94 miles

   Explanation: Substitute 50 into the equation from #1 for x and solve for y:

   $\dfrac{(50)^2}{1248.92} - \dfrac{y^2}{8751.08} = 1$; $2.002 - \dfrac{y^2}{8751.08} = 1$; $\dfrac{y^2}{8751.08} = 1.002$; $y^2 = 8768.58$; $y = 93.64$.

   So the ship is almost 94 miles from the shore.

Practice problems: *(Answers on page: 466)*

1. Suppose 2 Loran stations, T_1 and T_2, are positioned 250 miles apart and the signals they are sending travel 186,000 miles per second. A ship, traveling along a hyperbola with the stations as a foci, records a .00032 second time difference between the signals. Write the equation of the hyperbola that contains the ship.

2. Use the situation in problem #1 to determine the distance of the ship from the shore when it is 75 miles east of the y-axis.

Review questions: *(Answers to odd questions on page: 466)*

1. Suppose 2 Loran stations, T_1 and T_2, are positioned 150 miles apart and the signals they are sending travel 195,000 miles per second. A ship, traveling along a hyperbola with the stations as a foci, records a .00024 second time difference between the signals. Write the equation of the hyperbola that contains the ship.

2. Use the situation in problem #1 to determine the distance of the ship from the shore when it is 40 miles east of the y-axis.

Identifying a Conic

- You can determine whether an equation describes a conic section and which conic section an equation describes by completing the square for the x and y variables and factoring.
- **Review:** The standard equation for a **parabola** centered at (h, k) is $(x - h)^2 = 4p(y - k)$.
- **Review:** The standard equation for a **circle** centered at (h, k) is $(x - h)^2 + (y - k)^2 = r^2$.
- **Review:** The standard equation for an **ellipse** centered at (h, k) is $\dfrac{(x-h)^2}{a^2} + \dfrac{(y-k)^2}{b^2} = 1$.
- **Review:** The standard equation for a **hyperbola** centered at (h, k) that opens to the left and right is $\dfrac{(x-h)^2}{a^2} - \dfrac{(y-k)^2}{b^2} = 1$.

  For a hyperbola centered at (h, k) that opens upwards and downwards, the standard equation is $\dfrac{(y-k)^2}{b^2} - \dfrac{(x-h)^2}{a^2} = 1$.

Example By completing the square, we can recognize whether or not an algebraic expression is a conic section. $$4x^2 + 9y^2 - 16x - 36y + 16 = 0$$ Complete the square: $$4(x^2 - 4x + 4 - 4) + 9(y^2 - 4y + 4 - 4) + 16 = 0$$ $$4(x - 2)^2 - 16 + 9(y - 2)^2 - 36 + 16 = 0$$ $$4(x-2)^2 + 9(y-2)^2 = 36$$ This is an ellipse $\boxed{\dfrac{(x-2)^2}{9} + \dfrac{(y-2)^2}{4} = 1}$	Express the equation in a standard form through some algebraic manipulation. First, collect x-terms and the y-terms. Factor out any constants within each group. Complete the square for x and also for y. Move the unattached constants to the other side of the equation. Divide by the constant coefficients of each square. Now you have the equation in standard form! This particular equation describes an ellipse.
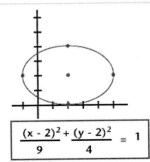 $$\dfrac{(x-2)^2}{9} + \dfrac{(y-2)^2}{4} = 1$$	Let's review how to graph the ellipse. First, find its center. In this case the center is $(2, 2)$. The a^2 tells you to go 3 units to the sides. Similarly, the b^2 tells you to go 2 units up and down. With these points plotted, it's a snap to sketch in the ellipse.

Sample problems:

1. Express the following equation in standard form, identify the conic, and state the location of its center or vertex: $-9x^2 + 4y^2 = 36$.

Solution: $\dfrac{y^2}{9} - \dfrac{x^2}{4} = 1$; hyperbola with center $(0, 0)$

Explanation: The equation appears to be a hyperbola since it is similar to $\dfrac{y^2}{a^2} - \dfrac{x^2}{b^2} = 1$.

Switch the x and y terms and divide the equation by 36: $\dfrac{4y^2}{36} - \dfrac{9x^2}{36} = \dfrac{36}{36}$; $\dfrac{y^2}{9} - \dfrac{x^2}{4} = 1$.

Therefore, it is an up/down hyperbola with center at $(0, 0)$.

2. Express the following equation in standard form, identify the conic, and state the location of its center or vertex: $x^2 - 6x + y^2 + 8y = 5$.

Solution: $(x-3)^2 + (y+4)^2 = 30$; circle with center $(3, -4)$

Explanation: The equation appears to be a circle. Complete the square for x and y:
$(x^2 - 6x + 9) + (y^2 + 8y + 16) = 5 + 9 + 16$. Factor and simplify: $(x-3)^2 + (y+4)^2 = 30$.
Therefore, since this equation is in the form $(x-h)^2 + (y-k)^2 = r^2$, the conic is a circle and the center is $(3, -4)$.

3. Express the following equation in standard form, identify the conic, and state the location of its center or vertex: $x^2 - 10x - 8y + 17 = 0$.

Solution: $(x-5)^2 = 8(y+1)$; parabola with vertex $(5, -1)$

Explanation: The equation appears to be a parabola since x is squared, but y is not.

So, manipulate the equation to express it in the standard form of a parabola, $(x-h)^2 = 4p(y-k)$.
Move the y-term and the constant term to the right side: $x^2 - 10x = 8y - 17$.
Complete the square for x: $x^2 - 10x + 25 = 8y - 17 + 25$. Factor and simplify: $(x-5)^2 = 8y + 8$.
Factor an 8 out of the right side: $(x-5)^2 = 8(y+1)$. So, the conic is a parabola and the vertex is at $(5, -1)$.

Practice problems: *(Answers on page: 466)*

1. Express the following equation in standard form, identify the conic, and state the location of its center or vertex: $-x^2 + 4y^2 - 6x - 8y - 21 = 0$.

2. Express the following equation in standard form, identify the conic, and state the location of its center or vertex: $9x^2 + 36y^2 - 36 = 0$.

3. Express the following equation in standard form, identify the conic, and state the location of its center or vertex: $2x^2 - 8x - 20y = 52$.

Review questions: *(Answers to odd questions on page: 467)*

1. Express the following equation in standard form, identify the conic, and state the location of its center or vertex: $-4x^2 - 12y^2 + 16x - 36y + 5 = 0$.

2. Express the following equation in standard form, identify the conic, and state the location of its center or vertex: $3x^2 - 12x + 3y^2 - 6 = 0$.

3. Express the following equation in standard form, identify the conic, and state the location of its center or vertex: $3y^2 - x + 15y + 11 = 0$.

4. Express the following equation in standard form, identify the conic, and state the location of its center or vertex: $x^2 - 6x - 4y^2 + 12y - 5 = 0$.

5. Express the following equation in standard form, identify the conic, and state the location of its center or vertex: $x^2 - 4y + 8 = 0$.

Name That Conic

- You can determine whether an equation describes a conic section and which conic section an equation describes by completing the square for the x and y variables and factoring.
- The standard equation for a **parabola** centered at (h, k) is $(x - h)^2 = 4p(y - k)$.
- The standard equation for a **circle** centered at (h, k) is $(x - h)^2 + (y - k)^2 = r^2$.
- The standard equation for an **ellipse** centered at (h, k) is $\dfrac{(x-h)^2}{a^2} + \dfrac{(y-k)^2}{b^2} = 1$.

- The standard equation for a **hyperbola** centered at (h, k) that opens to the left and right is $\dfrac{(x-h)^2}{a^2} - \dfrac{(y-k)^2}{b^2} = 1$. For a hyperbola centered at (h, k) that opens upwards and downwards, the standard equation is $\dfrac{(y-k)^2}{b^2} - \dfrac{(x-h)^2}{a^2} = 1$.

Example **Original Equation:** $\quad 9x^2 - 25y^2 - 18x + 50y = 0$ Complete the square: $9(x^2 - 2x + 1 - 1) - 25(y^2 - 2y + 1 - 1) = 0$ $9(x - 1)^2 - 9 - 25(y - 1)^2 + 25 = 0$ $9(x\text{-}1)^2 - 25(y\text{-}1)^2 = -16$ $\dfrac{9(x-1)^2}{-16} + \dfrac{25(y-1)^2}{16} = 1$	What conic section does this equation represent? First collect the x and y terms together. Factor any constants from each group. Watch out for those negative signs! Then, complete the square. Remove any unattached constants to the other side of the equation. Divide everything by the constant coefficients. Things are starting to look more familiar now.
$\dfrac{9(x-1)^2}{-16} + \dfrac{25(y-1)^2}{16} = 1$ $\boxed{\dfrac{(y\text{-}1)^2}{(\frac{4}{5})^2} - \dfrac{(x\text{-}1)^2}{(\frac{4}{3})^2} = 1}$	To finish things off, use a compound fraction to put the constant coefficients entirely in the denominators. You can see that the equation is now in the standard form for a hyperbola that opens upwards and downwards.
   $\boxed{\dfrac{(y\text{-}1)^2}{(\frac{4}{5})^2} - \dfrac{(x\text{-}1)^2}{(\frac{4}{3})^2} = 1}$	To graph the hyperbola, notice first that its center is at $(1, 1)$. Then, the coefficient of $(4/5)^2$ under the y term tells you to go up and down from the center by 4/5 units. With these points plotted, you can make a rough graph of the hyperbola.

Sample problems:

1. Identify the type of conic section represented by $3x^2 - 30x - 4y + 67 = 0$.
   Solution: Parabola
   Explanation: Since the x-term is squared, but the y-term is not, the conic must be a parabola. The same result is obtained when the equation is expressed in standard form by separating the terms and completing the square: $3x^2 - 30x = 4y - 67$; $3(x^2 - 10x) = 4y - 67$; $3(x^2 - 10x + 25)4y - 67 + 75$; $3(x-5)^2 = 4y + 8$; $(x-5)^2 = \dfrac{4}{3}(y + 2)$. So, this is the standard form of a parabola, $(x - h)^2 = 4p(y - k)$.

2. Identify the type of conic section represented by $x^2 + 22 = 10x - y^2 - 2y$.
   Solution: Circle
   Explanation: The equation contains x^2 and y^2, so it is not a parabola. It appears to be a circle or an ellipse since x^2 and y^2 will have the same sign when on the same side of the equation. Write the equation in standard from. First, move the y-terms to the left and the constant to the right, and then complete the square twice: $x^2 - 10x + y^2 + 2y = -22$; $x^2 + 10x + 25 + y^2 + 2y + 1 = -22 + 25 + 1$. Factor and simplify: $(x-5)^2 + (y+1)^2 = 4$. The equation is in the form $(x - h)^2 + (y - k)^2 = r^2$, so the conic is a circle.

3. Identify the type of conic section represented by $3x^2 - 18y^2 = 36$.
   Solution: Hyperbola
   Explanation: The equation appears to be a hyperbola since x^2 and y^2 have opposite signs. Divide the equation by 36 to write the equation in the standard form of a hyperbola, $\dfrac{x^2}{a^2} - \dfrac{y^2}{b^2} = 1$: $\dfrac{3x^2}{36} - \dfrac{18y^2}{36} = \dfrac{36}{36}$; $\dfrac{x^2}{12} - \dfrac{y^2}{2} = 1$; $\dfrac{x^2}{(\sqrt{12})^2} - \dfrac{y^2}{(\sqrt{2})^2} = 1$. Thus, the conic is a hyperbola.

Practice problems: *(Answers on page: 467)*

1. Identify the type of conic section represented by $x^2 + y^2 - 14x + 6y = 42$.

2. Identify the type of conic section represented by $15y^2 + 14x^2 = 90$.

3. Identify the type of conic section represented by $-2x^2 + 3x + 7y = 0$.

Review questions: *(Answers to odd questions on page: 467)*

1. Identify the type of conic section represented by $3x = 2y^2 + 7y - 11$.

2. Identify the type of conic section represented by $4x^2 - 6x + 9y^2 + 15y - 1 = 0$.

3. Identify the type of conic section represented by $3x^2 + 15x - 3y^2 = 0$.

4. Identify the type of conic section represented by $\dfrac{(x-7)^2}{20} + \dfrac{(y+3)^2}{20} = 1$.

5. Identify the type of conic section represented by $15y^2 + 14x^2 = 90$.

Answer Key:

Algebraic Prerequisites

Using the Cartesian System *p.19*

Practice: **1.** True   **2.** quadrant IV   **3.** $(-2, 2)$

Review: **1.** False   **3.** $(5, -5)$ **5.** the fourth quadrant

Thinking Visually *p.21*

Finding the Distance between Two Points *p.22*

Practice: **1.** 14.8   **2.** $5\sqrt{7}$ **3.** $(1997, 7900)$

Review: **1.** $(-3, -7)$ **3.** 17.37   **5.** 14.8

Finding the Second Endpoint of a Segment *p.24*

Practice: **1.** $\left(\frac{1}{2}, -1\right)$ **2.** 10   **3.** $(3n+1, -n)$

Review: **1.** $(1, 12)$ **3.** 1   **5.** $\left(\frac{2z}{3}, 0\right)$

Collinearity and Distance *p.26*

Practice: **1.** yes   **2.** no   **3.** yes

Review: **1.** yes   **3.** yes   **5.** yes

Triangles *p.27*

Practice: **1.** True   **2.** yes   **3.** no

Review: **1.** yes   **3.** no   **5.** no

Finding the Center-Radius Form of the Equation of a Circle *p.29*

Practice: **1.** $(x-3)^2 + (y+2)^2 = 5$ **2.** $x^2 + y^2 = 25$ **3.** False

Review: **1.** $(x+4)^2 + (y-2)^2 = 25$ **3.** $x^2 + (y-3)^2 = 9$ **5.** $(x-4)^2 + (y-2)^2 = 9$

Finding the Center and Radius of a Circle *p.31*

Practice: **1.** $(3, -1)$; $r = \sqrt{13}$ **2.** $\left(\frac{1}{3}, \frac{2}{3}\right)$; $r = 2$ **3.** $\left(\frac{2}{3}, \frac{1}{2}\right)$; $r = 1$

Review: **1.** $(3, -4)$; radius $= 4\sqrt{2}$ **3.** $(-2\sqrt{3}, -\sqrt{3})$; radius $= 3$ **5.** $\left(\frac{1}{2}, -\frac{1}{3}\right)$; radius $= \frac{1}{2}$

Decoding the Circle Formula *p.33*

Practice: **1.** $(2, 0)$; $r = 3$ **2.**   **3.** $(-4, 1)$; $r = \sqrt{5}$

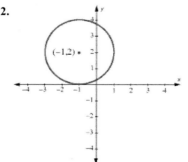

Review: **1.** $(3, 4)$; radius $= \sqrt{3}$ **3.** $(9, 3)$; radius $= 6$ **5.** $(0, -4)$; radius $= 121$

Solving Word Problems Involving Circles *p.34*

Practice: **1.** $(7, -7)$ and $(-1, 1)$ **2.** $(x-4)^2 + (y-1)^2 = 25$ **3.** $\left(x - \dfrac{1}{2}\right)^2 + \left(y - \dfrac{1}{2}\right)^2 = \dfrac{1}{2}$

Review: **1.** $(x-3)^2 + (y-5)^2 = 8$ **3.** $73 = (x-1)^2 + (y+2)^2$ **5.** 20

Graphing Equations by Locating Points *p.37*

Practice: **1.**
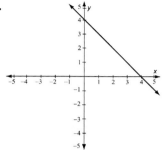
2.
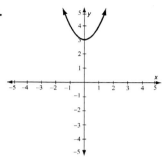
3.
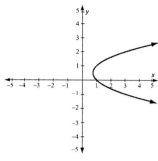

Review: **1.**
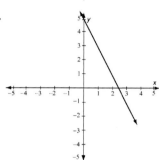
3.
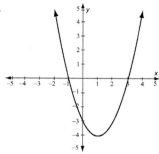
5.
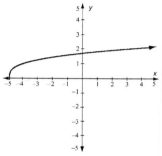

Finding the x- and y-Intercepts of an Equation *p.40*

Practice: **1.** $1, -3$ **2.** $\dfrac{5}{3}$ **3.** 2 or -2

Review: **1.** -8 **3.** $0, 3$ **5.** 3

Functions and the Vertical Line Test *p.42*

Practice: **1.** False   **2.** True   **3.** True

Review: **1.** Yes   **3.** False   **5.** True

Identifying Functions *p.45*

Practice: **1.** y is a function of x **2.** y is not a function of x **3.** y is a function of x

Review: **1.** y is a function of x **3.** y is not a function of x **5.** y is a function of x

Function Notation and Finding Function Values *p.47*

Practice: **1.** $\dfrac{a^2 + 2a + 3}{a + 1}$ **2.** $x^2 + 2hx + h^2 - 2x - 2h$ **3.** $x + 1$

Review: **1.** 0   **3.** 4   **5.** $\dfrac{2x - 5}{6x}$

Determining Intervals Over Which a Function Is Increasing *p.49*

Practice: **1.** $(0, \infty)$ **2.** $(-\infty, \infty)$ **3.** $(-3, 1)$

Review: **1.** $(0, \infty)$ **3.** $(-\infty, \infty)$ **5.** $(2, 3)$

Evaluating Piecewise-Defined Functions for Given Values *p.53*

Practice: **1.** $(-\infty, -1]$ and $[1, \infty)$ **2.** $-\dfrac{1}{3}$ **3.** -2

Review: **1.** $(0, 1)$ **3.** -10 **5.** -8

Solving Word Problems Involving Functions *p.55*

Practice: **1.** 64 units^2 **2.** $V = \dfrac{4}{3}\pi\left(\dfrac{S}{4\pi}\right)^{\frac{3}{2}}$ **3.** $A = 10w - w^2$

Review: **1.** 55 units^2 **3.** $\dfrac{C^2}{4\pi}$ **5.** $4x(5-x)(4-x)$

Finding the Domain and Range of a Function *p.57*

Practice: **1.** $-\infty < x < \infty$ **2.** $x \le 6$ **3.** domain: $x < 15$; range: $y \ge -3$

Review: **1.** $y \ge 4$ **3.** All real numbers   **5.** All real numbers

Domain and Range: One Explicit Example *p.62*

Practice: **1.** All real numbers except -4 **2.** All real numbers ≥ 5 **3.** Domain: $\mathbb{R}$; Range: $y \le 0$

Review: **1.** All real numbers   **3.** domain: All real numbers   **5.** domain: All real numbers except 3
                                          range: All real numbers   range: All real numbers except 0

Satisfying the Domain of a Function *p.64*

Practice: **1.** $x \ge -5$ **2.** $\mathbb{R} \setminus \{-3\}$ **3.** $x < 5 \setminus \{-4\}$

Review: **1.** $\mathbb{R} \setminus \{4\}$ **3.** $-3 \le x \le 3$ **5.** $[-2,3) \cup (3,\infty)$

An Introduction to Slope *p.66*

Finding the Slope of a Line Given Two Points *p.66*

Practice: **1.** $-\dfrac{9}{2}$ **2.** 1 **3.** -1

Review: **1.** $\dfrac{1}{3}$ **3.** $\dfrac{13}{22}$ **5.** $\dfrac{1}{3}$

Interpreting Slope from a Graph *p.68*

Practice: **1.** undefined   **2.** increase   **3.** decrease

Review: **1.** -8 **3.** increase   **5.** decrease

Graphing a Line Using Point and Slope *p.70*

Practice: **1.** $(0, 8)$ **2.** 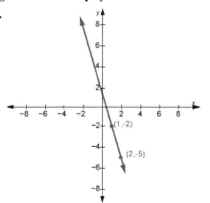   **3.** No

Review:

1.

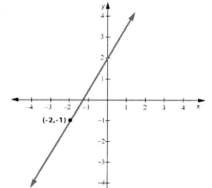

3.

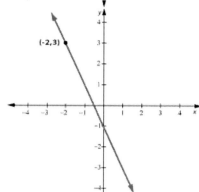

5.

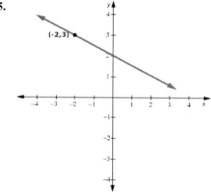

Writing an Equation in Slope-Intercept Form *p.72*

Practice: **1.** $y = \dfrac{4}{3}x - 1$ **2.** $m = -1$ and $b = 2$ **3.** $y = 3x$

Review: **1.** $y = -3x + 4$ **3.** $y = \dfrac{2}{3}x - 2$ **5.** $y = \dfrac{1}{3}x$

Writing an Equation Given Two Points *p.74*

Practice: **1.** $y = 22x + 29$ **2.** $y = -x$ **3.** $y = \dfrac{14}{13}x - \dfrac{37}{13}$

Review: **1.** $y = 2x$ **3.** $y = -2x$ **5.** $y = -\dfrac{1}{3}x + 7$

Writing an Equation in Point-Slope Form *p.75*

Practice: **1.** $y = 4(x - 3)$ **2.** $y - 5 = -2(x + 1)$ **3.** $y - 2 = 3(x + 3)$

Review: **1.** $y - 5 = 4(x - 2)$ **3.** $y = -(x - 4)$ **5.** $\left(y + \dfrac{2}{3}\right) = \dfrac{5}{3}\left(x - \dfrac{3}{4}\right)$

Matching a Slope-Intercept Equation with Its Graph *p.77*

Practice: **1.** Yes   **2.** Yes   **3.** $y = -\dfrac{3}{4}x + 4$

Review: **1.** Yes   **3.** $y = \frac{3}{2}x + 3$ **5.** Yes

Slope for Parallel and Perpendicular Lines *p.81*

Practice: **1.** 2   **2.** −2   **3.** $y = -\dfrac{3}{2}x + 5$

Review: **1.** $\dfrac{1}{2}$ **3.** $y = \dfrac{5}{2}x + \dfrac{1}{2}$ **5.** $y = -\dfrac{1}{2}x - \dfrac{11}{2}$

Graphing Some Important Functions *p.84*

Practice: **1.** $f(x) = \sqrt{x}$ **2.** $y = x^2$ **3.** I and IV

Review: **1.** False   **3.** $y = x$ **5.** True

Graphing Piecewise-Defined Functions *p.85*

Practice: **1.** $[0, \infty)$ **2.**
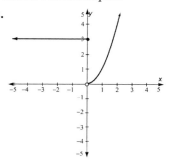
3.
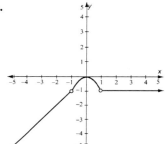

Review: **1.** 3   **3.** All positive numbers.   **5.**
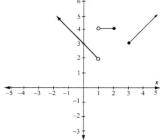

Matching Equations with Their Graphs *p.88*

Practice: **1.** $y = |x|$ **2.** $x = y^2$ **3.** $y = \dfrac{1}{x}$

Review: **1.** $y = x$ **3.** $y = x^3$ **5.** $y = 2^x$

Shifting Curves along Axes *p.92*

Practice:
1. Add +2 to the function's expression;
   therefore $f(x) = x^2 - 2$ becomes $f(x) = x^2$
2. Add +3 to the expression
3. $y = x^2$

Review: **1.** Add +7 to the function   **3.** True   **5.** $y = (x - 6)^2 - 2$

Shifting or Translating Curves along Axes *p.94*

Practice: 1. $f(x) = \dfrac{5}{4}\left(x - \dfrac{9}{2}\right)^2 + \dfrac{7}{4}$ **2.** $f(x) = 2(x+3)^2 - 5$ **3.** $b = 4;\ c = -14$

Review: 1. $f(x) = 5(x - 2\frac{1}{2})^2 - 1$ **3.** $f(x) = -(x + 3\frac{2}{5})^2 + 3$ **5.** $b = 0$ and $c = 6$

Stretching a Graph *p.95*

Practice: 1. True   **2.** False   **3.** True

Review: 1. True   **3.** False   **5.** The curve becomes narrower and gets flipped upside down

Graphing Quadratics Using Patterns *p.97*

Practice: 1. $y = \dfrac{10}{3}(x+7)^2$ **2.** $y = (x - 3.25)^2 + 1.5$ **3.** $y = (x+8)^2 - 3$

Review: 1. $y = 4(x+2)^2 + 5$ **3.** $y = -(x+3)^2 + 4$ **5.** $y = (x+8)^2 - 3$

Determining Symmetry *p.99*

Practice: 1. $(4, -1)$ and $(-5, 0)$ **2.** $(-2, 0)$ and $(5, 1)$ **3.** Odd

Review: 1. $(-3, -2)$ and $(0, -1)$ **3.** $(-13, 4)$ and $(7, 1)$ **5.** Neither

Reflections *p.101*

Practice: 1. $(-5, 2)$, $(1, 7)$, and $(0, 2)$ **2.** $(a-1, b-d)$ and $(d-c, e)$ **3.**

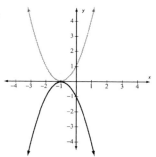

Review: 1. $(-10, -2)$, $(1, 3)$, and $(0, 0)$ **3.** $(2a+x, y-1)$ and $(z-w, -1-z)$ **5.**

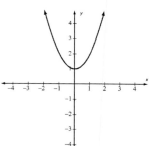

Reflecting Specific Functions *p.103*

Practice: 1. $(-1, 3)$ and $(1, 3)$ **2.** $g(x) = -2x^2 + x - 1$ **3.** $g(x) = \dfrac{1 + x^3}{x^2}$

Review: 1. $(2, -6)$ and $(-2, -6)$ **3.** $g(x) = x^3 + x^2 - x$ **5.** $g(x) = 1 + x - x^3$

Deconstructing the Graph of a Quadratic Function *p.105*

Practice: 1. 2 units to the left and one unit down   **2.** $(-5, 0)$, maximum   **3.** $y \geq -3$

Review: 1. $\frac{1}{2}$ units to the right and three units up   **3.** $(7, 1)$, minimum   **5.** $y \leq 2$

Nice-Looking Parabolas *p.107*

Practice: 1. down, $(0, 5)$ **2.** up, $(2, 0)$ **3.** up, $(-3, -7)$

Review: 1. up, $(0, -8)$ **3.** down, $(3, -2)$ **5.** up, $(-1, 1)$

Using Discriminants to Graph Parabolas *p.108*

Practice:
1. False, the discriminant is positive.
2. the vertex is on the *x*-axis and the parabola opens down
3. the dicriminant is >0

Review: **1.** False, the discriminant is zero. **3.** True **5.** the discriminant is 0 and *a* is negative

Maximum Height in the Real World *p.111*

Practice: **1.** $7.5\,\text{sec}.$ **2.** 5 sec., 400 ft. **3.** 10 seconds

Review: **1.** \$500 **3.** $1\frac{7}{8}$ second **5.** 2.5

Finding the Vertex by Completing the Square *p.113*

Practice: **1.** $\left(\frac{1}{4}, -\frac{15}{16}\right)$ **2.** $(-2, 9)$ **3.** $\left(\frac{1}{4}, -\frac{11}{4}\right)$

Review: **1.** $(1, 5)$ **3.** $(-1, -1)$ **5.** $\left(\frac{1}{2}, 1\right)$

Using the Vertex to Write the Quadratic Equation *p.115*

Practice: **1.** $y = (x-3)^2 + 1$ **2.** $y = 2(x+3)^2 - 5$ **3.** $y = 3x^2 - 6x + 1$

Review: **1.** $y = (x-4)^2 + 1$ **3.** $y = 5(x+1)^2 + 2$ **5.** $f(x) = 3x^2 - 18x + 1$

Finding the Maximum or Minimum of a Quadratic *p.117*

Practice: **1.** 1 **2.** $-\frac{35}{64}$ **3.** True

Review: **1.** 2 **3.** -6.05 **5.** $\frac{25}{12}$

Graphing Parabolas *p.118*

Practice:
1. vertex: $(0, 0)$; direction: up; *x* and *y*-intercepts: $(0, 0)$
2. vertex: $(4, 0)$; direction: up; *x*-intercept: $(4, 0)$; *y*-intercept: $(0, 8)$
3. vertex: $\left(-\frac{1}{3}, \frac{16}{3}\right)$; direction: down; *x*-intercept: $\left(-\frac{5}{3}, 0\right)$ and $(1, 0)$; *y*-intercept: $(0, 5)$

Review:
1. vertex: $(0, 0)$; direction: up; *x* and *y*-intercepts: $(0, 0)$
3. vertex: $(-1, -7)$; direction: up; *x*-intercepts: $-1 \pm \sqrt{7}$; *y*-intercept: $(0, -6)$
5. vertex: $\left(\frac{3}{2}, \frac{3}{2}\right)$; opens down; *x*-intercepts: $\frac{3 \pm \sqrt{3}}{2}$; *y*-intercept: -3

Using Operations on Functions *p.121*

Practice: **1.** $28x^3 - 7x^2$ **2.** $10x + 10$ **3.** $3x^2 + 7x + 6xh - 7h + 3h^2 - 3$

Review: **1.** True **3.** $\frac{1}{(x-5)}, \ x \neq \pm 5$ **5.** $4x^3 - x^2 - 7x + 3$

Composite Functions *p.122*

Practice: **1.** 16 **2.** 9 **3.** $\frac{5}{4}$

Review: **1.** 4 **3.** $2x^2 + 11$ **5.** 15

Components of Composite Functions *p.124*

Practice: **1.** $180x^2 + 240x + 80$ **2.** $x^2 - 10x + 30$ **3.** $-3x^2 - 6x + 6$

Review: **1.** -50 **3.** $18x^2 - 48x + 35$ **5.** $12x^2 + 12x + 8$

Finding Functions That Form a Given Composite *p.125*

Practice: **1.** $g(x) = 3x - 1, f(x) = 2x^2$ **2.** $g(x) = x^2, f(x) = -x^2 + 5x$ **3.** $g(x) = x^3, f(x) = \frac{1}{2}x^2 - 3x + 1$

Review: **1.** $g(x) = 1 - x, f(x) = 3x^5$ **3.** $g(x) = 2x, f(x) = 3x^6 + 3x^3 - x$ **5.** $g(x) = x^4, f(x) = x^2 - x$

Finding the Difference Quotient of a Function *p.127*

Practice: **1.** $5h^2 + 10hx + 2h$ **2.** $2x + h + 2, h \neq 0$ **3.** $4x + 2h - 3, h \neq 0$

Review: **1.** $h^2 + 2hx$ **3.** $2x + h - 6, h \neq 0$ **5.** $-3x^2 - h^2 - 3hx + 5, h \neq 0$

Understanding Rational Functions *p.128*

Practice:
1. Domain: all real numbers x such that $x \neq 4$
   Range: all real numbers y such that $y \neq -2$
2. Domain: all real numbers x such that $x \neq -2$
   Range: all real numbers y such that $y \neq -3$
3. $y = 0$ and $x = 0$

Review:
1. Domain: all real numbers x such that $x \neq 2$
   Range: all real numbers y such that $y \neq 3$
3. Domain: all real numbers x such that $x \neq -4$
   Range: all real numbers y such that $y \neq -3$
5. $y = -2$ and $x = 3$

Basic Rational Functions *p.132*

Practice: **1.**
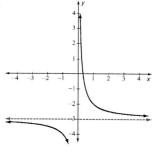

2.
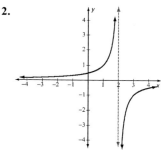

3.
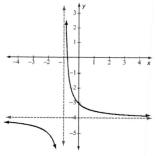

Review: **1.**
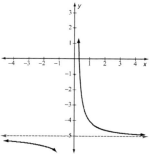

3.
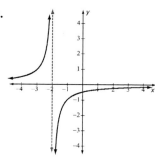

5.
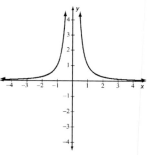

Vertical Asymptotes *p.134*

Practice: **1.** $x = -7$ **2.** $x = 3$ and $x = -3$ **3.** no vertical asymptotes

Review: **1.** $x = 0$ **3.** $x = 5$ and $x = -5$ **5.** no vertical asymptotes

Horizontal Asymptotes *p.136*

Practice: **1.** $y = 0$ **2.** $y = 0$ **3.** $y = \dfrac{1}{4}$

Review: **1.** $y = 0$ **3.** $y = 1$ **5.** does not exist

Graphing Rational Functions *p.138*

Practice: **1.**

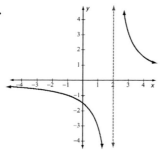

2.

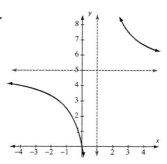

3.

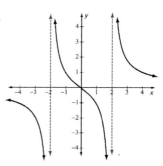

Review: **1.**

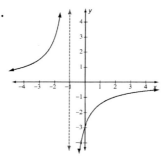

3.

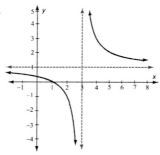

5.

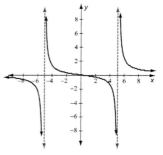

Graphing Rational Functions: More Examples *p.140*

Practice: **1.**

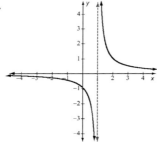

2.

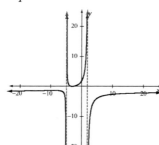

3.

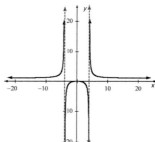

Review: **1.**

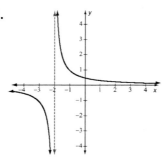

3.

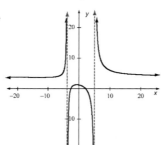

5.

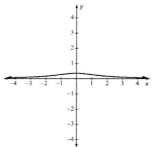

Understanding Inverse Functions *p.143*

Practice: **1.** −4   **2.** −3   **3.** 5

Review: **1.** 12   **3.** 5   **5.** 17.5

The Horizontal Line Test *p.144*

Practice: **1.** yes   **2.** False   **3.** True

Review: **1.** No   **3.** False   **5.** False

Are Two Functions Inverses of Each Other? *p.146*

Practice: **1.** Yes, the two functions are inverses. **2.** True **3.** True

Review: **1.** Yes **3.** No **5.** True

Graphing the Inverse *p.149*

Practice: **1.**

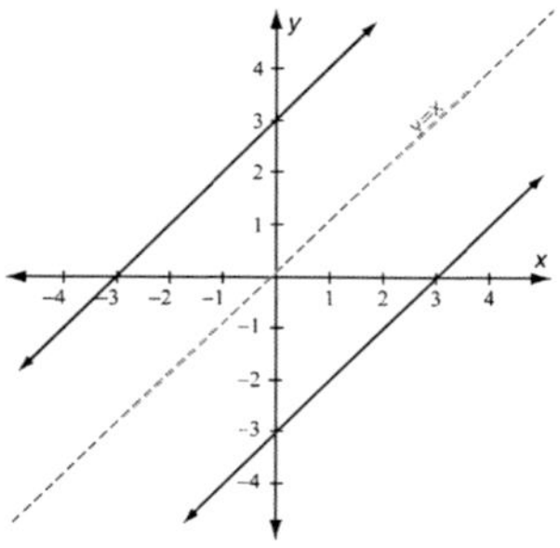

2.

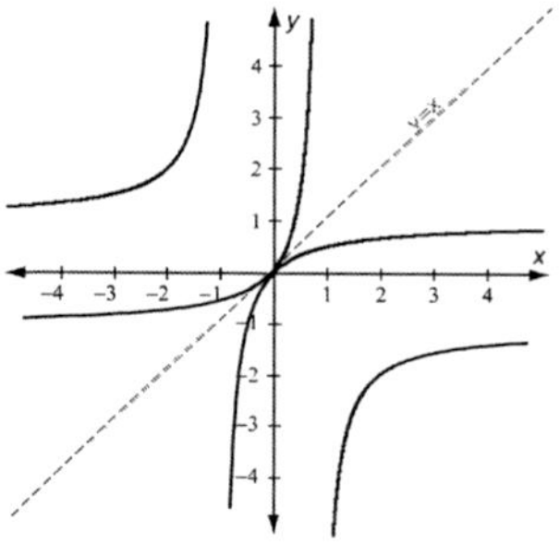

3.

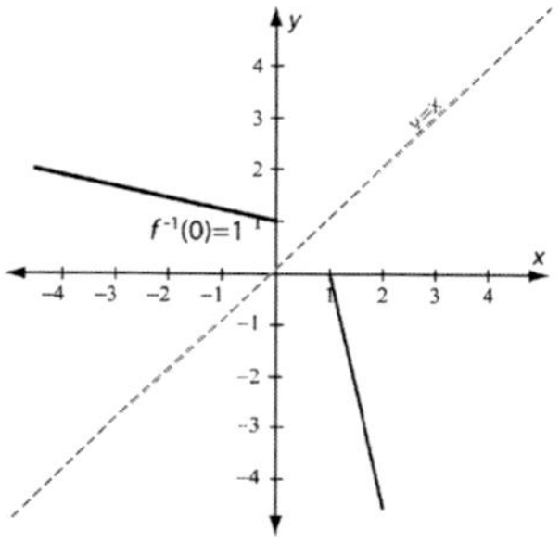

Review: **1.**

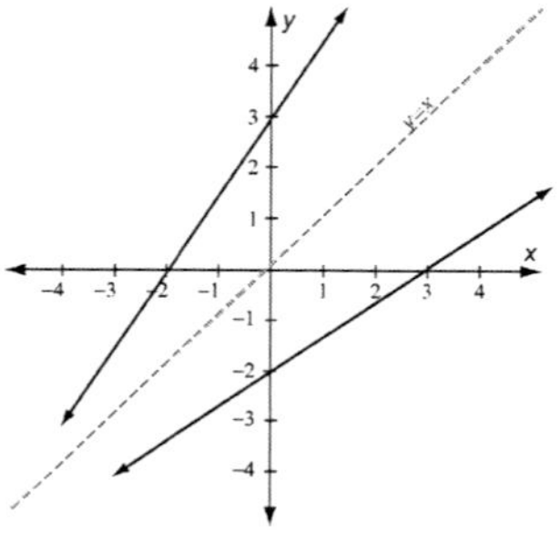

3.

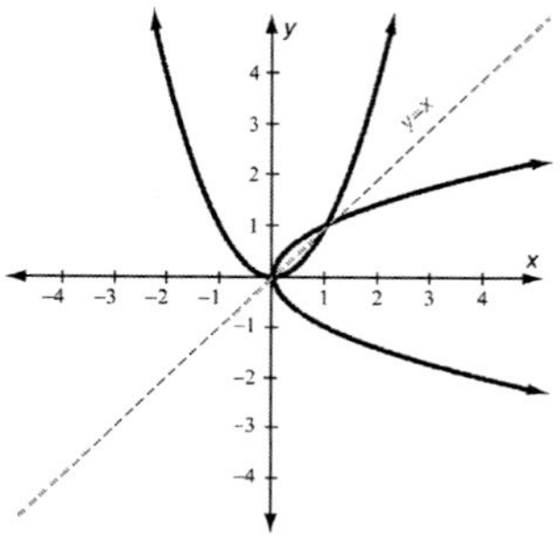

5.

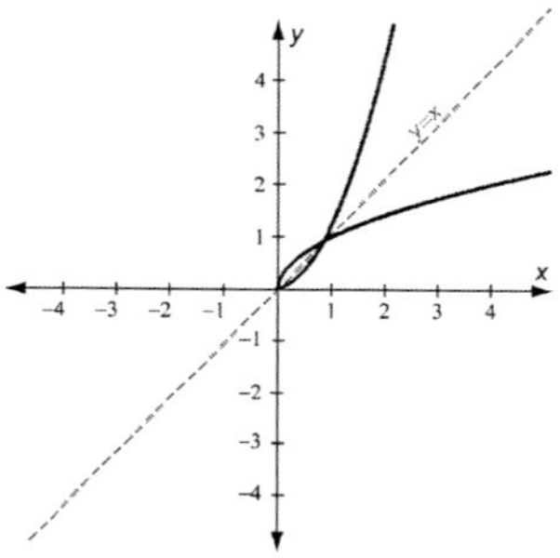

Finding the Inverse of a Function *p.153*

Practice:

1. $g^{-1}(x) = \dfrac{5}{2} - \dfrac{7x}{6}.$
2. The function is not invertible because it is not one-to-one.
3. $p^{-1}(x) = 5x^2;$
   $p^{-1}(3) = 45$ feet;
   If the period is 3 seconds
   then the length is 45 feet.

Review: **1.** $f^{-1}x = \frac{1}{2}(x-1);\ f^{-1}(5) = 2$

3. $f^{-1} = \sqrt{\dfrac{(x+5)}{2}},\quad x \geq -5$

5. $t^{-1}(5)$ is how many rescuers are required to find a hiker in 5 hours.
$t^{-1}(5) = \dfrac{80}{x}$ again; $t^{-1}(5) = 16$ rescuers

Finding the Inverse of a Function with Higher Powers *p.155*

Practice:

1. $f^{-1}(x) = \dfrac{\sqrt[3]{x}}{3} - 5$ and $f^{-1}(-8) = -\dfrac{17}{3}$
2. $f(x)$ is not invertible because it is not one-to-one
3. $T^{-1}(1)$ is the amount of poison (grams) in the blood 1 hour after ingestion.
   $T^{-1}(x) = 2 - \dfrac{x^4}{500}$
   $T^{-1}(1) = 1.998$ grams

Review:

1. $f^{-1}(x) = 1 + \sqrt[3]{2x}$ and $f^{-1}(4) = 3$
3. $f(x)$ is not invertible because it is not one-to-one

5. $S^{-1}(10)$ is the power produced by a 10 mph wind.

$S^{-1}(p) = \frac{p^3}{20}$.

$S^{-1}(10) = 50$ watts.

The Trigonometric Functions

Finding the Quadrant in Which an Angle Lies *p.161*

Practice: **1.** Quadrant I **2.** Quadrant III **3.** True

Review: **1.** Quadrant II **3.** Quadrant I **5.** False

Finding Coterminal Angles *p.163*

Practice: **1.** False **2.** False **3.** 285°

Review: **1.** True **3.** True **5.** –173°

Finding the Complement and Supplement of an Angle *p.165*

Practice: **1.** False **2.** $180° - x$ **3.** 32.7°

Review: **1.** False **3.** 122° **5.** 36°

Converting between Degrees and Radians *p.167*

Practice: **1.** $\frac{540}{\pi}°$ **2.** –1200° **3.** $\frac{2\pi}{3}$ radians

Review: **1.** $\frac{\pi}{4}$ rad **3.** $\frac{11\pi}{15}$ rad **5.** 1 radian

Using the Arc Length Formula *p.168*

Practice: **1.** 1.75 meters **2.** 19.635 ft **3.** 2.749 in.

Review: **1.** The length of the arc **3.** 0.586 ft **5.** 9.00 in

An Introduction to the Trigonometric Functions *p.171*

Practice: **1.** False **2.** $\frac{4}{3}$ **3.** $\frac{5}{17}$

Review: **1.** True **3.** $\frac{7}{5}$ **5.** $\frac{1}{4}$

Evaluating Trigonometric Functions for an Angle in a Right Triangle *p.175*

Practice: **1.** $\frac{16}{\sqrt{31}}$ **2.** $\frac{\sqrt{55}}{3}$ **3.** $\frac{9\sqrt{3}}{2}$

Review: **1.** $\frac{5}{4}$ **3.** $\frac{\sqrt{61}}{5}$ **5.** False

Finding an Angle Given the Value of a Trigonometric Function *p.178*

Practice: **1.** 30° **2.** $\frac{\pi}{6}$ rad **3.** $\frac{\pi}{3}$ rad

Review: **1.** $\frac{\pi}{3}$ rad **3.** $\frac{\pi}{3}$ rad **5.** 30° or $\frac{\pi}{6}$

Using Trigonometric Functions to Find Unknown Sides of Right Triangles *p.181*

Practice: **1.** 11.4 **2.** 5.6 **3.** 47.0 ft

Review: **1.** tangent **3.** 8.6 **5.** 427 ft

Finding the Height of a Building *p.184*

Practice: **1.** 1300 ft   **2.** 69 yd   **3.** 27 feet

Review: **1.** True   **3.** 3239 ft   **5.** 0.265 miles

Evaluating Trigonometric Functions for an Angle in the Coordinate Plane *p.187*

Practice: **1.** True   **2.** $\dfrac{4}{5}$ **3.** $\sin\theta = -\dfrac{\sqrt{5}}{5};\ \cos\theta = \dfrac{2\sqrt{5}}{5}$

Review: **1.** $\dfrac{4}{3}$ **3.** Quadrant IV   **5.** $\dfrac{4}{5}$

Evaluating Trigonometric Functions Using the Reference Angle *p.189*

Practice: **1.** $10°$ **2.** $\dfrac{1}{2}$ **3.** True

Review: **1.** $30°$ **3.** $50°$ **5.** $\dfrac{1}{2}$

Finding the Value of Trigonometric Functions Given Information about the Values of Other Trigonometric Functions *p.191*

Practice: **1.** $\sin\theta = -\dfrac{12}{13};\ \cos\theta = \dfrac{5}{13}$ **2.** $\sin\theta = \dfrac{4}{5};\ \tan\theta = -\dfrac{4}{3}$ **3.** $-\sqrt{2}$

Review: **1.** Quadrants I and III   **3.** $\dfrac{2}{\sqrt{5}}$ **5.** $\dfrac{1}{2}$

Trigonometric Functions of Important Angles *p.193*

Practice: **1.** 1   **2.** $-\sqrt{3}$ **3.** 1

Review: **1.** 0   **3.** $\dfrac{\sqrt{3}}{2}$ **5.** $\dfrac{\sqrt{3}}{3}$

An Introduction to the Graphs of Sine and Cosine Functions *p.195*

Practice: **1.** $y = \sin x$ **2.** 3   **3.** 6π

Review: **1.** False   **3.** True   **5.** True

Graphing Sine or Cosine Functions with Different Coefficients *p.198*

Practice:

1. 4

2. The period is $\dfrac{2\pi}{5}$, and the amplitude is 2.

3. True

Review: **1.** 4π **3.** 2   **5.** False

Finding Maximum and Minimum Values and Zeros of Sine and Cosine *p.200*

Practice: **1.** 3   **2.** -2 **3.** 35

Review: **1.** 4   **3.** 3   **5.** 5

Solving Word Problems Involving Sine or Cosine Functions *p.202*

Practice: **1.** 4 feet per second   **2.** 68.18 mi   **3.** 3.5 hours

Review: **1.** 1,584 mph   **3.** Cannot be determined   **5.** 97°F

Graphing Sine and Cosine Functions with Phase Shifts *p.204*

Practice: **1.** 3 to the right   **2.** True   **3.** True

Review: **1.** False **3.** $\dfrac{\pi}{2}$ units to the left **5.** 4 to the left

Fancy Graphing: Changes in Period, Amplitude, Vertical Shift, and Phase Shift *p.206*

Practice: **1.** $\dfrac{\pi}{6}$ to the left **2.** $y = 4\cos(x-3) + 2$ **3.** $y = 3\sin(x-\pi) - 1$

Review: **1.** down 4 units **3.** True **5.** False

Graphing the Tangent, Secant, Cosecant, and Cotangent Functions *p.208*

Practice: **1.** $\dfrac{\pi}{2}$ **2.** $x = k\pi$ (multiples of π) **3.** True

Review: **1.** π **3.** $x = k\pi$ (multiples of π) **5.** True

Fancy Graphing: Tangent, Secant, Cosecant, and Cotangent *p.211*

Practice:
1. True
2. $\dfrac{\pi}{3}$
3. The graph of $y = 2\sec x$ is stretched vertically by 2 and the graph of $y = 2\sec x$ has a period change from 2π to π.

Review:
1. $\dfrac{\pi}{6}$
3. False
5. The coefficient 3 stretches the graph vertically by a factor of 3 and the negative flips it.

Identifying a Trigonometric Function from its Graph *p.214*

Practice: **1.** $y = \cot x + 1$ **2.** False **3.** True

Review: **1.** $y = -\sec x$ **3.** $y = -\tan x - 3$ **5.** True

An Introduction to Inverse Trigonometric Functions *p.218*

Practice: **1.** True **2.** $-1 \le t \le 1$ **3.** True

Review: **1.** True **3.** False **5.** $-\dfrac{\pi}{6} < y < \dfrac{\pi}{6}$

Evaluating Inverse Trigonometric Functions *p.221*

Practice: **1.** $78°$ **2.** $30°$ **3.** $\dfrac{3\pi}{4}$

Review: **1.** 0.853 **3.** No such number exists. **5.** $\dfrac{\pi}{4}$

Solving an Equation Involving an Inverse Trigonometric Function *p.223*

Practice: **1.** $\dfrac{\pi}{2} + 2\pi n$ **2.** $-\dfrac{\pi}{4} + \pi n$ **3.** $\dfrac{5\pi}{6} + 2\pi n$ and $\dfrac{7\pi}{6} + 2\pi n$

Review: **1.** -2 **3.** πn **5.** $\dfrac{5\pi}{3} + 2\pi n$ and $\dfrac{\pi}{3} + 2\pi n$

Evaluating the Composition of a Trigonometric Function and Its Inverse *p.225*

Practice: **1.** $-\dfrac{\pi}{3}$ **2.** $\dfrac{\pi}{3}$ **3.** $\dfrac{\pi}{6}$

Review: **1.** 1.7 **3.** $\dfrac{\pi}{3}$ **5.** $-\dfrac{\pi}{6}$

Applying Trigonometric Functions: Is He Speeding? *p.228*

Practice: **1.** 5.3 mi   **2.** 60.7 mph   **3.** This horse is slower by 5.86 mph.

Review: **1.** 1492.8 ft   **3.** 0.0695 miles   **5.** 3.93 mph over the speed limit

Trigonometric Identities

Fundamental Trigonometric Identities *p.237*

Practice: **1.** True   **2.** False   **3.** $4x^2 + 12x + 9$

Review: **1.** True   **3.** True   **5.** $25x^2 - 30x + 9$

Finding All Function Values *p.239*

Practice: **1.** $\dfrac{\sqrt{3}}{2}$ **2.** $\dfrac{\sqrt{5}}{2}$ **3.** $-\sqrt{35}$

Review: **1.** $\sqrt{3}$ **3.** .86   **5.** 2

Simplifying a Trigonometric Expression Using Trigonometric Identities *p.241*

Practice: **1.** $\sin^2 x$ **2.** $\sin^2 t$ **3.** 1

Review: **1.** $\sec\theta$ **3.** $\tan^2 x$ **5.** 1

Simplifying Trigonometric Expressions Involving Fractions *p.243*

Practice: **1.** $1 + \cot\theta$ **2.** $\cot^2 \theta$ **3.** $\dfrac{1}{\cos^2 x \sin^2 x}$

Review: **1.** 1   **3.** $\tan^3 \theta$ **5.** 1

Simplifying Products of Binomials Involving Trigonometric Functions *p.245*

Practice: **1.** $2 + \cot^2 \theta$ **2.** $\tan^2 t \cdot \sin^2 t$ **3.** $\cot^2 \theta - 1$

Review: **1.** $-\cos^2 x$ **3.** $\tan^2 x - \sin^2 x$ **5.** $\left(\cot^2 x\right)\cos^2 x$

Factoring Trigonometric Expressions *p.247*

Practice: **1.** $2(\cos\theta + 2)(\cos\theta + 3)$ **2.** $\csc\theta$ **3.** $1 + \cot a$

Review: **1.** 1   **3.** 1   **5.** 1

Determining Whether a Trigonometric Function Is Odd, Even, or Neither *p.248*

Practice: **1.** Even   **2.** Odd   **3.** The function is odd.

Review: **1.** Odd   **3.** Neither   **5.** Neither

Proving an Identity *p.250*

Practice: **1.** True   **2.** True   **3.** True

Review: **1.** True   **3.** True   **5.** True

Proving an Identity: Other Examples *p.253*

Practice: **1.** $\csc^2 \theta - \csc^2 \theta \sin\theta = \cot^2 \theta$ **2.** $\dfrac{1}{\cot x} + \cot x = \dfrac{1}{\sin x \cos x}$ **3.** $\dfrac{1 + 2\tan^2 x + \tan^4 x}{1 - \tan^2 x} = \dfrac{\sec^4 x}{1 - \tan^2 x}$

Review: **1.** $\tan x$ **3.** $\tan^2 x + \sin^2 x$ **5.** $\csc\theta - \cot\theta$

Solving Trigonometric Equations *p.255*

Practice: **1.** $x = \dfrac{\pi}{4} + 2\pi n$ and $x = \dfrac{7\pi}{4} + 2\pi n$ **2.** $x = \pi + 2\pi n$ **3.** πn

Review: **1.** $x = \pi + 2\pi n$ **3.** True **5.** $\dfrac{\pi}{4} + \pi n$

Solving Trigonometric Equations by Factoring *p.258*

Practice: **1.** $\theta = 0, \dfrac{\pi}{6}, \dfrac{5\pi}{6}$, or π **2.** $x = 0, \dfrac{\pi}{4}, \pi$, or $\dfrac{5\pi}{4}$ **3.** $x = 0, \dfrac{\pi}{2}$, or π

Review: **1.** $x = 0$ or π **3.** $x = 0, \dfrac{\pi}{2}, \pi, \dfrac{3\pi}{2}$, or 2π **5.** $x = \dfrac{\pi}{3}, \pi, \dfrac{5\pi}{3}$

Solving Trigonometric Equations with Coefficients in the Argument *p.260*

Practice: **1.** $\dfrac{\pi}{12}, \dfrac{5\pi}{12}, \dfrac{13\pi}{12}$, or $\dfrac{17\pi}{12}$ **2.** $\dfrac{3\pi}{4}$ **3.** $\dfrac{4\pi}{9}, \dfrac{8\pi}{9}$, or $\dfrac{16\pi}{9}$

Review: **1.** $\dfrac{\pi}{12}, \dfrac{5\pi}{12}, \dfrac{7\pi}{12}, \dfrac{11\pi}{12}, \dfrac{13\pi}{12}, \dfrac{17\pi}{12}, \dfrac{19\pi}{12}$, and $\dfrac{23\pi}{12}$ **3.** $\dfrac{\pi}{6}, \dfrac{5\pi}{6}, \dfrac{7\pi}{6}$, and $\dfrac{11\pi}{6}$ **5.** π

Solving Trigonometric Equations Using the Quadratic Formula *p.262*

Practice:
1. .373, 1.721, 2.467, 3.815, 4.561, and 5.909 radians
2. 3.553 or 5.872
3. 0.196, 1.375, 3.338, or 4.516

Review: **1.** 1.922, 2.791, 5.064, and 5.933 radians **3.** True **5.** 1.179 or 5.104

Solving Word Problems Involving Trigonometric Equations *p.264*

Practice: **1.** $\dfrac{1}{3}$ **2.** 4.429 seconds **3.** $t = .2793 + \dfrac{\pi}{2}n$ for $0 \le n \le 38$

Review: **1.** 15° **3.** 13 seconds **5.** 5.854 seconds

Identities for Sums and Differences of Angles *p.266*

Practice: **1.** $\dfrac{\sqrt{2} - \sqrt{6}}{4}$ **2.** $\dfrac{-\sqrt{2} - \sqrt{6}}{4}$ **3.** -1.31

Review: **1.** True **3.** $\dfrac{\sqrt{6} + \sqrt{2}}{4}$ **5.** 0.43

Using Sum and Difference Identities *p.268*

Practice: **1.** $\dfrac{\sqrt{6} + \sqrt{2}}{4}$ **2.** $-2 + \sqrt{3}$ **3.** $-\dfrac{63}{16}$

Review: **1.** $\dfrac{\sqrt{6} - \sqrt{2}}{4}$ **3.** $2 + \sqrt{3}$ **5.** $\dfrac{16}{65}$

Using Sum and Difference Identities to Simplify an Expression *p.270*

Practice: **1.** 0 **2.** $\dfrac{\sqrt{3}}{3}$ **3.** $\dfrac{1}{2}$

Review: **1.** $\dfrac{1}{2}$ **3.** $\dfrac{\sqrt{3}}{2}$ **5.** $\cos x$

Confirming a Double-Angle Identity *p.271*

Practice: **1.** $\sqrt{3}$ **2.** $\dfrac{12}{13}$ **3.** $\cos^2 2x$

Review: **1.** 0 **3.** $\dfrac{120}{119}$ **5.** $\dfrac{24}{25}$

Using Double-Angle Identities *p.273*

Practice: **1.** $0, \pi$ **2.** $0, \pi, \frac{\pi}{6}, \frac{5\pi}{6}$ **3.** 0

Review: **1.** $\frac{\pi}{4}, \frac{3\pi}{4}, \frac{5\pi}{4},$ or $\frac{7\pi}{4}$ **3.** $\frac{2\pi}{3}$ or $\frac{4\pi}{3}$ **5.** $\frac{\pi}{2}$ or $\frac{3\pi}{2}$

Solving Word Problems Involving Multiple-Angle Identities *p.275*

Practice: **1.** $2y$ **2.** $\frac{\pi}{2}$ **3.** $\frac{\pi}{4}$ or $45°$

Review: **1.** $x = 5\cos\theta, y = 5\sin\theta$ **3.** $x = 20\cos\theta, y = 20\sin\theta$ **5.** $72\sin\theta\cos\theta$

Using a Cofunction Identity *p.279*

Practice: **1.** $-\tan x$ **2.** $\tan x$ **3.** $-\sin x$

Review: **1.** $\sin x$ **3.** $\sin x$ **5.** $-\tan x$

Using a Power-Reducing Identity *p.282*

Practice: **1.** $\cos 2t$ **2.** $\frac{\pi}{8}, \frac{3\pi}{8}, \frac{5\pi}{8},$ or $\frac{7\pi}{8}$ **3.** $\frac{3 - 4\cos 2t + \cos 4t}{3 + 4\cos 2t + \cos 4t}$

Review: **1.** $\left(\frac{1}{2}\right)(\sin t - \sin t \cos 2t)$ **3.** $\left(\frac{1}{8}\right)(-1 + \cos 4t)$ **5.** $\frac{3 - 4\cos 2t + \cos 4t}{12 + 16\cos 2t + 4\cos 4t}$

Using Half-Angle Identities to Solve a Trigonometric Equation *p.284*

Practice: **1.** $\frac{1}{7}$ **2.** $\frac{\sqrt{26}}{26}$ **3.** $\frac{\sqrt{2 - \left(\sqrt{2 + \sqrt{3}}\right)}}{2}$

Review: **1.** $\frac{\sqrt{2 + \sqrt{3}}}{2}$ **3.** $\sqrt{2} - 1$ **5.** $\frac{\sqrt{\left(2 + \sqrt{2}\right)}}{2}$

Applications of Trigonometry

The Law of Sines *p.289*

Practice: **1.** $a = 73$ mm, $b = 200$ mm   **2.** 237 mm   **3.** 4.3

Review: **1.** 13.5m   **3.** 2.87 cm   **5.** 22.0 in

Solving a Triangle Given Two Sides and One Angle *p.291*

Practice: **1.** $25.7°$ **2.** $31°$ **3.** $a = 22.2, b = 36.5$

Review: **1.** $64.19°$ **3.** $a = 23.67$ in, $A = 80.34°$ **5.** $b = 20.5$ in and $B = 78.65°$

Solving a Triangle (SAS): Another Example *p.293*

Practice: **1.** $\angle 1 = 109°, \angle 2 = 71°$ **2.** $104.88°$ or $21.12°$ **3.** $12.89 < a < 15.75$

Review: **1.** $C = 50.61°, b = 17.10$ ft   **3.** $12.76°$ or $105.24°$ **5.** no solution

The Law of Sines: An Application *p.296*

Practice: **1.** 103.95 m   **2.** 189 miles   **3.** $53.21'$

Review: **1.** 1615 ft   **3.** 11.5 miles   **5.** 14 miles

The Law of Cosines *p.300*

Practice: **1.** An angle and its two adjacent sides   **2.** 5.04 **3.** 6.6

Review: **1.** 3.6 **3.** 11.67 **5.** 12.12 m

The Law of Cosines (SSS) *p.302*

Practice:
1. $34.8°$

2. 53.13°

3. $\gamma = 114.974°$, $\alpha = 22.191°$, and $\beta = 42.835°$

Review: **1.** 22.33° **3.** 36.1° **5.** 34.047°

The Law of Cosines (SAS): An Application *p.304*

Practice: **1.** 3.4 mm **2.** 14.5 cm **3.** 114.57 km

Review: **1.** 3460 m **3.** 3.1 cm **5.** 424.5 km

Heron's Formula *p.306*

Practice: **1.** 63 **2.** 242.9 sq. in. **3.** 309.0 mm^2

Review: **1.** 54 in^2 **3.** 42 cm^2 **5.** 10859.3 sq ft

An Introduction to Vectors *p.309*

Practice: **1.** $< 9,5 >$ **2.** Vectors **a** and **w**. **3.** $\langle 6,-2 \rangle$

Review: **1.** $< 2,5 >$ **3.** $< 7,10 >$ **5.** $< -4,2 >$

Finding the Magnitude and Direction of a Vector *p.313*

Practice: **1.** 329.036° **2.** 273.8° **3.** 3

Review: **1.** $\sqrt{41}$ **3.** $3\sqrt{2}$ or 4.24 **5.** 234.46°

Vector Addition and Scalar Multiplication *p.315*

Practice: **1.** $\langle -18,22 \rangle$ **2.** $\langle -4,16 \rangle$ **3.** $\langle 0,-6 \rangle$

Review: **1.** $\langle 9,-21 \rangle$ **3.** $\langle 6,-9 \rangle$ **5.** $\langle 23,-13 \rangle$

Finding the Components of a Vector *p.317*

Practice: **1.** $(-\sqrt{3},-1)$ **2.** $(-15,15)$ **3.** $\langle -6.31,-9.01 \rangle$

Review: **1.** $\langle 5,5\sqrt{3} \rangle$ **3.** $\langle 6\sqrt{2},6\sqrt{2} \rangle$ **5.** $\langle 9.66,-2.59 \rangle$

Finding a Unit Vector *p.321*

Practice: **1.** $\left\langle \dfrac{-3\sqrt{58}}{58},\dfrac{-7\sqrt{58}}{58} \right\rangle$ **2.** $\langle 1,0 \rangle$ **3.** 1

Review: **1.** $\left\langle -\dfrac{5}{13},\dfrac{12}{13} \right\rangle$ **3.** $\left\langle -\dfrac{\sqrt{2}}{2},\dfrac{\sqrt{2}}{2} \right\rangle$ **5.** $\left\langle \dfrac{7}{25},\dfrac{-24}{25} \right\rangle$

Solving Word Problems Involving Velocity or Forces *p.323*

Practice: **1.** $90\langle -\sqrt{3},1 \rangle$ **2.** 225° **3.** 119.8

Review: **1.** $\langle 125,125\sqrt{3} \rangle$ **3.** $v = \langle 12.7,27.2 \rangle$ **5.** The plane is moving 493 mph on a bearing of 33.4°

Complex Numbers and Polar Coordinates

Introducing and Writing Complex Numbers *p.329*

Practice: **1.** $2i\sqrt{5}$ **2.** $9 + 3i\sqrt{2}$ **3.** $30i\sqrt{3}$

Review: **1.** $11i$ **3.** $7 + i$ **5.** $2\sqrt{5}(5i + 7)$

Rewriting Powers of i *p.330*

Practice: **1.** i **2.** $-i$ **3.** -1

Review: **1.** 1   **3.** $-i$ **5.** -1

Adding and Subtracting Complex Numbers *p.331*

Practice: **1.** $8i - 3$ **2.** $-4i + 3$ **3.** $14i + 42$

Review: **1.** 3   **3.** $-3 - 7i$ **5.** i

Multiplying Complex Numbers *p.333*

Practice: **1.** $21 + 20i$ **2.** 6   **3.** $-3 - 7i$

Review: **1.** $2i$ **3.** $12i$ **5.** $7 + 6i$

Dividing Complex Numbers *p.334*

Practice: **1.** $\dfrac{12}{13} + \dfrac{5}{13}i$ **2.** $\dfrac{11}{10} + \dfrac{13}{10}i$ **3.** $\dfrac{67}{113} + \dfrac{12}{113}i$

Review: **1.** $\dfrac{1}{5} + \dfrac{1}{5}i$ **3.** $\dfrac{3}{5} - \dfrac{4}{5}i$ **5.** $\dfrac{27}{61} + \dfrac{8}{61}i$

Graphing a Complex Number and Finding Its Absolute Value *p.336*

Practice: **1.** 5   **2.** False.   **3.** $5\sqrt{5}$

Review: **1.** True   **3.** 10   **5.** $\sqrt{290}$

Expressing a Complex Number in Trigonometric or Polar Form *p.338*

Practice: **1.** $7\left(\cos 270° + i\sin 270°\right)$ **2.** $5\sqrt{2}\left(\cos\dfrac{3\pi}{4} + i\sin\dfrac{3\pi}{4}\right)$ **3.** $-2\sqrt{2} - i2\sqrt{2}$

Review: **1.** $4\sqrt{2}\left(\cos 45° + i\sin 45°\right)$ **3.** $9(\cos 90° + i\sin 90°)$ **5.** -3

Multiplying and Dividing Complex Numbers in Trigonometric or Polar Form *p.340*

Practice: **1.** $8(\cos 210° + i\sin 210°)$ **2.** $3\left(\cos(-240°) + i\sin(-240°)\right)$ **3.** $-1 - i\sqrt{3}$

Review: **1.** $12(\cos 150° + i\sin 150°)$ **3.** $15\left(\cos 90° + i\sin 90°\right)$ **5.** -24 or $-24 + 0i$

Using DeMoivre's Theorem to Raise a Complex Number to a Power *p.343*

Practice: **1.** $64\left(\cos 120° + i\sin 120°\right)$ **2.** $32(\cos 150° + i\sin 150°)$ **3.** $8(\cos 270° + i\sin 270°)$

Review: **1.** $16(\cos 500° + i\sin 500°)$ **3.** $16(\cos 1200° + i\sin 1200°)$ **5.** $-32 - 32i\sqrt{3}$

Roots of Complex Numbers *p.345*

Practice:

1. $5, \dfrac{-5 + 5i\sqrt{3}}{2}, \dfrac{-5 - 5i\sqrt{3}}{2}$

2. $\sqrt[6]{2}\left(\cos\dfrac{\pi}{4} + i\sin\dfrac{\pi}{4}\right), \sqrt[6]{2}\left(\cos\dfrac{7\pi}{12} + i\sin\dfrac{7\pi}{12}\right),$

$\sqrt[6]{2}\left(\cos\dfrac{11\pi}{12} + i\sin\dfrac{11\pi}{12}\right), \sqrt[6]{2}\left(\cos\dfrac{5\pi}{4} + i\sin\dfrac{5\pi}{4}\right),$

$\sqrt[6]{2}\left(\cos\dfrac{19\pi}{12} + i\sin\dfrac{19\pi}{12}\right), \sqrt[6]{2}\left(\cos\dfrac{23\pi}{12} + i\sin\dfrac{23\pi}{12}\right)$

3. $3\sqrt[8]{2}\left(\cos\dfrac{3\pi}{16} + i\sin\dfrac{3\pi}{16}\right), 3\sqrt[8]{2}\left(\cos\dfrac{11\pi}{16} + i\sin\dfrac{11\pi}{16}\right),$

$3\sqrt[8]{2}\left(\cos\dfrac{19\pi}{16} + i\sin\dfrac{19\pi}{16}\right), 3\sqrt[8]{2}\left(\cos\dfrac{27\pi}{16} + i\sin\dfrac{27\pi}{16}\right)$

Review:

1. True

3.
$$2\left(\cos\frac{2\pi}{3}+i\sin\frac{2\pi}{3}\right)$$

5.
$$\sqrt[6]{2}\left(\cos\frac{7\pi}{12}+i\sin\frac{7\pi}{12}\right),\ \sqrt[6]{2}\left(\cos\frac{5\pi}{4}+i\sin\frac{5\pi}{4}\right),\ \sqrt[6]{2}\left(\cos\frac{23\pi}{12}+i\sin\frac{23\pi}{12}\right)$$

More Roots of Complex Numbers *p.349*

Practice:

1. $2,-2,2i,-2i$

2. $-5,\dfrac{5-5\sqrt{3}}{2},\dfrac{5+5i\sqrt{3}}{2}$

3. $1,\dfrac{1+i\sqrt{3}}{2},\dfrac{-1+i\sqrt{3}}{2}-1,\dfrac{-1-i\sqrt{3}}{2},\dfrac{1-i\sqrt{3}}{2}$

Review: **1.** $1,i,-1,-i$ **3.** $-4,2+2i\sqrt{3},2-2i\sqrt{3}$ **5.** $0.855+1.481i,-1.710,0.855-1.481i$

Roots of Unity *p.351*

Practice: **1.** $1,\ -\dfrac{1}{2}+\dfrac{i\sqrt{3}}{2},\ -\dfrac{1}{2}-\dfrac{i\sqrt{3}}{2}$ **2.** $0.5-0.866i$ **3.** $-0.5+0.866i$

Review:

1. $\cos 0+i\sin 0,\ \cos 36+i\sin 36,\ \cos 72+i\sin 72,\ \cos 108+i\sin 108,\ \cos 144+i\sin 144,$
$\cos 180+i\sin 180,\ \cos 216+i\sin 216,\ \cos 252+i\sin 252,\ \cos 288+i\sin 288,$
$\cos 324+i\sin 324$

3. $-\dfrac{1}{2}+\dfrac{\sqrt{3}}{2}i$

5. 2

An Introduction to Polar Coordinates *p.354*

Practice: **1.** negative $x-$axis   **2.** Quadrant II   **3.** Quadrant I

Review: **1.**    **3.** Quadrant IV   **5.** Quadrant I

Converting between Polar and Rectangular Coordinates *p.356*

Practice: **1.** 2 $(-2.4,-1.8)$

Review: **1.** $\left(2\sqrt{2},45°\right)$ **3.** $\left(2,2\sqrt{3}\right)$ **5.** True

Graphing Simple Polar Equations *p.358*

Practice: **1.** $(x-2)^2+y^2=4$ **2.**

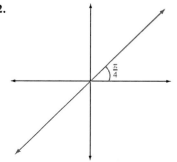

Review: **1.** False **3.** $x^2 + (y - 6)^2 = 36$ **5.**

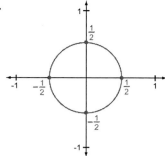

Exponential and Logarithmic Functions

An Introduction to Exponential Functions *p.363*

Practice: **1.** True **2.** $c(x)$ **3.** $f(x)$

Review: **1.** 0.06157 **3.** False **5.** $g(x) = \dfrac{1}{3}^x$

Graphing Exponential Functions: Useful Patterns *p.364*

Practice: **1.** Neither **2.** $h(x) = 8^x$ **3.** For all x-values

Review: **1.** $h(x) = 6^x$ **3.** $g(x) = 4^x$ **5.** $g(x) = \left(\dfrac{3}{2}\right)^x$

Graphing Exponential Functions: More Examples *p.366*

Practice:
1. True
2. Shift to the left 1 unit and up 3 units.
3. $y = 4^x + 2$

Review: **1.** $b(x) = 9 \cdot 3^x$ **3.** $f(x) = 6^x$ is shifted to the left 8 units to form $g(x)$ **5.** $y = 2^{x-1} - 6$

Using Properties of Exponents to Solve Exponential Equations *p.368*

Practice: **1.** $x = \dfrac{3}{7}$ **2.** $x = 8$ **3.** $x = \dfrac{1}{10}$

Review: **1.** $h = 8$ **3.** $x = -1.2$ **5.** $x = \dfrac{4}{3}$

Finding Present Value and Future Value *p.369*

Practice: **1.** 613,136.41 yen **2.** \$1,160.18 **3.** \$16,286.10

Review: **1.** \$212,557.18 **3.** \$4,646.43 **5.** \$100,418.07

Finding an Interest Rate to Match Given Goals *p.371*

Practice: **1.** 7.29% **2.** 21.8% **3.** 3.37%

Review: **1.** 4.19% **3.** 15.6% **5.** 5.7%

e *p.373*

Applying Exponential Functions *p.374*

Practice: **1.** 254 people **2.** 8.6% **3.** 11.3%

Review: **1.** 2.3 billion **3.** 82.2 % **5.** 59.8 %

An Introduction to Logarithmic Functions *p.375*

Practice: **1.** −1 **2.** True **3.** −3

Review: **1.** 2   **3.** −3   **5.** $\dfrac{2}{3}$

Converting between Exponential and Logarithmic Functions *p.377*

Practice: **1.** $\log_6 36 = 2$ **2.** $\log_m k = z$ **3.** $16^{\frac{1}{4}} = 2$

Review: **1.** $7^0 = 1$ **3.** $10^{-2} = 0.01$ **5.** $\log_4 0.125 = -\dfrac{3}{2}$

Finding the Value of a Logarithmic Function *p.378*

Practice: **1.** −2   **2.** 6   **3.** $-\dfrac{1}{8}$

Review: **1.** 7   **3.** 1   **5.** −1

Solving for x in Logarithmic Equations *p.380*

Practice: **1.** No solution   **2.** $x = \dfrac{4}{5}$ **3.** $x = \dfrac{4}{3}$

Review: **1.** $x = 10$ **3.** $x = 8$ **5.** $x = \dfrac{1}{4}$

Graphing Logarithmic Functions *p.381*

Practice: **1.** True   **2.** (1, 0)   **3.** $g(4) = -7$

Review: **1.**   **3.** (1,0)   **5.** $f(x)\log_{10} x$

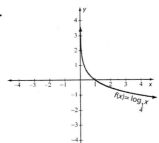

Matching Logarithmic Functions with Their Graphs *p.384*

Practice: **1.** $y = \log_9(7x)$ **2.** The curve is shifted 2 units to the right.   **3.** 1

Review: **1.** False   **3.**   **5.**

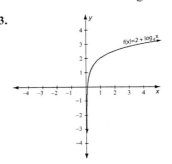 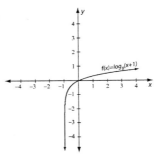

Properties of Logarithms *p.387*

Practice: **1.** $\log_1 x + 3\log_1 y$ **2.** $1 + \log_2 p - \log_2 q$ **3.** $\log_6(x-2) - \log_6 y$

Review: **1.** $\log_4 j + \dfrac{1}{6}\log_4 k$ **3.** $3\log_5 x - 1$ **5.** $\log_2 t - 3$

Expanding a Logarithmic Expression Using Properties *p.389*

Practice: **1.** $\dfrac{1}{2}\cdot\log_{10} 2 + \dfrac{1}{2}\cdot\log_{10} p - 6\log_{10} h$ **2.** Cannot be expanded or simplified.   **3.** $3 + 4\log_2 t - \log_2 3 - 2\log_2 n$

Review: **1.** $2\log_4 d + 7\log_4 g - 1 - 3\log_4 m$ **3.** Cannot be expanded or simplified.   **5.** $\frac{1}{3}\cdot\log_e a - \frac{1}{3}\cdot\log_e b$ or $\frac{(\log_e a - \log_e b)}{3}$

Combining Logarithmic Expressions *p.391*

Practice: **1.** $\log\sqrt[4]{\left(a^2 x\right)} - 3$ **2.** $\log_6\left[\dfrac{y^3}{(y+5)}\right] + 2$ **3.** $1 + \ln\dfrac{x^5}{8}$

Review: **1.** $\log_b(a-t)$ **3.** $\log_2\left(\sqrt{u^3}\cdot\sqrt[4]{w^3}\right)$ **5.** $\ln\left(\dfrac{x^2 y^4}{z^3}\right)$

Evaluating Logarithmic Functions Using a Calculator *p.393*

Practice: **1.** 0.7597 **2.** 4.4031 **3.** -4.5659

Review: **1.** 1.5465 **3.** -0.1761 **5.** 3.2308

Using the Change of Base Formula *p.395*

Practice: **1.** $\dfrac{\log\frac{1541}{3.29}}{\log 20}$ **2.** $\dfrac{\ln 0.287}{\ln 4}$ **3.** True

Review: **1.** $\dfrac{\ln 20}{\ln 9}$ **3.** $\dfrac{\log 35}{\log 9}$ **5.** $\dfrac{\log 8}{\log\frac{1}{2}}$

The Richter Scale *p.396*

Practice: **1.** 6.95 **2.** 7.87 **3.** 6.73

Review: **1.** 6.48 **3.** 7.31 **5.** 8.26

The Distance Modulus Formula *p.398*

Practice: **1.** 4.502 **2.** 5.57 parsecs   **3.** 2.2 million light years

Review: **1.** 5.11 **3.** 28.97 parsecs   **5.** 93 million light years

Solving Exponential Equations *p.399*

Practice: **1.** $x = \pm 2$ **2.** $x = -0.5544$ **3.** $x = -4.0107$

Review: **1.** $x = 2$ **3.** $x = -\dfrac{1}{2}$ **5.** $x = -3.212$

Solving Logarithmic Equations *p.401*

Practice: **1.** 5 **2.** 5 **3.** 3

Review: **1.** 17 **3.** 3 **5.** -4.3891

Solving Equations with Logarithmic Exponents *p.402*

Practice: **1.** 1 **2.** $\dfrac{1}{3}$ **3.** $\dfrac{3}{10}$

Review: **1.** 3 **3.** $\dfrac{3}{2}$ **5.** 103

Compound Interest *p.404*

Practice: **1.** \$12,555.40   **2.** 6.2% **3.** 17 years

Review: **1.** 7.9 years   **3.** 2.285 years   **5.** \$11,410.66

Predicting Change *p.406*

Practice: **1.** $.01$ moles per liter   **2.** 2004 **3.** 1998

Review: **1.** 1245.8 **3.** 15 watts   **5.** 63.41%

An Introduction to Exponential Growth and Decay *p.408*

Practice: **1.** 60,744   **2.** 14.5 years   **3.** 1957 and 1958

Review: **1.** 30,248   **3.** 19,700   **5.** 785 pounds

Half-Life *p.410*

Practice: **1.** 88%   **2.** 2.0 hours   **3.** 9.797 grams

Review: **1.** 16 years   **3.** 45.8%   **5.** $A(t) = 80e^{-.00578t}$

Newton's Law of Cooling *p.412*

Practice: **1.** 49 degrees   **2.** 102 minutes   **3.** $T(t) = 40 + 35e^{-0.01352t}$

Review: **1.** $133°F$ **3.** 83°   **5.** about 1 hour

Continuously Compounded Interest *p.414*

Practice: **1.** \$39,967   **2.** $4\frac{1}{2}$ years   **3.** 7 years

Review: **1.** 7.4%   **3.** 9.1%   **5.** The 8% account will double faster.

Conic Sections

An Introduction to Conic Sections *p.419*

An Introduction to Parabolas *p.420*

Practice: **1.** True   **2.** 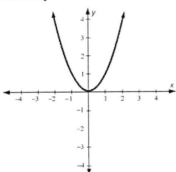   **3.** True

Review: **1.** direction: parabola opens up, vertex: $(-1, 0)$.   **3.** True   **5.** True

Determining Information about a Parabola from Its Equation *p.422*

Practice: **1.** vertex $(0,0)$; focus $\left(\frac{3}{8},0\right)$ **2.** focus: $(0,-1)$; directrix: $y = 1$ **3.** focus: $\left(\frac{1}{2},0\right)$

Review: **1.** vertex $(0,0)$; focus $\left(0,\frac{1}{32}\right)$ **3.** Focus: $\left(0,-\frac{1}{3}\right)$, directrix: $y = \frac{1}{3}$ **5.** $\left(-\frac{3}{4}, 0\right)$

Writing an Equation for a Parabola *p.424*

Practice: **1.** $y^2 = -12x$ **2.** $(x-3)^2 = 8(y-5)$ **3.** vertex: $(3,-5)$; focus: $(4,-5)$

Review: **1.** $x^2 = 6y$ **3.** $(2,3)$ **5.** $(y+5)^2 = 20(x-2)$

An Introduction to Ellipses *p.425*

Practice:
1. Center: $(4,-3)$; Minor axis: 2
2. Center: $(-2,0)$; Major axis: $2\sqrt{7}$; Minor axis: 4

3.

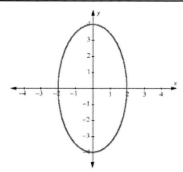

Review: 1. $(x-5)^2 + \dfrac{(y+3)^2}{4} = 1$ center: $(5,-3)$ **3.** Major axis $= 16$; minor axis $= 2\sqrt{15}$ **5.** $(-4, 1)$

Finding the Equation for an Ellipse *p.428*

Practice: 1. $\dfrac{x^2}{169} + \dfrac{y^2}{144} = 1$ **2.** $\dfrac{x^2}{4} + \dfrac{y^2}{9} = 1$ **3.** $(-4,0)$

Review: 1. $\left(\sqrt{3},0\right)$ and $\left(-\sqrt{3},0\right)$ **3.** $\dfrac{x^2}{9} + \dfrac{y^2}{25} = 1$ **5.** $(1,0)$

Applying Ellipses: Satellites *p.431*

Practice: 1. $(\pm 3\sqrt{3},\ 0)$ **2.** $(0,\ \pm 5)$ **3.** $5,249$ miles

Review: 1. $(8,0)$ and $(-8,0)$ **3.** $(4+2\sqrt{2},-3)$ and $(4-2\sqrt{2},-3)$ **5.** $\dfrac{x^2}{18^2} + \dfrac{y^2}{14^2} = 1$

An Introduction to Hyperbolas *p.433*

Practice:
1. $y = \pm 5x$
2. $(0,\pm\sqrt{29})$
3. Foci: $(\pm 2\sqrt{5},\ 0)$; Asymptotes: $y = \pm 2x$

Review: 1. $\left(\pm\sqrt{34},0\right)$ **3.** $(\pm 3,0)$ **5.** $(0,\pm 3)$

Finding the Equation for a Hyperbola *p.435*

Practice: 1. $\dfrac{x^2}{36} - \dfrac{y^2}{64} = 1$ **2.** $y^2 - \dfrac{x^2}{8} = 1$ **3.** $\dfrac{x^2}{16} - \dfrac{y^2}{\frac{400}{9}} = 1.$

Review: 1. $\dfrac{x^2}{49} - \dfrac{y^2}{25} = 1$ **3.** $\dfrac{y^2}{9} - \dfrac{4x^2}{9} = 1$ **5.** $\dfrac{x^2}{16} - \dfrac{y^2}{12} = 1$

Applying Hyperbolas: Navigation *p.437*

Practice: 1. $\dfrac{x^2}{885.66} - \dfrac{y^2}{14739.34} = 1$ **2.** Approximately 281 miles

Review: 1. $\dfrac{x^2}{547.56} - \dfrac{y^2}{5077.44} = 1$

Identifying a Conic *p.439*

Practice: 1. $\dfrac{(y-1)^2}{4} - \dfrac{(x+3)^2}{16} = 1$; hyperbola with center $(-3,1)$ **2.** $\dfrac{x^2}{4} + y^2 = 1$; ellipse with center $(0,0)$.   **3.** $(x-2)^2 = 10(y+3)$; parabola with vertex $(2,-3)$

Review:

1.

$$\frac{(x-2)^2}{12} + \frac{\left(y+\frac{3}{2}\right)^2}{4} = 1; \text{ ellipse with center } \left(2, -\frac{3}{2}\right)$$

3.

$$\left(y+\frac{5}{2}\right)^2 = \frac{1}{3}\left(x+\frac{31}{4}\right); \text{ parabola with vertex } \left(-\frac{31}{4}, -\frac{5}{2}\right)$$

5. $x^2 = 4(y-2);$ parabola with vertex $(0,2)$

Name That Conic *p.441*

Practice: **1.** Circle   **2.** Ellipse   **3.** Parabola

Review: **1.** Parabola   **3.** Hyperbola   **5.** Ellipse

Glossary:

absolute value	the measured distance on a number line from one location to the origin (0).
absolute value with greater than	all the solution values are outside the endpoints away from zero; $|A| > B$ means $A < -B$ or $A > B$
absolute value with less than	all the solution values are between the endpoints and zero: $|A| < B$ means $-B < A < B$
adding complex numbers	combine like terms, the real numbers with themselves and the imaginary numbers with themselves
adding polynomials	combining all like terms in an algebraic expression
algebra of functions	process of adding, subtracting, multiplying or dividing functions with functions
amplitude	half the difference between the maximum and minimum values of a periodic function; in effect, the maximum displacement of a periodic function from equilibrium
and	connector used with inequalities to indicate that the solution set will include only values which satisfy both inequalities in the problem; sometimes referred to as an intersection.
angle of depression	the angle measured downwards from the horizontal to a point or an object
angle of elevation	the angle measured upwards from the horizontal to a point or an object
approximation	a line or curve created to approximately represent the pattern produced by graphing single pieces of data on a plane.
arc	a portion of a circle or other curve
argument	the expression that a function operates on
arithmetic sequence	an ordered collection of numbers in which the difference between any two consecutive terms is a constant (d); these sequences follow the pattern $a_n = a_1 + (n - 1)d$
asymptote	a line that the graph of a function approaches but never reaches. Asymptotes can be either horizontal or vertical
augmented matrix	an array for a system of equations which utilizes as elements both the coefficients of the variables and the constants in the equations
average	one number used to represent a group of values, calculated by adding all the values in the group then dividing by the number of values included in the group
axis of symmetry	the imaginary line that passes through the vertex of a parabola and is parallel to the axis along which the curve is opening
b	variable used to represent the y-intercept in the slope-intercept equation for a line.
base	the number or variable to which an exponent is attached
bearing	the direction of an object measured clockwise from north; also called compass direction
binomial	an algebraic expression composed of two monomial terms linked by addition or subtraction
cancellation	dividing both a numerator and a denominator by the same number so long as the numbers being divided are either both in the same fraction or are in fractions which are multiplying with each other.
Cartesian coordinates	the ordered pair, usually (x,y), that designates the location of a point on a Cartesian plane
Cartesian plane	the flat surface created by two number lines which intersect at right angles
Center of a circle	the fixed point that is a set distance from each point in the set of points that is the circle; usually designated as the ordered pair (h, k) where h is the x-value and k is the y-value of the point.
circle	the set of all the points at a fixed distance, the radius (r), from a specified point, the center (h,k); a completely symmetrical figure

clearing the denominator	practice of elminating a radical from the denominator of a fraction
coefficient	a constant multiplying with an algebraic variable
collinear	any two or more points that fall on the same line
common denominator	a number that can be used as the denominator for every fraction in a problem; generally it is the lowest multiple common to all the existing denominators in the problem
compass direction	the direction of an object measured clockwise from north; also called bearing
complement	the positive angle that, when added to a given angle, results in a right angle
completing the square	the process of isolating on one side of the equation the terms containing the variable being solved for, then adding the value necessary for that side to be a perfect square to both sides of the equation, then factoring or taking the square root of both sides, and finally performing arithmetic as needed to solve for the variable.
complex fraction	a fraction which has one or more fractions in its numerator, denominator or both.
complex number	a value composed of both a real number and an imaginary number. Complex numbers are often written in the form $a + bi$, where a is the real number and bi is the imaginary number.
complex plane	a coordinate system for graphing complex numbers where the horizontal axis is the real axis and the vertical axis is the imaginary axis
composite function	a function that results from first applying one function, and then another.
composition	multiple functions acting on each other in a specified order.
compound inequality	two inequalities linked by *and* or *or*
compound interest formula	$A = P(\ 1 + {}^{r}/_{m}\ )^{mt}$
conic section	any curve which is derived by intersecting a cone with a plane, such figures include: the point (the plane touches the tip of the cone) line (the plane is tangent to the side of the cone) parabola (the plane intersects the cone parallel to its side) circle (the plane intersects the cone parallel to the base of the cone) ellipse (the plane intersects the cone at an angle), and hyperbola (the plane intersects the cone vertically).
conjugate pair	a pair of numbers of the form $a + b$ and $a - b$ where a or b (or both) is often a radical or imaginary number
consecutive even numbers	even numbers that follow one another when counting, i.e., 2, 4, 6, ... or x, x + 2, x + 4, ...
consecutive numbers	numbers that follow one another when counting; i.e., 3, 4, 5, ... or x, x + 1, x + 2, ...
consecutive odd numbers	odd numbers that follow one another when counting, i.e., 3, 5, 7, ..., or 2x + 1, 2x + 3, 2x + 5, ..., or x, x + 2, x + 4 ... given that x is an odd number
constant	a number which always has the same value, i.e., 7; the value in a function which does not change
constant velocity	a constant change in position with respect to time; traveling a distance over some amount of time at an even speed, can be determined using a formula that specifies that speed equals distance traveled divided by time used travelling
coordinate plane	a plane on which points can be identified using a set of values that uniquely specifies their location
cosine	one of the six trigonometric functions, denoted cos. In a right triangle, the cosine of an angle is equal to the adjacent side divided by the hypotenuse.
coterminal angles	angles that have the same initial and terminal sides. Coterminal angles have measures that differ by a multiple of 360°.
Cramer's rule	a process utilizing determinants to solve systems of linear equations
cross-multiplying	a practice used to eliminate denominators when one or more fractions are found in an equation; the procedure involves multiplying the common denominator from one side of the equation with the numerators on the other side of the equation with the result that the multiplying denominator disappears into the receiving numerator

curve fitting	superimposing a line or curve over the graph of single points of data to approximately represent the pattern produced in the graph
decreasing	a function or an interval for a function whose value is becoming smaller as viewed on its graph from left to right; a function may decrease over some intervals but not others
degree	the highest power used in any of the terms of an algebraic expression
degree of polynomial	highest power used in any of the terms of the algebraic expression
denominator	number or expression on the bottom, or doing the dividing, of a fraction
dependent system	a group of three equations in three unknowns that has an infinite number of solutions; the planes for the three equations intersect in a line
dependent variable	the quantity in an algebraic expession whose value changes as calculations are made subsequent to one or more substitutions for the independent variable, i.e., the variable whose value "depends" on what is substituted in for the other, or "independent," variable.
Descartes' rule of signs	a method for determining the number of positive and negative real roots for a polynomial; first arrange the polynomial in descending order with the highest power first, then substitute in "x" and note the number of times the sign changes between terms, then repeat the process using "-x". In each case the number of real number solutions of the type substituted will equal the number of sign changes or that number minus some even number.
determinant	|D|, det(D), a number, or scalar, that represents the value of a matrix
dimension of a matrix	the number of rows "x" the number of columns
direct proportion	two or more quantities increase or decrease in the same way to the same degree, each in accordance with its size
direct variation	two or more quantities increase or decrease in the same way to the same degree, each quantity in accordance with its size
direction angle	the angle measured counterclockwise from the positive x-axis to a vector
distance modulus formula	$M = 5\log r - 5$; used in astronomy to find large distances.
distributive property	(of multiplication over addition), $a(b + c) = ab + ac$, where a, b, and c are real numbers.
domain	the set of all values that the independent variable for a function, usually x, can use in that function
domain of a rational	the set of all values available for the variable such that the denominator of the rational never equals zero
e	the base of the natural logarithm, approximately 2.71828; a number important in calculating population growth, decay, and many other practical things, also known as Napier's number
elimination	a process for solving systems of equations by combining two of the equations in such a way that one of the variables adds or subtracts away, with steps following to solve the new equation(s) for the remaining variable(s) until a value has been discovered for each variable in the system.
empty set	a solution with no values which indicates that there are no numbers which satisfy the equation or inequality
equation	a mathematical sentence in which one term or expression is linked, using "=", to another of exactly the same value
equation of a line	$ax + by = c$
even function	a function whose graph is symmetric about the y-axis; a function $f(x)$ that satisfies the expression $f(-x) = f(x)$.
exponent	the superscripted number or term attached to the right side of an algebraic term or parentheses (the base) which indicates how many times the base is expected to multiply with itself in the problem
exponentiation	the practice of using exponents, or superscripted numerical indicators, rather than writing what is required in words

extraneous root	a value found for the variable that cannot be considered part of the solution because it gives a false statement when substituted into the original equation.
factor theorem	the expression (x - c) must be a factor of a polynomial, p(x), if it divides into the polynomial with a remainder of zero; for (x - c) to be a factor of f(x), f(c) = 0.
factorial (n!)	(n!) a process of multiplying the given integer with every positive integer smaller than itself
factoring	process for solving algebraic expressions by reversing multiplication to discover the elements which produced the expression; steps include first "unmultiplying" any number or variable which is common to all the terms in the expression, then looking for ways to group terms in multiplying expressions, then breaking up higher-power terms
Fibonacci sequence	a series of numbers that starts out with 1 and 1, then each succeeding term is the sum of the two terms that precede it; the early terms in the sequence are 1, 1, 2, 3, 5, 8, 13, ...; the sequence is found many times in nature.
FOIL method	a process for multiplying two binomial expressions: multiply the two First terms (F), then the two Outer terms (O), then the two Inner terms (I), and finally the two Last terms (L). Finish by combining like terms.
formula	a generalized equation in one or more variables used to measure a characteristic or action in every situation of its kind
fraction	a division problem written vertically with the number on top (numerator) being divided by the number on the bottom (denominator)
function	a set of ordered pairs in which any given x-value is paired with exactly one y-value; an expression for which each x-value produces exactly one y-value
function notation	f(x) read "f of x." If a value, say 2, is substituted into the function for x, then f(x) becomes f(2) and is read "f at 2;" "f(x)" is used instead of "y" to show that the y-value varies depending on the choices made for x.
Gauss-Jordan method	a process for solving linear equations which uses matrix manipulations such as flipping the order of rows, multiplying rows by constants, and replacing a row by the sum of two rows
graph	a visual representation of data on a line or plane, or in a higher-dimensional space
graphing inequalities	graph the inequality as an equation which divides the plane into two regions and show the graph as a broken line unless the "equal to" is part of the inequality, then pick a point off the curve and substitute it into the inequality checking to see if what results is a true statement. If the statement is true, shade in the region which included that point for that region will contain all the points and only those points which make the statement true while, if the statement is false, shade in the opposite region knowing that its points are those needed for the solution set.
greater than	(>) a linking concept which indicates that the number or expression on the left side of a mathematical sentence is larger than the number or expression on the right side of the sentence.
greatest integer function	assigns as the y-value the greatest integer that is less than or equal to the value produced by each x, graphs as a "step function" meaning that its graph appears in short horizontal bars rising one after another when viewed from left to right
grouping with exponents	setting all the bases within a term which carry the same exponent within parentheses to which the exponent is attached
half-angle identity	a trigonometric identity used to rewrite trigonometric functions of angle A/2 in terms of angle A.
harmonic motion	the motion of an object that moves back and forth regularly
Hooke's law	provides a formula to measure the distance a spring stretches and shows that the distance varies directly with the force applied
horizontal axis	measures horizontal distance from the origin on a plane; it is usually designated by x and referred to as the x-axis.

horizontal line test	a test to determine whether a function is one-to-one. The horizontal line test states that if every horizontal line that intersects the graph of a function does so at most once, then the function has an inverse.
hyperbola	consists of the set of points the difference of whose distance from two fixed points (foci) is constant
identity	an equation that is true for all meaningful values of the variable(s) involved
identity matrix	the array which will produce the given matrix when the given matrix multiplies with the identity matrix; an array made up of 0s and 1s such that the 1s form a diagonal from upper left to lower right in the array, and 0s fill in all the other places in the array
imaginary number	the square root of a negative number
imaginary part of a complex number	the part of a complex number measured along the imaginary axis in the complex plane; the imaginary part of the complex number $a + bi$ is b
inconsistent system	a group of three equations in three unknowns that has no solution; i.e., the planes for the three equations do not intersect
increasing	a term used to describe the behavior of a function over an interval. A curve is increasing if $f(x_1) < f(x_2)$ whenever $x_1 < x_2$; a graph that appears to be rising when viewed from the left to the right; In calculus, a function is increasing over an interval if the first derivative is positive over that entire interval.
independent system	a group of three equations in three unknowns that has exactly one solution; i.e., the planes for the three equations intersect in a single point
independent variable	the quantity in an algebraic expression whose value must be set before the value of the entire expression can be determined
indirect proportion	two or more quantities increase or decrease in opposite ways to the same degree each in accordance with its size; sometimes called inverse proportion
induction	a method of proving a list of statements is true by showing that the first statement is true, then showing that if one of the statements is true then the next one that follows is also true; i.e., each time one fact is shown to be true it proves the next one is true; when using this method first show the statement is true for n = 1, then assume that the statement is true for n = k and show that it is true for = k + 1 thereby proving that the statement is true for every n.
inductive sequence	an ordered collection of numbers which uses a pattern based upon previous terms
inequality	the concept that one side of a mathematical sentence is a different size than the other side, generally denoted with the less than and greater than symbols
infinity	the value derived by adding one more to the value at each end of the number line thereby extending the number line one more unit in either direction. The ability to keep performing this extension process for the number line means that the possible number values never end either as very large numbers or as very small numbers.
intercept	the point(s) at which a line or curve crosses one of the axes of the plane
interval	the range of values on a number line which are solutions for a given variable in a given problem situation; the range of x-values for a function over which the graph of the function is being considered in some aspect
interval notation	[a,b] indicates that the variable can be any of the values between the two given numbers including the end numbers. (a,b) indicates that the variable can be any of the values between the two given numbers except the end numbers.
inverse function	a function which undoes another function; if g(x) is the inverse of f(x), then g[f(x)] = x; not all functions have an inverse
inverse matrix	the array which will produce the identity matrix when multiplied with a given matrix; to have an inverse a matrix must be nonsingular; i.e., its determinant will be other than zero.
inverse proportion	two or more quantities increase or decrease in opposite ways to the same degree each quantity in accordance with its size; sometimes called indirect proportion or inverse variation

inverse trigonometric function	a function that undoes a trigonometric function; e.g. arcsine, arccosine, arctangent
inverse variation	two or more quantities increase or decrease in opposite ways to the same degree each quantity in accordance with its size; also called indirect proportion
investment problem	usually a word problem related to interest on sums of money
k	the constant of change, a value used with variation problems; a value fixed within each type of problem depending on the materials and situations involved in the problem
least common denominator (LCD)	(LCD) the smallest multiple common to all the denominators in the problem
less than	(<) a linking concept which indicates that the number or expression on the left side of a mathematical sentence is smaller than the number or expression on the right side of the sentence
less than or equal to	(<) a linking concept which indicates that the expression on the left of the mathematical sentence is smaller than or the same size as the expression on the right side of the sentence
like term	all monomials in an expression which contain exactly the same variables each to the same degree
line	the shortest distance between two points in Euclidean geometry; the straight path passing through and beyond any two points
linear equation	a mathematical sentence in which all variables are at the first power level, the equation graphs as a line
linear function	a function whose graph is a line
linear programming	a process for using systems of inequalities to determine maximum and minimum possibilities in business and other concrete situations; each inequality is graphed and the region bounded by the system is noted, then the vertex points of this region are substituted into the function to determine the maximum and minimum points
linear system of equations	solving a group of linear equations for a solution to each variable that is common to every equation in the group
linear work problem	usually a word problem designed to calculate work performed at an average rate over a period of time by one or more workers
ln A	the natural logarithm evaluated at A; the logarithm with base e evaluated at the number A
logarithmic function	function which has a logarithm as one of the elements; never equals zero; all of these functions graph to the same basic shape with the only unique pieces being the x-intercept and the altitude the curve attains.
major axis	the long axis of an ellipse
mathematical induction	a method of proving a list of statements is true by showing that the first statement is true, then showing that if one of the statements is true then the statement that follows is also true; i.e., each time one fact is shown to be true it proves the next one is true; when using this method to prove something first show the statement is true for n = 1, then assume that the statement is true for n = k and show that it is true for n = k + 1 thereby proving that the statement is true for every n
matrices	more than one matrix
matrix	a rectangular block or array of numbers
maxima	the plural form of maximum; the points on a graph where the function changes from increasing to decreasing
maximum	a point where a function attains its greatest value on an open interval; the high point on the graph of a curve; the point where a function which has been increasing in value begins to decrease; in calculus, the point in an open interval where the derivative of a function changes from positive to negative
midpoint of a line	the point that lies equidistant from the two endpoints of the line segment
minima	the plural form of minimum; the points on a graph where the function changes from decreasing to increasing

---

minimum	a point where a function attains its smallest value on an open interval; a low point on the graph of a curve; the point where a function which has been decreasing in value begins to increase; in calculus, the point in an interval where the derivative changes from negative to positive
minor axis	the short axis of an ellipse
mixture problem	usually a word problem designed to calculate quantities or strengths of substances mixed together
monomial	an algebraic term composed of numbers and variables that multiply or divide with each other, but do not add or subtract with each other
multiplicative identity	the number which multiplies with the given number for a product that is the given number; i.e., 1
multiplicative inverse	the number which multiplies with the given number for a product of 1
multiplicity	number of times a specific value is used as a solution for a polynomial
multiplying binomials	the process of multiplying individually each term in one binomial with each term in the other binomial followed by combining like terms
multiplying matrices	creating a new matrix by multiplying elements in the columns of one matrix with elements in the rows of the other matrix; for two matrices to be able to multiply, the number of columns in the left matrix must match the number of rows in the right matrix; the solution matrix will have the same number of rows as the left matrix and the same number of columns as the right matrix
multiplying polynomials	the process of multiplying individually each term in one polynomial with each term in the other polynomial followed by combining like terms
multiplying with exponents	since exponents actually count how often the base numbers multiply with themselves, multiplying with exponents involves adding the exponents attached to the same bases within a multiplication problem
Napier's number	the number e, or the base of the natural logarithm
natural log	a logarithm with base e
negative exponent	requires that the reciprocal of its base number be used in the problem
negative slope	indicates that the line falls, or loses value, when viewed from left to right.
nonlinear system of equations	a group of equations, all of which graph something other than a line, which are being processed for solutions that work in all the equations
nonsingular determinant	the value for a matrix equal to something other than zero
nth roots	the complex nth roots of a number k are those complex numbers z that satisfy the equation $z^n = k$. There are n complex nth roots of any number.
number line	a scale that represents the sequence of numbers from the smallest values and negative infinity on the left end to the largest values and positive infinity on the right end.
numerator	the number on top, or being divided, in a fraction
odd function	a function whose graph is symmetric about the origin; a function $f(x)$ that satisfies the equation $f(-x) = -f(x)$
one-to-one function	a function which satisfies the horizontal line test; every y-value output by the function comes from exactly one x-value input into the function
or	used with inequalities to indicate that the solution set will include values which satisfy one or the other inequalities, but not necessarily both; sometimes referred to as a union
order of operations	established practice for deriving consistent answers when doing arithmetic that requires whatever arithmetic is enclosed within parentheses be done first, followed by the arithmetic required to satisfy exponents, followed by multiplication and division from left to right across the expression, followed by addition and subtraction across the expression

ordered pair	two numbers in the form (x, y), usually representing the coordinates of a point; the two numbers which locate a point on the Cartesian plane by indicating with the first number (x) the horizontal distance of the point from the origin and with the second number (y) the vertical distance of the point from the origin
origin	the center of the rectangular or Cartesian coordinate system, located at $(0,0)$; the point of intersection of the two number lines used to create a Cartesian plane
parabola	one of the conic sections; the set of points equidistant from a fixed point (the focus) and a fixed line (the directrix)
parallel	indicates that two lines or planes will never intersect; i.e., they have no points in common; predicted by two lines having the same slope and different y-intercepts
partial fraction	a fraction which represents part of a more complicated fraction and which uses as its denominator one factor from the denominator of the more complicated fraction; one element of a process using a system of linear equations to simplify a complicated fraction as the sum of a group of simpler fractions
Pascal's triangle	a group of numbers which form and are derived from a unique pattern such that every row starts and ends with 1 while all the other terms are derived by adding the two elements above their position in the triangle
period	the smallest length of time or distance along the x-axis required for a periodic function to repeat itself
periodic function	a function that repeats itself
perpendicular	a concept that indicates that two lines or planes intersect at right angles; predicted when the slopes of two lines are the negative reciprocals of each other, which is to say that their slopes will multiply to give the answer -1.
phase shift	a horizontal translation of a periodic function
pi	(p) an irrational number, approximately equal to 3.14159..., that is the ratio of the circumference of a circle to its diameter ($p = C/d$).
piecewise function	function which is defined differently across various intervals of the x-axis with the result that its graph may be discontinuous and present more than one type of curve
pitch	a measure of the steepness with which a line or curve increases or decreases over an interval
plane	a two-dimensional surface considered to have height and width, but no depth; a plane is created whenever two axes intersect
plotting a point	the process of locating a point on a number line or axis system
point	a location in space with no width, depth or height; a location specified on the Cartesian plane by the ordered pair (x,y) which details the point's horizontal and vertical distance from the central point $(0,0)$
point of inflection	a point on a curve where the concavity changes; also called an inflection point
polar axis	the number line used to measure change in distance on the polar plane
polar coordinate system	a system for locating points on the plane by specifying their angle from a polar axis and their distance from a central point
polynomial	a sum of monomials; monomial terms linked by positive and negative signs
polynomial function	a function defined by a polynomial expression; often described by its degree n where n is a nonnegative integer
position function	a function describing the position or location of an object as a function of time t
positive slope	indicates that the line rises, or gains value, when viewed from left to right
power	an exponent attached to a base; the power of a polynomial or function equals the largest exponent attached to a variable in the expression
power-reducing identity	a trigonometric function used to rewrite powers of trigonometric identities

probability	a mathematical measurement as to the likelihood that a given event will occur
proving an answer	using the value found for each variable, substitute into the equation to validate they create a true mathematical sentence
Pythagorean theorem	the sum of the squares of the lengths of the legs of a right triangle equals the square of the length of the hypotenuse; $a^2 + b^2 = c^2$
quadrant	one of the four regions of the Cartesian plane. Starting with quadrant I in the upper-right, they are counted counterclockwise.
quadratic equation	a mathematical sentence which contains one variable to the second degree; an equation whose graph presents a parabola
quadratic function	a function defined by a quadratic, or second-degree expression; a function whose graph presents a parabola
radical	a notation indicating that the number under the symbol is to be reduced to the root prescribed by the index
radicand	the value or expression under a radical sign
radius	the distance from the center of a circle to any point on the circle
range	the set of all output values that can be taken by a function; the set of all values possible for the dependent variable of a function
rational	a number written in fraction form
rational exponent	a small superscripted number attached to a base number or term which is in fraction form whose numerator stipulates the power of the base and whose denominator stipulates what root of the base is desired
rational expression	a fraction with a polynomial in the numerator, the denominator, or both
rational function	a function in the form of a fraction with a polynomial in the numerator and another in the denominator, with the stipulation that the polynomial in the denominator is not equal to 0
real element of a complex number	the part of a complex number measured along the real axis in the complex plane. The real part of the complex number $a + bi$ is a.
rectangular coordinate plane	the plane containing the rectangular coordinate system
rectangular coordinate system	a system for locating points on the plane by specifying their horizontal and vertical components
rectangular coordinates	the ordered pair (x,y) used to denote the location of points on a Cartesian plane
rectangular form of a complex number	the a + bi form of a complex number, as opposed to the trigonometric form; also called standard form
recursive sequence	an ordered collection of numbers which uses a pattern based upon previous terms; an inductive sequence
reference angle	the positive, acute angle formed by the terminal side of an angle and the x-axis
reflecting a curve	this procedure turns a graph matching every point (x, y) with a point (x, -y) if the reflection is over the x-axis or matching every point (x, y) with a point (-x, y) if the reflection is over the y-axis
region	for graphing, one of the four quadrants of the Cartesian plane; for inequalities, one of the several areas created by the graphs of the related equations one of which, and possibly its boundaries, contains all the solution values for the inequality or system of inequalities.
relation	a set of ordered pairs in which any given x-value may be paired with multiple y-values; an equation that does not necessarily satify the vertical line test (as opposed to a function)
remainder theorem	if a polynomial p(x) is divided by (x - c), then the remainder will be p(c); this concept is useful for determining factors in that their remainder is always zero
right circular cylinder	the shape of a can with a round top and bottom that are the same size with its sides perpendicular to the top and bottom

root	a number derived when a given number is reduced according to its exponents; an x-value where a function or polynomial is equal to zero; also called a zero
roots of unity	the complex roots of 1, or the solutions to the equation $z^n = 1$. There are n nth roots of unity.
scalar	a single number which can multiply with a matrix or vector
sequence	an ordered collection of numbers
shifting a curve	adding a value to the equation of a curve with the result that the curve moves to a new location on its plane
similar	having the same shape and proportions
sine	one of the six trigonometric functions, denoted sin. In a right triangle, the sine of an angle is equal to the opposite side divided by the hypotenuse.
singular determinant	an array value equal to zero
sinusoidal	having the shape or characteristics of a sine curve
slope of a horizontal line	this value is zero because the difference between the y-values in the numerator is zero
slope of a vertical line	this value is undefined because the difference between the x-values in the denominator is zero
solution set	all the values that satisfy the terms required for an equation or inequality to be valid
solving an equation	finding the value(s) for the variable(s) that makes an equation true
solving an inequality	determining the set of values that can be used by the variables so that the inequality is a true statement
spiral	a path in a plane traced around a central point while continuously receding from or approaching it
square matrix	an array with the same number of rows as columns
standard form of a complex number	a + bi; also called rectangular form as opposed to the trigonometric form
step function	a function that graphs its values as short horizontal bars rising or falling one after another when viewed from left to right
substitution method	a process for solving systems of equations by distilling two of the equations to a value for one of the variables, then substituting that value back into one of the original equations to help solve for another variable, until a value has been discovered for each variable in the system
subtracting polynomials	changing the signs on the subtracting terms, then combining like terms; distributing the negative sign as appropriate, then combining like terms
supplement	an angle that, when added to a given angle, results in a straight angle
symmetry	when half the graph of a function is an exact mirror image of the other half
synthetic division	a shorthand method for dividing polynomials when the divisor is in the form (x + c). This method works only when the coefficient of x equals 1
system of inequalities	a group of inequalities or a group of inequalities mixed with equations
system of linear equations	a group of equations that is processed for solutions that work in all the equations
tangent	one of the six trigonometric functions, denoted tan. In a right triangle, the tangent of an angle is equal to the opposite side divided by the adjacent side.
terminal side	the position of the ray sweeping out an angle after rotation through the angle
transitive property	a concept for comparing numbers which states that if one number is larger than a second number, and the second number is larger than a third number, then the first number is also larger than the third number. The same property holds true if the numbers are smaller than each other. Other transitive properties exist (such as one for the equality of numbers).

translation	movement of the graph of an entire curve in some direction; sometimes called a shift
trigonometric function	a function of angle measure based on the ratios of the sides of right triangles; the six trigonometric functions are sine, cosine, tangent, cosecant, secant, and cotangent
trigonometric identity	an equation involving trigonometric functions that is true for all meaningful values of the variable involved
trinomial	an algebraic expression composed of three monomial terms linked by addition or subtraction
undefined	a rational expression whose value cannot be determined because its denominator has a value equal to zero.
ungrouping with exponents	removing a set of parentheses around a group of terms by attaching the parentheses' exponent to each individual term within the group
union	the solution set for two inequalities linked by "or"; a set formed by combining the elements of two or more sets
unit vector	a vector that has a magnitude of 1
variable	an unknown value in an expression or equation that is usually represented by a letter
variation	when two or more quantities increase or decrease in relation to each other
vector	a mathematical object made up of a magnitude (length) and a direction
velocity	the speed and direction of the motion of an object; the rate of change of position with respect to time.
vertex	(h, k) is the turning point of a parabola; the vertex is the minimum point if the parabola opens up along the y-axis or the maximum point if the parabola opens down along the y-axis; the coordinates of the vertex can be discovered by using information from the standard equation, h = -b/2a; k = f(h)
vertical axis	a scale to measure vertical distance from the origin on a plane; usually designated by y and referred to as the y-axis.
vertical line test	used to determine if a relation is a function; if a vertical line passes through the graph of a relation more than once at any specific point, then the relation fails the vertical line test and is not a function
vertical shift	the rigid motion (or translation) of the graph of a function upwards or downwards; changing the location of an entire curve upwards or downwards from its original location or from the origin on a Cartesian plane
volume	a measurement of 3-dimensional space; involves multiplying the three dimensions of the object as in height x width x depth for a rectangular prism, or pi x radius x radius x height for a right cylinder
word problem	a sentence or paragraph presenting a mathematical situation to solve; the solution procedure involves defining variables, discerning known facts, creating an equation, solving the equation, and checking the answer
x	letter most commonly used as a variable in algebraic expressions
x-axis	the number line used to measure horizontal change on a Cartesian plane
x-intercept	the x-value where a graph crosses or touches the x-axis
x-value	the number used for x within a given point (x,y) to indicate where the point is located horizontally on the Cartesian plane; in general, the value of the variable x
y-axis	the number line used to measure vertical change on the Cartesian plane
y-intercept	the y-value where a graph passes through or touches the y-axis
y-value	the number used for y in a given point (x,y) to indicate where the point is located vertically on the Cartesian plane; in general, the value of the variable y
zero of a function	an x-value where a function equals zero; the point(s) at which a function has an x-intercept

zero of a polynomial function   an x-value where a polynomial p(x) is equal to zero, i.e. any number c that satisfies p(c)=0; any point where the graph of a polynomial crosses or touches the x-axis